Children's Literature

DISCOVERY FOR A LIFETIME

THIRD EDITION

BARBARA D. STOODT-HILL

JOHN TYLER COMMUNITY COLLEGE

LINDA B. AMSPAUGH-CORSON

UNIVERSITY OF CINCINNATI

PEARSON

Merrill
Prentice Hall

Upper Saddle River, New Jersey
Columbus, Ohio

Library of Congress Cataloging in Publication Data

Stoodt, Barbara D.
  Children's literature: discovery for a lifetime / by Barbara D. Stoodt-Hill and Linda B.
 Amspaugh-Corson.—3rd ed.
    p. cm.
  Includes bibliographical references and index.
  ISBN 0-13-118185-8
  1. Children's literature—Study and teaching (Elementary) 2. Children—Books and
reading. I. Amspaugh, Linda B. II. Title.

LB1575.S86 2005
372.64—dc22   2004044541

Vice President and Executive Publisher: Jeffery W. Johnston
Editor: Linda Ashe Montgomery
Editorial Assistant: Laura Weaver
Development Editor: Dawne Brooks
Production Editor: Mary M. Irvin
Production Coordination: Lea Baranowski, Carlisle Publishers Services
Design Coordinator: Diane C. Lorenzo
Cover Designer: Ali Mohrman
Cover Images: Corbis
Production Manager: Pamela D. Bennett
Director of Marketing: Ann Castel Davis
Marketing Manager: Darcy Betts Prybella
Marketing Coordinator: Tyra Poole
Photo Credits: Anthony Magnacca/Merrill, 164; all other photos by Barbara Stoodt-Hill.
Art Credits: See page 386

This book was set in Times Roman by Carlisle Communications, Ltd. It was printed and bound by Courier Kendallville, Inc.
The cover was printed by Phoenix Color Corp.

Pearson Prentice Hall™ is a trademark of Pearson Education, Inc.
Pearson® is a registered trademark of Pearson plc
Prentice Hall® is a registered trademark of Pearson Education, Inc.
Merrill® is a registered trademark of Pearson Education, Inc.

Pearson Education Ltd.   Pearson Education Australia Pty. Limited
Pearson Education Singapore Pte. Ltd.   Pearson Education North Asia Ltd.
Pearson Education Canada, Ltd.   Pearson Educación de Mexico, S. A. de C. V.
Pearson Education—Japan   Pearson Education Malaysia Pte. Ltd.

10 9 8 7 6 5 4 3 2 1
ISBN: 0-13-118185-8

To my husband, James M. Hill,
Love, Barbara

To Sarah Price, Kyle Neu, Matthew Price,
and Andrew Price, with much love,
Grandma Barbara

To my husband, Jim Corwin, with love,
Linda

Preface

The virtues of literature are well established. Publishers, libraries, and bookstores offer a grand array of children's books. Many programs tout the importance of reading books as well as listening to books read aloud. Athletes, movie stars, and politicians urge children to read, and various programs provide books to children for their reading pleasure.

In spite of this widespread approval of literature, there is a quandary. Every U.S. state has some form of objectives or standards that students need to achieve. This may lead some teachers to force-feed facts to students, just so they will succeed. If teachers focus on preparing students for tests, it reduces their read-aloud time and the time to create literature experiences that will enhance their growth and development. Research supports the idea that optimizing children's literary experiences enhances their learning and knowledge retention.

This book is the product of our many experiences as teachers, professors, parents, and grandparents. Our goal is to help teachers, librarians, and parents infuse literature into children's lives and to promote a lifelong interest in books. Our theme is "literature for a lifetime." We hope to prepare teachers in children's lives to:

- choose books that will enhance children's learning and development.
- implement literature in the classroom that will support the curriculum.
- know which books children will respond to.
- share literature with children in authentic ways that stimulate their responses.
- infuse literature into elementary classrooms and homes.
- identify books that portray children with special needs so that their classmates will understand these needs.
- use computer programs and the Internet to enhance literary experiences.
- use multimedia in creating literary experiences.
- choose literature that will develop children's cultural consciousness.

THE ORGANIZATION OF THE TEXT

To provide guidance in reaching the goal of helping all children discover literature for a lifetime, we present information in this text in the following order.

Chapters 1 through 3 create a foundation for understanding and appreciating children's literature, as well as ways of incorporating literature in classrooms and libraries. These chapters also provide guidance for selecting children's books.

Chapters 4 through 11 explore the formats and genres of children's literature in picture books, poetry, traditional literature, fantasy, realistic fiction, historical fiction, nonfiction, and biography. Authors and illustrators are emphasized through profiles that appear throughout the book. In these profiles, we hope to acquaint students with authors and illustrators and their works, as well as offer models for classroom study.

Chapter 12 introduces literature for children who experience the daily challenges of physical, sensory, or emotional disabilities. Chapter 13 focuses on sharing multicultural literature inclusive of children from various cultures. These chapters serve a two-fold purpose. First, they afford children opportunities to identify with those who have had similar experiences. Second, they give readers opportunities to appreciate their own culture and the cultures of others.

Chapters 14, 15, and 16 present ways of nurturing children's engagement with, and response to, literature. Chapter 14 engages children with literature through oral and silent reading experiences; Chapter 15 explains how to encourage children's responses to literature. Finally, Chapter 16 presents sample guides and units that teachers have used in developing classroom experiences with books.

Each chapter opens with a list of key terms, guiding questions, and vignettes, which give examples of teachers and children involved with literature. These vignettes serve as classroom models for others. Throughout the book, additional authentic classroom experiences are meant to develop deeper cognitive and affective understandings and aesthetic awareness.

Each chapter concludes with *Thought Questions* and *Research and Application Experiences* that align IRA/NCTE standards (objectives) to the experiences. Also included at the end of each chapter are annotated bibliographies of cited books and recommended books that include genre identifications and suggested grade levels. Where appropriate, asterisks (*) indicate books that will appeal to reluctant readers.

NEW TO THIS EDITION

Users of the second edition of *Children's Literature: Discovery for a Lifetime* will find that this third edition reflects major revisions in every chapter and several important pedagogical changes.

- All activities in this edition have been aligned to IRA/NCTE standards and guidance on how to use the activity to advance the literary skills.
- Traditional literature and fantasy are now presented in separate chapters.
- Nonfiction and biography are now introduced in separate chapters.
- Chapter 13, "Literature for Children in All Cultures," has been revised in philosophy and organization. It explores multicultural and international children's literature in cultural groups of books that teachers can use in broad-based units of study.
- Author and illustrator profiles have been placed throughout the text.
- Picture books for middle-grade students are one focus in Chapter 4.
- The genre and format chapters include book clusters (text sets) that can be used to develop classroom experiences.
- All bibliographies and references have been thoroughly updated to reflect the latest children's books.

SUPPLEMENTS

Supporting this third edition are three supplements that we hope professors and students will find valuable.

- An updated **Instructor's Manual,** available electronically, contains chapter outlines, teaching tips, suggested test items, and model syllabi. Instructors may contact their local Merrill/Prentice Hall representative to obtain this supplement.
- Extensive bibliographies have been placed on a dual-platform, searchable **CD database** packaged free with every copy of the text. Instructors and students can easily use this software to search for children's books by author, title, illustrator, genre, subject, reading interest level, publisher, copyright year, and combinations thereof. Furthermore, readers can save comments on existing entries and enter bibliographic information for other titles of their choosing. This software will be an indispensable professional resource for years to come.
- A free **Companion Website** allows online posting of syllabi and has an interactive study guide, links to Web-based resources, a message board, and numerous other features. Instructors and students may access the Companion Website at

www.prenhall.com/stoodt

We hope that our enthusiasm will stimulate you to read to children, talk about books with them, and acquaint them with the joy of literature that will last them a lifetime.

ACKNOWLEDGMENTS

We wish to express our sincere appreciation for the support and encouragement of our editor, Linda Montgomery. We would also like to thank the following reviewers: Susan Knell, Pittsburgh State University; Barbara N. Kupetz, Indiana University of Pennsylvania; Deborah Overstreet, University of Southwestern Louisiana; Robert F. Smith, Towson University; Pat T. Sharp, Baylor University; and Barbara Stein, University of North Texas.

EDUCATOR LEARNING CENTER:
AN INVALUABLE ONLINE RESOURCE

Merrill Education and the Association for Supervision and Curriculum Development (ASCD) invite you to take advantage of a new online resource, one that provides access to the top research and proven strategies associated with ASCD and Merrill—the Educator Learning Center. At **www.EducatorLearningCenter.com** you will find resources that will enhance your students' understanding of course topics and of current educational issues, in addition to being invaluable for further research.

HOW THE EDUCATOR LEARNING CENTER WILL HELP YOUR STUDENTS BECOME BETTER TEACHERS

With the combined resources of Merrill Education and ASCD, you and your students will find a wealth of tools and materials to better prepare them for the classroom.

RESEARCH

- More than 600 articles from the ASCD journal *Educational Leadership* discuss everyday issues faced by practicing teachers.
- A direct link on the site to Research Navigator™ gives students access to many of the leading education journals, as well as extensive content detailing the research process.
- Excerpts from Merrill Education texts give your students insights on important topics of instructional methods, diverse populations, assessment, classroom management, technology, and refining classroom practice.

CLASSROOM PRACTICE

- Hundreds of lesson plans and teaching strategies are categorized by content area and age range.
- Case studies and classroom video footage provide virtual field experience for student reflection.
- Computer simulations and other electronic tools keep your students abreast of today's classrooms and current technologies.

LOOK INTO THE VALUE OF EDUCATOR LEARNING CENTER YOURSELF

A four-month subscription to Educator Learning Center is $25 but is FREE when used in conjunction with this text. To obtain free passcodes for your students, simply contact your local Merrill/Prentice Hall sales representative, and your representative will give you a special ISBN to give your bookstore when ordering your textbooks. To preview the value of this Web site to you and your students, please go to **www.EducatorLearningCenter.com** and click on "Demo."

Brief Contents

Contents

Children's Literature

Introduction to Children's Literature

KEY TERMS

character	theme
literature	touchstone
plot	trade books
story grammar	

GUIDING QUESTIONS

Think about a book you enjoyed as a child. Can you remember the title or the major character's name? What did you like about this book? What children's books have you read in the last year? Have you ever read a book to an elementary school child? Think about the following questions as you read this chapter.

1. How is children's literature different from adult literature?

2. What are the most significant values of children's literature in children's lives?

3. What kinds of literary knowledge do teachers need?

Monsieur Noel, the teacher in Susie Morgenstern's *A Book of Coupons*, told his fourth-grade students, "My gift to you is the story, the characters, the words, the ideas, the style, the emotions. Once you have read the book all of these things will be yours for life" (p. 17). According to Betsy Hearne (1999), "The power of story is not to be denied. In prehistoric caves, during Irish famines, in Nazi concentration camps, stories were as important as food . . . . Children's literature is the inheritance of this tradition" (pp. 4–5).

In this chapter, we create a foundation for those concerned with fostering children's literary experiences by exploring the nature of children's literature and its value in children's lives.

In the opening vignette, a first-grade teacher reads Coleen Salley's trade book, *Epossumondas,* to her class. A *trade book* is written to spark an audience's general interest, in contrast with a textbook, which is written for specific instructional purposes. The teacher, Mary Wooster, selected a noodlehead folk tale *Epossumondas* because the children had already heard other variants of this tale. The language in the story is catchy, and the central character is an appealing diaper-wearing, pacifier-sucking baby opossum.

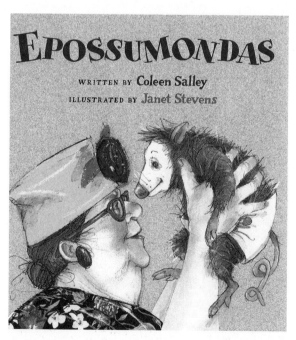

Epossumondas tries to please his Mamma and Aunty.

Mary Wooster watched as her first graders settled on the story rug, then held up *Epossumondas* and said, "This kind of story is called a folk tale because it is a tale story-tellers told before it was written. The main character, Epossumondas, is pictured on the book cover. What can you learn about Epossumondas from his picture?"

William volunteered, "He's a baby opossum."

"Why do you think he is a baby?"

Kendall said, "Because he has a pacifier in his mouth."

Grayson added, "He's wearing a diaper, and that's what babies do."

"I just noticed something about the book title", Katie said. "It's about a opossum, and the word *possum* is inside the name Epossumondas."

Mary responded, "That is very good thinking, Katie. Now I will read the story to you. While I am reading, think about whether the story is real or make-believe and how to tell which it is."

She began, "Epossumondas was his mama's and his auntie's sweet little patootie. They just loved him to death"(unnumbered pages). By the end of this page, there were peals of laughter at the word *patootie,* which the children chanted in chorus. By the fourth page they recognized that the story events formed a pattern. They anticipated that Epossumondas would get in trouble when he followed his mama's instructions.

Andrew volunteered, "His mama told him to put the cake on his head under his hat, then he put butter under his hat and I know what will happen."

"What do you think will happen, Andrew?" Mary asked.

"It'll melt all over him, for sure."

Then the children anticipated the result of each piece of mama's advice and laughed before the page was turned.

When Mary finished, she asked, "Is this story real or make-believe?"

Kendall immediately shouted, "Make-believe!"

"Why do you think that?" Mary asked.

"Well, the mama and auntie were real people and the baby was a opossum. No baby in a diaper with a pacifier would be allowed to run around with cake, butter, and a puppy," Kendall responded.

Christie added, "Animals can't talk like the ones in this story did."

Mary asked, "What was the funniest part of this story?"

The children chorused, "The part where he put the puppy in the water and wrapped leaves around it!"

Then Mary asked, "What else did you like about this story?"

Melissa answered, "I liked the way we could figure out what was going to happen next."

"I liked the trick Epossumondas played on his mama when he stepped in all of her pies," Andrew replied.

Kyle spoke up and said, "I liked the word *patootie,* and the phrase 'You haven't got the sense you were born with'."

"I really liked the pictures of the animals that Epossumondas talked to. . . ." Will said, "And the whole book was funny!"

What Is Children's Literature?

There has been a striking increase in the number of children's books published over the last two decades, as well as their use in elementary classrooms (Serafini, 2003). This time period is often considered the "Golden Age" of children's literature, which makes it important to learn about the body of children's literature, as well as the authors and illustrators who create children's books.

Children's literature is literature that children can relate to and appreciate. A more formal explanation of *literature* is thought, experience, and imagination shaped into oral or written language that may include visual images. Literature entertains listeners and readers, while at the same time giving them access to the accumulated experience and wisdom of the ages. Children's literature explores, orders, evaluates, and illuminates the human experience—its heights and depths, as well as its pains and pleasures. Memorable children's authors skillfully engage readers with information, language, unique plots, and many-faceted characters.

Children's literature relates to their experiences and is told in language they understand; therefore, they respond to it. The major difference between children's literature and adult literature is the more limited life experience reflected in the audience. Authors consider their audiences' experiences and their life events as they create order and form in their writing.

Literature contributes to readers' growing experiences by extending and enriching their knowledge while stimulating reflection. "Offering stories to children is the way our print-dominated society carries on a habit even older than writing and as common as bread—telling stories and listening to them" (Meek, 1977, p. 36). Stories are a natural part of life. Constructing stories in the mind is a fundamental way of making meaning. Through stories and language, humans record, explain, understand, and control their experience. They also come to know their world (Wells, 1998).

Stories are behind the nightly news, the comics, and the 11 o'clock sports report. When you ask a friend about her experiences in a hurricane, she creates a narrative to tell what happened, helping both of you understand her experience. Through telling, retelling, believing, and disbelieving stories about one another's past, future, and identity, we come to know each other.

The Power of Literature

Isolating and identifying the values of children's literature is a daunting task because literature affects our lives so deeply. Literature motivates readers to think, enhances language and cognitive development, stimulates thinking, motivates readers to learn to read and to continue reading, and accelerates learning (Pressley, 2001). It takes readers beyond everyday experiences, broadening their world knowledge, developing their imaginations and senses of humor, and enabling them to grow in humanity and understanding. Books can expand readers' knowledge and experience, entertain, help readers solve problems, and play a significant role in children's developmental journey (Galda, Ash, & Cullinan, 2001). From this beginning, we can distinguish some of the major values of children's literature—enjoyment, aesthetics, understanding, imagination, information and knowledge, cognition, language, and learning (Gallas, 2000).

Throughout the book we focus on learner-centered literary experiences with quality children's

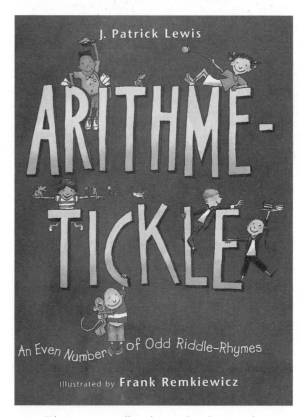

These poems will make you laugh at math.

books. The literature suggested in this text establishes *touchstones* or benchmarks that are quality standards to which you can compare the books you read. These touchstones will help you select inspiring literature for children that stimulates their responses and becomes a standard for selecting books.

Readers who enjoy literature read more and are oblivious to any quality other than enjoyment. Stories and poems enchant readers; however, readers also appreciate new, fascinating information acquired from nonfiction. For example, children respond to the comedic elements in David Wisniewski's *The Secret Knowledge of Grown-Ups,* in which children learn the truth about grown-ups' instructions. They learn why grown-ups say "Eat your vegetables," and "Comb your hair," and "Drink your milk." A well-written informational book piques readers' interest in new topics and whets their appetite for more knowledge. In her book *Brooklyn Bridge,* Lynn Curlee captures the strength and stability of this engineering masterpiece through language and illustrations. For example, "The broad roadway linking Brooklyn with Manhattan hangs by a complex web of metal ropes from four gigantic cables, each thicker than a very large man's waist"(p. 1). The subject is further dramatized in illustrations featuring straight lines, large size, a limited range of color, and views from various perspectives around New York.

Children appreciate poetry, too. Poetry captures the essence of children's experiences and ideas in succinct language that appeals to them. Jack Prelutsky's *Scranimals* is guaranteed to delight readers. This popular children's poet created a mythical Scranimal Island inhabited by hybrid scrambled animals created by combining vegetables, amphibians, birds, and fish. The elegant wordplay features such characters as "The Potatoad" and "The Cardinalbacore."

Superb writers first and foremost share their creative writing with readers. Those children who enjoy authors' creations will come back for more. Books that obviously preach or teach are too didactic for children's tastes. Unless they can relate to the ideas and experiences expressed, children will not listen to the voice of such a book, and often do not finish reading it.

Appreciating Aesthetics in Literature

Fiction, nonfiction, and poetry are artistic interpretations of experiences, events, and people. Picture books and book illustrations add the dimension of visual art, which interacts with language to tell a story, create a poem, or impart information. Aesthetics pertain to the beauty readers perceive in a literary work. Literature is verbal art that helps readers appreciate the beauty of language, thereby adding new dimensions to their lives.

Enhancing Understanding

Books stimulate readers' emotional responses. They often identify with characters, giving them a deeper involvement with the story. In this way, reading becomes a meaningful experience. For instance, readers chuckle over the outlandish teacher capers in *Hooray for Diffendoofer Day!* by Dr. Seuss, Jack Prelutsky, and Lane Smith. In Elissa Guest's *Iris and Walter: The Sleepover,* children understand Iris's feelings when she decides not to sleepover, even though she was excited about the invitation.

Readers gain insights about the life of a youngster with attention deficit disorder when Joey tells the story himself in Jack Gantos' *Joey Pigza Loses Control.* Joey is going to visit his father, but his dog throws up on the dashboard of his mom's car. However, mom saves the situation when she whispers "Call me. . . . Call often so I can say I love you."

As they read, children begin to realize that people around the world share their hopes, dreams, and fears. Through stories, they learn about happiness, sadness, fears, warm family relationships, death, and loneliness. Indeed, they learn that many life experiences are universal. In Marilyn Sachs' book, *The Four Ugly Cats in Apartment 3D,* 11-year-old Lily must locate homes for kittens. Her problems resonate with many children's experiences.

Today's authors address death, birth, anger, mental illness, alcoholism, and brutality in explicit terms. Adults who have not read recently published children's books may find the realism shocking; nevertheless, contemporary realism contributes to children's self-understanding. In *The Same Stuff as Stars,* Katherine Paterson writes about Angel and her brother, Bernie, whose father is in jail. The children's mother abandons them with their invalid great-grandmother. However, Angel's strength of spirit enables her to persevere in the face of these devastating problems.

Reading about story characters' feelings and actions develops children's abilities to understand and appreciate how others feel. Children who come to understand and appreciate various cultures are more likely to understand the shared aspects of human life and to appreciate the cultures that comprise the United States, as well as the world at large. In *Love to Langston,* a biography in poetry, Tony Medina gives readers insight into the life of Langston Hughes and the importance of his writing in all of our lives.

Developing Imagination

Imagination is a creative, constructive power that is intimately related to higher-order thinking skills. Every aspect of daily life involves imagination. People imagine as they talk and interact with others, make choices and decisions, analyze news reports, or assess advertising and entertainment. Critical and creative thinkers strive to develop or invent novel, aesthetic, and constructive ideas (Beyer, 1995; Wilks, 1995).

Literature educates the imagination because it illustrates the unlimited range of the human imagination and extends readers' personal visions of possibilities (Frye, 1964; Gallas, 2000). Literature stirs and stretches the imagination, providing new information, ideas, and perspectives so that readers can imagine possibilities. In this way, it expands the readers' ability to express imagination in words and images.

Many children's books inspire creative thought. The imaginary worlds that writers create help readers understand the real world. In Janet Lisle's *How I Became a Writer and Oggie Learned to Drive,* we learn about Archie, who decides to write a book of stories he told his brother. Writing becomes a coping device for him during his parents' divorce. Amanda has an imaginary world in Rod Clement's *Just Another Ordinary Day.* Amanda lives an ordinary life in all ways except she wakes up to the blaring clash of a gong instead of an alarm clock. She rides to school with a neighbor—a Tyrannosaurus. One of her classmates is an alien and her cat Fluffy is no ordinary pet. This book connects real and make-believe worlds, making imaginary worlds acceptable to children. Fantasy is explored in Chapter 7.

Increasing Information and Knowledge

Children find the real world and real events fascinating. Reading enables them to participate in experiences that go far beyond learning mere facts, because trade books give readers a sense of people, times, and places that textbooks do not. For example, in *The Young Adventurer's Guide to Everest: From Avalanche to Zopkio,* Jonathan Chester, a Himalayan climber and photographer, introduces his personal experiences replete with significant details.

Fine nonfiction writers not only increase their readers' world knowledge, but they expand the readers' thinking about the many concepts introduced in their books and subject matter textbooks (Pressley, 2001). Nonfiction encourages them to question and think critically. Often readers discover new nonfiction interests, as well as new facets they discover as they explore the topics in greater depth. The author Laurence Pringle introduces fascinating living animals and birds in *Strange Animals, New to Science.* Many nonfiction books are introduced in Chapter 10.

Stimulating Cognition

Literature is a way of thinking that serves as a source of knowledge and a sounding board for children's reasoning. It plays a role in developing a sharp and critical mind (Langer, 1995). All literature, stories, and poems, as well as nonfiction, stimulate thinking by giving readers substance for reflection. Literature can provoke readers to analyze, synthesize, connect, and respond thoughtfully, which facilitates cognitive development. Gordon Wells (1998) points out that humans construct stories to make sense of information, and stories are the means by which we enter into a shared world, which is broadened and enriched by the stories we exchange with others.

Literature is a forum that offers readers diverse perspectives on familiar topics by giving them a safe medium for trying different roles, imagining new settings, and puzzling out unique problem solutions. Many books model thinking processes such as problem solving, inferencing, evaluative thinking, relational thinking, and imagining. Readers of Jon Scieszka's *Math Curse* will be stimulated to discover the many times they confront mathematical reasoning in their lives.

Providing a Language Model

Language and thinking are so closely interrelated that "the ability to think for one's self depends upon one's mastery of the language" (Didion, 1968, p. 14). Children need many opportunities to interact with others using language that is essential to acquiring higher-order thinking (Healy, 1991). Children master language through social activities such as conversations, hearing and telling stories, and discussing the books they hear and read.

Literature creates a language foundation for listening and reading comprehension. Writers create richer language models than conversation can because they tend to use elaborate sentences and sumptuous words, whereas speakers employ the same few words again and again.

Leo Lionni used exquisite language in many of his books (Lionni, 1963). For example, his book *Swimmy* includes a lobster that walks like a "water-moving machine" and an "eel with a tail that is too long to remember." This writing expands children's language repertoire, enabling them to develop greater facility in thinking, imagining, reading, and writing.

Foundations of Literature

The values of literature emerge in children's lives when they have coherent, planned experiences with carefully selected literature. The following principles have emerged from research and experience:

1. Pleasure is the primary reason for involving literature in classrooms. Enjoyment attracts children to literature and reading. However, using literature as a drill for facts or skills can eliminate the enjoyment. We believe in the transactional perspective; that meaning is constructed in the transaction between a particular reader and a particular text (Rand, 2002; Rosenblatt, 1978; Rosenblatt, 1995; Serafini, 2003).

2. Literature programs should have a coherent structure. "Literature can be used as a way of understanding the world, or appreciated as a work of art that has value in and of itself"(Serafini, 2003).

3. Literature programs give students opportunities to appreciate the author's language, meaning cues, and literary conventions. Three principles are frequently used to organize literature programs: genre studies (categories of literature), elements of literature studies (plot, character, setting, style, theme), and authors and illustrators studies (recognized writers in the field of children's literature, and artists who illustrate children's books). Literary genre, elements, and authors are discussed more fully in Chapters 2 and 3.

4. Children's response to literature is an important part of the literary experience. Response refers to readers' feelings about a work of literature. "Each time we talk about a book we discover our sense of it, our ideas about it, our understanding of what it is and means, even the details we remember have changed and shifted and come to us in different arrangements, different patterns" (Chambers, 1983, p. 167). Readers' responses are cultivated through giving them occasions to read, discuss and discover, consider, represent, and reread to make their own meanings. Figure 1.1 illustrates the reader response transaction. Chapter 15 explores responses to literature.

5. Literature programs should balance literature studies with readers' response. Authors and readers create meaning together. Readers use the author's words to make a book come alive by using the author's meaning cues, extracting and constructing meaning as they interact with text and relate it to life as they know it.

Literature and Reading Instruction

The most commonly reported goals of reading and language arts instruction are helping students read for understanding, developing strategic learners, and helping students become engaged in reading. Interesting literature increases students' willingness to

---

FIGURE 1.1 Literary response continuum.

BOOK READER

| Uninterested, does not finish book | Somewhat interested | Enjoys book, finds it satisfying | Excited, wants to share feeling about book | Finds book totally absorbing |

put forth the energy to learn and cultivates their desire to read. For instance, discovering humorous stories moves many children to read, and reading such stories aloud is a good means of engaging children's interest. For example, *The True Story of the 3 Little Pigs* and *The Stinky Cheese Man and Other Fairly Stupid Tales,* both by Jon Scieszka, are guaranteed to tickle everyone's sense of humor and motivate them to read more.

Reading instruction usually combines language and literature-rich activities to enhance meaning, understanding, and love of literature with explicit teaching of skills as needed to develop proficient readers (Baumann, Hooten, & White, 1999; Rand 2002; Sensenbaugh, 1997). Reading instruction focuses on words, comprehension, and quality content. Literacy is based on reading materials that develop comprehension through meaningful reading, writing, and discussion about what is read and written (Baumann et al., 1999; International Reading Association and the National Association for the Education of Young Children, 1998; Rand, 2002; Weaver, 1998).

Literature and Language Arts

The language arts include speaking, listening, reading, and writing. Children's literature is essential to teaching and learning the language arts. Much of the content for teaching speaking, listening, reading, and writing is derived from children's books. Reading to children builds their sense of story and enhances their understanding of the ways authors structure and organize text. Moreover, literature builds knowledge. An instance of this is seen in Debra Frasier's book *Miss Alaineus: A Vocabulary Disaster.* The importance of words is illustrated dramatically when a student misunderstands one of the teacher's weekly vocabulary words, but the student finally figures it out and handles her mistake with humor.

Writers usually are avid readers. Prominent authors advise young writers that reading is an indispensable trait for learning to write (Gallo, 1977). Literature provides writers with a source of ideas and inspiration, as well as a means to create models for organizing ideas in text; therefore, immersing children in literature prepares them for writing.

Reading enlarges children's sensitivity to and understanding of language, thereby enabling them to choose the words and create the syntax that best express their thoughts. Fiction, nonfiction, and poetry help readers remember what they have read, promote their sense of the ways in which discourse may be structured, and discover patterns for structuring their own writing.

Research reveals that the stories children write reflect the characteristics of their reading materials. Children whose reading reflects a wide range of writing structures, complex sentence patterns, and rich vocabulary exhibit these characteristics in their own writing, whereas those who read simple, repetitious stories write in a simple, repetitive style. Reading and discussing a wide variety of stories seems to help students discover the ways authors create meaning in written language, as these children are more sensitive to plot, character, setting, and writing style than their less well-read peers (Calkins, 1986; Graves, 1983).

Literature and Curriculum

Literature gives students access to the accumulated experience, knowledge, and wisdom of the past. Integrating literature in the curriculum enhances learning in all subject areas regardless of the prevailing philosophy of learning.

Literature and the Content Areas

Literature supports learning across the curriculum because it widens the reader's world beyond the immediate

Audrey and Don Wood have written and illustrated many books. Readers return again and again to Little Penguin's Tale, only to discover that some of us can just hear a story—and others have to experience it.

time and place. Reading is an instrument for accessing ideas and information. Moreover, it gives students opportunities to interact with one another and to understand the ways that others think and respond. For example, students who read are able to generate hypotheses and cultivate multiple perspectives, ways of thinking that are used in all subject areas (Bruner, 1986).

Integrated instruction enables students to see the connectedness of separate subjects. An integrated curriculum is one in which teachers plan for students to learn language at the same time they are learning something else, which may be science, social studies, math, or art, or even a project such as planning an assembly program. Acquiring knowledge is a process of making connections and finding patterns (Short, 1993; Vygotsky, 1978). This is why integrated instruction, thematic and topical units, and literature-based instruction support optimal learning. For example, *Nibbling on Einstein's Brain: The Good the Bad & the Bogus in Science* by Diane Swanson explores science knowledge in interesting ways that help readers connect what they already know with new information.

Integrated instruction enables learners to make connections and find patterns throughout their lives,

carrying ideas from one subject to another. Literature provides students the content to generate hypotheses and to understand different perspectives. Literature is an excellent vehicle for interrelating and integrating science and social studies. Consider Claudia Logan's book *The 5,000 Year Old Puzzle: Solving a Mystery of Ancient Egypt,* which takes readers beyond mere facts and descriptions. They learn how real archaeologists conduct an actual dig. They learn about mummies, life in ancient Egypt, and the kinds of equipment needed on a dig. Students also get a picture of how archeologists think and communicate.

Literature is a means of enriching mathematics understandings and concepts. Novels, poetry, and nonfiction develop logic, problem solving, and mathematics concepts. In *The King's Chessboard,* which is based on an ancient Indian folk tale, David Birch demonstrates the squaring of numbers. J. Patrick Lewis's *Arithmetickle* contains an even number of odd riddle-rhymes that provide brain-teasing mathematics fun. Readers develop concepts, computation skills, logic, and fun.

Concepts of biology emerge in *A Drop of Water: A Book of Science and Wonder,* which Walter Wick illustrated with photographs of the various forms of water. History and social studies concepts are illustrated in Ken Mochizuki's *Passage to Freedom: The Sugihara Story,* which tells how a Japanese diplomat helped Jewish refugees during World War II. These and other nonfiction books enhance children's subject matter.

Literature and the Fine Arts

Writers are verbal artists who use language as their medium; other artists search for truth in visual art, music, and drama. Literature cultivates children's appreciation of the fine arts. They learn about music from books such as Toyomi Igus's *I See the Rhythm,* which illustrates the rhythms of work songs, jazz, and swing. Vincent van Gogh is the subject of Laurence Anholt's *Camille and the Sunflowers,* which introduces some of van Gogh's masterpieces.

Children respond to and extend the books they read, as shown in pictures painted by children who read *Camille and the Sunflowers.* One child may create a mural to express appreciation of a book, while another may paint or draw a picture to illustrate feelings

Sage's spelling disaster helps her learn.

Sarah painted this picture after reading Camille and the Sunflowers.

about a story or poem. Still others may use music to re-create the mood of a story or poem.

Curriculum Standards

There is widespread concern in the United States about the curriculum knowledge and student performance. As a result, many states and professional organizations have developed standards and high-stakes tests that define what students should know in a specific content subject. The tests are used to appraise students' progress toward achieving those standards or goals. For example, language arts standards define what students should know about language and be able to do with language (NCTE & IRA, 1996). *Standards for the English Language arts* jointly developed by the International Reading Association and the National Council of Teachers of English are shown in Figure 1.2. Throughout this book, we relate literature and standards to building this foundation for learning.

The curriculum standards movement has become a force in education because, in many states, students must achieve specified scores in order to pass to the next grade level, not to mention graduate from high school. Moreover, the "high-stakes" tests create tension for both teachers and students. However, teachers recognize that an education involves more than memorizing facts specified in the various standards. In fact, students need to create cognitive connections among facts in order to understand and remember them.

An example of a book that creates connections among facts is Judith St. George's picture book, *So You Want to Be President*. This trade book helps children learn more about the U.S. Presidents than merely memorizing their names and terms of office ever could. The author uses humor to convey information. For instance, she compares the spending habits of some Presidents as well as their personalities, and includes "backroom" facts that will stick with the readers. The illustrator, David Small, uses cartoons to further develop the humorous tone, which could lead to a lesson about creating cartoons and a study of political cartoons.

Creating Effective Literary Experience

Hearing literature read aloud is the usual introduction to literary experience. Genre, elements of literature, and authors/illustrators can be introduced through read-aloud experiences, which are discussed in Chapters 2 and 3, as well as in Chapter 14. These experiences and subsequent literature reading experiences can be structured through teacher and librarian (media specialist) planning. Children can participate in reading circles, reading discussions, Internet programs, taped books, and videos. Many teachers plan units with their students.

The Unit Approach

Teachers may choose from a diverse collection of literary and artistic styles to build students' in-depth understandings of themes, topics, and concepts. For instance, a thematic unit focusing on courage amplifies children's understanding of ideas such as moral courage, physical courage, integrity, and responsibility.

Subject-matter units address topics, such as farm life, problem solving, or the circus, rather than themes. In developing these units, teachers select a variety of materials that enrich students' understanding of the unit focus.

FIGURE 1.2   IRA/NCTE Standards for the English language arts.

✳

The vision guiding these standards is that all students must have the opportunities and resources to develop the language skills they need to pursue life's goals and to participate fully as informed, productive members of society. These standards assume that literacy growth begins before children enter school as they experience and experiment with literacy activities—reading and writing, and associating spoken words with their graphic representations. Recognizing this fact, these standards encourage the development of curriculum and instruction that make productive use of the emerging literacy abilities that children bring to school. Furthermore, the standards provide ample room for the innovation and creativity essential to teaching and learning. They are not prescriptions for particular curriculum or instruction.

Although we present these standards as a list, we want to emphasize that they are not distinct and separable; they are, in fact, interrelated and should be considered as a whole.

1. Students read a wide range of print and nonprint texts to build an understanding of texts, of themselves, and of the cultures of the United States and the world; to acquire new information; to respond to the needs and demands of society and the workplace; and for personal fulfillment. Among these texts are fiction and nonfiction, classic and contemporary works.

2. Students read a wide range of literature from many periods in many genres to build an understanding of the many dimensions (e.g., philosophical, ethical, aesthetic) of human experience.

3. Students apply a wide range of strategies to comprehend, interpret, evaluate, and appreciate texts. They draw on their prior experiences, their interactions with other readers and writers, their knowledge of word meaning and of other texts, their word identification strategies, and their understanding of textual features (e.g., sound-letter correspondence, sentence structure, context, graphics).

4. Students adjust their use of spoken, written, and visual language (e.g., conventions, style, vocabulary) to communicate effectively with a variety of audiences and for different purposes.

5. Students employ a wide range of strategies as they write and use different writing process elements appropriately to communicate with different audiences for a variety of purposes.

6. Students apply knowledge of language structure, language conventions (e.g., spelling and punctuation), media techniques, figurative language, and genre to create, critique, and discuss print and nonprint texts.

7. Students conduct research on issues and interests by generating ideas and questions, and by posing problems. They gather, evaluate, and synthesize data from a variety of sources (e.g., print and nonprint texts, artifacts, people) to communicate their discoveries in ways that suit their purpose and audience.

8. Students use a variety of technological and informational resources (e.g., libraries, databases, computer networks, video) to gather and synthesize information and to create and communicate knowledge.

9. Students develop an understanding of and respect for diversity in language use, patterns, and dialects across cultures, ethnic groups, geographic regions, and social roles.

10. Students whose first language is not English make use of their first language to develop competency in the English language arts and to develop understanding of content across the curriculum.

11. Students participate as knowledgeable, reflective, creative, and critical members of a variety of literacy communities.

12. Students use spoken, written, and visual language to accomplish their own purposes (e.g., for learning, enjoyment, persuasion, and the exchange of information).

Chapter 14 explores various kinds of units that relate to specific themes or topics to generate teaching units.

Story Elements

Story elements are another approach to understanding literature. *Story elements* include plot, character, setting, theme, and style. *Plot* is the sequence of events in a story. The *characters* are the people or personified animals or objects that are responsible for the action in the story. Characters and story events occur in a *setting,* the place and time of the story. As the story un-folds, a central meaning or theme emerges; this central meaning is usually a universal idea or truth. For example, one of the lasting truths expressed in E. B. White's *Charlotte's Web* is the concept of loyalty in friendship; like many books, this one has several layers of meaning so that readers may identify other themes that are meaningful to them. (The elements of literature are explained in Chapter 2.)

Themes are important ideas or universal understandings that evolve from reading a work or works of literature. One of several themes emerging from Maurice Sendak's *Where the Wild Things Are* is escaping in one's imagination. Max escapes when he gets in trouble for acting like a wild thing. Ruth Krauss's *A Very Special House* explores a similar theme. In this instance, the protagonist escapes to a house where he can do all of the things that are not allowed at home. Thematic understandings emerge gradually from reading a variety of related materials; therefore, thematic units are organized around all types of literature, including fiction, nonfiction, and poetry.

Story grammars, a means of exploring story elements, are organized around setting, story problem, attempts to solve the problem, and problem resolution. Figure 1.3 illustrates a story grammar.

The Teacher and Children's Literature

Teachers, librarians, and parents choose appealing books that motivate children to read. They also motivate children by reading books aloud (Hearne,1999). "Motivation to read depends on the adults' attitudes as well as the book's magic" (Hearne, 1999). Reading the first chapter of a book is often enough to motivate children to continue reading.

Teachers and librarians need to create a warm, literate environment where children have time to read each day. Many children in our hectic modern world have limited opportunities to read outside school because they attend after-school programs and/or are involved in a variety of activities. Thus, schools must play a pivotal role in providing books, as well as time, to read. A warm, literate environment should include an inviting physical setting. The physical environment may feature an attractive book-browsing center, book displays, and bulletin boards for authors' pictures and book jackets. Children are more likely to read when surrounded by inviting reading materials, which teachers can provide through school materials or long-term book loans from public libraries. Many teachers purchase secondhand books and paperbacks for their classroom book collections. All of these materials should be displayed in ways that invite children to pick them up.

Teachers and librarians can encourage children's response to literature by providing children with many opportunities to discuss stories, as well as through listening, reading, writing, and the fine arts.

FIGURE 1.3   Story grammar.

Title:
Author:

Setting (who, where, when):

Time

Character

Place

Problem:

Efforts to solve the problem (also called events):

1.

2.

3.

4. (number of events vary)

The resolution:

Summary

This chapter introduced children's literature as literature that children understand and enjoy. Moreover, the text established the importance of literature in elementary classrooms, as a means of exploring and seeking meaning in human experience. Children's literature includes all types of books that entertain and inform children, including picture books, traditional literature, realistic fiction, historical fiction, biography, fantasy, poetry, and nonfiction, among other media such as narratives, videos, verbal stories, and the fine arts. The content of children's literature is limited only by the experience and understanding of the reader. Successful teachers involve their students with literature daily by reading aloud and providing time for students to read on their own.

Literature has many personal values for children. Foremost among these are entertainment, aesthetics, thinking, and imagination. Learning is an important value of literature in elementary classrooms. Fine books can contribute to learning in language arts, social studies, science, mathematics, and fine arts. Literature knowledge enables teachers and other adults to select appropriate literature and to guide literature experiences.

Thought Questions

1. Write your own definition of *children's literature.*
2. How does literature develop children's imagination?
3. Which values of literature are most important, in your opinion?
4. How is a good children's book like a good adult book? How is it different from an adult book?
5. What do you think you need to learn in order to teach children's literature?
6. Could the same criteria be used to evaluate both adult and children's literature? Why or why not?
7. Do you think computers and software will replace literature?
8. What touchstone or benchmark books have you discovered?

Research and Application Experiences

1. Interview three of your friends to determine their favorite childhood books, and then interview three children. Compare their responses.
2. Read three new children's books (published within the last five years). How are they like the ones you read as a child? How are they different? Make file cards for each of these books to start your children's literature file.
3. Interview three teachers. Ask them how often they read aloud and what books they choose to read aloud.
4. Read several books by the same author to help you become acquainted with a children's author. What did you learn about the author from his or her writing? Look up the author on the Internet and add that information to what you have already learned. Add these books to your children's literature file.
5. If you are participating in an internship experience accompanying this course, observe the following in your classroom:
   a. How often does the teacher read aloud?
   b. What does the teacher read aloud?
   c. How often do the children independently read trade books?

6. Read one of the children's books mentioned in this chapter and compare your response to the book with the author's comments about it.
7. If you are participating in an internship experience related to this course, ask the students to identify their favorite authors.

Children's Literature References and Recommended Books

Note: Books designated with an asterisk (*) are recommended for reluctant readers.

Anholt, L. (1994). *Camille and the sunflowers.* New York: Barron's. (2–4). HISTORICAL FICTION.

Based on an actual encounter, this picture book tells how Camille made friends with Vincent van Gogh.

Birch, D. (1988). *The king's chessboard* (D. Grebu, Illus.). New York: Dial. (2–4). MODERN FANTASY.

The wise man asks for an unusual reward: a grain of rice for the first square on his chessboard, double the amount on the second, and so on.

Chester, J. (2002). *The young adventurer's guide to Everest: From avalanche to zopkio.* Toronto, CA: Greystone Books. (4–8). NONFICTION.

The true story of climbing Mount Everest.

Clement, R. (1997). *Just another ordinary day.* New York: HarperCollins. (2–4). MODERN FANTASY.

Amanda lives an ordinary life except that she has unusual neighbors, school, and so forth.

Curlee, L. (2001). *Brooklyn Bridge.* New York: Atheneum Books. (3–8). INFORMATIONAL PICTURE BOOK.*

The story of how the Brooklyn Bridge was built. Superb text and illustrations make this a fascinating read.

Frasier, D. (2000). *Miss Alaineus: A vocabulary disaster.* New York: Harcourt. (2–4). CONTEMPORARY REALISTIC FICTION.*

Sage misheard and misunderstood a weekly vocabulary word. In the end she has a new appreciation for words.

Gantos, J. (2000). *Joey Pigza loses control.* New York: Scholastic. (4–8). CONTEMPORARY REALISTIC FICTION.*

The protagonist has attention deficit disorder. In this story, he visits his recovering alcoholic father to get acquainted.

Guest, E. H. (2002). *Iris and Walter: The sleepover* (C. Davenier, Illus.). New York: Gulliver/Harcourt. (1–3). PICTURE BOOK/CONTEMPORARY FICTION.

Iris is excited about a sleepover with Walter, but at bedtime she wants to go home.

Igus, T. (1998). *I see the rhythm* (M. Wood, Illus.). San Francisco: Children's Book Press. (3–8). INFORMATIONAL BOOK.*

The author and illustrator teach readers about the rhythms of hip-hop, work songs, jazz, swing, and gospel music.

Krauss, R. (1954). *A very special house* (M. Sendak, Illus.). New York: HarperCollins. (K–3). FANTASY.

The boy in this story escapes in his imagination to a house where he can do the things that are not allowed in his home.

Lewis, J. P. (2002). *Arithmetickle* (F. Remkiewicz, Illus.). New York: Harcourt. (2–6). POETRY.

This book is an even number of odd riddle-rhymes.

Lionni, L. (1963). *Swimmy*. New York: Pantheon. (K–2). MODERN FANTASY.

After a fierce tuna eats his family, Swimmy sets out to see the world and escape the big fish.

Lisle, J. T. (2002). *How I became a writer and Oggie learned to drive*. New York: Philomel. (4–8). REALISTIC FICTION.

Eleven-year-old Archie decides to write a book of stories which becomes a coping device as he deals with his parents' divorce.

Logan, C. (2002). *The 5,000 year old puzzle: Solving a mystery of ancient Egypt*. New York: Farrar. (3–6). NONFICTION.

The story of an archaeological expedition that took place in 1924.

Medina, T. (2002). *Love to Langston* (R. G. Christie, Illus.). New York: Lee & Low. (4–9). POETRY.

Superb poetic biography of Langston Hughes.

Mochizuki, K. (1997). *Passage to freedom: The Sugihara story* (D. Lee, Illus.). New York: Lee & Low. (3–6). BIOGRAPHY.

A true story of how a Japanese diplomat helped Jewish refugees during World War II.

Morganstern, S. (2001). *A book of coupons*. New York: Viking. (3–5). CONTEMPORARY REALISTIC FICTION.*

The fourth-grade class has a new teacher, Monsieur Noel. He turns out to be an unusual teacher that does not fit their expectations.

Paterson, K. (2002). *The same stuff as stars*. New York: Clarion. (5–9). REALISTIC FICTION.

Angel is accustomed to caring for herself and her brother because her father is in jail and her mother is irresponsible.

Prelutsky, J. (2002). *Scranimals* (P. Sis, Illus.). New York: Greenwillow. (1–5). POETRY.

This poet introduced a mythical Scranimal Island through his poems about hybrid animals.

Pringle, L. (2002). *Strange animals, new to science*. (3–6). NONFICTION.

The animals introduced in this book are all recently discovered on Earth.

Sachs, M. (2002). *The four ugly cats in apartment 3D* (R. Litzinger, Illus.). New York: Atheneum. (3–5). REALISTIC FICTION.

When a neighbor dies, Lily has to find homes for his four loud, stray cats. She finally finds homes for all but one.

Salley, C. (2002). *Epossumondas*. (J. Stevens, Illus.). New York: Harcourt. (1–3). TRADITIONAL LITERATURE.

This noodlehead story is about a opossum who makes mistakes because he tries to follow mama's instructions.

Scieszka, J. (1989). *The true story of the 3 little pigs* by A. Wolf (L. Smith, Illus.). New York: Viking. (K–6). MODERN FANTASY.*

Mr. A. Wolf gives his version of what happened to the three little pigs. Of course, he was grossly misjudged in the original story.

Scieszka, J. (1992). *The stinky cheese man and other fairly stupid tales* (L. Smith, Illus.). New York: Viking. (K–6). MODERN FANTASY.*

This is a collection of fractured fairy tales that delight all ages.

Scieszka, J. (1995). *Math curse* (L. Smith, Illus.). New York: Viking. (All ages). CONTEMPORARY REALISTIC FICTION.

This book tells of the problems of living in a world where math is so important.

Sendak, M. (1963). *Where the wild things are*. New York: Harper & Row. (K–2). MODERN FANTASY.

Max is wild, so his mother sends him to bed without dinner. He escapes, but returns to where he is loved.

Seuss, Dr., with Prelutsky, J., & Smith, L. (1998). *Hooray for Diffendoofer day!* New York: Knopf. (K–6). MODERN FANTASY.*

Introduction to Children's Literature **15**

A parody of school, where the teachers teach children to think. The book also demonstrates the writing process.

St. George, J. (2000). *So you want to be President* (D. Small, Illus.). New York: Philomel. (2–6). NONFICTION.

This author and illustrator have created a funny book full of information about U.S. Presidents.

Swanson, D. (2001). *Nibbling on Einstein's brain: The good the bad & the bogus in science* (W. Clark, Illus.). Toronto: Annick Press. (4–7). NONFICTION.*

The author identifies the characteristics of good science and those of bad science. She identifies examples of each and presents facts in amusing ways that are enhanced with cartoon illustrations.

White, E. B. (1952). *Charlotte's web* (G. Williams, Illus.). New York: Harper & Row. (3–6). MODERN FANTASY.

Charlotte the spider saves Wilbur the pig's life with a unique solution to his problem.

Wick, W. (1997). *A drop of water: A book of science and wonder.* New York: Scholastic. (1–4). INFORMATIONAL BOOK.

Beautiful photographs illustrate the various forms of water and the water cycle.

Wisniewski, D. (1998). *The secret knowledge of grown-ups.* New York: Lothrop, Lee & Shepard. (K–4). PICTURE BOOK/MODERN FANTASY*

Readers learn the truth about things parents say to children such as, "Drink your milk," from secret files.

References and Books for Further Reading

Baumann, J., Hooten, H., and White, P. (1999, September). Teaching comprehension through literature: A teacher-research project to develop fifth graders' reading strategies and motivation. *The Reading Teacher, 53,* 38–51.

Beach, R. (1993). *Reader-response theories.* Urbana, IL: National Council of Teachers of English.

Bear, D. R., & Templeton, S. (1998). Explorations in developmental spelling: Foundations for learning and teaching phonics, spelling, and vocabulary. *The Reading Teacher, 52,* 222–242.

Beyer, B. (1995). *Critical thinking.* Bloomington, IN: Phi Delta Kappa.

Bruner, J. (1986). *Actual minds, possible worlds.* Cambridge, MA: Harvard University Press.

Calkins, L. (1986). *The art of teaching writing.* Portsmouth, NH: Heinemann.

Chambers, A. (1983). *Introducing books to children.* Boston: Horn Book.

Didion, J. (1968). *Slouching toward Bethlehem.* New York: Delta-Dell.

Frye, N. (1964). *The educated imagination.* Bloomington: Indiana University Press.

Galda, L., Ash, G. E., Cullinan, B. (2001, April). Research on children's literature. *Reading Online, 4* (9), 1–42.

Gallas, K. (2000, Winter). Why do we listen to stories? *New Advocate, 13,* 35–40.

Gallo, D. (1977). Teaching writing: Advice from the professionals. *Connecticut English Journal, 8,* 45–50.

Graves, D. (1983). *Writing teachers and children at work.* Portsmouth, NH: Heinemann.

Healey, J. M. (1991). *Endangered Minds.* New York: Simon & Schuster.

Hearne, B. (1999). *Choosing books for children.* Urbana, IL: University of Illinois Press.

International Reading Association and the National Association for the Education of Young Children. (1998). *Learning to read and write: Developmentally appropriate practices for young children.* Newark, DE: International Reading Association.

Langer, J. A. (1995). *Envisioning literature: Literary understanding and literature instruction.* New York: Teachers College Press.

Meek, M. (1977). Introduction. In M. Meek, A. Warlow & G. Barton (Eds.), *The cool web: The pattern of children's reading.* London: Bodley Head.

National Council of Teachers of English and International Reading Association. (1996). *Standards for the English language arts.* Urbana, IL: National Council of Teachers of English.

Paterson, K. (1981). *The gates of excellence: On reading and writing books for children.* New York: Dutton.

Pressley, M. (2001, September). Comprehension instruction: What makes sense now, what might make sense soon. *Reading Online, 5* (2). 3–35

Rand Corporation. (2002). *Reading for understanding: Toward an R and D program in reading comprehension.* Washington, D.C.: Rand Corporation.

Rosenblatt, L. M. (1978). *The reader, the text, the poem: The transactional theory of the literary work.* Edwardsville: Southern Illinois University.

Rosenblatt, L. M. (1995). *Literature as exploration* (5th ed.). New York: Modern Language Association.

Sensenbaugh, R. (1997). Phonemic awareness: An important early step in learning to read. *ERIC Clearinghouse on Reading, English, and Communication Digest*, 119, 1–4

Serafini, F. (2003, February). Informing our practice: Modernist, transactional, and critical perspectives on children's literature and reading instruction. *Reading Online, 6* (6), 1–7

Short, K. (1993). Making connections across literature and life. In K. Holland, R. Hungerford, & S. Ernst (Eds.), *Journeying: Children responding to literature* (284–301). Portsmouth, NH: Heinemann.

Vygotsky, L. (1978). *Mind in society.* Cambridge, MA: Harvard University Press.

Weaver, C. (1994). *Reading process and practice.* Portsmouth, NH: Heinemann.

Weaver, C. (1998). *Reconsidering a balanced approach to reading instruction.* Urbana, IL: National Council of Teachers of English.

Wells, G.(1998, September). Some questions about direct instruction: Why? To whom? How? And when? *Language Arts, 76,* 27–35.

Wilks, S. (1995). *Critical and creative thinking.* Portsmouth, NH: Heinemann.

Understanding Literature 2

KEY TERMS

antagonist	nonfiction
chapter books	picture books
climax	poetry
conflict	plot
denouement	protagonist
elements of literature	realistic fiction
episode	schemata
fantasy	setting
foreshadowing	story grammar
historical fiction	style
literary convention	theme
literary genre	traditional literature

GUIDING QUESTIONS

What literary genres were your favorites in childhood? How have your tastes changed since childhood? What do you remember about the plot of recent books you have read?

1. What genre of literature is your favorite? Why is this your favorite?

2. Think about the plot and characters in the last book you read. How would you describe the plot? Who was the principal character? How was the character revealed?

3. How do the genre, plots, and characters in adult books differ from those in children's books?

4. How do the elements of literature influence readers' understanding of the books they read?

Genre is a French word that means kind or type. A genre approach to exploring literature emphasizes the pattern or structure of literary works that gives readers a structure for thinking about and understanding literature. Each genre has universal *literary conventions* that are elements of form, style, or content (Morner & Rausch, 1991). Books belonging to a specific genre share characteristics in plot, characters, settings, tone, mood, and theme (Van Vliet, 1992).

Genre patterns create rules for literary elements that are the same for children's literature and adult literature. As you read, refer to the touchstone books introduced throughout the chapter. The following vignette illustrates how teachers introduce a book and develop genre understanding with third-grade children. Research shows that students' ability to understand text and their motivation to read is increased when a teacher or librarian introduces a book (Koskinen et al., 1999).

Genre in Children's Literature

Children's literature is usually classified into these *literary genres*: contemporary realistic fiction, histori-

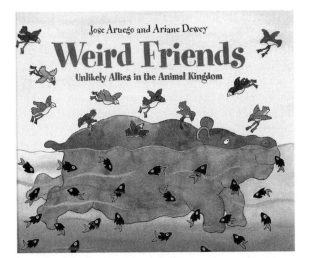

These weird friends help one another.

cal fiction, modern fantasy, traditional literature, poetry, biography, and informational books. Table 2.1 summarizes the basic distinguishing characteristics of each genre. Picture books include all genre; the stories in these books are told with words and pictures. Chapter books also belong to all genre. Experiences with literature enable children to recognize that nonfiction differs from fantasy. For example, authors of fantasy use elements of make-believe: perhaps a place where magical things happen, a futuristic time setting, or another fantastic element the author chooses to invent. They make unbelievable events acceptable to readers. Kevin Brockmeier created an appealing fantasy in the book *City of Names* by placing unbelievable events in an everyday setting and creating realistic characters who accepted these strange events.

Through reading and listening to a broad range of genres, children develop *schemata* (cognitive networks of knowledge and experience) that facilitate their understanding of literature (Applebee, 1978). This knowledge enables them to focus on the ways

Amanda spoke up, "I think it's fantasy because it couldn't happen."

"Why do you think that, Amanda?"

"Because there is no such thing as a clown fish or a horse mackerel, or a Portuguese man-of-war."

Andrew argued, "I disagree, because I saw a Portuguese man-of-war at the beach."

"I don't think that animals help each other like they do in this book," Lucy added.

Juanita asked, "How could we find out whether these animals actually exist?"

"Let's look it up on the world wide web," Joe said.

Tyler suggested, "We could use the Encarta Encyclopedia on the computer."

After doing some research, the children concluded that the book was based on real information; therefore, it could have happened. The following list of realistic characteristics was generated by the children:

- They tell real facts.
- They explain things like how animals help one another.
- They tell correct information.

Juanita placed the book on the reading table, so the children could read it and look at the pictures.

authors create stories, poems, and information. Children develop schemata and implicit understandings of genre through hearing and reading books with plot, character, setting, theme, and style. They use these schemata to construct meaning and predict outcomes (Kucan & Beck, 1996).

Picture books are perhaps the most recognizable book format in children's literature. In these books the story is told through pictures and words; neither could exist without the other, although wordless picture books tell their stories entirely in pictures. An incredibly funny fantasy, *The Boy Who Was Followed Home*, by Margaret Mahy features Robert, who was delighted when a hippo followed him home. His parents' agitation increased when 43 hippos arrived within days, but the solution to this problem delighted Robert and no one else.

Chapter books are short books that are excellent for younger children. These books, intended for children who are novice readers, feature simpler text and fewer illustrations than picture books. *Iris and Walter: The Sleepover* by Elissa Guest is a story told in four chapters. Iris and Walter are best friends and they look forward to a first sleepover, but Iris becomes homesick at bedtime.

Fantasy is characterized by one or more imaginary elements, such as a make-believe world, characters who have magic powers, time magic, or imaginary events. Imaginative language and visuals

TABLE 2.1

Distinguishing characteristics of various genres.

Genre	Distinguishing Characteristics
Contemporary Realistic Fiction	Could happen in the contemporary world
Historical Fiction	Set in the past
Modern Fantasy	Could not happen in the real world; science fiction is fantasy set in the future
Traditional Literature	Based on the oral tradition, the stories are spread through word of mouth rather than print
Poetry	Intense, imaginative writing in rhythmic language structured in shorter lines and verses
Biography	Based on the life of a person who has made a significant contribution to a culture
Informational Books	Present information, explain

mesh in Monika Bang-Campbell's *Little Rat Sets Sail*. Little Rat envisions the worst possible fate as she bravely embarks on sailing lessons which, of course, are imaginary. On her first sail she is joined by an engaging group of animal characters ensconced in life vests.

The characters in *contemporary realistic fiction* could be real, the settings could exist, and the plots could happen, although they are products of an author's imagination rather than actual history or fact (Morner & Rausch, 1991). *Third Grade Stinks!* by Colleen McKenna is a realistic fiction chapter book. In this story, Gordie's plans for third grade include sharing a locker with his friend, Lamont, but he is sabotaged when the new teacher assigns Lucy Diaz to the locker instead. Gordie makes plans to remove Lucy from his locker, but he is foiled at every turn.

In *historical fiction*, the author tells a story associated with historical events, characters, incidents, or time periods. However, historical setting alone is not enough to make the book worthwhile; it has to be a good story as well. The historical fiction in Brenda Woods' *The Red Rose Box* begins with life in the 1950s small town of Sulphur, Louisiana. When the central character, Leah Jean Hopper, visits Los Angeles, she discovers a whole new world of freedom where "Jim Crow" laws do not exist. The carefully developed historical settings for this story are in direct contrast with those found in fantasy. Historical fiction is discussed in Chapter 9.

Traditional literature is based on oral tradition: stories such as *Cinderella* which were passed from one generation to the next by word of mouth and were not written until the scholars collected these tales (Morner & Rausch, 1991). Among the oral conventions traditional stories share are formulaic beginnings and endings: "Once upon a time" and "They lived happily ever after." The settings are created in a sentence or two and the characters are stereotypes. *The Brave Little Seamstress*, Mary Pope Osborne's retelling of the Grimm Brothers' tale of the brave little tailor, features a little seamstress who is a stereotyped "good" character. The little seamstress tricks silly giants and foolish kings in order to acquire a knight and a castle. Traditional literature is discussed in Chapter 6.

Poetry is described as intense and imaginative literature. Poets strive to capture the essence of an experience in imaginative language. Christopher Myers captures the essence of a black street cat's life as it prowls through city thoroughfares in his poetic book, *Black Cat*. His focused and vivid free verse expresses the gritty reality of urban life, creating a greater concentration of meaning than is found in prose. Poetry differs visually from other types of literature in that it generally has short lines that may or may not rhyme and is written in verse form. Poetry is discussed in Chapter 5.

Nonfiction is organized and structured around main ideas and supporting details that present information and explain it in several styles, such as description, cause and effect, sequential order, comparison, and enumeration. Authors of nonfiction books identify key ideas and themes to grab readers' attention and motivate them to read more about the topic. Because informational books focus on actual events, places, people, and facts, authors and illustrators often use photographs and realistic drawings to illustrate these materials. For example, Donna Jackson used photographs of bugs to illustrate the fascinating book, *The Bug Scientists*, which encourages students to learn about the most successful creatures on the planet. Nonfiction is discussed in Chapter 10.

The vignette in the box on page 22 shows Jeremy, a fifth-grade student, using his knowledge of literary elements when reading a novel. Jeremy is an active reader

Only a scientist could love these bugs.

VIGNETTE

Jeremy Hamilton closed his copy of Robert Burleigh's *Black Whiteness* and thrust his hand in the air. His fifth-grade teacher, Robert Morse, asked, "What is it, Jeremy?"

"This book has just one character, but it has more than one conflict."

"Why do you think this?" asked Mr. Morse.

"Well, he fought the environment in the Antarctic, but he also battled loneliness, and he was so sick that he almost died, so he fought illness."

"Do you think *Black Whiteness* has more conflicts than other books you have read?" Mr. Morse responded.

Well, I just read *The Great Gilly Hopkins*," Jeremy said. "I guess it had several conflicts too, but there were more characters in it."

"What were the conflicts in that book?" Mr. Morse asked.

"Well Gilly had conflicts with Mrs. Trotter, Agnes, her teacher, and the social worker. Her mother and grandmother had conflicts. Oh! I just remembered. Gilly had conflicts within herself, too," he asked. "But, Richard Byrd's conflicts were not with people, they were with things that weren't obvious."

Mr. Morse asked, "Do Richard Byrd's conflicts seem less important than Gilly's?

"No, if anything they seem more important because they almost took his life and the conflicts were more difficult to battle than more concrete conflicts," Jeremy responded.

"How do you think the conflicts changed Richard Byrd?"

whose understanding of the language of narrative and narrative structure gave him this confidence (Tierney, 1990). He has developed a frame of reference for genre. Based on this, he anticipated that the story and the story conflict would make sense and he expected the author to say something of consequence, thereby focusing his comprehension (Adams & Collins, 1986).

Teachers use their knowledge of literary elements to guide students' explorations of the elements of fiction and nonfiction. The teacher in the vignette encouraged Jeremy to compare *Black Whiteness: Admiral Byrd Alone in the Antarctic* with a book of recognized quality to enlarge his understanding. Comparing and contrasting the ways that ideas are expressed in various literary forms and the characters, plots, settings, styles, and themes in a variety of books cultivate students' understanding of the *elements of literature* and enhance their appreciation of how the literary experience operates. Jeremy's teacher could have suggested that he enrich his understanding through comparing this book with fiction, nonfiction, biographies, or poetry on the same topic.

Literary Elements

Joseph Conrad (1922) states that the novelist's aim is "to make you hear, to make you feel—it is, before all, to make you see." Authors employ narrative style to help readers see their stories (Hardy, 1977). In much the same way that readers use their own lives as a basis for understanding literature, writers create plot, character, setting, and theme out of their own experiences. Authors create coherent sequences highlighting dramatic events to tell an exciting story. Even when telling true or nonfiction stories, writers organize the events that would otherwise be too chaotic to form a coherent story. In the process, they take liberties with reality, just as memories do when we reflect on experiences. We remember the high points in life—the dramatic events.

Plot

A *plot* is a chain of interacting events, as in our own lives. Each of us is involved in many plots as our lives unfold. These various plots, based on our own experiences, are the raw material for stories. Each story leads to another because life happens that way. Children need books where the story is at the center of the writer's attention, and where the plot matters (Wadham, 1999). The plot holds the story together, making it a critical element in fiction. Wyndham and Madison (1988) describe plot as "a plan of action devised to achieve a definite and much desired end—through cause and effect" (p. 81). Their definition is similar to Giblin's (1990), who calls plot the blueprint of the story, or the path it will follow from beginning to end.

In developing plot, the author weaves a logical series of events explaining why events occur. In *Where the Wild Things Are,* Maurice Sendak tells readers that Max was sent to bed without his supper because he acted like a "wild thing," which initiated the cause-and-

Gooney Bird Greene

LOIS LOWRY *Illustrated by* Middy Thomas

Gooney Bird Greene likes to be in the middle of things.

effect chain in this adroitly woven plot. "A well-crafted plot, like some remarkable clockwork, can fascinate us by its sheer ingenuity" (Alexander, 1981, p. 5). Credible plots unfold gradually, building a logical cause-and-effect sequence for story incidents. Story events inserted without adequate preparation make a contrived and uninteresting plot. Interesting plots usually have unique characteristics to grab children's attention.

Story characters act out the causes and effects of story incidents. *Cause* establishes the main character's line of action to solve a problem, get out of a situation, or reach a certain goal; *effect* is what happens to the character as a result of the action taken. Storytellers can make all sorts of imaginary events credible by laying the groundwork for them (Alexander, 1981). *Foreshadowing* is the groundwork that prepares for future story events through planted clues in situations, events, characters, and conflicts. In *Gooney Bird Greene* by Lois Lowry, foreshadowing occurs immediately when Gooney Bird arrives in the second grade from Paris (Texas), sporting an unusual hair style, unusual clothing, and an unusual lunch. Then she an-

nounces, "I want a desk right smack in the middle of the room because I like to be right smack in the middle of everything." This dramatic entrance signals that Gooney Bird is a character to watch.

Conflict

Story conflicts increase tension to arouse suspense (Giblin, 1990). The characters in stories with interesting plots have difficulties to overcome, problems to solve, and goals to achieve. Believable conflicts and problems provide the story with shape, movement, tension, and drama. *Conflict* is "the struggle that grows out of the interplay of two opposing forces in a plot" (Holman & Harmon, 1986, p. 107). One of these opposing forces is usually the main character in the story, who struggles to get what he or she wants and is vigorously opposed, either by someone who wants the same thing or by circumstances that stand in the way of the goal (Wyndham & Madison, 1988).

A conflict implies struggle, but it also suggests that motivation exists behind the conflict or a goal that can be achieved through the conflict. The central problem or conflict must remain out of the main character's reach until near the end of the story. Nevertheless, readers are aware that a fateful decision is at hand that will precipitate a crisis in the principal character's affairs, although the outcome of this struggle is never certain.

Chris Van Allsburg creates an unusual and suspenseful conflict in *Jumanji*. Tension is introduced early in the story through a note warning the principal characters that once they begin playing a jungle-adventure board game they cannot stop until the game is completed. Heedless of the warning, the children play the game, which rapidly gets out of hand as a python appears on the mantle and a rhinoceros crashes through the living room. They desperately need to stop the game—their parents are returning and the house is in chaos!

Types of conflict. *Jumanji* introduces the struggle against another person or situation, which is one of the four major types of conflict that writers commonly use. These types of conflict are summarized in the following list:

1. a struggle against nature;
2. a struggle against another person, usually the antagonist;

3. a struggle against society; and

4. a struggle for mastery by two elements within the person (Holman & Harmon, 1986).

Although the four types of conflict are distinct in literature, most stories have more than one type of conflict. In *Hatchet*, Gary Paulsen tells the story of a boy fighting to obtain food and shelter to survive (struggle with nature) after he survives a crash that kills the pilot of the plane. His struggle is one of trial and error because he lacks the knowledge that would help him, but his perseverance enables him to survive. This character also experiences internal conflicts due to his parents' divorce plans.

Mikey Donovan, the protagonist in Graham Salisbury's *Lord of the Deep*, experiences complex situations that produce several conflicts. Mikey's idolized stepfather makes an unethical decision shaking Mikey's faith, which creates Mikey's internal conflict. A conflict between man and nature develops on the fishing boat due to the mighty struggle between a fisherman and the marlin.

Climax

The protagonist's most intense struggle occurs at the *climax*, which is the highest point of interest in the story, the point at which readers learn how the conflict is resolved. A strong conflict keeps readers turning pages to discover whether the protagonist makes the right decision. Richard Peck's book, *A Year Down Yonder*, is a real page turner. Several conflicts and a zany grandma keep this hilarious story, set is 1937, moving. As the depression is winding down, Mary Alice, the protagonist, lives with crazy Grandma Dowdel because her father lost his job. Mary Alice faces many conflicts, such as sleeping in the attic alone, attending a hick town school where she is known as a rich girl from Chicago, and having a Grandma who expects her to be an accomplice in her outrageous schemes. By the climax, Mary Alice discovers she is a strong person who loves her Grandma.

Denouement

Denouement is the falling action that occurs during the unwinding of the story problem after the climax. This part of the story ties up the various threads of the plot into a satisfying, logical ending, although not neces-

sarily a "happily ever after" ending. Jack and his tiger, Lily, live in a lovely apartment and do everything together in Diane Goode's *Tiger Trouble*. Their life is perfect until the terrible day when a grumpy new landlord demands that Lily move out of the building. However, Lily saves the day when she catches burglars who are robbing the grumpy man. The denouement is satisfying because Lily becomes a hero.

Types of plot

Dramatic and episodic plots are the most common types of plot structure, but several others also appear in children's books, such as parallel plot and cumulative plot. These are often associated with traditional literature and picture books.

Dramatic plot. **Dramatic plots** establish setting, characters, and conflicts with fast-moving action that grabs children's attention and creates enough tension to hold their interest until the exciting climax. (Figure 2.1 illustrates a dramatic plot line.) Vivien Alcock creates a good dramatic plot in the mystery *Stranger at the Window*. She quickly establishes tension when 11-year-old Lesley sees a strange child peering at her from the attic next door. The tension in this book grows when three neighbor children accuse Lesley of hallucinating. However, their secret is soon revealed—they are hiding a frightened illegal immigrant.

Episodic plot. **Episodic plots** are quite similar to dramatic plots. The major difference is that in an episodic plot each chapter or part has its own "mini-plot," or a story within the main story. Each *episode* or incident is at least loosely linked to the same main character or characters, has a problem relating to the total book, and is unified by the common theme of

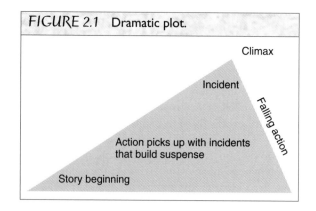

FIGURE 2.1   Dramatic plot.

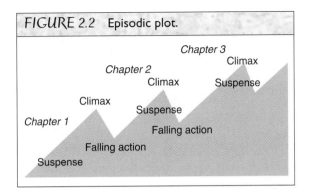

FIGURE 2.2 Episodic plot.

the main story. (Figure 2.2 illustrates an episodic plot.) In Susan Wojciechowski's *Beany Goes to Camp*, Beany resists going to camp; nevertheless, she is doomed to go there. Through a series of episodes Beany grows to like her cabinmate and discovers camping is all right.

Parallel plot. *Parallel plots* include two plots that unfold side by side. These plots usually are intertwined into a single story as the book winds down, so that the intertwining may occur near the story's climax. Carl Hiaasen used parallel plots to tell the story of *Hoot*. One plot line is told from the point of view of a middle school boy named Roy, and the other plot line develops from the point of view of a policeman named Dana. The connection between the plots gradually emerges as the story evolves.

Cumulative plot. *Cumulative plots* unfold through a pattern of repetition in which characters or events are added to each other, with each new character or event paralleling a previous character or event, building toward a climax that solves the problem. Cumulative plot stories, which usually appear in traditional literature or picture books such as *The Three Little Pigs* often contain repeated refrains.

Circular plot. *Circular plots* unfold with the story starting in one place before departing from that point, the climax then returns to the beginning point. The central character usually leaves the beginning point to solve a problem. He or she may return to the beginning because the problem is resolved. *Gold Fever* by Verla Kay illustrates a circular plot. Jasper, a farmer, decides that he would rather dig for gold than farm. He leaves for the California gold fields, but discovers that digging for gold is harder than farming. He returns to his farm with a sense of contentment.

Characters

Skillful authors create believable, memorable characters (Holman & Harmon, 1986). Readers care about believable characters with whom they can identify and feel truly involved. A variety of strategies make characters live and breathe in readers' minds. One is telling the details of a character's thoughts, feelings, motivations, and attitudes. Another is depicting characters in ways that are consistent with their social background, educational level, and age. Portraying the human qualities, emotions, desires, hopes, dreams, and motivations that distinguish characters as individuals creates memorable characters.

Characters are essential to stories because they propel the plot. They are the driving force behind the story that makes things happen and the actors who direct and act out the plot. In Patricia Reilly Giff's *Pictures of Hollis Woods,* readers meet an artistic girl, Hollis Woods, who has lived in foster homes her entire life. She is a moving force in the story. Hollis has run away from every foster home, including the one home that she liked and where she was wanted. As she is driven to yet another foster home, Hollis plans to once again run away. However, she discovers that she likes her foster mother, an elderly artist named Josie. Hollis then realizes that she must attend school in order to remain in Josie's home.

Developing characters

Like many chapter books, *What Jamie Saw* by Carolyn Coman includes several characters, but the *protagonist,* Jamie, is the focus of the plot. As the central character, Jamie is presented in greater detail than the other characters. Such detailed information usually leads readers to identify with and follow this character throughout the story. Jamie is a well-developed protagonist with three-dimensional characteristics. He has a complex, multifaceted personality that readers come to know as they learn about his individual traits through the trouble in his life, which never runs smoothly. If there were no trouble, there would be no story (Wyndham & Madison, 1988).

Many readers can relate to Jamie's fear of Van in *What Jamie Saw* after he wakens Jamie by throwing his baby sister. Van is the *antagonist* in this story, the character who is in conflict with the protagonist. The antagonist is sometimes a villain and sometimes a foil character, one whose traits provide a complete contrast to those of the protagonist. An antagonist lends excitement and suspense to a story, but is developed with less detail than a protagonist.

Supporting characters

Not all the characters are developed with the same depth as the protagonist. Supporting characters are flat because they lack the depth and complexity of a real person. These characters are built around a single dominant trait or quality representing a personality type (Morner & Rausch, 1991). Flat characters are needed as part of the interactive background; their primary function is to advance the protagonist's development. Fully portraying these characters would make the story too complex for children. Supporting characters often include the protagonist's best friend, a teacher, or parents. In *What Jamie Saw,* his mother, teacher, baby sister, and Earl are flat characters.

Some flat characters are stereotypes who lack individualizing characteristics and instead represent traits generally attributed to a social group as a whole (Morner & Rausch, 1991). They exhibit a few traits representative of conventional mothers, fathers, friends, or teachers and are developed quickly with brief bits of information so that drawing their characters does not interrupt the story flow. In traditional literature, all characters are stereotypes representing traits such as good, evil, innocence, and wisdom.

Dynamic and static characters

Dynamic characters. *Dynamic* or *developed characters* change significantly during the course of a story as incidents cause their personalities to emerge and expand. In *What Jamie Saw,* seeing Van throw his baby sister forever changes Jamie, and his continuing nightmares about the experience show its dramatic force.

Static characters. *Static* or *delineated story characters* are the opposite of developed characters. They seem impervious to experience and remain essentially the same throughout the story. These are the "Peter Pan" characters who never grow up. The principal character in Astrid Lindgren's *Pippi Longstocking* is static. Pippi, a 9-year-old Swedish girl, is well-rounded and fully described. She lives alone with a monkey and a horse and has many novel adventures. Pippi never changes; she remains irrepressible as ever.

Character interaction

Authors may use any number of characterizations that work together to create vivid and interesting stories. In Stephanie Tolan's *Surviving the Applewhites*, Jake Semple clashes with everyone he encounters. After he is kicked out of every school he enters, Jake is enrolled in the Applewhites' home school. Jake's character is revealed through his encounters with the Applewhite family. For example, E. D. Applewhite contrasts with Jake. E. D. is an orderly, responsible, hardworking student. Through his relationship with 4-year-old Destiny, Jake learns to be responsible for a child. One of his greatest insights occurs when he realizes that Destiny will never become a juvenile delinquent because he has nothing to rebel against.

Getting to know the story characters

Readers come to know characters the way they come to know an acquaintance—from the way the person talks and acts, the way the characters interact with others, and their reactions to and thoughts about the character. Character traits are revealed through a number of narration techniques. First-person narration, in which the main character is usually the narrator, allows readers to infer traits from what the main character says and how others react. Similarly, a limited narrator may tell the story from the main character's point of view. An omniscient narrator, however, may tell all about the main character and also tell about others from their points of view.

Patricia Reilly Giff reveals Hollis Woods, the central character in *Pictures of Hollis Woods*, through her conversations with a social worker; her foster parent, Josie; and the cat, Henry; as well as her thoughts about her past year living with the Regan family. At the end of this book, Hollis returns to the Regan family and, through their actions and conversations, readers learn how much she loves them and they love her.

The book *Surviving the Applewhites* includes a wide array of characters who interact with Jake Semple. Jake's thoughts in the following extract reveal how he views himself:

> Jake was beginning to feel he was disappearing altogether. Nobody except E. D. and Destiny noticed when he swore. Nothing he's done before to show people who he was and what he stood for worked here. He couldn't even chill out the way he used to. No TV to watch. His Walkman was useless without earphones.

If he dared to smoke where he could be seen, some-body was sure to snatch away his cigarette. (p. 85)

Authors often use conversations to help readers know characters; manner of speaking and subject matter are revealing, especially when combined with the characters' actions. A character's traits may be revealed through conversation with another character.

In the following extract, Jake is talking with E. D. Applewhite.

"Better not light that thing," she said.

The boy reached into his pocket and pulled out a yellow plastic lighter. "You can't have a smoke-free environment outdoors," he said.

"We can have it anywhere we want—this is our property, all sixteen acres of it."

Jake looked her square in the eye and lit the cigarette. He took a long drag and blew the smoke directly into her face so that she had to close her eyes and hold her breath to keep from choking on it. (pp. 5–6)

Character traits, descriptions, and actions are usually developed through illustrations and language in picture books. In these books, the words and the pictures are integrated to reveal character. Kathryn Lasky's *Marven of the Great North Woods,* is set in Duluth, Minnesota, in 1918. Marven's family sends him away to keep him safe from the raging influenza epidemic. Readers see Marven going off alone on a train headed for a logging camp, not knowing if he will ever see his family again. The illustrations show a small boy among the enormous woodsmen, and the endless snow creates a feeling of lonliness.

Setting

Setting is the story's time and place. Vivid settings give a story reality; they give readers a sense of being there. The importance of setting varies from story to story. In some it creates the stage for the characters' actions, whereas in others it is indefinite, a universal setting that is secondary to the story. The story itself dictates the importance of setting.

When creating setting, authors choose a location (an urban, rural, or small town and a country) and time (past, present, or future). Contemporary settings take place in the here and now, whereas historical settings occur in a time and place that previously occurred. Historical settings often require extensive research. In *Fair Weather*, Richard Peck researched the 1893 Columbian

Exposition to create authentic images. He found actual photographs of the Exposition to use in the book.

Once the general location and time are identified, authors decide on the details of a specific time and place: perhaps a very specific designation such as a certain district in London, England, in the summer of 1993, or a more universal setting requiring fewer details and a more indefinite time and place. Time and location dictate many of the story's other details: the type of home and furniture, the scenery, and the flora and fauna of the surrounding countryside. The social environment, foods, newspapers, magazines, and games are all aspects of the setting.

In fantasy, the time and place of a story may be a make-believe setting that no one has ever seen. Writers of fantasy create imaginary worlds, people, and events. For instance, Philippa Pearce creates a clock that strikes 13, signaling the appearance of a garden that does not exist at other times, in *Tom's Midnight Garden*. This fantasy garden is a playground for Tom and his friend, who is an old woman during the day and a young girl at night when she plays in the garden.

Illustrations develop setting in some books, whereas others portray it through words. Some stories are closely tied to the setting, whereas others are not. Kate Banks' book *And if the Moon Could Talk* is closely related to setting; Georg Hallensleben's paintings combine with the language to convey the mood of nightfall.

Settings for fantasy are a special challenge: authors must not only imagine places and times that do not exist, but they must make readers see them, as Donn Kushner does in the following excerpt from *A Book Dragon*:

Nonesuch was—and still is, for that matter—the last of a family of dragons that lived over five hundred years ago in a limestone hill, honeycombed with caverns. . . . The dark mouth of the family's cavern opened towards an ugly tangled scrub forest that ended, at the lap of the hill, in an evil bog. (p. 2)

Mood

The mood or tone of a story is created through the setting. The author uses words and the artist uses illustrations to create the feelings readers should experience. Consider the following excerpt from Ruth White's *Sweet Creek Holler*:

The holler was skinny between the mountains. The road was chiseled out of the side of one mountain base. . . . Houses were stuck on the sides of the hills, many with stilts underneath to prop them up level. Some were made of cinder blocks, a few were white-board, or brick, but most of them were tar-paper shacks. (p. 6)

The words and phrases used here—such as *skinny, chiseled, stuck, sides of the hills,* and *tar-paper shacks*—create a feeling for the hard life in a depressed area of the United States. These words and phrases express the author's interpretation of the significance of the place and time. Moreover, the author's language reflects the tone and theme of the story.

Theme

The *theme* is defined as the point, the message, or the central idea that underlies a book. In poetry, fiction, and drama, it is the abstract concept that is made concrete through the characters, plots, mood, and images created. The theme of a story has both a subject and a predicate; it tells what the book means. Another way of explaining theme is that it expresses "lessons about life" (Barton, 2001). For example, in Kate DiCamillo's *Because of Winn-Dixie,* one theme is Opal's yearning for the mother she has never known. Another theme is the way Opal creates a community of friends who give her support and fellowship. The author posits this message which has both a subject (Opal's yearning) and a position (friends giving) on the subject (Holman & Harmon, 1986).

Fine writers weave theme subtly into their stories. Children, like adults, prefer authors who trust their readers to infer theme from story events, characters, and setting rather than preaching or explicitly stating the theme. Patricia Reilly Giff expresses the theme of searching for a place to belong in *Pictures of Hollis Woods.* Two other themes emerge from this story: the importance of family and the importance of artistic vision and creativity. Every event and every character in the story resonates with these themes.

Multiple themes

Literature usually has multiple themes. Moreover, different readers discover different messages in the same story, because readers' schemata influence the themes they identify in a specific book (Barton, 2001). Carl Hiaasen's *Hoot* contains several themes. First, Roy Eberhardt, the protagonist, is the new kid in school—again. Second, he stumbles into an effort to save en-dangered burrowing owls from bungling adults. Third, he discovers that school bullies do serve a greater purpose in the world. Fourth, he makes friends as he works to save the burrowing owls. Carl Hiaasen, the author, points out that he wrote the book as a parody of the state of Florida because he reveals the good and bad of that state. Children may also discover other themes in this novel.

The most common themes in children's books are associated with fundamental human needs, including:

1. the need to love and be loved;
2. the need to belong;
3. the need to achieve;
4. the need for security—material, emotional, spiritual; and
5. the need to know (Wyndham & Madison, 1988).

These universal themes are expressed through the ideas, characters, plots, and settings developed in fiction, nonfiction, and poetry.

Children's response to theme

Building meaning is a complex developmental process. A 3-year-old understands a story differently than an 8-year-old; younger children can, however, identify theme. In kindergarten, children are "able to identify thematically matched books 80% of the time for realistic fiction and 35% for folktales, thus indicating that thematic identification is a fairly early developmental strategy," although older children are better able to talk about the themes in stories (Lehr, 1991, p. 67).

Themes are subject to readers' interpretation; therefore, they are open to individual responses. Nevertheless, the dominant idea or theme should be apparent to readers. Individuals respond differently to the same story because response is based on individual experience; readers use their schemata to interpret and understand the material. Individuals remember what is important to them and see what they expect to see or are capable of seeing. Readers who have experiences with their fathers' girlfriends may interpret *Totally Uncool* by Janice Levy in different ways: those who have had positive experiences with the new people in their parents' lives would respond differently from those who have had negative experiences. The varying responses of students are explored in greater depth in Chapter 15.

Many stories offer readers opportunities to respond at different levels of understanding. They can take as much or as little from literature as their developmental levels and experiential backgrounds permit. For example, Carl Hiaasen's book *Hoot* has several thematic layers. At the highest level, readers may recognize the story as satire revealing "the good, the bad, and the screwy state of Florida" (dust jacket). Readers at another level will identify the struggles of a boy who has been the "new kid" many, many times. Another theme is the way children have to guide bungling adults in some situations.

Theme and topic

Theme is concerned with the central idea, or meaning, of a literary work. Topic, however, may be thought of as the general subject of discussion or discourse. For example, a topic or subject could be "Saving endangered animals" (*Hoot*), while a "life lesson" would be Hollis's yearning to belong to a family. No proper theme is simply a subject or an activity.

Style

Authors express their *style* through the language they use to shape their stories: the words they choose, the sentences they craft, the dialogue they create, and the amount and nature of the descriptive passages. Authors arrange words in ways that express their individuality. "Style is a combination of the two elements: the idea to be expressed and the individuality of the author" (Holman & Harmon, 1986, p. 487). No two styles are exactly alike. Ultimately, the author's use of language determines the lasting quality of a book.

Language devices

Author style is most apparent in the language devices used to achieve special effects or meanings, stimulating their readers through use of figurative language, imagery, allusion, hyperbole, understatement, and symbolism. Readers then use these devices to infer and connote individual interpretations based upon their experiential background. *Connotation* refers to an association or emotional response a reader attaches to a particular word that goes beyond the dictionary definition, or *denotation*; it is a meaning drawn from personal experience. For example, many people associate warm, loving feelings with the word *mother* that go far beyond the literal denotation of a female parent.

Figurative language. Figurative language is connotative, sensory language that incorporates one or more of the various figures of speech such as simile, metaphor, repetition, and personification (Holman & Harmon, 1986). Figurative language is used to develop character, show mood, and create setting. Katherine Paterson uses figurative language to great effect in *The Great Gilly Hopkins.* Gilly moves to Mrs. Trotter's home, the latest in a long line of foster homes. There she meets William Ernest, another foster child living in the same home: "He was rattling the tray so hard that the milk glass was threatening to jump the edge" (p. 47). Paterson's figurative language vividly shows that William Ernest is a scared, nervous, timid person.

Her figurative language also creates mood when she describes Gilly's new foster home: "Inside, it was dark and crammed with junk. Everything seemed to need dusting" (p. 4). The words *dark, junk,* and *dust* have connotative meanings for most people that conjure visions of a dank, uninviting place. This clearly gives the reader a sense of Gilly's negative feelings about her new foster home without explicitly stating "Gilly had negative feelings about her new home," which is a drab and uninteresting way of conveying meaning.

Imagery. Sensory language widens the mind's eye and helps the reader build images that go beyond the ordinary to new and exciting experiences. These experiences can be the sensory kind in which one sees or hears new things, or they can be an intellectual kind in which one thinks new things. Dr. Seuss's book *Hooray for Diffendoofer Day!* illustrates the role of imagery. In this noisy book the pages are full of movement and unusual, dramatic characters such as the teacher who teaches yelling and the one who teaches smelling!

Allusion. *Allusion* is a figure of speech that makes indirect reference to a historical or literary figure, event, or object (Holman & Harmon, 1986). In *The Great Gilly Hopkins*, Gilly alludes to godfathers and the Mafia in reference to William Ernest, but it is the direct contrast to William Ernest's timid personality that makes the idea even funnier. "An inspiration came to [Gilly]. . . . It was William Ernest. She laughed out loud at the pleasure of it. Baby-Face Teague, the frog-eyed filcher. Wild-eyed William, the goose-brained godfather. . . . The midget of the Mafia" (p. 48). Paterson also uses allusion to describe Mrs. Trotter: "Trotter smiled impatiently and closed the door quickly. When she turned back toward Gilly, her face was like Mount Rushmore stone" (p. 97), thereby demonstrating that Trotter is impassive to Gilly's efforts to antagonize her.

Hyperbole.   *Hyperbole* is exaggeration used to make a point, as shown in this passage: "Gilly gave her the 300-watt smile that she had designed for melting the hearts of foster parents. 'Never better!' She spoke the words with just the right musical lilt" (p. 48). In this instance, the size and impact of Gilly's smile and the sound of her voice are exaggerated to make the point that she is trying to be congenial with her foster parent.

Understatement.   *Understatement* is almost the opposite of hyperbole. It plays down a situation or person and is often used for comic effect. Gilly deliberately wrecks her own hair with chewing gum to antagonize Mrs. Trotter, who ignores it. Gilly then shakes her head dramatically to draw attention, to which Mrs. Trotter calmly says, "You got a tic or something, honey?" (p. 18). Mrs. Trotter's understatement creates a comical situation—she appears not to notice Gilly's dreadful hair—which is embellished as Gilly tries to remove the chewing gum, further ruining her hair.

Symbolism.   *Symbols* express deeper meanings in children's literature (Barton, 2001). They can be persons, objects, situations, actions, or words that operate on two levels of meaning. A symbol has both a literal meaning—a concrete meaning—and an inferential meaning, one that is implied. Gilly's mother is described as a "flower child," which literally refers to someone who lived a free-spirited lifestyle in the 1960s, but Paterson uses the phrase as a symbol in two separate instances: (1) "Miss Ellis suddenly looked tired. 'God help the children of the flower children,' she said" (p. 119); and (2) "Her hair was long, but it was dull and stringy—a dark version of Agnes Stokes's, which had always needed washing. A flower child gone to seed" (p. 145). In the first instance, Paterson implies that the children of flower children need help that will not be forthcoming from these free spirits. The second suggests that Gilly's mother is stuck in an adolescent stage of development and continues to live as she did in her younger days, in spite of the fact that she is growing older.

Point of view

Point of view is the perspective or stance from which the author tells a story. It is the eye and mind through which the action is perceived (Morner & Rausch, 1991). The point of view determines the vocabulary, sentences, and attitudes expressed. Essentially, authors can use two general narrative points of view, first person and third person. A first-person narrator actually appears within the story and tells the tale using the pronoun "I." The first-person point of view has some advantages; one is its conversational nature, which makes readers feel they know the narrator. First-person narrators tell the reader what they are thinking and feeling, giving readers an intimate experience. Plot, setting, and character are more likely to be unified when the main character says, "This is what happened to me, this is where it happened, this is how I felt" (Sebesta & Iverson, 1975, p. 78).

Linda Sue Park chose first-person narration for the central characters in *When my Name was Keoko*. This stylistic choice is appropriate because she is narrating her own experiences and those of her brother in a parallel plot. Each person tells of his or her experiences during the Japanese occupation of Korea during World War II, at which time all Koreans had to choose a Japanese name.

A third-person narrator, unlike a first-person narrator, stands outside the story and tells the tale using pronouns such as *he, she,* and *they*. Third-person narration has two commonly used variations: omniscient perspective and limited omniscient perspective. Children's literature most frequently uses omniscient perspective to tell stories.

With omniscient perspective, the narrator sees all, knows all, and reveals all to the reader. This narrator has access to and reveals the thoughts and motives of all the characters; knows the present, past, and future; and also comments on or interprets the actions

A visual journey reveals America's beauty.

of all of the characters. A major advantage of this style lies in the freedom a narrator has in unfolding the story. For instance, authors can speak directly to readers, telling whatever they choose to tell or speaking over the heads of the characters in an aside to help readers understand the significance of an event or a character (Sebesta & Iverson, 1975). The omniscient style appears in this quotation from Betsy Byars' *Little Horse*, "Instead of pushing him toward the rocks as he had hoped, the swirling current bore him around the bend" (p.12). Throughout this story, the narrator makes asides to the reader that reveal his or her feelings.

Narrators with limited omniscience, however, focus on the thoughts of a single character and present the other characters externally (Morner & Rausch, 1991). In this approach, the author typically follows one character throughout the story. The reader knows only what this one character knows and sees only those incidents in which that character is involved. Judy Cox uses this style in her book *Third Grade Pet.* Rosemary, the main character, is revolted when the class chooses a rat as a pet, but it gets worse. She is chosen to be "Rat keeper, for a whole week. It was like a nightmare come true" (p. 41). Rosemary changes her mind about the rat as she cares for it.

Literary Experiences that Enhance Understanding

Literary experiences can motivate children to read, as well as enhance their understanding. Getting to know authors, as well as their experiences, writing techniques, and interests, are among the most powerful literary experiences. Authors make their stories come alive with details, stylistic devices, genre, and the elements of literature. What writers create comes from hearsay, incidents, people, places, and truths they have experienced. Betsy Byars (1993) says, "I always put something of myself into my books, something that happened to me. Once . . . a wanderer came by the house and showed me how to brush my teeth with a cherry twig. That went in *The House of Wings.*"

Many writers describe themselves as storytellers. Paula Fox (1991) says:

> I am a storyteller and I have been one for more than 30 years. When I finish one story, I watch the drift in my head, and very soon am thinking about another story. All one's experience shapes one's stories.

VIGNETTE

MY FIRST AUTHOR VISIT

Watching children in a local bookstore waiting to meet an author brought to mind my own first meeting with an author, Elizabeth Yates, at Ohio State University in the summer of 1963. She told about discovering the tombstone in a church cemetery that piqued her curiosity and her research that led her to write *Amos Fortune: Free Man.* I listened spellbound, as did everyone in the large audience.

Later someone asked where she got the ideas for her other books, and she shifted to talk about a forthcoming book, *Carolina's Courage,* and a buffalo-hide doll belonging to a little girl she knew. The doll, a family heirloom, was handed down from generation to generation along with the story of its origins. This doll and the family story became the impetus for *Carolina's Courage.* Later she told the story of another book that was based on a short newspaper clipping.

Of course, I eagerly read every book that Elizabeth Yates wrote. I thought about the ways she found ideas for her stories and the research she did to validate these stories. But, most of all, the beauty of her language and voice in telling the stories made me want to help children experience the same excitement I felt that day. . . .

However, readers expect authors to take them "there" to help them recreate the writer's reality; what matters is what they make of it—what they do with it.

Simply reporting incidents and characters as they took place is not enough to draw in readers; the author must create illusions with the facts. Illusion—what writers make of their experiences—must convince readers that it is reality by resonating with their emotions and moving them to new feelings and insights (Alexander, 1981). The preceding vignette illustrates how getting acquainted with authors enhances the literary experience.

Discussion as Literary Experience

Although reading seems like a solitary activity, its social aspects become apparent when readers discuss their literary experiences. When a group of seven or eight students discusses a book they have all read, they stimulate one another to think about the story, enhancing the understanding and response of each person in the group. Moreover, each time a different group of children discusses a story, they bring up ideas that no one has mentioned.

Literary Experiences

The best literature-based activities are those that grow naturally out of the literature and relate to the plot, theme, setting, characters, or style of the book. Activities that grow out of the literature encourage students to think critically and enable readers to demonstrate or share their response to the book. Later chapters discuss experiencing literature in much greater detail.

When working on developing an understanding of genre, select titles that are clear examples of the genre being studied. Picture books are useful for developing genre activities because they are appealing as well as clear and direct examples for teaching genre. They are also useful for developing an understanding of plot, theme, style, characterization, setting, and style. The suggested activities are suitable for individuals, pairs, small groups, or whole classes. Figure 2.3 is a map of literary activities.

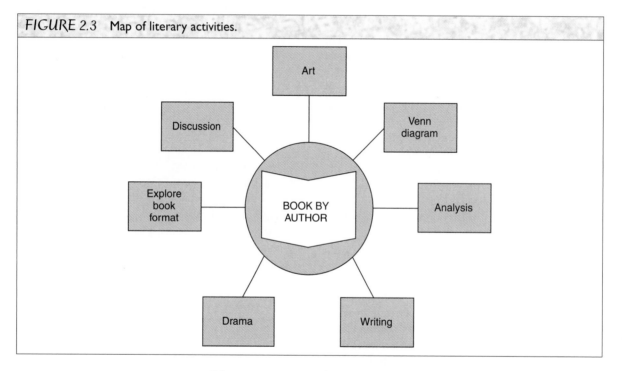

FIGURE 2.3   Map of literary activities.

Classroom Activities

ACTIVITY 2.1   LITERARY ELEMENTS

(IRA/NCTE Standards: 3, 6, 11. Develop comprehension, genre, elements of literature, and vocabulary in this specific book, science and conservation.)

This activity deals with analyzing the literary elements of a piece of realistic fiction. Although all of the elements are mentioned here, in an actual classroom you would probably choose to discuss only one of the elements, such as plot, characterization, or setting. This realistic fiction could be compared with a fantasy to clarify the genre characteristics.

Book: *Hoot* by Carl Hiaasen

1. Introduce the book, asking questions to help students predict the elements.

   A. What might the title indicate about the story?

   B. What can the dust jacket help you predict about it?

   C. Where do you think the story takes place? Who is the main character? How old is the main character?

2. Have students silently read the story.

3. Discuss the story with the students, encouraging them to think about the plot. Discuss the parallel plot in this book.

   A. Describe Roy at the beginning of the story. How does he change in the story? What events caused him to change?

   B. Describe Officer Delenko at the beginning of the story. How has he changed at the end of the story?

   C. Why did Roy say, "Dana was just a big stupid bully; the world was full of them"?

   D. What is the theme of this story? What makes you think this is the theme?

   E. What is the climax in this story? Did the story end the way you thought it would?

   F. What are the comical events in this story?

   G. Now that you have read the story, what do you think the significance of the title is?

   H. Describe Carl Hiaasen's writing style in this book.

4. Use extension activities to allow students to respond to the story.

   A. Make a time line for this story that shows its key events.

   B. Write a note to the President thanking him for the visit.

   C. Write a review for this book that will cause another person to want to read it.

   D. Read *Surviving the Applewhites* and compare the characters with those in *Hoot* or read *Mary Ann Alice* by Brian Doyle and compare the plots in these stories.

ACTIVITY 2.2   STORY GRAMMAR

(IRA/NCTE Standards: 3, 11, 12. Comprehension, genre, elements of literature, and vocabulary.)

A *story grammar* is a set of rules that describes the possible structures of well-formed stories (Rumelhart, 1975; Stein & Glenn, 1979). Most researchers agree that story grammars include character, setting, a problem or conflict, and a series of one or more episodes. Story grammars give readers a way of describing and discussing what they read, which helps refine their comprehension and gives them a means of organizing their recollections.

The story grammar in this activity is based on Audrey Wood's *The Red Racer*. In this book, Nona has an old, worn-out bicycle; the neighborhood kids call it a junker. She wants a new Deluxe Red. Nona's parents say they will not buy a new bicycle. After studying this story grammar have students create a story grammar to learn about plot (see Figure 2.4).

FIGURE 2.4   Story grammar.

Book:	*The Red Racer* by Audrey Wood
Setting:	Any small town in the United States; contemporary.
Characters:	Nona, her parents, neighborhood kids, adult neighbors.
Problem:	Nona needs a new bicycle, but her parents won't buy one.
Efforts to solve the problem (also called events):	1. Nona put the bike in the town dump. 2. Nona pushed the bike off the pier. 3. Nona put the bike on the railroad tracks.
Resolution:	Nona's bike is not crushed by the train. Her parents fix up her bicycle to make it look new like a Red Racer.

ACTIVITY 2.3   COMPARE CHARACTERS OR SETTING, IN A VENN DIAGRAM.

(IRA/NCTE Standards: 2, 3. Compare/contrast to comprehend.)

In this example, the characters are compared from *The Other Way to Listen* by Byrd Baylor and *Gold Fever* by Verla Kay (see Figure 2.5).

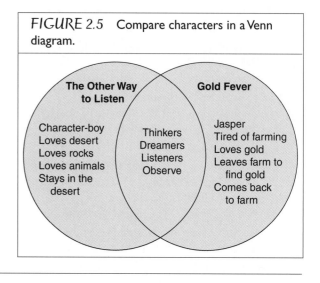

FIGURE 2.5   Compare characters in a Venn diagram.

The Other Way to Listen
Character-boy
Loves desert
Loves rocks
Loves animals
Stays in the desert

Thinkers
Dreamers
Listeners
Observe

Gold Fever
Jasper
Tired of farming
Loves gold
Leaves farm to find gold
Comes back to farm

ACTIVITY 2.4   STORY INTRODUCTION

(IRA/NCTE Standards: 2, 3, 4, 5, 6, 12. Summarize, synthesize, and persuade.)

Amber and Essie are sisters who can't agree whether their dad stole anything when he forged a check and went to jail. In spite of their arguments, they take care of each other because their mother works to keep the family together. Amber and Essie are exuberant, sometimes too much so, because they break a bed with their bouncing. What do you think their mother will do about this? Do you think their father will come home? Conclude this book talk by reading the first poem in the book (see Figure 2.6).

FIGURE 2.6   Suggested Individual Literary Experiences.

Teachers can suggest these activities for students to perform individually or in groups of two or three.

1. Prepare discussion questions for the book. (Students may need to be given models of open-ended questions until they become adept at creating such questions.)
2. Prepare a Venn diagram that compares and contrasts this book with another.
3. Prepare a diorama of an important scene or setting from the book.
4. Act out a scene from the book.
5. Prepare a poster or commercial for the book.
6. Keep a reading journal summarizing each day's reading and responding to the reading experience.
7. Prepare a story grammar or story map. (See the model in this chapter.)
8. Draw a plot line for the story. (See the models in this chapter.)

ACTIVITY 2.5   LEARNING ABOUT PLOT

(IRA/NCTE Standards: 2, 3, 6, 12. Compare/contrast, comprehend, and discussion.)

Listen to a taped book such as Richard Peck's *A Year Down Yonder* and compare it to the book. Discuss the two versions. This taped book is from Dial publishing company and can be obtained from any public library. Draw a plot line for the taped book. (See the models in this chapter and Figure 2.7.)

FIGURE 2.7   Elements of Fiction.

PLOT

1. Does the plot grab the reader's attention and move quickly?
2. Are the story events sequenced logically, so that cause and effect are clear?
3. Is the reader prepared for story events?
4. What is the conflict in this story (e.g., character with another character, character and society, character and a group, within the character)?
5. Is there a climax?
6. Is the denouement satisfying?

CHARACTER

1. Does the main character seem like a real person?
2. Is the main character well-rounded with character strengths and weaknesses revealed? (In a shorter story fewer traits are exhibited.)
3. How are character traits revealed (e.g., conversation, thoughts, author tells reader, actions)? Does the author rely too much on a single strategy?
4. Does the character grow and change?
5. Is the character a delineated character?
6. Are the character's conversations and behavior consistent with age and background?

SETTING

1. Where does this story take place?
2. When does this story take place?
3. How are time and place related to the plot, characters, and theme?
4. Is this a universal setting?

THEME

1. What is the theme?
2. Is the theme developed naturally through the actions and reactions of story characters?
3. Does the author avoid stating the theme in words (except in traditional literature)?
4. Is the abstract theme made concrete by the story?

STYLE

1. What stylistic devices characterize the author's writing (e.g., connotation, imagery, figurative language, hyperbole, understatement, allusion, symbol)?
2. What is the mood of the writing (e.g., gloomy, happy, evil, mysterious)?
3. What point of view is used?
4. Is the point of view appropriate to the story?

Summary

Genres are literature classifications with each member of a classification exhibiting common characteristics. Genre classifications give teachers, librarians, and students the language to discuss and analyze books. The genres of children's literature include: traditional literature, modern fantasy, contemporary realistic fiction, historical fiction, biography, poetry, and informational literature; all these categories of genres have the same characteristics as adult literature.

Initially, readers like or dislike the books they read for indefinable reasons; readers respond emotionally to literature. Through many experiences with stories, they gradually discover the elements that comprise literature: story, plot, characters, setting, theme, and style. As their experience with literature grows, they develop schemata, cognitive structures that enable them to make sense of what they read and to anticipate what the author will say, thus enriching their understanding. Children's understanding of literature exceeds their ability to verbalize story knowledge, but concerned adults can help them expand their appreciation and understanding. As one of those concerned adults, your understanding of the elements and organizational patterns of fiction discussed in this chapter will assist you in choosing books and planning literary experiences. Figure 2.7, *Elements of Fiction,* reviews the elements of fiction and suggests some questions to ask yourself when reviewing a piece of literature.

Thought Questions

1. What value do the elements of literature have for students?
2. What is author style? Identify the components of style.
3. Compare a picture book character with a character in a novel. How do they differ in development and the amount of detail included?
4. What themes have you discovered in the children's books you have read thus far?
5. Why do you think teachers choose to read fiction aloud more often than nonfiction?

Research and Application Experiences

1. Choose a fiction book to read and identify each of the elements of literature in that book. Map the story grammar of the book.
2. Choose a nonfiction book and identify the patterns of organization in it.
3. Compare two characters in two different realistic fiction books.
4. Compare a poem, a story, and a nonfiction book that are on the same topic.
5. Survey an elementary school class. Ask the students to identify the structures in various types of literature. Which type of literture do the students seem to know the most about? Why do you think this is true?
6. Identify any weaknesses revealed, keeping in mind that fewer traits are exhibited in a shorter story.

Children's Literature References and Recommended Books

Note: Books designated with an asterisk (*) are recommended for reluctant readers.

Alcock, V. (1998). *Stranger at the window.* Boston: Houghton Mifflin. (4–6). CONTEMPORARY REALISTIC FICTION.

Lesley is drawn into a mystery after seeing a strange child in the attic window of the house next door. The tension and mystery mount as the neighbors accuse her of hallucinating.

Aruego, J., & Dewey, A. (2002). *Weird friends: Unlikely allies in the animal kingdom.* New York: Gulliver Books\Harcourt. (1–3). NONFICTION.

This picture book shows animals who are helped by others. For example, the clown fish is protected by the poisonous sea anemone.

Bang-Campbell, M. (2002). *Little Rat sets sail* (M. Bang, Illus.). New York: Harcourt. (2–3). FANTASY.

Little Rat did not have a choice about sailing lessons because her parents signed her up. She envisions potential disasters, but she does take the lessons and learns to sail in spite of her fears.

Banks, K. (1999). *And if the moon could talk* (G. Hallensleben, Illus.). New York: Farrar, Straus & Giroux. (PreK–2). CONTEMPORARY REALISTIC FICTION.

The illustrations and the text capture the world outside a child's room at bedtime. The paintings that illustrate the text show the darkening sky as dusk falls.

Baylor, B. (1978). *The other way to listen* (P. Parnall, Illus.). New York: Scribners. (3–6). PICTURE BOOK, POETRY.

The poetry creates the feeling of a desert where the central character listens to his surroundings.

Briggs, R. (2002). *Ug: Boy genius of the Stone Age.* New York: Knopf. (3–6). FANTASY.

Ug lives in the Stone Age, but he has big ideas. He doesn't like living in caves or stone trousers. The illustrations contribute to the fun in this ridiculous prehistoric time.

Brockmeier, K. (2002). *City of names.* New York: Viking. (5–7). FANTASY.

Howie, a fourth grader, receives the incorrect book from a book-club order. This book, *The Secret Guide to North Mellwood,* leads Howie on fantastic adventures.

Burleigh, R. (1998). *Black whiteness: Admiral Byrd alone in the Antarctic* (W. L. Krudop, Illus.). New York: Atheneum. (4–8). BIOGRAPHY.*

This exquisite book tells about the six months that Admiral Richard Byrd stayed alone in an underground house in Antarctica.

Byars, B. (2002). *Little horse* (David McPhail, Illus.). New York: Holt. (1–3). FANTASY.*

This beginning chapter book is the story of a little horse who accidentally fell into a stream and washed away. His survival adventures began as he was washed down the river.

Coman, C. (1995). *What Jamie saw*. Arden, NY: Front Street. (4–7). CONTEMPORARY REALISTIC FICTION.*

After Van throws his baby sister, Jamie and his mom move to a place where he feels isolated, but he practices his magic tricks and learns how to take care of his mom and sister.

Cox, J. (1998). *Third grade pet* (C. Fisher, Illus.). New York: Holiday House. (K–4). REALISTIC FICTION.

Rosemary is shocked when her class chooses a rat for a class pet, but things get worse when she is chosen to take care of the rat.

DiCamillo, K. (2000). *Because of Winn-Dixie*. New York: Scholastic. (4–7). REALISTIC FICTION.*

Opal tries to learn about her mother, but her father is reluctant to reveal any information about her. Opal finds a dog and friends who help her understand her father and her situation.

Doyle, B. (2002). *Mary Ann Alice*. Toronto: Doublas & McIntyre. (4–7). REALISTIC FICTION.

The central character has the soul of a poet and a deep interest in geology.

Giff, P. R. (2002). *Pictures of Hollis Woods*. New York: Random House. (4–7). REALISTIC FICTION.

Hollis is a foundling who really wants to belong to a family. She finally finds her place in the world.

Goode, D. (2001). *Tiger trouble*. New York: Scholastic. (K–2). PICTURE BOOK, FANTASY.

Jack and Lily, his tiger, do everything together until the sad day when a grumpy man buys their apartment building and tells them that the tiger has to leave. Fortunately, Lily saves the grumpy man and stays.

Guest, E. (2002). *Iris and Walter: The Sleepover*. Gulliver (K–2). CHAPTER BOOK/REALIST FICTION.

Iris and Walter look forward to their first sleepover.

Hiaasen, C. (2002). *Hoot*. New York: Knopf. (4–7). REALISTIC FICTION.

Roy faces the usual "new kid" drill in middle school, but he also encounters a mystery that leads to new friendships and a campaign to save burrowing owls.

Jackson, D. (2002). *The bug scientists*. New York: Houghton Mifflin. (3–6). NONFICTION.

The author says "Small is beautiful" for bug scientists. She points out that bugs are the earth's best

fliers and farmers, who have survived and adapted for 350 million years.

Kay, V. (1999). *Gold fever* (S. D. Schindler, Illus.). New York: Putnam. (2–5). HISTORICAL FICTION.

Jasper, a farmer, sees men rushing to the California gold fields, so he decides it would be easier to dig gold than to farm. He finds out this is not true and returns to his farm.

Kushner, D. (1987). *A book dragon* (N. R. Jackson, Illus.). New York: Holt, Rinehart and Winston. (4–6). MODERN FANTASY.

Nonesuch, the dragon, has adventures in a cathedral, in London, and in a bookshop.

Lasky, K. (1997). *Marven of the Great North Woods* (K. Hawkes, Illus.). New York: Harcourt Brace. (2–4). HISTORICAL FICTION.

A true story of how one family protected a child from the influenza epidemic that struck the United States in 1918.

Levy, J. (1999). *Totally uncool* (C. Monroe, Illus.). Minneapolis, MN: Carolrhoda. (3–6). CONTEMPORARY REALISTIC FICTION.*

Dad's new girlfriend is "totally uncool." She has some downright alarming traits such as a kitchen floor that is too shiny. But she does have some redeeming qualities, such as clapping the loudest.

Lindgren, A. (1950). *Pippi Longstocking* (F. Lamborn, Trans., L. S. Glanzman, Illus.). New York: Viking. (2–4). MODERN FANTASY.

In this translation from Swedish, Pippi lives alone with a monkey and a horse. While doing what she pleases, she has many unusual adventures.

Lowry, L. (2002). *Gooney Bird Greene* (M. Thomas, Illus.). Boston: Houghton Mifflin. (1–4). REALISTIC FICTION.*

When Gooney Bird Greene arrives in second grade, she is obviously a unique character that intrigues her classmates, who want to learn all about her.

Mahy, M. (1994). *The boy who was followed home* (S. Kellogg, Illus.). (K–3). PICTURE BOOK, FANTASY.

To his delight, a young boy is followed home by a hippopotamus.

McKenna, C. (2001). *Third grade sinks!* (S. Roth, Illus.). New York: Holiday House. (2–4). REALISTIC FICTION.

Gordie plans to share a locker with his friend in third grade, but the teacher assigns a girl. He tries to get rid of her.

Myers, C. (1999). *Black cat*. New York: Scholastic. (All ages). POETRY.*

This poem about a slinky black cat and its urban lifestyle captures the visual and sound imagery of life on the street.

Osborne, M. P. (2002). *The brave little seamstress* (Giselle Potter, Illus.). New York: Schwartz/Atheneum. (K–3). PICTURE BOOK, TRADITIONAL LITERATURE.

This story is a retelling of the Grimm fairy tale, *The Brave Little Tailor*. The tailor is now a seamstress who proves she can overcome all sorts of villians to win a castle and a prince.

Park, L. S. (2002). *When my name was Keoko*. New York: Clarion. (5–8). HISTORICAL FICTION.

A narrative about a real family's experiences during the Japanese occupation of Korea during World War II.

Paterson, K. (1978). *The great Gilly Hopkins*. New York: Crowell. (4–6). CONTEMPORARY REALISTIC FICTION.

Gilly, a foster child, moves to a new foster home and attempts to outdo Mame Trotter, who wisely wins her over. However, Gilly has adjustment problems.

Paulsen, G. (1987). *Hatchet*. New York: Viking Penguin. (5–7). CONTEMPORARY REALISTIC FICTION.*

Brian survives an airplane crash and spends the next 54 days trying to survive with only the hatchet his mother gave him.

Pearce, P. (1958). *Tom's midnight garden*. Philadelphia: Lippincott. (4–7). MODERN FANTASY.

A time fantasy wherein a girl and boy play when the clock strikes 13.

Peck, R. (2000). *A year down yonder*. New York: Dial. (4–7). REALISTIC FICTION.

A zany grandma presents challenges to her grandaughter.

Peck, R. (2001). *Fair weather*. New York: Dial. (5–8). HISTORICAL FICTION.

This is the story of a family visiting the Columbian Exposition in Chicago in 1893. They have a life changing experience.

Salisbury, G. (2001). *Lord of the deep*. New York: Delacorte. (5–8). REALISTIC FICTION.

Mikey Donovan is learning the ins and outs of running a fishing charter boat from his stepfather. However, he painfully discovers that his idol has feet of clay when his stepfather makes a less-than-honest decision.

Sendak, M. (1963). *Where the wild things are*. New York: Harper & Row. (K–2). MODERN FANTASY.

Max is wild, so he is sent to bed without supper. He escapes in his imagination, but discovers that he wants to return.

Seuss, Dr., with Prelutsky, J., & Smith, L. (1998). *Hooray for Diffendoofer day!* New York: Knopf. (K–6). MODERN FANTASY.*

The story of a zany school where teachers view education differently.

Tolan, S. (2003). *Surviving the Applewhites*. New York: HarperCollins. (4–7). REALISTIC FICTION.*

Jake Semple has been thrown out of every school he ever attended when he lands in the Applewhite's Creative Academy, also known as "home schooling." The Applewhite clan totally confuses Jake in this hilarious book.

Van Allsburg, C. (1981). *Jumanji*. Boston: Houghton Mifflin. (2–4). MODERN FANTASY.

Children play a board game that they cannot stop playing.

White, R. (1988). *Sweet creek holler*. New York: Farrar, Straus & Giroux. (4–8). HISTORICAL FICTION.

This book portrays life in a 1948 Appalachian town, focusing on Ginny and her best friend.

Wojciechowski, S. (2002). *Beany goes to camp* (S. Natti, Illus.). New York: Candlewick. (2–4). REALISTIC FICTION.

Beany's parents insist that she go to summer camp. She feels doomed, but she makes friends and eventually enjoys the experience.

Wood, A. (1996). *The red racer*. New York: Simon & Schuster. (1–3). CONTEMPORARY REALISTIC FICTION.

A dream of owning a shiny, new bicycle leads this character to take extreme measures, but it all ends well.

Woods, B. (2002). *The red rose box*. New York: Putnam. (5–8). CONTEMPORARY REALISTIC FICTION.

Leah Jean Hopper, who lives in the 1950s' small town of Sulphur, Louisiana, discovers that "Jim

Crow" laws do not exist in Los Angeles. Her travel experiences lead to her discovery of real freedom.

References and Books
for Further Reading

Adams, S. M., & Collins, A. (1986). A schema-theoretic view of reading. In H. Singer & R. Ruddell (Eds.), *Theoretical models and processes of reading* (pp. 404–425). Newark, DE: International Reading Association.

Alexander, L. (1981). The grammar of story. In B. Hearne & M. Kaye (Eds.), *Celebrating children's books* (pp. 3–13). New York: Lothrop, Lee & Shepard.

Applebee, A. (1978). *The child's concept of story.* Chicago: University of Chicago Press.

Barton, J. (2001). *Teaching with children's literature.* Norwood, MA: Christopher-Gordon.

Byars, B. (1993). Writing for children. *Speech.* Durham, NC: Southeastern Children's Writers Association.

Conrad, J. (Ed.) and Simmons, A. (Ed.). (1922). Preface to a career. In *The nigger of the Narcissus* (p. x). New York: Doubleday.

Fox, P. (1991, September). Writing: The village by the sea. *Book Links, 1,* 48–50.

Giblin, J. (1990). *Writing books for young people.* Boston: The Writer.

Hardy, B. (1977). Narrative as a primary act of mine. In M. Meek, A. Warlow, & G. Barton (Eds.), *The cool web: The pattern of children's reading* (pp. 12–23). London: Bodley Head.

Holman, C. H., & Harmon, W. (1986). *A handbook to literature* (4th ed.). New York: Macmillan.

Koskinen, P., Blum, I., Bisson, S., Phillips, S., Creamer, T., & Baker, T. (1999, February). Shared reading, books, and audiotapes: Supporting diverse students in school and at home. *The Reading Teacher, 52* (5), 430–444.

Kucan, L., & Beck, L. (1996, June). Four fourth graders thinking aloud: An investigation of genre effects. *Journal of Literacy Research, 32* (2), 269–287.

Lehr, S. (1991). *The child's developing sense of theme.* New York: Teachers College Press.

Morner, K., & Rausch, R. (1991). *NTC's dictionary of literary terms.* Lincolnwood, IL: National Textbook.

Rumelhart, D.E. (1975). Notes on a schema for stories. In D. G. Bobow & A. M. Collins (Ed.), *Representation and Understanding* (pp. 573–603.) New York: Academic Press.

Sebesta, S., & Iverson, W. J. (1975). *Literature for Thursday's child.* Chicago: Science Research Associates.

Stein, N.L. & Glenn, C. G. (1979). An analysis of story comprehension in elementary school children. In R.O. Freedle (Ed.), *New directions in discourse processing* (pp. 53–101). Norwood, NJ: Ablex.

Tierney, R. (1990, March). Redefining reading comprehension. *Educational Leadership, 47,* 37–42.

Van Vliet, L. (1992). *Approaches to literature through genre.* Phoenix, AZ: Oryx.

Wadham, T. (1999). Plot does matter. *The Horn Book, LXXV,* 445–450.

Wyndham, L., & Madison, A. (1988). *Writing for children and teenagers.* Cincinnati, OH: Writer's Digest Books.

Connecting Children and Literature

3

KEY TERMS

audio books

bibliotherapy

Caldecott Medal

catharsis

censorship

Children's Choices

literary criticism

Newbery Award

videos

GUIDING QUESTIONS

How do you choose books to read? Do you read different types of books on vacation than for class? Do you read best-sellers? Who are your favorite authors? Examining your personal criteria for selecting books will help you better understand how to choose books for others, especially children. How would you feel if you were denied the right to read a book that you really wanted to read? As you read this chapter, keep in mind these questions:

1. What are some appropriate criteria adults can use when selecting books for children?

2. How can you identify the books that are most likely to engage the children that you will teach?

3. What factors are most likely to influence children's response to literature?

4. Why is censorship such an important issue for adults in choosing children's books?

Teachers, librarians, and parents have a plethora of choices among the children's books available today. According to *Children's Books in Print 1998, 29th edition*, there are 126,600 children's trade books in print, with approximately 5,000 new books added to this number each year. Since children's literature has assumed greater importance in education, extensive collections of quality children's literature have appeared in elementary schools (Serafini, 2001). Therefore, identifying books that cultivate children's desire to read is essential. The vignette on the following page illustrates a teacher's efforts to stimulate his students' interest in literature.

Selecting Children's Literature

As stated in Chapter 1, the foundation of this text is the transactional theory, which is the understanding that meaning is constructed in the transaction between an individual reader and a specific text (book, film, tape, etc.) (Rosenblatt, 1978). Readers bring their prior knowledge and experiences to the text and construct meaning as they interact with the text. The books children read, the videos they watch, the audiotapes they hear, the computer programs they use, and the Internet sites they visit become a part of their literary experiences. Exposing children to a wide variety of literature helps them develop a sense of literary quality. In addition, providing many opportunities for children to select literature that appeals to their own interests, purposes, and motivation encourages them to read widely. Moreover, consistently reading books that resonate with their experiences and interests helps chil-

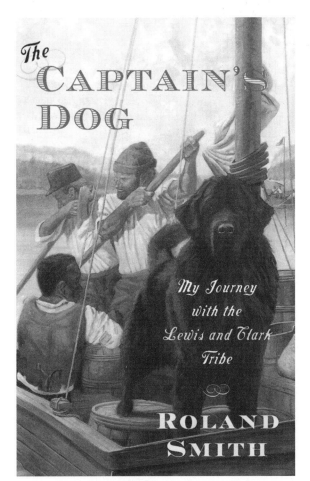

Seaman had more adventures than most dogs.

dren build reading fluency. *Literary criticism* is concerned with selecting quality literature for students.

Current literary criticism falls into three categories: work (text)-centered criticism (focused on the quality of the work [text or media]; child-centered criticism (focused on children's response to the work [text or media]; and issues-centered criticism (focused on the appropriate presentation of various social, cultural, and political

VIGNETTE

When he was planning his lesson, Jim Smith glanced at his calendar and realized that it was November 1, and at least half of his class continued to read well below grade level. Jim knew their best hope for acquiring reading fluency lay in extensively reading books they enjoyed.

At the beginning of the school year, the class took an interest inventory, but they had joked around rather than completing it. He considered engaging them in a group discussion, but realized they might not seriously discuss their interests. Instead, he decided to identify books that appealed to this age group, book-talk the books, and identify those that sparked their interests. He also planned to read books aloud to the class. After consulting *Great Books for Boys* (Odean, 1998), *The Read-Aloud Handbook* (Trelease, 1995), *Once Upon a Heroine* (Cooper-Mullin & Coye, 1998), *Children's Reference Plus* (Bowker, 1991), and *The Bulletin* from the University of Illinois, he identified three books to read aloud: *Slake's Limbo* by Felice Holman, *Hatchet* by Gary Paulsen, and *Scorpions* by Walter Dean Myers. He started the read-aloud sessions with *Slake's Limbo*. When his students pleaded "keep on reading, please," he knew he was on the right track. They were interested! He searched for other books with the same appeal. After obtaining copies from the public and school libraries, Mr. Smith prepared brief synopses of each book, book-talked the books, and created a display so the students could choose the ones they wanted to read.

He continued reading aloud, observing the students' responses and gathering ideas for other displays. The students read more and more and with increasing fluency as the school year progressed.

issues in the work [text or media]). All three categories are important when choosing literature for children: A book may present social issues accurately while failing to achieve excellence in storytelling, while a book of excellent literary quality may not appeal to children's interests. A comprehensive approach emphasizes the importance of finding a good fit between reader and story. Current research indicates that the contexts in which books are presented and the opportunities to respond to them are significant aspects of literary engagement (Beckett, 1997; Galda, Ash, & Cullinan, 2002).

Literary Quality as a Selection Standard

We should put books in children's hands that are worthy of them—books of honesty, integrity, and vision. There is no room for cutesy books, dull books, or books that talk down to children (Hearne, with Stevenson, 1999). What qualities does a truly great children's book have? Why do so many children return to these books year after year? First of all, they tell splendid stories that resonate with children's experiences and their imaginations. Books like Margaret Mahy's *The Boy Who Was Followed Home* tell stories that delight children. In this story, Robert is thrilled when a hippopotamus follows him home, but the 43 hippos who gather on his family's lawn complicate the situation. A witch is called in to convince the animals to leave, leading to an unexpected climax.

Second, appealing literature has memorable and well-drawn characters, who live on in our adult minds—consider Peter Pan and Captain Hook. Another unforgettable character is Tsynq Yr, an alien who crashes to earth and is forced to inject his mind into a skunk's body in Pamela Service's *Stinker from Space*. Look for this book in the library and you will find only well-worn copies . . . unless they are all checked out.

Third, many great books unite memorable text with vivid illustrations. Books such as Beatrix Potter's *The Tale of Peter Rabbit* and Maurice Sendak's *Where the Wild Things Are* illustrate this union of text and illustration. The true classics of literature are books that remain popular because children want to read them.

Award Books and Recommended Reading Lists

Award books and recommended reading lists are very helpful since most of us do not have the time to read all of the books in print. Although the majority of awards and lists are composed by adults rather than children, they provide a beginning place for identifying worthwhile literature.

Newbery Award

Newbery Awards are given to books that have outstanding literary quality. Each year this award goes to the author of a book published in the United States that represents the most outstanding contribution to the field of children's literature. This prestigious award is named after John Newbery, the first British publisher of books intended expressly for children. The Newbery Award represents artistic achievement and carries significant respect in the literary community.

A 15-member committee of the Association for Library Service to Children of the American Library Association determines the winners. Although the award is given to only one book, others are identified as Honor books. (See the Appendix for a list of winners and some Honor books.) Criteria for the award are shown in Figure 3.1. Newbery Award books are fine examples of literature; as noted, however, adults rather than children select them. Research indicates that many Newbery titles are beyond the reading ability of elementary children. In fact, Shafer (1976) found the readability of almost one-third of the Newbery titles to be fifth grade or higher; therefore, they are best presented as read-alouds to interested children. This trend continues in recent Newbery Award winners, which are young adult books rather than juvenile stories.

Caldecott Medal

The *Caldecott Medal,* named for the great British illustrator Randolph Caldecott, is awarded annually to the illustrator of the most distinguished picture book published in the United States. (See the Appendix for the list.) The medal is awarded for excellence in artwork, and for the effective interaction of text and illustrations (see Figure 3.2). Books featuring a wide range of media have won the Caldecott Medal; watercolor, pen and ink, and collage have all

This award winner is a great read.

FIGURE 3.1 Criteria for the Newbery Award.

1. In identifying distinguished writing in a book for children, committee members must:

a. consider:
- interpretation of the theme or concept
- presentation of information, including accuracy, clarity, and organization
- development of plot
- delineation of characters
- delineation of setting
- appropriateness of style

NOTE: Because the literary qualities to be considered will vary depending on content, the committee need not expect to find excellence in each of the named elements. The book should, however, have distinguished qualities in all the elements pertinent to it.

b. consider excellence of presentation for a child audience

2. Each book is to be considered as a contribution to literature. The committee is to make its decision primarily on the text. Other aspects of a book are to be considered only if they distract from the text. Such other aspects might include illustrations or overall design of the book.

NOTE: The committee should keep in mind that the award is for literary quality and quality of presentation for children. The award is not for didactic intent or for popularity.

From: Peterson, L. K. & Solt, M. L. (1982). *Newbery and Caldecott Model and Honor Books,* p. 399. New Providence, NJ: Bowker.

been represented. Caldecott Medal winners are typically suitable for younger children, but some, such as Chris Van Allsburg's *The Polar Express,* appeal to all age groups. The Caldecott committee also names Honor books.

Robert F. Sibert Informational Book Award

Established in 2001, the Robert F. Sibert Informational Book Award is given annually to the author of the most distinguished informational book published during the preceding year. The award honors Robert F. Sibert, the long-time President of Bound to Stay Bound Books and is sponsored by the company. The American Library Association administers the award. See the Appendix for a winners' list.

Other awards

Although the Newbery Award and the Caldecott Medal are the best-known of all children's book awards, a number of additional awards are presented each year to exemplary children's books. (See the Appendix for a list.) The following list identifies a few of these.

- The Hans Christian Andersen International Medal is awarded to living authors and artists by the International Board on Books for Young People.
- The International Reading Association presents the Children's Book Award to authors with unusual promise.
- The Laura Ingalls Wilder Award is given to authors or illustrators who have made lasting contributions to children's literature.
- The Boston Globe/Horn Book Award is presented to authors of fiction and nonfiction and to illustrators.

FIGURE 3.2 Criteria for the Caldecott Medal.

1. In identifying a distinguished picture book for children, committee members must:

   a. consider the excellence of:
   - execution in the artistic technique employed
   - pictorial interpretation of story, theme, or concept
   - appropriateness of style of illustration to the story, theme, or concept
   - delineation of plot, theme, characters, setting, mood, or information through the pictures

   b. consider the excellence of presentation in recognition of a child audience

2. The only limitation to graphic form is that the form must be one that may be used in a picture book (film photography is not considered, but still photography is).

3. Each book is to be considered as a picture book. The committee is to make its decision primarily on the illustrations, but other components of a book are to be considered, especially when they make a book less effective as a children's picture book. Other components might include elements such as the written text or the overall design of the book.

   NOTE: The committee should keep in mind that the award is for distinguished illustrations in a picture book and for excellence of pictorial presentation for children. The award is not for didactic intent or for popularity.

From: Peterson, L. K., & Solt, M. L. (1982). *Newbery and Caldecott Medal and Honor Books*, p. 400. New Providence, NJ: Bowker.

A celebration of illustrators and artists.

- The Coretta Scott King Award is given to the best books for children about the Black experience.
- The Pura Belpré Award is given to the best books for children about the Latino experience.
- The Consortium of Latin American Studies Programs (CLASP) gives the Americas Award in recognition of books that authentically and engagingly portray Latin America, the Caribbean, or Latinos in the United States.
- The Orbis Pictus Award recognizes outstanding nonfiction books. The National Council of Teachers of English sponsors this award.

Selection Aids

A number of educational organizations offer lists of recommended books that include great books, good books, and classics. For instance, the American Library Association compiles lists of notable books. The Teachers' Choices project, administered by the International Reading Association, identifies outstanding trade books for children and adolescents that effectively enhance the curriculum. The books listed are identified by regional teams of teachers who field test between 200 and 300 books annually and compile a list of 30 books categorized as primary (Grades K–2), intermediate (Grades 3–5), and advanced (Grades 6–8). Books are selected on the basis of literary quality and presentation.

The Child Study Children's Book Committee of Bank Street College also compiles an annual list. Each year the Children's Book Council works with the National Science Teachers Association and the National Council for the Social Studies, respectively, to compile "Outstanding Science Trade Books for Children" and "Notable Children's Trade Books in the Field of Social Studies." These annotated bibliographies are published in the periodicals *Social Education* and *Science and Children*. The reference, *Adventuring with Books*, which is published by the National Council of Teachers of English, categorizes books in ways that teachers find very helpful.

School Library Journal publishes lists and book reviews: for instance, "Reference Book Roundup" annually appears in the May issue. In addition to these lists, children's books are regularly reviewed and recommended in periodicals such as *The Horn Book, The Horn Book Guide to Children's and Young Adult Books, The Bulletin of the Center for Children's Books, The Reading Teacher, Journal of Reading*, and *Language Arts*.

The Internet is a superb source of information about children's books, videos, recordings, and computer programs. *The Children's Literature Web Guide* is an invaluable resource for identifying good books. *The Bulletin of the Center for Children's Books*, The American Library Association, *Smithsonian Magazine*, and Cooperative Children's Book Center (School of Education, University of Wisconsin-Madison) all maintain Web sites.

Adults will find a number of reference books to consult when choosing books for children. The following list identifies some of the best of these guides.

- Bowker, R. R. (Ed.). (2003). *Subject guide to children's books in print*. New York: Bowker.
- Hearne, B., with Stevenson, D. (1999). *Choosing books for children: A commonsense approach*. Urbana, IL: University of Illinois.
- *The Horn Book Guide* is published twice a year. Boston, MA: Horn Book.
- Isaacson, R., Hellas, F., & Yaakov, J. (annual). *Children's catalog*. New York: Wilson.
- Liggett, T. C., & Benfield, C. M. (1995). *Reading rainbow guide to children's books*. Chicago: Citadel Press.
- McClure, A., & Kristo, J. (Eds.). (2002). *Adventuring with books: A booklist for preK through grade 6, 13th edition*. Classroom teachers, librarians, and professors are involved in reviewing these books. Urbana, IL: National Council of Teachers of English.
- Winkel, L. (Ed.). (Biannually). *The elementary school library collection: A guide to books and other media*. Philadelphia: Brodart Foundation.
- Zarnowski, M., Kerper, R., & Jensen, J. (Eds.). (2002). *The Best in Children's Nonfiction, The Reading, Writing and Teaching Orbis Pictus Award Books*. Urbana, IL: National Council of Teachers of English.*

---

*Note: This list of references are not repeated in the end-of-chapter References list.

This book is a winner with students.

Criticism of Award Books and Reading Lists

Children's book awards and recommended lists have been criticized on several counts. First, such awards may be given to books appealing to only a small segment of the population, selected not on the basis of popularity with children but only on the basis of literary quality, which can differ dramatically from individual to individual. This can create the problem of elitism.

Second, many children's favorites are outstanding works that did not receive Newbery Awards, such as the *Little House* books by Laura Ingalls Wilder and *Charlotte's Web* by E. B. White. However, *Charlotte's Web* was recognized as an Honor book by the Newbery Award Committee.

Third, the vast majority of awards and lists reflect the standards and taste of adults; they should be viewed as resources rather than prescriptions for children's reading. Ohanian (1990) points out the dangers of such lists:

> Rather than including children in some sort of common cultural foundation, they exclude [children] from the rich possibilities of language and literature. . . . Lists . . . end up driving the curriculum, making us forget the needs of individuals. (p. 176)

Betsy Hearne (1999) also stresses the importance of personal appeal and involvement in selecting children's books. She suggests that adults choose books that meet their standards but that also appeal to children. She maintains that children's responses to books are as important as experts' recommendations. The power of personal attraction to a book cannot be underestimated. During their school years, children will read many types of literature, and the appeal of some books will not be apparent to adults.

Child-Centered Criticism: What Do Children Like to Read?

Many teachers advocate children's free choice of literature as an important element for promoting reading in classrooms. Some suggest that children themselves should be the ultimate critics of their literature, that children's preferences for certain kinds of books not only should be honored, but also should form a basis for evaluating books. Children's reading selections frequently include series books such as R. L. Stine's *Goosebumps* series and the *American Girl* series, as well as books based on television shows and movies. In research, thousands of teachers and librarians compiled bibliographies of what their students read, revealing that "the respondents became momentarily addicted to both the series and comic books. . . . These materials seem to be as much a part of one's literary maturation as are the children's classics" (Carlsen & Sherrill, 1988, p. 16).

How do we explain the popularity of such books? First, they possess predictable language, action, and characters. This predictability, coupled with following the same characters' adventures through several books, creates a familiarity that many children enjoy. Second, children identify readily with the characters in these books. Although the characters are often one-dimensional, they do possess the larger-than-life characteristics of mythological heroes that are important in traditional literature (Purves & Monson, 1984). Although these characters are clichés, they sustain children in the same ways that *Cinderella* and *Little Red Riding Hood* do (Purves & Monson, 1984).

Series books do have value for young readers. "The experience of making patterns, putting stories together, extrapolating and confirming may be providing a crucial step toward more substantial reading" (Mackey, 1990, p. 44). Teachers can help children recognize similarities between series book characters and those found in myths, legends, and other traditional literature.

Outstanding authors have written series, such as R. K. Rowling's *Harry Potter* series and Brian Jacques's *Redwall* series. These books attract many children to reading, developing both motivation and fluency along with other values. Series books add to "the reservoir of experiences and ideas created from the sum total of all their reading"; the richer this reservoir of experience and ideas, the more effective children's transactions with literature will become over time (Purves & Monson, 1984).

What Attracts Children to Certain Books?

Content is typically regarded as the most important criterion children use in selecting books. Studies over a period of years yield surprisingly consistent results about the topics that appeal to children (Wolfson, Manning, & Manning, 1984). The general interests of children of all ages include animals, humor, action, suspense, and surprise. Research indicates that reading ability affects reading interests (Swanton, 1984). Lehman (1991) studied nine award-winning books that appeared on the *Children's Choices* list (published annually by the International Reading Association in *The Reading Teacher*). After analyzing and categorizing the theme, style, and structure of each, she generalized the following:

1. Substantial differences do exist among award-winning books children do and do not prefer.
2. Children prefer predictable qualities, optimistic tone, and a lively pace.
3. Children prefer action-oriented structures and complete plot resolutions.
4. Children do not choose books with unresolved endings, tragic tones, or slow-paced, introspective plots.

Many children are attracted to books by an author or artist whose work they have previously enjoyed.

Readers of all ages from preschool through college seek out known and enjoyed authors and illustrators, and correspondingly, they may avoid others due to negative experiences (Stoodt-Hill, 1999). For example, the *Harry Potter* series by J. K. Rowling could be termed a phenomenon with middle-grade children, who eagerly wait for the publication of each new book in the series. Harry Potter actually has universal popularity since it appeals to younger children and adults, as well as middle-grade students. The zany illustrations in Steven Kellogg's books makes them popular with the young picture book crowd. Jack Prelutsky's poetry is well-known; therefore, each new book he writes is welcomed by elementary school children.

Understanding the attraction of known authors suggests that teachers and librarians should be aware of current authors and illustrators so they can make them available to children. Author and illustrator visits attract children to their works. Getting acquainted with artists and illustrators through in-depth studies is also highly motivating for children.

Reading Interest Research

The majority of research into children's reading interests is dated, but the most pertinent is summarized here to help concerned adults think about the reading interests of children.

The physical appearance of books is important to children. Type size, style, illustrations, and cover design influence their choice of books. Children in Grades 3 through 8 select books on the basis of appearance, author, recommendation, or some combination of these factors. Older children base their decisions on peer recommendations and the information on the book jacket (Burgess, 1985). Elementary children prefer paperback to hardcover when selecting books (Campbell, 1990). Illustrations are important to children's choices at all grade levels. Young children generally prefer colored illustrations. Even middle school students prefer books with illustrations to those without (Robbins, 1982).

Story elements

Children express preferences based on story structures and elements. Abramson (1980) analyzed the plot structure of 50 picture books on the Children's Choices list. He found that children most frequently chose picture books with one of three plot structures:

1. a main character who confronts a problem and attempts to solve it,
2. a story that unfolds incident by incident, and
3. characters who have opposing viewpoints or who experience the same thing in different ways.

Sebesta's (1979) analysis of the Children's Choices list indicated that children's favorites had fast-paced plots, detailed information and descriptions, and a variety of plot structures. Books with a strong theme and with characters who had warm relationships appeared frequently on the list.

Children's characteristics that influence reading interests

Many factors influence children's reading interests, including age, developmental appropriateness, gender, home environment, reading ability, and readability.

Age. Age is clearly related to reading interests. Children's book preferences gradually change as they mature. For example, younger children exhibit narrow reading interests because they have had fewer life experiences and thus have not developed a range of interests. Research indicates that younger children enjoy fairy tales, animals, make-believe, and stories about children.

Children in Grades 4 through 6 consistently exhibit a wider range of interest than their younger counterparts. As children mature they become more interested in realistic literature (Purves & Beach, 1972). Elementary students enjoy adventure stories, fantasies, social studies and history, mysteries, animals, and humor (Pieronek, 1980). Students between the ages of 10 and 13 generally are more interested in recreational reading and develop a broader range of interests because they dip into many genres that reflect their range of experiences. In fact, students at this age probably indulge in more recreational reading than they will at any time during their educational lives. As students progress through school, the academic and social demands of their lives leave less and less time for recreational reading. Table 3.1 summarizes the research regarding elementary and middle school students' preferences.

Developmental appropriateness. Current theory suggests that children are in the process of becoming literate from birth and are capable of learning to understand written language before attending school (Adams, 1990). Schlager (1978) examined the relationship between child development and children's

TABLE 3.1
Elementary and middle school reading preferences.

Topic	Title	Author
Adventure	Bandit's Moon	Sid Fleischman
Animal stories	Not My Dog	Colby Rodowsky
Fantasy	Cougar	Helen V. Griffith
History	Foster's War	Carolyn Reeder
Humor	Granville Jones, Commando	Natalie Honeycutt
Mystery	Sammy Keyes and the Skeleton Man	Wendelin Van Draanen
Social Issues	Nowhere to Call Home	Cynthia DeFelice

literature, analyzing the relationship between the characteristics of middle childhood (ages 7 through 12) and the children's book choices. She found a clear correlation between popular books and the developmental characteristics of middle childhood; the children's interest was aroused by the developmental characteristics displayed by the main characters in the story rather than the literary quality of the books. Table 3.2 summarizes children's stages of development and the developmental characteristics for each stage, as well as books appropriate to each level.

Gender.   Although the role of gender in reading interests is unclear because of the individual nature of children's reading interests, research indicates that these differences become more prominent at about age 9 (Haynes, 1988), with the greatest number of differences appearing between ages 10 and 13. Sex stereotypes in reading preferences have been observed in preschool children as well as school-age students (Kopp & Halverson, 1983). Boys prefer the main characters to be male and girls prefer them to be female. Table 3.3 summarizes the gender differences in children's reading interests.

Home environment.   The home, school, teacher, and community are all powerful influences on children's interests, motivations, and development. Children who express an interest in literature come from homes with environments supportive of literacy: books are avail-

able, parents read for themselves and to their children, and they all use the public library. Teachers observe that children who are read to at home enter school with greater interest in books than children who lack these experiences (Stoodt-Hill, 2003).

An increasing number of studies point to the positive effects of teachers' influence on children's reading interests. Fielding, Wilson, and Anderson (1986) found that avid readers belong to communities of readers that begin at home but expand to include peers and teachers. In fact, teachers have observed that peers have the greatest influence on students' reading at all ages (Stoodt-Hill, 2003). Hiebert, Mervar, and Person (1990) found that second graders whose classrooms contained many trade books, and where the teachers commonly used literature, gave more detailed reasons for their book selections and had specific books in mind when they visited the library.

Reading ability.   The influence of reading ability on reading interest is unclear due to mixed research conclusions. Swanton (1984), however, found that gifted readers prefer mysteries, fiction, science fiction, and fantasy, whereas average readers prefer mysteries, comedy/humor, realistic fiction, and adventure. Style may contribute to the differences in reading preferences; for example, some authors write in abstract language, which appeals to some children, whereas other children prefer authors who use concrete language. Readers with higher ability select longer books than those with less reading ability.

Readability.   *Readability* refers to the reading level of a book. This level should be considered not only by teachers, parents, and librarians when selecting books for children to read, but by children themselves as they select books to read on their own. Readability formulas provide a rough measure of a book's range of difficulty based on the number of difficult words and the average sentence length. Children can use a simple method to independently check the difficulty of a particular book. The "five-finger test" simply involves selecting a page in a book and counting on the fingers of one hand the number of unknown words. If a child finds five or more unknown words on the page, the book may be too difficult. Books with too many unknown words daunt even the most determined readers.

Some children's books include information regarding the readability level on the dust jacket or

TABLE 3.2

Appropriate literature for each developmental stage.

Age and Stage	Characteristics	Book Types	Sample Books
0–6 prereading	acquire language rapidly understand simple concepts, environmental print, signs, brand names	concept	*Planting a Rainbow*, Lois Ehlert *Airport*, Donald Crews
	recognize letters, numbers, their own names	alphabet	*A. B. See*, Tana Hoban *One Day Two Dragons*, Lynne Bertrand
	enjoy listening to stories	simple, predictable	*Goodnight Moon*, Margaret Wise Brown *Brown Bear, Brown Bear*, Bill Martin, Jr.
	engage in pretend reading	wordless books	*The Snowman*, Raymond Briggs *Deep in the Forest*, Brinton Turkle
6–7 initial reading	learn letters and associate them with words	easy to read	*Mine's the Best*, Crosby Consall *A Dark, Dark Tale*, Ruth Brown
	develop concepts of print bring meaning to print	animal books	*Go Dog Go*, P.D. Eastman *Little Bear*, Else Minarick
		predictable	*Hop on Pop*, Dr. Seuss
7–8 confirmation fluency	read to increase fluency	high-frequency words	*Frog and Toad*, Arnold Lobel *Henry and Mudge*, Cynthia Rylant *Babar's Little Circus Star*, Laurent de Brunhoff
		nonfiction	*Going on a Whale Watch*, Bruce McMillan
9–12	read for knowledge, information, ideas, and experiences	more complex and sophisticated fiction	*Lon Po Po*, Ed Young *Bunnicula*, Deborah & James Howe *Tuck Everlasting*, Natalie Babbitt
	word meanings and prior experiences are important	nonfiction	*Honest Abe*, Malcah Zeldis *The Hospital Book*, James Howe
	longer, more complex sentences		*Whales and Dolphins*, Steve Parker *A Medieval Feast*, Aliki *A Walk on the Great Barrier Reef*, Caroline Arnold
			The Great Little Madison, Jean Fritz

TABLE 3.3
Gender differences in children's reading interests.

Boys' Interests	Girls' Interests
Male characters	*Female characters*
Nonfiction topics	*Fiction topics*
■ science	■ families
■ animals	■ home
■ history	■ romance
■ biography	■ historical fiction
■ geography	■ mystery/adventure
■ sports	■ fantasy
■ cars	■ multiethnic
■ war	*Nonfiction topics*
■ machines	■ sports
■ applied science	■ arts
■ adventure	■ multiethnic

cover. The designation "RL 4.0" means that the book is written at a fourth-grade reading level. This does not mean the book is appropriate for every fourth grader, however, because reading abilities in a fourth-grade classroom may range from first to seventh grade. Moreover, children must be able to pronounce 98 to 100 percent of the words and answer 90 to 100 percent of the questions asked about the book if they are to read with understanding. Therefore, if the book is to be independently read, it might well be appropriate for an average reader in fifth grade. Developmentally appropriate literature is summarized in Table 3.2.

Identifying Reading Preferences and Interests

Literature preferences and interests are highly individual phenomena that change from reader to reader and book to book (Galda, et al., 2001). Understanding readers, the texts they choose to read, and the contexts in which they read is very complex. Therefore, observations, discussions, and book-talks are the best ways to identify books that will energize children's reading. Observations regarding the engaging books that students choose to read and making notes about their choices are the most valid ways to identify their reading interests. Teachers can identify individual children's reading interests through techniques like the following:

1. Observe children as they engage in classroom activities, noting and recording interests exhibited during class assignments, oral discussions, group projects, and so forth.
2. Conduct informal discussions with the children themselves, their parents, peers, and others, which will reveal some interests.
3. Book-talk a group of books, observe the students' responses to these books, and make notes about the books that the students responded to.
4. Conduct interest inventories, which take a variety of forms, asking children directly about their reading interests. Children can list their favorite book titles, respond to questions through a multiple-choice format, or complete sentence starters (illustrated in Figure 3.3).
5. Encourage children to choose books independently and observe their choices.

Bibliotherapy

Bibliotherapy literally means "helping with books." A book may present a story or information about a problem. Historically, doctors, therapists, and other health-care professionals have used bibliotherapy. According to Bernstein (1989), bibliotherapy involves the "self examination and insights gained from reading" (p. 159). It can help children meet their most basic human needs such as love, belonging, esteem, and self-actualization.

Bibliotherapy is based on identification, catharsis, and insight. Through *identification*, readers associate themselves with story characters, thereby recognizing similarities to their own lives. Sometimes talking about the problems that book characters encounter enables children to discuss their own difficulties. *Catharsis* is the emotional release that occurs when readers identify with a character. Some readers orally express their response, while others find writing about their experience leads to and facilitates discussion. Readers can develop *insight*, which is a form of self-discovery, as a result of responding to literature. Insight leads to attitudinal and behavioral changes (Stephens, 1981).

FIGURE 3.3   Interest inventory.

1. I like to read _____.

2. I go to the library every _____.

3. I like to read when _____.

4. I like to read more than I like to _____.

5. I like to watch television every _____.

6. I like television shows about _____.

7. Books about sports are _____.

8. I think horse stories are _____.

9. I think mysteries are _____.

10. My favorite author is _____.

11. Books bore me when _____.

12. I read funny stories about _____.

13. When I have spare time, I _____.

14. I like to read in _____.

15. Good books make me feel _____.

16. The best books are about _____.

17. I own _____

    _____

    _____

    _____

    _____ books.

18. My favorite video is _____.

19. The best taped book I have heard is _____.

20. I read _____
    because my friend told me about it.

Scoring: Score one point for each positive answer.

Positive answers are answers that indicate the student enjoys reading and has identifiable reading, listening, and viewing interests.

13–17 = child has positive attitude toward reading.

9–12 = child has average interest in reading.

1–8 = child needs guidance in developing greater interest in reading.

For the child experiencing the fear, loneliness, and confusion created by the loss of a parent, a book such as Jill Krementz's *How It Feels When a Parent Dies* may be helpful. This book is a collection of interviews with children who describe their feelings about this traumatic event. A child who has recently experienced this loss may identify with all of the children in the book or with the feelings of one particular child. Identification may help the child feel less alone with the grief and may ultimately result in catharsis and insight. This process can enhance children's sense of self, thereby contributing to their self-esteem.

Children's response to books is central to the concept of bibliotherapy, but we cannot accurately predict the response of a particular individual to a particular book. Teachers often find that a book that appealed to a previous class holds no interest for the current year's class. Often a book that one individual does not enjoy is of particular interest to another person. For instance, one student commented to a teacher that she had enjoyed a certain book more than any other she had ever read. The teacher was puzzled because, in her opinion, the book had no redeeming qualities. The student explained, however, that she had blamed herself for her mother's suicide until she read this book, in which the same tragic event had happened. The student developed insight about her own life through reading this book. Unfortunately, such responses are not predictable, showing that teachers can make suggestions, but children should ultimately choose books that appeal to them and seem to meet their needs.

Bernstein (1989) suggests guidelines for selecting books to use therapeutically in the classroom:

1. Allow children to select their own books.

2. Discuss books with the students; the adults should listen with empathy rather than sympathy.

3. Use group discussions to help children generate new solutions to problems. Group discussions should focus on expressing and clarifying feelings. Children who are uncomfortable with discussing feelings should not be forced into revelations.

Media-Based Literature

Audio books, electronic books, television, movies, Internet sites, and videos provide legitimate forms of literature that are here to stay. High-quality media actively involve children with the literature they are experiencing—an advantage that children may carry into other literary experiences. *Reading Rainbow*, which is aired on local PBS stations, is an example of a superb television show for children.

The availability of media-based literature is growing rapidly: Listening Library now offers more than 200 unabridged children's recordings. Although these media do not replace books, they do offer a different dimension, and narrators and actors can make stories come alive for children. Many children will go on to read books they have been exposed to through various media; others will not because the media offer an alternative route to literature they could not access otherwise. Videos such as *The Very Hungry Caterpillar* (Disney) offer animation and music to enhance this well-loved story. The various genres of children's literature are represented in videos. The *James Marshall Library* (Children's Circle/Scholastic) includes popular fairy tales that primary-grade children will enjoy. Videos include feature-length films such as *Beethoven Lives Upstairs*. The *Children's Literature Web Guide* on the Internet can direct you to multimedia materials that have been evaluated by parents' groups and the American Library Association.

The growth of literature available on the computer has surged since CD–ROM drives have been added to computers. *Living Books*, featuring children's authors such as Mercer Mayer, are very popular (Random House/Broderbund). *Busy Town* by Richard Scarry has received the Parents Award for Quality (Paramount International). Microsoft published some of the *Magic School Bus* titles on CD–ROM, which children find fascinating. The interactive, involving nature of computerized books adds to their popularity and their value for children.

Media-based literature should not be based on offering alternative editions of existing books; rather, it should offer additional dimensions. Some writers create original literature for CD–ROM rather than converting existing literature to a media format. Shelley Duvall writes computer-based adventure stories centered on Digby, a little dog with a big bark (Sanctuary Woods). *Where in the World Is Carmen Sandiego?* (Broderbund) is an interactive detective story that also provides geography lessons to participants. *Freddi Fish and the Case of the Missing Kelp Seeds* (Humongous Entertainment) is another entertaining and original computer story.

Some exceptional *audiobooks* for upper elementary students are Jamake Highwater's *Anapao* (Recorded Books) and Gary Paulsen's *Canyons* (Bantam Doubleday Dell Audio). Peter Coyote narrates *Canyons*, a parallel story of two boys, one contemporary and one an Apache who lived a century earlier. Audio recording is the perfect medium for *Anapao*, which was intended to be read aloud, as this recording captures the distinctive style of Native American storytelling. Listening to the recording of *Island of the Blue Dolphins* brings the story alive even for those who have read it many times before.

Some of these media stories will become classics for future generations. Certainly the movie *Fantasia* is a Disney classic, and Disney's *Jungle Book* has led to a resurgence of interest in the original writing of this wonderful story, popularizing Rudyard Kipling's book for a new generation. Raffi, a singer and storyteller, is a superstar to many in the younger set, who flock to his concerts, listen to his audiotapes, and watch his videos.

Evaluating Media-Based Literature

The American Library Association reviews and evaluates media for children. Consulting their reviews and standards can be very helpful to librarians and teachers. The standards for literature identified earlier in this chapter are also applicable to media presentations of literature. Some children's bookstores and companies that distribute media to schools will allow teachers to try out or preview their materials, which is an advantage because catalog descriptions and advertising materials cannot predict how the children will respond. In addition to trying before buying, the following guidelines should be helpful in selecting media-based literature.

1. The literature must tell a good story or a wonderful poem or give accurate, interesting information (check the guidelines established in the genre chapters).
2. The literature must actively involve viewers or listeners.
3. The literature should convey the essence of the literature so that plot, theme, characterization, and setting are authentic, although the style may differ according to the medium.
4. The literature should meet all of the standards set for written literature; for instance, informational literature should meet nonfiction standards and the difference between theory and fact should be apparent.
5. The literature should have all illustrations in scale and accurately identified.

6. The literature should not be simplified so that it loses literary quality; literature prepared for film, computer, video, and so forth may require changes but these can be achieved without loss of quality.

7. The literature should not trivialize the story, for instance, by making the presentation too "cute."

Exploring Literature

The ways that literature is presented influences children's literary response. How books are read and what is read, frequency of read-alouds, and active discussions build children's reading interests and response to literature (Galda, et al., 2001). Reading books aloud and discussing them helps students construct meaning. Increasing the connections that students can make with literature content (including media-based) through discussion and response activities also increases comprehension and appreciation.

Media-based literature is easy to present: it can be done as easily as turning on a switch. It should always, however, be a part of a planned literary experience. Parents, teachers, or librarians presenting the literature should share the experience with the children. First, creating a context for the experience by introducing the piece and helping the children see connections to themselves will help ensure their active involvement and response; afterward, adults can discuss the experience with the children and share their responses. Discussion and opportunities to respond are just as important for media as for books. The suggestions in Chapter 15 will be helpful in planning responses to literature.

Issues-Centered Criticism of Children's Literature: Censorship

A book becomes part of the curriculum when all students in a class are assigned the same book. When literature is used as part of the curriculum, it can be a catalyst for intense reactions. After all, the things we read make us who we are by presenting our image of ourselves as girls and women, or as boys and men. Children's literature is perhaps the most influential genre in this regard. The stereotypes and worldview embedded in these stories become accepted knowledge.

As literature has been recognized as an important influence in children's lives, the literature itself has changed. Today's books use realistic language, includ-

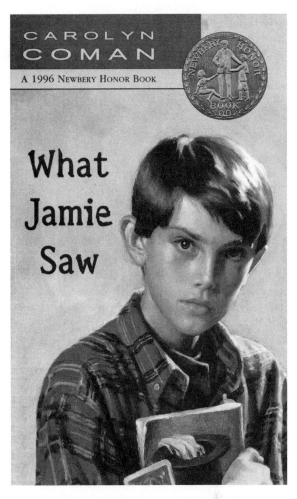

Jamie confronted violence in this suspenseful story.

ing nonstandard English and expletives. Formerly taboo topics such as drugs, sex, homosexuality, fights, death, and divorce are now found in children's books (McClure, 1995). Coincidentally, our culture is becoming more conservative in the face of national concern for values and morals, which stimulates censors to believe that they must protect children from influences they consider evil or harmful.

Until they are faced with it, many teachers and librarians tend to believe that censorship only happens in other places. Many adults believe children's literature comprises simple stories populated with charming magic, toys, and animals. However, the nature of objectionable content often depends on the reader's perceptions. The *Harry Potter* books have been targeted for more complaints than any other books in recent memory (American Library Association, 2003). These

FIGURE 3.4   Examples of censored books.

Book	Author	Alleged Reason for Censorship
Scary Stories to Tell in the Dark	Alvin Schwartz	Witchcraft/occult/satanic
Missing May	Cynthia Rylant	References to spirits, ghosts
Bridge to Terabithia	Katherine Paterson	Use of words *Lord* and *hell*
The Great Gilly Hopkins	Katherine Paterson	Remarks about God and religion
Starring Sally J. Freedman as Herself	Judy Blume	Questions adults
Daddy's Roommate	Michael Wilhoite	Concerns gay parents
Heather Has Two Mommies	Leslea Newman	Concerns lesbian parents
My Puppy Is Born	Joanna Cole Word	Uses word *mating*
Noah's Ark	Peter Spier	Piles of manure on ark
Stonewords	Pam Conrad	Concerns New Age philosophy
My Special Best Words	John Steptoe	Has child on toilet

complaints are based on concerns about magic and wizards in these stories; nevertheless, these books have intensified children's interest in fantasy, making it an immensely popular genre. Additional examples of censored books are listed in Figure 3.4.

Censorship is usually based on removing a book from circulation because of sexual references, profanity, sexism, racism, ageism, nudity, drugs, or violence. Censors focus on books they consider harmful or evil, and they seek to protect children from these books (McClure, 1995). However, efforts to censor the harmful or evil influences of books are based on the censors' own biases. For example, liberals want books that avoid racist or sexist stereotypes; conservatives fear books that permit characters to question God, parents, or teachers. At the same time, proponents of intellectual freedom believe that children should have free access to ideas and the right to examine and challenge ideas (McClure, 1995).

Where do we draw the line? Should no book be challenged? In contrast, if every book is challenged, whose values will be the basis for challenging books in libraries and schools? Certainly, parents have the right to question reading material assigned to their children, but should they determine what other children read? Does anyone have the right to determine what others will or will not read? These are not easy questions to answer; nevertheless, they must be addressed. We recommend that adults seek out and read books that are worthy of children's attention and offer them as alternatives to unacceptable books. The following sections examine some of the specific issues related to censorship.

Racial and Ethnic Issues

This section addresses some aspects of evaluating children's books to ensure appropriate portrayal of the diversity in our culture. Positive and accurate portrayals of minority cultures are important in children's literature, which contributes to their social/cultural development. In addition to evaluating books for literary quality, adults need to consider whether they (a) provide diversity and range of representation, (b) avoid stereotyping, (c) use appropriate language, and (d) have appropriate cultural perspectives.

In order to address diversity and range of representation, children's books should portray minorities in a wide variety of economic circumstances, lifestyles, and occupations. Consistent portrayal of Asian Americans as studious scientists or engineers stereotypes them in a way that is just as inaccurate and damaging as portraying all Latinos as poor migrant workers. Members of particular cultural groups must be regarded as unique individuals with their own values, beliefs, and opinions, not merely as representatives of those groups. In research (Costello, 1992; Harris, 1994) regarding African American children's literature, parents expressed their concern for an accurate portrayal of their culture, lives, and concepts of beauty that looked like their own children (Costello, 1992). Violet Harris (1994) considers the portrayal of the African American experience in this country when identifying culturally conscious books.

In order to avoid stereotyping, authors should refrain from using certain items that traditionally have been associated with particular ethnic groups, such as *sombreros*. The customs and values of each group should be accurately portrayed. Illustrations should capture the distinctive characteristics of a particular group and should portray scenes including individuals from many cultures. Characters of color should be readily recognizable as members of a particular racial or cultural group.

Appropriate Language

Language comprehension is essential to effective communication; therefore, authors must use appropriate language that avoids stereotypes and derogatory labels for racial and ethnic groups. Appropriate language portrays racial and ethnic characters as three-dimensional individuals who have positive roles in stories, poems, and nonfiction. Many authors use words and phrases that reflect the language of the cultural group in the book. To facilitate readers' comprehension, these authors often include a glossary or dictionary at the end of the book. Jewell Coburn's *Domitila: A Cinderella Tale from the Mexican Tradition* illustrates how writers introduce language that facilitates comprehension. The publisher's note, the glossary, and a recipe communicate the ethnic roots of this story.

Culturally conscious literature tells stories from the perspective of the culture. It depicts characters as capable of making their own decisions and meeting their own needs without the intervention of White benefactors. Non-White characters are represented as being equal to White characters, not subservient or inferior.

Gender Stereotyping Issues

Evaluation of children's books includes attention to gender stereotyping. Many children's books have traditionally depicted women only in traditional roles such as housewives, reflecting the culture that existed at the time they were written. Traditional literature sometimes portrays helpless, vulnerable female characters waiting for strong, capable men to rescue them, as in the Grimm Brothers' *Snow White* and *Cinderella*.

Although we often point to such works as examples of female stereotyping, they also stereotype men as perpetually strong, capable, and competent. When reading such works, the context of the literature should be examined so that students have the means of understanding the gender stereotyping reflected in some literature. Students should have opportunities to compare contemporary gender portrayals with more traditional portrayals. In contemporary literature, women are presented in a variety of occupations, deriving satisfaction from

their achievements, and are described as intelligent, independent, and strong. Modern folk tales are reversing the stereotyping found in the aforementioned examples from this genre. Robert Munsch provides a view of a contemporary princess who takes charge of her own life in *The Paper Bag Princess;* other stories, such as Betsy Hearne's *Seven Brave Women* and Jeanette Winter's *My Name Is Georgia*, portray women as strong and capable.

Nonstereotyped men and boys are portrayed as sensitive human beings with a wide range of emotions. In addition, males as well as females should be portrayed in a variety of occupations, including those traditionally reserved for women. Books such as Gary Paulsen's *Hatchet* show an adolescent boy learning to survive in the wilderness while coping with his parents' divorce. Although he lacks the skills and knowledge needed, he uses trial-and-error strategies to survive. In *On My Honor*, Marion Dane Bauer describes a young man's emotional struggle to deal with his friend's death.

Addressing Censorship

The American Library Association is a rich source of material regarding censorship. Their Internet site, **www.ala.org/alaorg.html**, has many references to guide librarians and teachers as they learn about censorship and ways of addressing it. The American Library Association sponsors Banned Books Week and provides a *Resource Guide* for schools. They also offer Library Advocacy Training and sponsor the Freedom to Read Foundation. The Coalition Against Censorship also maintains a Web site that offers information and resources for people who must navigate the shoals of censorship.

Teachers and librarians may find censors challenging books that have significant literary value, so they should be sensitive to community feelings regarding literature. To avoid challenges, they can introduce the literature to parents and offer them opportunities to preview books by including parents in meetings and committees. The National Council of Teachers of English offers a CD-ROM resource entitled *Challenged Books*, which provides rationales for more than 200 literary works that have been frequently challenged and removed from classroom and library shelves. Materials for Grades K–12 are included; however, the work emphasizes middle school and high school levels. M. Jerry Weiss (1989) and the International Reading Association's Intellectual Freedom Committee offer the following professional strategies for addressing censorship issues.

1. Communicate with parents regarding their concerns about certain books. This might include forming a book discussion group for parents so that they can read and discuss children's books.

2. Provide a variety of books for children so that if parents prefer their child not to read a specific book, plenty of others are available from which to choose. A well-balanced library collection will contain many books about a given subject.

3. Clearly state and write down the school's adoption and purchasing policy for classroom and library books. The school may create an advisory board to assist in decisions about purchasing books and include parents on the board. Provide forms for parents to complete when they have concerns about a book with room to detail specific objections.

4. A school review committee should consider objections to books by using the questionnaire in Figure 3.5, or a similar one, to guide deliberations regarding objections.

FIGURE 3.5   Questionnaire for concerned parents.

1. Have you read the entire book?
2. What is the teacher's purpose for using this material?
3. Identify the specific passages that you find objectionable.
4. In your view, what problems would reading this material cause?
5. What action do you think should be taken?
6. Can you suggest an acceptable substitute?

Classroom Activities

Response activities in this chapter focus on award books, as well as the authors and illustrators of these books. In this section, you will find activities that encourage students to concentrate on criteria for writing and illustrating the books they read. All of the following activities lend themselves to small group or whole class experiences. Some teachers and librarians have had the children work in groups and present their award winners and their reasons for choosing the particular book or books.

ACTIVITY 3.1   PREDICTING THE NEWBERY AWARD

(IRA/NCTE Standards: 1, 2, 6, 7, 12, reading comprehension, literary genre, employing literary criteria, literary response.)

Identify books published in the current year and have the students apply the Newbery Criteria to the books and identify their favorite to win the award. When the awards are announced they can compare their favorites with the award winners and honor books. Some states also give state awards to outstanding books. Students may contact their school librarian to investigate this award as well. The Newbery and Caldecott award winners are announced in newspapers, on television, and in professional journals following the winter meeting of the American Library Association.

ACTIVITY 3.2   PREDICTING AWARDS

(IRA/NCTE Standards: 1, 2, 6, 7, 12, reading comprehension, literary genre, employing criteria, literary response.)

Follow the same procedure for potential Caldecott winners, Orbis Pictus Books, and Coretta Scott King Award books.

ACTIVITY 3.3   NEWBERY AND CALDECOTT FAVORITES

(IRA/NCTE Standards: 1, 2, 6, 7, 12, reading comprehension, literary genre, employing criteria, literary response.)

Students may read past Newbery and Caldecott Medal books, as well as Orbis Pictus and Coretta Scott King Award books to identify their favorites and the qualities that made these books winners. They may include honor books in this activity as well.

ACTIVITY 3.4   WHICH GENRE IS MOST POPULAR

(IRA/NCTE Standards: 5, 6, 7, 8, 12.)

Read the award winning books and identify the genre receiving the most awards and the one with the fewest awards.

ACTIVITY 3.5   AWARD WINNING CHARACTERS

(IRA/NCTE Standards: 5, 6, 7, 8, 12.)

Compare the central characters in two award winning books.

ACTIVITY 3.6   AWARD WINNING THEMES

(IRA/NCTE Standards: 5, 6, 7, 8, 12.)

Read award winning books and identify the frequently occurring themes.

ACTIVITY 3.7   WHICH AUTHORS AND ILLUSTRATORS HAVE WON MULTIPLE AWARDS?

(IRA/NCTE Standards: 5, 6, 7, 8, 12.)

Identify an author or illustrator who has had multiple award winning books and/or honor books and do an author profile of the author or illustrator.

Summary

Carefully selected literature engages readers' minds, interests, and feelings. Choosing well-written, interesting books for classrooms and libraries is basic to creating successful literature programs. Such a large number of children's books are published each year, and these books vary so widely in quality, that book selection is too important to be left to chance. Carefully selected literature engages readers' minds, interests, and feelings. Considerations in selection include interests, age, grade, and developmental stage. Books should be evaluated from a variety of perspectives, including references and Web sites. Censorship denies children free access to books, which does not prepare them to make responsible choices or to promote their intellectual growth.

A broad collection of excellent literature drawn from all genres is the cornerstone of literary experience. Selected books should appeal to both readers and listeners. In selecting books, consider the elements that make a story, a poem, or an informational book excellent literature. Children's reading interests are important considerations in choosing literature (see Figure 3.6).

When stocking a library or media center, remember that literature is not confined to print. Media such as films, videos, audiotapes, filmstrips, recordings, puppets, dramatizations, and storytelling are forms of literary experience. Experiencing literature through various media expands background knowledge, deepens students' response, and strengthens their understanding.

Thought Questions

1. What factors should you consider when selecting children's books?
2. Summarize the research related to children's reading interests in your own words.
3. What books did you enjoy as a child? How old were you when you enjoyed these books? How do you think these books related to your development?
4. Why is avoiding books that have gender or racial stereotyping important?
5. Describe some ways that teachers, parents, and librarians can promote children's reading interests.

Research and Application Experiences

1. Select several books for a child with whom you are well-acquainted. Consider the criteria listed in Figure 3.6. Which of these criteria did you apply when choosing these books? Which were least important?

FIGURE 3.6   Guidelines for Literature Selection.

Remember to consider not only literary quality when selecting children's books but children's reading interests and issues as well. This will help create a well-balanced literary experience for the children.

1. Is the book of high literary quality?
   a. Fiction
      - Is the plot well developed?
      - Are characters well drawn and memorable?
      - Does the setting accurately reflect the time and place?
      - Is the theme significant?
      - Is the book carefully crafted and well written?
   b. Nonfiction
      - Is the author qualified to write this book?
      - Is the information clearly organized and presented?
      - Is the information accurate?
      - Is this book appropriate to a child audience?
2. Does the book appeal to children's reading interests?
3. Does the book avoid stereotyping on the basis of race, sex, age, and other discriminatory factors?
4. Is the book's readability level appropriate to the audience that is expected to read it?
5. Is the book's physical format appealing to children?
6. Will this book enhance the child's personal growth and development?
7. Will this book contribute to the child's development as a reader?
8. Will this book help foster a love of reading in this child?
9. Am I creating an environment that will help promote love of literature?

2. Read three Newbery and three Caldecott books. Evaluate each one according to the award criteria, then rank the books according to your own evaluation.

3. Interview children who have read Newbery or Caldecott winners. Find out which were their favorites and why.

4. Imagine that a parent has challenged you for using a particular children's book. Role-play the meeting you would have with him or her.

Children's Literature References and Recommended Books

Note: Books designated with an asterisk (*) are recommended for reluctant readers.

Bauer, M. D. (1986). *On my honor*. New York: Clarion. (4–7). REALISTIC FICTION.

A boy must cope with guilt and self-blame when his friend drowns.

George, J. C. (1972). *Julie of the wolves*. New York: Harper & Row. (5–7). CONTEMPORARY REALISTIC FICTION.

This is a survival story set in the Alaskan wilderness.

Grimm, J., & Grimm, W. (1972). *Snow White and the seven dwarfs* (N. E. Burkert, Illus.). New York: Farrar, Straus & Giroux. (2–4). TRADITIONAL LITERATURE.

A classic version of this tale.

Grimm, J., & Grimm, W. (1987). *Cinderella*. New York: Holiday. (1–3). TRADITIONAL LITERATURE.

This is an older version of the well-known folk tale.

Hearne, B. (1997). *Seven brave women* (B. Andersen, Illus.). New York: Greenwillow. (2–6). NONFICTION BOOK.*

This is the story of women who expressed their bravery in different ways.

Holman, F. (1986). *Slake's limbo*. New York: Aladdin. (5–7). REALISTIC FICTION.*

Slake goes underground in the subway system when life overwhelms him above ground.

Krementz, J. (1981). *How it feels when a parent dies*. New York: Knopf. (3–6). INFORMATIONAL BOOK.

This book tells a child's feelings about a parent's death.

Mahy, M. (1986). *The boy who was followed home* (S. Kellogg, Illus.). New York: Dial. (K–2). FANTASY.

When a hippopotamus follows Robert home, he is very pleased. The story becomes more complicated when 43 hippos appear on the lawn, but a witch casts a spell to solve the problem.

Munsch, R (1992). *The paperbag princess*. Toronto, Canada: Annick Press. (6–10). FANTASY.

Elizabeth, a beautiful princess, rescues her prince from a dragon, but the prince is dismayed at her appearance.

Myers, W. D. (1988). *Scorpions*. New York: Harper & Row. (5–7). REALISTIC FICTION.

Family tragedies force Jamal to grow up quickly.

Paulsen, G. (1987). *Hatchet*. New York: Viking Penguin. (5–7). REALISTIC FICTION.*

Brian survives an airplane crash and spends the next 54 days trying to survive with only the hatchet his mother gave him.

Potter, B. (1934). *The tale of Peter Rabbit*. New York: Frederick Warne. (PreK–2). PICTURE BOOK, MODERN FANTASY.

The classic tale of a naughty rabbit.

Reeder, C. (1998). *Foster's war*. New York: Scholastic. (4–8). HISTORICAL FICTION.

This is the story of 11-year-old Foster, who has conflicts about his father, his best friend, and his older brother who is in the air corps.

Rowling, J. K. (1999). *Harry Potter and the chamber of secrets* (M. GrandPré, Illus.). New York: Levine. (4–6). MODERN FANTASY.

Harry Potter is an orphaned wizard who attends the Hogwarts School for Witchcraft and Wizardry.

Sendak, M. (1963). *Where the wild things are*. New York: Harper & Row. (PreK–2). PICTURE BOOK, MODERN FANTASY.

A boy visits the land of wild things.

Service, P. (1988). *Stinker from space*. New York: Scribners. (4–6). SCIENCE FICTION.

In this very funny science fiction story, the central character crashes into earth and injects himself into a skunk in order to save his life.

Van Allsburg, C. (1985). *The polar express*. Boston: Houghton Mifflin. (K–4). MODERN FANTASY.

The Christmas train to the north pole story has become a classic.

White, E. B. (1952). *Charlotte's web* (G. Williams, Illus.). New York: Harper. (3–6). MODERN FANTASY.

This classic book describes the friendship between Charlotte and Wilbur, a spider and a pig.

Winter, J. (1998). *My name is Georgia*. San Diego: Silver Whistle/Harcourt Brace. (1–4). BIOGRAPHY.

This is the story of artist Georgia O'Keeffe, who saw the world in her own way.

Multimedia References

Children's circle. Scholastic offers a variety of titles for primary grades.

Reading rainbow. Public Broadcasting System. Individual videos of programs can be ordered and teachers can videotape them to use in their own classes.

The very hungry caterpillar. Disney (Based on the picture book by E. Carle). (PreK–2). MODERN FANTASY.

Recorded Books

Highwater, J. *Anapao*. Recorded books. (4–6). CONTEMPORARY REALISTIC FICTION.

Paulsen, G. *Canyons*. Bantam Doubleday Dell Audio. (3–6). CONTEMPORARY REALISTIC FICTION. Listening Library has a large variety of titles available.

Computer Software

Duvall, S. *Digby* (several titles). Sanctuary Woods. (PreK–2). MODERN FANTASY.

Freddi Fish and the case of the missing kelp seeds. Humongous Entertainment. (K–2). MODERN FANTASY.

Magic school bus. Various titles. Scholastic. (K–4). MODERN FANTASY, INFORMATIONAL.

Mayer, M. Various titles. Random House/Broderbund. (PreK–2). MODERN FANTASY.

Scarry, R. *Busy town*. Paramount International. (PreK–1). Activities about neighborhoods and building.

Where in the world is Carmen Sandiego? Broderbund. (1–3). INFORMATIONAL.

References and Books for Further Reading

Abramson, R. (1980). An analysis of children's favorite picture storybooks. *The Reading Teacher, 34,* 167–170.

Adams, J. J. (1990). *Thinking and learning about print*. Cambridge, MA: MIT Press.

American Library Association. (2003). *Challenged Books*. Chicago: ALA.

Beckett, S. L. (1997). Introduction: Reflections of change. In S. L. Beckett, *Reflections of change: Children's literature since 1945* (pp. ix–xi). Westport, CT: Greenwood.

Bernstein, J. E. (1989). Bibliotherapy: How books can help young children cope. In Bernstein *Books to help children cope with separation and loss* (2nd ed., pp. 166–178). New York: Bowker.

Bowker, R. R. (Ed.). (1991). *Children's reference plus*. New York: Bowker.

Burgess, S. A. (1985). Reading but not literature: The ChildRead survey. *School Library Journal, 31,* 27–30.

Campbell, R. (1990). *Reading together*. London: Open University.

Carlsen, G. R., & Sherrill, A. (1988). *Voices of readers: How we came to love books*. Urbana, IL: National Council of Teachers of English.

Cooper-Mullin, A., & Coye, J. M. (1998). *Once upon a heroine*. Chicago: Contemporary Books.

Costello, J. H. (1992). *An inquiry into the attitudes of a selected group of African Americans towards the portrayal of African Americans in contemporary children's literature*. Unpublished doctoral dissertation, University of North Carolina at Greensboro.

Fielding, L. G., Wilson, P., & Anderson, R. (1986). A new focus on free reading: The role of trade books in reading instruction. In T. Raphael (Ed.), *The contexts of school-based literacy* (pp. 149–169). New York: Random House.

Galda, L., Ash, G., & Cullinan, B. (2001, April). Research on childen's literature. *Reading Online, 4* (9), 1–4.

Harris, V. J. (1994). No invitations required to share multicultural literature. *Journal of Children's Literature, 20,* 9–15.

Haynes, C. (1988). Explanatory power of content for identifying children's literature preferences. *Dissertation Abstracts International,* 3617. University Microfilms, No. DEW8900468.

Hearne, B., with Stevenson, D. (1999). *Choosing books for children: A commonsense approach.* (3rd Ed.). Urbana, IL: University of Illinois.

Hiebert, E. H., Mervar, K., & Person, D. (1990). Children's selection of trade books in libraries and classrooms. *Language Arts, 67,* 758–763.

Kopp, J. J., & Halverson, C. (1983). Preschool children's preferences and recall for stereotyped versus non-stereotyped stories. *Sex Roles, 9,* 261–272.

Lehman B. A. (1991). Children's choice and critical acclaim: A united perspective for children's literature. *Reading Research and Instruction, 30,* 1–20.

Mackey, M. (1990). Filling in gaps: The baby sitters club, the series book, and the learning reader. *Language Arts, 67,* 484–489.

McClure, A. (1995). Censorship in children's books. In S. Lehr (Ed.), *Battling dragons: Issues and controversies in children's literature.* Portsmouth, NH: Heinemann.

Odean, K. (1998). *Great books for boys.* New York: Ballantine.

Ohanian, S. (1990). How to create a generation of aliterates. In K. Goodman, L. Bird, & Y. Goodman (Eds.), *Whole language catalog* (p. 76). New York: American School.

Pieronek, F. T. (1980). Do basal readers reflect the interests of intermediate students? *The Reading Teacher, 33,* 408–412.

Purves, A., & Beach, R. (1972). *Literature and the reader: Research in response to literature, reading interests, and the teaching of literature.* Urbana, IL: National Council of Teachers of English.

Purves, A., & Monson, D. (1984). *Experiencing children's literature.* Glenview, IL: Scott Foresman.

Robbins, P. (Ed.). (1982, November 22). *National Geographic books for world explorers.* Presentation to Children's Literature Association, Washington, D.C.

Rosenblatt, L. M. (1978) *The reader, the text, the poem*: *The transactional theory of the literary work.* Edwardsville, Southern Illinois University.

Schlager, N. (1978). Predicting children's choices in literature: A developmental approach. *Children's Literature in Education, 9,* 136–142.

Sebesta, S. (1979). What do you people think about the literature they read? *Reading Newsletter, 8,* 3.

Serafini, F. (2001). *The reading workshop: Creating space for readers.* Portsmouth, NH: Heinemann.

Shafer, P.J. (1976, May). The readability of Newberry Award and Caldecott Medal books. *Language Arts, 53,* 557–559.

Stephens, J.W. (1981). *A practical guide in the use and implementation of bibliotherapy.* Great Neck, NY: Todd & Honeywell.

Stoodt-Hill, B. (1999). *How children choose their books.* Unpublished research paper.

Stoodt-Hill, B. (2003). *Children's Reading Interests and Reading Success.* Unpublished research paper.

Swanton, S. (1984). Minds alive! What and why gifted students read for pleasure. *School Library Journal, 30,* 99–102.

Trelease, J. (1995). *The read-aloud handbook.* New York: Penguin Books.

Weiss, M.J. (1989). International Reading Association stands out against censorship. *Reading Today, 6,* 6.

Wolfson, B., Manning, G. & Manning, M. (1984). Revisiting what children say their reading interests are. *The reading world 14,* 81–82.

Picture Books: Visual and Verbal Art

4

KEY TERMS

benchmark	picture book
illustrated book	visual literacy
medium	wordless picture book

GUIDING QUESTIONS

1. What was your favorite picture book when you were a child? Why did you like this book?

2. Why are picture books unique works of art?

3. Why are picture books valuable for all ages?

4. Who is your favorite picture book illustrator?

Most children's first experiences with literature are with picture books. However, more and more picture books are appearing in middle school classes because they present complex ideas and concepts in an easy-to-access format. In picture books, images and ideas come together in a unique and exciting art form that adults and children can explore at many levels (Kiefer, 1995)."A picture book has a collective unity of story-line, theme, or concept, developed through the series of pictures of which the book is comprised" (Matulka, 2002). Fine picture books give children a window on the wider world, enabling them to know and learn things outside their own limited experience. In picture books, authors may tell stories, share poems, or convey information.

This chapter includes examples of excellent picture books available to enrich your understanding of picture books and their value in children's lives. This chapter introduces picture books in a genre organization because all literary genre appear in the picture book format. *Benchmarks* or standards of quality are represented in the exemplary books discussed in this chapter. We suggest that you read some of these books to develop your own taste and standards of quality. Your ability to distinguish between outstanding picture books and those of lesser quality will increase with experience.

The Nature of Picture Books

Picture books are a form of artistic expression that is ideally suited to reinterpreting and re-presenting the world to an audience (Lewis, 2001). Pictures and text in picture books function as different forms of communication; each is incomplete without the other (Nikolajeva & Scott, 2001). The vignette on the following page illustrates using the combination of narrative and illustration to tell a story. When the children recognized the nursery rhyme figures, they were connecting the illustrations with prior experiences. After seeing the map, the children realized it would help them understand the characters' travels.

Caldecott Medalist Ed Young (1990) believes "there are things that words do that pictures never can, and likewise, there are images that words can never describe." Picture books are "as close to drama or a thirty-two page movie, as it is to either literature or

First-grade teacher Jane Fredericks began class with "Hey Diddle Diddle, the Cat and the Fiddle. . . " At this point, several first graders joined in chanting the nursery rhyme. After they said, "and the dish ran away with the spoon," she opened the book *And the DISH Ran Away with the SPOON* by Janet Stevens and Susan Crummel. She showed the children the double-page spread of the characters from this nursery rhyme and they chanted it again. Then she explained, "This story begins like the one we just chanted, but it changes. I will read it and you listen for the change." She then turned the page and read, "They didn't come back!"

"It changed when they didn't come back," Riley said.

"Who do you think didn't come back?" Jane queried.

Jason answered, "The dish and the spoon."

"Why do you think that?" Jane asked.

"Because the rhyme says the dish ran away with the spoon," Andrew replied.

"Very good thinking," Jane said. "Now I'll read what the animals thought about their missing friends."

"Why do we need the dish and the spoon anyway?"

"Why don't we just change their part?"

"cat yawned."

"we could end it 'and the cow took a nap until noon.'"

Randall volunteered, "They thought they didn't need the others."

Jane continued reading until. . . . . .

"Look, there's a map in the book!" Kendra said.

JANET STEVENS AND SUSAN STEVENS CRUMMEL

And the DISH Ran Away with the SPOON

illustrated by Janet Stevens

The dish and the spoon ran away . . . will they come back?

"Can I see the map?" Jason asked.

"I want to see where they are and where they are going,"

"I'll put a copy of the map on the board, so you can follow their travels," responded Jane.

As she continued, the children could see each stop the animals made on the map.

After she completed reading, Jane asked the children to identify the two problems in the story.

Emily responded, "The dish and the spoon ran away, so the others couldn't do the rhyme without them."

"When they found the dish it was broken, so they had to get it fixed," Sarah said.

"There was another problem," Kendall mentioned.

Jane asked, "Can you tell us about the other problem?"

(continued)

"Yes, they had to hurry back to get home in time to do the rhyme."

After the class discussed the solutions to the various problems in the story, Emily pointed out that the story contained many other Mother Goose rhymes. The children decided to read the various rhymes and continued the study for two weeks, including dramatizing of the rhymes. Several of the children wanted to draw maps like the one in the story, so they drew maps for the other rhymes. The story introduced directions that were incorporated in the maps. On the following day, Jane introduced David Wiesner's picture book *The Three Pigs*, because it provided an excellent comparison with *And the DISH Ran Away with the SPOON*. This single picture book provided opportunities to address several standards of learning. (IRA/NCTE Standards: 2, 3, 6. Comprehension, following directions, and comparing. Maps are a social studies topic.)

art" (Wood, & Wood 1986, p. 556). Pictures stimulate dramatic, active responses in children that compare with their responses to theater or film. Researchers have found that illustrations contribute to readers' understanding, as well as to intellectual and emotional development (Kiefer, 1995). Although the text itself is brief, the interaction of text and illustrations makes picture books complex literature. Since picture books usually contain 2,000 words or fewer, with 60 words per page and only 32 pages per book, the author can only give the bare bones of a story (Ardizzone, 1980). These textual constraints mean that writers must be downright stingy with their words, while creating characters, setting, plot, and theme, along with enough suspense to make readers turn the pages. Each double-page spread must lead readers to turn the page.

The blending of text and art is shown in Eve Bunting's *In the Haunted House*. Only 280 words were used in telling this story; the entire book takes only 10 minutes to read. Susan Meddaugh's art amplifies the rhythmic language, while creating visual and auditory images. The plot begins with: "This is the house where the scary ones hide." Two pairs of sneakers, one large and one small, introduce the characters. Readers follow the sneakers through the story, as they build suspense and move the plot along. The text increases suspense with: "An organ is playing a funeral air. It's

playing and playing, but nobody's there." Then readers see an organ, a spider, an arrow, and sneaker-clad feet. Implied questions increase the drama: What is this house? Who is wearing the sneakers? Ghosts, witches, and bats appear, communicating a spooky mood that the sneakers extend (see Figure 4.1).

The illustrations contrast a confident character with a timid character, thereby developing humor. The text goes on: "Faces that don't look like faces at all." The pictures show running feet, and the tension mounts. A mummy appears, but readers see only the shadows. A werewolf gargles in the bathroom, and the sneakers run downstairs and outside. The characters step "into the day that's asparkle with sun." The text concludes, "Halloween Houses are so much fun!" Readers see a father and daughter; the father pauses and wipes his brow (see Figure 4.2). The falling action shows a little girl stepping through the front door of the haunted house. In true picture book style, readers encounter an interesting twist at the story's end.

Illustrators

Illustrators are artists who create visuals that tell or interpret stories. Illustrators consider the nature of the story or subject as they make careful selections of color, technique, and style. The key to "telling stories

FIGURE 4.1 In a true picture book like this one, the illustrations tell as much about the story as do the words.

FIGURE 4.2   Halloween Houses are so much fun!

Halloween Houses are so much fun!

with pictures" is creating a flow of graphic images that is readable, coherent, and obviously related to the text (Shulevitz, 1985). Artists strive to evoke the essence of a work rather than to simply "make pictures." Christopher Myers chose photographs of Harlem and Brooklyn as backgrounds for bold collage art to illustrate *Black Cat*. The art and rhythmic poetry stimulates readers to explore their own feelings. Christlow (1999) demonstrated the differences in artists' interpretations of literature by following two illustrators as they created dramatically different illustrations for *Jack and the Bean Stalk*. Janet Stevens is an accomplished artist who has used her talents in many picture books. Her skill is evident in two of our favorite books: *And the DISH Ran Away with the SPOON* and *Jackalope*.

Illustrated books

Illustrated books have fewer illustrations; these illustrations simply depict characters, story events, or setting. The text can stand alone to tell the story; the illustrations merely help readers visualize characters and so forth. The *Harry Potter* books are illustrated books, as are both Luis Lowry's *Gooney Bird Greene* and *Frindle* by Andrew Clements. All of these books are enhanced with pictures of characters and story events. The vast majority of illustrated books are for children above second grade.

Picture book art

Artists combine visual elements and artistic media to create styles expressing their thoughts, feelings, and interpretations. Authors choose words and sentences to create text, while artists choose style, *medium*, technique, and color to interpret a particular piece of literature. Artistic styles are summarized with examples in Table 4.1, and popular media are summarized in Table 4.2. Color has a sensuous, emotive appeal that conveys temperature, personality, and emotion in illustrations. *The Napping House* by Audrey and Don Wood illustrates the use of color. The book begins with blue to indicate a rainy day, but yellow increases in the pictures as the rain stops and the sun comes out. Illustration lines may be thin, which provide a lighter, more fragile appearance, while thick lines convey weight and strength. Artists combine elements of color, line, and texture into a balanced, satisfying pattern between pictures and text (see Figures 4.3, 4.4 and 4.5).

Uri Shulevitz used the elements of art and of narrative to illustrate *Snow*. The book begins with gray skies and gray buildings styled with vertical pointed lines. On the following pages, the people are dressed in muted colors. As the snow begins to fall, the white snow softens the vertical, pointed lines of the houses. Gradually, the buildings become less forbidding as the roofs lighten and splashes of color enliven the illustrations, and finally the town is all white. Shulevitz uses dark and light to create the mood in the spare text. The author uses lively words such as *circling*, *swirling*, *spinning*, *twirling*, *dancing*, *playing*, and *floating* to describe the mood of the season's first snowfall.

Types of Picture Books

Up to this point we have discussed the integration of picture and language in picture books; however, some picture books have no language. *Wordless picture books* or visual stories are told entirely through pictures. This format is very appealing for today's children, whose experiences with television and film orient them to visual communication. Teachers find wordless picture books invaluable for telling stories. These books also develop vocabulary, comprehension, and critical reading (Cianciolo, 1990).

Wordless picture books delight all age groups, address all subjects, and belong to all genres. Illustrators

TABLE 4.1
Artistic styles commonly used in picture books.

Style	Example
Cartoon	
The artist uses a cartoon style based on line drawings.	*Meanwhile*—by Jules Feiffer
Expressionism	
The artist expresses strong emotions with vivid colors.	*The Red Racer* by Audrey Wood
Folk or primitive art	
The artist uses bold lines and colors.	*A Gift for Abuelita* by Nancy Luenn, illustrated by Robert Chapman
Impressionism	
The artist suggests or gives an impression.	*Between Earth & Sky* by Joseph Bruchac, illustrated by Thomas Locker
Realistic	
The artist depicts subjects as they actually appear.	*Home Run* by Robert Burieigh, illustrated by Mike Wimmer

TABLE 4.2
Popular media for illustrations in children's picture books.

Medium	Example[*]
Pastels	*The Polar Express* by Chris Van Allsburg
Watercolors	*The Shaman's Apprentice* by Lynne Cherry and Mark Plotkin, illustrated by Lynne Cherry
Handmade paper and stencils	*Mama Cat Has Three Kittens* by Denise Fleming
Watercolor and color pencils	*Pigs* by Gail Gibbons
Cut paper collage	*Top Cat* by Lois Ehlert
Oil	*Home: A Journey Through America* by Thomas Locker and Candace Christiansen, illustrated by Thomas Locker
Oil on wood	*The Pilgrims of Plimoth* by Marcia Sewall
Gouache[**]	*Arrow to the Sun* by Gerald McDermott
Digital painting	*Swimming Lessons* by Betsy Jay, illustrated by Lori Osiecki
Photographs and cut paper	*Black Cat* by Christoper Myers

[*] When one name is listed as author, the author both wrote and illustrated the book.
[**] Gouache is an opaque watercolor created by using a white base with tempera.

FIGURE 4.3 A rainy day in *The Napping House.*

FIGURE 4.5 A rainbow in *The Napping House.*

in the napping house,
where no one now is sleeping.

FIGURE 4.4 The sun comes out in *The Napping House.*

Jerry enjoys reading to his children.

of wordless picture books use their artistic talents to create character, setting, plot, theme, and style without using any words at all. Each frame or page leads readers to the next. David Wiesner tells a visual story in the wordless picture book *Sector 7*, which recounts the story of a boy who visits the Empire State Building on a school field trip. On the observation deck, the boy makes friends with a cumulus cloud. Wiesner's art created a magnificently constructed cloud station (Hearne, 1999).

Among the artists who create wonderful wordless picture books are Raymond Briggs, John Goodall, Pat Hutchins, Peter Spier, and Paula Winter. Peter Spier explores many aspects of rain in his book by the same name. It opens with raindrops on the title page and goes on to portray rain in many ways: from splashing raindrops to the glistening drops caught in a spider's web to children's delight in playing in the rain. Spier captures a rainy-day mood that makes the reader think of cozily enjoying cookies and cocoa while warm and dry inside—and he never writes a single word.

Picture books for the youngest readers

Literature is important during the preschool years, which are a remarkably active period for children to learn about oral and written language. Young children learn how and why people read, the basics of story structure, and the means for making meaning in written and oral language. Books such as Jean Ekman Adams' *Clarence and the Great Surprise* and Jennifer Ward and T. J. March's *Somewhere in the Ocean* develop picture book appreciation, language, and story structure. Children who hear by Nancy Kaufmann's story *Bye, Bye!* will learn about saying good-bye on the first day of school. The benefits of literature for young children are summarized in Figure 4.6. Concept books, counting books, and alphabet books are identified in Figure 4.7

Saying goodbye can be difficult on the first day of school.

Picture books for older students

Picture books can play important roles in the development of older students. Teachers will find that picture books appeal to all ages because "the best children's writers say things to a five-year-old that a fifty-year-old can also respect" (Hearne, 1999, p. 9). Both a 5-year-old and a 50-year-old appreciate picture books, albeit in different ways. For instance, the sheer beauty of the oil paintings of various U.S. locations found in *Home: A Journey through America* gives it ageless appeal. Although the comedy of David Wisniewski's *The Secret Knowledge of Grown-Ups* appeals to all ages, young children will probably miss some of the humor; therefore, the humor will probably appeal to children in Grade 2 and above.

An entirely different picture book style appears in Jules Feiffer's *Meanwhile*, which is illustrated with cartoons. Raymond, the main character, learns to use the word *meanwhile* to escape difficult situations. This wonderful book will appeal to all ages. *Purple Mountain Majesties* (Younger, 1998), a nonfiction picture book that tells the story of Katharine Lee Bates and "America the Beautiful," is a superb choice for children in Grades 3 through 5 and beyond. Picture books have many layers of meaning, some of which resonate most readily with older students. Furthermore, picture books are an excellent choice for introducing concepts, literary elements, genre, and writing. Besides, they are just plain fun. The following lesson snapshot illustrates a middle school class using a picture book.

Genre in the Picture Book Format

Realistic fiction, modern fantasy, traditional literature, biography, historical fiction, poetry, and informational books are all genres of children's literature found in picture books. Picture books must be alive enough to grab readers' attention and hold it (Hearne, 1999). The picture books we include in this section will achieve this goal. In the following segment, we address each genre.

Realistic Fiction

As you read earlier in this text, realistic fiction has characters like people we know. Settings are contemporary and the characters encounter problems that occur in actual

FIGURE 4.6   The benefits of literature for kindergarten and preschool.

Choosing appropriate literature and sharing it effectively with children gives them the benefits of literature. They learn that reading and writing are prominent parts of their world and that these abilities will help them accomplish many things. Meaningful experiences with literature help children learn many things:

1. To enjoy, appreciate, and respond to fine literature. *And If the Moon Could Talk* by Kate Banks and *Mama Cat Has Three Kittens* by Denise Fleming are superb early literary experiences.

2. To develop understanding of story structure by parts such as beginnings, middles, and endings. Introduce books such as *Max's Dragon Shirt* by Rosemary Wells and *Piggies* by Don and Audrey Wood.

3. To interpret literature and understand what the author is saying to readers. Introduce *I Lose My Bear* by Jules Feiffer and *Gramma's Walks* by Anna Grossnickle Hines, which are books that young children can interpret.

4. To communicate more effectively. Using Kevin Henkes's *Chrysanthemum* shows the importance of sounds, vocabulary, and language for children, and *Little Penguin's Tale* by Audrey Wood includes language play.

5. To broaden their understanding of cultural consciousness and individual differences. Read *More, More, More, Said the Baby* by Vera Williams and *Abuela* by Arthur Dorros.

6. To build interests and encourage children to think. Read *What Can You Do in the Sun?* by Anna Grossnickle Hines.

7. To recognize sequence. Introduce Ellen Walsh's *Mouse Count,* which demonstrates counting and uncounting, and *Arlene Alda's 1 2 3,* illustrating number shapes in photos.

8. To understand and appreciate different forms of literature (fiction and nonfiction). Introduce an informational book such as *Water* by Frank Asch, poetry such as *Dancin' in the Kitchen* by Wendy Gelsanliter and Frank Christian, nursery rhymes, and fiction such as *Cat Up a Tree* by John and Ann Hassett.

9. To enhance their development in all areas, social, emotional, linguistic, cognitive, and physical. Read Kathy Henderson's *The Baby Dances,* a book young children will enjoy. Children who have looked for their mothers will relate to *Little Fish Lost* by Nancy Van Laan.

10. To introduce a wide variety of experiences and specific facts about the world. *Way Out in the Desert* by T. J. Marsh and Jennifer Ward introduces desert animals in a rhyming counting book.

11. To develop children's cultural literacy. Nursery rhymes such as Michael Foreman's *Mother Goose* introduce children to well-known literary figures such as Mother Goose and Little Boy Blue.

12. To create a bond with parents and caregivers. Any book read with a child develops bonds, but books such as Sue Heap's *Cowboy Baby* are especially good because they show a warm relationship between father and son.

FIGURE 4.7   Concept books, counting books, and alphabet books.

Concept Books

Bang, M. *When Sophie Gets Angry—Really, Really Angry. . . .* Scholastic, 1999.

Cobb, V. *I Face the Wind.* HarperCollins, 2003.

Dodds, D. A. *Where's Pup?* Dial, 2003.

Emberley, E. *Thanks, Mom.* Little, 2003.

Florian, D. *A Pig Is Big.* Greenwillow, 2000.

Rockwell, A. *Big Wheels.* Walker, 2003.

Schaefer, L. *This Is Rain* (J. Wattenberg, Illus.). Greenwillow, 2001.

Schwartz, A. *What James Likes Best.* Atheneum, 2003.

Yolen, J. *How Do Dinosaurs Get Well Soon?* Scholastic, 2003.

Counting and Math Concepts

Hoberman, M. *The Looking Book: A Hide-and-Seek Counting Story.* Little, 2002.

Newman, L. *Dogs, Dogs, Dogs!* Simon & Schuster, 2003.

Noonan, J. *Mouse by Mouse: A Counting Adventure.* Dutton, 2003.

Parker, V. *Bearum Scarum.* Viking, 2002.

Reiser, L. *Ten Puppies.* Greenwillow, 2003.

Schulman, J. *Countdown to Spring!: An Animal Counting Book.* Knopf, 2002.

Yorke, J. *My First Number Book.* DK, 2003.

Alphabet Books

Arnosky, J. *Mouse Letters: A Very First Alphabet Book.* Clarion, 1999.

Catalanotto, P. *Matthew A.B.C.* Atheneum, 2002.

Demarest, C. *Firefighters A to Z.* McElderry Books, 2000.

Dodd, E. *Dog's ABC: A Silly Story about the Alphabet.* Dutton, 2002.

Rose, D. *Into the A, B, Sea: An Ocean Alphabet* (S. Jenkins, Illus.). Scholastic, 2000.

Shahan, S. *The Jazzy Alphabet.* Philomel, 2002.

Sobel, J. *B Is for Bulldozer: A Construction ABC.* Harcourt, 2003.

Sloat, T. *Patty's Pumpkin Patch.* Putnam, 1999.

Lesson Snapshot

Lisa James read the book *So You Want to be President* by Judith St. George and David Small because it received the Caldecott Medal. As Lisa read, it occurred to her that the book might interest her sixth-grade students who were studying political cartoons and Presidents. To introduce the book, she showed the book cover to the class and asked the students to identify the four Presidents on the cover (the cover is Mt. Rushmore). After the class identified George Washington, Thomas Jefferson, Theodore Roosevelt, and Abraham Lincoln, she asked the students how they identified the Presidents. In class discussion, the students distinguished the exaggerated characteristics that made the Presidents identifiable, such as Roosevelt's glasses and mustache, Lincoln's nose and chin, and so forth. Lisa then showed the double-page spreads in the book and asked the students to identify as many of the Presidents as possible. The students recognized a number of them.

Lisa asked, "Would you want to be President?"

Some of the students answered, "Yes, because you could do whatever you want, live in the White House, travel in Air Force 1, and have lots of vacations. You get a lot of money." However, others responded, "No, everyone criticizes you all the time. It's too hard to be President. There are wars, shootings, and all the other countries that don't cooperate."

Then Lisa read the book. Following the reading, the students discussed these points:

A. positive and negative aspects of being President;
B. unusual characteristics of the Presidents;
C. the pros and cons of being President; and
D. creating cartoons of the Presidents.

Following the reading and discussion, the students chose Presidents to be subjects of their cartoons. They decided to branch out and create cartoons for local notable people, including the principal.

life situations. The plots are based on real life events. The boy and girl in Marc Simont's book, *The Stray Dog*, are just like many children who discover a stray dog. They name the dog Will and play with him until it is time to leave. The following Saturday they return to the picnic grounds just in time to save the dog from the dogcatcher. Mr. Simont captured the essence of this actual family experience in both illustrations and language and was awarded a Caldecott Honor Medal for it. The cat in Maggie Smith's *Desser the Best Ever Cat* is also a stray who is adopted into a family. Readers see the cat's antics and the affection between the cat and his family, but then he grows old and dies. After mourning, the family chooses a kitten and the girl tells it about Desser. Both of these books will stimulate a discussion of family pets, as well as writing about pets.

Another family story, *Full, Full, Full of Love* by Trish Cooke, features Jay Jay, who looks forward to Sunday dinner at Grandmother's when the family gathers around the dining room table. Family also plays an important role in Mary Hoffman's *Amazing Grace*. Grandparents play an important role in picture book realistic fiction, as seen in Juan Felipe Herrera's *Grandma and Me at the Flea/Los meros meros remateros*. This story is set at a Fresno flea market, where a Mexican American boy and his grandmother sell things. Juanito discovers the flea market is a community of people who help one another. The warmth, energy, and excitement of the flea market are captured in the illustrations. Children will enjoy making pictures to illustrate their family activities after savoring these books.

Nadia Wheatley's picture book, *Luke's Way of Looking*, gives realistic fiction an imaginative angle. The protagonist, Luke, looks at things differently than all the boys in his class. When the teacher looks at Luke's paintings, he goes ballistic! Then Luke discovers a museum and his world changes. Many imaginative children have experienced Luke's problem in their actual school life. Another familiar school situation illustrates children's creative flair in Debra Frasier's *Miss Alaineus*. Sage, a fifth grader, misunderstood one of the weekly spelling words. To her embarrassment, miscellaneous became Miss Alaineus on her spelling paper. Many of us can remember making such spelling errors, but Sage's solution would not have occurred to many of us.

Picture Book Fantasy

Picture book fantasy has elements of make-believe, but readers enjoy good fantasy so much that they want to believe it is true. Fantasy is especially popular in picture books because authors and illustrators often use animal characters in order to communicate important ideas and solve problems. In *A Nice Party* by Elle van Lieshout and Erik van Os, Gus, a bear, does not want a birthday party because his family throws the worst parties. He explains that his grandmother squeezes and tickles him and his cousins eat the whole cake before he can make a birthday wish. His friend, Boris, suggests that they go fishing and leave a note for the family to drop off his presents. The illustrator shows two delighted bears fishing, while the family has a wonderful time, so everyone is happy. Adults who are parents have probably heard similar complaints from their children.

A bear is also an important character in Jon Agee's book *Milo's Hat Trick*. Milo is a magician who has failed miserably in his chosen profession. However, he has one last chance . . . he must get a rabbit to jump out of his hat. He finds a bear instead, but the bear cooperates. Now he has a bear in his hat; all he has to do is whistle and the bear jumps out to the crowds' astonishment. Milo encounters several problems, but his solutions are revealed through the illustrations.

Henry P. Baloney is a different kind of magican in Jon Scieszka and Lane Smith's *Baloney (Henry P.)*. Henry P. is from another planet, but he has problems just like earthlings. He has to come up with a very good excuse for being late, or he will have permanent lifelong detention. Imagination serves Henry P. well because he creates amazing adventures and near misses. Strange words appear in the text because Henry uses words from many languages. Thankfully, the authors provide a DECODER page to help readers. Did Henry's magic work? Miss Bugscuffle was not taken in by the tale, but she explained the day's assignment was to compose a tall tale, and suggested that Henry get busy writing his story. The artist created Henry with green skin color, large eyes, and pointed ears that are clearly from another galaxy, as is his teacher, Miss Bugscuffle.

Some picture book fantasies feature children in unusual situations, often including unusual characters. Tina, the girl in Richard Waring's *Alberto the Dancing Alligator*, received an egg for a gift, which hatched into an alligator. Tina enjoyed spending time with her pet, especially dancing the Tango. Unfortunately, the alligator fell into the toilet and descended to the world underneath the city. He had fun for a while, but when he tried to return home, he climbed into other peoples' bathrooms. The rumor spread that 1,000 alligators were on the loose and all bathrooms were at risk, resulting in expert alligator hunters going after the alligator. How did Tina save her friend? Read this fantastic book and find out. Children will enjoy think-

Alberto has adventures in the sewer system.

ing of ways to save Alberto from the alligator hunters, as well as Alphonse in the next story.

Louis, the protagonist in Steven Kellogg's *The Mysterious Tadpole*, received a tadpole as a gift, which he named Alphonse. This pet only ate cheeseburgers, so he quickly grew into a giant. You can imagine the panic Alphonse caused when he visited the high school pool and scared the swim team. The authorities were called in, only to discover that Alphonse is the Loch Ness monster. However, Louis loves him and is determined to save his pet, which he does.

Picture Book/Poetry

Children are naturally drawn to the rhythmic nature of poetry. They enjoy exploring poetry through sound and sight. Tony Johnston's *Gopher Up Your Sleeve* is a collection of witty rhyming text and hilarious illustrations. Readers meet Eve, who has a gopher up her sleeve, and Claire, who has a hamster in her hair. In addition, an octopus falls in love with a bathtub mat. Each poem and picture is funnier than the one before. The humorous interaction of picture and poem continues in Calef Brown's *Dutch Sneakers and Flea Keepers*. In this collection of 14 "stories," readers meet a runaway waffle and donut beetles marching across Sugar Beach. They will find a mysterious fish, tattlesnakes, and seven bad teeth! Animals are a popular subject for children, and Tony Johnston wrote to this interest in *It's About Dogs*. Children love the poems, but Ted Rand's brilliant watercolor illustrations make them remain in children's memories.

Nina Payne and Adam Payne created *Four in All*, which is a true marriage of language and art. A child's epic adventure is depicted in this exquisite book. The poet used only 56 common nouns to tell about the world's symmetry and beauty, while the artist created cut-paper collage to join the language. Winter is the subject of Dori Chaconas' story poem, *On a Wintry Morning*. Primary grade children enjoy the repeated refrains, and the watercolor and pastel paintings create a winter mood. Lee Bennett Hopkins has created a gastronomic and visual delight in *Yummy! Eating Through a Day*. These dietary poems are fun to read, as well as to see, thanks to the vibrant paintings accompanying them.

Picture Book/Traditional Literature

Traditional literature consists of the written form of stories that grew from the oral tradition. Selecting the picture books to include in this group was a challenge because they are a popular format for traditional stories. *Jack and the Beanstalk* is a good place to begin because there are so many wonderful interpretations of this classic tale. Professional storyteller Richard Walker wrote a quirky, humorous version that we enjoy. Niamh Sharkey created offbeat, outlandish artwork to tell the tale. In this version Jack is not lazy, but rather looking for adventure. He loves magic and the story ends with a merry dance. Another favorite version of this story is Raymond Briggs' *Jim and the Beanstalk*. In this version Jim climbs a beanstalk and meets an aging giant who needs teeth, hair, and glasses. Both of these tales will stimulate students to invent their own versions of this tale. Jim Harris's *Jack and the Giant: A Story Full of Beans* is a western version of *Jack and the Beanstalk*. Jack is a cowpoke and his ma, Annie Okey-Dokey, live on a desert ranch. The zany illustrations make this story a delightful read.

An unfamilar Grimm tale was the basis for Natalie Babbitt's *Ouch*. Fred Marcellino's rich pictures create the mood and help to tell the tale. Young Marco, the central character, started out as an ordinary baby, but the king feared he would marry his daughter. He took the baby, placed him in a box, and threw the box into the water. The baby was saved and in the process became acquainted with the princess. All of the king's efforts to eliminate him fail. Of course, in the end they lived happily ever after, but not so the king.

Steven Kellogg is a talented reteller of traditional tales and tall tales. A favorite with many readers is *Sally Ann Thunder Ann Whirlwind Crockett*. At birth Sally could out-talk, out-grin, out-scream, out-swim, and out-run any baby in Kentucky. She stunned a hungry grizzly bear and made a lasso out of six rattlesnakes. She rescued Davy Crockett, who then proposed to her. These are only a few of the feats attributed to this remarkable woman. Another bigger-than-life great American hero, *John Henry*, is featured in Julius Lester's picture book. This steel-driving man raced a steam drill to cut through a mountain as big as "hurt feelings." John Henry was a humble man whose philosophy is revealed in this statement "What matters is how well you do your living."

Picture Book/Historical Fiction

Historical fiction addresses actual events and ways of living, and picture books are an advantageous format for this genre because the artist can create settings that are authentic to the time. Avi's book, *The Silent Movie*, portrays immigrant life of 100 years ago. The black and white illustrations create the mood of a silent movie, while accurately depicting the time period. Diane Goode used soft colors in pen and wash illustrations to create the country setting for Cynthia Rylant's book, *Christmas in the Country*. Rylant tells about her childhood and everyday life in *Christmas in the Country*, which is a follow-up to her earlier book, *When I was Young in the Mountains. Freedom School, Yes!* by Amy Littlesugar is based on the 1964 Mississippi Freedom School Summer Project. The author shows Jolie the protagonist's transformation as she becomes committed to learning about her heritage. The church where Freedom School was to meet was burned, which was only one of the tragedies connected with this story. Middle school students will enjoy this book.

My Nine Lives by Clio, an historical fiction book, is based upon Clio the cat's journal documenting her nine lives. Clio begins life #1 in Mesopotamia 3000 B.C. She recreates life as she experienced it in those times, such as living in a temple and enjoying the usual cat foods of milk and fish. Life #2 was in China around 1500 B.C., and life #3 was in Rome around 600

B.C.. Life #4 was at sea with Norse sailors in the year 1000 A.D. Life #5 was in England 1300. Each lifetime has an authentic setting, with her life continuing into the present day. This book will stimulate writing and thinking; however, children above second grade will understand the concepts better than younger children.

Picture Book/Biography

The picture book format is ideal for telling about a person's life because both the author and the artist can characterize the individual. Lesa Cline-Ransome chose this format for her biography of baseball legend *Satchel Paige*. The narrative has an oral quality that is ideal for a read-aloud. The bold and glowing colors of the illustrations bring his achievement to life. The early life of Michael Jordan and his pursuit of a dream are the focus of *Salt in His Shoes*, written by his sister, with help from his mother. This partial biography focuses on Jordan's determination to play basketball.

The life and art of Romare Bearden is presented in Claire Hartfield's book *Me and Uncle Romie: A Story Inspired by the Life and Art of Romare Bearden*. The biography is told through fictionalized diary entries written by James, who is visiting Harlem from North Carolina. James discovers the wonders of his uncle's art and explores the wonders of Harlem. The rich illustrations are Romare Bearden's collages. This is a wonderful picture book for introducing different points of view, art, and diary or journal writing.

According to Barbara Kerley, there was a time when almost no one in the world knew what a dinosaur looked like. That was before a Victorian artist named Waterhouse Hawkins, whose story is revealed in *The Dinosaurs of Waterhouse Hawkins*. Hawkins spent over 30 years building the first awe-inspiring life-size dinosaur models. His passion and courage created an extraordinary legacy for us. Brian Selznick created a visual masterpiece with paintings to tell the story of this complex, fascinating individual. Dinosaur lovers of all ages will love this book.

Nonfiction

Informational picture books are popular with writers and readers because illustrations clarify and illustrate nonfiction. Large colorful illustrations with heavy lines illustrate Kate and Jim McMullan's *I Stink*. The unusual garbage truck narrates information, and explains that he eats trash. He describes himself using smell, sight, and sound along with accompanying sound effects. Younger children will enjoy the roars, crushing, compacting, and most of all, the BURP. The garbage truck concludes with the alphabet in garbage: A is apple cores, and B is banana peels, and so forth. An unusual voice also narrates Diane Siebert's book *Cave*. The narrator is the cave itself. Its evocative language and luminous paintings collaborate to create a cool, dark, mysterious feeling. The cave describes mazes, colonies of bats, majestic columns, and secret worlds below ground. Children of all ages will enjoy this book, which is especially effective for introducing children to caves when they are planning a visit below ground.

Who acts as both a baby-sitter and a burglar alarm? In Jose Aruego and Ariane Dewey's *Weird Friends*, a bird called a water thick-knees does this for the crocodile, while another weird friendship exists between the clown fish and the poisonous sea anemone. In fact, these weird friendships are necessary for the survival of many animals. The exquisite, detailed pictures give the relationships visual impact. Animal behavior is also the subject of naturalist Jim Arnosky's *Field Trips*. He shows readers how to hunt bugs, track animals, watch birds, and walk on shores. Black and white drawings based on his own field research illustrate this book. He encourages readers to sharpen their observation skills and encourages them to draw and record each day's watch.

Visual Literacy

Visual literacy is the ability to comprehend and evaluate illustrations and the visual elements of media and artistic style the artist uses (Camp & Tompkins, 1990). Visual texts are not as simple as they appear; they are complex, multilayered texts that communicate meaning (Moline, 1995). Illustrations convey meaning to readers and viewers because they are the artist's rendering of plot, theme, setting, mood, and character.

We know that children respond to visual texts to construct both cognitive and affective meaning (Kiefer, 1995). Children who have many opportunities to describe, compare, interpret, and value illustrations in picture books learn to interact with visual information (Stewig, 1992). For instance, focusing on an illustration and describing it clearly and completely is a good beginning. The *I Spy* books by Walter Wick and

Jean Marzollo are excellent beginning books for kindergarten children, who enjoy examining these puzzles and later creating their own. They also enjoy books like Joan Steiner's *Look-Alikes, Jr.*.

Involving children in experiences that require comparing two or more versions of the same story, such as *Cinderella*, *Stone Soup*, or *Goldilocks*, builds their visual literacy. *The Marvelous Mouse Man* by Mary Ann Hoberman is a new and different version of the *Pied Piper of Hamlin*, providing a delightful comparison to the original. Teachers should provide children opportunities to focus on illustrations, describe them, and compare them. As children explore the work of various artists, they will develop preferences for illustrators and styles of art.

Selecting and Evaluating Picture Books

What makes a picture book an outstanding example of the format and genre? This question is at once simple and complex, just as are fine picture books. Creating superb picture books is not easy, due to the short and simple text that must be interesting while retaining freshness and quality through many readings. Picture books have well-drawn characters, suspenseful plots, authentic settings, and accurate information, all factors that contribute to literary excellence in the various genre of literature. The art is integrated with the narrative and is appropriate to the mood and subject matter. Arnold Lobel (1981) established the most important standard: "A good picture book should be true. That is to say, it should rise out of the lives and passions of its creators" (p. 74).

The Internet can be invaluable in helping media specialists (librarians) and teachers in locating and evaluating books. The National Center for Children's Illustrated Literature, located in Abilene, Texas, sponsors exhibits and educational programs, and also maintains a Web site. The site currently located at **www.nccil.org/children** has illustrations, biographies, and teaching activities. The Children's Literature Web Guide is a rich source of information; most publishers of children's picture books such as Houghton Mifflin, Random House, Rising Moon, and Simon & Schuster maintain Web sites that include book information, author information, and teaching ideas. Web locations and addresses often change, so we suggest that you include key words into your search engine that will pull up a list of Web sites for you to explore.

In choosing picture books to read, consider the visual components of color, line, shape, space, texture, and perspective (Lacey, 1986), as well as the standards suggested for that particular genre, because picture books encompass all genres. The best indicators for picture books that children will enjoy, however, are these qualities:

1. The book is appropriate for the age and stage of development of the potential readers or listeners. Fine picture books are works of art appropriate for a broad range of students.
2. Children can identify with the main character. Consider whether the main character is developed as a rounded character or a stereotype. (Stereotypes are appropriate characters in traditional literature, of course.)
3. Children can understand the plot, which has an identifiable climax and an identifiable ending. Stories have beginnings, middles, and endings.
4. The theme grows out of characters, and the plot is appropriate for children.
5. The story is told in interesting, expressive language with simple narrative, and the author avoids long descriptions—it is a "page turner."
6. Nonfiction is accurate and presented in an interesting, authentic style.
7. The illustrations enrich the text, are integrated with the text, and are appropriate to the mood and subject matter.

Classroom Activities

Picture books are written to be read-aloud while the listeners look at the pictures, creating an integral part of the literary picture book experience. (Chapter 14 gives information regarding oral presentations of literature.) Children often cluster in a group to listen so that they can better see the illustrations, frequently asking the teacher to read it again; they do benefit from multiple hearings. Placing the book nearby where children can pick it up and pore over the pictures at their own pace builds their interest in literature and reading. This section presents strategies and activities to engage students with picture books, encourage response, and develop visual literacy. Many of the suggestions focus on the illustrations and careful observations of them. Although these activities are based on picture books, they are also applicable to other literature.

ACTIVITY 4.1   READING A PICTURE BOOK TO CHILDREN

(IRA/NCTE Standards: 3, 4, 6. Listening comprehension, oral language, and visual literacy.)

1. Introduce the book. An introduction can motivate listeners and anticipate the ideas in the book. Show students the cover and title, and tell them the author's and illustrator's names.

2. Read the story aloud to give students the opportunity for appreciative listening. Make sure that all the children have the chance to view the pictures as you read.

3. Discuss the story with the children, stimulating them to think about the story. Discussion following appreciative listening enhances understanding. Ask them what things they noticed in the book. Encourage children to compare themselves and their experiences to the picture book and its illustrations. Does the main character look like them? Act like them? Would they do the same things the character did? Would they like to have the character as a friend?

4. Use extension activities to allow students to respond to the story and enrich their understanding. Exploring how the author and artist express meaning in text and illustrations is useful. Comparing and contrasting experiences are very helpful to learning.

ACTIVITY 4.2   COMPARING FOLK TALE VARIATION

(IRA/NCTE Standards: 1, 3, 6, 11. Understanding of print and nonprint texts. Use a variety of strategies to understand, interpret, and evaluate figurative language and participate in a literacy community.)

Studying various versions of the same story facilitates children's understanding and response. Traditional literature is especially appropriate for this experience because many children know these tales that have been told, retold, and illustrated in many ways. Figure 4.8 shows one way that an artist interpreted the traditional tale of Little Red Riding Hood. Compare the interpretations of the wolf illustrator with that of other illustrators. Of course, the other characters and the setting can be compared as well. Examine the art in each version, including the line, shape, texture, color, value, and layout used in each version. Find other versions of this story for children to compare. A good example comparing various interpretations of the Little Red Riding Hood tale follows. Trina Schart Hyman drew on her childhood love of the Little Red Riding Hood story when creating her Caldecott Honor book. Her elegantly detailed illustrations are rich in color, and she framed the text and illustrations with elaborate designs of flowers, hearts, and plaids, while

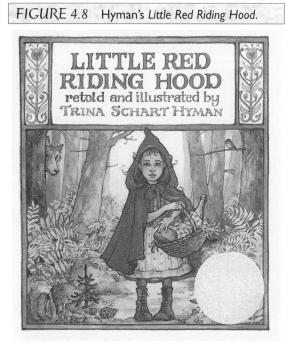

FIGURE 4.8 Hyman's *Little Red Riding Hood.*

the characters are soft and rounded. The wolf is soft and fuzzy looking. In Beatrice Schenk de Regnier's version, Edward Gorey used a more primitive style: his long, sharp lines for drawing Red Riding Hood, the mother, the wolf, and the grandmother contrast with Hyman's softer characters. Gorey's spare, simple settings create a vastly different mood than the lushness of Hyman's illustrations. In this version, the wolf looks lean and mean.

Lon Po Po: A Red-Riding Hood Story from China, a Caldecott Medal winner translated by Ed Young, is a Chinese version of the Red Riding Hood story, although it does not have a Red Riding Hood character. In this version, three little children stay at home while their mother goes to visit their grandmother, Po Po. The wolf plans to eat the children while their mother is away, but they outwit him. Young renders a more realistic treatment of the wolf than either Hyman or de Regniers, as his wolf is more dangerous looking than the others.

1. Older students can do the previous activity as a writing activity.

2. Students can create their own versions of Red Riding Hood (or another favorite).

3. Students can compare the written text of various versions of Red Riding Hood.

4. Additional aesthetic experiences can involve making puppets, drawing or painting pictures, painting friezes, designing bulletin boards, creating posters, and doing craft projects.

5. Retelling stories through creative drama and storytelling gives children opportunities to respond to the language of picture books. Encourage students to relate prior knowledge to picture clues to construct understanding.

6. Writing stories, poems, or informative pieces based on picture books gives children additional literary experiences. They could even develop their own illustrations to accompany their written responses.

7. Choosing music that fits the mood of a book extends the aesthetic experience.

ACTIVITY 4.3   DEVELOPING A UNIT OF STUDY ON THE TOPIC OF DOGS

(IRA/NCTE Standards: 3, 6, 11.)

Select several appropriate books for a teaching unit on dogs, which could extend over a week or more. A partial list of good picture books about dogs appears at the end of this activity. Although this unit focuses on dogs, the topic could be virtually anything—trees, giants, boys, girls, teachers, mothers, or fathers.

1. Introduce the book you have selected to the children and encourage them to make predictions from the title and the cover of the book or from the opening sentences.

2. Read the story aloud to give them the opportunity for appreciative listening. Ask them to think about the pictures of the dog in the book and what the text says about the dog. Ask them to think about how this dog is similar to dogs they know or have seen.

3. Discuss the story with the children and encourage them to think about the story. Ask appropriate questions to start discussion, such as:

   a. Do the pictures look like real dogs or make-believe dogs?

   b. How is this dog special (unique)?

   c. What things did the dog do in the story?

   d. What is special about the things the dog did?

   e. Does this dog remind you of any dog that you know?

   f. How is the dog different from dogs that you know?

   g. If you could talk to the author or illustrator, what questions would you like to ask?

4. Use extension activities to allow students to respond to the story.

   a. After reading several books to the children and letting them enjoy the illustrations, have them think of ways to compare and contrast dogs. They may suggest things such as size, color, personality (some dogs are gentle, some are not), whether they are real or make-believe, and so forth.

   b. Have students draw pictures of their favorite dog and tell or write why this is their favorite.

   c. Have students tell or write about the dog they would like to have as a pet and explain why.

   d. Ask older students to compare the dog characters by creating grids such as the one in Figure 4.9.

   e. Ask students to write about the things that make dogs good pets or ways of caring for pet dogs.

   f. Suggest that children make up stories about dogs that they can tell aloud, dictate to the teacher, or write on their own.

The following are suggested picture books to use in a unit on dogs.

- *The First Dog* by Jan Brett
- *Dogs in Space* by Nancy Coffelt
- *A Dog Like Jack* by DyAnne DiSalvo-Ryan
- *Nobody's Dog* by Charlotte Graeber
- *Dogs Don't Wear Sneakers* by Laura Numeroff
- *Martha Calling* by Susan Meddaugh
- *A Home for Spooky* by Gloria Rand
- *SPEAK: Children's illustrators Brag About Their Dogs* by Michael J. Rosen, Ed.
- *Guard the House, Sam!* by Charnan Simon
- *It's Hard to Read a Map with a Beagle on Your Lap* by Marilyn Singer

FIGURE 4.9 **Grid for comparing characters, in this case dogs.**

Title	Dog's Looks	Dog's Personality	Dog's Actions	Dog's Likable Characteristics

ACTIVITY 4.4   EXPLORING A SINGLE BOOK IN DEPTH

(IRA/NCTE Standards: 3, 4, 11.)

Book: *What! Cried Granny: An Almost Bedtime Story* by Kate Lum, illustrated by Adrian Johnson.

Story Synopsis: Patrick is sleeping over at Granny's. He comes up with many reasons to delay going to bed. He says he cannot go to bed because he does not have a bed, or a blanket, or a teddy bear. So Granny solves the problems. She chops down a tree to build a bed, shears a sheep and weaves a blanket, and stitches up an enormous bear. Her efforts take all night, but they give Patrick a new excuse because "it's morning."

The illustrations are collage-like figures, and the background is in vibrant color. The illustrator included whimsical details, such as a dog and the colors Granny paints with.

1. Introduce the book.

   a. Hold the book up, read the title, and ask the children if they have ever slept over with their grandparents.

   b. Ask what they think will happen in this story about Patrick's sleepover at Granny's.

2. Read about half of the story aloud. Ask the children what they think will happen next. They should be able to explain why they predict as they do, using details from the story for support.

3. Complete the story and compare the outcome with their predictions both before and halfway through.

4. Discuss the story with the children, encouraging them to think about the story.

   a. Which picture in the book do you like the best? Why?

   b. What was the funniest thing that Granny did?

   c. Why did Granny make things for Patrick?

   d. Did this story really happen? Why or why not?

   e. How did Granny feel when Patrick could not go to sleep because it was morning?

   f. How did Patrick feel when he found out it was morning?

   g. What was your favorite part of the story?

5. Discuss the illustrations in this book. Prepare to discuss the illustrations by holding up the book and looking at each page to examine the illustrations.

   a. Ask the children to identify their favorite illustrations.

   b. Have them identify their favorite details in the pictures.

   c. Ask them what color they like best in the illustrations.

   d. Ask if they can think of another book that has illustrations similar to these. (Lois Ehlert and others use collages.)

6. Use extension activities to allow students to respond to the story.

   a. Introduce the word *exaggerate* to first or second graders, and discuss the ways that exaggeration is related to this story. Ask the children if they have ever used exaggeration.

   b. Compare this story with *Just Another Ordinary Day* by Rod Clement. Ask how these stories are alike and how they are different. Ask students how exaggeration is related to this story. Ask students why they think Amanda exaggerated in her imagination. You can compare both of these books to Steve Kellogg's *Paul Bunyan*.

   c. Have the children tell about or draw pictures of the funniest thing that ever happened with a grandparent.

ACTIVITY 4.5   ARTIST/ILLUSTRATOR PROFILES

Studying illustrators yields many benefits to young readers. Readers who know something about the person who illustrated a picture book have a better understanding of it. Finding connections between books and their creators challenges children to think in new ways, which widens their life experiences. Artists often project their own experiences into their work. The accompanying profile of Paul Zelinsky demonstrates this.

A Biographical Profile: Paul O. Zelinsky

Paul O. Zelinsky is a versatile artist who has won three Caldecott Honor medals and a Caldecott Medal in 1997.

Zelinsky's artistic talent emerged early in life, although he considered becoming an astronomer, a ventriloquist, a scientist, and another Frank Lloyd Wright rather than an illustrator. However, after completing his master's degree, Zelinsky realized he was destined to illustrate children's books.

He once used art to create identity and stability during his many moves as his father relocated from one college to another. Now he adjusts his style to give each book a distinctive character. He says, "I don't like to do the same thing over and over." Variety in medium and technique keeps his work interesting and fresh (National Center for Children's Illustrated Literature n. d.). Moreover, Zelinsky is a meticulous artist who researches subject matter carefully so he can authentically depict the era of the book he is illustrating.

In discussing his work, Zelinsky shares a story about his great-grandmother who started oil painting and painted a picture of the witch's house from the story *Hansel and Gretel* for his sister. He has this picture and cherishes its character and air of mystery. He realized early in his illustrating career that he wanted to create that feeling in a whole book of *Hansel and Gretel*. Of course, his illustrations for *Hansel and Gretel*, which was retold by Rika Lesser, culminated in a Caldecott Honor book in 1985. In 1987 his work for Grimm's *Rumpelstiltskin* was honored with another Caldecott Honor book designation. His third Caldecott Honor book was *Swamp Angel* by Anne Isaacs in 1995. Grimm's *Rapunzel*, which was published in 1997, brought him the Caldecott Medal. However, *The Wheels on the Bus* is the personal favorite of this author, just as it is the favorite of many young children.

———

This biographic profile drew on information from the dust jackets of Paul O. Zelinsky's books and from the National Center for Children's Illustrated Literature Web site.

ACTIVITY 4.6   EXPERIMENTING WITH MEDIA

(IRA/NCTE Standards: 10, 11, 12.)

Students can experiment with the media that artists use and make their own picture books. You may choose to involve the art teacher in this experience and explore media such as paint, collage, chalk, photographs, pencil, lithograph, watercolor, fabric, or quilt paintings. Students could create a picture book or photographic essay using photographs they have taken. They can create a composition based on the photographs, write the text, make a cover, and bind the book.

ACTIVITY 4.7   ILLUSTRATING A TEXT

(IRA/NCTE Standards: 3, 6, 7.)

Read a picture book to the class without showing them the pictures, then ask them to create appropriate illustrations to accompany the story. Compare their illustrations with those in the book.

ACTIVITY 4.8   CREATING A STORY MAP

(IRA/NCTE Standards: 6, 7, 12.)

Create a story map using a format similar to the one shown in Figure 4.10 for a picture book or a wordless picture book. Both the illustrations and the narrative will contribute to the story map. (See Chapter 15 for more information on story maps.)

FIGURE 4.10   Blank story map.

Setting: (time, place, character)
Problem:
Efforts to Solve the Problem: 1.   2.   3.
Resolution:

ACTIVITY 4.9   RECITING IN UNISON

(IRA/NCTE Standards: 6, 7, 8.)

After students have listened to a picture book of a traditional story, have them read the refrain in unison from a chart you have prepared. Paul Galdone's picture book versions of traditional stories such as *The Little Red Hen*, *Henny Penny*, and *The Three Little Pigs* are good choices for this activity because he includes refrains in the story narrative. Many of the children will then join in to read the entire story.

ACTIVITY 4.10   USING ILLUSTRATIONS TO LEARN MORE ABOUT STORIES

(IRA/NCTE Standards: 5, 6.)

Students can examine the illustrations in a book to glean information that is not presented in the story. Answering questions like the following will guide their studies (Stewig, 1992). These questions and their answers are based on an illustration from *Chicken Little* by Steven Kellogg.

1. What can we tell from the characters' clothing? (The animals are wearing clothing, which suggests that the story is make-believe. They are not wearing cold-weather clothing, so it is probably not winter.)

2. Where do you think Chicken Little is going? Why? (She is carrying a lunch box and pencil, which suggest that she is going to school.)

3. How did the fox happen to see Chicken Little? (He is using binoculars.)

4. Why does the fox have a book in the car? (It is a poultry recipe book: He is planning to cook Chicken Little.)

5. What can we infer about the time of year? (It is probably fall, because school is in session, but it is not cold yet, because the leaves are green and acorns are on the tree.)

6. How does the fox plan to kill Chicken Little? How do you know? (With a hatchet, because the picture of his imagination shows one.)

7. What do we learn about the fox? (He likes to eat chickens.)

Summary

Children are usually introduced to literature through picture books; however, they are valuable literature for all ages. Picture books are complex art forms that include all genre of literature. In picture books, the text and illustrations interact to tell a story or convey information (nonfiction). Neither pictures nor text tell the story alone. The brevity of picture books force authors to choose their words carefully and the artists' work becomes very important to telling a good story. Many illustrators are artists who experiment with a variety of styles, media, and colors to achieve the interpretation they feel is appropriate for the text. Picture books are important literature because they introduce literature to children and they also introduce the various genre to students.

Thought Questions

1. What is a picture book? Why is it a format rather than a genre?

2. Identify your favorite picture book illustrations. Why are these illustrations favorites?

3. What are the advantages of using picture books with older students?

4. How can you use picture books to extend children's aesthetic experience?

5. How do language and illustrations interact in picture books?

6. Why do artists choose to illustrate children's books?

Research and Application Experiences

1. Read three picture books to a group of children. Ask them to choose their favorites and explain why they are favorites.

2. Choose a picture book and identify its beginning, middle, and ending.

3. Read *Talking with Artists* (vol. 3), compiled and edited by Pat Cummings (1998), or *Side by Side* by Leonard Marcus (2001). Which team of artist and writer do you especially enjoy? How could you use these books in your classroom?

4. Visit a children's bookstore and study the picture books. Which genre was represented with the most books? Can you identify any trends in the subject matter?

5. Create a picture book of your favorite traditional story.

6. Write a book and have a friend illustrate it. What problems in interpretation did you encounter?

7. Create a list of picture books that parents could read to their children.

Children's Literature References and Recommended Books

Note: Books designated with an asterisk (*) are recommended for reluctant readers.

Adams, J. E. (2001). *Clarence and the great surprise.* Flagstaff, Arizona: Rising Moon. (PreK–1). PICTURE BOOK, FANTASY.

Clarence, a purple horse, and a city pig pack their bags and begin a new adventure in this book.

Agee, J. (2001). *Milo's hat trick.* New York: Hyperion. (3–6). FANTASY.

Milo learns to be a magician, but a bear comes out of his hat.

Arnosky, J. (2002). *Field trips.* New York: Harper-Collins. (All ages). PICTURE BOOK, NONFICTION.

Jim Aronsky, a naturalist, has created a guidebook for field trips to develop observation and recording skills.

Aruego, J., & Dewey, A. (2002). *Weird friends.* New York: Harcourt. (All ages). PICTURE BOOK, NONFICTION.

This book is subtitled "Unlikely Allies in the Animal Kingdom" and it explores interdependent relationships between animals.

Avi. (2003). *The silent movie* (C. B. Mordan, Illus.). Atheneum. (All ages). PICTURE BOOK, HISTORICAL FICTION.

This unusual picture book is illustrated with black and white images that follow one after another to tell the story of an immigrant family alone in the big city. Readers have the feeling of watching a silent movie.

Babbitt, N. (1998). *Ouch!* (F. Marcellino, Illus.). New York:HarperCollins. (All ages). PICTURE BOOK, TRADITIONAL.

In this little known Grimm tale, Marco begins life as an ordinary boy.

Briggs, R. (1970). *Jim and the beanstalk.* New York:Coward-McCann Inc. (All ages). PICTURE BOOK, TRADITIONAL LITERATURE.

Jim meets an aging giant at the top of the beanstalk. He needs teeth, hair, and glasses, so Jim helps him.

Brown, C. (2000). *Dutch sneakers and flea keepers.* Boston: Houghton Mifflin. (All ages). PICTURE BOOK, POETRY.

A delightful collection of poetry.

Bruchac, J. (1996). *Between earth & sky* (T. Locker, Illus.). New York: Harcourt. (2–5). TRADITIONAL LITERATURE.

This collection of Native American legends is illuminated with beautiful paintings.

Bunting, E. (1990). *In the haunted house* (S. Meddaugh, Illus.). New York: Clarion. (K–3). PICTURE BOOK, REALISTIC FICTION.

Father and daughter visit a haunted house.

Burleigh, R. (1998). *Home run* (M. Wimmer, Illus.). San Diego: Silver Whistle. (3–4). PICTURE BOOK, BIOGRAPHY, POETRY.*

This book tells about the career of Babe Ruth.

Chaconas, Dori. (2000). *On a wintry morning.* (S. Johnson, Illus.). New York: Viking. (K–2). POETRY.

The subject of this story poem is winter. The poet creates a winter mood with words and illustrations.

Clement, R. (1998). *Just another ordinary day.* New York: HarperCollins. (1–3). PICTURE BOOK, FANTASY.

A young girl goes through an ordinary day with extraordinary flair.

Clements, A. (1996). *Frindle* (B. Selznick, Illus.). New York: Simon & Schuster. (3–5). REALISTIC FICTION.

Nick decides to call his pen a frindle, which creates an uproar in his school.

Cline-Ransome, L. (2003). *Satchel Paige* (J. E. Ransome, Illus.). New York: Aladdin. (2–4). BIOGRAPHY.

Satchel Paige, the first black pitcher in the major leagues is the subject of this anecdotal profile.*

Cooke, T. (2003). *Full, full, full of love.* (P. Howard, Illus.). New York: Candlewick. (K–2). REALISTIC FICTION.

Jay Jay loves Sunday dinner at his grandmother's house because all of the family gathers around the table.

de Regniers, B. S. (1972). *Red riding hood* (E. Gorey, Illus.). New York: Atheneum. (1–3). PICTURE BOOK, TRADITIONAL LITERATURE.

This version of the traditional tale is told in verse.

DiSalvo-Ryan, D. (1999). *A dog like Jack.* New York: Holiday. (K–2). CONTEMPORARY REALISTIC FICTION.

The story of a very special dog.

Feiffer, J. (1997). *Meanwhile —*. New York: Harper-Collins. (2–6). PICTURE BOOK.

Raymond discovers that meanwhile . . . can take him somewhere else, so he finds it a useful device in this comedic adventure.

Frasier, D. (2000). *Miss Alaineus*. New York: Harcourt. (2–5). REALISTIC FICTION.

Sage misunderstood one of the words on her spelling list, which led to great embarassment. Sage, however, thought of a creative solution.

Harris, J. (1997). *Jack and the giant: A story full of beans*. Flagstaff, AZ: Rising Moon. (1–4). TRADITIONAL.

A Western version of Jack and the Beanstalk.

Hartfield, C. (2002). *Me and Uncle Romie*. New York: Dial. (All ages). PICTURE BOOK, BIOGRAPHY.

This is the story of Romare Bearden, the artist, told from a child's point of view.

Herrera, J. F. (2002). *Grandma and me at the flea/Los meros meros remateros* (A. DeLucio-Brock, Illus.). San Francisco: Children's Book Press. (1–3). REALISTIC FICTION

Juanito learns about flea markets when he and his grandmother sell wares at one. He learns that it is a community with warmth, energy, and excitement.

Hoberman, M. (2002). *The marvelous mouse man*. (L. Freeman, Illus.). New York: Harcourt. (1–3). PICTURE BOOK.

A marvelous version of the "The Pied Piper of Hamlin."

Hoffman, M. (1991). *Amazing Grace* (C. Binch, Illus.). Dial. (1–3). CONTEMPRARY REALISTIC FICTION.

A young girl loves dramatizing stories.

Hopkins, L. B. (2000). *Yummy! Eating through a day*. (R. Flower, Illus.). New York: Simon & Schuster. (K–3). PICTURE BOOK, POETRY.

Poems about eating.

Hyman, T. S. (Reteller). (1983). *Little Red Riding Hood*. New York: Holiday House. (1–3). PICTURE BOOK, TRADITIONAL LITERATURE.

This version of Red Riding Hood is a traditional version.

Jay, B. (1998). *Swimming lessons* (L. Osiecki, Illus.). Flagstaff, AZ: Rising Moon. (1–3). PICTURE BOOK, CONTEMPORARY REALISTIC FICTION.

Jane's Momma signs her up for swimming lessons, but Jane tells her that she does not want to learn how to swim.

Johnston, T. (2000). *It's about dogs*. New York: Harcourt. (1–6). POETRY.

A collection of poems about dogs.

Johnston, T. (2002). *Gopher up your sleeve*. Flagstaff, AZ: Rising Moon. (All ages). PICTURE BOOK, POETRY.

Comic poetry about outlandish animals.

Jordan, D., with Jordan, R. (2000). *Salt in his shoes: Michael Jordan in pursuit of a dream* (K. Nelson, Illus). New York: Simon & Schuster. (All ages). PICTURE BOOK, BIOGRAPHY.

Michael Jordan's family shares parts of his personal story to show the importance of following your dreams.

Kaufmann, N. (2003). *Bye, bye!* (J. Spetter, Illus.). Asheville, NC: Front Street. (K–1). REALISTIC FICTION.

A young child has a hard time saying good-bye to his father on the first day of school.

Kellogg, S. (1995). *Sally Ann Thunder Ann Whirlwind Crockett*. New York: Morrow. (All ages). PICTURE BOOK, TALL TALE.

When she was born, Sally Ann could out-talk, out-grin, out-scream, out-swim, and out-run any baby in Kentucky. She became an American frontier legend when she rescued Davy Crockett from eagles.

Kellogg, S. (Reteller). (2000). *Paul Bunyan*. New York: William Morrow. (PreK–3). PICTURE BOOK.

A newer version of this tall tale.

Kellogg, S. (2002, Reissue). *The mysterious tadpole*. New York: Dial. (All ages).

Louis receives a tadpole for his birthday. The cheeseburger eating tadpole quickly outgrows his surroundings which creates a huge problem.

Kerley, B. (2001). *The dinosaurs of Waterhouse Hawkins* (B. Selznick, Illus.). New York: Scholastic. (All ages). PICTURE BOOK, BIOGRAPHY.

Waterhouse Hawkins studied dinosaurs at a time when most people had no idea of what they looked like. He spent more than 30 years constructing model dinosaurs.

Lester, J. (1994). *John Henry* (J. Pinkney, Illus.). New York: Dial. (All ages). PICTURE BOOK, TRADITIONAL.

John Henry, a great American hero, was a "steel-driving" man who battled a steam drill to cut through a mountain.

Littlesugar, A. (2001). *Freedom School, yes!* (F. Cooper, Illus.). New York: Philomel. (2–4). REALISTIC FICTION.

Jodie attended Freedom School and learned about her heritage.

Lowry, L. (2002). *Gooney Bird Greene* (M. Thomas, Illus.). Boston: Houghton Mifflin (1–4). REALISTIC FICTION.*

When Gooney Bird Greene arrives in second grade, she is obviously a unique character that intrigues her classmates, who want to learn all about her.

Luenn, N. (1998). *A gift for Abuelita* (R. Chapman, Illus.). Flagstaff, AZ: Rising Moon. (1–4). PICTURE BOOK, CONTEMPORARY REALISTIC FICTION.

This family story focuses on the Day of the Dead's Memorial Day celebrated in many Mexican-American communities.

McMulllen, K. (2002). *I stink.* New York: Cotler Publishing. PICTURE BOOK, FANTASY.

A talking garbage truck tells readers about his job.

Myers, C. (1999). *Black cat.* New York: Scholastic. (1–3). PICTURE BOOK, REALISTIC FICTION.*

The story of a cat living on the streets of New York told in a rap.

Priceman, M. (1998). *My nine lives by Clio.* New York: Atheneum. (3–up). PICTURE BOOK, HISTORICAL FICTION.

Clio is a cat whose nine lives have spanned centuries and cultures. This fascinating book is told through the cat's diaries.

Raczek, L. T. (1999). *Rainy's powwow* (G. Bennett, Illus.). Flagstaff, AZ: Rising Moon. (2–4). PICTURE BOOK, CONTEMPORARY REALISTIC FICTION.

Rainy is planning to dance at the Thunderbird Powwow, but she has a problem. In this story, Rainy learns to listen to and follow her own heart.

Rylant, C. (1982). *When I was young in the mountains* (Diane Goode, Illus.). Dutton. (All ages). PICTURE BOOK, BIOGRAPHY.

Cynthia Rylant wrote about growing up in the mountains with her grandparents.

Rylant, C. (2002). *Christmas in the country* (D. Goode, Illus.). Orchard. (All ages). PICTURE BOOK, BIOGRAPHY.

Cynthia Rylant tells about everyday life during her childhood, as well as holiday rituals.

Schneider, H. (2000). *Chewy Louie.* Flagstaff, AZ: Rising Moon. (PreK–K). PICTURE BOOK, REALISTIC FICTION.

Chewy Louie begins as a small black dog who gradually chews more and more and larger and larger things. His owner fears that Chewy Louie will be sent away because of his bad habits.

Scieszka, J. & Smith, L. (2001). *Baloney.* (Henry P.). New York: Viking. (2–4). PICTURE BOOK/FANTASY.

Henry P. Baloney is an alien who has the same problem as earth children. He has to think of a good excuse for being late to class otherwise he will have permanent lifelong detention.

Shulevitz, U. (1998). *Snow.* New York: Farrar, Straus & Giroux. (K–2). PICTURE BOOK.

In this book, snow transforms a town, and a boy and his dog celebrate the first snowfall.

Siebert, D. (2000). *Cave.* (W. McLoughlin, Illus.). New York: Harper Collins. (2–up). PICTURE BOOK/NONFICTION.

The cave narrates this book, creating the mood and feeling of a cave through narration and illustrations.

Simon, C. (1998). *Guard the house, Sam!* Chicago: Children's Book Press. (K–2). CONTEMPORARY REALISTIC FICTION.

Sam is the dog charged with guarding his home.

Simont, M. (2001). *The stray dog.* New York: HarperCollins. (1–3). REALISTIC FICTION.

A picnicing family meets and plays with a stray dog. They return a week later to find him and save him from the dogcatcher.

Smith, M. (2001). *Desser the best ever cat.* New York: Knopf. (K–3). REALISTIC FICTION

A girl recalls her cat's life from kitten to old age.

Spier, P. (1982). *Peter Spier's rain.* New York: Doubleday. (PreK–3). PICTURE BOOK.

The artist explores rain from many perspectives.

Steiner, J. (1999). *Look-alikes, jr.* (T. Lindley, Photog.). Boston: Little, Brown. (PreK–2). PICTURE BOOK.

Everyday places are constructed from a variety of objects, such as pencils and crackers. Children can identify over 700 objects.

Stevens, J., & Crummel, S. T. (2001) *And the dish ran away with the spoon* (Stevens, J. Illus.). New York: Harcourt. (1–3). PICTURE BOOK, NURSERY RHYME.

A new version of the old rhyme.

Stevens, J., & Crummel, S. T. (2003). *Jackalope*. New York: Harcourt. (1–3). PICTURE BOOK.

A plain old hare gets horns from a fairy godrabbit and a cranky coyote.

St. George, J. (2000). *So you want to be President* (D. Small, Illus.). New York: Philomel. (2–up). PICTURE BOOK, NONFICTION.

The author and illustrator have profiled Presidents' quirks that make them human and memorable.

Van Allsburg, C. (1985). *The polar express*. Boston: Houghton Mifflin. (K–4). PICTURE BOOK.

A boy discovers the spirit of Christmas after traveling to the North Pole on the polar express and meeting Santa Claus.

van Lieshout, E., & van Os, E. *A nice party* (P. Gerritsen, Illus.). Asheville, NC: Front Street (1–3). PICTURE BOOK, FANTASY.

Gus dreads his birthday because his family has awful birthday parties; with the help of his best friend, he solves this problem.

Walker, R., & Sharkey, N. (1999). *Jack and the beanstalk*. New York: Bareboot Books. (1–3). TRADATIONS.

A different version of this traditional tale. Jack loves magic, so he proudly trades the cow for beans. The illustrations for this version are also unique.

Ward, J., & Marsh, T. J. (2000). *Somewhere in the ocean* (K. Spengler, Illus.). Flagstaff, AZ: Rising Moon. (P–2). PICTURE BOOK, INFORMATION, NUMBERS.

Exquisite illustrations of sea animals with counting.

Waring, R. (2002). *Alberto the dancing alligator* (H. Swain, Illus.). New York: Candlewick. (2–5). PICTURE BOOK, FANTASY.

Tina and her Alberto the Alligator love to dance until Alberto is accidently flushed. When he tries to return home, he sets off a panic in the city. This many layered book will appeal to many ages.

Wheatley, N., & Ottley, M. (2001). *Luke's way of looking*. LaJolla, CA: Kane/Miller. (2–4). PICTURE BOOK, REALISTIC FICTION.

Luke's art is not acceptable in his school, but he discovers a museum and realizes that his art is wonderful.

Wick, W. (1998). *Walter Wick's optical tricks*. New York: Cartwheel/Scholastic. (3–6). INFORMATIONAL BOOK.*

A wonderful collection of optical illusions.

Wiesner, D. (1999). *Sector 7*. New York: Clarion. (1–3). PICTURE BOOK.

This wordless book tells the story of a boy who visits the Empire State Building on a school field trip. On the observation deck of the building, the boy makes friends with a cumulus cloud.

Wiesner, D. (2001). *The three pigs*. New York: Clarion Books. (1–4). PICTURE BOOK, FANTASY.

The three little pigs of the old, old story wander in and out of other traditional tales.

Wisniewski, D. (1998). *The secret knowledge of grown-ups*. New York: Lothrop, Lee & Shepard. (K–4). PICTURE BOOK, MODERN FANTASY.

Secret files that grown-ups have hidden from children for thousands of years are opened to reveal knowledge to children such as why they say, "Eat your vegetables."

Wood, A. (1984). *The napping house* (D. Wood, Illus.). New York: Harcourt Brace. (K–2). PICTURE BOOK, MODERN FANTASY.

A child and some animals fall asleep on Granny's bed; they nap until a flea bites a mouse, and then they break the bed.

Wood, A. (1996). *The red racer*. New York: Simon & Schuster. (1–3). PICTURE BOOK.

Nona has an old bicycle, but she wants a new red racer. When her parents say no because it costs too much, Nona sets out to solve her problem.

Young, E. (Trans.). (1989). *Lon Po Po: A Red-Riding Hood story from China*. New York: Philomel. (1–3). PICTURE BOOK, TRADITIONAL.

In this variation, the mother leaves her three daughters home and goes to visit the grandmother, and the wolf comes to the girls.

Younger, B. (1998). *Purple mountain majesties* (S. Schuett, Illus.). New York: Dutton. (2–5). PICTURE BOOK, HISTORICAL FICTION.

The story of the song "America the Beautiful."

References and Books for Further Reading

Ardizzone, E. (1980). Creation of a picture book. In S. Egoff, G. Stubbs, & L. Ashley (Eds.), *Only connect: Readings on children's literature* (pp. 289–298). New York: Oxford University Press.

Camp, D. J. & Tompkins, G. E. (1990). Show–tell in middle school? *Middle School Journal, 21*, 18–20.

Christlow, E. (1999). *What do illustrators do?* New York: Clarion.

Cianciolo, P. (1990). *Picture books for children* (3rd ed.). Chicago: American Library Association.

Cummings, P. (1998). *Talking with artists* (Vol. 3). New York: Bradbury.

Dillon, L., & Dillon, D. (1992b). Leo's story. In P. Cummings (Ed.), *Talking with artists* (pp. 22–23). New York: Bradbury.

Hearn, M. P. (1999). *David Wiesner: Master of incongruity*. Abilene, TX: National Center for Children's Illustrated Literature.

Hearne, B. (1999). *Choosing books for children: A commonsense approach*. Urbana, IL: University of Illinois Press.

Kiefer, B. (1995). *The potential of picturebooks*. Upper Saddle River, NJ: Merrill/Prentice Hall.

Lacey, L. E. (1986). *Art and design in children's picture books*. Chicago: American Library Association.

Lewis, D. (2001). *Reading contemporary picturebooks: Picturing text*. New York: Routledge/Falmer.

Lobel, A. (1981). A good picture book should. . . . In B. Hearne & M. Kaye (Eds.), *Celebrating children's books* (pp. 73–80). New York: Lothrop, Lee & Shepard.

Marcus, L. S. (2001). *Side by side*. New York: Walker.

Matulka, D. (2002) "Picturing books: A site about picture books." **http://picturingbooks.org.**

Moline, S. (1995). *I see what you mean*. York, ME: Stenhouse.

Nikolajeva, M., & Scott, C. (2001). *How picturebooks work*. New York: Garland.

Schwarcz, C. (1991). *The picture book comes of age: Looking at childhood through the art of illustration*. Chicago: American Library Association.

Shulevitz, U. (1985). *Writing with pictures: How to write and illustrate children's books*. New York: Watson Guptill.

Smith, L. H. (1991). *The unreluctant years*. New York: Viking.

Stewig, J. (1992). Reading pictures, reading text. *New Advocate, 5*, 11–22.

Wood, D., & Wood, A. (1986). The artist at work: Where ideas come from. *Horn book, 60*, 556–565.

Young, E. (1990). Caldecott acceptance speech. *Hornbook, 66*, 452–456.

Zelinsky [Online]. Available: **http://www.nccil.org/exhibit/zelinsky.html** [2000, March 23].

Poetry for Every Child

5

KEY TERMS

alliteration	meter
assonance	narrative poem
concrete poetry	nonsense poetry
epics	onomatopoeia
figurative language	personification
free verse	rhyme
haiku	rhythm
imagery	simile
metaphor	

GUIDING QUESTIONS

Think about your early experiences with poetry—did you enjoy them? Did anyone read poetry to you? What types of poems were your favorites? Do you think your early experiences affected the way you feel about poetry now? What was the last poem you read? Keep these questions in mind as you read.

1. What is poetry?

2. Why is poetry valuable in children's lives?

3. Who are some of the popular contemporary children's poets?

4. How can teachers engage children with poetry?

"Poetry . . . is something very close to dance and song" (Frye, 1964). Many people believe poetry is the highest form of literature, that somehow it stands above the novel, the drama, and the essay (Tiedt, 2002). Certainly, poetry represents literature in its most intense, imaginative, and rhythmic form, expressing and interpreting the essence of experience through language (Morner & Rausch, 1991; Perrine, 1969). A major difference between poetry and prose is its compactness. One word in a poem says much more than a single word in prose. The rich imagery of poetry permits a far greater concentration of meaning than what is found in prose (Morner & Rausch, 1991).

To tap this meaning, teachers and librarians choose poetry related to students' lives, experiences, and interests. Developing a broad acquaintance with children's poetry enables teachers to nurture children's appreciation. Teachers can experiment with various ways of sharing poetry to build children's responses. This chapter focuses on these aspects of poetry. Vignette one demonstrates one teacher's approach to poetry in the classroom.

Vignette two provides an example of poetry in a primary classroom.

The Nature of Poetry

The opening vignettes demonstrate classroom experiences with poetry, illustrating that linguistically simple poetry can have multiple layers of meaning. Poets' words "reflect subtle shadows, images, and symbols that lead children to see beyond the literal and surface-level meanings" (Cullinan, Scala, & Schroder, 1995, p. 3). Poetry tells stories as it does in *Carver: A Life in Poems*.

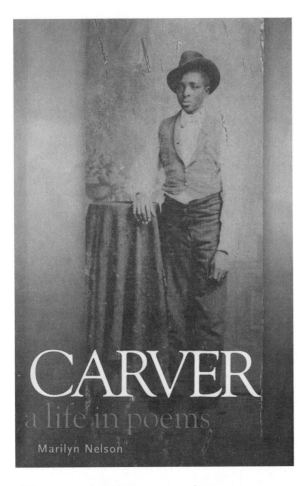

The many talented Carver was a botanist, inventor, painter, musician, and teacher.

Poetry is both emotional and intellectual. A poem can start us thinking and talking about feelings and subjects. It can also express feelings that we cannot put into words ourselves. Poetry's economy of expression is comparable to the terseness of a conversation between long-time friends—it relies on the ring of familiarity in voice inflections and images to create meaning. Paul Janeczko relies on conversational language to create the poems in *The Music of What Happens*.

VIGNETTE ONE

Chris Reed's sixth-grade class was engaged in a unit focusing on "Admirable People" when Marilyn Nelson's book, *Carver: a Life in Poems*, was honored by the Coretta Scott King Honor Award, the John Newbery Honor Award, and the Boston Globe-Horn Book Award, and was a National Book Award Finalist. After reading it, he decided this compelling work belonged in his unit.

Chris used a picture of George Washington Carver and a copy of the postage stamp honoring him to introduce this extraordinary individual. He then explained that Carver was born a slave, but he had lived a rich and complex life. Mr. Reed showed the students a jar of peanut butter and asked how it was related to Carver. A few of the students immediately guessed that Carver had created peanut butter. After explaining that this unusual biography consisted of Marilyn Nelson's poems, he told the students he was going to read the lyric poem "Out of 'Slave's Ransom'" orally. He then posed the following discussion questions on an overhead transparency. Chris read the poem again so the students could think about the questions.

1. What does this poem tell us about Carver?
2. Whose voice speaks in this poem?
3. Why is this poem titled "Out of 'Slave's Ransom'"?
4. What senses are used in telling this poem?
5. What are the four major images in this poem? Which of these is the most powerful image in your mind?
6. Why is this poem considered a lyric poem?

A lively discussion followed because the students disagreed about questions 4, 5, and 6.

(continued)

Chris assigned the poems, "Prayer of the Ivory-Handled Knife" and "Watkins Laundry and Apothecary" for the following day. After the second day's discussion, Chris gave the students the responsibility for presenting specific poems. They could read their poems orally or, if they preferred, audio or video tape their reading. They began a time line of Carver's life. The culmination of this book unit involved identifying the various poetic forms used in the book and researching the factors that made Carver an admirable person. At a later point during the year they compared this book with a narrative biography of Carver.

The poem "Locusts" was written by a student after reading *insectlopedia*.

Locusts

Eating is mostly what this insect does
Swerving around looking for food
Locusts
Swarming and exploring
Food every where and then gone
Born in North America
The nymph is still young
Looking for amusement
Soon it grows and sheds its dry skin
Growing to soon swarm like bees
But stinging the land instead of
innocent humans
They are energized and they swarm and
buzz everywhere rubbing and bumping
into each other mating season
Soon enough a great grassland is bare
A forest is soon a barren land
Covered with dead trees
Eating leaves at all costs
Consuming some of our lives in yield
Wishing for more to eat
More
More
More
Always more
Like a bull they charge to their red,
green leafs
Great green leafs full of water and flavor
Eating more and still not full
Consuming all the vegetation they can see
And for farmers there goes money

VIGNETTE TWO

Poetry fun in the primary grades is obviously different than in middle school or intermediate grades. Poetry has to move for these children because they are on the move. Rhythm, words, and humor are major attractions. Courtney Rogers, a second-grade teacher, chose "The Polliwogs" from Douglas Florian's *Lizards, Frogs, and Polliwogs*. As the children listened, they picked up on the rhythm and the wordplay. On the second reading they joined in chanting appealing words such as *polliwoggle and polliwiggle*; *wriggle*; *quiver and shiver*; and *jiggle, jog, and frog*. A number of the children moved with the words, thereby resembling a group of polliwogs.

Courtney then printed the poem on a large chart, so the children could read it themselves. She noticed the children copied the movement words on their own papers. Many of the children chose to draw pictures of polliwogs to accompany the words they wrote. As she expected, the students asked for more poems from this collection. This vignette demonstrates that children have a natural affinity for poetic language and language play. They relish inventing words and rolling them over their tongues. They respond to the rhythms of jump rope rhymes, advertising jingles, and rap music (McClure, 2002). Unusual combinations of words intrigue children who respond to their musical, rhythmic qualities.

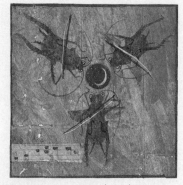

Insects can be poetic.

Groceries
Every thing for them
These beasts
Short horned grasshoppers
Swerving
Chewing
Eating
Flying
Locusts covering the sky like a solar
eclipse just as if we had no
Sun
The plants die
And so do we
Still they're pondering how to get more
food
Destroying countries
Swarming by the thousands
Eating and nothing more
Luckily, other insects aren't like that
Eating till nothing exists any more
They survive for a short while
Finally dying out when winter comes
Giving the land a much needed break.
by
Kyle Neu

Middle grade students integrate Insectlopedia
with science.

Poets use language in ways that not only re-create the rhythms of oral language, but also extend them to include novel and unusual applications. Poetry's rhythm, sound patterns, figurative language, compactness, and emotional intensity set it apart from prose. "You can't say anything much more briefly than a poem or folktale says it, nor catch a fact or feeling much more expressively" (Hearne, 1991, p. 107). *Imagery* enables poets to create dense meaning with a few words. Poets use words economically, choosing and polishing each one like a gem to create associations in readers' minds. This characteristic is illustrated in the lyrical text of Shaik's *The Jazz of Our Street*, which pulses with the rhythms and spirit of a jazz melody. The rhythm draws children to the jazz parade and they join in joyful movements, shimmying, shaking, and swaying. The band's beat has the "stamping and hauling we hear on our block every day."

Emotional Intensity

"The best poetry is a union of beauty and truth. . . . The best poets speak to us with beauty that we can appreciate and in truths we can understand" (Russell, 1991, p. 77). Poetry, rooted in the world of emotions as well as in the mind, is emotionally intense. Poets capture universal feelings by writing about experiences that have affected them in such a way that they believe the experiences will affect readers as well. The experiences may be everyday happenings that have been commemorated with an emotional intensity that meets the needs and interests of listeners and readers. For instance, Charlotte Zolotow expresses emotional intensity when she demands *Say It!* in the book of the same name. In this joyful book, a little girl and her mother celebrate the pleasure of walking on a beautiful autumn day.

> *"Say it," shrieked the little girl. "Say it*
> *say it say it!"*
> *"I love you," said her mother. "I love*
> *you I love you I love you!"*

Expressing Feelings and Moods

Poetic language may be unpretentious and the number of words limited, but the emotional intensity of poetry makes it a natural form for expressing feelings. *Honey, I Love, and Other Love Poems* by Eloise Greenfield shares an African-American child's love for members of her family and her enthusiasm for life.

Poetry voices many feelings and moods. In *Locomotion*, Jacqueline Woodson tells the sad story of Lonnie Collins Motion in poetic narrative. Lonnie, an orphan, lives with a foster parent who does not like boys. Through a school assignment to keep a poetry journal, Lonnie finds his poetic voice. The poems in his journal change as his poetic expression grows and as he finds comfort through writing. Feelings of racism, grief, loss, and growing up lead readers to consider these complex issues while remaining hopeful.

Paul Janeczko expresses the feelings of baseball players and fans in *That Sweet Diamond: Baseball Poems*. The poem "The Pitcher" is from this collection.

> ### The Pitcher
> *Standing*
> *alone*
> *above the rest*
> *in the center of the diamond*
> *his art is foolery,*
> *casting a spell,*
> *never showing the batter*
> *more than he needs to know*
> *for the moment*
> *it takes a slider, change, or*
> *tantalizing curve*
> *to break the heart*

Shel Silverstein addresses the fears and joys of childhood in his enormously popular book, *Where the Sidewalk Ends: The Poems & Drawings of Shel Silverstein*. His humor and zany illustrations help us examine our feelings with a light heart. "Sick," a popular poem in this collection, tells about a character who is gravely ill—until she realizes that it is Saturday.

Jill Bennett has compiled a diverse collection of lively family poems in *Grandad's Tree: Poems about Families*. These poems have themes of humor, affection, sorrow, and sibling rivalry. Nikki Grimes used a nontraditional perspective to create a biography in *Talkin' about Bessie: The Story of Aviator Elizabeth Coleman*. This poem is set in a family parlor with the voices of people mourning the passing of Elizabeth Coleman. Her family, friends, teachers, and siblings reflect on her life and steely character. They remember her drive to learn, and her resilience in the face of discrimination.

Poetry can be categorized according to various criteria; we have chosen to organize our discussion of poetry in these ways: poetic form, content, theme, and audience appeal.

Elements of Poetry

Poets use words in melodious combinations to create singing, lyrical qualities. Sound patterns and figurative language connote sensory images appealing to sight, sound, touch, and smell. These images build on children's experiences and relate to their lives. Nancy Van Laan used sensory winter experiences and poetic language in describing children's experiences with winter in *When Winter Comes*. Children's sensory feelings are captured by language such as "cold winds blow" and "snuggling deep" in a warm bed. In the illustrations, readers see the children and their loving parents walking through the landscape of a snowy day and returning to their warm home. In *Snow Music*, Lynne Rae Perkins tells about a dog, a boy, and a girl who are lost in the snow. However, they enjoy their trek through the snow by describing it in musical language. This poetry is perfect for choral reading.

Poetic Language

The words in a poem are carefully chosen to imply a range of ideas, images, and feelings. Each word implies and suggests more than it literally says. Poets create rich metaphors that summon hundreds of associations to stimulate readers' thoughts and emotions. Readers' individual connotative understandings are based on their emotional responses to words or concepts. For instance, readers who lived in the Blue Ridge Mountains will have richer responses to poetry about mountains than those who have never seen mountains. In Alarcón's book, *From the Bellybutton of the Moon and Other Summer Poems*, the poet's vivid images are built on his memories of summer vacations in Mexico. His experience leads him to compare the "Summer Sun" with a luminous orange, hanging from the tree.

Sensory language stimulates reader associations. This language arouses readers' senses and reminds them of concrete experiences. Poets continually search for fresh imagery to arouse the senses, a sample of which is shown in Table 5.1.

Sound Patterns

Children learn the sound patterns of language before they learn words; in fact, sound patterns appear to be instrumental in children's acquisition of language. The sounds of poetry attract young children, who realize early on that words have sounds as well as meanings. "They love to rhyme words, to read alliterative

	TABLE 5.1
	Examples of sensory language.

Sense	Imagery
Vision	Fire-engine red, gigantic, elongated
Touch	Soft, hard, rough
Sound	Crunch, rumble, squeak
Smell	Rotting leaves, wet dog, bread baking
Movement	Hop, skip, trudge
Taste	Sweet, salty, bitter

tongue twisters, to laugh at funny-sounding names" (Fleischman, 1986, p. 553). Sound patterns are a delight to the ear of everyone, young and old. Rhyme, alliteration, onomatopoeia, and assonance are several devices commonly used by poets to achieve these sound patterns, and are often combined to give sound effects to a poem.

The delightful sound patterns of nursery rhymes, combined with their brevity and simplicity, invite children to roll them over their tongues. "Hickory Dickory Dock" is a good example. Repeat it aloud to yourself or read it to a young child. Think about your own or the child's response to its patterns of sound. How many devices can you identify in this verse?

> *Hickory, dickory, dock,*
> *The mouse ran up the clock.*
> *The clock struck one,*
> *and down he run.*
> *Hickory, dickory, dock.*

Rhyme

Rhyme is one of the most recognizable elements in poetry, even though poetry does not have to rhyme. Rhyme is based on the similarity of sound between two words such as *sold* and *mold* or *chrome* and *foam*. "When the sounds of their accented syllables and all succeeding sounds are identical, words rhyme" (Morner & Rausch, 1991). A good rhyme, a repetition of sounds, pleases readers. It gives order to thoughts and pleasure to the ears (Livingston, 1991). Rhyme gives poetry an appealing musical quality.

The most common form of rhyme in poetry is end rhyme, so named because it comes at the end of the line of poetry (Morner & Rausch, 1991). End rhyme is il-

lustrated in Rhoda Bacmeister's poem "Galoshes." Internal rhyme occurs within a line of poetry and is illustrated in Karla Kuskin's poem "Hughbert and the Glue" in Arbuthnot's *Time for Poetry*. Rhyming patterns in poetry are grouped in stanzas. A common end rhyming pattern is to rhyme the last word in every other line. An example of this appears in Alice Schertle's book, *Advice for a Frog and Other Poems*. In this book, the poem "A Traveler's Tale" illustrates the end rhyme.

> *At length we found a land of mud and*
> *flowers.*
> *And slipped into the New World that*
> *was ours.*

The stanzas thus formed have special names depending on the number of lines in the rhyming pattern:

two lines: couplet
three lines: tercet
four lines: quatrain
five lines: quintet
six lines: sextet
seven lines: septet
eight lines: octave

Alliteration

Alliteration is achieved through repetition of consonant sounds at the beginning of words or within words. It is one of the most ancient devices used in English poetry to give unity, emphasis, and musical effect. Jack Prelutsky repeats the P sound in his poem, "Peanut Peg and Peanut Pete." This poem is found in *The Frog Wore Red Suspenders*.

Onomatopoeia

Onomatopoeia gives poetry a sensuous feeling. Onomatopoeia refers to words that sound like what they mean. For example, the word *bang* sounds very much like the loud noise to which it refers. In *Stories to Begin On*, Rhonda Bacmeister uses the words *splishes, sploshes, slooshes,* and *sloshes* in the poem "Galoshes" to create the sounds of walking in slush.

Assonance

Assonance is the close repetition of middle vowel sounds between different consonant sounds such as the long /a/ sound in *fade* and *pale*. Assonance creates near rhymes rather than true rhymes commonly found in improvised folk ballads (Morner & Rausch, 1991). Assonance gives unity and rhythmic effect to a line of poetry.

Rhythm

Rhythm is the patterned flow of sound in poetry created through combinations of words that convey a beat. Rhythm can set the sense of a story to a beat, but it can also emphasize what a writer is saying or even convey sense on its own. David McCord's "Song of the Train" in *Far and Few* demonstrates this. In traditional English poetry, rhythm is based on *meter*, the combination of accent and numbers of syllables (Morner & Rausch, 1991). Meter and rhythm are created when patterns of accented and unaccented syllables and of long and short vowels work together. Diane Siebert illustrates this meter in her book-length poem *Motorcycle Song*.

Wordplay

Wordplay is an inviting characteristic of children's poetry. The sound patterns in poetry create the playful language that children find pleasurable. They roll interesting words over their tongues and repeat them, savoring their flavor. Douglas Florian's wordplay is on display in *Laugh-eteria* and *Bing Bang Boing*, which are collections of humorous short verse. These lines from *Laugh-eteria* illustrate wordplay.

> *Hello, my name is Dracula.*
> *My clothing is all blackula.*

Figures of Speech

Writers use figures of speech, also called *figurative language*, to express feelings and create mental pictures (images). Figures of speech offer writers many possibilities for expressing thoughts and feelings. One of the major challenges in creating poetry is to choose figures of speech that offer fresh images and that uniquely express the writer. In fact, a poet's facility in using figures of speech is what makes the major difference between pleasant verse and fine poetry (Livingston, 1991). The best-known figures of speech are simile, metaphor, and personification.

Simile

A *simile* is a figure of speech using the words *like* or *as* to compare one thing to another. Most of you will recognize that "white as snow" is a simile, but it is so timeworn that it has become a cliché. Poets must be acute observers, seeing and hearing in new ways to offer fresh figures of speech. Look for the similes used by Valerie Worth in "Frog," a poem from her book *Small Poems*.

Metaphor

Metaphor, like simile, is a figure of speech comparing two items, but instead of saying something is *like* something else, metaphor says that something *is* something else. Langston Hughes uses metaphor to arouse the reader's feelings and imagination in his poem "Dreams," calling life a "broken-winged bird" and a "barren field! Frozen with snow." These metaphors create images that clarify our thoughts about dreams. The reader recognizes, of course, that life is not actually a bird or field (Livingston, 1991); however, these comparisons communicate vivid, unique images. In the following example, a poet gives spring the attributes of a baseball player, using the words *swings, pitches, throws, catches, slides, bunts*, and *tags*.

> *Spring brings out her baseball bat,*
> *swings it through the air,*
> *Pitches bulbs and apple blossoms,*
> *throws them where it's bare,*
> *Catches dogtooth violets, slides to meadow sweet,*
> *Bunts a breeze and tags the trees with green buds everywhere.*

Personification

Personification attributes human characteristics to something that does not actually have these qualities. Poets have a talent for endowing inanimate objects with life, as Myra Cohn Livingston does in the poems in her book, *A Circle of Seasons*: "Spring brings out her baseball bat, swings it through the air."

Types of Poetry

Free verse has become the most popular form for contemporary children's poetry, whereas older poetry follows traditional forms. Authorities divide poetry into three categories (i.e., narrative, dramatic, and lyric), although these elements are often combined in a single poem (Bagert, 1992). Poets choose and combine poetic forms to create a form that best tells their ideas and feelings. This means that attempts to categorize poems by type are usually impossible. This section examines poetic form and introduces examples to clarify understanding.

Narrative Poems

Narrative poems tell stories. The story elements—plot, character, setting, and theme—make narrative poems especially appealing because everyone enjoys a good story. Narrative poems that tell about the adventures of young characters or those who are childlike make compelling reading for children. Anne Isaacs' book, *Cat Up a Tree*, tells a humorous story in a narrative poem. Seven geographic regions and Washington, D.C., are the focus of Bennett Hopkins' collection of poems in *My America: A Poetry Atlas of the United States*. Narrative poems may be short or long. Book-length narrative poems are called *epics*. Byrd Baylor and her illustrator, Peter Parnall, share their love of the desert with readers in their illustrated epic, *The Other Way to Listen*.

Dramatic Poetry

Dramatic poetry often appears in the form of a monologue, in which a single character tells about a dramatic

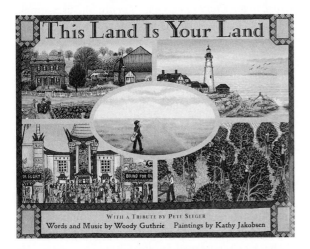

The poet and songwriter helps us appreciate the beauty of our country.

situation (Morner & Rausch, 1991). Many examples of dramatic form are found in traditional ballads. In a different vein, the poem found in Jane Medina's *My Name Is Jorge on Both Sides of the River: Poems* tells the story of a young Mexican boy who experiences humiliation at the public library and earns low grades.

Lyric Poetry

Lyric poems are short, personal poems expressing the poet's emotions and feelings. They speak of personal experience and comment on how the writer sees the world. Originally such poems were written to be sung to the music of a lyre, so it is not surprising that lyric poetry has a feeling of melody and song (Livingston, 1991). Lyric poetry is the most common form for children's poetry. It can be identified through the use of the personal pronouns *I*, *me*, *my*, *we*, *our*, and *us* or related words (Livingston, 1991).

Emotion, subjectivity, melodiousness, imagination, and description are distinguishing characteristics of dramatic poems (Morner & Rausch, 1991). Alice Shertle employs these characteristics when she writes about cats in *I Am the Cat*. She provides word pictures, as well as illustrations. Art and poetry also are paired in Nikki Grimes' book, *A Pocketful of Poems*. The voice in the book belongs to Tiana, who uses her favorite words and tells us, "I slip under its silver light/and pull it to my chin, like a quilt."

Haiku

Authentic *haiku*, a poetic form that originated in Japan, describes nature and the seasons. Haiku are patterned poems based on syllables, words, and lines. The first line contains five syllables, the second contains seven, and the third contains five for a total of 17 syllables in three lines. Matthew Gollub's book *Cool Melons—Turn to Frogs!: The Life and Poems of Issa* introduces haiku and the life of Issa, who is considered Japan's premier haiku poet.

Free Verse

Free verse differs from traditional forms of poetry in that it is "free" of a regular beat or meter (Morner & Rausch, 1991). Free verse usually does not rhyme, does not follow a predetermined pattern, and has a fragmentary syntax. Free verse incorporates many of the same poetic devices that writers of structured poetry employ, but writers of free verse are more concerned with natural speech rhythms, imagery, and meaning than with rhyme and meter.

Concrete Poetry

The form of *concrete poetry* is inseparable from the content. Concrete poetry merges visual, verbal, and auditory elements, arranging the words and letters to suggest something about the subject of the poem. For example, a poem about a rock might be written in the shape of a rock, or a poem about a cloud may be written in the shape of a cloud. In addition, several carefully selected words may be suspended on a mobile so that, as the air moves the mobile, the words move and a poem evolves, with each person seeing a different poem.

A marvelous collection of shape poems is found in J. Patrick Lewis' *Doodle Dandies: Poems That Take Shape*. Douglas Florian includes a room-shaped concrete poem, "The Gecko," in *Lizards, Frogs, and Polliwogs*.

Nonsense Poetry

Nonsense poetry ordinarily is composed in lyric or narrative form, but does not conform to the expected order of things. It defies reason. Nonsense poetry is playful; the meaning is subordinate to sound (Morner & Rausch, 1991). "Nonsense is a literary genre whose purpose is to rebel against, not only reason, but the physical laws of nature. It rejects established tenets and institutions, pokes fun at rational behavior, and touts destruction. It champions aberrations" (Livingston, 1981, p. 123).

Writers of nonsense poetry create unusual worlds in which objects and characters are recognizable but do absurd things and become involved in absurd situations. They know cows cannot jump over the moon, but they like the fun of such implausible antics as those in the following lines.

> *Hey diddle diddle*
> *The cat played the fiddle,*
> *The cow jumped over the moon.*

Edward Lear, the master of nonsense, wrote poems that appealed to all ages. Although his *Complete Nonsense Book* was published in 1948, it remains popular today. J. Patrick Lewis shows that he is an outstanding student of Lear in his book *Boshblobberbosh: Runcible Poems for Edward Lear*. Funky nonsense is the theme of Calef Brown's appealing book, *Polkabats and Octopus Slacks: 14 Stories*.

Nonsense writers use a variety of strategies in their craft. They invent words, as Laura Richards does in "Eletelephony." Alliteration is the technique Lear used in "Pelican Chorus." Personification lends itself well to nonsense verse, as animals, objects, and even pieces of furniture take on human characteristics. Exaggeration is a useful device to writers of nonsense, as Shel Silverstein shows in "Sarah Cynthia Sylvia Stout Would Not Take the Garbage Out," one of many nonsense poems in his book, *Where the Sidewalk Ends*.

Content of Poetry

The subject matter of poetry is unlimited, as poets find no activity too humble and no object of daily living too minor for poetry. For instance, Douglas Florian featured birthday cake in "Cake Mistake" from *Bing Bang Boing*.

Poetry embodies life and reveals its complexity; it is a part of the fabric of life. Poets look at ordinary things and events more closely than the rest of us and see the things we overlook. Constance Levy fosters new ways of seeing the everyday world in the poems featured in *A Crack in the Clouds and Other Poems*. She uses simple language and varied cadences to tell about cricket songs, icicles, weeds, and comets. Pat Mora's book, *Love to Mama*, features Latino poets, who celebrate mothers, grandmothers, and great-grandmothers—women who are always there for their families.

A plethora of poems on subjects ranging from garbage to fairy tales and from topics that are side-splittingly funny to serious are readily available. Teachers can find that poems fitting every mood, interest, and topic are available in any form. Content is more important than form when selecting poetry for children.

Although the range of content in poetry is far too broad to catalog here, we will highlight humor as one of the most popular subjects in children's poetry. Jack Prelutsky is a poet well-known for his zany poems. He uses splendid words such as *disputatious* and *alacrity*,

A Book of Nighttime Poems

STILL ∗ AS ∗ A ∗ STAR

selected by Lee Bennett Hopkins
illustrated by Karen Milone

This collection of poems and lullabies perfectly captures the dreamy nighttime mood when a child leans out of her window to gaze at the moon, and a boy dreams of giants up in the mountains.

and his poems have unexpected twists that delight his readers. Perhaps most important, all children (including boys, who are sometimes hard to interest in poetry) love his poems. His book, *Something Big Has Been Here*, has many ridiculous images to delight readers. In "The Turkey Shot Out of the Oven," a turkey shoots out of an oven because it is stuffed with unpopped popcorn. Then there is the character in "Denson Dumm" who planted light bulbs in his hair so that he would be forever bright. Like all of Prelutsky's books, however, this one offers a diverse range of topics, including serious poems such as "Don't Yell at Me."

Again, space constrains us from cataloging the variety of ways to treat subjects in poetry, but we will briefly discuss three poems on a topic elementary children love: dinosaurs. Each poet chose different stylistic devices to portray dinosaurs: the first two poems could be categorized as realistic fiction or even informational compositions because they communicate the

essence of actual dinosaurs, whereas the third poem is delightful fantasy.

The first poem, "When Dinosaurs Ruled the Earth" by Patricia Hubbell, uses repeated words to create rhythm and to tie the verses together. The phrases "teeth were made for tearing flesh, his teeth were made to gnash" creates auditory images, whereas later phrases establish visual images. This poet dramatizes the dinosaurs' sizes by comparing them with buildings and trees. Continuing on, the poet says that the dinosaurs have "pygmy brains."

In "Brachiosaurus," Jack Prelutsky, in his book *Tyrannosaurus Was a Beast*, describes the dinosaur as a "perpetual eating machine," and as "clumsy and slow." These phrases give us visual images. Prelutsky also points out that the dinosaur did not need "to be clever and wise." These phrases reiterate the idea of "pygmy brain" found in the first poem. However, Prelutsky uses fewer words and rhymes every other line in his poem, distinguishing his poem from Hubbell's "When Dinosaurs Ruled the Earth."

The third poem, "Dinosaur Dances," is bound to be a hit with children. In this poem, Jane Yolen writes about make-believe dinosaurs in costumes, dancing everything from a ballet to a hula. The poet creates a rhythmic beat with words and rhymes in the title poem, telling readers that "anything goes" at a prehistoric party with "lights low, couples doing Twist and Shout" and "hopping all about." Bruce Degen's illustrations create unusual images—clumsy dinosaurs dancing a refined minuet. Each of the poems in this book has a different dance beat, making it unique and delightful. The best of these poems makes toes tap and leads to movement.

Stimulating Children's Response to Poetry

Children's poetry has experienced a renaissance in recent years. Contemporary children's poets such as Jack Prelutsky, Paul Fleischman, Paul Janeczko, Eloise Greenfield, and Douglas Florian are very popular (Crisp, 1991). "More than ever before, poetry for children has climbed to its proper station" (Hopkins, 1998, p. 4). Teachers, librarians, and parents have the opportunity to choose from a wide variety of poems and poetry books to nurture children's interests.

Poetry speaks to the emotions and the intellect. It is pleasurable and comfortable, amusing and relaxing. Poetry can be an important part of children's literary life, clarifying and illuminating experience and enriching daily life. The rhythms of poetic language appeal to children; they stick in memory and children repeat the rhythms through marching, tapping, skipping, and so forth. They also enjoy repeating interesting rhymes again and again, savoring the feel of them on their tongues. Poetry lifts spirits and stimulates imaginations, stirring readers to communicate in interesting ways (Peck, 1979).

Poetry appreciation begins with the premise that it merits a prominent place in children's lives. "Poetry must flow freely in our children's lives; it should come to them as naturally as breathing, for nothing—nothing—can ring and rage through hearts and minds as does poetry" (Hopkins, 1998).

Adults who wish to engage children's interest in poetry will be pleased to learn that extensive technical knowledge is unnecessary. Although sometimes helpful, expertise regarding poetic form is not as important as having many experiences with interesting poetry. Response to poetry is largely a matter of ex-perience. Presenting a variety of poems gives children opportunities to identify their favorites, and with experience, adults can acquire a discriminating sense for the poetry, and may even discover an unrealized passion for it.

Poets and Their Poetry

Learning about the people who create poetry will motivate children to read more. When choosing a poet to study, the teacher may do read-alouds that focus on a single poet's works. However, children can immerse themselves in the work of a single poet, focusing on one they like very much. Children who lack experience with poetry may have to experience more poetry to find a favorite.

We chose Jack Prelutsky for a poet's profile because he is a favorite of children all over the United States with his keen sensitivity to children's fears, pleasures, and funny bones (Behr, 1995). This poet's profile was prepared with materials from the *Highlights' Teacher Net*, **www.teachingk-8.com** and *Children's Books and Their Creators* (Silvey, 1995).

A Biographical Profile: Jack Prelutsky

Jack Prelutsky says that he was probably a challenge to parents and teachers because schools and parents were not prepared for individuals with great creativity. His multifaceted talents are demonstrated by his various occupations, including musician, photographer, truck driver, entertainer, and sculptor.

When a publisher expressed an interest in his poems when he was really trying to sell his photographs, he was shocked. He did not like poetry due to his experiences in school. In fact, he thought poets were very strange people. Moreover, he grew up in a tough Bronx neighborhood where poets were generally considered boring, sissies, or dead.

Prelutsky's goal is to write fresh, contemporary poems with humor as a basic ingredient. He believes that life does not have to be so serious, so his poems are almost always humorous, and he throws in a good bit of nonsense. Prelutsky is recognized for his irreverent style, technical versatility, and awareness of what children like.

Prelutsky loves what he is doing, writing poems and traveling around the United States meeting and talking with children. He likes writing, travel, and people, and he likes to see how children are growing through his books. Among his more than 30 volumes are:

Rolling Harvey Down the Hill
The New Kid on the Block
The Baby Uggs Are Hatching
The Dragons Are Singing Tonight
Something Big Has Been Here

Selecting and Evaluating Poetry

Some poets and educators have selected exemplary poetry and suggestions for classroom activities:

Let's Do a Poem! by Nancy Larrick

Pass the Poetry, Please! by Lee Bennett Hopkins

Tiger Lilies, Toadstools and Thunderbolts: Engaging K–8 by Iris Tiedt

Students with Poetry by Iris Tiedt

The Place My Words Are Looking For by Paul Janeczko

Near the Window Tree by Karla Kuskin

Poem-Making: Ways to Begin Writing Poetry by Myra Cohn Livingston

One of the very best ways to cultivate confidence with poetry is through reading many poems and deciding which poems and poets you like the best. Once you have discovered a poem or a poet who speaks to you, look for more poems by the same poet. Through this process your own taste will evolve, and you will find it easier to share poetry that you really enjoy. Develop your own wide collection of poems, both for your own use and to engage children's interests.

Offer a variety of poems in read-aloud sessions. A particular poem or book, however, may not be for everyone. It is for the person who relates to the feelings and ideas expressed. In the introduction to *A Tune Beyond Us*, Myra Cohn Livingston (1968) cautions readers: "Every poem in this collection will not speak for you. But perhaps one, or two, will. And that will be enough" (p. iv).

The brevity of poems motivates some children. Despite their brevity, however, poems should be read at a leisurely pace to allow readers to savor the words and ideas (Hearne, 1991). Brevity and leisurely pace are features of Mary Ann Hoberman's book, *You Read to Me, I'll Read to You: Very Short Stories to Read Together*. This unique book "in two voices" uses rhyme, rhythm, and repetition in poetry. The end flap of this book says, "Here's a book with something new—You read to me! I'll read to you."

Children relish poetry in classrooms and other settings where it is cultivated as a natural happening, a part of daily life. Reading a poem to celebrate holidays, rainy days, snowy days, pets, funny incidents, and sad events gives children opportunities to read and listen.

Locating Poetry

Poetry appears in several types of books: anthologies, specialized collections, and book-length poems. Poetry anthologies are collections of poetry that include many types of poems on many subjects. One of the most comprehensive is *The Random House Book of Poetry for Children* (Prelutsky, 1983), edited by Jack Prelutsky and illustrated by Arnold Lobel, which includes poems arranged in broad categories. Specialized collections are books of poems that focus on a specific theme or topic. All of the poems in Jane Yolen's *Dinosaur Dances* relate to dinosaurs—more specifically, dancing dinosaurs. A lengthy single poem may be published as an entire book, usually a picture book, as is Byrd Baylor's *The Other Way to Listen*.

Evaluating anthologies can be especially difficult because the poems represent such a broad range of subject matter and style, but reviewing the table of contents and examining the literary quality of a few poems in different sections can identify the range of topics. An anthology can provide appropriate poetry at a moment's notice for everyday reading needs—holidays, weather, and daily incidents. Of course, one or two good anthologies cannot fulfill all the poetry needs of children, and poetry should be a part of planned experiences as well as incidental experiences. Table 5.2 presents several examples each of anthologies, specialized collections, and book-length poems.

Children's Preferences

Children's appreciation of poetry is enhanced when adults thoughtfully choose literature reflecting children's experiences and interests. Of course, asking children what they like has obvious value. Research suggests that visual appeal is a factor in children's choices. They like poetry that is generously spaced and tastefully illustrated (Sebesta, 1983). Fisher and Natarella (1982) report that primary-grade children's poetry preferences include narrative poems and limericks, poems about strange and fantastic events, traditional poems, and poems that use alliteration, onomatopoeia, and rhyming.

Intermediate-grade students like poems related to their experiences and interests, humorous poems, and those with rhythm and rhyme (Bridge, 1966). They respond better to contemporary poems than to traditional ones and also prefer poems that address

	TABLE 5.2	
	Examples of books of poetry	
Author	Title	Grade Level

Anthologies

Author	Title	Grade Level
Beatrice de Regniers	*Sing a Song of Popcorn*	K–8
Tomie dePaola	*Tomie dePaola's Book of Poems*	1–6
Jack Prelutsky	*The Random House Book of Poetry for Children*	1–8
Ann McGovern	*Arrow Book of Poetry*	3–7
Nancy Larrick	*Piping Down the Valleys Wild*	3–7

Specialized Collections

Author	Title	Grade Level
Zena Sutherland	*The Orchard Book of Nursery Rhymes*	Preschool–1
Valerie Worth	*Small Poems*	K–2
Mary Ann Hoberman	*Yellow Butter Purple Jelly Red Jam Black Bread*	K–3
Nancy Larrick	*Mice Are Nice*	K–3
Edward Lear	*Of Pelicans and Pussycats: Poems and Limericks*	K–4
Jack Prelutsky	*Something Big Has Been Here*	K–4
Aileen Fisher	*When it Comes to Bugs*	K–6
Karama Fufula	*My Daddy Is a Cool Dude*	1–5
Robert Froman	*Seeing Things: A Book of Poems*	1–6
Nancy Larrick	*On City Streets*	1–6
David McCord	*One at a Time*	1–6
Jack Prelutsky	*Rolling Harvey Down the Hill*	1–6
Paul Fleischman	*Joyful Noise: Poems for Two Voices*	2–6
Arnold Adoff	*Sports Pages*	4–7
Cynthia Rylant	*Waiting to Waltz: A Childhood*	4–8

Single-Book Poems

Author	Title	Grade Level
Nadine Bernard Westcott	*Peanut Butter and Jelly: A Play Rhyme*	K–2
Myra Cohn Livingston	*Up in the Air*	K–4
Robert Frost	*Stopping by Woods on a Snowy Evening*	1–6
Arnold Adoff	*All the Colors of the Race*	3–8
Byrd Baylor	*The Desert Is Theirs*	3–8
Byrd Baylor	*The Other Way to Listen*	3–8
George Ella Lyon	*Together*	K–6

familiar and enjoyable experiences, funny poems, and those telling a story (Terry, 1974). Narrative poems and limericks are the most popular form with fourth, fifth, and sixth graders, whereas haiku and free verse are among the least popular (Terry, 1974).

Later studies of children's poetry preferences are consistent with the earlier studies (Ingham, 1980; Simmons, 1980). The weight of research indicates that children prefer humorous poetry and poetry addressing familiar experiences. Children prefer poems by Shel Silverstein and Dennis Lee to traditional poetry (Ingham, 1980). It communicates, inspires, informs, and tells of things that are, were, may be, and will never be (Peck, 1979).

Finding Winners

After reviewing teachers' reports, Crisp (1991) found that the top 10 books of poetry in the 1980s were:

1. *Joyful Noise: Poems for Two Voices* by Paul Fleischman
2. *Under the Sunday Tree* by Eloise Greenfield
3. *Brickyard Summer: Poems* by Paul Janeczko
4. *Did Adam Name the Vinegarroon?* by X. J. Kennedy
5. *Knock at a Star: A Child's Introduction to Poetry* by X. J. and Dorothy M. Kennedy, editors
6. *American Sports Poems* by R. R. Knudson and May Swenson, compilers
7. *Poems for Jewish Holidays* by Myra Cohn Livingston, editor
8. *Fresh Paint: New Poems* by Eve Merriam
9. *Tyrannosaurus Was a Beast: Dinosaur Poems* by Jack Prelutsky
10. *A Visit to William Blake's Inn: Poems for Innocent and Experienced Travelers* by Nancy Willard

Honorable mentions on her list included:

- *Tomie dePaola's Book of Poems* by Tomie dePaola, compiler and illustrator
- *The Music of What Happens: Poems That Tell Stories* by Paul Janeczko, compiler
- *Dogs & Dragons, Trees & Dreams: A Collection of Poems* by Karla Kuskin
- *Overheard in a Bubble Chamber and Other Science Poems* by Lillian Morrison
- *Waiting to Waltz: A Childhood* by Cynthia Rylant
- *Small Poems Again* by Valerie Worth

Books of poetry such as these can serve as a beginning point for exploring poetry. Use the following questions to help you in selecting poetry:

1. Can children understand it?
2. Does the poem stir emotions such as humor, sadness, empathy, and joy?
3. Does the poem create sensory images such as taste, touch, smell, or sight?
4. Does the poem play with the sounds of language? Does the sound echo the senses (Cullinan et al., 1995; Lenz, 1992)?
5. Does the rhythm enhance the meaning? Does the poem bring the subject to life? (Literary critics agree that fine poets bring an experience or emotion to life, making it live for others.)
6. Will this poem motivate children to read other poetry?
7. Does the poem evoke a response in the listener/reader?

Using such guidelines, however, is no substitute for old-fashioned observation: Children's eyes light up over a splendid poem that speaks directly to them; they grimace over ones they do not like. The clearest signal that you have read a winner is, of course, a request to read it again.

Enriching Poetic Experiences

Children's responses to poetry are closely linked to the ways in which they customarily explore the world: observing and manipulating. As they explore the nature and parameters of language, poetry can give them access to specific characteristics or elements not found in their everyday experience (Parsons, 1992).

Surround children with poetry: Display poems, posters, and books related to classroom activities and studies. Place poem posters (that you or the children make and laminate) around the classroom. Recite or read poems whenever opportunities arise. Celebrate poets and poetry books that the children especially enjoy. Play tapes of poets reading their own work. Make up poems on the spur of the moment that fit classroom events and studies.

Poetry experiences begin with listening and chanting. Poetry comes to life when read or said out loud. Children enjoy repeating and intensifying the magic of poetry; they like to hear it again and again and object to changes in delivery or attempts to leave out verses (Parsons, 1992). Children love to chime in with the reader, clap with the rhythm, mime facial expressions, act out events, or just repeat the words. Such oral experiences intensify their appreciation of poetry.

The poet's use of unfamiliar words and combinations of words, definite rhythms, vocal stress on words and syllables, and even the ideas, however, can complicate reading poetry aloud. Practice reading poetry so you can read fluently, at a comfortable rate. A tape recorder can be helpful in practicing oral reading.

Children need to hear poetry daily, particularly appealing poems that help them develop an ear for the rhythm and sound of poetry. Daily poetry readings should be both incidental and planned. Incidental poetry reading occurs in conjunction with an event such as a birthday or a new baby in the family. Holidays and events such as the first day of spring and the first day of winter are good reasons to read a poem. Rain, sunshine, snow, and the first robin of the spring are all events to be marked with poetry. Planned poetry reading occurs when the teacher chooses poetry that fits the curriculum or develops thematic units with poetry; the diversity of subject matter and form in poetry makes such planning easy. A few unit suggestions are included at the end of this chapter.

Rhythm

Sound effects

Students can express the rhythms of poetry through sound effects. Teachers may organize a team to create background sound effects as a poem is read aloud (Larrick, 1991); for instance, for "The Merry-Go-Round Song," a sound effects team could re-create the up-and-down rhythm of a carousel by repeating the sounds OOM-pa-pa, OOM-pa-pa in the rhythm of the song. Encourage the children to vary the sound effects and work at identifying the most effective ones for poems they enjoy. Groaning, snapping fingers, stomping feet, and rubbing hands together may be appropriate sound effects for some poems. For other poems, students might make crying sounds, or laugh, moo, or cluck. They may even invent sounds.

Repetition

Young children enjoy repeating sounds, words, and phrases they hear. Joining in on the repeated lines in nursery rhymes, ballads, camp songs, spirituals, and traditional play rhymes is a fine way to involve them with poetry. Invite them to join in on the repeated parts during reading or singing such songs and rhymes as "The Muffin Man," "John Brown's Baby Had a Cold Upon His Chest," "The Wheels on the Bus Go Round and Round," or "He's Got the Whole World in His Hands."

Echo

Echoing lines and words are another way of inviting children into poetry. Repeated words or phrases can be

---

FIGURE 5.1   The Poor Old Lady Who Swallowed a Fly.

There was an old lady
who swallowed a fly.
I don't know why she swallowed a fly.
Perhaps she'll die.
There was an old lady who swallowed a spider;
that wriggled and jiggled and tickled inside her.
She swallowed the spider to catch the fly.
I don't know why she swallowed a fly.
Perhaps she'll die.
There was an old lady who swallowed a bird.
How absurd, to swallow a bird!
She swallowed the bird to catch the spider.
She swallowed the spider to catch the fly.
I don't know why she swallowed the fly.
Perhaps she'll die.
There was an old lady who swallowed a cat.
Think of that, she swallowed a cat!
She swallowed the cat to catch the bird.
She swallowed the bird to catch the spider.
She swallowed the spider to catch the fly.
I don't know why she swallowed the fly.
Perhaps she'll die.
There was an old lady who swallowed a dog.
She went the whole hog and swallowed a dog.
She swallowed the dog to catch the cat.
She swallowed the cat to catch the bird.
She swallowed the bird to catch the spider.
She swallowed the spider to catch the fly.
I don't know why she swallowed the fly.
Perhaps she'll die.
There was an old lady who swallowed a cow.
I don't know how she swallowed a cow!
She swallowed the cow to catch the dog.
She swallowed the dog to catch the cat.
She swallowed the cat to catch the bird.
She swallowed the bird to catch the spider.
She swallowed the spider to catch the fly.
I don't know why she swallowed the fly.
Perhaps she'll die.
There was an old lady who swallowed a horse.
She died of course.
Unknown

---

treated like an echo or a series of echoes (Larrick, 1991), as seen in the traditional folk song "Miss Mary Mack". The echo can be developed in a number of ways: one individual can read or recite the poem with another echoing the repeated words; or groups can do the parts instead of individuals. Another variation is to emphasize the beat on the repeated words by clapping with the chant on those words.

Choral reading

Activities such as repetition and echoing prepare children for choral reading of poetry. Many poems lend themselves to choral reading. "The Poor Old Lady Who Swallowed a Fly," shown in Figure 5.1, can be a choral reading involving two or three groups of students. Assign the various stanzas to different groups and have the repeated words chanted in unison by the entire group. You can literally find hundreds of poems for this and similar activities; the examples here are provided to give you an idea of what to look for. If you try a poem and it does not work out, try others until you find some that you and the students enjoy. Material for choral reading should be meaningful, have strong rhythm, have an easily discernible structure, and perhaps rhyme (McCracken & McCracken, 1983). Some good ones are:

- "The Pickety Fence" by David McCord, in *Far and Few, Rhymes of the Never Was and Always Is*.
- "The Umbrella Brigade" by Laura Richards in *Time for Poetry* by Karla Kuskin.
- "Godfrey, Gordon, Gustavus Gore" by William B. Rand in *Time for Poetry* by Karla Kuskin.
- "Yak" by William Jay Smith in *Oh, That's Ridiculous* by Jane Yolen.

Movement

The rhythm of poetry gives it a feeling of movement, making it difficult for children to be still when listening to it. "Poetry is not irregular lines in a book, but something very close to dance and song, something to walk down the street keeping in time to" (Frye, 1964). "Or jog down the trail keeping time to. Or do the dishes by. Or jump rope on the playground with" (Hearne, 1991). Being involved with poetry makes it more appealing. "Doing" creates opportunities for children to respond to, to participate in, and to be involved with the poetry. "Doing" can involve chanting, singing, dancing, tapping, and swinging to the rhythms of poetry (Larrick, 1991). Children appreciate the rhythmic aspect of poetry and rhymes. Tapping, clapping, and swinging arms with poetry sensitizes participants to the rhythms and involves them with poetry. They need opportunities to hop, skip, jump, and march to poetry. They enjoy trying out various assignments such as: "Walk with confi-

dence. Tiptoe stealthily. Walk flatfoot like a clown. Walk like a sad old man. Imagine you are picking up a heavy sack of apples and carry it on your shoulder. . . . Swim like a fish. Fly like a bird" (Larrick, 1991).

Movement is a natural introduction to poetry. Some traditional singing games such as "If You're Happy and You Know It, Clap Your Hands" and "The Wheels on the Bus Go Round and Round" are excellent vehicles for making students more aware of rhythm. Movement is an important element in Lillian Morrison's *Rhythm Road: Poems to Move To*. This fresh, inventive collection of nearly 100 poems is an excellent introduction to the genre and to motion for all ages. Morrison has arranged the poems in sections that include dancing, riding, watching water, and hearing music; other sections include the topics of living things, active entertainments, sports, work, television, technology, and the mind. When using this book in the classroom, read the poems aloud and encourage listeners to move with the sounds.

Lillian Morrison has accommodated the need for movement in much of the poetry she has written. *The Break Dance Kids* is just one of her books that stimulates poetic movement. *A Rocket in my Pocket*, compiled by Carl Withers, is a collection of rhythmic chants, songs, and verses that are part of U.S. folklore. The works in this volume also encourage movement.

Riddle-Poems

Riddle-poems delight young children and their brevity invites readers. The reader uses hints hidden in the verses and in illustrations. Such poems introduce a sense of fun and wordplay. In *Riddle-Lightful: Oodles of Little Riddle-Poems*, J. Patrick Lewis indirectly describes common objects such as a fire truck, a raisin, and a kite. Both children and adults enjoy solving the riddles in Brian Swann's *The House with no Door: African Riddle-Poems* and *Touching the Distance: Native American Riddle-Poems*.

Themes and Topics

One way of organizing poetry experiences and activities is through themes and topics. Topics are subjects that serve to focus and integrate classroom experiences, such as transportation, bridges, baseball, and so forth. Even houses can be topics for poetry as Mary Ann Hoberman demonstrates in her picture book, *A House Is a House for Me.* She explores the concept of houses with interesting ideas such as a glove (a house for a hand) and a hand (a house for money). Diane Siebert's book, *Train Song*, could be part of a transportation unit, along with her book *Truck Song*, or George Ella Lyon's picture book *A Regular Rolling Noah* and Robert Welber's *The Train*.

Themes of love, courage, patriotism, friendship, and so forth appear in poetry. It is often used to introduce themes and topics, and such units may include all types of literature or poetry. Chapter 16 discusses units in greater detail.

Quiet is Peter Parnall's theme in his book of the same name. In this book-length poem, a boy sprinkles apple cores and seeds on his chest while lying in the grass so that he can observe the life around him. A chipmunk, a mouse, a bumblebee, and a chickadee see the treats from different perspectives, shown in the charcoal-and-colored-pencil illustrations. After reading this poem, children may want to lie in the grass themselves, observing what happens and writing their own poems or stories about the experience. They could also examine the meaning of some other word in the same way that Parnall did in *Quiet*. Teachers who would like to expand this theme could use *The Other Way to Listen* by Byrd Baylor. Another book-length poem, *Train Song* by Diane Siebert, contrasts with Parnall's *Quiet*. The rhythm and rhyme of the rolling wheels of a train create the movement, sights, and sounds of a train. Richly colored paintings illustrate this picture book.

Animals, birds, and insects

Animals, birds, and insects are frequent subjects for poets and favorite subjects of children, and no shortage of books exist from which to build a topical unit. William Jay Smith's *Birds and Beasts* is both a poetry collection and an art book. Smith's poems and the graphic images created by Jacques Hnizdovsky's woodcuts combine to create a funny, lighthearted tone. Myra Cohn Livingston's *If the Owl Calls Again: A Collection of Owl Poems* views owls from many perspectives. Many readers will be surprised at the number of great poets from various cultures who have written about owls.

Insects are the topic of Paul Fleischman's Newbery Award book, *Joyful Noise: Poems for Two Voices*. These poems are wonderful fun in the classroom because two or more individuals must read them, and they can be the basis for creating choral readings. In these poems, sounds create the images, movements, and appearance of many insects. Douglas Florian writes about bugs that creep, crawl, and fly in *Insectlopedia*.

Holidays

Poetry is a natural part of holiday celebrations, and holidays are a good time for integrating poetry in classrooms. Almost every holiday or season has more than enough poetry written about it to serve as the basis for a unit of study at the appropriate time of year. Several poets and compilers have created holiday poems and collections, a few examples of which are in the following list.

- *New Year's Poems* by Myra Cohn Livingston
- *Valentine Poems* by Myra Cohn Livingston
- *Easter Poems* by Myra Cohn Livingston
- *Merrily Comes Our Harvest In* by Lee Bennett Hopkins
- *Best Witches: Poems for Halloween* by Jane Yolen
- *Halloween A B C* by Eve Merriam
- *Halloween Poems* by Myra Cohn Livingston
- *Hey-How for Halloween* by Lee Bennett Hopkins
- *Thanksgiving Poems* by Myra Cohn Livingston, ed.
- *Christmas Poems* by Myra Cohn Livingston, ed.
- *An American Christmas* by Diane Goode
- *Sing Hey for Christmas Day* by Lee Bennett Hopkins
- *A Visit from St. Nicholas and Santa Mouse, Too!* by Clement C. Mouse
- *Celebrations* by Myra Cohn Livingston

Discussion

Many people are unsure about discussing or asking questions about poetry. Poetry is art and many of us agree that it should not be overanalyzed, but does that mean it cannot be discussed or examined at all? Discussions of poetry should avoid overanalysis as well as overgeneralization. The best guide for poetry discussion comes from Perrine (1969).

1. Consider the speaker and the occasion. Discuss who wrote the poem, whether the speaker or character is the same person as the poet, and the point of view the poet uses.

2. Consider the central purpose of the poem. Discuss why the poet wrote it and what type of poem it is: a circus poem, a wildlife poem that celebrates nature, and so on.

3. Consider the means by which that purpose is achieved: rhythm, rhyme, imagery, or repeated words, phrases, or lines, and so on.

As children become fluent readers, they can prepare poems to read aloud either as individuals or as groups, implementing some of the suggestions in the activity section that follows. One way of generating student participation in poetry is to write a poem on a chart, then cut it apart and give each student the part they are to read. The parts can be numbered to assist the students.

Playing music as a background when reading poetry dramatizes it. Puppets, pantomime, and creative drama are appropriate activities for many poems because they tell stories. Nursery rhymes such as "Jack and Jill" or "Humpty Dumpty" are appropriate to these activities, as are many other poems. "The Poor Old Lady Who Swallowed a Fly" works well for puppets or drama. Children may experiment and explore with the sounds of poetry through their voices, create their own poetry, examine various themes, and relate poetry to the arts.

Classroom Activities

ACTIVITY 5.1   HUMOR

(IRA/NCTE Standards: 2,3,4,5,6,12. Language comprehension, figurative language, communication, range of literature and language use.)

Read orally or silently selected books and discuss them using the guide question.

Suggested Book List
- *Faint Frogs Feeling Feverish* by Lillian Obligado
- *If I Were in Charge of the World* by Judith Viorst
- *The New Kid on the Block* by Jack Prelutsky
- *Rolling Harvey Down the Hill* by Jack Prelutsky
- *The Complete Nonsense Book* by Edward Lear
- *Where the Sidewalk Ends* by Shel Silverstein
- *You Read to Me, I'll Read to You* by John Ciardi

Guiding Questions
1. What makes you laugh? Think about television shows, books, poems, and real-life events. Some people laugh at exaggeration, wordplay, jokes on other people, or unexpected events.
2. Can you think of other things that make people laugh? Make a list with your classmates.
3. Listen to the poems that your teacher reads. Which ones did you think were the funniest? Which ones were not funny?
4. How did the poet make you laugh? What techniques, elements, forms, and so forth did he or she use?
5. Why did the poet write this poem?
6. What poems made your classmates laugh? Why did they laugh?
7. Vote for the funniest poem or poems of those your teacher reads. Find out why these were the funniest.
8. Make a bulletin board display to tell the school about funny poems and the ways authors make them funny.
9. Find more funny poems and make a class book. Read funny poems to your family and friends to find out what poems make them laugh.

ACTIVITY 5.2 WEATHER

(IRA/NCTE Standards: 2, 3, 4. Language comprehension, figurative language, read a wide range of literature, and adjust language to communicate).

This activity focuses on the weather. After reading the books individually or in small groups, discuss or write using the guiding questions.

Suggested Book List
- *A Circle of Seasons* by Myra Cohn Livingston
- *Go with the Poem* by Lilian Moore
- *I Like Weather* by Aileen Fisher
- *Rain Talk* by Mary Serfozo
- *Rainbows Are Made: Poems by Carl Sandburg* by Lee Bennett Hopkins and Fritz Eichenberg
- *Season Songs* by Ted Hughes
- *Sky Songs* by Myra Cohn Livingston

Guiding Questions
1. What is your favorite kind of weather? Why?
2. What is your least favorite kind of weather? Why?
3. In the poem you have selected for study, what is the poet's favorite weather? How do you know?
4. How does weather in the poem make you feel?
5. Why did the poet write this poem?
6. How did the poet help you experience a particular kind of weather?
7. Compose a poem of your own that is parallel to one of those studied in this unit.

ACTIVITY 5.3 ANIMALS

(IRA/NCTE Standards: 2, 3, 4. Comprehension, read a wide variety of literature, figurative language, and adjust language to communicate.)

The focus of this activity is figurative language. Read the books orally in group and discuss using the guide questions.

Suggested Book List
- *Animals, Animals* by Eric Carle
- *A Gopher in the Garden and Other Animal Poems* by Jack Prelutsky
- *Birds and Beasts* by William Jay Smith
- *Cat Poems* by Myra Cohn Livingston
- *Circus! Circus!* by Lee Bennett Hopkins
- *Dinosaurs* by Lee Bennett Hopkins
- *My Mane Catches the Wind: Poems About Horses* by Lee Bennett Hopkins
- *Turtle in July* by Marilyn Singer
- *Tyrannosaurus Was a Beast* by Jack Prelutsky
- *Welcome to the Ice House* by Jane Yolen

Guiding Questions
1. What kinds of animals are good pets? Why?
2. Do you have a pet? What is it?
3. How does the poet feel about animals? How do you know?
4. What did the poet tell you about animals?
5. How did the poet tell you about animals?
6. Why did the poet write this poem?
7. What did you learn about animals from the poems your teacher read?
8. Which animal poem did you like best? Why?
9. Do you have different ideas about animals after hearing poems about them? How did your ideas change?
10. How are animals in poems similar to those in stories? How are they different?
11. Write a poem about your favorite animal.

ACTIVITY 5.4   POETRY FAIR

(IRA/NCTE Standards: 1, 2, 4, 5, 11. Students read a range of texts and genre for a variety of purposes including personal fulfillment, students communicate with a variety of audiences for different purposes.)

A poetry fair involves students reading aloud poetry they have written or poetry their favorite poets have written. They perform for an invited audience and they may also perform for other classes. Following are an invitation to a poetry fair that includes a poem written by the teacher and a program for the fair.

> When children love a poem,
> A story or a song...
> Their lives are blessed
> With love of words
> That lasts a whole life long.
>
> *M. Richardson*

> Recitations, choral speaking,
> and original poems
> presented by talented
> speakers and writers
>
> Thursday, June 12
> beginning promptly at 11:00
>
> We love applause,
> so friends and relatives
> are welcomed.

ACTIVITY 5.5   POETRY RELATED MEDIA

The internet site **www.poetry.com** will provide a variety of poetry-related sites including the Poetry Society of America.

For Teachers:
Refer to *Book Links, School Library Media Activities Monthly,* and *Tiger Lilies, Toadstools, and Thunderbolts: Engaging K–8 Students with Poetry* by Iris McClellan Tiedt, for additional ideas.

Summary

Poetry is compressed language and thought that implies more than it says. Poetry is literature in verse form. The good news about children's poetry is its plentiful supply. Current poetry addresses contemporary themes and experiences that children can appreciate. Children see poetic language as natural unless they have had negative experiences that turn off their interest in this form. Unfortunately, many adults view poetry with a mixture of awe and insecurity because they believe they must have academic knowledge in order to do justice to it in the home or the classroom. However, teachers, librarians, and parents can read poetry with and to children as an organic part of their daily experiences and celebrations. Oral read-aloud experiences are the best way to introduce poetry to children.

Adults should acquire a wide variety of poetry for students. They need a wide acquaintance with all forms and types of poetry so they can discover children's preferences. A wide-ranging collection of poetry enhances children's opportunities to find their favorites. Children enjoy the rhyme, humor, rhythm, and movement of poetry. Emphasizing meaning, response, and enjoyment is important when incorporating poetry into children's lives.

Thought Questions

1. How is poetry different from prose?
2. What are the major characteristics of poetry?
3. Why does poetry appeal to children?
4. How can you as a teacher build children's response to poetry?
5. Do you think poetry is natural for children? Why or why not?
6. How should poetry be presented in classrooms? Why?
7. Identify three strategies for presenting poetry that you plan to use as a classroom teacher. Why do you like these strategies?

Research and Application Experiences

1. Start a poetry file or collection for use in your classroom. This collection should relate to everyday events, holidays, and the curriculum.
2. Start a thematic collection of poetry. The themes you identify will depend upon the ages of the children with whom you will be working.
3. Compare the treatment of a single subject in poetry, prose, and informational writing.
4. Survey the teachers in an elementary school. Ask them how often they use poetry in their classrooms and what the children's favorite poems are. What conclusions can you reach based on your research?
5. Survey students at one grade level and ask them to identify their favorite poems. Create a graph that shows the titles, poets, and types of poems they enjoy most.
6. Practice reading three poems aloud. Tape yourself, so that you can realize your progress in the oral interpretation of poetry.
7. Examine three or more anthologies of poetry. Which one would you find most useful in the classroom? Why?

Children's Literature References and Recommended Books

Note: Books designated with an asterisk (*) are recommended for reluctant readers.

Alarcón, F. X. (1998). *From the bellybutton of the moon and other summer poems/Del ombligo de la luna y otros poemas de verano*. Chicago: Children's Press. (K–3). POETRY.

The poems in this collection, presented in Spanish and English, focus on summer vacations in Mexico.

Arbuthnot, M. (Ed.). (1951). *Time for poetry*. Chicago: Scott, Foresman. (K–8). POETRY.

This is an anthology of many types of poetry by a wide range of poets.

Bacmeister, R. W. (1940). *Stories to begin on* (T. Maley, Illus.). New York: Dutton. (1–3). POETRY.

This is a collection of poems for young children. "Galoshes" is included in the collection.

Baylor, B. (1978). *The other way to listen* (P. Parnall, Illus.). New York: Scribner's. (2–8). POETRY.

This is a book-length poem that explores ways of knowing. The theme is respect for all.

Bennett, J. (2003). *Grandad's tree: Poems about families* (J. Cairns, Illus.). Kihei, HI: Barefoot. (K–3). POETRY

This collection reflects a range of family experiences.

Brown, C. (1998). *Polkabats and octopus slacks: 14 stories*. Boston: Houghton Mifflin. (PreK–3). POETRY.*

Many adults have purchased this book for themselves. It is an exuberant, unforgettable collection of poems.

dePaola, T. (1988). *Tomie dePaola's book of poems*. New York: Putnam. (K–3). POETRY.

The poems in this collection are by the poet.

Fleischman, P. (1988). *Joyful noise: Poems for two voices* (E. Beddows, Illus.). New York: Harper. (3–6). POETRY.

These are poems about insects to be read by two people.

Florian, D. (1994). *Bing bang boing*. New York: Harcourt. (3–6). POETRY.*

This is a popular collection of humorous short verse. Children like the wordplay they discover in these poems.

Florian, D. (1998). *Insectlopedia*. New York: Harcourt Brace. (K–3). POETRY.*

Bugs that creep, crawl, and fly are the subjects of this poetry book.

Florian, D. (1999). *Laugh-eteria*. New York: Harcourt. (3–6). POETRY.*

This collection of humorous short verse is decorated with line drawings. The poems are about subjects that children know and love.

Florian, D. (2001). *Lizards, frogs, and polliwogs*. New York: Harcourt. (2–5). POETRY.

This is a "toadlly outrageous collection of twenty-one reptile and amphibian poems."

Gollub, M. (1998). *Cool melons—turn to frogs!: The life and poems of Issa* (K. G. Stone and K. Smith, Illus.). New York: Lee & Low. (3–6). POETRY.

This book is an introduction to an eighteenth-century Japanese haiku writer.

Greenfield, E. (1978). *Honey, I love, and other love poems* (D. & L. Dillon, Illus.). New York: Crowell. (1–4). POETRY.

This book of poems shares an African-American child's enthusiasm for love and family life.

Greenfield, E. (1988). *Under the Sunday tree* (A. Ferguson, Illus.). New York: Harper & Row. (1–5). POETRY.

This collection of poems focuses on family and the Caribbean Islands.

Grimes, N. (1999). *A Pocketful of Poems*. (J. Steptoe, Illus.). New York: Putnam. (2–4). POETRY.

Tiana uses her favorite words in free verse and haiku. Her poems are paired with illustrations.

Grimes, N. (2002). *Talkin' about Bessie: The story of aviator Elizabeth Coleman* (E. B. Lewis, Illus.). New York: Orchard. (4–6). POETRY.

A biography told through poetry using the perspectives of friends and family who are mourning Elizabeth Coleman's passing.

Heard, G. (2002). *The place I know: Poems of comfort*. New York: Candlewick Press. (1–6). POETRY.

These poems, selected to comfort children after 9/11, share feelings of fear, sadness, and most importantly, hope.

Hoberman, M. A. (1982). *A house is a house for me* (B. Fraser, Illus.). New York: Penguin. (PreK–2). POETRY.*

Rhyming verses tell about many kinds of houses.

Hoberman, M. A. (2001) *You read to me, I'll read to you: Very short stories to read together*. (K–2). POETRY.

Poems to read aloud in tandem.

Hopkins, L. B. (1989). *Still as a star: A book of nighttime poems* (K. Milone, Illus.). Boston: Little, Brown. (K–3). POETRY.

A collection of bedtime poems.

Hopkins, L. B. (2000). *My America: A poetry atlas of the United States* (S. Alcorn, Illus.). New York: Simon & Schuster. (3–7). POETRY.*

This anthology is arranged around seven geographic regions and Washington, D.C.

Hubbell, P. (1987). When dinosaurs ruled the earth (M. Tinkleman, Illus.). In L. B. Hopkins (Ed.), *Dinosaurs: Poems*. New York: Harcourt Brace Jovanovich. (3–6). POETRY.

A collection of dinosaur poems.

Hubbell, P. (1991). Bedtime and Miss Mary Mack. In N. Larrick (Ed.), *Let's do a poem!* New York: Delacorte. (K–3). POETRY.

A bedtime poem in a collection of poems to fit most occasions.

Hughes, L. (1932). Dreams. In *The dream keeper and other poems*. New York: Knopf. (3–7). POETRY.

This wonderful poem is ageless.

Isaacs, A. (1998). *Cat up a tree: A story in poems*. New York: Dutton. (K–3). POETRY.*

This book is a series of narrative poems that expresses how all of the participants feel about catching the cat.

Janeczko, P. B. (1988). *The music of what happens: Poems that tell stories*. New York: Orchard. (4–8). POETRY.

The poems in this book tell true stories about the lives of unknown people. Their lives create the music of what happens.

Janeczko, P. B. (1989). *Brickyard summer*. New York: Orchard. (5–7). POETRY.

The poems in this volume have a flavor of summer.

Janeczko, P. B. (1990). *The place my words are looking for: What poets say about and through their work*. New York: Bradbury. (4–8). POETRY.

An anthology of contemporary poets with comments by the poets.

Janeczko, P. B. (1998). *That sweet diamond: Baseball poems* (C. Katchen, Illus.). New York: Atheneum. (3–7). POETRY.

The poet has captured the tension of baseball players and the fans—everyone who is in the stadium for a big game.

Kennedy, X. J. (1982). *Did Adam name the vinegarroon?* (H. J. Selig, Illus.). Boston: David Godine. (1–3). POETRY.

This book includes poems about unusual animals.

Kennedy, X. J., & Kennedy, D. M. (Eds.). (1982). *Knock at a star: A child's introduction to poetry* (K. A. Weinhaus, Illus.). Boston: Little, Brown. (K–2). POETRY.

A collection of bedtime poems.

Knudson, R. R., & Swenson, M. (Eds.). (1988). *American sports poems*. New York: Orchard (4–6). POETRY.

Athletes and sports fans will enjoy these poems.

Kuskin, K. (1975). Near the window tree. New York: Harper. (4–6). POETRY.

Kuskin addresses childhood concerns and explains why she wrote each poem.

Kuskin, K. (1980). *Dogs & dragons, trees & dreams: A collection of poems*. New York: HarperCollins. (1–3). POETRY.*

Kuskin's introductions to the poems are an added asset in this book.

Lear, E. (1948). *The complete nonsense book*. New York: Dodd, Mead. (K–6). POETRY.

This book contains classic nonsense poetry.

Levy, C. (1998). *A crack in the clouds and other poems* (R. B. Corfield, Illus.). New York: McElderry. (4–6). POETRY.*

The poet uses simple language and varied cadences to tell about everyday things.

Lewis, J. P. (1998a). *Boshblobberbosh: Runcible poems for Edward Lear* (G. Kelley, Illus.). New York: Creative Editions. (4–6). POETRY.

The poet is a student of Lear's work, and he demonstrates his skill in creating nonsense in this book.

Lewis, J. P. (1998b). *Doodle dandies: Poems that take shape* (L. Desimini, Illus.). New York: Atheneum. (K–5). POETRY.

A collection of concrete poems.

Lewis, J. P. (1998c). *Riddle-lightful: Oodles of little riddle poems*. New York: Knopf. (3–5). POETRY.

This is a collection of 32 riddles using familiar objects and scenes.

Livingston, M. C. (1982). *A circle of seasons* (L. E. Fisher, Illus.). New York: Holiday House. (2–5). POETRY.

A collection of seasonal poetry.

Livingston, M. C. (1986). Poems for Jewish holidays (L. Bloom, Illus.). New York: Holiday House. (PreK–3). POETRY.

A collection of poems celebrating Jewish holidays.

Livingston, M. C. (1990). *If the owl calls again: A collection of owl poems* (A. Frasconi, Illus.). New York: McElderry. (3–6). POETRY.

All kinds of owl poems.

Livingston, M. C. (1991). *Poem-making: Ways to begin writing poetry*. New York: Harper. (5–8). POETRY.

This is a guide to creating poetry and includes excellent examples.

Lyon, G. E. (1986). *A regular rolling Noah* (S. Gammell, Illus.). New York: Bradbury. (1–3). POETRY, PICTURE BOOK.

The story of moving farm animals in a train, which compares the boxcar to Noah's ark.

McCord, D. (1952). *Far and few, rhymes of the never was and always is* (H. B. Kane, Illus.). New York: Little, Brown. (K–4). POETRY.

This collection includes many of McCord's best rhythmic poems, including "Song of the Train."

Medina, J. (1999). *My name is Jorge on both sides of the river: Poems* (F. V. Broeck, Illus.). Pennsylvania: Boyds Mills. (All ages). POETRY.

This narrative poem tells the story of a Mexican boy who is teased because of his language and is humiliated at the public library.

Merriam, E. (1986). *Fresh paint: New poems*. New York: Macmillan. (1–4). POETRY.

This collection has 45 poems whose subjects range from squat mushrooms to the new moon.

Mora, P. (2001). *Love to Mama* (P. Barragan, Illus.). New York: Lee & Low. (5 and older). POETRY.

This collection features Latino poets and celebrates family.

Morrison, L. (1981). *Overheard in a bubble chamber and other science poems* (E. de Lanux, Illus.). New York: Lothrop, Lee, & Shepard. (3–6). POETRY.

This collection of poems has a science theme.

Morrison, L. (1985). *The break dance kids*. New York: Lothrop. (3–6). POETRY.*

Morrison's poems have strong rhythms that invite people to move.

Morrison, L. (Selector). (1988). *Rhythm road: Poems to move to*. New York: Lothrop. (K–2). POETRY.*

Poems to move to. The topics include dancing, riding, watching water, hearing music, sports, work, and so on.

Nelson, M. (2001). *Carver: A life in poems*. Asheville, NC: Front Street. (5–9). POETRY.

This stunning collection of poems presents a biography of George Washington Carver.

Parnall, P. (1989). *Quiet*. New York: Morrow Junior Books. (3–6). POETRY.

This book-length poem explores the meaning of quiet.

Perkins, L. (2003). *Snow Music*. New York: Greenwillow. Poetry (K–3). POETRY.

Musical language and the soft focus illustrations give children a sense of snow.

Prelutsky, J. (Comp.). (1983). *The Random House book of poetry for children* (A. Lobel, Illus.). New York: Random House. (K–6). POETRY.

A large collection of thematically arranged poetry.

Prelutsky, J. (1988). *Tyrannosaurus was a beast: Dinosaur poems* (A. Lobel, Illus.). New York: Greenwillow. (K–4). POETRY.

Humorous poems about dinosaurs.

Prelutsky, J. (1990). *Something big has been here* (J. Stevenson, Illus.). New York: Greenwillow. (K–4). POETRY.*

This collection ranges from the boy who planted light bulbs in his hair to the more serious "Don't Yell at Me!"

Prelutsky, J. (2002). *The frogs wore red suspenders* (P. Mathers, Illus.). (1–4). POETRY.

Exuberant poems about people and animals living in far-flung places.

Richards, L. (1983). Eletelephony. In J. Prelutsky (Ed.) (A. Lobel Illus.), *The Random House book of poetry for children*. New York: Random House. (K–6). POETRY.

A funny, nonsense poem.

Rylant, C. (1984). *Waiting to waltz: A childhood* (S. Gammel, Illus.). New York: Bradbury. (3–6). POETRY.

These poems are autobiographical.

Schertle, A. (1995). *Advice for a frog and other poems* (N. Green, Illus.). New York: Lothrop. (K–4). POETRY.

This collection of poems pays tribute to some of nature's most remarkable animals.

Schertle, A. (1999). *I am the cat* (M. Buehner, Illus.). New York: Lothrop. (K–3). POETRY.

Humorous poetry, in narrative and haiku.

Shaik, F. (1997). *The jazz of our street* (E. B. Lewis, Illus.). New York: Dial. (1–5). POETRY.

This poetic story is set in New Orleans where jazz parades are common. The rhythmic language creates the feel of jazz music.

Siebert, D. (1984). *Truck song* (B. Barton, Illus.). New York: Crowell. (1–5). PICTURE BOOK, POETRY.

The rhythm of wheels on the road is expressed in this poem.

Siebert, D. (1990). *Train song* (M. Wimmer, Illus.). New York: Crowell. (1–5). PICTURE BOOK, POETRY.

A book-length poem written with the rhythm of train wheels. Movement, sights, and sounds of trains are expressed through rhyme and rhythm.

Siebert, D. (2002). *Motorcycle song* (L. Jenkins, Illus.). New York: HarperCollins. (3–5). POETRY.

Sibert uses rhythm and rhyme to create the rhythms of riding a motorcycle, a feeling that children enjoy.

Silverstein, S. (1974). *Where the sidewalk ends: The poems & drawings of Shel Silverstein*. New York: Harper. (5–12). POETRY.*

Humorous poetry exploring the joys and fears of childhood.

Smith, C. R. (2002). *Perfect harmony: A musical journey with the Boys Choir of Harlem*. New York: Hyperion. (1–6). POETRY.

These poems celebrate music-making, as well as the spirit and energy of music makers. The book is illustrated with photographs of the Boys Choir.

Smith, W. J. (1990). *Birds and beasts* (J. Hnizdovsky, Illus.). Boston: Godine. (3–6). POETRY.

Creative verses illustrated with woodcuts that enhance the humor.

Swann, B. (1998a). *The house with no door: African riddle-poems* (A. Bryan, Illus.). New York: Browndeer Press/Harcourt Brace. (1–4). POETRY.*

A collection of riddles from Africa.

Swann, B. (1998b). *Touching the distance: Native American riddle-poems*. New York: Browndeer Press/Harcourt Brace. (1–4). POETRY.*

A book of riddle-poems from Native-American cultures.

Van Laan, N. (2000). *When winter comes* (S. Gaber, Illus.). New York: Atheneum. (1–3) POETRY.

Sensory poetry about family winter experiences.

Welber, R. (1972). *The train* (D. Ray, Illus.). New York: Pantheon. (K–2). POETRY.

This book explores everyday things that frighten children such as trains and unexplained noises.

Willard, N. (1981). *A visit to William Blake's Inn: Poems for innocent and experienced travelers* (A. & M. Provensen, Illus.). San Diego: Harcourt Brace Jovanovich. (2–4). POETRY.

Poetry that reflects the innocence of children in earlier times.

Withers, C. (Comp.). (1988). *A rocket in my pocket: The rhymes and chants of young Americans* (S. Suba, Illus.). New York: Henry Holt. (K–4). POETRY.

A collection of rhythmic chants, songs, and verses.

Woodson, J. (2003). *Locomotion*. New York: Patnam. (4–8). POETRY.

This poetic narrative tells about Lonnie Collins Motion's poetry.

Worth, V. (1972). *Small poems* (N. Babbitt, Illus.). New York: Farrar, Straus & Giroux. (PreK–3). POETRY.

Small poems for young children, including "Frog."

Worth, V. (1978). *Small poems again* (N. Babbitt, Illus.). New York: Farrar, Straus & Giroux. (PreK–3). POETRY.

This is another volume of small poems.

Yolen, J. (1990). *Dinosaur dances* (B. Degen, Illus.). New York: Putnam. (1–4). POETRY.

This work includes poems about all kinds of dinosaurs who dance everything from ballet to chorus line.

Zolotow, C. (1980). *Say it!* (J. Stevenson, Illus.). New York: Greenwillow. (PreK–3). POETRY.

Mother and child play a language game as they walk through the autumn air.

References and Books for Further Reading

Bagert, B. (1992). *Act It Out: Making Poetry Alive.* In B. Cullinan (Ed.), *Invitation to read: More children's literature in the reading program*. Newark, DE: International Reading Association.

Behr, C. C. (1995). Jack Prelutsky. In A. Silvey (Ed.), *Children's books and their creators*. Boston: Houghton Mifflin.

Bridge, E. (1966). *Using children's choices and reactions to poetry as determinants in enriching literary experience in the middle grades* (University microfilm no. 67–6246). Philadelphia: Temple University.

Crisp, S. (1991). Children's poetry in the United States: The best of the 1980s. *Children's Literature in Education, 22,* 143–160.

Cullinan, B., Scala, M., & Schroder, V. (1995). *Three voices: An invitation to poetry across the curriculum*. York, ME: Stenhouse Publishers.

Fisher, C., & Natarella, M. (1982). Young children's preferences in poetry: A national survey of first, second, and third graders. *Research in the Teaching of English, 16,* 339–354.

Fleischman, P. (1986). Sound and sense. *The Horn Book, 62,* 551–555.

Frye, N. (1964). *The educated imaginations*. Bloomington: Indiana University Press.

Hearne, B. (1991). *Choosing books for children: A commonsense approach*. New York: Delacorte.

Hopkins, L. B. (1998). *Pass the poetry, please!* New York: Harper.

Ingham, R. (1980). *The poetry preferences of fourth- and fifth-grade students in a suburban setting in 1980*. Unpublished doctoral dissertation, University of Houston, Texas.

Larrick, N. (1991). *Let's do a poem!* New York: Delacorte.

Lenz, L. (1992). Crossroads of literacy and orality: Reading poetry aloud. *Language Arts, 69*, 597–603.

Livingston, M. C. (Ed.). (1968). Editor's note. In *A tune beyond us*. New York: Harcourt.

Livingston, M. C. (1981). Nonsense verse: The complete escape. In B. Hearne & M. Kaye (Eds.), *Celebrating children's books* (pp. 122–142). New York: Lothrop, Lee, & Shepard.

Livingston, M. C. (1991). *Poem-making: Ways to begin writing poetry*. New York: HarperCollins.

Livingston, M. C. (1997). *I am writing a poem about— A game of poetry*. New York: McElderry (3–6). POETRY.

McClure, A. A. (2002). Poetry. In A. McClure & J. Kristo (Eds.), *Adventuring with books: A booklist for PreK–Grade 6*. A. McClure and J. Kristo, Editors. Urbana, IL: National Council of Teachers of English.

McCracken, R., & McCracken, M. (1983). Chants, charts and 'chievement. In J. Cowen (Ed.), *Teaching through the arts* (pp. 44–50). Newark, DE: International Reading Association.

Morner, K., & Rausch, R. (1991). *NTC's dictionary of literary terms*. Lincolnwood, IL: National Textbook Company.

Parsons, L. (1992). *Poetry themes and activities*. Portsmouth, NH: Heinemann.

Peck, P. (1979). Poetry: A turn-on to reading. In J. Shapiro (Ed.), *Using literature and poetry affectively* (pp. 92–105). Newark, DE: International Reading Association.

Perrine, L. (1969). *Sound and sense: An introduction to poetry*. (3rd ed.). New York: Harcourt.

Russell, D. L. (1991). *Literature for children: A short introduction*. New York: Longman.

Sebesta, S. (1983). Choosing poetry. In N. Roser & M. Frith (Eds.), *Children's choices: Teaching with books children like* (pp. 56–70). Newark, DE: International Reading Association.

Silvey, A. (1995). *Children's books and their creators*. Boston: Houghton Mifflin.

Simmons, M. (1980). *Intermediate-grade children's preferences in poetry*. Unpublished doctoral dissertation, University of Alabama, Birmingham.

Terry, A. (1974). *Children's poetry preferences: A national survey of upper elementary grades*. Urbana, IL: National Council of Teachers of English.

Tiedt, I. M. (2002). *Tiger lilies, toadstools, and thunderbolts: Engaging K–8 students with poetry*. Newark, DE: International Reading Association.

Traditional Literature: Stories Old and New

6

KEY TERMS

ballad   legend
fable   myth
folk tale   pourquoi tales

GUIDING QUESTIONS

Consider the folk tales you heard as a child. What were your favorites: Goldilocks, Tom Thumb, Jack and the Beanstalk, or Cinderella? Do you think children continue to enjoy these stories? The following questions will guide your reading.

1. Why is traditional literature so popular?

2. Why does traditional literature have an oral history?

3. How are characters in traditional literature different from characters in realistic fiction?

Stories are a universal tradition, as all societies have literature in their culture. There is an African proverb that says, "When an old person dies, it is like an entire library has gone up in flames" (Steiner, 2001). These ageless stories are folk tales, traditional literature, and folklore. In times gone by, storytellers told stories to people gathered around campfires and to people who were working on everyday tasks. My grandmother told us stories while we shelled peas; this is how I learned about my Pennsylvania Dutch heritage. These tales reflect a people's concept of themselves—"their beliefs, hopes and fears, courage and humor, sense of delight in the odd, and fascination with the supernatural" (Miller, 1995, p. 22). The following vignette illustrates the value of these time-honored tales in classrooms today.

Traditional Literature

Traditional literature reflects the long folk memory stretching from ancient times to the present (Hunter, 1975). Traditional tales survived for centuries in the memories of storytellers who shared their personal versions of the same stories with different audiences, perpetuating them in much the same way a pebble sends ripples out in a pool. The Cinderella story alone has nearly 1,000 variants (Thompson, 1951). Traditional stories were committed to print after the brothers Grimm and Charles Perrault listened to storytellers and collected the tales. Children continue to delight in folk tales that are continually recreated by new voices (Hearne, 1999). Teachers and librarians today have an abundance of folk tales available in books, collections, the Internet, videos, and recordings (Steiner, 2001).

Primitive humans shared, celebrated, and remembered experiences through story, art, and dance. Storytellers entertained and instructed others with timeless tales of greed, jealousy, love, and the need for security as they relaxed around nightly campfires. Storytellers, bards, minstrels, poets, and rhymers of old were venerated; they were welcomed into palaces and huts alike and accorded places of honor. Storytelling has enjoyed a revival over recent decades with storytelling festivals popping up all over the globe (Jaffe, 1999). There is even a center for the "Preservation and Perpetuation of Storytelling" in Jonesboro, Tennessee.

Folk literature represents the accumulated wisdom and art of humankind springing from the many world cultures. *Folk tales* originate in humanity itself through stories of the "folk" that mirror the mores and values of the culture of origin. The oral origins of traditional folk tales make them different from other genres. The Native Americans called many of their tales "teaching stories." Children learned from cautionary tales how to behave. For example, *How the Fisherman*

Domitila is a Mexican Cinderella.

Jim Summers took advantage of his fourth graders' physical education class to check out the *Children's Literature Web Guide.* He found seven pages of material related to Cinderella stories, including different versions of the story, references, other Internet resources, and teaching ideas. This made his planning much easier. After the students returned, he directed them to their reading workshop groups, which the children eagerly joined. Mr. Summers said, "Last week, you read *Stone Soup* and *Nail Soup,* and quite a few of you asked to read more folk tales like these. I couldn't locate additional versions of *Stone Soup,* so I collected 'Cinderella' stories, since there are over 1,000 versions of that tale. You'll find several of these stories at each workstation. Scan the books and decide on one for your group to read and study." The workshop groups chose from the following books:

The Girl Who Wanted to Hunt by Emery Bernhard and Durga Bernhard

The Korean Cinderella by Shirley Climo

Fair, Brown & Trembling: An Irish Cinderella Story by J. Daly

"Cinderella" in *Little Book of Latin American Folktales* by Carmen Dearden

Tattercoats by Joseph Jacobs

The Way Meat Loves Salt by Nina Jaffe

Yeh-Shen: A Cinderella Story from China by Ai-Ling Louie

The Rough-Face Girl by Rafe Martin

(continued)

Cinderella: A Fairy Tale by Charles Perrault

The Turkey Girl: A Zuni Cinderella Story by Penny Pollock

Cendrillon: A Caribbean Cinderella by Robert San Souci

Smoky Mountain Rose: An Appalachian Cinderella by Alice Schroder

If the Shoe Fits by Laura Whipple

After reading and discussion, each group settled on a book to read.

"Why are these books called 'Cinderella' books?" Matt queried.

"They don't even have 'Cinderella' in the title. This one is called *The Rough-Face Girl*."

Mr. Summers answered, "That is a Native-American Cinderella. Each of these books is from a different country or culture."

"Oh! This one is from Siberia. Where is Siberia?" Shannon asked.

"And this one is from China," Melissa said.

"How do you think we should study these Cinderella stories?" Mr. Summers asked.

Cory suggested, "We need to figure out what countries our stories are from first."

"Good idea," Mr. Summers replied. "What other questions should we ask?"

Each group discussed the questions they should ask and compiled this list:

What country or culture did this story come from?

What is the main character's (i.e., Cinderella) name?

What kind of magic occurs?

Does every story have a prince?

How are the stories different?

How are the stories alike?

Can you think of any modern day Cinderellas?

How does the country of orgin make this Cinderella different?

How does each story begin and end?

Tricked the Genie: A Tale Within a Tale Within a Tale by Kitoba Sunami teaches that evil deeds beget more evil.

Folk tales feature impressive feats, such as escaping from powerful enemies, outwitting wicked people, earning a living, securing food, and protecting the weak. For example, *Little Plum,* a modern picture-book version of the Tom Thumb story by Ed Young, teaches that size has very little to do with success and ability. As you read folk tales, you will discover the far-reaching effects of tradition in current stories that have similar themes and plot structures. For example, the "Jack and the Beanstalk" story is a hero tale wherein a young boy overcomes a larger, stronger character to prove himself. Even though story characters' feats are imaginary, we enjoy believing they could happen. Traditional stories entertain as well as disseminate cultural beliefs to future generations.

The tales we enjoy today have been polished and edited as storytellers have shared stories from their own cultures using their own idioms, perspectives, and

Jack uses his golden lasso and the help of a buffalo to escape the beanstalk giant.

values. Every time a storyteller tells a tale, the story changes, giving rise to thousands of variations of a single tale that grows or shrinks over time as portions are expanded or omitted by different tellers. A folk tale is a living thing that outlives its creator; the names of the people who first told these tales are lost in the mist of time. Today's written versions are derived from those ancient stories; for this reason, folk tale creators are called retellers, collectors, and illustrators.

Retellers and illustrators continue to create many appealing books in this genre. Some of these are picture-book versions of single tales, while others are collections of folk tales. For example, *Ouch!*, Natalie Babbitt's retelling of a Grimm tale, is a single tale. In this story, Marco becomes king by using his wits. Jeanne Steig's *A Handful of Beans: Six Fairy Tales* is a collection of fairy tale retellings. Michael Hague's *Kate Culhane: A Ghost Story* satisfies intermediate graders' appetite for ghost stories. Primary-grade children will enjoy hearing the stories in Judy Sierra's *Can You Guess My Name? Traditional Tales Around the World*. This book includes three versions of each well-known tale.

Folk tales have been sources of controversy throughout history. They were controversial early in the nineteenth century because they did not provide direct, specific moral instruction (Saxby & Winch, 1987). More recently, parents and teachers have expressed concerns about the violence in folk tales; some versions of traditional stories have been rewritten to "launder" or "sanitize" them (Rothman, 1990). In some instances, the vocabulary of traditional tales is changed; in others, the plot is altered. For example, the wolf in a "Little Red Riding Hood" puppet show was sent to the zoo. Trickster tales are popular in many cultures, although they are objectionable to some adults. The sly trickster characters who use questionable tactics create examples that adults would prefer to avoid. "Brer Rabbit" stories and the wily coyote character in Native-American tales are trickster characters. Brer Rabbit represents the spirit of disorder in life (Hearne, 1999). Fortunately, strong traditional tales seem to be resilient and indestructible; they have withstood all assaults. Their popularity is ensured by their simplicity, directness, and fun.

The Contemporary Values of Traditional Literature

Traditional stories entertain modern children just as they once delighted children and adults around the campfires of long ago. Children of all ages enjoy folk tales as read-alones or read-alouds, and they love storytellers. The direct simplicity of these stories appeals to children. Over the years, many of the Caldecott Medal books have belonged to this genre, including Marcia Brown's *Cinderella* and Paul Zelinsky's *Rapunzel*. Enjoyment is a most valuable benefit of literature.

Readers learn about themselves through traditional stories, because characters can do things not permitted in real life (Dundes, 1965). Storytellers can comfort children or frighten them, depending upon the teller's purpose. They can express anger and frustration without fear of reprisal. When folk tale heroes celebrate overcoming monsters, giants, dragons, and other disreputable forces, they give us heroes, wise men, wizards, and magicians. Nothing in the entire range of children's literature—with rare exceptions—can be as enriching and satisfying to child and adult alike as the folk fairy tale. A child can learn more about people's inner problems and about solutions to his or her own (and our) predicaments in any society than can be found from any other type of story within his or her comprehension (Bettelheim, 1975, p. 76).

The language of traditional literature is an important part of childrens' literary heritage. Musical, rhythmic language, melodic refrains, and the characters' direct dialogue punctuated with quick action excite readers' and listeners' interest. Through listening to and reading these tales, children acquire language. Moreover, traditional stories provide them with writing models.

The form and content of folk tales, although grounded in vastly different cultures, are often remarkably similar, because people throughout the world share common human concerns. The details and modifications that appear in folk tale variations reflect the society or culture that produced them. For this reason, traditional stories give anthropologists a window into other cultures. Traditional literature is a rich source of content for multicultural studies and global education that will develop children's cultural consciousness (Schwartz, 1977). Renata Bini's *World Treasury of Myths, Legends, and Folktales: Stories from Six Countries* is a rich source of multicultural literature for all ages.

Leigh Casler's Native-American tale, *The Boy Who Dreamed of an Acorn*, tells us that children are searching for their place in the world and that all children have dreams. *The Lion's Whiskers: An Ethiopian Folktale* by Nancy Raines Day develops both cultural and personal understanding. Margaret MacDonald's *Fat Cat: A Danish Folktale* will delight primary children.

They like the Fat Cat's overeating character and his continuously cooking mouse friend. Children will enjoy dramatizing this hilarious story.

The African folk tale, *Why Mosquitoes Buzz in People's Ears* by Verna Aardema, is extremely popular, perhaps because we have all swatted mosquitoes. Richard Chase collected his *Jack Tales* from storytellers in the Appalachian Mountains, but they are variants of British tales. Ludmila Zeman adapted the thousand and one nights in *Sinbad's Secret,* which provides another cultural contrast to explore.

Elements of Traditional Literature

Traditional stories have the elements of character, plot, setting, theme, and style; however, they develop in different ways than other forms of fiction.

Character

Only a few characters are needed to tell folk tales. The good characters are totally good and the bad ones are altogether bad. These flat, stereotyped characters are clearly recognizable as symbols of good or evil, kindness or meanness. Each character is a stereotype representing a part of humanity such as courage, trickery, evil, or foolishness. The characters are introduced briefly, like Chanticleer in Helen Ward's *The Rooster and the Fox,* who is called "herald of the morning, pride of the farmyard" (p. 1). Good characters are rewarded and bad characters are punished, such as when the wolf villain in "Red Riding Hood" is killed to rescue the grandma he ate. These moralistic stories appeal to most of us, who tend to see people as completely good or completely bad. We all love to cheer when the "bad guys" get what they deserve and when dreams come true for good characters. Small, weak, hardworking characters are honored with riches, magical powers, palaces, and delicious banquets. Traditional literature teaches lessons such as the importance of the inner qualities of love and kindness. Seemingly weak characters have virtues that enable them to achieve success in the face of violence and cruelty. This theme appears in Bryce Milligan's *The Prince of Ireland and the Three Magic Stallions*. In this story, a stepmother seeks to remove her stepson, who is in line for her husband's throne.

When folk tale characters experience conflicts, they spring into action to solve the problem or end the conflict. Peasants, kings, princes, woodcutters, and fools dramatize a part of life such as seeking a fortune, finding a lost sibling or parent, or escaping danger. Magic often appears in folk tales, but it must be logical within the story framework. Listeners expect good characters to reign supreme while bad characters go down in infamy, so the good ones can live happily ever after.

Plot and Setting in Folk Tales

The minimal development and description in folk tale plots and settings lack subtle nuances. Plot and setting are sketched quickly and the stereotyped characters are dropped into place. Time is developed with stock phrases such as "once upon a time" and "long ago and far away." This brevity sets a stage for the story that would be difficult to improve upon. The setting may be a castle, a peasant's hut, or a forest, but again brevity is the key word. The setting is often symbolic; for example, a forest can be a symbol of confusion and losing one's way. The most important aspect of place in traditional literature is creating a backdrop for characters' actions.

Storytellers include just enough events to make the story interesting. Stories become boring when too many attempts are made to solve problems or conflicts; therefore, storytellers quickly introduce the conflict. Typically, there are three attempts to climb the glass mountain, three riddles to answer, three brothers who seek their fortune, or a beautiful maiden who has three wishes. Three is the magic number in the European tradition, while Asian folk tales have a magic number of four. Three or four attempts or incidents seem to be just the right number to make most stories interesting without dragging them out too long. Figure 6.1 illustrates the components of traditional tales and models a comparison of these tales that you may use in the classroom.

Typical story structures for traditional tales are sequential (beginning, middle, end), circular (ends up about where it began), and cumulative (additions and repetitions build the story). Figure 6.2, *Goldilocks and the Three Bears,* illustrates the sequential building of events to a quick resolution, and Figure 6.3 shows the circular structure of *The Little Red Hen.*

Theme

Traditional stories have significant themes illustrating cultural values and mores. Characters exhibit traits of humility, courage, honesty, patience, and demonstrate

Title	Characters	Setting	Villain	Hero/Heroine	Conclusion
FIGURE 6.1 Chart comparing *Molly Whuppie* to other traditional tales.					
Molly Whuppie	Three girls	Woods/giant's castle/king's castle	Giant	Molly	Molly saves herself and her sisters
Jack and the Beanstalk	Jack, his mother, the giant's wife, the giant	Giant's house	Giant	Jack	Jack saves himself and gets the means to support his mother
Hansel and Gretel	Hansel and Gretel, stepmother, father, and witch	Woods, witch's hut	Wicked stepmother and witch	Hansel and Gretel	Hansel and Gretel escape and get to eat all the food they want

that dreams come true for good characters. *The Fire: An Ethiopian Folk Tale* by Heinz Janisch is the story of a slave longing to be free that tells how he bravely achieves his freedom. This beautifully told tale is a spellbinding read-aloud.

Style

One of the hallmarks of folk tale styles is the formulaic beginnings used to establish setting and characters, as well as invite listeners: "long ago and far away" or "once there was and was not." Folk tales also have formulaic endings such as "they lived happily ever after" or the ending of *Three Billy Goats Gruff*, "snip, snap, snout; this tale's told out." The language style is succinct and direct. These stories are compact; they retain a sense of their oral language beginnings although they may be read. Some folk tales include stylistic devices such as rhymes, verses, or repetition. *The Marvelous Mouse Man* by Mary Ann Hoberman is a retelling of the Hamelin story told in rhyming text.

Types of Traditional Literature

According to Dundes (1965), folklore includes many forms such as myths, legends, folk tales, jokes, proverbs, riddles, chants, charms, blessings, curses, oaths, insults, retorts, taunts, teases, toasts, tongue-twisters, greetings, and leave-taking formulas. Many of these types of folklore are found in Gerald Milnes' *Granny, Will Your Dog Bite, and Other Mountain Rhymes*. To experience the folklore in this volume, Milnes, the reteller, collected the rhymes, songs, riddles, and so forth in West Virginia from a man who greeted him with, "Just throw your hat on the bed, spit on the

This story is a retelling of the Pied Piper of Hamelin.

fire, sit down on your fist, lean back against your thumb, and make yourself at home."

Folk poetry ranges from oral epics to autograph-book verse, epitaphs, latrinalia (i.e., writings on the walls of public bathrooms), limericks, ball-bouncing rhymes, jump-rope jingles, finger and toe rhymes, dandling rhymes (to bounce children on the knee), counting-out rhymes (to determine who will be "it" in games), and nursery rhymes.

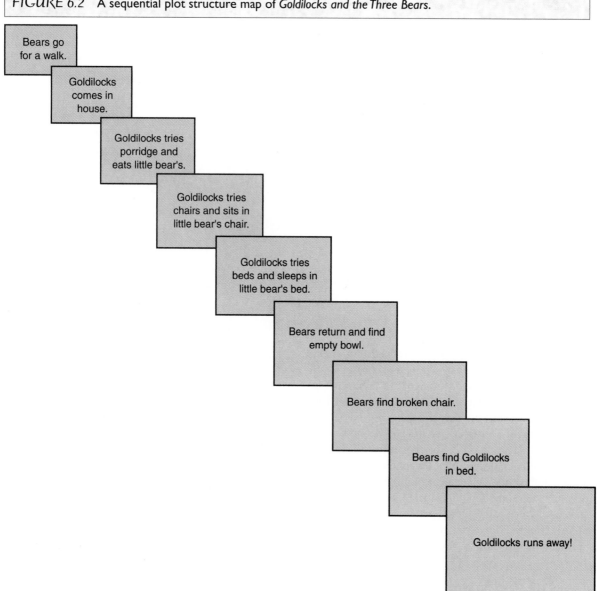

FIGURE 6.2   A sequential plot structure map of *Goldilocks and the Three Bears.*

Bears go for a walk.

Goldilocks comes in house.

Goldilocks tries porridge and eats little bear's.

Goldilocks tries chairs and sits in little bear's chair.

Goldilocks tries beds and sleeps in little bear's bed.

Bears return and find empty bowl.

Bears find broken chair.

Bears find Goldilocks in bed.

Goldilocks runs away!

Traditional literature is classified in various ways, and authorities differ in the terminology they use. However, folk tales (also called wonder tales and household tales) consist of all kinds of narrative originating in the oral tradition (Thompson, 1951). In this sense, the category of folk tales encompasses all traditional literature. Fairy tales, animal tales, myths, legends, tall tales, and ballads are all folk tales. The forms of folk tales, discussed in this section and summarized in Table 6.1, represent the majority of traditional literature in print for children today.

"New Folk Tales"

Authors who create alternate versions of classic folk tales are creating "new folk tales"; in fact, some people call these "fractured fairy tales." These stories are not true folk tales, but they are fun. Both children and

FIGURE 6.3   A circular plot structure map of *The Little Red Hen.*

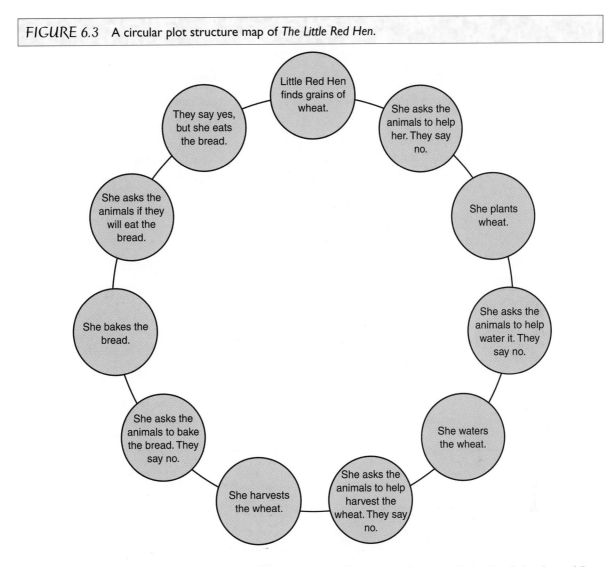

adults find these stories stimulating, and they are particularly good for stimulating writing experiences. The following are a few examples of these excellent stories.

Jim and the Beanstalk by Raymond Briggs

Porkenstein by Kathryn Lasky, illustrated by David Jarvis

The Frog Prince, Continued by Jon Scieszka, illustrated by Steve Johnson

The True Story of the 3 Little Pigs by Jon Scieszka, illustrated by Lane Smith

The Stinky Cheese Man and Other Fairly Stupid Tales by Jon Scieszka, illustrated by Lane Smith

Squids Will Be Squids by Jon Scieszka and Lane Smith

The Three Pigs by David Wiesner

Fairy Tales

Fairy tales are unbelievable stories featuring magic and the supernatural. Fairies, giants, witches, dwarfs, good people, and bad people in fairy tales live in supernatural worlds with enchanted toadstools and crystal lakes. Heroes and heroines in these stories have supernatural assistance in solving problems. "Snow White and the Seven Dwarfs" is a typical fairy tale.

TABLE 6.1

Common types of traditional literature.

Type	Characteristics	Example
Folk tales	giants, witches, magic, tasks, ogres	*Jack and the Beanstalk* *Goldilocks and the Three Bears*
Cumulative folk tales	repeat actions, refrains in sequence	*Henny Penny, Johnny Cake*
Fairy tales	magic and wonder	*Cinderella, Beauty and the Beast*
Animal tales	animals who outwit enemies	*Little Red Hen, Three Billy Goats Gruff*
Fables	animal stories that teach a lesson	*The Hare and the Tortoise*
Trickster tales	tales in which characters are able to dupe other characters (especially rabbits and coyotes)	*Brer Rabbit*
Noodlehead tales (humorous folk tales)	silly humans, stupid characters	*The Princess and the Pea, Simple Simon*
Myths	explain the origin of the world and natural phenomena	Greek myths
Pourquoi tales	explain why certain things are the way they are	*How the Snake Got Its Rattles* *How the Rabbit Got a Short Tail*
Legends	often based on historical figures with embellished deeds	*Robin Hood, King Arthur*
Tall tales	larger-than-life characters	*Daniel Boone, Paul Bunyan*
Ballads	rhyme and rhythm set to music	*Granny, Will Your Dog Bite, and Other Mountain Rhymes*

This version of the Three Pigs is quite different from the well-known tale.

Animal Tales

Folk tales often feature animals with human characteristics as the main characters. "The Little Red Hen" falls into this category of folk tale. *Fables* are ancient animal tales in which the animals symbolize humans, often to make a specific point or teach a moral lesson, which is explicitly stated at the end of the fable. Aesop's Fables are among the best-known fables in the Western culture, and Jataka Tales are well-known in the Eastern culture.

Trickster tales are also animal tales. The principal character in these stories is amoral, neither good nor bad. Tricksters laugh when they should not and are always "up to" something, but tricksters are charming, likable, and tend to escape punishment. The trickster's function in folk literature is to keep us from taking ourselves too seriously (Lester, 1988). Trickster tales appear in every culture, although the trickster animal varies among cultures. Brer Rabbit is a well-known trickster character for children in the United States. Native Americans identify the coyote as a trickster, and tales from the African tradition have a spider as trickster. The trickster in Amy MacDonald's *Please Malese! A Trickster Tale from Haiti* is a devious man who is trying to get brand new shoes.

Noodlehead Tales, Drolls, and Simpleton Tales

The principal character in these stories is an engaging fool. Fools are popular because they represent the underdog who wins, or the good-hearted person who triumphs. A common theme in noodlehead stories is the simpleton or fool who trades something of value for a worthless object. "Lazy Jack," one of the most famous of these characters, trades a cow for some worthless beans in one popular story. Of course, in the end the worthless objects turn out to be valuable—they grow into a giant beanstalk. This character catches the imagination of so many people that his story continues to live in retellings such as Shelley Fowles' *The Bachelor and the Bean*.

Myths

Myths are stories about gods and supernatural beings that explain human origins and natural events, and tie together relationships between humans and the supernatural. Myths occur in all cultures. Perhaps the best-known myths are *pourquoi tales*, also called why stories. These myths explain scientific things like why the rabbit has a short tail, why the elephant has a long trunk, and so forth.

Legends

Legends are closely related to myths, but the main characters are frequently based on actual historical figures, such as religious saints, rather than supernatural beings. Although usually based in truth about a person, place, or event, legends tend to embellish and embroider the truth in order to showcase a particular virtue so that the character's wonderful feats grow more amazing with each telling. For instance, King Arthur and his Knights of the Round Table exemplify chivalrous behavior, Joan of Arc exemplifies courage and convic-

tion, and Robin Hood and his Merry Men exemplify taking care of the poor. A famous American legend tells us that George Washington refused to lie about chopping down a cherry tree. Other legends explain rocks, mountains, and other natural features, as do the Australian writer Oodgeroo's stories about Mother Earth's features, as well as her legends about trees.

Published and unpublished legends exist throughout the United States; local and regional legends are especially interesting to students. *The Legend of Sleeping Bear,* by Kathy-Jo Wargin, will be familiar to people living in Michigan and those who have visited the Sleeping Bear Dunes.

Tall Tales

Tall tales are based on lies and exaggerations about larger-than-life characters such as Paul Bunyan, Fin M'Coul, John Henry, Mike Fink, Davy Crockett, Johnny Appleseed, and Daniel Boone. As with legends, some of the characters in tall tales actually lived, whereas others may be a composite of several people; many are entirely fictitious. These stories are probably the precursors of modern larger-than-life characters (Saxby & Winch, 1987) such as Crocodile Dundee of movie fame and Paul Zelinsky's picture book, *Swamp Angel.* Tall tale characters continue to capture our imaginations.

Paul Bunyan, a popular tall tale character, was probably created by the American lumbering industry. The University of Minnesota has a Paul Bunyan Collection of books, newspaper clippings, photos, phonograph recordings, and memorabilia. Steven Kellogg added to the Paul Bunyan tall tales with his picture book titled *Paul Bunyan.*

Ballads

Ballads are essentially dramatic poems that tell stories handed down from one generation to the next through song. These narrative poems have marked rhythm and rhyme. They may include passages of dialogue, a repeated chorus or refrain, and formalized phrases that recur from verse to verse. Ballads usually tell stories about heroes, murders, love, tragedies, and feuds. "The Streets of Laredo" is a ballad that tells of a cowboy's exploits (Sutherland & Livingston, 1984). "Stagolee" is an African-American hero who is the subject of both ballads and folk tales (Lester, 1969). The popular Australian ballad "Waltzing Matilda" tells about life in the Australian bush. Traditional ballads can introduce literature and poetry. Ballads introduce children to the themes of great literature and tune their ears to the rhythms of poetry.

Selecting and Evaluating Traditional Literature

The factors to consider when selecting and evaluating traditional literature are basically the same as for all literature. Some specific guidelines to keep in mind as you add to your collection are:

1. Does the book tell a good story?
2. Does the dust jacket or the foreword identify the book as traditional literature and tell the original cultural source of the selection? Does the reteller identify the source of the tale?
3. What characteristics of traditional literature does it have (e.g., formulaic beginning or ending, universal setting stated briefly, little or no description, etc.)?
4. Does the story have rapid plot development?
5. Are the characters symbolic? Can children relate to them?
6. Is the style simple and direct?
7. Does the story express universal values?

Classroom Activities

ACTIVITY 6.1   CHANTING

(IRA/NCTE Standards: 1, 3, 4. Building understanding of texts and cultures, comprehend and interpret, and use spoken and written language to communicate.)

Folk tales are ideal vehicles for teaching students to chant refrains. The "Little Red Hen" works well for this activity because it has repetitive events and repeated, rhythmic phrases. Write the repeated phrases on the chalkboard or on charts and encourage the children to join in on repeated parts as you read aloud. Show them the charts that will guide their part of the activity. Read the story with the children's assistance several times. Vary this activity by having them prepare to read the story and then have the other children join in on the refrain.

ACTIVITY 6.2   MAPPING

(IRA/NCTE Standards: 3,4,6. Comprehension, vocabulary, knowledge of story structure.)

Mapping is a good activity for developing understanding, even if the students will not be telling a story. This activity summarizes and organizes students' understanding of stories. You may have the students create their own maps using the model given in Figure 6.4.

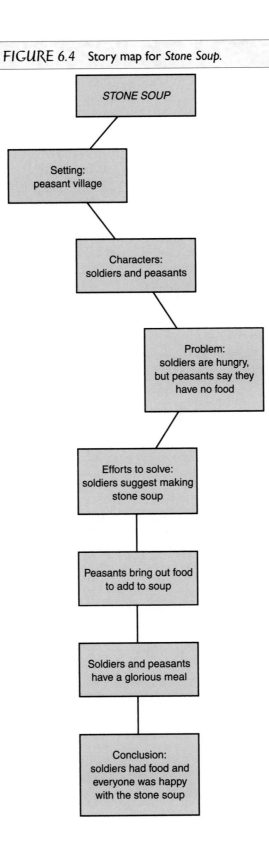

FIGURE 6.4 Story map for *Stone Soup*.

STONE SOUP

Setting:
peasant village

Characters:
soldiers and peasants

Problem:
soldiers are hungry,
but peasants say they
have no food

Efforts to solve:
soldiers suggest making
stone soup

Peasants bring out food
to add to soup

Soldiers and peasants
have a glorious meal

Conclusion:
soldiers had food and
everyone was happy
with the stone soup

ACTIVITY 6.3   STORYTELLING

(IRA/NCTE Standards: 2,4,9. Oral language/communication.)

Storytelling is a natural activity to use with traditional literature. The following guidelines help storytellers.

1. Let the children choose stories that they especially enjoy.
2. Have them learn their stories, but not memorize them. Tell them to initially be concerned with the outline of the story. After identifying the basic plot, they can list, map, or outline these elements with drawings. A story map is a graphic display showing the organization of events and ideas in the story (see Figure 6.4).
3. After the students have a map or plan for their stories, group them in pairs, so the pairs can tell their stories to each other from the map or plan.
4. Once they can remember their story outlines, ask them to elaborate on their storytelling using these techniques:
   A. Visualize the setting, the people, and the action. Think about what you would see, hear, and feel if you were there. Choose words that will make the story more vivid so that your listeners can visualize it as you do. Retell the story with the more vivid language.
   B. Think of ways that you can make the story more exciting for the audience and get them more involved.

ACTIVITY 6.4   COMPOSING FOLK TALES

(IRA/NCTE Standards: 5, 12. Writing to communicate and to accomplish students' purposes.)

Students can compose their own folk tales. This activity is a variation of one suggested by Livo and Rietz (1986). Write setting, character, and problem or conflict ideas on slips of paper and put each in a separate pile (all of the settings together, all the characters together, etc.). Organize students into groups of two or three and let each group draw one idea from each pile of slips. Then ask them to develop a spontaneous story using the setting, characters, and problem or conflict they selected. Once they are used to working this way, the activity can be varied by giving the students one slip of paper only, so they have a part of the story and must build the rest of it.

On the slips of paper you might write ideas such as:

1. Characters: mean witch, spider, trickster rabbit, good fairy.
2. Setting: enchanted forest, a peasant hut, a giant toadstool, a castle.
3. Problem: cannot break evil witch's spell, lost in a forest, cannot find family, hungry.

ACTIVITY 6.5   PREDICTION

(IRA/NCTE Standards: 3. Comprehension and vocabulary.)

Folk tales are quite predictable, so anticipation and prediction are good ways to involve children with the stories. Select a story such as *Henny Penny* or *The Three Billy Goats Gruff* by Paul Galdone or *Fin M'Coul: The Giant of Knockmany Hill* by Tomie dePaola. Introduce the story to the children, and ask them to predict what the story will be about from the title and the book cover. Then read the story aloud, stopping at various points in the story to ask them to predict what will happen next. After they predict, tell them to listen to determine whether their predictions were correct. When teaching *The Little Red Hen,* you might stop for predictions after each of these points in the story:

1. The hen asks for help planting the wheat.
2. The hen asks for help watering the wheat and pulling the weeds.
3. The hen asks for help cutting the ripe wheat.
4. The hen asks someone to take the wheat to be ground into flour.

5. The hen asks for help making the wheat into bread.
6. The hen asks for help eating the bread.

A variation of this activity might be to have the children write their predictions and then discuss them after the story is completed.

Children enjoy creating their own versions of folk tales.

ACTIVITY 6.6   ILLUSTRATING FOLK TALES

(IRA/NCTE Standards: 12. Interpreting written language.)

Many children enjoy creating their own illustrations for their favorite folk tales, many of which have variants that have been interpreted in various ways. Prepare them for this activity by presenting several picture-book versions of the same folk tale (see Figure 6.5 for a sample list). After the students examine the tales, ask them to identify the medium, style, colors, and lines used to illustrate the tale and why they chose these specific media, colors, and so forth. They may like to add the text to their illustrations and bind the stories to make their own books.

FIGURE 6.5   Illustrated folk tales to compare.

Brer Rabbit	*The Tales of Uncle Remus: The Adventures of Brer Rabbit* by Julius Lester, illustrated by Jerry Pinkney *The People Could Fly: American Black Folktales* by Virginia Hamilton, illustrated by Leo and Diane Dillon
The Three Billy Goats Gruff	*The Three Billy Goats Gruff* by Peter Asbjornsen, illustrated by Marcia Brown *The Three Billy Goats Gruff* by Paul Galdone
Jack and the Beanstalk	*Jim and the Beanstalk* by Raymond Briggs *Jack and the Beanstalk* by Tony Ross *Jack and the Bean Tree* by Gail E. Haley
Cinderella	*Yeh-Shen* by Ai-Ling Louie *Cinderella* by Charles Perrault, illustrated by Errol Le Cain *Cinderella* by Charles Perrault, illustrated by Marcia Brown *Cinderella* by the Brothers Grimm, illustrated by Nonny Hogrogian *Cinderella* by Paul Galdone

---

ACTIVITY 6.7   WRITING FOLK TALES

(IRA/NCTE Standards: 5, 6. Organizing and structuring writing, applying language conventions.)

Folk tales are exceptional models for writing. Folk tale studies can teach story parts (beginning, middle, end), story form, and story structure, as well as the elements of story grammar (i.e., setting, problem, actions, and resolution). Folk tales also provide models of story content. Through studying legends, myths, animal tales, fairy tales, and other folk tales, students can learn to understand and write them.

Introduce each type of folk tale to the students (i.e., fables, pourquoi tales, trickster tales, legends, myths, etc.) and give examples of each, then have the students identify additional examples of each type, specifying the characteristics that helped them identify the various types of folk tales. Ways of applying this activity to specific types of folk tales are listed below.

1. Have the students identify cumulative stories structured around repetition: *Bringing the Rain to Kapiti Plain* by Verna Aardema, *The Gingerbread Boy* by Paul Galdone, and *The House that Jack Built* by Janet Stevens are examples. Read or have the students read the tales aloud, then discuss the cumulative aspects of the stories. Write the repeated portions on the chalkboard or charts. They may want to act out the repeated lines. Have them identify these elements of cumulative stories:

   The stories are short.

   The stories have a strong rhythmic pattern.

   The story events are in a logical order and related to the preceding events.

   All of the story events are in a logical order and accumulated to the preceding events.

   All of the story events are repeated and accumulated until a surprise ending is reached.

   Book clusters provide a beginning point for activities and discussion, as well as materials for a variety of activities.

ACTIVITY 6.8   COMPARE FOLK TALE VARIANTS

(IRA/NCTE Standards: 7, 8, 9. Research, evaluate, and synthesize data, and use a variety of information resources, critical thinking, and diversity in language and culture.)

Variants exist for most popular tales. Compare variants by noting the similarities and differences in the various aspects of the story structure (e.g., setting, character, problem, resolution, and conclusion) and the way they are written or illustrated.

Read variants of a folk tale aloud for younger students, while older students can prepare their own charts to compare variants such as the one shown in Table 6.2.

TABLE 6.2
Comparison chart for folk tale variants.

Author/ illustrator	Main character	Setting	Other characters	Beginning	Problem	Ending
Jakob and Wilhelm Grimm Nonny Hogrogian Greenwillow, 1981	Cinderella	Germany	Stepmother Doves Hazel tree	Invitation to ball	Cinderella mistreated	Marries prince
Charles Perrault Marcia Brown Scribner's 1954	Cinderella	France	Stepmother Stepsisters	Invitation to ball	Cinderella mistreated	Marries prince

ACTIVITY 6.9   COMPARING WRITTEN AND FILM VERSIONS (THIS ACTIVITY CAN BE APPLIED TO ANY GENRE)

(IRA/NCTE Standards: 1, 6, 3, 8. Comprehension, vocabulary, and reading print and nonprint texts.)

Many traditional stories have been made into films, which children will enjoy watching as a class after having heard or read the book version. Class discussion after viewing the film can focus on questions such as:

1. What scenes were in the book that were not in the film?
2. Why did the filmmaker omit these scenes?

3. Were the characters the same in the book and the film?

4. How did the colors and art style vary between the two media?

5. Describe the overall differences between the two versions.

6. Why did these differences occur?

If a video recorder is available, students can film their own versions of the story.

ACTIVITY 6.10   AUTHOR PROFILES

(IRA/NCTE Standards: 4, 6, 8. Students adjust language, apply language knowledge, and create, critique, and discuss print and nonprint texts.)

Students will use a variety of technological and informational resources to access author information.

Choosing an author or reteller of traditional literature is difficult. John Bierhorst has written exceptional Native-American folk tales, Gale Haley is recognized for her interpretations of folk tales, and Ed Young has often retold Asian folk tales. Harold Courlander has collected tales from Native Americans, Haitians, and Africans, so his name is significant in traditional literature. Julius Lester has retold the Uncle Remus tales. Peter and Iona Opie have retold and interpreted classic fairy tales. Steven Kellogg is a masterful writer of tall tales, and Jon Scieszka fractures fairy tales with a sure hand. An increasing number of story retellers are publishing excellent versions of traditional tales so begin to get acquainted with your own favorites. We have selected John Bierhorst for our profile.

A Biological Profile: John Bierhorst

John Bierhorst is an American folklorist and adapter of Native-American literature for children. Many of his books have been recognized as Notable Books by the American Library Association.

As a child, Bierhorst never encountered Native-American culture in any of the books he read. He discovered his interest in writing while attending college, where his interest in anthropology contributed to his desire to study native cultures. These interests led him to create an anthology of songs, prayers, orations, and languages in *The Hungry Woman: Myths and Legends of the Aztecs*. He concentrates on the Iroquois in *The Woman Who Fell from the Sky: The Iroquois Story of Creation*. He has translated eight Charles Perrault tales, which provides a sense of his diverse skills. The books identified in this profile are merely representative of his work.

Summary

Traditional literature is rooted in the oral tradition. The stories, ballads, and tales in this genre are descendents of the original oral stories that have traveled all over the world from storyteller to storyteller, teaching listeners about life and about people. The favorite stories of the past continue to be popular today.

The characters, settings, and events in folk tales are symbolic, and they differ from other forms of fiction in that they teach more direct lessons. Other forms of literature develop themes more subtly, but folk tales have very obvious themes most of the time.

Tall tales and fractured fairy tales are included in this chapter because they are closely related to traditional literature. Tall tales are about superheroes of former times and their sources are unclear. Fractured fairy tales were created by authors as different versions of existing tales. Authors of traditional stories are considered retellers. They often collect stories in actual storytelling situations.

Research and Application Experiences

1. Develop a booktalk for introducing a folk tale to a group of children, and then read the tale to the children.
2. Analyze folk tales such as "Jack Tales," "Little Red Riding Hood," or "Sleeping Beauty" from different cultures and identify how the tale changes from culture.
3. Identify a folk tale that you especially enjoy and prepare to tell it to a group of children.
4. Read or tell a folk tale to a group of children, and then have them dramatize the tale.
5. Read two versions of a folk tale to children and ask them to identify their favorite and to explain the reasons for choosing that tale.

Children's Literature References and Recommended Books

Note: Books designated with an asterisk (*) are recommended for reluctant readers.

Aardema, V. (1975). *Why mosquitoes buzz in people's ears* (L. & D. Dillon, Illus.). New York: Dial. (All ages). TRADITIONAL LITERATURE.

A popular African folk tale.

Aardema, V. (1981). *Bringing the rain to Kapiti Plain*. New York: Dial. (All ages). TRADITIONAL LITERATURE.

A popular African folk tale.

Asbjornsen, P. C. (1957). *The three billy goats gruff* (M. Brown, Illus.). San Diego, CA: Harcourt. (K–3). TRADITIONAL LITERATURE.

Three goats want to eat grass, but a troll threatens them.

Babbitt, N. (1998). *Ouch! A tale from Grimm* (F. Marcellino, Illus.). New York: HarperCollins. (K–3). TRADITIONAL LITERATURE.

Marco is born into an unremarkable family, but uses his wits to become king.

Bierhorst, J. (2002). *Is my friend at home? Pueblo fireside tales* (W. Watson, Illus.). New York: Farrar. (K–3). TRADITIONAL LITERATURE.

These brief trickster tales are populated by Coyote and his friends.

Bini, R. (2000). *World treasury of myths, legends, and folktales: Stories from six countries* (M. Frodorow, Illus.). Abrams: Milan, Italy. (All ages). TRADITIONAL LITERATURE.

This book contains 33 stories from around the world.

Briggs, R. (1970). *Jim and the beanstalk*. New York: Coward-McCann. (1–4). TRADITIONAL LITERATURE.

The giant needs false teeth, glasses, and a wig in this version of the tale.

Brown, N. (1954). *Cinderella*. New York: Scribners. K–4. TRADITIONAL LITERATURE.

This version of Cinderella is based on the Charles Perrault tale.

Casler, L. (1994). *The boy who dreamed of an acorn* (S. Begay, Illus.). New York: Philomel. (3–6). TRADITIONAL LITERATURE.

A boy discovers that small, weak things have great power.

Chase, R. (1943). *Jack tales*. Boston: Houghton Mifflin. (All ages). TRADITIONAL LITERATURE.

These Jack tales are retold in an Appalachian dialect.

Climo, S. (1993). *The Korean Cinderella* (R. Heller, Illus.). New York: HarperCollins. (K–4). TRADITIONAL LITERATURE.

A variant of the well-known Cinderella tale.

Coburn, J. (1996). *Jouanah: A Hmong Cinderella* (A. O'Brien, Illus.). Fremont, CA: Shen's Books. (3–6). TRADITIONAL LITERATURE.

This is a Southeastern Asia Cinderella tale.

Coburn, J. (2000). *Domitila: A Cinderella tale from the Mexican tradition* (C. McLennan, Illus.). Fremont, CA: Shen's Books. (3–6). TRADITIONAL LITERATURE.

This is an authentic Mexican Cinderella version.

Daly, J. (2000). *Fair, Brown & Trembling: An Irish Cinderella story*. New York: Farrar. (K–3). TRADITIONAL LITERATURE.

In this version, Trembling must stay at home, while her sisters go to church.

Day, N. R. (1995). *The lion's whiskers: An Ethiopian folktale* (A. Grifalconi. Illus.). New York: Scholastic. (1–4). TRADITIONAL LITERATURE.

A loving stepmother risks death for her stepson. The illustrations show the lifestyle of Amhara people.

Dearden, C. (2003). *Little book of Latin American folktales*. Joronto, CA: Groundwood. (3–6). TRADITIONAL LITERATURE.

A collection of 10 Latin American tales including versions of well-known tales.

DePaola, T. (1981). *Fin M'Coul: The giant of Knockmany Hill*. New York: Holiday House. (1–3). TRADITIONAL LITERATURE.

This is an Irish folk tale.

Fowles, S. (2003). *The bachelor and the bean*. New York: Farrar. (1–4). TRADITIONAL LITERATURE.

A grumpy old bachelor is the central character who drops his last bean in a well, disturbing the imp of the well.

Galdone, P. (1979). *The three billy goats gruff*. New York: Clarion. (K–2). TRADITIONAL LITERATURE.

A well-illustrated telling of this tale.

Galdone, P. (1984). *Henny Penny*. New York: Clarion. (K–2). TRADITIONAL LITERATURE.

A retelling of the popular tale.

Hague, M. (2001). *Kate Culhane: A ghost story* (M. Hague, Illus.). New York: SeaStar. (3–6). TRADITIONAL LITERATURE.

A popular tale for storytellers. After staying too long in the graveyard, Kate Culhane needs help to escape.

Hamiltion, V. (1985). *The people could fly: American Black folktales* (L. & D. Dillon, Illus.). New York: Knopf. (4–8). TRADITIONAL LITERATURE.

A superb collection of folk tales.

Hickox, R. (1999). *The golden sandal* (W. Hillenbrand, Illus.). New York: Holiday House. TRADITIONAL LITERATURE.

This is a Middle Eastern version of the Cinderella story.

Hoberman, M. (2002). *The marvelous mouse man* (L. Forman, Illus.). New York: Harcourt. (All ages). (1–4). TRADITIONAL LITERATURE.

A new version of "The Pied Piper of Hamlin."

Isaacs, A. (1995). *Swamp Angel* (P. Zelinsky, Illus.). New York: Dutton. (1–4). TRADITIONAL LITERATURE.

The Swamp Angel is the larger-than-life heroine of this tall tale.

Janisch, H. (2002) *The fire: An Ethopian folk tale*. New York: Groundwood.

A pourquoi about the origins of fire.

Johnson, P. B. (2001). *Fearless Jack*. New York: McElderry. (2–4). TRADITIONAL LITERATURE.

This story is a version of the Appalachian tale "Jack the Giant Killer."

Kellogg, S. (1984). *Paul Bunyan*. New York: (1–4). TRADITIONAL LITERATURE.

Kellogg's retelling of the Paul Bunyan tall tale.

Lasky, K. (2002). *Porkenstein*. New York: Scholastic. (1–4). TRADITIONAL LITERATURE, FRACTURED FAIRY TALE.

Dr. Smart Pig was lonely after the wolf ate his brothers.

Lester, J. (1969). *Black Folktales*. (T. Feelings, Illus.). New York: Barron. (3–12). TRADITIONAL LITERATURE.

A collection of Black folktales including Stagolee.

Lupton, H. (2001). *The story tree: Tales to read aloud*. Kinev, HI: Barefoot. (K–2). TRADITIONAL LITERATURE.

This English collection features retelling of well-known tales.

MacDonald, A. (2002). *Please, Malese!: A trickster tale from Haiti* (E. Lisker, Illus.). New York: Farrar. (3–5). TRADITIONAL LITERATURE.

Malese plots to avoid work and get new shoes.

MacDonald, M. (2001). *Fat cat: A Danish folktale* (J. Paschkis, Illus.). Panama City LA: August House. (K–2). TRADITIONAL LITERATURE.

The story of an overeating cat and a mouse who cooks. The refrain invites participation.

Martin, R. (1992). *The rough-face girl* (D. Shannon, Illus.). New York: Putnam. (1–4). TRADITIONAL LITERATURE.

A Native-American version of Cinderella.

Milligan, B. (2003). *The prince of Ireland and the three magic stallions*. New York: Holiday House. (1–4). TRADITIONAL LITERATURE.

A prince of Ireland's stepmother seeks to eliminate her stepson from the throne.

Milnes, G. (1990). *Granny will your dog bite, and other mountain rhymes*. New York: Knopf. (3–6). TRADITIONAL LITERATURE.

A collection of unique rhymes.

Oodgeroo. (1994). *Dreamtime: Aboriginal stories* (B. Bancroft, Illus.). New York: Lothrop, Lee & Shepard. (3–8). TRADITIONAL LITERATURE.

Aboriginal folklore that Oodgeroo heard as a child.

Pollock, P. (1996). *The turkey girl: A Zuni Cinderella story* (E. Young, Illus.). Boston: Little Brown. (1–4) TRADITIONAL LITERATURE.

A Cinderella story.

San Souci, R. (1989). *The talking eggs* (J. Pinkney, Illus.). New York: Dial. (1–4). TRADITIONAL LITERATURE.

A colorful version of the Cinderella story.

Scieszka, J. (1989). *The true story of the 3 little pigs* (L. Smith, Illus.). New York: Viking. (All ages). FRACTURED FAIRY TALE.

The wolf tells his version of this story.

Scieszka, J. (1991). *The frog prince, continued* (S. Johnson, Illus.). New York: Viking. (All ages). TRADITIONAL LITERATURE/FRACTURED FAIRY TALE.

A new version of the traditional tale.

Scieszka, J. (1992). *The stinky cheese man and other fairly stupid tales* (L. Smith, Illus.). New York: Viking. (All ages). TRADITIONAL LITERATURE/FRACTURED FAIRY TALES.

New versions of well-known traditional tales.

Scieszka, J., & Lane Smith. (1998). *Squids will be squids*. New York: Viking. (2–6). TRADITIONAL LITERATURE/FRACTURED FABLES.

A collection including fresh morals and beastly fables.

Sierra, J. (2002). *Can you guess my name?: Traditional tales around the world* (S. Vitale, Illus.). New York: Clarion. (4–8). TRADITIONAL LITERATURE.

A storyteller shares her retellings of popular tales. This collection features variants of tales from Anglo-American to Xhosa, from Argentina to Swaziland.

Souci, R. (1998). *Cendrillon: A Caribbean Cinderella* (B. Pinkney, Illus.). New York: Simon & Schuster. (K–4). TRADITIONAL LITERATURE.

A version of the traditional Cinderella story.

Steig, J. (1998). *A handful of beans: Six fairy tales* (W. Steig, Illus.). New York: Harper. (K–4). TRADITIONAL LITERATURE.

This book features retellings of traditional tales.

Stevens, J. (1985). *The house that Jack built*. New York: Harcourt (K–2). TRADITIONAL LITERATURE, CUMULATIVE TALE.

This story is about building a house.

Sunami, K. (2002). *How the fisherman tricked the genie: A tale within a tale within a tale* (A. Hirao, Illus.). New York: Atheneum. (3–6). TRADITIONAL LITERATURE.

A fisherman releases a genie from a bottle, but the genie refuses to grant wishes.

Ward, H. (2002). *The rooster and the fox*. New York: Millbrook. (K–3). TRADITIONAL LITERATURE.

Chanticleer the rooster appears in this retelling of the traditional tale.

Wargin, K. (1998). *The legend of sleeping bear* (F. Van Frankenhuyzen, Illus.). Chelsea, MI: Sleeping Bear Press. (K–3). TRADITIONAL LITERATURE.

The story of the formation of the Sleeping Bear Dunes.

Whipple, L. (2002). *If the shoe fits: Voices from Cinderella* (L. Beingessner, Illus.). New York: McElderry. (2–4). TRADITIONAL LITERATURE.

The voices of Cinderella characters in poetry.

Wiesner, D. (2001). *The three pigs*. New York: Clarion. (2–5). TRADITIONAL LITERATURE/FRACTURED FAIRY TALES.

The pigs wander in and out of other tales.

Young, E. (1994). *Little plum*. New York: Philomel. (1–4). TRADITIONAL LITERATURE.

A new version of Tom Thumb.

Zelinsky, P. (1998). *Rapunzel*. New York: Dutton. (1–4). TRADITIONAL LITERATURE.

Zelinsky interpreted this Grimm tale with exquisite new illustrations.

Zeman, L. (2003). *Sinbad's secret*. Toronto, CA: Tundra. (3–6). TRADITIONAL LITERATURE.

A retelling of the thousand and one nights from Sinbad's point of view.

References and Books for Further Reading

Bettelheim, B. (1975, December 8). The uses of enchantment. *New Yorker,* 5.

Dundes, A. (1965). *The study of folklore*. Upper Saddle River, NJ: Prentice Hall.

Hearne, B. (1999). *Choosing books for children.* (3rd ed). New York: Delacorte.

Hunter, M. (1975). *Talent is not enough*. New York: Harper.

Jaffe, N. (1999). Global storytelling. *Book Links, 8,* 53.

Lester, J. (1988, Summer). The storyteller's voice: Reflections on the rewriting of Uncle Remus. *New Advocate, 1*, 143–159.

Livo, N. J., & Rietz, S. A. (1986). *Storytelling process and practice*. Littleton, CO: Libraries Unlimited.

Miller, S. (1995). American folklore. In A. Silvey (Ed.), *Children's books and their creators* (pp. 22–24). Boston: Houghton Mifflin.

Rothman, R. (1990, February 21). Experts warn of attempts to censor classic texts. *Education Week,* 5.

Saxby, M. T. & Winch, G. (1987). *Give them wings: The experience of children's literature*. South Melbourne, Australia: Macmillian.

Schwartz, A. (1977). Children, humor, and folklore. In P. Heins (Ed.), *Crosscurrents of criticism: Horn Book essays 1968–77* (pp. 214–215). Boston: Horn Book.

Steiner, H. (2001). Storytelling around the world. *Book Links, 10* (5), 40–48.

Sutherland, Z., & Livingston, M. C. (1984). *The Scott Foresman anthology of children's literature*. (8th ed.) Chicago: Scott Foresman.

Thompson, S. (1951). *The Folktale*. New York: Holt Rinehart Winston.

Modern Fantasy: Today's Magic

7

KEY TERMS

fantastic elements   modern fantasy

high fantasy   science fiction

GUIDING QUESTIONS

1. What was your favorite fantasy when you were a child? As you read, think about current fantasy that is similar to your favorite story.

2. Why is fantasy such an important genre of literature for children?

3. Why is fantasy so popular today?

4. What are the elements of fantasy?

"Fantasy is the ultimate literature of the imagination" (Greenlaw, 2001, p. 148). According to Albert Einstein, the power to imagine is more important than simple knowledge (Shlain, 1990). In fantasy, authors create extraordinary worlds and characters who challenge and expand our sense of the norm. Imagined worlds permit readers to explore the basic truths of our own world. In this way, good fantasy helps readers understand reality. The vignette on the following page illus-

trates the "Harry Potter" phenomenon, which has created world-wide interest in fantasy.

Modern Fantasy—The Literature of Imagination

Harry Potter has generated more reading than any book in recent memory. Moreover, its roots in magic, epic storytelling, myth, and folklore have generated a huge interest in reading fantasy literature (Whited, 2002). Fantasy exercises the imagination. It should be an important part of children's lives so they can dream and imagine, as those who cannot imagine cannot read (Eisner, 1992). We have to imagine to construct meaning through language.

Fantasy fulfills the human need to imagine alternate realities and to explore the unexplainable and the impossible (Woolsey, 2002). The *Harry Potter* stories enable readers to imagine alternate realities. Other stories, like Paul Fleischman's *Westlandia* and Betsy Byars' *Little Horse*, give children opportunities to use their imaginations to conceive of another reality.

Authors of fantasy have special writing challenges because "the more fantastic a piece of fiction is, the harder the writer must work to make it believable" (Hearne, 1999, p. 86). Writers must effortlessly use imaginary elements to create a seamless story so real that the reader cannot avoid accepting its *fantastic elements*. When creating fantasy, authors must adhere to strict rules; they cannot wave a wand to solve all of the dilemmas confronting the protagonist. Readers have to willingly suspend disbelief to

The only sounds in Will Livingston's fifth-grade classroom were those of turning pages. Reading workshop had that effect on his students: they really enjoyed reading.

THE AMULET OF KOMONDOR

ADAM OSTERWEIL
pictures by Peter Thorpe

This story begins with a strange store and a game of DragonSteel.

When he told them it was time to stop, Josh groaned, "Our group just finished *Harry Potter and the Order of the Phoenix* and we have read all of the other Harry Potter books. There just isn't anything as good as Harry Potter. We don't want to read anything else."

"What do you like about the Harry Potter books?" Will asked.

"The story is so interesting that I don't want to stop reading. Harry is like a real kid. He is very brave. I like the characters and the magic. They have adventures and learn how to use magic, but they can't cast spells in the world of Muggles. Quinton and James agree with me that they only want to read Harry Potter."

Will responded, "What genre is Harry Potter?"

"That's easy! It is definitely fantasy."

"Let me see if I can find some books that have some of the same qualities as Harry Potter. Then you can survey them and select another one to read," Will suggested.

Will checked several reviews and selected these titles.

The Amulet of Komondor by Adam Osterweil
Wanna Buy an Alien? by Eve Bunting
Space Race by Sylvia Waugh
Skelling by David Almond
Island of the Aunts by Eva Ibbotson

After surveying the books, the boys selected *Westlandia*. Josh said, "We are going to read *Westlandia*, but we don't think it will be as good as Harry Potter."

"Perhaps you could compare *Westlandia* with Harry Potter," Will suggested. "You might also enjoy studying the authors of both books."

join in the magic and believe the story could actually happen. Once they do that, they accept the magic that enables pigs to fly, animals to talk, entire villages to appear and disappear, and clocks to strike 13. The story cannot "clank," jarring the reader back to reality (Greenlaw, 1995).

Fantasy stimulates students to look at life and its problems in new ways (Britton, 1977). Through fantasy, children develop more open-minded attitudes that enable them to understand others' points of view. Fantasy stretches the imagination and encourages dreams, stimulating creative thinking and problem-solving abilities. Fantasy, of all the genres of children's literature, offers the greatest challenge and the greatest rewards to both readers and writers (Smith, 1988). This is why many have welcomed the blossoming of interest in fantasy since the arrival of Harry Potter.

Modern fantasy inherits the common themes of the struggle between good and evil, basic human values, and perseverance in the face of adversity from traditional literature. Many of its characters are symbols of good, beauty, and wisdom or of bad, ugliness, and evil. The characters' personalities are developed and children identify with their roles.

The Nature of Fantasy

Two things set excellent fantasy apart from other genres. First, the author must have a strongly realized personal vision, a perspective or belief about the meaning, significance, symbolism, and allegory. This leads to the moral, message, or lesson in the fantasy, which is the second aspect (Langton, 1977). For instance, L'Engle addresses the theological role of love in the conflict between good and evil. "The best stories are like extended lyrical images of unchanging human predicaments": in them, life and death, love and hate, good and evil, courage and despair are dramatized (Cook, 1969, p. 2).

The images, ideas, and possibilities in fantasy must, however, remain essentially true to life. The fantasy must maintain a consistent logic throughout so that readers believe that the magic and impossible happenings are plausible. Obviously, fantasy always includes at least one element of the impossible, one element that goes against the laws of the physical universe as we currently understand them (Alexander, 1991). Fantasy concerns things that cannot really happen, as well as people or creatures that do not really exist. Nevertheless, each story must have its own self-contained logic that creates

its own reality (Cameron, 1993). Authors need to draw boundary lines outside which the fantasy may not wander. For example, in E. B. White's *Charlotte's Web*, the animals talk among themselves, but not to the human beings. White created this logic at the outset of the story, and it is never violated. Although the author is free to create any specific boundaries or logic, writers of fantasy must be hardheaded realists. "What appears gossamer is, underneath, solid as prestressed concrete. Once committed to his imaginary kingdom, the writer is not a monarch but a subject" (Alexander, 1991, p. 143).

Fantasy has special qualities distinguishing it from other genres. It concerns things that cannot happen and worlds that cannot exist, yet each story has a self-contained logic that creates its reality, such as the other world fantasy that appears in C. S. Lewis's *The Chronicles of Narnia* and the land of unicorns that Bruce Coville created when he wrote *Into the Land of the Unicorns*. In some fantasy, visitors can come from other worlds, as in Alexander Key's *The Forgotten Door*. These visitors may cause us to see ourselves in new ways and to discover the importance of kindness and love.

Readers and Fantasy

Fantasy communicates a sense of truth. In addition, it tells us something about our world and ourselves. Fantasy gives children a means of verifying their understanding of the external world they share with others (their immediate world). It also gives children a means of examining their inner world and comparing it with others' inner worlds (Britton, 1977). For example, in Alexander Key's *The Forgotten Door*, readers confront their fear of the unknown and that which is different. A truth clothed in the fantastic is often easier to understand and accept than a baldly stated fact.

A theme of L'Engle's fantasy *A Wrinkle in Time* is good versus evil. Despite this basic moral or lesson, the author must avoid moral pronouncements; children do not tolerate them any better than do adults. Instead, these truths must emerge naturally from the story, providing insights about the human condition without preaching (Smith, 1988).

People vary in imaginative ability. Some readers take pleasure in the ingenuity of fine fantasy, whereas others read fantasy simply because it tells a good story. Some readers reject fantasy because it is not real. However, research shows that gifted children choose fantasy more frequently than other children (Swanton, 1984).

Nevertheless, experienced teachers recognize the need to cultivate children's taste for fantasy.

Reading fantasy aloud and engaging in related classroom activities will stimulate students' interest. In our experience, when a reader discovers a fantasy that speaks to him or her, it can open new reading interests. Madeline L'Engle's *A Wrinkle in Time* created this interest. When teaching fifth grade, we encouraged a student to read this book. He stated he didn't have time. However, after a teacher read it to his class, he ended up devouring all of L'Engle's books.

Types of Fantasy

Modern fantasy is perhaps the most richly varied of all genres, ranging from simple stories of magic to profoundly complex stories like those told in the *Star Wars* movies. These films are elaborate stories of good versus evil. The diversity of fantasy appeals to a broad range of readers with varying reading abilities and interests.

Classic fantasy includes some of the most popular fantasies of all times: *Winnie-the-Pooh* by A. A. Milne, *A Wrinkle in Time* by Madeline L'Engle, *A Bear Called Paddington* by Michael Bond, *Charlie and the Chocolate Factory* by Roald Dahl, and *The Wonderful Wizard of Oz* by Frank Baum. These authors have created fantasies that give current storytellers glass mountains to climb if they are to create equally worthwhile literature.

Stellaluna has both real and make-believe elements.

To organize our discussion of fantasy, we will categorize stories as animal fantasies, literary fairy tales, and enchanted realism. More complex fantasy, often called *high fantasy*, is grouped into heroic fantasy, time magic, and science fiction (Woolsey, 2002). These categories are arbitrary because many stories could belong to multiple categories. For example, *Charlotte's Web* is an animal fantasy, beginning in the real world, which then introduces the alternative animals' world. Moreover, the theme of friendship, as well as the comments on society, can give different perspectives on this fantasy.

Animal Fantasies

Animal fantasies are often the first stories that children encounter. In these stories, animals act and interact like human beings. For example, Helen Lester's *Three Cheers for Tacky* is an animal fantasy; Tacky the penguin has children's qualities and overcomes his problems with enthusiasm and his friend's support. The tiger in Anthony Paul's *The Tiger Who Lost His Stripes* has a case of "stripelessness." While searching for his stripes, he discovers selfishness, which he overcomes with ingenuity and intuition. The lively field mouse, Ragweed, is the central character in Avi's *Ragweed*. In this story, Ragweed sets out to explore the world. When he reaches the city, he meets F.E.A.R., a cat, but the street-smart Clutch helps him overcome F.E.A.R.

Young readers will enjoy the adventures of the inquisitive Little Horse in Betsy Byars' *Little Horse*. Little Horse fell into a stream and washed away from home. Through his adventures he realized that he was small, helpless, and alone, then help arrived making him feel secure and loved.

Literary Fairy Tales

Fantasy and traditional literature share the quality of make-believe, as well as many stylistic features, leading authors of fantasy to make extensive use of the folk tale style. Hans Christian Andersen, a shy man, used this style to tell stories about his own experiences in *The Wild Swans*, *The Ugly Duckling*, and *The Steadfast Tin Soldier*. He also chose this style when he wrote *The Emperor's New Clothes*, which comments on the falseness he observed in society.

Gary Schmidt used fairy tale style in his story, *Straw into Gold*. The hero of this story, Tousle, sets out

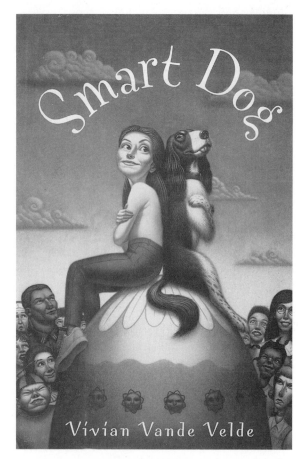

Amy saved Sherlock, a talking dog, who helped Amy solve a problem.

imal until she gives birth to her disfigured foal. The foal is a unicorn that plunges Heart, the mare, and the foal into danger. The medieval setting, the stereotyped characters, and the cliffhanger ending create a traditional feeling in this fantasy.

Enchanted Realism

Enchanted realism has elements of both fantasy and high fantasy. These stories include magical objects, characters, or events that appear in a realistic world, creating suspense and intrigue in the story (Woolsey, 2002).

Fantasy and high fantasy are present in *Lulu's Hat* by Susan Meddaugh. Lulu, the protagonist, is adopted into a family of magicians, but they believe she has no "real magic." However, Lulu discovers an old top hat that gives her magic powers and drops her into the world of magic. She acquires a dog named Hereboy and learns the secret of her past. She thereby achieves her goal of becoming a true magician.

Modern fantasy takes for granted not only the physical world and the real world that we see and feel, but also the supernatural world that presents all sorts of possibilities.

High Fantasy

High fantasy is a complex, philosophical form of literature that focuses on themes such as the conflict between good and evil. The complexity and abstractness of high fantasy includes detailed alternate or parallel worlds that authors create through dramatic plots, fully developed characters, geographies, languages, mythologies, histories, and traditions (Greenlaw, 2001).

Creators of fantasy write of myth and legend, of science and technology, and of human life—as it is lived, as it might be lived, and as it ought to be lived (Le Guin, 1979). The characters in high fantasy are often symbolic of good people who are entangled in an endless battle between good and evil, such as what occurs in each book of the popular *Harry Potter* series.

Heroic fantasy

The theme of Jackie Koller's *The Dragonling* is peace. At the beginning of the story, Darek hopes to slay a dragon, but instead he finds a baby dragon in the pouch of a dragon his brother killed. This discovery leads him

on a quest to solve the king's riddle, to find the queen, and to set the kingdom right. In the process, he discovers his special gift and a purpose in life. This story has strong ties to Rumpelstiltskin, since it shares riddles, finding a lost person, and discovering special gifts.

Eric Kimmel chose fairy tale style for his book, correct *Zigazak! A Magical Hanukkah Night*. The theme of good battling bad is apparent in this hilarious tale of two devils creating chaos on the first night of Hanukkah. Their magic makes dreidels dance, candles explode, and results in general chaos. However, the rabbi shows them that holiness can triumph over chaos.

The Unicorn's Secret: Moonsilver by Kathleen Duey tells the story of a girl and her unicorn. Heart, the heroine of this tale, is a foundling who is forced to work for an evil lord in this medieval setting. When Heart discovers a disfigured mare, she cares for the an-to see the dragons in a new light. In this high fantasy, the protagonist's goal changes and he strives to make peace between his people and the surviving dragons.

Brian Jacques' *Redwall* series has both heroic rodent characters and terrible villain characters in the never-ending battle between good and evil. *Triss* is the fifteenth book of this popular series. Children enjoy reading about the friendship, adventure, and mayhem of characters whose personalities seem like people they know, as well as the resolution of conflict and the fact that good prevails over chaos and peace reigns in the Abbey world.

Science fiction

What will life be like in 2050? How will we travel? Will there be colonies of earth people on Mars or some newly discovered planet? These are the kinds of themes explored in *science fiction*. In this imaginative literature, plausible events are depicted that are logical extrapolations from known facts. The story builds around events and problems that would not have happened at all without the scientific content (Gunn, 1975).

Sylvia Engdahl's *Beyond the Tomorrow Mountains* is an example of science fiction. This fantasy details the challenges of rebuilding a life in a different world after escaping an earth doomed to destruction. Lois Lowry's *The Giver* is another example of science fiction. In this book, Jonas, the protagonist, lives in a time when everything in life is controlled. Children are the same until they become Twelves, and then they are assigned to their adult jobs. Jonas is selected to receive the true memories of the pain and joy of life.

Vivien Alcock's *The Monster Garden* is splendid science fiction for children in third through fifth grade. In the story, matter produced in a young girl's father's lab grows into a kind-hearted and wise monster. However, Monny the monster suffers rejections when people in the community find her unacceptable because she is different. Her rescuer sadly releases Monny to find a better and kinder place.

Younger readers will identify with Henry P. in Jon Scieszka's *Baloney (Henry P.)*. Henry is an alien with an alien language, but he has problems just like any earth child, such as getting to school on time. When he is repeatedly late for school, the teacher rejects his complex excuse. Children may wonder what happens to an alien when his teacher punishes him.

A birthday present is magic in Eve Bunting's *Wanna Buy an Alien?* Ben's birthday space souvenirs present includes an invitation to visit the planet Cham. When a spaceship arrives near his house he faces a big decision: should he go or should he stay?

Time Magic

In time magic stories, children read about magic that moves the story to the past, or the future. Usually, a magic object launches time travel. One of my favorite time-based stories is Philippa Pearce's *Tom's Midnight Garden*. The action begins when Tom hears the grandfather clock strike 13, after which he plays with a girl who lived in the house long ago. She is actually the child who grew into the old woman who lives upstairs.

Jessie is the protagonist in Margaret Haddix's *Running Out of Time*. She is dismayed when she learns that it is not 1840, but rather 1996, and she has to venture into the future to save her friends' lives. Omri in Lynn Banks' *The Indian in the Cupboard* also ventures into the past. He discovers that a magic cupboard can change plastic toys into miniature people from the past, which leads to life and death adventures. In Mary Pope Osborne's *Dinosaur Before Dark*, Jack and Annie find a magic tree house that takes them back to the time of dinosaurs.

Elements of Fantasy

As with traditional literature, authors of fantasy use all of the normal stylistic devices to make readers believe in fantasy. They skillfully craft language that will cause readers to suspend their disbelief, inviting readers to enter their fanciful worlds. Authors must make their plots credible and consistent, and retain their inner logic, if readers are to believe in their fantasy.

Characters

Well-rounded, believable characters are essential in fantasy. To be believable, characters must be multidimensional creations who grow and develop through their experiences in the story. Meg, the protagonist in *A Wrinkle in Time*, is such a character. She is fearless at times and falters at others; nevertheless, she is courageous and determined to find her father at any cost. Meg learns lessons, changes, and develops throughout the book.

Readers come to know characters' personalities through their dialect, vocabulary, and speech rhythms. For instance, in *Eva*, Peter Dickinson creates much of the principal character's personality by revealing her thoughts. Eva awakens from a coma induced by an accident, thinking:

> Waking . . . strange . . . dream about trees? Oh, come back! Come. . . . Lost . . . . But so strange. . . Oh, darling, said Mom's voice, farther away now. There was something in it—had been all along, in spite of the happiness in the words. A difficulty, a sense of effort. (p. 35)

Dickinson creates mood through what is not said. Eva senses that something is not normal long before she or the readers realize exactly what has happened: Eva survived the accident because her brain was placed in the body of a chimpanzee. After Eva realizes that she is living in a chimpanzee's body, she thinks:

> Okay, it was better than dying, but that wasn't enough. You had to awaken and open your eyes and see your new face and like what you saw. You had to make the human greeting and the chimp greeting and mean them. (p. 31)

The principal character in a fantasy establishes the logic of the fantasy and helps readers enter into the make-believe realm by expressing a confidence and belief in the unbelievable events and characters. Eva recognizes her dilemma and suffers as she becomes more aware and must adjust to her situation. The fact that she is living in a chimpanzee's body is logical because her father is a researcher who studies them. Both the masterful characterization and Eva's reactions to the situation make readers believe.

Another technique authors use to entice readers into accepting make-believe is through characters who refuse to believe in fantasy, despite the fact that they may be fantasies themselves or at least taking part in a fantasy. In Philippa Pearce's *Tom's Midnight Garden*, strange events defy the laws of time. However, Tom has a difficult time finding a friend to discuss the words "Time No Longer" on the face of the grandfather clock. When the clock strikes 13, he finds a friend who convinces him to suspend disbelief until the mystery unfolds.

Setting

Detailed settings make readers believe in fantasy. Neil Gaiman uses graphic details in describing the characters and setting in *Coraline*. As the story unfolds, Coraline discovers a passageway to a home identical to her own, complete with two people who call themselves her "other parents." These characters look just like her parents except for the fact that their eyes are black buttons.

Peter Dickinson invites readers to believe in his stories by describing unusual characters, places, and events in detail. His skill is illustrated in *A Box of Nothing*:

> It took a whole day for the Burra's green arm to come to life again. In the meanwhile it made do with a monkey arm, which wasn't as useful. The table set firm at the same time, and the fridge out on the slope had "gone fossil." . . . By then James was almost used to eating food that cooked itself and watching a TV that switched itself off and on when it felt like it and sleeping on a living bed. (p. 47)

Plot

Characters and setting come together in an original plot to create excellent fantasy. Natalie Babbitt does this in *Tuck Everlasting*. In this story, the central characters drink from a secret spring, which allows anyone who drinks from it to live forever. The carefully drawn characters are as convincing as the setting of this make-believe world, creating a tightly wound novel.

One of the most common strategies that authors use for making a fantastic plot believable is beginning the story in reality and gradually moving into fantasy. Readers may not even realize the book is fantasy until later. Gaiman used this technique in *Coraline*. The mood is sunny and inviting when Coraline blithely explores her new neighborhood. This creates a dramatic contrast to the horror of her later environment.

Authors sometimes convince us to believe in their fantasy by having characters move back and forth between their real environment and the make-believe environment. In *Fog Magic*, Julia Sauer creates a character who lives in a normal home; however, she visits a make-believe village, Blue Cove, only when it is foggy. Philippa Pearce also uses this strategy effectively in *Tom's Midnight Garden*. Tom lives in a present-day house, but he visits in a long-ago garden and plays with an imaginary character when the old hall clock strikes 13, thus defying the natural laws of time. Tom does not realize the fantasy until he is leaving the house and garden to return.

A similar technique appears in Nicky Singer's *Feather Boy*. Robert Nobel is the central character who moves from a normal school situation to a nursing home for a class project, but then he is seized and or-

Can you imagine purchasing an Alien?

dered to walk to Chance House, an abandoned building that is haunted. Robert seems connected to the Chance House boy. The story moves back and forth between regular life and the mystic building.

Theme

Theme is a significant aspect of fantasy. Universal themes such as wishes and dreams, the struggle between good and evil, and the importance of lore are most common in modern fantasy. Symbolism is often used to help further the theme of a fantasy. In *Tuck Everlasting*, Babbitt uses Ferris wheels and other wheels as symbols of the cycle of the seasons and of life and death. The point of symbolism is that the hub of a wheel is a fixed point that is best left undisturbed, which supports Babbitt's major theme that "everlasting life can be a burden."

Style

The language authors use, which is one of the major components of style, is especially important in fantasy because authors must find a way to tell about places, things, and people that do not exist in such a way that readers will see them in their imagination. William Steig's elegant language easily accomplishes this. His animal fantasy *The Amazing Bone* tells about a "succulent" pig that "dawdled" on the way to school and seemed "destined" to become a fox's dinner. Steig always stays within the logic of his story while using his superb language styling. Pearl may talk to amazing bones, but she always remains a pig.

The point of view, determined by the person telling the story, is another aspect of style. A 12-year-old girl who travels back in time 100 years narrates *The Root Cellar*. The author, Janet Lunn, researched how people lived at that time. In Elizabeth Winthrop's *The Battle for the Castle*, two boys travel back in time to battle huge rats in order to save a palace. In the process, they learn about different kinds of courage.

The point of view, in some stories, switches from one character to another or to an omniscient storyteller. In *Wonderful Alexander and the Catwings*, Ursula K. Le Guin uses an omniscient point of view to tell about kittens who are born with wings that permit them to escape the city slums. The point of view changes when they go to the country and find children who will cherish them.

Selecting Fantasy

When selecting fantasy for your classroom, consider the following factors in addition to the guidelines for all literature.

1. Does it tell a good story?
2. What are the elements of fantasy in this story (e.g., setting, magic powers, time, etc.)?
3. How is this story different from the real world?
4. How has the author made the story believable?
5. What is the theme of this fantasy?

Fantasy in Classrooms

Reading aloud from fine fantasy develops children's appreciation for this genre; therefore, choose fantasies that have the broadest appeal and that are a good "read." A delightful read-aloud for younger listeners is Lloyd Alexander's *The Fortune-Tellers*. Children like the witty characters and the fortune-teller's interesting prophesies, as well as looking at the vivid, detailed illustrations. Another great read-aloud is Deborah and James Howe's *Bunnicula*. Harold, a dog who observed this story, wrote this hilarious book. After a rabbit arrives in the home, vegetables begin to appear that have been drained of their juices. The plot thickens when Chester the cat concludes that Bunnicula is a vampire rabbit and sets out to protect the family from a vampire attack.

Readers in the fifth and sixth grades enjoy the originality of plot and character in William J. Brooke's short stories featured in *Untold Tales*. One of the stories is a clever play, "A Prince in the Throat." The science-fiction piece "Into the Computer" is an entertaining and challenging story. Middle-grade readers who like ghost stories will like Patricia McKissack's *The Dark-Thirty: Southern Tales of the Supernatural*. These stories stir the imagination but are not so gruesome as to make children fearful.

Classroom Activities

More than other genre, fantasy needs to be introduced and read aloud. Introductions explain the context of the story and encourage listeners to predict story events.

ACTIVITY 7.1   FIND THE MAGIC

(IRA/NCTE Standards: 1,2,3. Comprehension, read a wide range of print and genre.)

The purpose of this activity is to identify the magic in a fantasy book. This activity can be conducted with individuals or groups. Younger students may work with one fantasy, while intermediate-grade students may compare various books.

Book: *The Amulet of Komondor* by A. Osterweil, Front Street, 2003.

Character/s	Setting	Magic	Plot	Theme
Joe and Katie	Strange mall store	DragonSteel game that transports them to Komondor via a CD	After buying a game, children have a hilarious trip to Komondor where they have to locate the five pieces needed for the game, so they can win and quit playing.	Good vs. evil; family and friendship

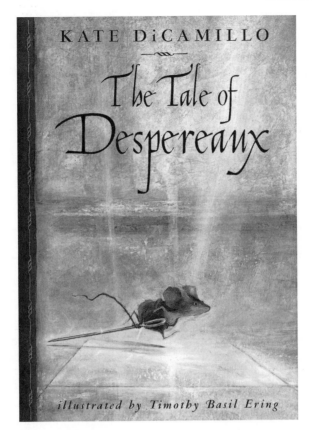

Despereaux is a popular read-aloud.

ACTIVITY 7.2   STORY INTERPRETATION

(IRA/NCTE Standard: 3. Comprehension.)

A discussion that includes questions like the following will help children comprehend fantasy.

Book Title _____

1. Who are the characters?
2. Describe the protagonist.
3. Where does the story take place?
4. When does the story take place?
5. What is the magic in this story?
6. What is the story's theme?

ACTIVITY 7.3   READING JOURNALS

(IRA/NCTE Standard: 4. Oral language/communication.)

Reading journals are important vehicles to facilitate children's response to fantasy, as well as other genres. At the close of each reading session, the students summarize and respond to the reading completed that day by writing in their journals. In addition to writing about what they read and responding to the reading, students should include any questions they have for subsequent discussions and identify words and phrases that are new to them or that need further exploration. Reading journals can be used during discussions to refresh their memory.

ACTIVITY 7.4   INQUIRIES

(IRA/NCTE Standards: 3, 4, 5, 7. Research, apply range of strategies, communication, and writing process.)

Exploring a topic or theme develops the children's response to fantasy. An inquiry may explore the fantastic elements such as time travel, miniature worlds, futuristic settings, and other strange happenings. Through comparing the plot, theme, characterization, setting, and style, students achieve a greater understanding and appreciation for fantasy. Other units may be developed around books with themes of peace, good versus evil, or other common fantasy ideas. Group or class charts can compare thematic development in different works.

An example of a topical study about dragons follows. We selected the topic of dragons because it can be developed with children of different ages. Additionally, most dragon books are in the fantasy genre, which is our focus. The objective of this study is to identify the element or elements of the impossible that the author created. Intermediate-grade students will extend this goal to include the strategy that authors use to make readers believe the impossible.

Introduction

Preview the read-alouds by asking what the children know about dragons. Show the students pictures of dragons, which you can locate in art books and from various museums' Web sites. The CD-ROM *The Dragon in Chinese Art* (CDR Software ed., 1998; C/W95/ww) is also very useful.

Ask primary-grade children if they have ever discovered anything exciting on a walk or while they were playing. Ask intermediate-grade students if they have ever seen a dragon dance or a dragon in art. After discussion, read aloud *Raising Dragons* for primary-grade students and *Behold... the Dragons!* to intermediate-grade students.

Discussion Questions: Primary Grades

1. What is the best part of this story? Why do you think that?
2. Which character is your favorite? Why?
3. Do you think you could find a dragon egg?
4. Would you like to have a dragon of your own? Why or why not?
5. How do you know this story is make-believe (fantasy)?
6. What did you learn from this story?
7. How did the author make you like the story?
8. Art and writing:
   A. The children could draw pictures of their own dragons and dragon eggs.
   B. They could write about the things they would do with a dragon as a friend.
   C. They could draw pictures of ways that dragons could help them.
9. Music and dance: Look up Chinese dragon dancing on the Internet.

Books for Further Study: Primary Grades

- *Dragon School* by Cara J. Cooperman
- *Aja's Dragon* by Diane Fisher
- *Dragon Poems* by John Foster
- *Custard the Dragon and the Wicked Knight* by Ogden Nash
- *Dragon's Fat Cat: Dragon's Fourth Tale* by Dav Pilkey
- *Elvira* by Margaret Shannon
- *Chin Chiang and the Dragon's Dance* by Ian Wallace

Discussion Questions: Intermediate Grades

1. Do you believe in dragons? Why or why not?
2. Where do dragons come from?
3. What new facts did you learn from *Behold . . . the Dragons!*?
4. Why are dragons so popular?
5. Why do you think dragons are important in so many cultures?
6. What mechanical things can be compared to dragons?
7. Do you think dragons are real? Why or why not?
8. Art and music: After studying dragon dancing, have the children do a dragon dance.
9. Social studies: Discuss the types of dragons found in the art, dance, and music of different cultures. How do they differ? How are they similar? Have the children create their own artistic expressions of dragons.
10. Inquiry: Ask the students to brainstorm and come up with questions they would like to study about dragons.
11. Literature: Have the students read at least one additional book about dragons, then discuss the fantasy in the book and the writer's strategies for creating fantasy.

Books for Further Study: Intermediate Grades

- *The Dragonslayers* by Bruce Coville
- *Dragon's Milk* by Susan Fletcher
- *The Reluctant Dragon* by Kenneth Grahame
- *The Book of Dragons* by Michael Hague
- *The Dragon of Lonely Island* by Rebecca Rupp
- *The Care and Feeding of Dragons* by Brenda Seabrooke
- *Backyard Dragon* by Betsy and Samuel Sterman
- *American Dragons: Twenty-Five Asian American Voices* by Laurence Yep

---

ACTIVITY 7.5   DISCUSSION

(IRA/NCTE Standards: 1, 2, 3, 5. Comprehension and oral language.)

Class discussion of fantasy is important to building children's understanding and response. Through discussion, students achieve a greater understanding and appreciation for fantasy.

Instead of leading the discussion, you may prefer to participate as a group member and let the students take turns starting the discussion, using significant questions such as, "What do you think?" and "Why do you think this?" The students may have enough questions in their journals to stimulate the discussion. However, they may need help in coming up with good open-ended discussion questions such as:

- What do you predict will happen next in the story?
- What did you learn about the characters, setting, and other parts of the story in today's reading?
- What experiences of your own did you remember in relation to today's reading?
- What other books could you compare this one to? Another approach is for students to individually complete discussion webs such as the one shown in Figure 7.1.

FIGURE 7.1   Example of a discussion web.

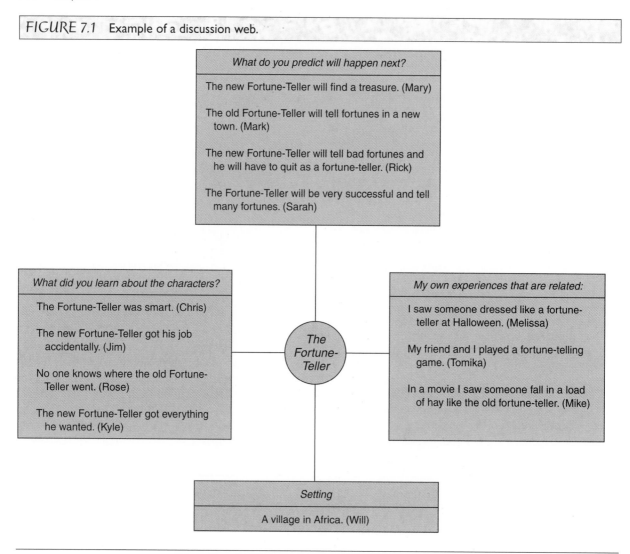

What do you predict will happen next?

The new Fortune-Teller will find a treasure. (Mary)

The old Fortune-Teller will tell fortunes in a new town. (Mark)

The new Fortune-Teller will tell bad fortunes and he will have to quit as a fortune-teller. (Rick)

The Fortune-Teller will be very successful and tell many fortunes. (Sarah)

What did you learn about the characters?

The Fortune-Teller was smart. (Chris)

The new Fortune-Teller got his job accidentally. (Jim)

No one knows where the old Fortune-Teller went. (Rose)

The new Fortune-Teller got everything he wanted. (Kyle)

The Fortune-Teller

My own experiences that are related:

I saw someone dressed like a fortune-teller at Halloween. (Melissa)

My friend and I played a fortune-telling game. (Tomika)

In a movie I saw someone fall in a load of hay like the old fortune-teller. (Mike)

Setting

A village in Africa. (Will)

Summary

Modern fantasy is the literature of imagination. Fantasy has magic that developed through events, objects, characters, time, and places. Fantasy is categorized into animal fantasy, literary fairy tales, enchanted realism, science fiction, and time magic.

The themes of fantasy are often concerned with the age-old battle between good and evil. Fantasy touches our deepest feelings, and in so doing, it speaks to the best and most hopeful parts of ourselves. It can help us learn the most fundamental skill of all—how to be human (Alexander, 1991, p. 43). The abstract, imaginative nature of fantasy educates children's imagina-tion, but children are more likely to appreciate it when teachers introduce the stories and read them aloud.

Thought Questions

1. What are the major characteristics of high fantasy?
2. How can teachers motivate children to read fantasy?
3. What are the major characteristics of fantasy?
4. Compare fantasy with fiction.
5. What are fantasy's values for children?

Research and Application Experiences

1. Develop a book-talk for introducing fantasy to a group of children.

2. Interview children at various grade levels and ask them to identify which fantasy books they have enjoyed. Ask them what they like about the particular books they enjoy.

3. Interview teachers, asking them to tell how many fantasies they read in one year to their class. What conclusions can you draw from this information?

4. Read a fantasy to a group of children or a class and then discuss the book. Tape the discussion so you can analyze its strengths and weaknesses.

5. Create a bibliography of fantasies for a selected grade level.

Children's Literature References and Recommended Books

Note: Books designated with an asterisk (*) are recommended for reluctant readers.

Alcock, V. (1988). *The monster garden*. New York: Delacorte. (3–6). FANTASY.*

Frankie discovers an experimental matter sample that she grows into a baby monster. She then has to be responsible for its well-being.

Alexander, L. (1992). *The Fortune Tellers* (T. S. Hyman, Illus.). New York: Dutton. (K–5). TRADITIONAL LITERATURE. *

The Fortune-Teller prophesies for his customers.

Andersen, H. C. (1986). *The emperor's new clothes* (D. Duntze, Illus.). New York: North South Books. (2–5). FANTASY.

The king shows off his new clothes, but only one boy points out that he actually has no clothes on.

Andersen, H. C. (1992). *The steadfast tin soldier* (F. Marcellino, Illus.). New York: HarperCollins. (K–3). FANTASY.

The story of a tin soldier's love for a paper doll.

Avi. (1999). *Ragweed* (B. Floca, Illus.). New York; Avon. (3–6). FANTASY.

Ragweed is the story of a field mouse who decides to explore the world and finds it can be a frightening place. This is part of the Dimwood Forest Series.

Avi. (2000). *Erth's birthday* (B. Floca, Illus.). New York: HarperCollins. (3–6). FANTASY.

Erth, a crotchey old porcupine, goes into the woods because his friends forgot his birthday. He unexpectedly becomes guardian for fox kits. This is a great read-aloud story.

Babbitt, N. (1975). *Tuck everlasting*. New York: Farrar, Straus & Giroux. (4–7). FANTASY.

Winnie Foster runs away from her parents and meets the Tucks, all of whom have drunk from the spring of everlasting life.

Banks, L. R. (1981). *The Indian in the cupboard*. New York: Doubleday. (4–6). FANTASY.

Omri's magic cupboard brings a toy Indian to life, which is the beginning of exciting life and death adventures. The themes emerging from this story are friendship, responsibility, and the importance of making serious decisions.

Baum, L. F. (1987). *The wonderful wizard of Oz*. New York: Morrow. (4–8). FANTASY.

Originally published in 1900, this book has been called the "first American fantasy." The land of Oz is inhabited by the Tin Man, the Scarecrow, the Cowardly Lion, and Dorothy.

Bond, M. (1960). *A bear called Paddington* (P. Fortnum, Illus.). Boston: Houghton Mifflin. (K–2). FANTASY.

A bear from darkest Peru visits London.

Brooke, W. J. (1992). *Untold tales*. New York: HarperCollins. (5–9). FANTASY.

A collection of short stories that build on clever wordplay and traditions.

Bunting, E. (2000). *Wanna Buy an Alien?* New York: Clarion. (3–6). SCIENCE FICTION.*

Ben's unusual birthday present creates problems. Part of the present is an invitation to visit an alien planet. When a spaceship lands to pick him up, he has to decide whether or not to go.

Byars, B. (2002). *Little Horse*. New York: Holt. (1–3). FANTASY.*

Little Horse accidentally falls into a stream and washes away from home. He discovers that he is small, lost, and lonely during his adventure.

Cooperman, C. J. (1997). *Dragon school* (J. Pierard, Illus.). New York: Pocket Books. (K–4). FANTASY.

Dragons have to learn how to be dragons in this school.

Coville, B. (1994). *Into the land of the unicorns*. New York: Scholastic. (3–6). FANTASY.

Cara's grandmother convinces her to jump into space and into the land of the unicorns where she discovers that she must save the unicorns from extinction.

Coville, B. (1995). *The dragonslayers* (K. Coville, Illus.). New York: Pocket. (3–6). FANTASY.

Princess Wilhelmina wants to kill a dragon to save her kingdom, so the feisty heroine goes on the mission in disguise.

Dahl, R. (1964). *Charlie and the chocolate factory* (J. Schindelman, Illus.). New York: Knopf. (2–6). FANTASY.

These unusual characters have vices that lead to their downfall.

Dickinson, P. (1985). *A box of nothing*. New York: Delacorte. (3–5). FANTASY.

James purchases a box of nothing for $0.00 in the Nothing Shop.

Dickinson, P. (1988). *Eva*. New York: Delacorte. (6–9). FANTASY.

The principal character survives an accident when her brain is implanted in the body of a chimp.

Duey, K. (2002). *The unicorn's secret: Moonsilver*. New York: Simon & Schuster. (3–6). FANTASY.

Heart adopts a mare that has a unicorn foal.

Engdahl, S. L. (1973). *Beyond the tomorrow mountains* (R. Cuffari, Illus.). New York: Atheneum. (4–8). FANTASY.

The story of a young man who is born after the earth is doomed to destruction.

Fisher, D. (1999). *Aja's dragon* (M. Levy, Illus.). New York: Mercury. (K–2). FANTASY.

Aja finds a colorful egg which he takes to school for show and tell. A bubble-blowing dragon hatches from the egg in his classroom.

Fleischman, P. (1999). *Westlandia* (K. Hawkes, Illus.). New York: Candlewick. (3–6). FANTASY.

Wesley creates a world in his back yard during summer vacation. Through this experience he finds a level of appreciation and social acceptance.

Fletcher, S. (1996). *Dragon's milk*. New York: Aladdin Paperbacks. (3–6). FANTASY.

The dragons in this book are capable of being good and loving. They have well-developed characters.

Foster, J. (Ed.). (1997). *Dragon poems* (K. Paul, Illus.). New York: Oxford University Press. (K–4). POETRY.

A collection of poems about dragons.

Gaiman, N. (2002). *Coraline*. New York: Harper-Collins. (4–7). FANTASY.

Coraline and her parents move to a new apartment and she discovers another identical apartment inhabited by people who look like her parents, except for their black button eyes.

Grahame, K. (1988). *The reluctant dragon* (M. Hague, Illus.). New York: Holt. (3–6). FANTASY.

The dragon in this story is lonely and wants to make friends. This is a simplified version of this wonderful story that may motivate students to read the original.

Haddix, M. (1997). *Running out of time*. New York: Alladin. (5–8). FANTASY.

A young girl tries to save her family from a deadly disease.

Haddix, M. P. (1998). *Among the hidden*. New York: Simon & Schuster. (4–6). FANTASY.

In a society where families are allowed to have only two children, a third child escapes discovery in an attic.

Hague, M. (Selector). (1995). *The book of dragons*. New York: Morrow. (3–6). FANTASY.

This is a wide-ranging collection of dragon stories.

Howe, D., & Howe, J. (1979). *Bunnicula* (A. Daniel, Illus.). New York: Atheneum. (3–5). FANTASY.

This is the story of a vampire rabbit.

Hurwitz, J. (2000). *PeeWee's tale* (P. Brewster, Illus.). New York: SeaStar. (1–3). FANTASY.

PeeWee, a guinea pig, survives in the wild with the help of a savvy squirrel. His reading skills are also helpful.

Ibbotson, E. (2000). *Island of the aunts* (K. Hawkes, Illus.). New York: Dutton. (4–6). FANTASY.

Three elderly aunts fear that no one will be left to carry on their legacy of caring for the magical and mystical animals they have rescued, so they make a plan.

Jacques, B. (1998). *Redwall*. London, England: Ace Books. (3–6). FANTASY.

The mice of Redwall battle Cluny the evil rat.

Key, A. (1965). *The forgotten door*. Philadelphia: Westminster. (4–6). FANTASY.*

A strange boy with unusual powers appears in a farming community. He seems to have come out of nowhere.

Kimmel, E. (2001). *Zigazak! A magical Hanukkah night* (J. Goodell, Illus.). New York: Doubleday. (1–3). FANTASY.

Two mischievous devils create chaos in this hilarious tale. They have a battle of wills with a crafty rabbi. Good overcomes the bad in this great read-aloud.

Koller, J. F. (1990). *The dragonling* (J. Mitchel, Illus.). New York: Little Brown. (3–5). FANTASY.

Darek hopes to slay a dragon until he discovers a baby dragon and nurtures it.

L'Engle, M. (1962). *A wrinkle in time*. New York: Farrar, Straus & Giroux. (5–8). FANTASY.

Meg and her brother set out to find their lost father and discover they must journey through time to find him.

Le Guin, U. (1988). *Wonderful Alexander and the Catwings*. (S. D. Schindler, Illus.). New York: Orchard. (1–3). FANTASY.

These wonderful cats can fly.

Lester, H. (1994). *Three cheers for Tacky* (L. Munsinger, Illus.). Boston: Houghton Mifflin. (1–3). FANTASY.*

Tacky the penguin is a bumbling character who tries to achieve greater skill through practice. His friends appreciate his individuality.

Lowry, L. (1993). *The giver*. Boston: Houghton Mifflin. (4–7). FANTASY.

This science fiction story is about a world where everything is under outside control. When the children become Twelves, they are assigned their adult jobs.

Lunn, J. (1983). *The root cellar*. New York: Scribner's. (4–8). FANTASY.

Twelve-year-old Rose is sent to live with her aunt in a country home on the shores of Lake Ontario where she discovers an overgrown root cellar.

Meddaugh, S. (2002). *Lu lu's hat*. New York: Houghton Mifflin. (3–5). FANTASY.

Lulu is adopted by a family of magicians.

McKissack, P. C. (1992). *The dark-thirty: Southern tales of the supernatural* (B. Pinkney, Illus.). New York: Knopf. (2–6). TRADITION LITERATURE.

A collection of scary stories.

Milne, A. A. (1926). *Winnie-the-pooh* (E. H. Shepard, Illus.). New York: Dutton. (PreK–4). FANTASY.

Classic stories of a bear who gets into great difficulties.

Nash, O. (1999). *Custard the dragon and the wicked knight* (L. Munsinger, Illus.). Boston: Little Brown. (K–2). POETRY.

Nash's funny story of a dragon and the knight who would defeat him.

Nolen, J. (1998). *Raising dragons* (E. Primavera, Illus.). New York: Silver Whistle. (K–3). FANTASY.

During a Sunday before-supper walk, a little girl discovers an egg that hatches into a baby dragon and becomes her best friend.

Osborne, M. P. (1992). *Dinosaur before dark*. New York: Random House. (2–4). FANTASY.

Jack and Annie discover a tree house that takes them to a time when dinosaurs lived.

Paul, A. (1995). *The tiger who lost his stripes* (M. Foreman, Illus.). New York: Harcourt. (PreK–2). TRADITIONAL LITERATURE.

General MacTiger awakens from a nap to discover that Python has stolen his stripes, and he must bargain with various animals to get them back.

Pearce, P. (1958). *Tom's midnight garden* (S. Einzig, Illus.). Philadelphia: Lippincott. (4–7). FANTASY.

A time fantasy that won the British Carnegie Medal. Tom is visiting an old house and discovers both a clock that strikes 13 and a mysterious garden.

Pilkey, D. (1992). *Dragon's fat cat: Dragon's fourth tale*. New York: Orchard. (K–2). FANTASY.*

A lovable dragon loses his cat and finds it again. This is a very popular story with young children.

Rowling, J. K. (1999). *Harry Potter and the prisoner of Azkaban*. New York: Levine. (4–8). FANTASY.

Harry Potter, a wizard, attends Hogwarts School of Witchcraft and Wizardry and is forced to spend summer vacations with his aunt, uncle, and cousin who detest him. The preceding books in this series are *Harry Potter and the Chamber of Secrets, Harry Potter and the Sorcerer's Stone, Harry Potter and the Goblet of Fire,* and *Harry Potter and the Order of the Phoenix.*

Rupp, R. (1998). *The dragon of Lonely Island* (W. Minor, Illus.). New York: Candlewick. (3–6). FANTASY.

Three children are on summer vacation with their mother when they discover a three-headed dragon. Each head tells an enthralling story.

Sauer, J. L. (1963). *Fog magic* (L. Ward, Illus.). New York: Viking. (4–6). FANTASY.

Ten-year-old Greta discovers the village of Blue Cove, only to realize that it exists only in the fog.

Sciezka, J. (2001). *Baloney (Henry P.)* (L. Smith, Illus.). New York: Viking. (1–3). SCIENCE FICTION, FANTASY.

Henry P. is an alien boy who faces an angry teacher because he is once again tardy to alien school.

Seabrooke, B. (1998). *The care and feeding of dragons*. New York: Cobblehill. (K–4). FANTASY.

Spike the dragon saves his human family from evildoers in this hilarious story.

Schmidt, G. (2001). *Straw into gold*. New York: Clarion. (3–6). FANTASY.

Tousle is a magical man who has special powers in this adventure reminiscent of Rumpelstiltskin.

Shannon, M. (1993). *Elvira*. New York: Ticknor & Fields. (1–3). FANTASY.

Elvira is an unusual dragon who prefers to avoid eating people.

Singer, N. (2002). *Feather boy*. New York: Delacorte. (5–8). FANTASY.

Robert Nobel leaves school to participate in a school project, but he is seized and forced to go to Chance House, which is haunted. His adventures begin there.

Steig, W. (1976). *The amazing bone*. New York: Farrar, Straus & Giroux. (2–4). FANTASY.

A succulent pig and a talking bone outwit a wily fox.

Sterman, B., & Sterman, S. (1993). *Backyard dragon* (D. Wenzel, Illus.). New York: HarperCollins. (3–6). FANTASY.

Children have an imaginary dragon in the backyard.

Wallace, I. (1984). *Chin Chiang and the dragon's dance*. New York: Atheneum. (K–2). INFORMATIONAL BOOK.

This book explains the Chinese dragon dance and includes excellent photographs.

Winthrop, E. (1993). *The battle for the castle*. New York: Holiday House. (4–6). FANTASY.

Two boys travel back to medieval times where they help battle large rats to save the castle.

Yep, L. (Ed.). (1995). *American dragons: Twenty-five Asian American voices*. New York: HarperCollins. (5–8). CONTEMPORARY REALISTIC FICTION, POETRY.

A collection of literature related to dragons.

References and Books for Further Reading

Alexander, L. (1991). The grammar of story. In B. Hearne & M. Kaye (Eds.), *Celebrating children's books* (pp. 3–13). New York: Lothrop, Lee & Shepard.

Britton, J. (1977). The role of fantasy. In M. Meek, A. Worlow, & G. Barton (Eds.), *The cool web: The pattern of children's reading*. London: Bodley Head.

Cameron, E. (1993). *The seed and the vision: On the writing and appreciation of children's books*. New York: Dutton.

Cook, E. (1969). *The ordinary and the fabulous*. Cambridge, England: Cambridge University Press.

Eisner, E. (1992). The misunderstood role of the arts in human development. *Phi Delta Kappan, 8*, 591–595.

Greenlaw, M. J. (1995). Fantasy. In A. Silvey (Ed.) *Children's books and their creators* (pp 234–236). Boston: Houghton Mifflin.

Greenlaw, M. J. (2001). Fantasy. In A. Silvey (Ed.), *Children's books and their creators* (pp. 234–236). Boston: Houghton Mifflin.

Gunn, J. (1975). *Alternative worlds: The illustrated history of science fiction.* Upper Saddle River, NJ: Prentice Hall. A & W Visual Library.

Hearne, B. (1999). *Choosing books for children: A commonsense approach.* New York: Delacorte.

Langton, J. (1977). The weak place in the cloth: A study of fantasy for children. In P. Heins (Ed.), *Crosscurrents of criticism: Horn Book essays 1968–1977* (pp. 143–159). Boston: Horn Book.

Le Guin, U. K. (1979). National book award acceptance speech. In S. Wood (Ed.), *The language of the night: Essays of fantasy and science fiction* (pp. 60–61). New York: Putnam.

Shlain, L. (1990). *Art and physics: Parallel visions in space, time and light.* New York: Morrow.

Smith, F. (1988). *Joining the Literacy Club: Further essays into education.* Portsmouth, NH: Heinemann.

Sutherland, Z., & Livingston, M. C. (1984). *The Scott/Foresman anthology of children's literature* (8th ed.). Chicago: Scott Foresman.

Swanton, S. (1984, March). Minds alive! What and why gifted students read for pleasure. *School Library Journal, 30,* 99–102.

Whited, L. (2002). *The ivory tower and Harry Potter: Perspectives on a literary phenomenon.* University of Missouri Press.

Woolsey, D. (2002). Fantasy literature. In A. McClare and J. V. Kristo (Eds.), *Adventuring with books.* (pp. 278–297). Urbana, IL: National Council of Teachers of English.

People Now: Contemporary Realistic Fiction 8

KEY TERMS

alternative family
structure

coming-of-age books

didacticism

contemporary realistic
fiction

series books

GUIDING QUESTIONS

Think about the following questions as you read through this chapter. Then, as you read contemporary realistic fiction books, try to identify with the characters and their issues and problems.

1. Can you make connections between any of the issues and problems presented in these realistic books and issues and problems that you may have experienced growing up?

2. Do you know any young people who are currently facing some of these problems?

3. What might be the reasons for putting contemporary characters in such a wide variety of settings?

4. Why is realistic fiction so popular with many readers?

Contemporary realistic fiction and historical fiction (Chapter 9) both describe events, people, and relationships as they actually might have happened. In these stories, problems are solved through hard work, persistence, and determined efforts rather than magic, as in fantasy. No fantastic elements, no magical spells, and no supernatural powers appear in this type of fiction. However, we do find occasional serendipities—because truth is often stranger than fiction. The characters succeed or fail as a result of their own strengths or weaknesses.

Contemporary realistic fiction addresses problems that are often faced in the real world. Readers can learn about the problems and the tragedies—and sometimes the comedies—of growing and living in today's world. As they identify with the characters, readers can walk in another person's shoes to learn about new experiences and situations.

As children and young adults read contemporary realistic fiction, they have opportunities to:

- gain insights about people and events that occur in the current time;
- learn how current events may influence young people;
- become aware of the similarities of the human spirit in all contexts; and
- experience the ways that people have survived and learned from their challenges.

Contemporary Realistic Fiction

The challenge for writers of realistic fiction is to combine characters, contemporary events, and actions in such a way as to create a memorable story with a theme that appeals to readers. The most memorable stories allow readers to identify with the characters' feelings. Perhaps most importantly, they are characters that readers care about. Creating believable events and settings make readers drawn into seeking resolution to the problems presented. The themes need to be ones that we care about; in other words, they need to be universal so readers can connect them with their own lives.

Furthermore, authors of *contemporary realistic fiction* must be committed to telling the truth. Fine literature portrays honest interpretations of events, characters, and conflicts. After all, "The world has not spared children hunger, cold, sorrow, pain, fear, loneliness, disease, death, war, famine, or madness. Why should we hesitate to make use of this knowledge when writing for them?" (Steele, 1973, p. 290). A growing number of people, however, believe that books for children and young adults need to be censored—or at least rewritten—to protect the children from the harsh realities portrayed or because the ideas conflict with their view of the world.

Robert Burch (1973) disagrees, stating,

> "If we could guarantee children that the world out there would be completely safe, then fine, we could afford to give them only stories that leave the impression. But until we can, in whatever we present as being realistic, is it not cheating for it to be otherwise?" (p. 284).

Well-written realistic fiction gives an honest depiction of life as perceived by the author. Young people, no less than adults, experience the effects of cruelty, war, segregation, separation, and a multitude of other stresses. How characters in these books deal with difficult issues can give readers insight for recognizing and dealing with conflicts that they may face in

VIGNETTE

During the fourth-grade team of teachers' weekly planning meeting, they discussed how the week had been particularly frustrating because of the upcoming holidays. Nora observed, "The kids simply did not want to read this week. All they wanted to do was talk."

Marty added, "I just read an article about reluctant readers—and our kids certainly have been reluctant recently. The article suggested that series books sometimes will get some kids reading when the award-winning books will not. The stories are predictable, the characters are not complex, and they seem to make reading easier."

Alice reminisced, "I remember reading the *Cherry Ames* books when I was a kid. They were my favorite books for about a year. Then I read a series of mysteries before I 'graduated' to award-winning books. I still like to read an occasional mystery, just for fun."

Always the pragmatist, Nora responded, "Using series books for the next couple of weeks sounds like a good idea to me. I'll bet, too, that some of the standards we need to meet could be accomplished by using series books. Let's plan activities we could use with them for the next few weeks." (See activities at the end of this chapter.)

their lives. Books can give them a vision of a better world as well as a vision of how they can be a part of changing their own world. One of the distinguishing characteristics of contemporary realistic fiction for children and young adults is the message of hope and the possibility that is always present. Even though life may be hard, survival and the possibility of better

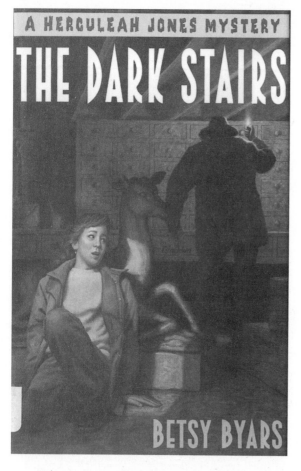

This story is in the popular Herculah Jones mystery series.

things are never out of the question. People, especially young people, need hope to be able to sustain the will to live, and contemporary realistic fiction encourages positive expectations of fulfillment. "Writings for young people are about maturing in the real world. The important thing is that things do change; whatever is can be made better" (Hamilton, 1992, p. 678).

Realistic fiction does not only deal with "heavy" issues, but also includes many books with non–life-threatening problems that authors deal with sensitively and with compassion—often with a touch of humor and lighhheartedness. For example, in *The Real True Dulcie Campbell,* Cynthia DeFelice presents Dulcie, who knows that she shouldn't be living on the farm because she is really a princess. After she retreats to her royal palace (the barn) to read, she begins to realize that maybe the life of a princess is not as great as it may

first appear and that home is a good place to be. Beverly Cleary's book *Ramona's World* is superb realistic fiction that focuses on the ever-feisty Ramona, a fourth grader adjusting to a baby sister.

This genre includes many *"series" books,* which satisfy the needs of readers to simply relax and enjoy a good read. Some examples of series books include Bill Cosby's popular *Little Bill* series, Karen Hesse's fine *Red Feather* series (*Lavender* is an example), and the *Babysitters Club* series by Ann Martin.

Similarities and Differences Between Contemporary and Historical Realistic Fiction

Although historical fiction and contemporary realistic fiction are different genres, they have many common features. Understanding these shared features is imporatant if one wants to classify some books into one genre or the other. Their *shared* characteristics include:

1. The plot contains events and incidents that could actually occur in the particular setting of the book. These events and incidents are possible, but need not be probable (Russell, 1994).
2. The characters demonstrate both strengths and weaknesses in their actions. They are not perfect.
3. The language used is typical of the language used in the setting, either in the past or the present.
4. The theme is one that readers can relate to. They can make connections between the ideas in the book and their own lives.

The primary *difference* between historical and contemporary realistic fiction is the setting. Historical fiction is set in a time other than the present. (See the section When Does the Present Become the Past? in Chapter 9.) Since the previous characteristics hold true in well-written historical fiction as well as in contemporary realistic fiction, sometimes classification into one genre or the other is difficult and depends on the reader's view.

Issues in Both Contemporary and Historical Realistic Fiction

Many adults do not understand the use of graphic reality as portrayed in some realistic fiction, and this is an important issue to consider for those who choose literature for children and young adults. Harris et al. (2001) found that preservice teachers tended to be conservative and did not introduce books into their classrooms that might be complex or controversial. However, many times teachers may be the only adults a student will trust, so it seems that teachers at least need to be familiar with books that portray important issues. Certainly, no books are "right" or "wrong" in and of themselves; the issue is whether a specific book is right or wrong for a specific reader. This implies that the adult should be familiar with both the book and the reader before making a recommendation.

Didacticism

Didacticism, or presenting obvious, heavy-handed moral messages or instructions, alienates many readers. Some authors find realistic fiction an irresistible platform for sharing their beliefs and values. Some believe young people lack values and should be taught through didactic literature. The issue here is not a concern for the specific values espoused, but the way in which they are presented. One of the differences between well-written fiction and poorly written fiction is the way beliefs and values are expressed. In well-written fiction, the beliefs and values are implicit. They emerge from the characters' actions, conversations, and decisions. In poorly written fiction, the theme or message gets in the way of the story itself.

Susan Sharp (1992) suggests, "It is the values and ideas we think children might miss if we don't assert them that leads us into didactic stories, [however,] in the works of the greatest writers, unresolved issues can make the best stories" (p. 696). Because didacticism usually alienates readers, we recommend avoiding didactic books when selecting or recommending literature.

Anne Devereaux Jordan (1997a) sums up the important issues relating not only to didacticism but also to realistic fiction in general:

> While realistic fiction is useful in conveying messages to readers, the reason to choose a particular book should be because it is well-written and pleasing to read; it enhances the reading experience. If we review the history of realistic fiction, we see that these are the books that have claimed the hearts of children generation after generation. Similarly, the books we have carried with us into adulthood are those that still delight us and reveal insights into our humanity at any age rather than being a sermon about a particular problem topical only during our youth. This is not to say that the

moral tale, or, today, the problem novel does not have a place, but that it must be recommended—unlike the rod of earlier days—sparingly if we are to develop a love of reading in young people. (p. 57)

Values Expressed in Realistic Fiction

Values portrayed in many realistic fiction books can be a major issue in children's literature. In Chapter 1 we introduced this issue, which cannot be resolved in a simple fashion. Certainly authors express values one way or another every time they write. Knowing this places greater responsibility on the adults who guide the reading of children and young adults. An open marketplace of ideas encourages children to think critically and express their own values. Certainly this multifaceted issue is an ongoing concern, and values are an especially important issue in realistic fiction. The depiction of families has moved from what was, at one time, seen as the typical family of two parents, children, pets, and grandparents close by to single-parent families, unwed mothers, and alcoholic family members. Should we pretend that these families and issues do not exist or should authors present a realistic picture of society today? Should authors allow the characters in children's books to use profanity? Would Gilly, the foster child in *The Great Gilly Hopkins*, be the same character if she did not use some profanity? The author, Katherine Paterson, is a minister's wife and the daughter of missionaries. She has Gilly use profanity as the way to demonstrate Gilly's characteristics; no amount of description would be as effective. No matter what the arguments are in favor of such realism or who writes it, some parents may object if their children are allowed to read books in which profanity is used.

Violence

Violence is an issue throughout our society and the depiction of violence in realistic fiction is a concern in selecting literature. Although violence appears in all genres of children's literature, it seems to appear most frequently in contemporary and historical realistic fiction, as well as in traditional literature. (See Chapter 6 for a discussion of violence in traditional literature.)

Can children's books exclude violence while realistically portraying life? Walter Dean Myers includes guns, gangs, and violence in his book *Scorpions* and depicts teachers and principals in a negative light. Nevertheless, this is a too-good-to-miss book that raises important issues for children in Grades 4 through 8. The author writes out of his own experience, which may be a reality for many youngsters in contemporary society.

The issue of violence in realistic historical fiction may also be a concern to some adults who choose books for readers. For example, the 2003 Newbery Award winner *Crispin,* by Avi, is set in fourteenth-century England. Violence was commonplace then and is included as an integral part of the plot.

Types of Realistic Fiction

The categories of realistic fiction in this section emerged from the literature itself in answer to this question: Is the struggle one in which the focus is on the main character's growth and development and in which the setting is almost incidental, or is the reason for the problem the result of societal events? Three broad categories emerged from the literature: (a) families, (b) challenges from outside the family, and (c) books to meet special interests. We developed subcategories based on the types of problems or themes within the books. We also found books that describe children with challenges—learning problems, emotional disabilities, physical handicaps, and so forth; these are described in Chapter 12.

Families

Stories grow out of authors' experiences and are greatly influenced by the times and values of the society in which they write. Taxel (1994) states, "Like other cultural artifacts, children's literature is a product of convention that it is rooted in, if not determined by, the dominant belief systems and ideologies of the times in which they are created" (p. 99). Family structure in books, both past and present, gives evidence of these belief systems and values.

Nuclear families

Although many families no longer consist of two parents and their children, this is still society's norm. Not surprisingly, then, we see this structure mirrored in numerous books. For some children and adults, these books confirm the belief that families provide needed support and guidance as children mature. Books in which the family interactions are the focus of the story have many variations. They range from "happily ever after" books to those with less-optimistic endings.

Beverly Cleary's books have a longstanding popularity with children and adults, and children can easily identify with many of the situations she presents. In *Beezus and Ramona,* Beezus learns that having bad thoughts about a pesky little sister who always seems to get her own way is quite normal. The entire Quimby family learns to adjust to Mr. Quimby's unemployment in *Ramona and Her Father,* and the feelings of unease, irritation, and worry are eventually resolved and replaced with joy, understanding, and insight. Some readers may think the solutions are too easy; others gain a sense of relief and comfort as problems are solved.

A book for younger readers, James Proimos' *The Loudness of Sam,* is a prime example of a book showing parents who accept their children without conditions. From the time he is born, everything Sam does

Woodrow learns that friendship helps him survive adversity.

is LOUD. His parents think this is wonderful and encourage him. Not until he visits his aunt in the city is his loudness considered a problem. However, by the time Sam goes home, even his aunt learns that being loud has some advantages.

Stereotypically, we often think of mother as being the ones who sing and rock their young children. In Tony Bradman's *Daddy's Lullaby*, the father spends warm, caring time with the baby.

Family problems

Blister, formerly Alyssa Reed, finds her family falling apart after the stillborn death of a sibling. Her mother falls into depression, her father leaves and gets a girlfriend, and they move to a new neighborhood. There appear to be too many problems for Blister to solve, even though she tries to do so, often inappropriately, but also with resiliency. Susan Shreve presents a realistic picture of a family dealing with many problems from the perspective of a 10-year-old.

Extended families

More and more books of realistic fiction are including relationships with grandparents, aunts, uncles, and other extended family members. Research by Janice S. McElhoe (1999) found that although grandparents are often presented stereotypically in picture books, many excellent books are available that include grandparents more realistically, which means that they are presented with both strengths and weaknesses.

Ruth White has written an incredible story describing the importance of family support in the Newbery Honor book *Belle Prater's Boy*. When Woodrow's mother, Belle, disappears, he moves in with his grandparents. His next door neighbors are his aunt, uncle, and cousin, Gypsy. As their friendship develops, both Gypsy and Woodrow learn to depend on each other and in the process come to terms with Belle's disappearance and the death of Gypsy's father.

Sharon Creech often writes of extended families. In *Chasing Redbird*, the extended family includes aunts and uncles. Zinny describes the two houses: "Strolling from our kitchen through the passage into Aunt Jessie and Uncle Nate's kitchen was like drifting back in time. On our side was a zoo of noises: . . . But when you stepped through the passage, suddenly you'd be in the Quiet Zone of Aunt Jessie's and Uncle Nate's house. . . " (p. 3). In *The Wanderer*, the extended family consists of uncles and cousins. Sophie persuades her parents and the uncles that she should be allowed to join the sailing expedition to visit their father/grandfather in England. Told from the diary entries of Sophie and her cousin Cody, there is more complexity and story layers than there first appears to be. Both of these books let the readers discover that there are surprises and responsibilities associated with growing up.

Alternative family structures

In many books published earlier, the typical family structure included two parents, children, and perhaps a few close family members. *Alternative family structures* were the result of a parent's death, often the mother. Contemporary realistic fiction published today portrays alternative family structures much more frequently, and death is not the sole reason for these changes. Divorce, desertion, or sexual preference of parents all create families that are not "typical." Homelessness, single-parent families, children raised by family members rather than parents, children whose parents are gay or lesbian, foster children, and families with stepparents are all portrayed with increasing frequency as family structures in this genre. The children and young people in these books struggle as they learn to survive. For some of the children, the struggle is physical; for others, it is emotional. In addition to the normal challenges of growing up, these children have extra responsibilities, different expectations, and circumstances over which they have no control. The ways they cope with these life conditions give readers insights about their own life.

Most of the characters in these books have some sort of family structure or adult support. Through their experiences, the characters begin to develop an understanding of themselves and those around them. They come to realize that they are not the only people in the world facing these problems, a realization that helps them feel connected to the world. Connectedness to others is a major theme in many of these books.

Single parents

Single parent families may be headed by mothers, fathers, or grandparents. Single-parent families often struggle. Money may be in short supply, and the family members often go without things they want or need. Thursday is the worst day of the week in Melrose Cooper's *Gettin' through Thursday*, because that is the day before payday. Andre worries that even though Mama has promised to have a party for him if he makes the honor roll, it will not occur because it happens on Thursday. To his surprise, this is a celebration that he will not forget.

Often it seems that the missing parent is the father in single parent families. In *What Every Girl (Except Me) Knows,* by Nora Raleigh Baskin, Gabby lives with her father. As she grows up, she realizes that she really needs a mother to learn how to be "womanly." She not only has no objection to her father getting married again, but she wishes he would do so soon. When the relationship between her dad and his girlfriend falls apart, Gabby learns that the solution to her problems will not come from someone else—it must come from within.

Before their abusive father dies, sixth-grade Ricky assumes much responsibility for his younger siblings since his mom is working to support them. After his father's death, Ricky gets in trouble for fighting. In order to spare his mother more anxiety, he makes a deal with the principal: in exchange for not telling his mother, he will miss recess and avoid fighting again. Because the boy he fought rode the same school bus he did, he wouldn't ride the bus. Rather than walking to school, he decides to run to and from school. In *Racing the Past* by Sis Boulos Deans, Ricky's life holds more promise because of his talent for running; because of it, he is able to dispel bad memories.

Children with lesbian or gay parents

Alternative family structures include children with lesbian or gay parents. For example, when Holly and her two moms move to a new community, Holly decides that she will assume a new identity. As Holly becomes closer with the popular group of girls, her "secret" is exposed with all of the expected consequences. Holly learns that honesty is better than trying to keep all of the untruths straight and that she can have real friends who accept her and her parents as they are. Refer to *Holly's Secret* by Nancy Garden. The reference is on page 171.

Stepfamilies

Children in stepfamilies face complex relationships. Laura has a hard time dealing with her mother's death, even after three years. She is resentful of her new stepmother and is determined to keep her mother's memory alive. She has a string of buttons, each symbolizing

an event in her mother's life. When the string breaks and she loses one button, her stepmother finds the missing button. This is the beginning of Laura's acceptance. Eve Bunting has again addressed important issues in this book, *The Memory String.*

Maggie visits her father, stepmother, and baby half-sister in Avi's *Blue Heron.* She anticipates tensions when she arrives, but does not realize the actual problems she will face. Her sick father has lost his job, he refuses to take his medicine, and then he has a serious car accident. Maggie's only peace during the summer comes from observing a blue heron. As she works with her stepmother to save her father, they begin to develop a positive relationship. In the end, all of the main characters develop greater self-awareness.

Angel has many responsibilities, but the library and a mystery man help her.

The protagonist, Margaret, in Stephanie Greene's *Falling into Place*, has to adjust to having three younger stepsisters; now that her stepmother is pregnant, Margaret finds it even more difficult. She goes to visit her beloved grandmother, who seems to be entering depression after the death of her husband and her move into a retirement community. As Margaret and her cousin Roy plan a party to help Gran meet new people, Margaret learns to accept her own family situation. She even gets to name the new baby. The believable characters in this story solve their problems realistically.

Living with foster parents or family members other than a parent

Many times children must live with foster parents or relatives who are not their parents. Sometimes parents die, some parents are dysfunctional, or war or military careers may separate children from either or both parents. There are also instances where siblings live together without parents.

Katherine Paterson's *The Same Stuff as Stars* is a compelling story about 11-year-old Angel, a child who has always assumed many more responsibilities than should be expected of her. Her father is in jail and her irresponsible mother has left her and her 7-year-old brother with their great-grandmother. Now Angel has even more responsibilities. She does have some support from the local librarian and the mystery man who introduces her to astronomy. *The Same Stuff as Stars* ends on a hopeful note but the reader assumes that life for Angel will never be easy.

Even though 15-year-old Katherine and her three younger siblings live with their mother, they essentially are living on their own. Their mother is an alcoholic who is unable to assume any responsibility for her children, while their father has left and started a new family. Katherine tries to keep up appearances and hold the family together so that Social Services will not become aware of their situation. She does this in the face of illness, lack of money and problems at school. When a teacher tries to be supportive, Katherine panics and makes unwise decisions. The ending in Heather Quarles' *A Door Near Here* is not "happily ever after," but life does become more manageable for the children.

In *Miracle's Boys,* we see the story of three young men whose mother, Miracle, has died of insulin shock,

through the eyes of the youngest, Lafayette. The eldest, Ty'ree, has turned down a scholarship so that he can support the boys and prevent Social Services from separating them. The middle brother, Charlie, has returned from a juvenile detention center and has almost become a stranger. Lafayette struggles with guilt and anger. Only because of their mother's enduring love, which allows the boys to hold on to their love for each other, are they able to carry on and have hope for the future. Jacqueline Woodson's novel, which won the 2001 Coretta Scott King Award, is a powerful testament to the bond among brothers.

Sharon Creech, in *Ruby Holler,* again envelopes the reader in a story in which the characters and setting seem so real that it is hard not to read the book in a single session. The "trouble twins," Dallas and Florida, are living in an orphanage; since thengs never worked out when they were sent to live with a variety of families, they are now back in the abysmal orphanage. A request for them comes from an elderly couple who each want one more adventure and want the twins to accompany them on their separate vacations. They do so and learn to trust Tiller and Sairy. The twists and turns of the plot are intriguing but healing and loving develop along with their relationships.

Pictures of Hollis Woods by Patricia Reilly Giff is another book in which the foster child begins to find healing with an older guardian. Hollis has run away from many foster homes and is sent to live with Josie, a retired art teacher. As Hollis and Josie begin to bond, Hollis begins to draw her experiences. She also begins to realize that Josie may be developing dementia and is determined to save herself and Josie. As Hollis looks back at her previous foster family, she is able to look at the circumstances under which she left. The two situations come together as Hollis searches for a family.

Generations of families

Grandparents play an integral part in the lives of many children. For children who are lucky enough to interact with their grandparents, as well as children who may not have grandparents around, these books show how interactions with family members of other generations can help children grow and gain insight. The first two examples give readers insight into a family over many years. The rest deal only with a single grandparent.

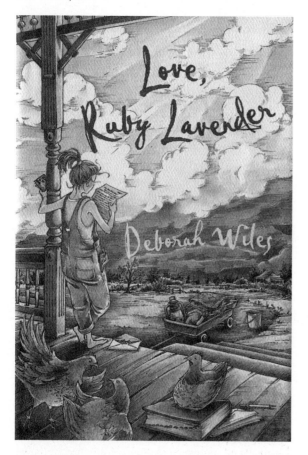

Ruby and her grandmother have adventures together.

In *Jericho,* Janet Hickman presents the lives of four generations of women, focusing primarily on GrandMin, the great-grandmother, and Angela, the great-granddaughter. GrandMin's mind is back in Jericho, the town where she grew up. She has only fleeting periods of living in the present and requires the help of her daughter, granddaughter, and Angela. Through a series of flashbacks, we see GrandMin's life from childhood through adulthood and we develop an understanding of the family.

Walter Dean Myers portrays the generations of survivors that make up the Lewis family in *The Glory Field.* He traces the family from living on the coast of Sierra Leone, West Africa, in 1753 to present-day Harlem, New York. They were slaves in 1864 during the Civil War. By 1900, they lived on eight acres of land called the Glory Field. By 1964, the family joined the Civil Rights Movement battle. Tommy finds the shackles that were on the legs of the first family member brought to this country and chains himself to the sheriff. In the final section, the Lewis family gathers for a last reunion at Glory Field, as a resort is going to be built there. Malcolm, a family member, attends the reunion and becomes custodian of the shackles that symbolize the common bond among all generations.

Sharon Creech introduces us to Rosie and her visually impaired friend, Bailey. As with many 12-year-olds, they often have misunderstandings and hurt feelings. However, when *Granny Torrelli Makes Soup,* eventually with the help of both young people, they are able to come to terms with their relationship through conversations, Granny's stories, and working together.

Miss Eula Garnet and her granddaughter Ruby have wonderful adventures together—stealing chickens, painting the house pink, and writing letters to each other. However, they also share their sadness about the death of Grandpa Garnet. When Miss Eula goes to visit her son to try to cope with her loss, Ruby feels abandoned. Although Ruby writes faithfully to her grandmother, she also needs to deal with situations close at hand. We see Ruby growing during this time as she learns to deal with individuals and situations that are sometimes difficult. *Love, Ruby Lavender* by Deborah Whiles is a humorous and touching look at relationship between an out-of-the-ordinary girl and her grandmother.

Family reunions are a wonderful time to build memories of generations of family members. Patricia Polacco, in *When Lightening Comes in a Jar*, helps readers understand the significance of simple family activities with generations of children.

For children who are close to their grandparents, death is particularly hard to accept. Mags and Cody have spent summers on their grandparents' farm. However, after Grandma's death, Gramps sold much of his property. Since new houses have been built where farmland was, the bluebirds no longer nest close by. The children take matters into their own hands, clean up the gardens, and purchase a bluebird nesting box. The assumption is that the bluebirds will return once their habitat has been restored. Deborah Hopkinson, in writing *Bluebird Summer*, has shown how activity can help heal broken hearts.

Challenges from Outside the Family

As children grow up, the family—whether nuclear or alternative—may come to assume less importance in children's lives while the peer group takes on greater importance. These changes represent the children's growing need for independence. Parents, siblings, extended family members, and other adults who have been the focus of a child's interactions may begin to fade into the background. In general, however, despite conflicts, many characters still see their families, especially parents, as integral partners in resolving problems. Other books address problems outside the family with peers, school, and non-family adults; the family is less involved as the characters seek to define who they are becoming. In these books, the support needed may be received from peers or other adults.

Many children are confronted by the death of a family member, friend, or pet. Adults often have a significant role in helping children cope with death. School becomes more important; characters must learn to face issues and resolve them through their own means. Other characters face emotional or physical challenges that they must meet by themselves, often without family or peers. Their ultimate survival depends on how they overcome the hardships. They may not have the support of adults or others; they may be alone by choice or because of circumstances beyond their control. Some of these books may be described as *"coming-of-age" books*—the character's future life depends on decisions made in the present time. The books for children and young adults reviewed here reflect these kinds of problems or conflicts. Of course, readers may place a book in a different category than is done here. As is true in life, many books cannot be neatly pigeonholed.

Peers

Ernie has always been an entrepreneur. His latest scheme for making money is to conduct pet funerals. With his friends, he is kept very busy—until his father finds out and his own pet dies. Doug Cooney uses humor in *The Beloved Dearly* to address some significant issues.

It is always a difficult experience when one's best friend moves away. Paula Danziger (author of many well-written books, including the *Amber Brown* books) and Ann M. Martin (author of the *Babysitters Club* series) have captured the essence of what this is like in their book, *P. S. Longer Letter Later.* Through the letters that Tara and Elizabeth write, readers learn how change affects families and individuals. Their friendship is strong, supportive, and long lasting, even if their primary interactions are through their writing.

In a follow-up book by Danziger and Martin, *Snail Mail No More,* Tara and Elizabeth use e-mail to communicate. They deal with a variety of problems, some significant, others fairly mundane. Tara's new baby sister, the death of Elizabeth's father, dating, babysitting, peer relations—all are shared through e-mail. Middle-school girls should find this book especially interesting.

Kissing Tennessee by Kathi Appelt is a collection of eight stories about students who are going to an eighth-grade dance. The focus is on the relationships between the boys and girls, but woven into each story are issues of substance—rape, abuse by parents, and sexuality. The dance is the centerpiece of all the stories and effectively ties them together.

Death

For many children and adults, the death of a beloved pet is a significant event in their lives. In *Goodbye Mousie*, a young boy finds his pet mouse "sleeping." Told from the perspective of the boy, we see how his father and family support him in this loss. Robie Harris has written a book that can be shared with younger readers but also is very appropriate for older ones as well.

When Sugar Plum's mom goes to work, Mis' Lela takes care of her. They spend pleasant and loving times together. Sugar Plum has a difficult time understanding what has happened when Mis' Lela dies. She does learn to remember the happy times spent together in Dorothy Carter's *Bye, Mis' Lela.*

T. A. Barron shares his family's reactions to the death of his father. The children do not understand where Grandpa is. Through talking about Grandpa and sharing important memories of the time he spent with each child, the entire family is able to come to a first acceptance of the death. *Where is Grandpa?* is a book for all ages.

Adjowa J. Burrowes' book, *Grandma's Purple Flowers*, is a wonderful tribute to the cyclical nature of life. When her grandma dies in the winter, the narrator misses her very much. However, by the time the spring comes, she appreciates the purple flowers that were among her grandma's favorites. She is able to relate the death to the seasons of nature. The cut-paper collage with watercolor illustrations add depth to this sensitive book.

The death of a child is especially difficult to deal with, both for parents and siblings. As Wenny and Will go to the store, Wenny is killed. Will writes to his sister, describing the difficulty the family has in coping. His parents are almost too affected by the death to be of help to Will. His father moves out for awhile and the pregnant mother tries to re-do Wenny's room for the new baby. Will's writing helps him go through the typical stages of grief. Janet Lee Cary's book, *Wenny has Wings*, would be an insightful book even for those children who have not experienced such a devastating loss.

Eve Bunting has written a haunting book about the unanticipated effects of a prank gone wrong. In *Blackwater*, 13-year-old Brian causes the death of the girl he wanted to date but is regarded as a hero because of his cousin's cover-up. Brian struggles with the nightmare of what to do—does he confess or let things ride without taking responsibility for his actions?

Some young children are afraid to go to school for the first time. In *I am NOT Going to School Today*, Robie Harris takes readers through the struggle of the first day of school fears. With supportive parents and the company of a favorite stuffed animal, the first-day fears are conquered.

Jack can't stand poetry—and that is what his teacher insists that he write. However, when his teacher has him write in his poetry journal, he not only learns to like the poetry of others (Robert Frost, Walter Dean Myers) but gains insight into the loss of his dog. Sharon Creech's *Love that Dog* lets readers see poetry (and a sensitive teacher) as a way to find out about oneself and life.

Survival

The young people in these books must rely on their own wits, intelligence, and strength to survive. Except for occasional intervals, they may not have family, peer, or other adult support. Survival may include a number of elements. The characters learn to pay attention to and take cues from animals, from the people around them, and from the environment as well. They must learn not to panic but to keep calm. In most of the stories that follow, characters may learn to trust themselves, as well as selected other people. They also need resilience and hope (Poe, 1999).

Literature circles give students opportunities to discuss the books they've read.

After Alex has been in serious trouble, her mother sends her to live with her father in International Falls, Minnesota. Her father is a biologist who is an authority on bald eagles. When Alex becomes stranded on an island, trying to save an eaglet, she must fight for her own life as well as that of the injured eaglet. The author, Mary Casanova, describes her own research with eagle experts and includes several Web sites. The well-written *When Eagles Fall* should appeal to both male and female readers.

Children and young adults often have little or no control over events that have a powerful impact on their lives. Ben Mikaelsen describes 12-year-old Santiago's struggle for survival after guerrilla soldiers strike his village in *Red Midnight*. Santiago and his 4-year-old sister take a sea kayak to escape to the United States. Their journey is beset by difficulties a person much older would be challenged by: sharks, soldiers, storms, and sun. Their survival and triumph is a tribute to their courage as well as to luck.

Books by Will Hobbs often seem to include life-threatening challenges. *Wild Man Island* is no exception. Andy Gallow ignores the rules set by his mother and the professional sea kayak guide as he leaves by himself to find the site of his father's death on the coast of Alaska. A storm leaves him marooned on Admiralty Island, where he discovers another person secretly living there. This Wild Man is also an archeologist, as was Andy's father, so there is interesting information presented about the first Americans who arrived in Alaska.

When Palmer LaRue turns 10, he is expected by his father, the boys in his class, and the community in general to become a *Wringer*, one who finishes killing the pigeons that were not killed by gunfire in the annual pigeon shoot. Palmer is taunted by the boys who see his aversion to wringing as a weakness they can use to their advantage. After Palmer adopts a pigeon, he knows that he must take a stand against tradition and defy his father and the others. In doing so, he not only develops a sense of respect for himself but begins to change the perspective of his father and some others in the community. Jerry Spinelli creates a realistic picture of conflict between an individual and his peers and family members.

Special Interest Books

Many children develop interests during the elementary years that they retain throughout their lives; others explore a different interest each month. Whichever is true of the children you are working with, literature is a means of exploring and expanding children's interests. Some of the special interest books are included in the section on series books. They may well fit into both this category and the one that follows.

Sports

This section identifies books that help readers look at sports from a broader perspective than that of who wins or loses. The games and game practice create events and contexts that show readers the importance of telling the truth, racial appreciation, and accepting one's weaknesses as well as strengths. Older readers may enjoy some of these books even if they are not involved in sports.

There seem to be more excellent books about baseball than about any of the other sports. As is true with other topics, baseball is the vehicle to create a story that demonstrates a significant theme. In Randy Powell's *Dean Duffy*, 17-year-old Dean must make some hard decisions about what direction he wants his life to take. Although he has been a baseball star in high school, he has had a two-year slump. His mentor has been able to get him a baseball scholarship, but Dean does not know if he is willing to take advantage of it to try to get out of his slump. His friends have a variety of other kinds of dilemmas, and he sees other alternatives. Only because of these situations is he finally able to come to some resolution about his future.

Two books by Will Weaver, *Striking Out* and *Farm Team,* chronicle the tensions that occur between responsibilities to oneself and responsibilities for work. Keeping a balance while growing up is difficult; it is even more difficult when there is not as much support as one really needs. Fourteen-year old Billy Baggs makes difficult decisions, during which readers learn about both baseball and farm life.

Some children learn to cope with failure through sports. Jason Ross is despondent when he is cut from the baseball team. He seeks coaching assistance from a school custodian in Alfred Slote's *Finding Buck McHenry*. This story includes some interesting history of players in the old Negro leagues.

Dean Hughes' *Team Picture* helps us understand a foster child's feelings through his interest in baseball. David puts his energy into pitching in his Pony League. However, he is struggling with the fact that his foster father, Paul, might start drinking again. This fear translates into unacceptable behaviors with his teammates until finally David begins to talk with, and trust, Paul. As he begins to get support from others, he is able to accept both friendship and the weaknesses within himself.

Two exceptional books about running are *Runner's Song* by Frank McLaughlin and *The Runner* by Cynthia Voigt. In *The Runner,* Jeannie is persistent about her goal of becoming a track champion, even though she has more than her share of trouble. After her father deserts her and her mother, they have little money to live on or to buy her special track shoes. She has trouble passing several of her classes, and confronts a family illness. However, with the support of her coach and her poetry, she is able to reach many of her goals.

In *Runner's Song,* Bullet Tillerman, the best runner on the school track team, has become a loner. He consistently feels boxed in by his father's unreasonable demands. When he finally learns a little about being a team player, he drops out of high school and joins the army. He finds running away did not solve his problems.

Basketball from a coach's perspective is the theme of Thomas J. Dygard's *The Rebounder.* The coach, Doug

Fulton, encounters a natural basketball player, Chris Patton, who refuses to play because he is afraid of injuring other players. Of course, Chris has a reason for these fears and eventually the student manager is able to help Chris work through them. Chris finally is able to join the team, having come to accept the fact that accidents do happen.

Three books by Australian author Markus Zusak chronicle the interactions between two brothers, but the whole family provides the context for the relationship. In the first book, *The Underdog*, Cameron and Ruben Wolfe fight and get into trouble together. Cam reflects on this and how the family is changing. In the second book, *Fighting Ruben Wolfe,* both boys enter the boxing ring in an attempt to earn money for the family. Ruben rarely loses; Cam rarely wins. When the boys are scheduled to fight each other, it is a bloody contest that changes both of them. In the third book, *Getting the Girl,* Cam falls for Ruben's former girlfriend. Octavia is the cause of the brother's first real conflict. The relationship changes as a result, with Cam realizing that he is not Ruben's shadow.

Mysteries

Mysteries are popular with children, although teachers, librarians, and parents have often regarded them with suspicious eyes, as they are concerned about their literary quality. Fortunately, children's mysteries include those by several notable authors such as Betsy Byars, Joan Lowery Nixon, Gary Paulsen, Phyllis Reynolds Naylor, and Virginia Hamilton. Adults can be assured of the quality of children's books by these authors.

Betsy Byars writes about Herculeah Jones, whose father is a police detective and mother is a private investigator, in *Dead Letter.* Herculeah finds a letter in the pocket lining of a coat she bought from a thrift shop. She and her friend, Meat, discover who the coat belonged to and discover who killed her. A more recent book, *Disappearing Act,* also raises interesting questions about who went where.

Joan Lowery Nixon is a well-known mystery writer and the only three-time winner of the Edgar Allan Poe Award. In *The Haunting,* Lia and her family move into Graymoss, the plantation that has been in their family since the Civil War. The diary of Lia's great-great-grandmother gives clues about the haunted house. In *The House on Hackman Hill,* strange events make people wonder what happened to Dr. Hackman.

Both of these great mysteries keep readers involved to the very last pages.

Animal stories

Eleven-year-old William's life seems to be falling apart. His parents separate, his dad gets engaged, and his grandfather dies. When he adopts an abandoned dog, Riley, things seem to get better. However, when Riley chases and injures a neighbor's horse, the local law states that the dog must be put to death. Williams works to get the community's support to save his dog. The problem is solved when a man offers to take Riley and train him. William realizes that even through he won't be able to keep his dog, the process of saving him has made him better able to deal with his loss and grief. Eve Bunting's *The Summer of Riley* is a perceptive and believable story.

Jean Craighead George has written several books in which Frightful, Sam Gribley's trained peregrine falcon, plays a major role. Although the first two books are told from the perspective of Sam (*My Side of the Mountain, On the Far Side of the Mountain*), *Frightful's Mountain* is primarily from Frightful's perspective. Since it is illegal to keep an endangered bird of prey, Sam must release Frightful into the forest. *Frightful's Mountain* is the account of how she survives on her own.

Jean Craighead George has written another animal story, very different from those above. *Look to the North: A Wolf Pup Diary* is written in journal form and includes facts as well as a story. The events of the wolves are described in relationship to nature.

Series books

In the children's and young adult section of many bookstores, series books may comprise the majority of books found on the shelves; in fact, you may find special sections devoted only to series books. What are series books? Anne Devereaux Jordan (1997b) suggests that these are the books that are read while in the bathtub: They are "usually not particularly well-written or intellectually taxing, but are heavy in suspense or action and cheap in cost so that it doesn't matter if they accidentally fall in the water" (p. 22).

Nonetheless, series books have an important role to play in making children lifelong readers. Brooks, Waterman, and Allington (2003) surveyed K–6 teachers about their students' preferences for series books. They found that series books seemed to have an important function in the development of reading proficiencies. "We suggest that virtually every avid reader we have ever met was able to recall one or more children's series that (was) devoured at some early point in the reading acquisition process" (p. 12).

The characteristics of series books are that they follow a set formula, have predictable plots with stereotypic characters who are often one-sided but who are able to solve all problems, and often are short and easy to read. These books often tend to be episodic. They obviously appeal to readers, both boys and girls, and are worthwhile in that they often encourage reluctant readers to start reading other books that may be more substantial. Although they are popular with a range of ages of children, many of them serve a particular need for second- and third-grade readers, who are moving from the learning-to-read stage to gaining fluency.

There is a relatively new series of books for children in the middle grades who are interested in sports. The *Broadway Ballplayers* by Maureen Holohan are books that have girls as the main characters. They are active in almost every sport: *Left Out* (baseball), *Friday Nights* (basketball), *Ice Cold* (ice hockey), *Don't Stop* (track), *Catch Shorty* (football), *Everybody's Favorite* (soccer), and *Sideline Blues* (volleyball). These books are written from a first-person point of view and emphasize that understanding and respecting people of a variety of socioeconomic backgrounds is an important aspect of sports as well as in life.

The *Cam Jansen Adventure* series, written by David Adler, includes books for readers who are making the transition from easy-to-read books to chapter books. Both Cam, who has a photographic memory, and her friend, Eric, are willing to take chances to solve the mysteries they seem to attract. An adventure doesn't wait long to begin in *Cam Jansen and the First Day of School.* In *Young Cam Jansen and the Double Beach Mystery*, Cam uses her photographic memory to solve this problem.

Other series books

The *Pony Pals,* Anna, Lulu, and Pam, always seem to be having adventures—or adventures find them. In *He's My Pony,* Anna has a hard time sharing her pony when the niece of a neighbor seems to be developing a special bond with the pony. *The Pony and the Haunted Barn* describes their adventure in a very different setting.

Cynthia Rylant has written a series of books in which three 9-year-old cousins go to live with their aunt for a year. The *Cobble Street Cousins* have a variety of experiences, all of which are creative and fun to read about. For example, in the first book, *In Aunt Lucy's Kitchen,* they keep busy baking cookies and doing a poetry and singing presentation as well as trying to do some matchmaking for their aunt. There are several other books in this series (*A Little Shopping, Summer Party, Wedding Flowers*) which will be enjoyed by girls in Grades 2 through 5.

The *Spencer's Adventures* books by Gary Hogg relate the zany ideas that Spencer has and that all seem to have happy endings. For example, in the series' fourth book, *The Great Toilet Paper Caper,* Spencer decides to get his name into the Gigantic Book of World Records by walking backward longer than anyone else has. When his teacher and the principal of the school recognize the fun of "Backwards Day" at school, the class decides to make the world's biggest roll of toilet paper so the principal will also get an award. Everyone has fun and wins awards.

David A. Adler writes about a fourth grader in his series about Andy Russell. In *School Trouble for Andy Russell,* Andy gets into trouble when someone plays jokes on the substitute teacher. In *Andy Russell, NOT Wanted by the Police,* Andy and his friend Tamika watch the neighbors' house while they are away. When something suspicious is going on, big trouble may be just around the corner.

The *Bluford* Series has become popular, especially with African-American middle-school students. It is a series of seven novels whose characters, both male and female, attend Bluford High. The books deal with issues that are significant to many students—relationships with family members and friends, stealing, bullying, and revenge. This series might well be the one to turn on many reluctant readers.

The "Alice" series by Phyllis Reynolds Naylor focuses on a young girl being brought up by her father and older brother after the death of her mother. In *The Grooming of Alice*, the twelfth in the series, Alice and her friends are getting ready to start high school in the fall. They are all concerned about their bodies, and want to be perfect. This leads to problems. Other significant issues are explored in the book, including the death of her favorite teacher. Many of the issues discussed in the book may primarily be of interest to girls; other books may be more suitable for boys.

Classroom Activities

Fiction in contemporary settings is particularly useful in developing children's understanding of themselves, their families, their cultural backgrounds, their values, and issues that may be addressed in the curriculum. Books of contemporary realistic fiction provide children with insights into the human condition in both serious and hu-morous ways. These books are favorites of many readers because they are often able to identify with the characters and the situations in which they live. More and more teachers are incorporating contemporary realistic fiction into reader's theater, literature study groups, read-alouds, storytelling, and informal drama in their classes.

ACTIVITY 8.1 USING SERIES BOOKS TO ENCOURAGE RELUCTANT READERS

(IRA/NCTE Standards: 3, 4, 5, 6, 7, 8, 11, 12. Make connections and visualize.)

The fourth-grade teachers brainstormed for the rest of their planning period as they discussed plans for their unit. They decided to use two series, the *Andy Russell* books by David Adler and the *Broadway Ballplayers* series by Maureen Holohan. They knew that they needed to address a variety of Standards for the English Language Arts so that they could justify this unit that might otherwise seem to be just for fun. Following is a brief description of what they decided to do during the 45-minute literacy session each day.

Day 1: Give a brief overview of the unit, including the rationale. Introduce the series of books to the children. Provide brief book-talks about each. Let the students take the books and review them, listing the top three choices they would like to read.

Day 2: Having matched students and their choices, share who will be in each of the six groups and what book each group will read. Give each group two copies of their book. Let each group plan their reading schedule; include paired reading, reading aloud, and silent reading. Discuss strategies they will use as they read (make connections and visualize). Give them time to read.

Day 3: Present the choices for their activities during the unit.

    A. Research the author, using the library and the Internet. Prepare a report and share it with the class.

    B. Create an art project, make a video, write a play based on the book, and so forth. (In-struction by teachers would be given depending on the group's needs.) Share them with the class.

    C. Research the sport in the *Ball Players* series or a topic in the *Andy Russell* series (such as gerbils). Present the information to the class.

Days 4–10: Perform reading, writing, and research, with instruction as appropriate.

Days 11 and 12: Presentations and written reports are due.

Books used:

Andy Russell Books

> *The Many Troubles of Andy Russell*
> *Andy and Tamika*
> *School Trouble for Andy Russell*
> *Parachuting Hamsters and Andy Russell*
> *Andy Russell, NOT Wanted by the Police*

The *Broadway Ballplayers* Books

> *Left Out*
> *Friday Nights*
> *Don't Stop*
> *Ice Cold*
> *Catch Shorty*
> *Everybody's Favorite*
> *Sideline Blues*

(Note: Each activity would be explained in greater detail for the students.)

ACTIVITY 8.2 COMPREHENSION CONNECTIONS

(NCTE/IRA Standards: 3, 5, 6.)

Because contemporary realistic fiction is a "tell it like it is" genre that deals with a broad range of topics, there are many books that can be used to supplement many topics in the curriculum. Because these books are enjoyable to read, provide insights about oneself and others, and increase understanding of events and issues, students are more likely to remember the content than if they just read from the textbook. This genre plays an important role in the curriculum because it puts the reader in the shoes of characters who have different experiences than they have had. Such experiences help children understand themselves and others. Realistic fiction encourages readers to reflect on themselves and on contemporary issues in ways that few others genres do.

Current events often are an impetus for further study. Issues about immigration and refugees are regularly in the news in many parts of the country. As students explore this topic, they are much more likely to make connections to their own lives and family situations by reading about characters who are close in age to them. In planning a unit about refugees, the following kinds of activities and books could be used.

1. Interview students in the school who came from another country.
2. Research why there are immigrants in this time period; contrast this with immigrants who came to this country in the past. This would be a good way to combine using books of contemporary realistic fiction and historical fiction. Nonfiction books could also be used.
3. Write articles about immigrants for the school newspaper.
4. Set up a debate in which arguments are raised about the numbers of immigrants who come to this country.

Contemporary realistic fiction books that could be used in this study:

Knight, Margy Burns. *Who Belongs Here?*
Mikaelsen, Ben. *Red Midnight*
Temple, Frances. *Tonight by Sea*

Summary

Contemporary realistic fiction books can be read to gain insight into one's own life or the lives of others. They can be used to convince reluctant readers that reading really is OK, or they can be read just for fun. Although some of these books may include content matter that some teachers may be uncomfortable with, they may be the topics that some children really need to read about. This is a very popular genre and one that can be utilized in all classrooms.

Thought Questions

1. What preparations will you make as you select books for use in your classroom? Does your school district have written guidelines for book selection? Does the district have an approved book list? Does the district have a policy that addresses what to do if a book is challenged by a parent or other adult? Is censorship an issue?
2. What policy, if any, exists in your school district about using specific textbooks or basal readers? If you are required to use a basal reader, how will you adapt it so your students can read authentic literature?
3. How can you integrate contemporary realistic fiction with the various curriculum areas?
4. What are your favorite contemporary realistic fiction books? Why?

Research and Application Experiences

1. Find movies that have been adapted from realistic fiction. After reading the books, make Venn diagrams that illustrate the similarities and differences in the book and film version of the story.

2. Identify an issue or topic. Using one of the resource books cited or other sources, identify books that are available on that topic. Compile an annotated bibliography for current or future use.

3. Read several of the contemporary fiction works that have received the Newbery or Newbery Honor Award. Explain why you think these books received the award.

4. Many realistic fiction books refer to school and school experiences as an integral part of the plot. Identify several of these books and analyze the portrayal of the school. Is it positive or negative? What are the implications of the portrayal?

Children's Literature References and Recommended Books

Note: Books with an asterisk (*) are recommended for reluctant readers. All of the books in this section are CONTEMPORARY REALISTIC FICTION unless otherwise noted. Approximate reading/interest levels are in parentheses ().

Adler, D. A. (2000). *School trouble for Andy Russell* (W. Hillenbrand, Illus.). New York: Harcourt. (1–3).*

When a substitute teacher comes, Andy gets in trouble.

Adler, D. A. (2001). *Andy Russell, NOT wanted by the police* (L. Franson, Illus.). New York: Harcourt. (3–4; 5–6).*

Andy and Tamika are house-sitting for a neighbor when there are strange events happening in the house.

Adler, D. A. (2002a). *Cam Jansen and the first day of school mystery.* New York: Viking. (1–4).*

Cam and Eric waste no time to have an adventure when school starts.

Adler, D. A. (2002b). *Young Cam Jansen and the double beach mystery.* New York: Viking. (1–4).

Another mystery solved by Cam!

Appelt, K. (2000). *Kissing Tennessee.* San Diego: Harcourt. (6–9).

Eight short stories of eighth graders going to a school dance.

Avi. (1992). *Blue heron.* New York: Bradbury. (4–7).

Maggie visits her father, stepmother, and baby half-sister and discovers problems she did not expect.

Avi. (2003). *Crispin.* New York: Hyperion. (5–9). HISTORICAL FICTION.

A young boy is being hunted and does not know why. His friend, Bear, helps save him.

Barron, T. A. (2002). *Where is grandpa?* (Chris Soentpiet, Illus.). New York: Penguin Putnam. (PreK–3).

When grandpa dies, each family member remembers time spent with him.

Baskin, N. R. (2001) *What every girl (except me) knows.* New York: Little Brown. (4–8).

Gabby hopes her single father will soon marry so she can have a mother to find out how to be womanly.

Betancourt, J. (2001). *He's my pony.* New York: Scholastic. (2–4).*

Anna is jealous of a neighbor's niece who likes to ride her horse in this *Pony Pals* series book.

Betancourt, J. (2002). *The pony and the haunted barn* (R. Jones, Illus.). New York: Scholastic. (2–4).*

Another *Pony Pals* series adventure.

Bradman, T. (2001). *Daddy's lullaby* (J. Crockcroft, Illus.). New York: Margaret K. Mc Elderry Books. (PreK–2).

A father comes home from work and spends time with his baby who is awake.

Bunting, E. (2000). *Blackwater.* New York: HarperCollins. (5–8).

A thoughtless prank predicates tragic consequences.

Bunting, E. (2000). *The memory string* (T. Rand, Illus.). New York: Houghton Mifflin. (K–3).

Each of Laura's buttons represents a memory of her deceased mother. Losing one is a traumatic experience.

Bunting, E. (2002). *The summer of Riley.* New York: HarperCollins. (3–6).

William's dog injures a neighbor's horse, which is against the law. William finds an alternative to killing the dog.

Burrowes, A. J. (2000). *Grandma's purple flowers.* New York: Lee & Low. (K–3).

A young girl's grandmother dies.

Byars, B. (1996). *Dead letter.* New York: Viking. (4–6).

Herculah Jones finds a letter from a dead woman in a coat pocket and finds out who killed her.

Byars, B. (2000). *Disappearing act.* New York: Puffin. (4–6).

Another mystery story.

Capote, T. (1996). *The Thanksgiving visitor* (B. Peck, Illus.). New York: Knopf. (5–8).

Buddy learns that there are more perspectives about life than his own.

Cary, J. L. (2002). *Wenny has wings*. New York: Atheneum. (3–6).

Will tries to find a way to adjust to the death of his younger sister.

Carter, D. (1998). *Bye Mis' Lela* (H. Stevenson, Illus.). New York: Farrar. REALISTIC FICTION. (K–4).

Sugar plum has difficulty understanding her babysitter's death.

Casanova, M. (2002). *When eagles fall*. New York: Hyperion. (6–10).

Alex goes to Minnesota with her father on a eagle-banding expedition.

Cleary, B. (1968). *Beezus and Ramona* (L. Darling, Illus.). New York: Morrow. (2–5).*

An old favorite: how do siblings work out relationships?

Cleary, B. (1977). *Ramona and her father* (A. Tiegreen, Illus.). New York: Morrow. (2–5).*

Ramona and her father have some problems to work out—each has difficulty looking at the other's perspective.

Cleary, B. (1999). *Ramona's world* (A. Tiegreen, Illus.). New York: Morrow. (2–5).*

Ramona adjusts to the birth of a new sibling.

Cooney, D. (2002). *The beloved dearly* (Tony Di Terlizzi, Illus.). New York: Simon and Schuster. (2–5).

Eddie and his friends conduct pet funerals to earn money.

Cooper, M. (1998). *Gettin' through Thursday* (N. Bennett, Illus.). New York: Lee & Low. (4–6).

Being poor is not easy and Thursday, the day before payday, is worst of all, especially when a party has been promised.

Cosby, B. (2000). *The day I saw my father cry*. (V. P. Honeywood, Illus.). New York: Cartwheel Books. (4–8).*

Child reflects on seeing his father cry.

Creech, S. (1997). *Chasing redbird*. New York: HarperCollins. (5–9).

Setting and attaining a personal goal is an important part of growing up. However, Zinny's goal may be impossible to achieve.

Creech, S. (1998). *The wanderer* (D. Diaz, Illus.). New York: HarperCollins. (5–9).

Sophie joins her uncles and cousins as they sail across the Atlantic to England.

Creech, S. (2001). *Love that dog*. New York: Harper-Collins. (4–8).

Jack is able to come to terms about the death of his dog through his poetry journal.

Creech, S. (2002). *Ruby Holler*. New York: Harper-Collins. (4–8).

Twin orphans find acceptance as they accompany an older couple on their adventures.

Creech, S. (2003). *Granny Torrelli makes soup*. New York: HarperCollins. (4–8).

Rosie and her friend Bailey mend their bad feelings as they work with Granny Torrelli.

Danziger, P., & Martin, A. M. (1998). *P.S. Longer letter later*. New York: Scholastic. (4–8).

When a best friend moves away, the friendship survives through letters.

Danziger, P., & Martin, A. M. (2001). *Snail mail no more*. New York: Scholastic. (4–8).

As the e-mail each other, friends deal with serious and not-so-serious problems.

Deans, S. B. (2001). *Racing the past*. New York: Henry Holt. (5–9).

After Ricky's father dies, he doesn't want to bother his mother with the trouble he gets in at school. He and the principal come to an agreement and Ricky no longer can ride the bus. Instead, he races the bus.

DeFelice, C. C. (2002). *The real, true Dulcie Campbell* (R. W. Alley, Illus.). New York: Farrar, Straus & Giroux. (K–3).

Dulcie thinks she is a princess and shouldn't have to live on a farm.

Dygard, T. J. (1994). *The rebounder*. New York: Morrow. (5–9).

A basketball coach discovers why a "natural" player refuses to be on the team.

Garden, N. (2000). *Holly's secret*. New York: Farrar, Straus & Giroux. (4–7).

When Holly moves, she tries to keep it secret that she has two moms.

George, J. C. (1988). *My side of the mountain*. New York: Dutton. (4–7).

In this enduring favorite, Sam becomes self-sufficient in the house he creates in the roots of a tree.

George, J. C. (1990). *On the far side of the mountain*. New York: Dutton. (4–7).

The sequel to *My Side of the Mountain* tells what happens when Sam's sister joins him on the mountain.

George, J. C, (2001a). *Frightful's mountain*. New York: Penguin Putnam. (4–7).

Sam discovers that he must release his pet peregrine falcon into the wilds. This is Frightful's story.

George, J. C. (2001b). *Look to the north: A wolf pup diary* (L. Washburn, Illus.). New York: Dutton. (4–7).

A journal account of the lives of young wolves.

Giff, P. R. (2002). *Pictures of Hollis Woods*. New York: Random House. (5–7).

Hollis has lived in lots of foster homes and finally finds one where she wants to stay.

Greene, S. (2002). *Falling into place*. New York: Clarion. (3–6).

A blended family is difficult to deal with, so Margaret goes to stay with her grandmother.

Harris, R. (2001). *Goodbye Mousie*. New York: McElderry. (K–2).

When a pet mouse dies, a young boy gets support and help from his dad.

Harris, R. (2003). *I am NOT going to school today* (J. Ormerod, Illus.). New York: McElderry. (K–12).

With the support of his family and his stuffed animal, a young boy goes to kindergarten for the first time.

Hesse, K. (1993). *Lavender* (A. Glass, Illus.). New York: Holt. (1–4).*

Codie wonders if she will still be special after her aunt has a baby.

Hickman, J. (1994). *Jericho*. New York: Greenwillow. (4–7).

Four generations of girls and women learn about and from one another.

Hobbs, W. (2002). *Wild Man Island*. New York: HarperCollins. (5–9).

Andy is stranded on an island in Alaska.

Hogg, G. (1997). *The great toilet paper caper* (C. Slack, Illus.). New York: Scholastic. (2–4).

Spencer and his friends have a variety of very humorous adventures in the *Spencer's Adventures* series.

Holohan, M. (2000–2001). The *Broadway Ballplayers* series. New York: Pocket Books. (3–7).

A group of girls, active in most sports—baseball, soccer, hockey—tell their stories.

Hopkinson, D. (2001). *Bluedbird summer*. New York: Greenwillow. (2–5).

Two grandchildren help their grandfather after the death of his wife.

Hughes, D. (1996). *Team picture*. New York: Atheneum. (4–7).

David cannot control events around him, so he concentrates on his pitching.

Jacobson, J. (2001). *Winnie (dancing) on her own*. Boston: Houghton Mifflin. (3–6).

Winnie's best friends want her to take dancing lessons with them. She doesn't want to but is convinced that she needs to if she wants to continue being friends with them.

Johnson, L. L. (2002). *Soul moon soup*. New York: Front Street Books. (6–9).

Phoebe, who is homeless, is sent to live with her grandmother for the summer.

Martin, A. M. (1983–2002). The *Babysitters Club* Series. New York: Scholastic. (3–5).*

A series of books about young girls growing up together.

McLaughlin, F. (1998). *Runner's song*. New York: Northbush. (7–10).

Deserted by her father, Jeannie and her mother must make sacrifices. A runner, Jeannie tries to concentrate on becoming a champion and discovers new interests and purposes.

Mikaelsen, B. (2003). *Red midnight*. New York: HarperCollins. (5–8).

Two children sail to America after their village is attacked by guerrillas.

Myers, W. D. (1998). *Scorpions*. New York: Harper & Row. (5–8).

Jamal is forced into taking on the leadership of a Harlem gang when his brother goes to jail.

Myers, W. D. (1994). *The glory field*. New York: Scholastic. (5–9).

This book traces the Lewis family from 1753 in Sierra Leone, West Africa, to present-day Harlem, New York.

Naylor, P. R. (2000). *The grooming of Alice*. New York: Atheneum. (6–9).

Alice and her friends have many issues to address in the summer before starting high school.

Nixon, J. L. (2000). *The Haunting*. New York: Delacorte. (5–9).

Moving into a plantation that is supposed to be haunted provides a mystery.

Nixon, J. L. (2001). *The house on Hackman's Hill*. New York: Delacorte. (5–8).

What happened to Dr. Hackman? Who can explain the strange events that are happening?

Paterson, K. (1978). *The great Gilly Hopkins*. New York: Crowell. (4–7).

Gilly is a hardened child of the foster care system until she lives with Trotter, a foster parent. She finally meets her biological mother and comes face-to-face with reality.

Paterson, K. (2001). *The same stuff as stars*. New York: Clarion. (4–8).

Angel is an 11-year-old who has had to grow up too fast. She and her brother have been left with their elderly great-grandmother.

Polacco, P. (2001). *Mr. Lincoln's way*. New York: Penguin Putnam. (3–6).

The class bully learns some profound lessons from the principal.

Polacco, P. (2002). *When lightening comes in a jar*. New York: Penguin Putnam. (3–6).

At family reunions, collecting fireflies connects the generations.

Powell, R. (1995). *Dean Duffy*. New York: Farrar, Straus & Giroux. (6–10).

Dean Duffy must make some hard decisions about his future. Will he be able to overcome his slump and learn to play baseball professionally?

Proimos, J. (1999). *The loudness of Sam*. New York: Harcourt. (PreK–3).

Sam has been loud since birth. He visits his aunt who thinks he should be quiet, until the time Sam gets ready to leave.

Quarles, H. (1998). *A door near here*. New York: Delacorte. (6–9).

Four siblings try to make it on their own after their father leaves and their mother becomes alcoholic.

Rylant, C. (2000–2002). The *Cobble Street Cousins* series (W. A. Halperin, Illus.). New York: Simon & Schuster. (2–4).

Three cousins stay with their aunt while their parents are away.

Schraff, A. (2000–2001). The *Bluford* Series. West Berlin, NJ: Townsend Press. (5–8).

A series of seven books about African-American high school students and their families.

Shreve, S. (2001). *Blister*. New York: Scholastic. (3–6).

Blister's family disintegrates after the stillborn death of a sister. Blister is able to bounce back because of her positive attitude.

Slote, A. (1991). *Finding Buck McHenry*. New York: HarperCollins. (5–8).

When Jason is cut from the baseball team, he seeks coaching assistance from the school's custodian.

Spinelli, J. (1997). *Wringer*. New York: HarperCollins. (5–8).

LaRue knows that when he is 10, he will be expected to take part in the annual pigeon shoot; he does so in an unexpected manner.

Voigt, C. (1985). *The runner*. New York: Atheneum. (7–10).

A powerful book in which family conflicts are intense. Bullet takes much of his frustration out by running, which ultimately leads to his death.

Weaver, W. (1993). *Striking out*. New York: HarperCollins. (5–8).

This book addresses the way Billy balances baseball with responsibilities for work.

Weaver, W. (1995). *Farm team*. New York: HarperCollins. (5–8).

With Billy's father in jail, the balance between work and baseball is even more crucial.

White, R. (1996). *Belle Prater's boy*. New York: Farrar, Straus & Giroux. (4–8).

When Belle Prater disappears, her son Woodrow goes to live with his grandparents, next door to his cousin. The cousins develop a close and supportive relationship.

Whiles, D. (2001). *Love, Ruby Lavender*. San Diego: Harcourt. (4–7).

> Ruby and her grandmother have many adventures until the grandmother goes to Hawaii to visit a new grandchild.

Woodson, J. (2000). *Miracle's boys*. New York: Penguin Putnam. (6–10).

> After their mother dies, three siblings try to live on their own.

Zusak, M. (1998). *The underdog*. New York: Scholastic. (6–10).

> In a working class family, life is not easy. Cam and his brother Ruben get into trouble together.

Zusak, M. (2000). *Fighting Ruben Wolfe*. New York: Scholastic. (6–10).

> Ruben and Cam fight professionally to earn money for the family. Finally, they must fight each other.

Zusak, M. (2002). *Getting the girl*. New York: Scholastic. (6–10).

> Cam falls for his brother's ex-girlfriend and bears the brunt of his brother's anger.

References and Books for Further Reading

Brooks, G. W., Waterman, R., & Allington, R. (2003). A national survey of teachers' reports of children's favorite series books. *The Dragon Lode, 21*, 8–14.

Burch, R. (1973). The new realism. In V. Haviland (Ed.), *Children and literature: Views and reviews*. Glenview, IL: Scott Foresman.

Copenhaver, J. (1993). Instances of inquiry. *Primary Voices, K–6*, 6–12.

Daniels, H. (1994). *Literature circles: Voice and choice in the student-centered classroom*. York, ME: Stenhouse.

Hamilton, V. (1992). Planting seeds. *The Horn Book, 57*, 674–680.

Harris, V. J., et al. (2001). Controversial issues in children's literature. *The New Advocate, 15*, vii–viii.

Jordan, A. D. (1997a). *Follow the gleam: Teaching and learning genre with children and young adults, Part I*. Brandon, VT: Esmont.

Jordan, A. D. (1997b). *Follow the gleam: Teaching and learning genre with children and young adults Part II*. Brandon, VT: Esmont.

McElhoe, J. S. (1999). Images of grandparents in children's literature. *New Advocate, 12*, 249–258.

Poe, E. A. (1999). Reading to survive. *Signal, 23*, 3.

Russell, D. L. (1994). *Literature for children: A short introduction*. (2nd ed.). White Plains, NY: Longman.

Sharp, S. (1992). Why didacticism endures. *The Horn Book, 68*, 694–696.

Steele, M. (1973). Realism, truth and honesty. In V. Haviland (Ed.), *Children and literature: Views and review*, Glenview, IL: Scott Foresman.

Taxel, J. (1994). Political correctness, cultural politics, and writing for young people. *New Advocate, 1*, 93–107.

People Then: Historical Fiction

9

KEY TERMS

historical fiction	issues
historical periods	KWWL charts
immigration	

GUIDING QUESTIONS

Historical fiction books share many similarities with contemporary realistic fiction. Because historical situations often resonate with situations children and young adults find themselves in today, this is a favorite genre for many readers, especially those who have an interest in history. As you read, think about the following questions and the kinds of connections readers can make with the characters.

1. What are some of the similarities between the problems presented in contemporary realistic fiction (see Chapter 8) and the problems presented in historical fiction books?

2. Why are the problems presented in historical fiction related to those currently faced by young people?

3. Why is the setting so important for historical fiction books?

4. Why might some books in this genre be challenged, censored, or banned?

5. Why do you think that some historical periods have many more books written about them than other periods? What are the implications for children and teaching?

6. What subject do you think is most neglected in historical fiction? Why might this be so?

"History is the collection of stories people tell about the past to explain the present, and the most memorable stories usually center on the actions and dreams of remarkable human beings" (Ives & Burns, 1996). Historical fiction is the genre that tells stories that are based on fact but nonetheless are fictionalized. Simply stated, historical fiction is the genre in which the story takes place long enough ago that the setting is considered "historical." However, the story must also be realistic, including events and actions that could have actually occurred. As is true for contemporary realistic fiction, no magical or make-believe elements can be used to allow problems to be solved. (See Chapter 8 for a description of the similarities between contemporary and historical fiction.) The characters, although imagined, must act in a realistic manner consistent with how individuals might have thought and acted at the time. They may interact with actual historical figures, but no made-up conversations can occur with those figures. The setting, including the language used, must accurately represent the time period.

Jean Fritz brings to life explorers who changed the map of the world.

The attitudes and behaviors must reflect those of the historical times rather than those of the present. This means that some readers may regard aspects of a particular story as racist, stereotyped, or condescending, an unfair criticism if what is described would have been realistic in that time and setting. The themes in historical fiction are similar to the themes of any good literature: They must connect with the life, dreams, and heart of the reader.

FIGURE 9.1 KWWL charts can be helpful in reading and understanding historical fiction.			
K What we already KNOW	**W** What we WANT to know	**W** WHERE can we find what we want to know?	**L** What did we LEARN?

Historical Fiction

"The more things change, the more they stay the same." This familiar quotation is a good description of *historical fiction,* the genre discussed in this chapter. When reading these books, you may notice that many of the themes and events found in them are similar to those found in contemporary realistic fiction. Often, only the details and the contexts have changed; the events remain parallel.

Katherine Paterson (1992), author of many award-winning children's books, notes: "I've been writing a chapter this year for a book entitled *The World in 1492*. My assignment is 'Asia in 1492.' What I discovered about the world in 1492 and Asia in 1492 was that it looked depressingly like the world in 1992" (p. 165).

In both historical and contemporary realistic fiction, events reflect what has happened or could have happened. The similarities exist because, throughout time, the same kinds of events occur again and again.

The interactions among people of different eras are also similar. Some people in the past were governed by greed and self-interest, just as some people are today. Mean-spiritedness and the desire to take advantage of those who may be weaker are traits not limited to any historical era—these characteristics certainly are evident in historical fiction as well as in contemporary realistic fiction. However, one also reads about characters in past and present settings who exemplify many positive characteristics. They are compassionate, unselfish, and benevolent. Characters are most realistic when they have a reasonable mix of good and not-so-good characteristics—because then they are most like real people.

What makes historical fiction unique? The major difference between this genre and that of contemporary realistic fiction is the setting and the time period. These impact the story because they influence the language used, the interactions among people, the social traditions displayed, the cultural behaviors, and the conflicts that occur. Rosemary Sutcliff (1973) suggests that "the way people act is conditioned by the social custom of their day and age—even the way they think and feel" (p. 308). When writing about a setting that is historically quite different from the present, authors obviously must include more details about the context. This can cause problems for the authors. If too much detail is provided about the setting and the time period, readers may lose interest in the book itself (Enciso, 2000). The integration of these details into the story is a distinguishing characteristic between well-written historical fiction and that which is merely mediocre.

Choice of characters, both the main characters and those who support them, is also particularly important. Placing fictional characters in actual events and creating actions and conversations for them is acceptable; doing the same with actual historical people is not. An author must have documentation of the characters' actions and conversations in order to use them in historical realistic fiction.

Historical fiction has additional characteristics that distinguish it from realistic fiction:

1. The details describing the historical setting are portrayed so that readers comprehend what it was like in that particular time period. This allows them to be drawn into the times.
2. The actions, thoughts, conversations, and feelings accurately reflect the historical period.
3. Although actual historical events may be used, no conversations or actions of actual people are included unless the conversations or actions can be documented.
4. There are descriptions of, or references to, historical events that are documented or events that could have occurred in the time period.

Issues in Historical Fiction

Experts do not all agree on how historical fiction is defined. For example, some authors suggest that an author must write about a time other than his or her own Adamson (1987) and Jordan (1997). However, there have been many books written by individuals describing their lives as they grew up or traumatic experiences they experienced. For example, the Laura Ingalls Wilder books are accounts of Laura's years growing up. Are they really historical fiction? Should they be considered memoirs instead? Enciso (2000) suggest that because this series of books may actually have been co-authored by Laura and her daughter, Rose, they should be considered historical fiction. Other books of memoirs are considered nonfiction. "It is not surprising, then, that the line between historical fiction and nonfiction is a blurred one at best" (Enciso, 2000).

Some of the events in this genre's books are unpleasant, but they reflect real life in a particular historical era. A few of the books deal with the uglier side of life. Death and dying, cruelty and abuse, racism and sexism are integral elements of many plots. Hester Burton (1973), author of several books of historical fiction, reflects: "History is not pretty. The Nazi concentration camps aside, I think people were far more cruel to each other in times past than they are today. The law was certainly more cruel. So was poverty. So was the treatment of children. The brutality of times past may shock the oversensitive" (p. 303).

As you read books in this genre, you will discover that addressing sensitive *issues* often seems to be more acceptable in historical fiction than it is in contemporary realistic fiction. For example, two of Avi's books, *Night Journeys* and *Encounter at Easton,* describe events in the late 1700s. The community is trying to find two runaway bondsmen. Twelve-year-old Peter wants to help find them to get the reward; then he finds out that the runaways are children his own age. Elizabeth was branded with an "M" on her thumb because she stole food; Robert was sentenced because he

Marika is a young girl in Budapest during the 1930s.

helped her. Elizabeth died trying to escape; Robert survived. Clearly, this is not a pretty picture but the immediacy of the abuse seems to be lessened because of its historical setting.

Because of the realistic nature of historical fiction, some parents and educators may try to limit the choices of books available for children to read. They may feel that they have a duty to screen readers from what they believe is objectionable. This happens in large part because, as Sutcliff (1973) suggests, the "child is liable to absorb ideas from books which may remain with him for the rest of his life, and even play some part in determining the kind of person that he is going to become" (p. 306). When adults decide the content is unsuitable for a group of readers, this is an overt form of censorship.

A more subtle form of censorship occurs in both contemporary and historical realistic fiction when authors choose which societal issues and events to write about. For example, during World War II, little quality children's literature was written about the war that was occurring. "Pulp war stories" appeared in which "war is reduced to a simple adventure story in which good is pitted against evil" (Hunt, 1994, p. 199). Not until the mid-1960s, when many authors who grew up during World War II began to write, did readers have opportunities to identify with characters who experienced the events and interactions that could have occurred during the war years.

Hunt continues:

> Writers for children generally mirror very accurately the mood and expectations of the country. Although most adults (including writers) were aware the inevitability of U.S. involvement in World War II, a reluctance to think about the implications kept even distant echoes of it out of most children's books except for propagandistic adventures. . . . It was only when those children grew up that they wrote, for the next generation after them, about the experiences of the 1940s—perhaps because it was only then, a quarter of a century and more later, that their readers were ready to hear about it. (p. 205)

The contention might be made, however, that only then were the adults ready for the children to hear about these experiences.

Not all books of this genre, however, are so intense. Many present life experiences have to do with the everlasting conflicts inherent in growing up, of relationships in families, and the problems of peer relationships. For example, Katherine Paterson's *Preacher's Boy* tells the story of Robbie Hewitt from Decoration Day 1899, when a girl's bloomers mysteriously appear on a flag pole until the eve of January 1, 1900, the beginning of a new millennium.

When Does the Present Become the Past?

Readers are often confused when attempting to classify books as contemporary realistic fiction or historical fiction: Just when does the present become the past? Books that were contemporary when they were published may, over time, become historical. Children who are currently in the third grade think of the historical past as any time before they were born. Adults have very different perspectives regarding the historical past. Many books are easy to classify. Scott O'Dell places *My Name Is Not Angelica* in 1733; in *Waiting for Anya,* Michael Morpurgo uses a World War II setting. Both of these books are clearly historical fiction. However, *Snail Mail No More* by Paula Danziger and Ann Martin and the Herculeah Jones mysteries by Betsy Byars are set in the present. These are obviously contemporary realistic fiction.

Various children's literature experts employ different schemes for categorizing books as historical or contemporary fiction. Some authors classify anything set after World War II as contemporary fiction (Norton, 1995; Russell, 1994), whereas other authors classify everything up until the Gulf War as historical fiction (Cullinan & Galda, 1994; Huck, Hepler, & Hickman, 1993; Reed, 1994). Perhaps the most sensible solution is for readers to decide whether the book is contemporary or historical, which permits them to use their experience and judgment as they respond to a book. As long as readers can support a classification, it should be honored.

Organizing the Categories of Historical Fiction

To be most easily used, books of historical fiction need to be in categories. Readers who want to read about a particular era need to be able to quickly and efficiently find those books. However, this genre also has many books that have important themes that may not be related to a particular time; their themes are more universal in nature. Although most of the subcategories in this chapter are based on a modification of the historical periods Crabtree, Nash, Gagnon, and Waugh (1992) describe, two other categories emerged: families and friends, and survival and growing up. The themes and events in these categories are not dependent on any specific time era, even though the setting is long ago. The books in these two categories typify the idea that the more things change, the more they stay the same.

Recently, *series* of historical fiction books have been published. They share many of the characteristics of the series books described in Chapter 8. However, there are notable differences between the historical series books and other series books. These books are written by different authors, all of whom have earned a reputation for quality writing. They are set in many different historical periods, do not have the same plots, nor do they have the same characters. Most are written in journal or diary form. They are of great interest to middle school readers and are good for reluctant readers. They will be described here rather than in the historical eras section later in this chapter.

The *Dear America* series is written in the format of diaries of young adolescent girls who could have lived during particular times of history. Included in each book is an epilogue so that readers have an idea of "what happened next," a historical note that provides factual information about the times, and pictures of original documents, maps, and photographs. Readers gain insight about what life might have been like for girls their own ages long ago. Some of the books in this series include the following. *Love Thy Neighbor: The Tory Diary of Prudence Emerson* by Ann Turner takes place in Greenmarsh, Massachusetts, in 1774. Prudence and her family are Tories, who are loyal to the British king. Reading about this perspective, which is often not understood nor written about, provides background for understanding the American Revolutionary War. Megan McDonald writes about moving from Missouri to Mexico and life on the trail in *All the Stars in the Sky: The Santa Fe Trail Diary of Florrie Mack Ryder*. In 1848, traveling was not easy; the hardships as well as the good events are recounted from the perspective of Florrie. We sometimes forget that, as late as 1873, immigrants were moving to this country in search of religious freedom—as well as land of their own.

The *My Name Is America* series is written to appeal to boys in the middle school. Many of the time periods are the same but the books are the journals kept by boys. This series also includes historical notes, with illustrations and maps. Sid Hite writes a compelling story of 16-year-old Rufus, who sees the battle of Fredericksburg in 1862. Rufus writes "Maybe that's what war is. You lose when you lose and lose when you win" in *The Journal of Rufus Rowe: A Witness to the Battle of Fredericksburg*. A period of time that often seems to be skipped in the study of American History is the late 1800s. In *The Journal of Finn Reardon: A Newsie*, we read the insights of a young man who supports his family after his father dies by peddling newspapers. Susan Campbell Bartoletti provides a picture of life in 1899: gangs, a strike, and no school for the newsies!

The *My America* series differs from those previously described because each book is part of a "miniseries." For example, Kathryn Lasky has written *Hope in My Heart, Sofia's Immigrant Diary, Book One,* and *Home at Last: Sofia's Immigrant Diary, Book Two.* These two books chronicle Sofia's arrival in America from Italy, when she is separated from her parents and quarantined, to when she is reunited with her parents in the North End of Boston in 1903.

A "mini-series" for boys is Sharon Dennis Wyeth's *Corey's Underground Railroad Diary.* In Book 1, *Freedom's Wings,* Corey describes his daily life as a slaved child in Kentucky and then his escape on the Underground Railroad; in Book 2, *Flying Free,* Corey details his life in Canada as a freed person; in Book 3, *Message in the Sky,* Corey plans a way to help one of his old friends escape from slavery.

Families and Friends

Historical fiction often centers on family stories. The family unit reflects the culture, issues, and way of life in a historical setting. For Amen McBee, life is good at the end of the 19th century as she and her sisters explore the family estate, learn to use the new Kodak camera, and get new siblings. However, Amen worries about a neighbor who keeps trained doves. Her interactions with him have a great impact on her. Betsy Byars' *Keeper of the Doves* gives insight into this period in history.

In the 1940s, baseball was one of the country's favorite sports. Girls were playing as much as boys. In *Players in Pigtails*, Shana Corey shares the story of how one girl follows her dream and is a player in the All-American Girls Professional Baseball League. The illustrations by Rebecca Gibbon make this book even more attractive to those who like to read about girls and baseball.

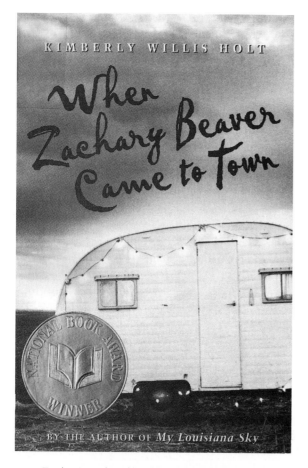

Zachary is abandoned in a small Texas town of the 1960s.

whom she is working. He goes and helps with the farming; in the process, he is able to trust and love again because of Gunar, Olaf, and, of course, his grandmother. *Alida's Song* is partly autobiographical, as well as a tribute to the impact of a loving grandmother.

Janell has always had a special relationship with her grandfather. After her grandma dies, Grandpap comes to live with Janell and her family. When he buys a 1962 Cadillac convertible, he lets Janell drive—on the sly. When a neighbor moves into Grandpap's old place, the family is most upset—but when Janell is able to drive the neighbor to the hospital and saves his life, everyone comes to terms with who they are and their place in the community. Kimberly Willis Holt has shared a bit of mid-century Americana in her book, *Dancing in Cadillac Light.*

Another book by Kimberly Willis Holt, *When Zachary Beaver Came to Town,* looks at life in a small Texas town during the late 1960s. Nothing much happens in Antler—until the fattest boy in the world is abandoned there in a trailer. Toby and his friend Cal first look at Zachary as a freak but then become his friend. After Toby's mom abandons him and Cal's brother dies in Vietnam, the boys have a falling out. Their responsibilities for Zachary Beaver help to heal the rift.

Survival and Growing Up

This literature is frequently called "coming of age" literature because it tells stories of young people who overcome obstacles and become more mature in the process.

Crispin, Avi's 2003 Newbery Award winner, is set in 14th-century England. After his mother dies, "Asta's son" is accused of murdering the local priest who first told him his name. Crispin is wanted "dead or alive" for reasons unknown to him. He escapes and becomes friends with Bear, the traveling juggler. Their secrets and their trust in each other bind them together through situations where each could be killed. Crispin's identity is revealed at the end. This is truly a very intense survival book.

Michael Cadnum has written several books that take place in the Viking era, including *Raven of the Waves*. In this book, the boys of the village were all trained as warriors, eager to go on their first voyage. Lidsmod is no different; when Hego is injured, he gets his chance. After the crew has burned and sacked villages, Lidsmod's feelings change when he must watch

Isabelle Anderson's father died in 1942. Since then, Isabelle's mother has had an increasingly difficult time coping. She finally sends Isabelle to one aunt and uncle and her sisters to another aunt and uncle. Although the three girls seem to be able to make the transition to living in the country, they want to go back home. Isabelle steals money from her aunt and uncle and gets on the bus, after meeting her older sister, and goes home. There are even more adjustments there. Their mother has sold their house, has married, and is expecting a baby. In Anne Yivisaker's *Dear Papa*, readers can identify with a young girl who experiences many changes in her life that she is trying to cope with.

Gary Paulsen writes of a teenaged boy who is struggling in school, working part-time jobs, and trying to avoid his alcoholic parents. His grandmother invites him to spend a summer with her and the two farmers for a 13-year-old captive with a withered arm. Both boys mature and change under the conditions of battle.

In *Daughter of the Wind,* Michael Cadnum shows that during Viking times physical force ruled and that revenge was an acceptable means of justice. The relationship between Hallgerd, who is kidnapped from her home, and Gauk, a young warrior, is a part of this story that focuses on both adventure and friendship.

Historical Periods

(*Note:* See the section on series books for titles that also fit in these time periods.)

The story characters in various *historical periods* face many of the same challenges as those in the previous section—growing up with or without families, establishing relationships with peers and adults, and surviving on their own. However, these young people have no control over the events that affect them. Slavery, war, economic hardships, and political upheavals change their entire way of life and create new challenges.

The books in this section are organized chronologically, but considerable overlap occurs in the years included in the various categories. History resists neat categorization.

Pre-Colonial Era

Pedro's Journal by Pam Conrad and *I Sailed with Columbus* by Miriam Schlein tell about Columbus's voyages from a cabin boy's point of view. In both books, the cabin boy is aware that Columbus is keeping two sets of records, and each is ashamed of the mistreatment of the natives. Overall, each writer gives a relatively positive view of Columbus and his goals. We find similarities in the authors' descriptions of events, although they differ in the emphasis placed on some events, so both books suggest interesting possibilities for critical comparison reading.

Jane Yolen offers a very different perspective of Columbus in *Encounter.* A native boy dreams of strangers who are coming to the village and the problems they will bring with them, but because he is only a child, the elders ignore him. When the strangers arrive, he and several others are taken captive. He is able to escape, but disease and colonization doom his people.

Being a member of a tribe in which members get an adult name by demonstrating an ability to use a bow and arrow is not a good thing—especially if one's vision is poor. Walnut cannot count the number of fingers on an upraised hand but learns that, by listening, he is able to know more about the setting than those who can see. He earns the name *Sees Behind Trees* and, as he supports other tribe members, he grows in confidence and strength. Michale Dorris has written a book that makes the reader ponder the issues presented.

Colonial Era

Two books for younger readers describe the life of the Pilgrims soon after coming to the New World. Gary Bowen uses the diary of 13-year-old Christopher Seals, an indentured orphan who stays with the Brewster family, in *Stranded at Plimoth Plantation, 1626,* to describe the challenges endured. Cheryl Harness presents an interesting and carefully researched account of a fictional family designed to be representative of the Pilgrims who arrived on the *Mayflower* and their struggles. The detailed drawings and bibliography make *Three Young Pilgrims* a particularly interesting book.

A new series of books for middle grade readers—*Colonial Williamsburg: Young Americans* by Joan Lowery Nixon has been published. *Ann's Story: 1747* tells of 9-year-old Ann, who would rather help her father, who is a doctor, than learn the proper duties of a young woman. There are historical notes on a variety of topics, maps, and recipes. *Caesar's Story: 1759* tells of a young slave and a white child growing up as friends. However, as each gets older, the slave family is separated and Caesar must become the personal servant of the boy who was once his best friend. In *Maria's Story: 1773,* after the death of her father, Maria's mother must take over the family printing business. However, Maria's mother is in danger of losing her business because of the anti-British articles that she prints. In *John's Story: 1775,* the war is imminent. John's family is divided about what to do— seek peace or fight for their rights. Seeing the war from these different perspectives provides middle school students with an understanding of the complexity of war and how it affects families.

By the late 1600s, Salem, Massachusetts, was the setting for the ugly events known as the Salem witch trials. Ann Rinaldi writes graphically of the context in which they occurred and about the effects on the accusers, those accused, and those who were part of this community. *A Break with Charity: A Story About the Salem Witch Trials* is fascinating reading for older readers.

In Kathryn Lasky's book *Beyond the Burning Time,* Mary Chase's widowed mother is named a witch and sentenced to hang. Although they are terrified, Mary and her brother are determined to save their mother, who is imprisoned under terrible conditions while awaiting execution. In the end, their mother must have her foot amputated, but she escapes and the family starts a new life in Bermuda. This carefully researched book includes interesting documentation.

Monday and her mother come to New York from their home in Madagascar in 1760 to prove that Uncle Frederick, who has been sold as a slave, is actually a free man. Sharon Dennis Wyeth did extensive research about the African Americans who were living at that time; *Once on this River* is a spectacular book with a surprising ending.

There are many stories of white children being taken captive by Indians. One such book, *The Ransom of Mercy Carter* by Caroline B. Cooney, tells the story of one child who decides to stay with her Indian family, even when she has the chance to be ransomed and returned to the English. From February 1704, when her village is attacked, to May 1705, Mercy thinks of returning to those she knew in Deerfield. When the chance actually comes to return, she (and 29 other children who have become members of the tribe that adopted them) decides that she prefers the Indian families.

Nicholas Young runs away from his father and the butcher and stows away on Captain James Cook's ship, going on a three-year voyage around the world. The story, told in Nicholas' diary, recounts the discoveries made by naturalist Joseph Banks and Captain Cook. Because Nicholas is literate, he is able to be a part of both the crew and to help Joseph Banks. *Stowaway,* by Karen Hesse, is based on records and journals written at the time. The book includes maps, a list of those on the ship, the ship's itinerary, and a glossary.

Revolutionary War Era

Children's authors have written about many of the dimensions of the Revolutionary War, including the colonists, the loyalists, the Native Americans, adults, children, and many others. Literature helps children understand complex periods of history such as this by helping them identify with the characters and their emotions as they hear or read the stories of this period.

The Great Big Wagon that Rang: How the Liberty Bell was Saved by Joseph Slate is a book for younger readers. Slate uses rhythmic prose to tell the story of a farmer who sells his produce and then carries the Liberty Bell home in his wagon to hide it from the British.

When the Revolutionary War began, both the British and the colonists wanted the Native Americans to fight with them. This caused great problems for Coshmoo, a Delaware Indian boy, and Daniel, a young settler, who are best friends. Sally Keehn clearly illustrates in *Moon of Two Dark Horses* that taking sides in any conflict often means making life-threatening decisions.

A similar situation occurs in Joseph Bruchac's *The Arrow Over the Door.* Samuel is resentful of his family's Quaker pacifism at a time when everyone takes sides. Stands Straight is an Abenaki whose family has been killed by colonists. The Abenakis are trying to decide if they will fight on the side of the British or the colonists. The Abenakis join the Quakers at worship and the two boys interact. The story is told by the two boys, with each telling his side. The book is based on an actual incident and the author provides additional historical information.

As is demonstrated in Sally Lunn's *The Hollow Tree,* not all people, even those in the same family, were supporters of the American Revolution. Phoebe's father joins the Patriots and is killed in one of the early battles. Her favorite cousin, Gideon, joins the Loyalists and is captured and killed by the Patriots. Although Phoebe refuses to take sides, she honors Gideon's request to take a secret message to Fort Ticonderoga but on the way helps a patriot spy escape. Although she is regarded as a traitor by the Loyalists, Phoebe is able to make them understand her actions and lives with them in Canada after the war ends.

Ann Rinaldi has written several books for older readers about the Revolutionary War era. All of these books have strong female characters who provide insights that may allow a clearer understanding of the times. *The Fifth of March: A Story of the Boston Massacre* shows that every issue has at least two perspectives. Rachel Marsh is a Patriot and an indentured servant girl for John Adams, but she falls in love with a young British soldier. Her conflicting feelings require her to make very difficult decisions. In *The Secret of Sarah Revere,* readers are given a picture of the tensions that occur in the family of Paul Revere before and during the war. In *Finishing Becca: A Story About Peggy Shippen and Benedict Arnold,* 14-year-old Becca serves as the personal maid of Peggy Shippen.

Historical evidence suggests that Peggy may have manipulated Arnold into becoming a traitor. When most of us think about the Revolutionary War, we think of events that took place in Boston and the Northeast.

Building and Expansion

Following the Revolutionary War and continuing well into the 1900s, the United States expanded and grew in remarkable ways. Some of these expansions were the result of events that today's Americans are not proud of; others demonstrate the best qualities that we still celebrate. For many people, America was a land of opportunity, and with hard work and persistence, people could have better lives. Other families and groups were discriminated against and their ways of living were destroyed. This category of books covers a large span of time and cuts across several historical eras.

One of the events during this time period was the War of 1812. Caroline's brother Charlie was supposed to have died at sea. She didn't believe it and tried to find out what really happened. She found out the truth but it was not what she expected. K. M. Kimball's *The Star-Spangled Search* describes the intrigue associated with any war, making it very realistic.

Two books for younger readers tell of families who moved from the northeast to the west. In *Sunsets of the West,* a picture book by Tony Johnston, the pictures and text convey both the difficulties of the trip as well as the feeling of satisfaction the family had as they accomplished their goal. Eve Bunting presents a thoughtful story of Zoe and her family, who move to the prairies of the Nebraska Territory. Zoe's mother is especially sad, so the two sisters surprise her by finding a clump of *Dandelions* and planting it on the roof of their soddie. The illustrations imply that, once the dandelions have taken root and spread and the fields are planted, there is acceptance and even enjoyment of this new life.

Gary Paulsen has written a series of five books about Francis Tucket, a 14-year-old going west with his family on the Oregon Trail. Francis *(Mr. Tucket)* is captured by Pawnees and escapes only with the help of Mr. Grimes. In the second book, *Call Me Francis Tucket,* he rescues a young girl and her younger brother. The three of them are captured by outlaws in *Tucket's Ride.* They find ancient treasures in *Tucket's Gold.* Finally, in *Tucket's Home,* they are still seeking Francis's family but have several challenges before they head home. The adventures take place from 1847 to 1849 and present a picture of what it may have been like for the adventurous person of that time.

Also going west, between 1850 and 1929, were the Orphan Trains—trains that carried children from the East Coast to the West, where they were thought to be adoptable and/or needed as workers. Eve Bunting's *Train to Somewhere* chronicles the story of Marianne, who is the last child to be chosen from the train. Adopted by an elderly couple who initially had wanted a boy, she finally finds love and acceptance.

Karen Cushman tells the story of *Rodzina,* who, at age 12, has decided that she can live by herself. On the Orphan Train, Rodzina unwillingly befriends several other children, goes through some very traumatic experiences, and finally bonds with Miss Doctor, who had been sent as the guardian with the orphans. Readers will gain much insight into what it is like to be lonely and abandoned as they identify with Rodzina.

Rodzina, an abandoned girl, rides the orphan train.

In 1840, New England was developing transportation canals. Young Etta, an orphan who ran away from her foster home, finds an abandoned cabin near the new canal. She convinces Walter, who is hiding from his abusive alcoholic father, to let her live there, too. They develop a tense friendship but learn to work together. Etta finds a place of her own and helps to protect the locks from the local farmers, whose land has been taken to build the canal. Carol Otis Hurst's *Through the Locks* reflects some of her family history.

Civil War Era

The themes of slavery and the Civil War are inextricably tied together and influence the entire history of our nation. Slavery was a pivotal issue before, during, and after the Civil War. Understanding this period in history allows readers to understand current events better. The attitudes and interactions among the people living during this time, the risks they took for themselves and others, and the decisions they made have had long-term effects on all of us.

Escaping from slavery is an important element in many books written about this time period. Jip tumbled off a wagon when he was a young boy. He could never understand why his mother never stopped to pick him up. He lives in the town's poor farm, doing what is expected of him, but always wondering about his past. A stranger inquires about Jip, which raises more questions about who he is and where he comes from. With the help and support of his teacher and her friend, Jip goes to safety and finds the answers to his questions. Katherine Paterson has created a fascinating book describing *Jip: His Story*.

Katherine Ayers shares a way that abolitionists could aide slaves in escaping from their masters in *Stealing South*. Will had been a part of the Underground Railroad for years. When he knew he did not want to continue to be a farmer he bought a wagon and planned to become a peddler. On his last trip as a conductor on the Underground Railroad, the runaway slave convinced him to go to Kentucky as a slave stealer, find his younger brother, and bring him north before he was sold down south. Stealing slaves is a perspective that we often do not read about.

In *Nightjohn* and *Sarny: A Life Remembered*, Gary Paulsen describes how the human spirit survives even under the greatest adversity. Dismemberment was the punishment for teaching slaves how to learn

to read and write. Nightjohn is tortured but still his mission is to teach others to read. Sarny learns to read and, when she finally becomes a free woman, she passes on the gift of literacy that she received from Nightjohn.

Many times, the patriotism of young people is so great that they will lie about their age to join the army. Fourteen-year-old Thrasher tries to prove to his father that he has courage by enrolling in the Confederate Army. He experiences the misery of war and returns with an injury. His father then accepts him as a man, but at what price? Susan Bartoletti presents Thrasher's misery in *No Man's Land: A Young Soldier's Story*.

For at least two years, 15-year-old Sarah has been planning to run away from her abusive father. When he makes plans for her to marry the widower next door, she must leave sooner than she planned. She cuts off her hair, disguises herself as a young man, and joins the Union Army. She is successful as a male nurse until her disguise is discovered. She is given the alternative of being punished or of being a spy for Allen Pinkerton. Ann Rinaldi's *Girl in Blue* gives readers a behind-the-scenes look at how spying helped the Union win the war.

A little-known aspect of the Civil War occurred with General Grant's General Order #11, in which all Jews were commanded to evacuate the territory for violating trade regulations. Hannah and her family lose everything they have. After very difficult experiences, they are finally allowed to return to Holly Springs, Mississippi, to start over. *The War Within* by Carol Matas includes a copy of the Orders, as well as the letter sent to Abraham Lincoln asking that they be revoked.

Many readers are familiar with Mildred Taylor's books about the Logan family. *The Land*, set in the time of Reconstruction following the Civil War, is the prequel to *Roll of Thunder, Hear my Cry*. Cassie Logan's grandfather had a difficult time growing up because of his mixed racial heritage. However, he was able to get an education and was determined to work so that he could own his own land. This book presents readers with an understanding of how important land was to those who were treated unjustly.

Industrialization

The Civil War forwarded the movement toward industrialization and the peace made raw materials available. The industrial movement, however, was built on the labor of men, women, and even children who were in many ways enslaved to the factory owners and managers. In *The Bobbin Girl,* Emily Arnold McCully writes about 10-year-old Rebecca, a bobbin girl in a textile mill. Working conditions are awful, and when the owners of the mill plan to lower the already too-low wages, she must decide whether to join the strike or continue working.

A mining story takes place in Utah in the early 1900s. After Tommy's dad was killed in a mining accident, Tommy drops out of school at age 11 to work in the mines himself. However, he begins to develop his true talent, which is singing and composing songs. He is conflicted by what other people want him to be—union worker, miner, song writer, and student. *Rockbuster* by Gloria Skurzynski presents an intense picture of the times when unions were becoming a force in the mining industry.

Industrialization often means that some craftspeople will give up their craft to work in a factory. In *Basket Moon,* Mary Lyn Ray tells the story of a young boy whose family made baskets to sell in the city. He accompanies his father on a selling trip and is made fun of by the local boys. When they return home, he wants his father to stop making baskets and tries to destroy the baskets already made. Because of the wise advice of Big Joe, he decides that he will carry on the tradition of making baskets. The Author's note says that, by the 1950s, baskets were being replaced by cardboard, bags, and plastic, so few families continued to make baskets.

Immigration

Many who came to the United States during the *immigration* movement fled lives of injustice and poverty to come to work in U.S. factories and farms. *Nory Ryan's Song* by Patricia Reilly Giff provides the background for why many people immigrated. Ireland was in the midst of the potato famine. There was great hunger, cold, and need. Finally, Nory's father sent tickets to come to America. The choice to go was not easy, because of Nory's commitment to Anna.

A present-day immigration story is Eve Bunting's *How Many Days to America? A Thanksgiving Story.* A family from an unnamed Caribbean country leaves their country and heads for America and freedom. They crowd into a small fishing boat and set off under the cover of night, encountering thieves and soldiers, but finally reach the shores of the United States.

The 20th Century: Wars, Issues, and Events

The 20th-century wars provide the subject for many books, but more of these books focus on World War II than World War I, the Korean War, the Vietnam War, or the more recent Gulf War. Perhaps this is because everyone living during World War II was involved at some level, and it drastically changed people's lives. Also, authors tend to write about their childhood experiences and memories, so this far-reaching event became the subject of many books. This section includes a sampling from several of these wars, but consult a card catalog or a computer database to locate books that fit your educational needs.

World War I

Gloria Skurzynski portrays life in the United States of World War I through the lives of two boys in *Goodbye, Billy Radish.* In a steel town of 1917, the men who are not soldiers work 12 hours a day, seven days a week. Boys as young as 14 work these long shifts as well. The heavy work schedule leads to factory accidents and deaths, but accidents are not the only threat to life: A dreaded flu epidemic sweeps through the United States and takes Billy's life.

Pam and her father raise homing pigeons—rare ones that are able to fly at night. After her father goes off to fight in World War I, Pam is in charge of the pigeons. When she finds some of her pigeons missing, she is afraid they are being stolen and used as spies for the enemy. Elizabeth McDavid Jones' *The Night Flyers* is part of the *American Girl History Mysteries* series.

World War II

Many fine pieces of literature exist that focus on this period. A number of these books show the war's impact on different people. The themes in this section are concerned with the prejudice that fear creates, the importance of freedom, and the courage to prevail in the face of great difficulty.

The prejudice against Germans during World War I was prevalent throughout the United States during World War II as well, and that prejudice extended to the Japanese living on the West Coast. Because of fear and prejudice, Japanese Americans were interned in camps located in remote areas of the United States. Yoshika Uchida brings these events to life in *The Bracelet, Journey to Topaz,* and *Journey Home,* fictional accounts based on her own family's experiences. In *The Bracelet,* a book for younger readers, Emi, a second grader, and her Japanese-American family are sent to an internment camp. They first live in a horse stall at a former racetrack; they are later transferred to an internment camp in Utah. Both *Journey to Topaz* and *Journey Home* are for older readers. *Journey to Topaz* describes life in the internment camp through Yuki's eyes. She vividly describes their fears, the privations of living in the camp, and their desire to prove their loyalty to the United States. *Journey Home* tells about the mistreatment the Japanese Americans faced once they were released and returned home. This great injustice in American history is commemorated in a mural that depicts the internment of 120,000 Japanese Americans, which in turn inspired Sheila Hamanaka to write the picture book *The Journey: Japanese Americans, Racism, and Renewal.* The text accompanying the dramatic illustrations in this book describes the indignities and degradation suffered by these innocent people.

Three books tell the stories of the war in Europe. A young Austrian girl, Greta, arranges to take piano lessons against her mother's wishes, from a piano teacher whose past is very much a secret. When the Nazis come, she finds out that he is a famous German pianist who helped many Jewish musicians escape from Germany. The Nazis want to punish him but Greta helps him escape. *Play to the Angel* by Maurine F. Dahlberg presents a picture of pre-war Austria and how it changed when the war began.

Martha Attema writes a powerful book set in Holland from 1943 to 1945. Janke's family (except for her mother) and friends are all very much involved in the resistance movement. She falls in love with Helmut, a young German soldier, who later rescues her from the Nazis when she is captured. After the war, Janke is rejected by her family and friends because of her love for Helmut. She makes the decision to go to Canada to join him. *When the War Is Over* presents a very clear picture of the resistance movement but is also very much a story of developing relationships.

Several books recount what it was like to live in the United States during this time. It is interesting that in two of them the focus is Oswego, New York, where there is a war shelter for refugees. Miriam Bat-Ami's story *Two Suns in the Sky* (a Scott O'Dell Award winner) is told from the perspective of the two main characters: Chris, who lives in Oswego, and Adam, a Yugoslavian Jew who escapes from the Nazis. When Chris defies her father and goes to the shelter, she and Adam fall in love. Their relationship causes both of them to rethink their lives and to reconsider their goals.

Norma Fox Mazer's book, *Good Night, Maman,* begins in France where Karin, her mother, and her brother are hidden in a small attic room. When told that they must leave, the three of them walk to Italy where they are given refuge. Finally, when Karin and her brother must leave for the United States, their mother is too weak to go with them. The children are sent to Fort Ontario in Oswego, where they are safe. Karin writes letters to her mother, letters that tell of her experiences and feelings. When she finally learns of her mother's death, she knows that she must just keep going, regardless of the past.

The winner of the 2001 Scott O'Dell Award for Historical Fiction, *The Art of Keeping Cool* by Janet Taylor Lisle, tells a story of how one family copes with World War II in the United States. After Robert's dad has gone to fight in the war, Robert and his mom move from Ohio to Rhode Island to stay with his father's family. Many issues are addressed—family secrets, community relationships, the war itself, and the treatment of a reclusive German painter who becomes a kind of mentor to Elliot, Robert's cousin. Robert does a lot of growing up as he is forced to deal with issues of life and death.

Vietnam War

The Vietnam War is a little-understood chapter in U.S. history; nevertheless, it has had an influence on all of our lives.

In *The Wall,* Eve Bunting portrays a boy and his father searching for a name at the Vietnam Veterans Memorial. This picture book helps children understand the significance of the wall from the perspective of a disabled veteran, a mourning couple, and children on an outing.

Another picture book, which is really not intended for young children, is *Patrol: An American Soldier in Vietnam* by Walter Dean Myers. In it Myers, aided by Ann Grifalconi's collages, lets readers share what it was like to be in Vietnam, in constant danger, and always tired. This is a very powerful picture of war.

Events and Issues in the 20th Century

Natural events, over which we have little control, happen all the time, as do events caused by human error or mistaken judgment and events caused by attitudes and tradition that impact what individuals and groups may or may not be allowed to do. These types of events are reflected in the literature in this genre.

In 1913, the medical profession was not able to cope with epidemics. The response of those who wanted to avoid illness was often to physically move from the area. In *The Name of the Child,* Lloyd has been sent to relatives in the country—but even there, he is in danger. He must drive himself and a baby away from his aunt and uncle's home to try to avoid illness. Marilynn Reynolds' book presents a picture to children about responsibility and relationships.

The Ku Klux Klan's impact was insidious and evil. Nowhere was that more apparent than in a small Vermont town where no one was really safe from them. We can identify with the residents of the town as each tells of his or her experiences. *Witness* by Karen Hesse is a powerful book for readers of all ages.

In 1925, it was not unusual to have a one-room school in which students in Grades 1 through 8 attended. Ida Bidson and her younger brother went to such a school. Near the end of the school year, the regular teacher had to leave to take care of her ill mother. The head of the school board decided that he would not hire a new teacher for that short period and that the students would have to redo the year. The students decided that eighth-grade Ida should be the teacher so that they could take their exams and get credit for the year. *The Secret School* by Avi is a tribute to student responsibility.

The Great Depression made life difficult for most people. It was not unusual for city dwellers to send their children to live with relatives who lived in the country. Richard Peck tells about Mary Alice's year spent with Grandma Dowdel in *A Year Down Yonder.* Grandma is not a typical grandparent, as we learned from Peck's previous book, *A Long Way from Chicago.* This time she and Alice prevent her privy from being overturned; they plan revenge on a classmate who bullies Alice and they do a variety of good deeds. This humorous book is a good choice for a read-aloud.

Events leading up to and including the Civil Rights Movement are some of the most significant in our country's history. Many books have been written on the issues involved, the effects on people, and the results of the efforts taken by individuals, families, and institutions. Rural Alabama was a difficult place to live in the times before the Civil Rights Movement, especially for an intelligent 12-year-old black girl. *Francie* is a dreamer who tutors a 16-year-old who can't read. When the boy is accused of attacking a white man,

Francie courageously speaks up for him, endangering herself and those she loves. This book by Karen English was a Coretta Scott King Honor book.

When Meg starts a new school in 1954, she experiences racism because she is Black and most of the other students are white. She uses her favorite sport, baseball, as a means of dealing with her relationships with others. *Mayfield Crossing* by Vaunda Micheaux Nelson helps readers identify with what it feels like to be the outsider.

The Civil Rights Movement gained much publicity and momentum with the Montgomery bus boycott, which was a part of the lives of Alfa and his family. When they are accused of stealing their employer's money, they work very hard to clear their names and regain their dignity. Harriette Gillem Robinet allows readers to feel what it must have been like for a "colored" family living at that time in *Walking to the Busrider Blues.*

In a thoroughly enjoyable story, Christopher Paul Curtis lets readers become a part of the Watson family on a trip to see their grandparents in Alabama. This was a difficult time—1963—for an African-American family to travel south, where schools, parks, and playgrounds, as well as hotels and restaurants, were segregated. *The Watsons Go to Birmingham—1963* helps readers experience the social conditions at that time and appreciate the changes that have been made.

Historical Fiction in the Classroom

Books of historical fiction are frequently used to turn historical facts and statistics into living human experience (Tunnell & Ammon, 1993). They help create emotional connections so that readers understand the realities of times other than their own; they can feel the joys, triumphs, and hopes, as well as the pain, suffering, and despair of others. Trade books can be used as the primary resource, with textbooks used as supplementary materials when integrating curriculum studies.

The National Council of the Social Studies and the National Center for History in the Schools (1994) have developed standards for children in kindergarten through Grade 12. These standards include teaching suggestions, and trade book examples such as using "historical fiction such as *Trouble at the Mines* by Doreen Rappaport to investigate the strikes in the coal mines and the organizing efforts of Mother Mary Jones" (1993, p. 154). The Web site for the National Council of the Social Studies, **www.NESS.org,** is very helpful, offering suggestions for teachers and updated lists of trade books for the social studies.

An increasing number of historical fiction books have been put on audiotapes, which can be used in several ways. First, students whose reading levels may not match their interest levels are able to listen to the sories for purely recreational purposes. These same students will be able to participate in literature circles if they are able to listen to the tapes while they read the books. Second, if teachers recommend these audio books and share titles with the parents of their students, families can listen to them while on car trips and can discuss the ideas they hear. Third, using these books as models, students can record their favorite books to be shared with audiences of their choice. Audio books are a very flexible teaching resource.

Examples of Audio Books

When Zachary Beaver Came to Town (Author: Kimberly Willis Holt). Listening Library: ISBN: 0-8072-8393-2.

A Year Down Yonder, (Author: Richard Peck). Listening Library, ISBN: 0-8072-8750-4.

The Land (Author: Mildred D. Taylor). Listening Library, ISBN: 0-8072-0619-9.

Roll of Thunder, Hear my Cry (Author: Mildred D. Taylor). Listening Library: ISBN: 0-8072-0622-9.

Nory Ryan's Song (Author: Patricia Reilly Giff). Listening Library: ISBN: 0-8072-8728-8.

Witness (Author: Karen Hesse). Listening Library: ISBN: 0-8072-0593-1.

Resources for Teachers

As teachers, we want to help our students make connections with other time periods and cultures. Using historical fiction is one way to do this, of course. These books can provide emotional links between readers, events, and people of other times and places. A recently published series of books, not designed for use by young people but by adults who are going to write about particular time periods of the past, certainly presents clear pictures of these historical times. These books describe foods and drinks, how to furnish a house, how much things cost, employment, and language as it was used at the time. These books could most effectively be used by teachers as they build up their own background of information or with older students—perhaps sixth grade and up—because they give an accurate presentation of the way life really was. For example, common slang terms and their definitions are given—and these include some words some people might find objectionable. Nonetheless, they are well worthwhile for teachers' use, even those who might not feel comfortable sharing them with their students.

The Writer's Guide to Everyday Life in Renaissance England: From 1485–1649 (Emerson, 1996).

The Writer's Guide to Everyday Life in the 1800s (McCutcheon, 1993).

The Writer's Guide to Everyday Life in the Middle Ages: The British Isles from 500 to 1500 (Kenyon, 1995).

The Writer's Guide to Everyday Life in Regency and Victorian England: From 1811–1901 (Hughes, 1997).

The Writer's Guide to Everyday Life in the Wild West: From 1840–1900 (Moulton, 1998).

The Writer's Guide to Everyday Life in Colonial America: From 1607–1783 (Taylor, 1997).

Classroom Activities

ACTIVITY 9.1   FROM SLAVERY TO CIVIL RIGHTS

(IRA/NCTE Standards: 3, 4, 5.)

Beginning with the KWWL charts developed in the opening vignette, Ms. Alexander and her class participated in an ongoing theme cycle. They read widely from a variety of genres—including biography, informational books, poetry, realistic fiction, and historical fiction, as well as reference books such as encyclopedias and textbooks. They used the Internet to supplement the information found in these books. Based on what they found, they created a time line and added dates throughout the year as they discovered significant events. The book *Oh,*

Freedom! Kids Talk About the Civil Rights Movement with the People who Made it Happen was an important source of dates for the time line as well as a resource for other books, series books, and videos about the times. One group of students decided that they would do interviews as the students did in this book, but instead of a book format, they wrote their own newspaper.

All students wrote letters; some to public figures to determine if discriminatory practices were happening in their cities, others to solicit information about the proposed upcoming Underground Railroad Museum, and others to family members who lived out of town to collect their remembrances. The letter writing was a continuing project for the whole year.

When a group of students found the book *Bull Run* by Paul Fleischman, they did a reader's theater presentation for the other sixth-grade classes. They did read-alouds of biographies to younger classes during Black History Month, which inspired them to write their own autobiographies.

During their language arts periods, Ms. Alexander provided much instruction, so the students reviewed and relearned many literacy strategies for both reading and writing. These students read, discussed, wrote, shared, did interviews, listened to people—recorded and in person—and asked questions for which they wanted answers. They self-evaluated the information they got and made decisions about the quality of their own work and the work of their peers. In doing all of these activities, they learned about themselves, how to conduct investigations, and the process of inquiry as well as improving their literacy abilities—all of which will serve them well as life-long learners. In the process, all of the IRA/NCTE Standards for the English Language Arts were accomplished because the students needed the skills for practical purposes, not just for doing well on the end-of-the year required test.

The titles of a few of the books used in this unit, which were found not only by Ms. Alexander but by the students themselves, meet a variety of reading levels and interests. When doing a theme cycle, it is possible to include many kinds and levels of books.

Steal Away by Jennifer Armstrong

Barefoot: Escape on the Underground Railroad by Pamela Duncan Edwards

The Last Safe House by Barbara Greenwood

Oh, Freedom! by Casey King and Linda Barrett Osborne

. . . If You Traveled on the Underground Railroad by Ellen Levine

Christmas in the Big House, Christmas in the Quarters by Patricia McKissack and Fredrick L. McKissack

The Glory Field by Walter Dean Myers

Once on this River by Sharon Dennis Wyeth

ACTIVITY 9.2   DIARIES AND JOURNALS: A UNIT OF STUDY

(IRA/NCTE Standards: 1, 3, 4, 5, 7, 11, 12.)

Many historical fiction books are written in diary or journal form; others may include letters as an integral part of the story. Discuss why so many of the books are written in this format. Have students participate in literature study groups in which they read journal/diary books for the introduction to this unit. Then challenge children to find, read, and share as many other diary/journal books as they can find. These books may include memoirs and other nonfiction books.

Encourage students to write their own journals/diaries about their lives. Have them make the assumption that children of their ages will be reading their journals/diaries 50 years from now. What will they need to include so that future readers will have the context necessary to understand the current times? What events are important and which have little or no significance? To be able to do this, the students will have to do some research. At the conclusion of this unit, invite other classes and parents in to share the books and their own journals/diaries.

This unit of study models how social studies and language arts can be integrated into a lesson.

Summary

Historical fiction books are read and enjoyed by most people because of the connections that they can make between their life and the lives of people in other times and places. We can relate to the characters' problems, joys, and sorrows because these are the feelings of the human condition. In addition, teachers find this to be a very useful genre because there are so many connections that can be made in the curriculum.

Teachers should exercise care, however, and inform parents when choosing these books. Many of these books depict events and conditions that may be considered violent, racist, or stereotyped. Parents can be involved in classroom activities, such as listening and discussing the books and the ideas in the books with their children.

Thought Questions

1. Discuss ways of integrating literature with social studies textbooks.
2. Identify your favorite historical fiction books.
3. Why do you think that some historical periods have more books written about them than other periods? What are the implications for children and teaching?
4. Why is World War II a popular subject of current historical fiction?
5. How does setting in historical fiction differ from setting in other genres?
6. What themes appear most often in historical fiction?

Research and Application Experiences

1. How does historical fiction help readers understand themselves?
2. Compare historical fiction and contemporary realistic fiction.
3. How does historical fiction make history come alive? Provide examples to illustrate your answer.
4. What have you learned about your own cultural/ historical background from historical fiction?
5. Historical fiction shows how events relate to each other. Identify at least one historical fiction book that does this.

Children's Literature References and Recommended Books

Note: All books in this section are HISTORICAL FICTION unless otherwise noted. The number in parentheses indicate the approximate interest level for each book.

Armstrong, J. (1992). *Steal away*. New York: Orchard Books. (4–6).

Susannah and a new friend, Bethlehem, a slave, escape to the north and become life-long friends.

Attema, M. (2002). *When the war is over*. Victoria, BC: Orca. (7–10).

A Dutch resistance worker falls in love with a German soldier.

Avi. (1994a). *Encounter at Easton*. New York: Beech Tree. (4–7).

The sequel to *Night Journeys* tells what happened to the bondsmen.

Avi. (1994b). *Night journeys*. New York: Beech Tree. (4–7).

This story is set in the late 1700s and focuses on the search for and treatment of two escaped bondsmen, who happen to be young children.

Avi. (2001). *The secret school*. New York: Scholastic. (4–6).

When the teacher leaves, one of the students becomes the teacher in this one-room school house.

Avi. (2003). *Crispin: The cross of lead*. New York: Hyperion. (6–10).

People are trying to kill Crispin, an orphan, for reasons he does not understand. His friendship with a juggler saves his life.

Ayers, K. (2001). *Stealing south: A story of the Underground Railroad*. New York: Dell. (4–6).

Instead of just being a peddler, Will goes south to bring back the brother of an escaping slave.

Bartoletti, S. C. (1999). *No man's land: A young soldier's story*. New York: Blue Sky. (5–7).

A young southern boy joins the Confederate Army and gains his father's respect.

Bartoletti, S. C. (2003). *The journal of Finn Reardon: A newsie. New York City, 1899*. New York: Scholastic. (3–6).

The story of a boy who supports his family by selling newspapers; a book in the *My Name Is America* series.

Bat-Ami, M. (1999). *Two suns in the sky*. Chicago: Front Street/Cricket Books. (5–8).

> Chris falls in love with Adam, who is kept in the Emergency Refugee Shelter during WWII.

Baures, M. D. (2003). *Land of the buffalo bones: The diary of Mary Elizabeth Rodgers*. New York: Scholastic. (4–6).

> A book in the *Dear America* series, told by a Minnesota girl in 1873.

Bowen, G. (1994). *Stranded at Plimoth Plantation, 1626*. New York: HarperCollins. (2–4).

> The daily life of an indentured orphan boy at Plimoth Plantation is told.

Bruchac, J. (1998). *The Arrow Over the Door*. New York: Dial. HISTORICAL FICTION (4–8).

> A little known story about Indians and Quakers.

Bunting, E. (1988). *How many days to America? A Thanksgiving story* (B. Peck, Illus.). New York: Clarion. (K–3). CONTEMPORARY REALISTIC FICTION.

> This book is a reminder that, even today, immigrants come to the United States to escape repression and danger in their own countries.

Bunting, E. (1990). *The wall* (R. Himler, Illus.). New York: Clarion. (4–8). CONTEMPORARY REALISTIC FICTION.

> A boy and his father visit the Vietnam Veterans Memorial to search for a name. During the visit they encounter many other people who are also looking for names.

Bunting, E. (2000). *Train to somewhere* (R. Himler, Illus.). New York: Houghton Mifflin. (1–3).

> An orphan hopes to find her mother as she goes west on the Orphan Train but is chosen by a loving elderly couple.

Bunting, E. (2001). *Dandelions*. New York: Harcourt. (1–3).

> A family travels to the Nebraska Territory but are sad until they have dandelions growing on their soddie roof and see their farm come to life.

Byars, B. (1996). *Dead letter*. New York: Viking. (4–6). CONTEMPORARY REALISTIC FICTION.

> Herculeah Jones solves a mystery after she finds a letter in the lining of her coat.

Byars, B. (2002). *Keeper of the doves*. New York: Viking. (5–8).

> At the end of the 1800s, Amen finds out about the peculiar neighbor who raises doves.

Cadnum, M. (2001). *Raven of the waves*. New York: Orchard. (7–10).

> A young Viking warrior goes on his first voyage.

Cadnum, M. (2003). *Daughter of the wind*. New York: Orchard. (7–10).

> Hallgerd, a young Viking woman, is kidnapped.

Conrad, P. (1991). *Pedro's journal*. Honesdale, PA: Boyds Mill. (4–6).

> Pedro is a cabin boy on Columbus's ship. His journal reveals his observations and feelings about the adventure.

Cooney, C. B. (2001). *The ransom of Mercy Carter*. New York: Dell. (5–8).

> Mercy and some of her family and friends are captured during an Indian attack. She lives with the tribe and chooses to stay with them even though a ransom is brought for her.

Corey, S. (2003). *Players in pigtails* (R. Gibbon, Illus.). New York: Scholastic. (1–4).

> A young girl joins the All-American Girls Professional Baseball League in the 1940s.

Curtis, C. P. (1995). *The Watsons go to Birmingham—1963*. New York: Delacorte. (5–7).

> The story of an African-American family who visits their family in the segregated south.

Cushman, K. (2003). *Rodzina*. New York: Clarion. (4–7).

> A 12-year-old girl travels on the Orphan Train but no one seems to want her.

Dahlberg, M. F. (2000). *Play to the angel*. New York: Penguin Putnam. (5–7).

> Greta takes piano lessons from a mysterious teacher in pre-war Austria.

Danziger, P., & Martin, A. (2001). *Snail mail no more*. New York: Scholastic. (4–8). CONTEMPORARY REALISTIC FICTION.

> As they e-mail each other, best friends deal with serious and not-so-serious problems.

Dorris, M. (1996). *Sees behind trees*. New York: Hyperion. (5–8).

> Having poor vision presents a variety of obstacles for Walnut, a Native American boy, until he learns how to "see" with his ears.

Edwards, P. D. (1997). *Barefoot: Escape on the Underground Railroad* (H. Cole, Illus.). New York: HarperCollins. (1–4).

Animals help an escaped slave on the Underground Railroad.

English, K. (2000). *Francie*. New York: Farrar, Straus & Giroux. (5–9).

The story of a poor African-American girl living in the rural south who never gives up hope for a better life.

Fleischman, P. (1993). *Bull run* (D. Frampton, Illus.). New York: HarperCollins. (4–7).

Perspectives of both Northerners and Southerners about Bull Run are presented.

Freedman, R. (1983). *Children of the wild west*. New York: Clarion. (3–6). INFORMATIONAL BOOK.

The book documents life in the American West from 1840 to the early 1900s.

Giff, P. R. (2000). *Nory Ryan's song*. New York: Random House. (4–7).

People are starving to death in Ireland because of the potato famine; as a result, many people immigrate to the United States.

Greenwood, B. (1998). *The last safe house* (H. Collins, Illus.). San Francisco: Kids Can. (3–6). HISTORICAL FICTION, INFORMATIONAL BOOK.

This book, a combination historical fiction and informational book, describes the Underground Railroad.

Hamanaka, S. (1990). *The journey: Japanese Americans, racism, and renewal*. New York: Orchard. (5–8). HISTORICAL FICTION, INFORMATIONAL BOOK.

This book depicts the mural commemorating the internment of Japanese Americans during World War II.

Harness, C. (1992). *Three young Pilgrims*. New York: Bradbury. (1–4).

A fictionalized account of a family who comes to America on the *Mayflower* and their struggles to survive as well as their pleasures.

Hesse, K. (2000). *Stowaway*. New York: Scholastic. (5–7).

A boy hides on a ship until it is out of port, then joins the crew.

Hesse, K. (2001). *Witness*. New York: Scholastic. (5–8).

Activities of the Ku Klux Klan mean that no one is safe in a small Vermont town in 1924.

Hite, S. (2003). *The journal of Rufus Rowe: A witness to the battle of fredericksburg*. New York: Scholastic. (5, 6, 7+).

Rufus runs away from home and witnesses the battle at Fredericksburg; A book in the *My Name Is America* series.

Holt, K. W. (1999). *When Zachary Beaver came to town*. New York: Random House. (5–7).

Toby and Cal befriend the fattest boy they have ever met.

Holt, K. W. (2001). *Dancing in Cadillac light*. New York: Putnam. (5–7).

When Grandpa moves in and buys a Cadillac, Janell's life changes forever.

Hurst, C. O. (2001). *Through the locks*. New York: Houghton Mifflin. (4–7).

Two young children learn to live together, earning a living by protecting a section of canal locks.

Johnston, T. (2002). *Sunsets of the west* (T. Lewin, Illus.). New York: Putnam. (1–3).

A pioneer family moves from New Hampshire to the west.

Jones, E. McD. (1999). *The night flyers*. New York: Pleasant Company. (4–6).

Pam's pigeons are of interest to a number of people during WWI; an *American Girl History Mystery*.

Keehn, S. M. (1995). *Moon of two dark horses*. New York: Philomel. (4–6).

Cooshmoo, a Delaware Indian boy, and Daniel, a young settler, have been friends a long time. However, their friendship is severely tested during the Revolutionary War.

Kimball, K. M. (2001). *The star-spangled search*. New York: Simon & Schuster. (4–7).

There is a mystery surrounding the supposed death of Caroline's brother. She finds out what really happened.

King, C., & Osborne, L. B. (1997). *Oh, freedom! Kids talk about the Civil Rights Movement with the people who made it happen* (J. Brooks, Illus.). New York: Knopf. (3–8). INFORMATIONAL BOOK.

Factual descriptions of aspects of the Civil Rights Movement and interviews of those who were involved.

Lasky, K. (1996). *Beyond the burning time*. New York: Blue Sky. (5–8).

The widow Virginia Chase is named a witch and sentenced to hang. Her children succeed in saving her life.

Lasky, K. (2003a). *Hope in my heart: Sofia's immigrant diary, book one*. New York: Scholastic. (3–6).

Sofia is separated from her family when they come to Ellis Island in 1903.

Lasky, K. (2003b). *Home at last: Sofia's immigrant diary, book two*. New York: Scholastic. (3–6).

Sofia is reunited with her family.

Levine, E. (1988). *. . . If you traveled on the Underground Railroad* (L. Johnson, Illus.). New York: Scholastic. (3–5). INFORMATIONAL BOOK.

Questions and answers about the Underground Railroad.

Lisle, J. T. (2000). *The art of keeping cool*. New York: Atheneum. (6–8).

Robert and his mom go to live with his dad's parents during the war. Family secrets and community fears are discovered.

Lunn, J. (1997). *The hollow tree*. New York: Penguin Putnam. (6–10).

Phoebe's cousin is hanged as a British spy; she struggles between Patriot and Tory loyalties.

Matas, C. (2001). *The war within: A novel of the Civil War*. New York: Aladdin. (6–8).

The property of Jews was confiscated because of General Grant's General Order #11. This book presents a perspective not always known about the Civil War.

Mazer, H. (2001). *A boy at war: A novel of Pearl Harbor*. New York: Simon & Schuster. (5–8).

Adam is fishing with friends in Pearl Harbor when they see his father's ship get blown up.

Mazer, N. F. (1999). *Good night, Maman*. San Diego: Harcourt Brace. (5–8).

Karin and her family flee the Nazis. She and her brother become refugees in Oswego, New York.

McCully, E. A. (1996). *The bobbin girl*. New York: Dial. (K–4).

Ten-year-old Rebecca works in a textile mill, where she must decide whether to go on strike when the owners threaten to lower wages.

McDonald, M. (2003). *All the stars in the sky: The Santa Fe Trail diary of Florrie Mack Ryder*. New York: Scholastic. (4–8).

Florrie's diary describes the family's trip from Missouri to New Mexico.

McKissack, P. C., & McKissack, F. L. (1994). *Christmas in the big house, Christmas in the quarters* (J. Thompson, Illus.). New York: Scholastic. (4–9).

A recounting of what Christmas was like for white people and black slaves in 1859 in the south.

Morpurgo, M. (1991). *Waiting for Anya*. New York: Viking. (4–8).

French villagers help Jewish children escape the Nazis during World War II.

Myers, W. D. (1994). *The glory field*. New York: Scholastic. (6–10).

The book traces generations of an African-American family from 1753 in Sierra Leone to the present.

Myers, W. D. (2002). *Patrol: An American soldier in Vietnam* (A. Grifalconi, Illus.). New York: HarperCollins. (4–7).

A day is presented in the life of a soldier.

Nelson, V. M. (2001). *Mayfield crossing*. New York: Puffin. (3–6).

Meg experiences racism as she tries to play baseball with the white kids in 1950.

Nixon, J. L. (2000a). *Ann's story: 1747*. New York: Delacorte Press. (4–6).

Ann wants to be a doctor instead of learning to be a proper young woman.

Nixon, J. L. (2000b). *Caesar's story: 1759*. New York: Delacorte Press. (4–6).

Caesar goes through the transition from being a friend to a white boy to becoming his personal servant.

Nixon, J. L. (2001a). *John's story: 1775*. New York: Delacorte Press. (4–6).

John's family is divided about whether to seek peace or go to seek independence from England.

Nixon, J. L. (2001b). *Maria's story: 1773*. New York: Delacorte Press. (4–6).

Maria's family runs a publishing house; they must decide about the kinds of articles they will choose to publish.

O'Dell, S. (1989). *My Name is not Angelica*. Boston: Houghton Mifflin. (5–8). HISTORICAL FICTION.

The story of two young people who are sold into slavery.

Paterson, K. (1996). *Jip: His story*. New York: Lodestar. (4–6).

Jip is abandoned as a small child; finding out who he is presents grave dangers.

Paterson, K. (1999). *Preacher's boy*. New York: Clarion Books. (4–7).

We see the change of centuries, 1899–1900, from the humorous perspective of Robbie.

Paulsen, G. (1993). *Nightjohn*. New York: Delacorte. (5–9).

When Nightjohn is caught teaching slaves to read, which is illegal, he is tortured.

Paulsen, G. (1995–2002). *The Tucket adventures*. New York: Yearling. (4–7).

Francis Tucket has a series of adventures in these five books as he and his family are on the Oregon Trail.

Paulsen, G. (1997). *Sarny: A life remembered*. New York: Delacorte. (5–9).

Sarny, whom Nightjohn taught to read, becomes a free woman. She helps other people become literate.

Paulsen, G. (1999). *Alida's song*. New York: Delacorte. (5–8).

A grandmother provides stability for her grandson on the farm for a summer.

Paulsen, G. (2000). *Soldier's heart*. New York: Laurel Leaf. (6–10).

Fifteen-year-old Charley thinks being in the Union Army will be a big adventure. Instead, he learns of the horrors of war.

Peck, R. (2000). *A long way from Chicago*. New York: Dial. (4–8).

Joey and Mary Alice spend summers with their unusual grandmother.

Peck, R. (2001). *A year down yonder*. New York: Dial. (4–8).

A family from the country is invited by an aunt to visit the 1893 World's Columbian exposition. The grandfather accompanies his grandchildren with humorous consequences.

Rappaport, D. (1987). *Trouble at the mines* (J. Sandin, Illus.). New York: Crowell. (5–7).

Families and children get involved in a strike in Arnot, Pennsylvania, in 1898.

Ray, M. L. (1999). *Basket moon*. Boston: Little Brown. (1–4).

A young boy has to decide if he will follow his family's path as basket makers or find another kind of life.

Reynolds, M. (2002). *The name of the child* (D. Kilby, Illus.). Victoria, British Columbia: Orca. (1–3).

During a flu epidemic, Lloyd must be especially brave as he saves a baby's life.

Rinaldi, A. (1992). *A break with charity: A story about the Salem witch trials*. San Diego: Harcourt Brace. (6–10).

When Susanna finds out why people are accused of being witches, she must decide if she wants to share what she knows and put her family in danger, or if she should not say anything and let the hysteria continue.

Rinaldi, A. (1993). *The fifth of March: A story of the Boston Massacre*. San Diego: Harcourt Brace. (6–10).

Rachel Marsh, an indentured servant for John Adams, falls in love with a British soldier.

Rinaldi, A. (1994). *Finishing Becca: A story about Peggy Shippen and Benedict Arnold*. San Diego: Harcourt Brace. (4–6).

Benedict Arnold may have become a traitor to the country because of the influence of Peggy Shippen.

Rinaldi, A. (1995). *The secret of Sarah Revere*. San Diego: Harcourt Brace. (6–10).

Sarah, daughter of Paul Revere, takes on the responsibility of keeping her family together while her father is away.

Rinaldi, A. (1998). *Cast two shadows: The American Revolution in the south*. San Diego: Harcourt Brace. (6–8).

Caroline, who lives in South Carolina, has difficulty coming to terms with the deaths, the takeover of their land, and the imprisonment of her father during this war.

Rinaldi, A. (2001). *Girl in blue*. New York: Scholastic. (6–8).

To escape an abusive father, Louisa runs away and enlists in the Union Army as a boy.

Robinet, H. G. (2000). *Walking to the bus-rider blues*. New York: Simon & Schuster. (4–6).

The Montgomery bus boycott impacts the lives of Alfa's family, just as it does the other black families.

Schlein, M. (1991). *I sailed with Columbus* (T. Newsom, Illus.). HarperCollins. (4–7).

A cabin boy tells his story about sailing with Columbus.

Skurzynski, G. (1992). *Goodbye, Billy Radish*. New York: Bradbury. (4–7).

During World War I, even boys had to work long hours in steel factories. They were not safe places for workers of any age.

Skurzynski, G. (2001). *Rockbuster*. New York: Antheneum. (7–9).

>Tommy's father was killed in the mines; Tommy works there, too, but really wants to sing and compose songs.

Slate, J. (2002). *The great big wagon that rang: How the Liberty Bell was saved* (C. Spearing, Illus.). New York: Marshall Cavendish. (1–3).

>A farmer saves the Liberty Bell from being stolen by hiding it in his wagon after market.

Taylor, M. D. (1976). *Roll of thunder, hear my cry*. New York: Dial. (5–9).

>Members of the Putnam family face overt racism.

Taylor, M. D. (2001). *The land*. New York: Penguin Putnam. (4–8).

>This prequel to Taylor's other books shows how important owning land is to former slaves.

Turner, A. (2003). *Love thy neighbor: The Tory diary of Prudence Emerson*. New York: Scholastic. (4–6).

>We see what it may have been like to be a Tory girl at the time of the American Revolution.

Uchida, Y. (1971). *Journey to Topaz* (D. Carrick, Illus.). New York: Scribner's Sons. (4–7).

>This story of a Japanese-American family sent to an internment camp shows how they prove their loyalty to the United States.

Uchida, Y. (1978). *Journey home* (C. Robinson, Illus.). New York: Atheneum. (4–7).

>The sequel to *Journey to Topaz* describes the mistreatment the Japanese Americans faced once released from the internment camps.

Uchida, Y. (1993). *The bracelet* (J. Yardley, Illus.). New York: Philomel. (2–5).

>Emi and her family are moved to internment camps after the bombing of Pearl Harbor.

Wallace, I. (1999). *Boy of the deeps*. New York: DK Publishing. (4–7). HISTORICAL FICTION.

>Boys as well as men worked underground in the mines; when a cave-in occurs, James survives because he and his father work together.

Wyeth, S. D. (1998). *Once on this river*. New York: Knopf. (5–9). HISTORICAL FICTION.

>Monday learns about the horrors of slavery as she and her mother try to win the freedom of her uncle, who has been enslaved even though he is a free man.

Wyeth, S. D. (2002a). *Flying free: Corey's Underground Railroad diary, book 2*. New York: Scholastic. (3–5).

>Corey and his family make a new life for themselves in Canada.

Wyeth, S. D. (2002b). *Freedom's wings: Cory's Underground Railroad diary, book 1*. New York: Scholastic. (3–5).

>Cory escapes from the farm where he is a slave in Kentucky.

Wyeth, S. D. (2003). *Message in the sky: Corey's Underground Railroad diary, book 3*. New York: Scholastic. (3–5).

>Corey becomes a conductor on the Underground Railroad.

Yivisaker, A. O. (2002) *Dear papa*. New York: Candlewick Press. (4–6).

>Isabelle and her sisters are sent to live with relatives after their father dies.

Yolen, J. (1992). *Encounter* (D. Shannon, Illus.). New York: Harcourt Brace Jovanovich. (4–9).

>A young Taino boy has a nightmare about the arrival of Columbus to the island where his tribe lives. The future fulfills his worst fears.

References and Books for Further Reading

Adamson, L. G. (1987). *A reference guide to historical fiction for children and young adults*. Westport, CT: Greenwood Press.

Burton, H. (1973). The writing of historical novels. In V. Haviland (Ed.), *Children and literature: Views and reviews*. Glenview, IL: Scott Foresman.

Crabtree, C., Nash, G. B., Gagnon, P., & Waugh, S. (Eds.). (1992). *Lessons from history: Essential understandings and historical perspectives students should acquire*. Los Angeles: University of California.

Cullinan, B., & Galda, L. (1994). *Literature and the child* (3rd ed.). Fort Worth, TX: Harcourt Brace.

Emerson, K. L. (1996). *The writer's guide to everyday life in renaissance England: From 1485–1649*. Cincinnati, OH: Writer's Digest Books.

Enciso, P. E. (2000). Historical facts and fictions: Representing and reading diverse perspectives on the past. *The New Advocate, 13,* 279–296.

Huck, C., Hepler, S., & Hickman, J. (1993). *Children's literature in the elementary school* (5th ed.). Dubuque, IA: Wm. C. Brown.

Hughes, K. (1997). *The writer's guide to everyday life in Regency and Victorian England: From 1811–1901.* Cincinnati, OH: Writer's Digest Books.

Hunt, C. C. (1994). U.S. children's books about the World War II period: From isolationism to internationalism, 1940–1990. *The Lion and the Unicorn, 18,* 190–208.

Ives, S., & Burns, K. (1996). Introduction. In D. Duncan, *People of the west* (pp. vi–vii). Boston: Little, Brown.

Jordan, A. D. (1997). *Follow the gleam: Teaching and learning genre with children and young adults, Part II.* Brandon, VT: Esmont.

Kenyon, S. (1995). *The writer's guide to everyday life in the middle ages: The British Isles from 500 to 1500.* Cincinnati, OH: Writer's Digest Books.

McCutcheon, M. (1993). *The writer's guide to everyday life in the 1800s.* Cincinnati, OH: Writer's Digest Books.

Moulton, C. (1998). *The writer's guide to everyday life in the wild west: From 1840–1900.* Cincinnati, OH: Writer's Digest Books.

National Council of the Social Studies and National Center for History in the Schools. (1994). *Social studies standards.* Los Angeles: University of California.

Norton, D. (1995). *Through the eyes of a child* (2nd ed.). Upper Saddle River, NJ: Merrill/Prentice Hall.

Paterson, K. (1992). Daughters of hope. *Horn Book, 69,* 164–170.

Perez-Stable, M. A., & Cordier, M. H. (1994). *Understanding American history through children's literature.* Phoenix, AZ: Oryx.

Reed, A. (1994). *Reaching adolescents: The young adult book and the schools.* New York: Merrill/Macmillan.

Russell, D. L. (1994). *Literature for children: A short introduction* (2nd ed.). White Plains, NY: Longman.

Sutcliff, R. (1973). History is people. In V. Haviland (Ed.), *Children and literature: Views and reviews* (pp. 305–312). Glenview IL: Scott Foresman.

Taylor, D. (1997). *The writer's guide to everyday life in colonial America: From 1607–1783.* Cincinnati, OH: Writer's Digest Books.

Tunnell, M., & Ammon, R. (Ed.). (1993). *The story of ourselves: Teaching history through children's literature.* Portsmouth, NH: Heinemann.

Truth Is Stranger than Fiction: Nonfiction

10

KEY TERMS

concept books

experiment and
    activity books

exposition

informational books

life-cycle books

GUIDING QUESTIONS

1. What kinds of information interested you as an elementary student? Did you find books in the library on this subject?

2. What are the major characteristics of nonfiction?

3. What are the most important values of nonfiction?

4. Identify the characteristics that distinguish excellent nonfiction.

We live in an information age fueled by a flood of knowledge. Information drives our society. We gulp it, gobble it, and wait for the next wave to come. As a result, nonfiction literature is more important in all our lives than ever before, as today's children will have to read and understand massive amounts of information throughout their lives. Furthermore, this information will quickly become obsolete. We must put the right books into children's hands to spark their interests. This requires a solid knowledge of nonfiction, whether it is in a book, a computer program, or an Internet site. The vignette on the following page illustrates how nonfiction is used in one classroom.

The Changing Face of Nonfiction

One of the most exciting trends in children's literature today is the burgeoning informational book market. Nonfiction whets children's appetites for more literature, as demonstrated in the opening vignette where the children demonstrated how factual content fascinated and motivated their interests. Tony Stead (2002) examined the kinds of content that readers commonly encountered and found that 80 percent was nonfiction. Nonfiction not only provides rich experiences, but has implications for life-long learning (Walmsley, 1994).

Several developments have contributed to the changing place of nonfiction in children's literature. First, today's nonfiction is exciting and creative. It is well-written, well-researched, has attractive layouts, and addresses a wide range of subject matter. Nonfiction authors comb archives, look at documents, gather photographs, interview, research topics on the Internet, and read books in order to piece together their own work. In writing *The Great Fire*, Jim Murphy gathered information about the Chicago fire from letters, journals, published accounts, and other sources. To breathe life into this information, he wrote about the fire from the points of view of four individuals (Jensen, 2001).

Jim Collier, the teacher of a fourth/fifth-grade combination class, decided to introduce literature circles in January of the school year. He knew this would be a stimulating change for his students. With literature circles, students could select trade books appropriate to their individual reading levels. He studied Harvey Daniels' *Literature Circles: Voice and Choice in Book Clubs and Reading Groups* (2002) and made his own plan.

Jim's students worked in groups at tables, with each group of students having a stack of informational books and a list of group-generated questions. One group of students, who were deeply involved in a discussion of bridges, worked on these questions:

What kind of bridge is the best?

Why do bridges have different shapes?

What kinds of things go across bridges?

Why did one book call bridges "bare utilities"?

Why did another book call bridges "durable monuments"?

Why did one book say "And this bridge just soars. It carries dreams"?

Students referred to different books as they completed their questions, including *Brooklyn Bridge* by Lynn Curlee, *Bridges: From my Side to Yours* by Jan Adkins, *Bridges* by Etta Kaner, and *Building Toothpick Bridges* by Jeanne Pollard. As the group put the finishing touches on their work for the day, one boy was asked, "What was the most interesting thing that you learned about bridges?"

He pointed to an illustration in the book he

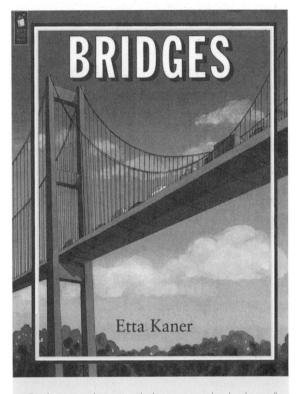

Bridges may be a simple log or complex bridges of suspension, arch, and cantilever.

was reading and said, "I learned about a lot of bridges. People have built bridges throughout history. I want to know more about covered bridges." Then a classmate added, "I liked *Brooklyn Bridge*. I liked reading the text, and looking at the illustrations made me see the beauty of bridges. I really want to see it. Now I want to read books about other famous bridges."

Another indication that nonfiction is assuming a place of greater prominence in the world of children's literature consists of the awards for nonfiction. The Horn Book Graphic Gallery competition honors outstanding nonfiction books for excellence in design. The National

Council of Teachers of English bestows the Orbis Pictus Award to an outstanding children's nonfiction book each year, and the American Library Association honors nonfiction with the Sibert Medal.

Trends in Current Nonfiction

James Cross Giblin (1987), author and publisher of numerous nonfiction children's books, identifies four factors that characterize recent nonfiction. The first of these is a clear focus on a single aspect of the subject. Lynn Curlee chose to focus on a single bridge in her book, *Brooklyn Bridge* rather than writing a general bridges book. Focused books are a contrast to general coverage books. Focused books include more detail, which enables authors to tightly create written text that holds readers' attention more than a more generalized text, which is similar to encyclopedia. Lynn Curlee has written rich descriptive text in *Brooklyn Bridge*, which enables readers to appreciate the monumental effort involved in creating this magnificent bridge. She includes facts and figures at the end of the text which draw the interest of many students. Illustrations and text grab readers' interest in this book. Both color and line create the feeling of an enormous, rugged structure in the illustrations. Furthermore, the illustrations give readers additional perspectives for appreciating the bridge.

The Value of Nonfiction

Nonfiction has a reputation for being dull enough to put an owl to sleep (Harvey, 1998). However, nonfiction has changed dramatically in current times. The contrast in quality of writing on the same topic is illustrated in these passages from a textbook and a trade book:

Textbook.

"So the Pilgrims decided to look for a place where they could have their own church and also live as English men and women.

After thinking about a number of places, the Pilgrims decided to go to North America. . . .

In 1620, about a hundred people crowded onto a small ship called the Mayflower" (McAuley & Wilson, 1987, p. 69).

Trade book.

"The Sparrowhawk's crew set sail from London in hopes of reaching Jamestown, Virginia. Amongst the 26 passengers, mostly Irish servants, were Masters Fells and Sibsey. I was indentured to Captain Sibsey by my unscrupulous uncle. On November 6 our ship crashed in fog on what the captain told us was a New England shore" (Bowen, *Stranded at Plimoth Plantation, 1626*, p. 1).

The values of nonfiction for children are examined in this section.

Provides information

Informational books provide up-to-date facts. Students can explore timely topics such as global warming in books such as Laurence Pringle's *Global Warming*. The color illustrations, maps, graphs, and text present this topic in ways that children can comprehend, as well as increase their awareness of issues as they impinge on the global community.

Expands background knowledge

Through wide reading on content area topics, children learn associated concepts and terms. Nonfiction books present topics in greater depth and detail than textbooks. Social studies textbooks tell facts about Hitler, but James Cross Giblin's compelling narrative, *The Life and Death of Hitler*, traces his rise and fall. Nonfiction gives children a rich context for understanding many aspects of some real time, place, animal, person, or event, thereby enhancing their schemata.

Promotes exploration

A good book simulates direct experience—it makes the child want to go out and experience the observation or discovery firsthand (Harvey, 1998). Many of today's nonfiction books for young readers promote firsthand discovery by explaining how to participate in particular activities through clear, easy-to-follow directions. For example, in *Simple Simon Says: Take One Magnifying Glass*, Melvin Berger provides easy directions for a variety of fascinating experiments whereby children examine fingerprints, dollar bills, and crystals with a magnifying glass.

Nonfiction books summarize and organize information. In *Give Me Liberty! The Story of the Declaration of Independence*, Russell Freedman chronicles the events associated with the writing and signing of this document. He includes a detailed description of the militia, as well as ordinary citizens. The appendix includes interesting

Books Derived from Original Documents and Journals

Books derived from research involving original documents and journals interest children because of their authenticity. Dennis Fradin's *The Signers: The 56 Stories Behind the Declaration of Independence* provides a reference for the Declaration of Independence based on original documents. Students will find Pete Nelson's *Left for Dead: A Young Man's Search for the USS Indianapolis* inspirational. Hunter Scott used documents and journals to uncover the real story behind the World War II sinking of the *USS Indianapolis*.

Photographic Essays

Photographic essays are an increasingly important form of informational book. Color photography lends an air of authenticity to the information in Kathleen Zoehfeld's *From Tadpole to Frog*. In this book, the photographs provide visual clues to the meaning. Sandra Markle used striking, colorful photographs in *Growing Up Wild: Wolves* to make readers feel as though they are present in the wolves' den.

Reference Books and Periodicals

Reference works are available for virtually all areas of information, including encyclopedias, bibliographies, dictionaries, atlases, and almanacs that appear in print, on CD, and on the Internet, for all age groups. References are necessary for developing students' information-location skills.

The Children's Animal Atlas by David Lambert explains how animals have evolved, where they live today, and why so many are in danger. *The Children's Atlas of Exploration*, by Antony Mason and Kay Lye, enables readers to follow in the footsteps of the great explorers. Mason's *The Kingfisher First Picture Atlas* represents the trend to publish reference books for younger students. Encyclopedias on CD-ROM are an exciting addition to traditional reference works. When using these reference materials, students may actually listen to a speech or piece of music. They can also see people and machines moving, as well as many exciting innovations.

Some reference works are recommended for all age groups, such as *Exploring Your World: The Adventure of Geography* (Donald Crump, Ed.). Specialized bibliographies such as Mary Anne Pilger's *Science Experiments Index for Young People* include science activities and experiments drawn from 700 books. *The Kingfisher Young People's Encyclopedia of the United States* (William Shapiro, Ed.) has contents that reflect the school curriculum.

Innovative Informational Books

The *Magic School Bus* series by Joanna Cole is well-known among school children and teachers because Ms. Frizzle, the teacher in the series, wears outrageous clothes and drives a magic school bus on incredible journeys. This humorous approach to science is popular. Two well-received titles in this series are *The Magic School Bus: In the Time of the Dinosaurs* and *The Magic School Bus on the Ocean Floor*.

Sue Davidson and Ben Morgan's book, *Human Body Revealed*, is unique in the spectacular quality and quantity of images and the use of transparent templates, which allow readers to peel away layers and see the interactions among body systems.

Selecting and Evaluating Informational Books

Certain qualities distinguish excellent informational books from mediocre ones. First and foremost, the best informational books make us think. Facts abound in our information-dense world, but books that make readers think are uncommon. The qualities of excellent nonfiction include: thought-provoking text; literary style; technique; and the authority of the author; as well as the accuracy, appropriateness, and attractiveness of the book.

Thought-Provoking Text

Fine nonfiction raises questions in readers' minds, thereby making connections to other topics and experiences. Moreover, it encourages readers' curiosity and wonder (Jensen, 2001). A book that raises questions in many children's minds is *Weird Friends: Unlikely Allies in the Animal Kingdom* by Jose Aruego and Ariane Dewey. They are amazed to discover that animals help materials related to the Declaration of Independence, as well as a replica of it. Christopher Manson's book, *Uncle Sam and Old Glory: Symbols of America*, explains each symbol in detail. The text is informative, interesting, and serves as a springboard to further reading.

As students read nonfiction, they develop a basis for organizing ideas and writing in the nonfiction genre. For example, Albert Marrin's *Dr. Jenner and the Speckled Monster: The Search for the Smallpox Vaccine* traces the history of smallpox, including its weapon potential. The author includes books to read and Web sites. A topical book like this will stimulate children to read and write about their interests.

Types of Nonfiction

Informational books appear in a variety of formats: concept books, nature identification books, life-cycle books, experiment and activity books, books derived from original documents and journals, photographic essays, and reference books and periodicals. They focus on many subjects, including the arts, animals,

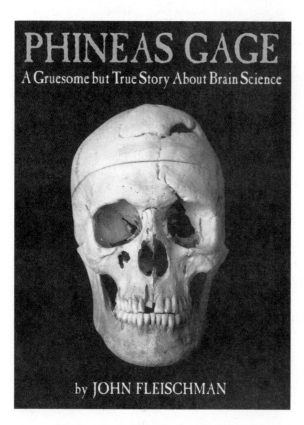

Phineas Gage had a hole in his head.

mathematics, man-made objects, language, se life cycle, and every other topic imaginable.

Concept Books

Concept books explore both concrete and a ideas. For example, *Desert Trek: An Eye-O Journey Through the World's Driest Places* by Le Rochais will change students' concept of The author explores desert vegetation and a dispelling the notion that deserts are vast, wastelands. David Schwartz's book, *Millions t sure*, develops the concept of millions, as well ear, weight, and volume measurements.

Nature Identification Books

Nature identification books, as the name implie children's attention on the natural world. Jim Ar book, *Wild and Swampy: Exploring with Jim A* explores southern swamps. Readers are encour make their own wildlife sketches. Another typ ture is examined in Carole Vogel's *Nature's Fu witness Reports of Natural Disasters.* Su reports of devastating natural events, as well views and photographs, are the focus of this bc

Life-Cycle Books

Life-cycle books trace the growth of anim plants. In *River of Life*, Debbie Miller explores of life in and along an Alaskan river, includin worms, dragonflies, and a brown bear. Miller' richly evokes vivid images and the illustra paintings enhance the language.

Experiment and Activity Books

Experiment and activity books, another cate nonfiction, provide children with hands-or ration of a variety of concepts. Such books safety precaution statements, lists of sequent to follow, lists of required materials or equipm an illustration of the finished project. A good of this type of book is Vicki Cobb's *You Gotta Absolutely Irresistible Science*, which include dozen experiments with observations and cle ings about potential problems.

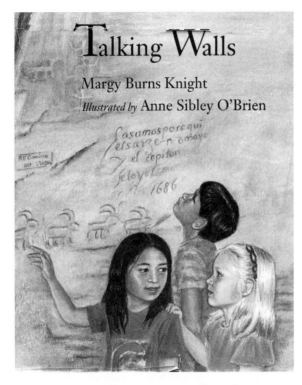

These walls communicate effectively.

one another and begin to look for additional animals that can help one another.

Style

Literary style refers to a subtle concept, the author's use of language, that is sometimes called voice. Nonfiction prose should engage readers with a distinctive, interesting voice. Factual accuracy and currency are very important, but rich language, appropriate terminology, and an interesting, stimulating style bring topics to life (Jensen, 2001). To achieve this, authors combine factual information with literary devices. A concise style that presents facts in simple, direct language is appropriate for most informational books. Nonfiction authors use correct terminology, and do not talk down to their readers.

Jim Arnosky's writing has an appealing, unmistakable voice. He opens readers' eyes to the natural world through his informal style, drawings, and suggestions. Readers feel they are joining in his experience. In his book *Field Trips: Bug Hunting, Animal Tracking, Bird Watching, Shore Walking with Jim Arnosky*, he opens

readers' eyes to a variety of habitats and explains what to look for, what equipment to take, and how to document discoveries.

Technique

Closely related to style is the literary technique authors employ to make their subjects interesting. Nonfiction authors use all of the techniques fiction writers use, including narrative, metaphor and simile, relating known information to new information, imagery, and "hooks" to engage readers' interest.

In *Think of an Eel*, Karen Wallace compares eels to familiar things to help children who probably have never seen an eel understand what they are like:

> *Think of an eel.*
> *He swims like a fish.*
> *He slides like a snake. . . .*
> *He looks like a willow leaf,*
> *clear as a crystal. . . .*
> *He eats like a horse.*

Authors often use the journalistic device of a "hook" to capture children's interest. An example is found in *To Space & Back*, "Launch morning. 6 . . . 5 . . . 4. . . . The alarm clock counts down. 3 . . . 2 . . . 1. . . . Ring! 3:15 A.M. Launch minus four hours" (Ride & Okie, p. 14). The countdown, juxtaposed with the alarm-clock ring, draws children's interest. It also relates the unfamiliar countdown with the familiar ring of an alarm clock.

Authority

The author's qualifications for writing an informational book are usually given on the back flap of the book jacket or the book itself. Readers can consult reviews in journals such as the *Horn Book, Language Arts,* and the *Bulletin of the Center for Children's Books* to learn more about an author's expertise.

Some authors of informational books are not experts in the fields they have chosen as subjects. For example, on the copyright page of the book *Volcano: The Eruption and Healing of Mount St. Helens*, Patricia Lauber acknowledges the help of 13 individuals, including geologists, naturalists, and foresters, in writing the book.

Accuracy

Accuracy is essential in nonfiction. Clear, correct, and up-to-date facts and concepts are the hallmarks of fine children's nonfiction, and illustrations, diagrams, charts, maps, and other material in the book should meet these requirements as well. Checking the copyright date will help determine the currency of information. Accuracy of information can be checked with a recent encyclopedia or a current textbook. It includes distinguishing between theories and facts and making clear that various points of view exist regarding controversial subjects.

Another consideration in selecting and evaluating nonfiction is the author's use of anthropomorphism, which is attributing human characteristics to animals or objects. Authors use this technique because they are trying to make the text more interesting, but it is often unnecessary.

Appropriateness

The concept of appropriateness in informational books encompasses several issues. Excellent informational books suit their audience. The literary style corresponds to the subject and the audience for which the book is intended. *Meltdown: A Race Against Nuclear Disaster at Three Mile Island: A Reporter's Story* by Wilborn Hampton illustrates appropriate style. In vivid narrative, the author provides relevant information about Three Mile Island and the accident that occurred there. The writer creates suspense as he chronicles what people in various positions were doing to respond to the emergency situation. A glossary, list of resources, and index are included.

Clearly organized text enables children to understand the author's presentation of information. An author may organize the text by moving from the familiar to the unfamiliar, moving from the general to the specific, or through a question-and-answer format. A common organizational pattern is presenting facts in chronological order. Gordon Morrison identifies the changes and activities that occur chronologically over weeks and months in *Pond*.

Bibliographic data, which includes tables of contents, indices, glossaries, appendices, and lists of related readings, help children understand the information presented. These aids can help readers locate specific information within a book. Effective bibliographic aids

Young children enjoy nonfiction, too.

provide the starting point for gathering additional information on a particular topic.

Attractiveness

Attractiveness or appeal is important to children, who are more likely to pick up an attractive book. Television and videos have conditioned children to visual images and fast-paced information with dramatic impact. Illustrations prepare readers to understand the text while photographs add a sense of direct reporting and authenticity. Nonfiction illustrations range from photographs to paintings to line drawings.

Leonard Everett Fisher (1988), who has illustrated many nonfiction books, explains his purpose in illustrating nonfiction:

> Today what interests me . . . is giving youngsters a visual memory of a fact rather than just the fact. I am trying to present a factual mood. The Tower of London, for instance, is a creepy place, and if I can establish the creepiness of the place so that the youngster gets an unsettled feeling about the tower. . . . I'm trying to create the emotion of the history, the dynamics of history, together with the facts of history. I'm trying to communicate what events in history felt like. (p. 319)

Nonfiction in the Classroom

Reading nonfiction aloud establishes children's familiarity with it and enables them to read with confi-

Classroom Activities

ACTIVITY 10.1   DATA CHARTS

(IRA/NCTE Standards: 1, 3, 5, 7, 8, 10, 11, 12. Comprehension, writing, higher order thinking.)

Data charts are excellent tools for summarizing data from multiple sources for writing. Read Tomie DePaola's *The Quicksand Book* as preparation for data organization and presentation. Data charts help students integrate collected information (Hennings, 1994; Stoodt, 1989). The steps in preparing a data chart are:

1. Identify the topic, problem, or question.

2. Brainstorm questions regarding the topic, problem, or major question, which become the labels for each column.

3. Identify the sources of information in the left-hand column.

4. Have the students complete the chart (see Figure 10.2).

FIGURE 10.2   Data chart for summarizing data from different sources.

BOOK TITLE	QUESTIONS			
	What kinds of elephants are there?	What do elephants eat?	How large do elephants grow?	How dangerous are elephants?
Elephant Crossing by Toshi Yoshida				
Kingfisher Animal Atlas				
Zoo magazine				

ACTIVITY 10.2   WHAT ABOUT BATS? (4TH GRADE–UP)

(IRA/NCTE Standards: 1, 3, 4, 5, 6, 7, 8, 10, 11, 12. Higher order thinking skills, comprehension, research in print and nonprint texts, communicate to various audiences, range of strategies, apply knowledge, use language.)

This research project was the outcome of a student's question about the bat houses he saw while on vacation. He asked, "Why do people want to have bats in their yards? They're dirty, they drink blood, and they get in your hair and give you rabies." Several of the students in the class agreed with him, so this is the unit the teacher and the students planned.

1. *Objective:* Students will research the questions posed by their classmates.

A. Do bats drink blood?

B. Do bats get in humans' hair?

C. Why are bats considered dirty?

D. Do bats carry rabies?

E. How well can bats see? Is it accurate to say someone is as blind as a bat?

2. *Objective:* Students will develop these basic concepts:

A. Bats are the only mammals that fly.

B. Nearly 1,000 kinds of bats are found in the world.

C. Some bats navigate by sight and some use sound waves.

D. Bats eat vast quantities of insects every night.

E. Some bats are essential for the pollination and reseeding of important plants—bananas, cashews, avocados, and figs, to name a few.

F. Bats are some of the most helpful and fascinating creatures in the world.

G. Bats need to be protected because through ignorance and fear many of them are being destroyed.

H. Bats, whose wings are very much like human hands, belong to the scientific order *Chiroptera*, which means "hand-wing" in Latin.

The students learned so much from researching these questions that they wanted to learn more about bats and ways to protect them. They decided to complete the following projects.

1. Build a model of a bat's wing to show the fingers and thumb.

2. Build models of various kinds of bats.

3. Research the bat as a symbol of good fortune and wisdom in China. Paint illustrations and be prepared to explain why the bat is a symbol of good fortune.

4. Find out about the construction of bat houses and build one.

5. Choose your favorite bat and find out all you can about this particular bat. Write a report, a story, or a poem about your bat.

6. Write a newspaper article about bat protection. Why do bats need protection? What can be done to protect bats? How can we spread the word about protecting bats?

Suggested Books

- *Shadows of Night: The Hidden World of the Little Brown Bat* by Barbara Bash
- *Zipping, Zapping, Zooming Bats* by Ann Earle
- *Bats* by Gail Gibbons
- *Beautiful Bats* by Linda Glaser
- *Bats: Night Fliers* by Betsy Maestro
- *Bats: Mysterious Flyers of the Night* by Dee Stuart

ACTIVITY 10.3   BOOK-TALKS

(IRA/NCTE Standards: 1, 2, 12.)

Students will read and understand many genres, and read for a variety of purposes.

Book-talks will spur students to read. Books like *Gotcha! Nonfiction Booktalks to Get Kids Excited About Reading* by Kathleen Baxter and Marcia Kochel and *Gotcha Again!* by the same authors are invaluable aids for teachers and librarians.

Book-talk A. "Kids Are Valuable People"

Lyddie is proof that kids can change things. She worked in a tavern for 50 cents a week, which was paid to her mother. She then worked in a factory and was treated like a slave. When she stood up for her rights, she was fired and had no place to go.

(Show the students photos from *Kids at Work* by Russell Freedman and *Kids on Strike* by Susan Bartoletti. Have available *Kids with Courage: True Stories About Young People Making a Difference* by Barbara Lewis and *Lyddie* by Katharine Paterson.)

The kids in these books have worked in terrible conditions. They knew they lacked power, but they resisted inhumane treatment. Who do you think has the most power? The kids or the bosses? The children in *Kids at Work* were also working in terrible conditions. How do you suppose they tried to make conditions better? In *It's Our World, Too!*, there are stories of kids doing remarkable things throughout history: newspaper boys who went

on strike for better pay, children who led slaves to freedom, youngsters who protested working conditions. Some of the kids in *Kids Have Courage* expressed their courage through fighting crime; others took social action, while others tried to save the environment.

ACTIVITY 10.4   VISUAL LITERACY

(IRA/NCTE Standards: 1, 2, 3, 4, 6, 7, 8, 11, 12. Language comprehension, visual literacy, knowledge, comprehending various texts, and critical thinking.)

This is a model guide for developing visual literacy. The activity is based on ideas from *Visual Interpretation of Children's Books* (Goldstone, 1989), *Stop, Look, and Write!* (Leavitt & Sohn, 1964), and *Images in Language, Media and Mind* (Fox, 1994). The guide is applied to Pam Conrad's *Prairie Visions: The Life and Times of Soloman Butcher*.

1. Introduce the selected photograph or illustration. Explain its significance and its source. After learning this strategy, students can choose their own photo or illustration.

2. Students may work in pairs, small groups, or individually to answer questions like the following. They may write their answers or make notes for class discussion.

    Where do you think this picture was taken?

    What does it illustrate?

    What does the picture tell about the lives of the people (or animals)?

    Why were the horses on the roof of the house (specific to this book)?

3. Describe the overall impression of the illustration. Is the picture dark and dreary or light and sunny? Is it colorful, sad or happy, lively or quiet?

4. Students should label the people, animals, and objects. For example, students could label different individuals, the shelter, and the horses in *Prairie Visions: The Life and Times of Solomon Butcher.*

5. Students can describe the items, people, activities, structures, and so forth in the photograph or illustration. A list for a photograph in *Prairie Visions* would include the many items crowded into it.

6. Consider the things catalogued in steps 3 to 5 and draw inferences about the people in the book. How did they live? Where did they go to school? What did they eat? What were their homes like? What did they do for recreation?

7. When students complete their inferences, read the book aloud. Students may write a paragraph about their conclusions and support them with references to the illustrations and text.

ACTIVITY 10.5   PROFILING AN AUTHOR

(IRA/NCTE Standards: 3, 4, 5, 6, 7, 11, 12. Comprehension, interpretation, critical thinking, use a variety of resources, and use language to achieve purposes).

Learning about authors and their interests helps readers understand how they get story ideas. After studying an author or illustrator through one of the methods described in previous activities, students can write biographical profiles. The profile of Jim Arnosky focuses on his ways of bringing the natural world to life.

A Biographical Profile: Jim Arnosky

Jim Arnosky has an uncanny connection to nature. He communicates a reverence for and a passionate love of nature using realistic illustrations and lyrical text. He thinks of himself as a naturalist; perhaps this is why his writing leads readers to explore nature and to learn from their own experiences. His best research is done through observation and journals. Visiting different places and comparing them is a part of his research. He believes that doing is the best learning.

His books have been cited for excellence by: Bank Street College of Education; the John Burroughs Association, the National Council of Teachers of English, the National Science Teachers Association, and *Smithsonian* magazine. He has a Web site at **www.jimarnosky.com**.

His excellent books include:

Arnosky's Ark
Beaver Pond, Moose Pond
One Whole Day—Wolves
Watching Desert Wildlife
Wild and Swampy

Summary

Nonfiction includes biography and informational literature. In the past, this genre has been overlooked, but its quality and quantity are increasing. Children find these books interesting because they answer children's natural questions about the world around them. Children comprehend nonfiction better when they have opportunities to hear it read aloud, as well as read it.

Children can learn about people who have been leaders and people who have made contributions to all aspects of life from biography. Curriculum areas are enriched with nonfiction. These books also give students the background necessary to understand the facts presented and to relate these facts to their experiences.

Thought Questions

1. Why is nonfiction particularly appealing to many children?
2. Why do you think some authors specialize in the nonfiction genre?
3. How does a nonfiction author ensure accuracy and authenticity in a work?

Research and Application Experiences

1. Compare three informational books on the same topic. What are the differences in the facts presented? What are the similarities?
2. Compare three biographies of the same person's life. What are the similarities? What are the differences?
3. Identify a topic you would like to know more about. Then identify the types of information you would collect about the topic. Create a data chart for the topic.
4. Read a nonfiction book and write a synopsis of it. Then evaluate it and list the standards you used. What were the book's strong points? What were its weak points?
5. Prepare a book-talk for a nonfiction book you enjoy. Give the book-talk to a group of children or to a group of classmates.
6. Find a nonfiction author on the Web and learn why he or she chooses to write nonfiction. Find out how the author chooses his or her topics. Write an author profile.
7. Find Jim Aronsky's Web site and ask him questions that you or your students would like to have answered.
8. Select a topic that you would like to explore in a classroom and use the Internet to identify books and create a bibliography.

Children's Literature References and Recommended Books

Note: Books designated with an asterisk (*) are recommended for reluctant readers.

Adkins, J. (1997). *Bridges: From my side to yours.* Toronto, Canada. Kids Can Press. (4–7). NONFICTION.

This illustrated book provides a guide to building models that are suitable for elementary students.

Adler, D. A. (1999). *How tall, how short, how far away* (N. Tobin, Illus.). New York: Holiday. (1–3). NONFICTION.

An interesting book of measurement.

Agee, J. (2000). *Who ordered the Jumbo Shrimp and other oxymorons.* New York: HarperCollins. (3–6). PICTURE BOOK.

A collection of illustrated oxymorons.

Agee, J. (2002). *Palindromania.* New York: Farrar. (4–6). NONFICTION.

A collection of palindromes.

Anderson, L. (2000). *Tea for ten.* New York: Farrar. (1–3). NONFICTION.

The author portrays the various efforts to locate King Arthur.

Arnosky, J. (2000). *Wild and swampy: Exploring with Jim Arnosky.* New York: HarperCollins. (All ages). NONFICTION.

The author takes readers into southern swamps and shows young naturalists how to record their observations.

Aronsky, J. (2002). *Field trips: Bug hunting, animal tracking, bird watching, shore walking with Jim Arnosky.* New York: HarperCollins. (4–7). NONFICTION.

The author opens readers' eyes to the natural world and a variety of habitats.

Aruego, J., & Dewey, A. (2002). *Weird friends: Unlikely allies in the animal kingdom.* New York: Harcourt. (2–5). NONFICTION.

Some animals assist others, which benefits both of them.

Bartoletti, S. (1999). *Kids on strike!* Boston: Houghton Mifflin. (4–8). NONFICTION.

This book focuses on children who have been exploited in the United States and their collective power in resisting.

Bash, B. (1993). *Shadows of night: The hidden world of the little brown bat.* San Francisco: Sierra Club Books for Children. (1–3). INFORMATIONAL BOOK.*

The author provides interesting bat facts illustrated with color photographs.

Berger, M. (1989). *Simple Simon says: Take one magnifying glass.* New York: Scholastic. (K–3). INFORMATIONAL BOOK.

This activity book helps children use magnification to get a different view of the world.

Bowen, G. (1994). *Stranded at Plimoth Plantation, 1626* (G. Bowen, Illus.). New York: HarperCollins. (2–5). INFORMATIONAL BOOK, HISTORICAL FICTION.*

This story is told through the journal entries of a 13-year-old boy who is stranded at Plimoth Plantation until he can find passage to Jamestown.

Brown, R. (2001). *Ten seeds.* New York: Knopf. (1–3). NONFICTION.

This is an appealing counting book.

Chertok, B., Hirshfeld, G., & Rosh, M. (1994). *Learning about ancient civilizations through art.* New York: Scholastic. (3–6). NONFICTION.

This book illustrates the art of ancient civilizations.

Cobb, V., (1999). *You gotta try this! Absolutely irresistible science* (T. Kelley, Illus.). New York: Morrow. (3–6). INFORMATIONAL BOOK.

Experiments for students accompanied by appropriate warnings and observations.

Cole, J. (1986). *The magic school bus at the waterworks* (B. Degen, Illus.). New York: Scholastic. (K–4). INFORMATIONAL BOOK, MODERN FANTASY.

The magic school bus travels to the waterworks.

Cole, J. (1992). *The magic school bus on the ocean floor* (B. Degen, Illus.). New York: Scholastic. (K–4). INFORMATIONAL BOOK, MODERN FANTASY.

The indomitable Ms. Frizzle takes her class to the ocean floor.

Cole, J. (1994). *The magic school bus: In the time of the dinosaurs* (B. Degen, Illus.). New York: Scholastic. (K–4). INFORMATIONAL BOOK, MODERN FANTASY.

Ms. Frizzle's class visits a dinosaur dig.

Conrad, P. (1989). *Prairie visions: The life and times of Solomon Butcher.* New York: HarperCollins. (4–8). BIOGRAPHY.

This book is based on the life of a frontier photographer in Nebraska during the 1800s.

Crump. D. (Ed.). (1994). *Exploring your world: The adventure of geography*. New York: National Geographic Society. (3–6). NONFICTION.

The author explores geography as it relates to children.

Curlee, L. (2001). *Brooklyn Bridge*. New York: Simon & Schuster. (3–8). NONFICTION.

The author describes the bridge, and tells its history. The magnificent illustrations are stunning.

Curlee, L. (2003). *Capital*. New York: Simon & Schuster. (2–6). NONFICTION.

Five important structures in Washington D.C. are presented in this book. A map and drawings contribute to the book.

Davidson, S., & Morgan, B. (2002). *Human body revealed*. New York: DK Publishing. (4–7). NONFICTION.

Spectacular quality and quantity of images make this book fascinating.

dePaola, T. (1992). *The quicksand book*. New York: Putnam. (All ages). NONFICTION.

This book describes and explains quicksand and how to deal with it.

DesJarlait, P. (1995). *Patrick DesJarlait: Conversations with a Native American artist* Minneapolis: Runestone Press. (3–8). BIOGRAPHY.

The artist talks about his life and art.

Dewey, J. (2002). *Paisano, the roadrunner*. Millbrook. (3–6). NONFICTION.

A true story of a family of roadrunners.

Earle, A. (1995). *Zipping, zapping, zooming bats* (H. Cole, Illus.). Chicago: Scott Foresman. (K–4). NONFICTION.

This book shows the value of bats in our world and decreases the fear of bats.

Fleischman, J. (2002). *Phineas Gage: A gruesome but true story about brain science*. Boston: Houghton Mifflin. (All ages). NONFICTION.

The true story of a man whose brain was injured, which led to advances in our understanding of the brain.

Fradin, D. (2002). *The signers: The 56 stories behind the Declaration of Independence*. New York: Walker. (4–8). NONFICTION.

This book examines the lives of the signers of the Declaration of Independence.

Frank, M. (2001). *Understanding September 11th: Answering questions about the attacks on America*. New York: Viking. (4–8). NONFICTION.

This is a reference book organized around a question-answer format.

Freedman, R. (1994). *Kids at work*. Boston: Houghton Mifflin. (4–8). NONFICTION.

This book explores child labor during the industrial era.

Freedman, R. (2000). *Give me liberty! The story of the Declaration of Independence*. New York: Holiday House. (3–6). NONFICTION.

This book chronicles the events leading up to the writing and signing of the Declaration of Independence.

Gibbons, G. (2000). *Bats*. New York: Holiday House. (1–4). INFORMATIONAL BOOK.*

This well-written book uses scientific terms in a natural history approach to dispel myths about bats.

Giblin, J. C. (2000). *The amazing life of Benjamin Franklin* (M. Dooling, Illus.). New York: Scholastic. (4–7). BIOGRAPHY.

The author focuses on the amazing accomplishments of Franklin.

Giblin, J. C. (2002). *The Life and Death of Adolf Hitler* New York: Clarion. (5–6; 74). BIOGRAPHY.

This biography shows the complexity of Hitler's personality.

Glaser, L. (1998). *Beautiful bats*. Brookfield, CT: Millbrook. (K–4). NONFICTION.

This book describes the little brown bat with basic informaiton and full color illustrations.

Hampton, W. (2001). *Meltdown: A race against nuclear disaster at Three Mile Island: A reporter's story*. Cambridge, MA: Candlewick Press. (5–12). NONFICTION.

This book describes the efforts to contain this disaster.

Hart, A. & Mantell, P. (1994). *Kids make music!* Charlotte, VT: Williamson. (K–4). NONFICTION.

This book illustrates the various ways children can make music.

Hart, K. (1994). *I can paint!* Portsmouth, NH: Heineman. (2–5). NONFICTION.

This book illustrates color and painting.

Hastings, S. (1993). *The firebird* (R. Cartwright, Illus.). Cambridge, MA: Candlewick Press. (3–6). NONFICTION.

This work is based on the famous Russian composition.

Heller, R. (1990). *Merry-go-round: A book about nouns*. New York: Grosset & Dunlap. (1–3). NONFICTION.

Picture book of nouns.

Heller, R. (1995). *Behind the mask: A book about prepositions*. New York: Grosset & Dunlap. (2–4). NONFICTION.

Picture book about prepositions.

Heller, R. (1997). *Mine, all mine: A book about pronouns.* New York: Grosset & Dunlap. (2–5). NONFICTION.

Picture book of pronouns.

Hoban, T. (1999). *Let's count.* New York: Greenwillow. (1–3). NONFICTION.

This is a counting book.

Jenkins, J. (1992). *Thinking about colors.* New York: Dalton. (1–3). NONFICTION.

This book relates color to artistic modern expression.

Kaner, E. (2002). *Bridges.* (P. Cupples, Illus.). New York: Simon & Schuster. (4–7). NONFICTION.

This is a historical treatment of the art and science of bridge building, beginning with log bridges and concluding with technical marvels.

Lambert, D. (1992). *The children's animal atlas.* Brookfield, CT: Millbrook. (2–5). NONFICTION.

This documents animal evolution and the dangers of extinction.

Lauber, P. (1986). *Volcano: The eruption and healing of Mount St. Helens.* New York: Bradbury. (3–6). INFORMATIONAL BOOK.

Photographs and text describe the events before, during, and after the eruption of Mount St. Helens.

Le Rochais, M. (2001). *Desert trek: An eye-opening journey through the world's driest places.* New York: Walker. (3–6). NONFICTION.

The author shows that deserts are not vast empty spaces. The animals and vegetation give a different picture of deserts.

Lewis, B. (1992). *Kids with courage: True stories about young people making a difference.* Minneapolis, MN: Free Spirit. (5–8). NONFICTION.

A collection of inspiring stories about kids fighting crime, taking social action, heroes, and saving the environment make up this anthology.

Logan, C. (2002). *The 5,000-year-old puzzle: Solving a mystery of ancient Egypt.* New York: Farrar. (3–6). NONFICTION.

This book is written in diary form, as readers travel with the central character on a "dig."

Maestro, B. (1994). *Bats: Night fliers* (G. Maestro, Illus.). New York: Scholastic. (1–3). INFORMATIONAL BOOK.*

The author includes interesting bat information for the younger reader.

Manson, C. (2000). *Uncle Sam and Old Glory: Symbols of America.* New York: Atheneum. (3–6). NONFICTION.

The author explains the meaning each symbol.

Markle, S. (2001). *Growing up wild: Wolves.* New York: Atheneum. (All ages). NONFICTION.

The author uses large, colorful photographs to make this book exciting.

Markle, S. (1997). *Discovering Graph Secrets: Experiments, Puzzles, and Games Exploring Graphs.* New York: Atheneum (3–6). NONFICTION.

Learning activities and games for math.

Marrin, A. (2002). *Dr. Jenner and the speckled monster: The search for the smallpox vaccine.* New York: Dutton. (3–6). NONFICTION.

The history of the deadly smallpox disease.

Martin, B. (1994). *The Maestro plays.* New York: Henry Holt. (1–3). NONFICTION.

This book introduces children to an orchestra.

Masoff, J. (2001). *Everest: Reaching for the sky.* New York: Scholastic. (1–5). NONFICTION.

Photographs help readers experience the ascent to Everest.

Mason, A. (1994). *The Kingfisher first picture atlas.* New York: Kingfisher. (1–4). INFORMATIONAL BOOK.

A picture-book atlas for younger students.

Mason, A., & Lye, K. (1993). *The children's atlas of exploration.* Brookfield, CT: Millbrook. (3–6). INFORMATIONAL BOOK.

This book documents the routes of great explorers.

Micklethwait, L. (1994). *A child's book of art.* New York: Dorling Kindersley. (1–5). NONFICTION.

This book introduces masterpieces that children can enjoy.

Miller, D. (2000). *River of life.* New York: Clarion. (1–4). NONFICTION.

This book describes an Alaskan river, as well as the plants and animals that live in it and along the shore.

Montgomery, S. (2002). *Encantado: Pink dolphin of the Amazon.* Boston: Houghton Mifflin. (4–7). NONFICTION.

The captivating story of a trip down the Amazon to see little-known animals. The author includes facts, maps, and unsolved mysteries.

Morrison, G. (2003). *Pond.* Boston: Houghton Mifflin (K–2). NONFICTION.

This book identifies the changes and activities that occur over days and weeks.

Murphy, J. (1995). *The great fire.* New York: Scholastic. (4–8). NONFICTION.

The well-documented story of the Chicago fire.

Nelson, P. (2002). *Left for dead: A young man's search for the USS Indianapolis*. New York: Delacorte. (4–8). NONFICTION.

Pete Nelson tells the story of searching to learn what happened to his father.

Old, W. (2002). *To fly: The story of the Wright Brothers* (R. Parker, Illus.). (3–6). NONFICTION.

Readers learn about the Wright Brothers' struggle to achieve manned flight.

Osband, G., & Andrew, R. (1991). *Castles*. New York: Orchard. (2–5). INFORMATIONAL BOOK.

This book describes how castles are built.

Parr, T. (2000). *The feelings book*. New York: Little Brown. (1–3). NONFICTION.

This book helps children put their feelings in words.

Paterson, K. (1991). *Lyddie*. New York: Lodestar. (4–7). HISTORICAL FICTION.

This story portrays the life of a New England factory girl who labors in slave-like conditions.

Pilger, M. A. (1988). *Science experiments index for young people*. Englewood, CO: Libraries Unlimited. (3–8). INFORMATIONAL BOOK.

The book is a specialized biography of science activities and experiments.

Pollard, J. (1995). *Building toothpick bridges*. New York: Dale Seymour. (5–8). NONFICTION.

A guide for an architectural approach to building a bridge. Students compute load bearing, and so forth.

Posada, M. (2002). *Ladybugs: Red, fiery, and bright*. Minneapolis: Carolrhoda. (1–3). NONFICTION.

This book describes the ladybug's life cycle.

Pringle, L. (1990). *Global warming*. New York: Arcade. (4–6). INFORMATIONAL BOOK.

The author offers a detailed explanation of global warming.

Pringle, L. (1991). *Living treasure: Saving Earth's threatened biodiversity* (I. Brady, Illus.). New York: Morrow. (4–6). INFORMATIONAL BOOK.

This informational book summarizes and organizes information about our planet's unique organisms.

Prokofiev, S. (1987). *Peter and the wolf* (R. Cartwright, Illus.). New York: Holt. (1–5). NONFICTION

This book tells the famous Russian story.

Ride, S., & Okie, S. (1986). *To space & back*. New York: Lothrop, Lee & Shepard. (2–5). NONFICTION.

This book documents an astronaut's life.

Ryan, P. M. (2002). *When Marian sang* (B. Selznick, Illus.). New York: Scholastic. (1–4). BIOGRAPHY.

This book shows how Marian Anderson overcame humble beginnings and prejudice to sing.

Say, A. (1993). *Grandfather's journey*. Boston: Houghton Mifflin. (3–6). BIOGRAPHY.

The author compares his life with his grandfather's.

Schmandt-Besserat, D. (1999). *The history of counting*. New York: Morrow. (4–6). NONFICTION.

This book discusses the counting systems from several cultures.

Schwartz, D. (2003). *Millions to measure* (S. Kellogg, Illus.). New York: HarperCollins. (2–5). NONFICTION.

This book helps readers learn about measurement concepts.

Shapiro, W. E. (Ed.). (1994). *The Kingfisher young people's encyclopedia of the United States*. New York: Kingfisher. (3–6). INFORMATIONAL BOOK.

This work has entries reflecting the school curriculum.

Stuart, D. (1994). *Bats: Mysterious flyers of the night*. Minneapolis: Carolrhoda. (1–4). INFORMATIONAL BOOK.

This is an informative book about bats.

Sturges, P., & Laroche, G. (1998). *Bridges are to cross* (P. Sturges, Illus.). (3–5). NONFICTION.*

The author presents bridges and the things they carry from around the world.

Tang, G. (2001). *The grapes of math: Mind-stretching math riddles*. New York: Scholastic. (All ages). NONFICTION.

Calculation becomes an enthralling game in this book.

Tang, G. (2002). *The best of times: Math strategies that multiply*. New York: Scholastic. (2–5). NONFICTION.

A book of multiplication fun.

Turner, R. (1992). *Portraits of women artists for children: Mary Cassatt*. Boston: Little, Brown. (3–8). NONFICTION.

Themed collection of portraits.

Vogel, C. (2000). *Nature's fury: Eyewitness reports of natural disasters*. New York: Scholastic. (4–7). NONFICTION.

The author includes background information and summaries about events, including survivors' reports of natural events.

Wallace, K. (1993). *Think of an eel* (M. Bostock, Illus.). Cambridge, MA: Candlewick Press. (1–4). INFORMATIONAL BOOK.

> The author describes the characteristics and life cycle of the eel.

Zaslavsky, C. (2001). *Number sense and nonsense.* Chicago: Chicago Press. (3–6). NONFICTION.

> An inviting book addressing a variety of topics such as odd and even numbers, prime and composite number, and so forth.

Zoehfeld, K. W. (2002). *From tadpole to frog.* New York: Scholastic. (1–3). NONFICTION.

> Full-color photographs document tadpole development.

References and Books for Further Reading

Ballantyne, M. M. (1993). The effects of narrative and expository discourse on the reading comprehension of middle school-aged good and poor readers (University Microfilms No. 94–06, 749). Dissertation Abstracts International 54, 4046.

Baxter, K., & Kochel, M. (1999). *Gotcha! Nonfiction booktalks to get kids excited about reading.* Englewood, CO: Libraries Unlimited.

Baxter, K., & Kochel, M. (2002). *Gotcha again! More nonfiction booktalks to get kids excited about reading.* Englewood, CO: Libraries Unlimited.

Daniels, H. (2002). *Literature circles: Voice and choice in book clubs and reading groups.* Portland, ME: Stenhouse.

Duthie, C. (1994). Nonfiction: A genre study for the primary classroom. *Language Arts, 71,* 588–595.

Fisher, L. E. (1988). The artist at work: Creating nonfiction. *The Horn Book, 78,* 315–323.

Ford, D. (2002, May/June). More than the facts: Reviewing science books. *The Horn Book 78,* 265–271.

Fox, S. (1994). *Media and mind.* Alexandria, VA: ASCD.

Giblin, J C. (1987). A Publisher's Perspective. *Horn Book, 63,* 104–107.

Goldstone, F. (1989). Visual interpretation of children's books. *Reading Teacher, 42,* 592–595.

Greene, M. (1992). Texts and margins. In M. Boldberg & A. Phillips (Eds.), *Arts as education.* Cambridge, MA: Harvard Educational Review. Reprint Series No. 24, 1–18.

Harvey, S. (1998). *Nonfiction matters.* York, ME: Stenhouse.

Hennings, D. (1994). *Language arts.* Boston: Houghton Mifflin.

Jensen, J. (2001). The quality of prose in Orbis Pictus Award books. In M. Zarnowski, R. Kerper, & J. Jensen (Eds.), *The best in children's nonfiction.* Urbana, IL: National Council of Teachers of English, 2–21.

Leavitt, J., & Sohn, D. (1964). *Stop, look, and write!* New York: Bantam.

McAuley, K., & Wilson, R. H. (1987). *The United States: Past to present.* Lexington, MA: D. C. Heath.

Meltzer, M. (1994). *Nonfiction for the classroom.* New York: Teachers College Press.

Pappas, C. C., Kiefer, B., & Levstik, L. (1990). *An integrated language perspective in the elementary school.* White Plains, NY: Longman.

Shanahan, T. (1992). Nine good reason for using children's literature across the curriculum. In T. Shanahan (Ed.), *Distant shores resource packages, IV* (pp. 10–22). New York: McGraw Hill School Division.

Stead, T. (2002). *Is that a fact?* Portland, ME: Stenhouse Publishers.

Stoodt, B. (1989). *Reading instruction* (2nd ed.). New York: HarperCollins.

Stoodt, B., & Amspaugh, L. (1994, May). Children's response to nonfiction. A paper presented to the Annual Meeting of the International Reading Association, Toronto, Canada.

Walmsley, S. A. (1994). *Children exploring their world: Theme teaching in elementary school.* Portsmouth, NH: Heinemann.

Whitin, P., & Whitin, D. (2002). Mathematics in our world. In A. McClure & J. Kristo (Eds.), *Adventuring with books,* (13th ed.). Urbana, IL: National Council of Teachers of English.

Biography: Fascinating Real Life

KEY TERMS

authentic biography
autobiography
biographical fiction

biography
fictionalized biography

GUIDING QUESTIONS

1. How do biographies differ from other genres?

2. Did you have a favorite biography as a child?

3. What values does biography have for children?

Aunt Clara Brown was an unusual pioneer.

Biography is the story of a life, the "history of the life of an individual" (Lukens, 1995). Reading a well-written biography becomes an absorbing human encounter with a person whose achievement is out of the ordinary. That person may be famous, as in Andrea Pinkney's *Ella Fitzgerald,* or infamous, as in James Cross Giblin's *The Life and Death of Hitler,* or unknown to the general public, as in Lois Lowery's *Aunt Clara Brown: Official Pioneer.* We can learn from all of these people. Teachers can excite students' interest in biography, as the vignette on the following page illustrates. The vignette is a personal reflection showing the roots of my life-long love of biography.

218

The Wright Brothers were pioneers in flight.

Learning About Life in Biography

Reading a well-written *biography* becomes an absorbing human encounter with a person and his or her interesting life. Tapping the life experiences of others helps students learn about their own life. They will discover people who overcame obstacles such as ignorance, poverty, misery, fear, and hate, which shows us how to overcome problems (Zarnowski, 1990). For example, *Tallchief: America's Prima Ballerina* is a first person account of Maria Tallchief's courage and tenacity in the face of adversity, resulting in the accomplishment of her dreams.

Biography subjects do not live isolated lives. Rather, their lives are shaped through their interactions with other people and through events that form the backdrop of their story. As Milton Meltzer said, "when you write biography, you present history through the prism of a single life, a life, that is, of course, connected to other lives " (Meltzer, 1981, p. 15). These elements are apparent in Mary Collins' *Airborne: A Photobiography of Wilbur and Orville Wright*. She focuses on the Wright brothers and their lives in the

VIGNETTE

Picture this. . . , Monday, 10 A.M., in a one-room school with six rows, one for each grade. This scene is from rural Ohio of the 1940s. A teacher-fired stove stands at the right side of the classroom, with a bucket of water with tin cups for the students and an outhouse in back of the school. It's read-aloud time! The teacher, Miss Minshall, removes a book from the corner of the desk and continues reading from the Lincoln biography started the preceding week. The story was Lincoln's courtroom defense of an accused murderer. I held my breath as she read The Testimony of the first witness, "I saw him do it in the light of the full moon." However, Lincoln proved he was innocent when the Farmers Almanac showed there was no full moon on the night in question. Awestruck at Lincoln's brilliance, this first grader began reading biographies of Lincoln, then ventured into stories of Benjamin Franklin, another hero. Recently, she read a brand new biography of Franklin with the same relish as long ago.

Postscript: I now realize that Miss Minshall read from adult biographies and translated the text into language that young children could understand. This was an important factor because the few biographies of that era were poorly written and lacked research. When Miss Minshall read biography, she focused on myths that appealed to children, such as George Washington and the cherry tree. She also read from American history and the daily newspaper. When she read about German casualties, we cheered. She told us that was wrong because these were innocent civilians who probably did not want to fight. Perhaps she chose these subjects because this was the time of World War II, but biography and history have remained my major reading interests throughout life. I owe this to my first-grade teacher. She proved teachers can make a difference!

The Stetson hat helped win the West.

close-knit Wright famiy, their bicycle shop, their flight experiments, and their ultimate success at Kitty Hawk. In clearly written, lively prose, the author reveals the Wright brothers as individuals.

Some biographies reveal a great deal about the times and places in which an individual or individuals lived. In *Boss of the Plains,* Laurie Carlson explains how John Batterson Stetson invented his famous hat after he saw that the hats men wore in the east were useless in the west's heat and wind.

Writing Biography

Accuracy and authenticity are the hallmarks of fine biography. Biographers must research their subjects carefully, then assume an attitude or theme regarding the subject, which guides them in selecting the events and details to include. The writer then shapes the biography to make the subject come alive.

Biography may appear to be a simple writing task, essentially a reporting of actual people, events, and life stories. However, the writer has to decide the amount of detail to include, whether to use illustrations, which friends or enemies of the subject to write about, and

many other details. Biographers use many of the same techniques as other storytellers: They "set their scenes descriptively, develop their characters completely, and give us the impression of life unfolding " (Zarnowski, 1990, p. 6). Finally, they determine which facts to include and which to exclude. For example, in *Charles A. Lindbergh: A Human Hero,* James Cross Giblin chose to recognize this man's controversial Nazi sympathies.

Types of Biography

One of the most important decisions a biographer must make is the type of biography to write: complete or partial, single or collective.

Complete Biography

Complete, or cradle-to-grave, biographies describe a subject's life from birth to death as James Cross Giblin does in *The Life and Death of Hitler.* Single biographies can address the theme of an individual's life. The theme of Giblin's *The Amazing Life of Benjamin Franklin* was Franklin's amazing accomplishments.

Walter Dean Myers chose to write a complete biography of Muhammad Ali in *The Greatest: Muhammad Ali* because a complete biography enabled him to show all the accomplishments of this complex man. This fascinating book is difficult to put down once you start reading it because the writer chronicles Ali's early years in poverty, and shows how his determination led to success.

A complete biography was also the choice of Tom Lalicki when he wrote about the complex character, Harry Houdini, in *Spellbinder: The Life of Harry Houdini.* The theme of this biography was Houdini's ability to spellbind people both on and off the stage. The author researched his subject carefully, and was able to include many little-known details about Houdini, including the fact that his real name was Erich Weiss. Marfe Delano tells the story of Edison's life through photographs in *Inventing the Future: A Photobiography of Thomas Alva Edison.*

Partial Biography

When biography focuses on a portion of the subject's life, it is a partial life story. In this instance, the biographer focuses on a particular time or specific event in a subject's

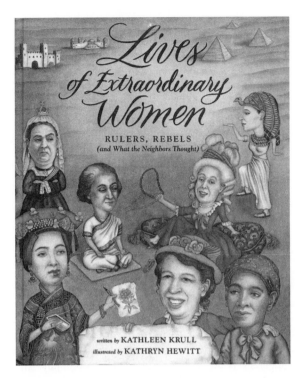

These Women triumphed over adverse attitudes and conditions.

life. For example, Alice and Marten Provensen described the events of the year 1492 in da Vinci's life, when they wrote *Leonardo da Vinci: The Artist, Inventor, Scientist.* During this year of his life, he developed a flying machine, created a statue, studied the heavens, and painted the Mona Lisa. Ruby Bridges chronicled the year that she was one of the first Black children to integrate segregated schools in her book, *Through My Eyes.* William Miller's picture book *Zora Hurston and the Chinaberry Tree* tells of one little-known episode in the childhood of the renowned writer Zora Nele Hurston. Another picture book, Edith Kunhardt's *Honest Abe,* depicts only major events in the life of Abraham Lincoln through unforgettable primitive paintings and simple language. The text and illustrations are uniquely suited to the historic events in Lincoln's life.

Collective Biography

Collective biographies focus on the lives of several subjects with a connection among them. Kathleen Krull's *Lives of Extraordinary Women Rulers, Rebels (and What the Neighbors Thought)* is the story of 20 women who triumphed over adverse attitudes and conditions. She identifies the unique characteristics of each woman, and each one's individuality is clear. Liza Ketchum wrote a collective biography about women who made their mark on the West of the 1800s, *Into a New Country: Eight Remarkable Women of the West.* Each of these women made unique and unexpected contributions to people of the west, such as two sisters who helped the Omaha Indians.

Autobiography

Autobiographies are actually written by the book's subjects. For example, in *Through My Eyes* Ruby Bridges chronicles her life as a 6-year-old, when she was one of the nation's first Black children to attend school in the deep south. Helen Lester shares her life story in *Author: A True Story,* and tells of considering herself an author at three years of age. Lester explains how much time and work is involved in getting a book published. Teachers can introduce some of her very popular books with this autobiography.

Authentic Biography and Fictionalized Biography

Interpreting an individual's life is a very important decision on the biographer's part. The author may adhere to the facts in *authentic biography* or dramatize the subject's life through *fictionalized biography.* In authentic biography, the only facts included are those verifiable through research. Any dialogue must be able to be substantiated by historical documents (Russell, 1994). Biographer Jean Fritz (1990) explains her stance: "I would make up nothing, not even the dialogue, and I wouldn't even use dialogue unless I had a source. I would be honest. If there was a fact I wasn't sure of, or if it was unknown, I would say so" (p. 25).

Most children's biography is fictionalized, which represents a middle position between strict adherence to known facts and completely invented narrative. In this case, "facts are the bricks with which a biographer builds" (Coolidge, 1974, p. 141). In fictionalized biography, dialogue and events can be invented based upon historical documents (Sutherland & Arbuthnot, 1991). In Barbara Brenner's *On the Frontier with Mr. Audubon,* the story of Audubon's journey down the

Mississippi in 1821 is told through an imaginary journal created as if his real-life assistant made the entries.

Selecting and Evaluating Biography

Many current biographies are of excellent quality. When selecting biography, consider the following guidelines:

1. *Subject.* The subject should be relevant to students and their interests or studies.
2. *Accuracy.* The information should be well-researched and documented. Authors should include a bibliography and source notes.
3. The information should be clearly presented.
4. The book should use photographs, drawings, and paintings that support the text, orient the reader, and build interest.
5. The writing style should make the subject interesting. Using descriptions, anecdotes, and details create interest in readers.

Subject

James Cross Giblin explains that, when choosing subjects for biography, he is drawn to complicated people, which he then he has to make understandable and meaningful to young people. He adds that he is fascinated with the complexities of human nature (Harris & McCarthy, (2002).

For many years, the subjects of children's biographies were historical figures. However, more and more writers are now choosing to write about a broader range of subjects (Lukens, 1995). For instance Linda Lowery's biography *Aunt Clara Brown: Official Pioneer* tells the dramatic story of Clara Brown, a former slave who traveled to Colorado to find a better life. Ultimately she became the first official Colorado pioneer who was neither white nor male. In an unusual collective biography, Andrew Glass chose to write about *Bad Guys: True Stories of Legendary Gunslingers, Sidewinders, Fourflushers, Dry Gulchers, Bushwhackers, Freebooters, and Downright Bad Guys and Gals of the Wild West,* exploring the characters of individuals like Jessie James and Billy the Kid. For a picture-book biography, Don Brown chose Mack Sennett as his subject in *Mack Made Movies*, explaining how Sennett applied slapstick techniques to the movies.

Members of minority cultures have often been omitted from biography and history. For many years, American children learned history minus Black people, women, Hispanics, and Native Americans (Hearne, 1990, p. 136). However, newer biographies include a broader range of subjects. For example, the biography, *When Marian Sang* by Pam Munoz Ryan brings Marian Anderson, the great American singer, to life. She grew up in humble circumstances and was rejected by schools of music, but Eleanor Roosevelt arranged for her to sing at the Lincoln Memorial in 1939 after she was rejected by another group.

Accuracy

Accuracy is the linchpin of excellent biography. The best biographers conduct exhaustive research to document their books. Russell Freedman carefully researched "the greatest woman athlete of all time" to write the book *Babe Didrikson Zaharias: The Making of a Champion.* His theme in this biography was the subject's impact on the image of American women. He used many photographs to show her in motion. His research provided details and quotes that he used to capture her personality. For instance, "She ran the soles off a pair of tennis shoes every two weeks" (p. 10). He details Didrikson's prizes and statistics in the many sports she played.

Biographers often choose to use the main characteristic of a subject as a focal point and theme for their writing. Freedman has done this in his biographies of Abraham Lincoln and Eleanor Roosevelt. Jean Fritz focused on Revere's compulsive activities in *And Then What Happened, Paul Revere?* Her theme and style in this biography meld together seamlessly: Her short sentences and informal tone mimic Revere's compulsive, breathless speech.

The goal of biographers is to create characters who come alive for children. To achieve this, a biographer selects facts that effectively tell the subject's story and help children feel they know the character described. Authors use various devices to help us understand their subjects. In *George Washington's Teeth* by Deborah Chandra and Madeleine Comora, the authors use humor, wit, and sympathy in helping children understand Washington's problems with his teeth. This interesting book is historically accurate and includes the sources the authors used in telling the tale.

Another stylistic technique for helping readers "see" a subject is telling the story from a child's point of view. Allen Say compares his life and his grandfather's life in the Caldecott Award-winning book *Grandfather's Journey,* telling about his grandfather's journey to the United States and his return to Japan. His grandfather loved both countries, and when he was in one country he yearned for the other.

Theme

Biographers identify a unifying thread or theme to bind the characterization of their subject together. Identifying a theme determines which facts to include and exclude and shapes the authors' interpretation of their subjects. The theme of Lesa Cline-Ransome's *Satchel Paige* was Paige's genuine love of baseball. In Andrea Pinkney's *Ella Fitzgerald: The Tale of a Vocal Virtuosa,* the author focuses on Ella Fitzgerald's vocal talents. This theme appears in the illustrations, as well as the text. The biographer's theme often appears in the biography title.

Style

Children find it easier to understand biography that reads like a story, albeit a real-life story. Children generally enjoy facts woven into narrative style, but the biographer must do the research needed to create authenticity. Research involves examining the subject's daily life, food, games, clothing, and conversation. The language created in conversation should be appropriate to the era, and discussions must reflect the issues of the time. Some of the vocabulary used may be foreign to young readers and impede their understanding. Jean Fritz (1990) explains that she does not omit important words just because they may be strange to young readers. In addition, some authors include glossaries to help children.

Teaching Strategies for Biography

Biography is an excellent means for enhancing language arts and social studies. Perhaps the most important contribution of teachers and librarians is providing excellent biography and reading it aloud to children at all levels.

Classroom Activities

ACTIVITY 11.1   DRAMA AND ROLE-PLAYING

(IRA/NCTE Standards: 3, 6, 7, 8, 9, 10, 11, 12. Language arts, comprehension, vocabulary, response, knowledge, reading, and writing.)

Creative drama is an excellent learning experience for students who are reading biographies. They can learn a great deal from role-playing or dramatizing biographies, as well as nonfiction. They may also act out events from nonfiction. Dramatizing a historical figure helps students develop a better understanding of the character. Another drama activity involves conducting television interviews. One student prepares questions while another prepares to be the character, considering the style of dress, issues of the day, and so forth. A camcorder or a tape recorder will add to the feeling of conducting a television interview.

ACTIVITY 11.2   DATA CHART FOR BIOGRAPHY—TIGER WOODS

(IRA/NCTE Standards: 1, 3, 5, 7, 8, 10, 11, 12.)

1. Identify the subject for the biographical study.
2. Identify the categories of information that you expect to appear in a biography.
3. Identify the sources of information in the left-hand column, as shown in Figure 11.1.
4. Have the students complete the chart. Older students can create their own charts on a computer.

FIGURE 11.1   A Biographical Study of Tiger Woods.

Biography	Childhood	Family	Personality	Theme	Honors	Photos
Tiger Woods by William Durbin	precocious; played golf as toddler	close; father taught		precocious childhood		newspaper
Tiger Woods: Golf's Shining Young Star by Bill Gutman	brief discussion		emphasize	stardom	youngest golfer ever to win the Masters	color photos
Tiger Woods: Golf Superstar by David Collins	introduced as an infant who became a famous toddler	faced prejudice and bullying	emphasized positive attitude and demeanor	intelligence, athletic ability, and personality	skill	full color illustrations

ACTIVITY 11.3   COMPARING BIOGRAPHIES: BENJAMIN FRANKLIN

(IRA/NCTE Standards: 1, 2, 3, 6. Read a variety of print and nonprint texts from a range of genres; use a wide range of strategies to comprehend for a variety of purposes; and apply language knowledge to critique and discuss text.)

This activity may be completed with print biographies, as well as biographical material from the Internet. Students may establish their own categories for comparison, as shown in Figure 11.2.

FIGURE 11.2   A Biographical Study of Benjamin Franklin.

Title & Author	Family	Theme	Honors	Inventions	Science	Publisher
B. Franklin, Printer by D. Adler, Holiday, 2001.	husband and father	our greatest American; his glory and humble pride; what he means to our country today	ambassador; helped write the Declaration of Independence			his proudest title; includes passages from his newspaper
Ben Franklin's Almanac: Being a True Account of the Good Gentleman's Life by C. Fleming, Atheneum, 2003.*		a tribute to Franklin's complexity	ambassador; author of the Declaration of Independence	includes anecdotes	includes anecdotes	includes anecdotes
Who Was Benjamin Franklin? by D. Fradin, Grossett & Dunlap, 2002.	one of 17 children	fascinating founding father; creative; inventive mind; contributed to culture, politics, and society	diplomat	national postal system, bifocals, volunteer fire department, public library	identifies contributions	

*Each of these books is an important contribution to children's literature. However, the Fleming book is exceptional in that it is done in a scrapbook style and provides unusual material related to Franklin's life.

ACTIVITY 11.4   PROFILING A BIOGRAPHER

(IRA/NCTE Standards: 3, 4, 5, 6, 7, 11, 12. Comprehension, interpretation, critical thinking, use a variety of resources, and use language to achieve purposes.)

Learning about authors and their interests helps readers understand how they get story ideas. After studying an author or illustrator through one of the methods de-scribed in previous activities, students can write biographical profiles.

A Biographical Profile: Jean Fritz

Jean Fritz's biography from Penguin Putnam Books for young readers calls her biographies, "refreshingly informal." Her widely acclaimed biographies have been described as unconventional, good-humored, witty, irrepressible, and extraordinary. Jean Fritz is an original and lively thinker who is recognized as a master of her craft. The majority of her writing is nonfiction and biography.

When asked about her choice of subjects, she suggests that she may write about the United States because she grew up in China, and she has discovered that American history is packed full of stories and people. She points out that every person has his or her own stories and she likes to find out about them. She wants readers to realize that past times were as exciting and fun as present times.

Fritz enjoys research very much because it involves reading and traveling. She wants to find the truth, so that she never makes up anything in her books. Research also turns up surprises, such as the fact that young Patrick Henry was remembered for wearing clean underwear. Her research has provided adventures, including her trip to London when she wrote about King George III. She has received these awards: Regina Medal by the Catholic Library Association; the Laura Ingalls Wilder Award by the American Library Association; and the Knickerbocker Award for Juvenile Literature from the New York State Library Association for her body of work. A list of her books follows:

> You Want Women to Vote, Lizzie Stanton?
>
> Bully for You, Teddy Roosevelt
>
> The Great Little Madison
>
> Surprising Myself (autobiography)
>
> Can't You Make Them Behave, King George?
>
> What's the Big Idea, Ben Franklin?
>
> Harriet Beecher Stowe and the Beecher Preachers
>
> Traitor: The Case of Benedict Arnold

Note: The materials for this author profile were drawn from Internet sites: Penguin Putnam Books for Young Readers; Children's Book Council; Carol Hurst's Children's Literature Site.

Summary

Biography is the story of a person's life. Children learn about their own life through the lives of people who have made contributions to the world. These lives give students models of people who have overcome adverse conditions to succeed. Students also learn, from biographies of people who are not admirable, to avoid certain behaviors. Biography enriches curriculum areas because students can read about leaders in the various subject areas. These books give students the background necessary to understand the life and times of famous, infamous, and unknown people.

Thought Questions

1. Why is theme important in biography?

2. How are biography and nonfiction related?

3. How does a biographer ensure accuracy and authenticity in a work?

Research and Application Experiences

1. Create a special interest bibliography for a specific grade level based on an individual that would fit into the curriculum at the chosen grade level. These individuals might include scientists, politicians, Presidents, and so forth.

2. Compare three biographies of the same person's life. What are the similarities? What are the differences?

3. Prepare a book-talk for a biography you enjoy. Present the book-talk to a group of children or to a group of classmates.

4. Find a biographer on the Web and learn why he or she chooses to write biography. Find out how the author chooses his or her subjects. Write an author profile.

Children's Literature References and Recommended Books

Note: Books designated with an asterisk (*) are recommended for reluctant readers.

Brenner, B. (1977). *On the frontier with Mr. Audubon* (G. Lippincott, Illus.). New York: Coward, McCann, and Geoghegan. (4–8). BIOGRAPHY.

Audubon's experiences are detailed, as told by his apprentice.

Bridges, R. (1999). *Through my eyes*. New York: Scholastic. (4–6). AUTOBIOGRAPHY.

This book chronicles the year Ruby Bridges was one of the first Black children to integrate schools.

Brown, D. (2003). *Mack made movies*. New York: Roaring Brook. (1–4). NONFICTION.*

A picture-book biography of film pioneer Mack Sennett.

Carlson, L. M. (1998). *Boss of the plains: The hat that won the west* (H. Meade, Illus.). New York: DK Publishing. (1–4). INFORMATIONAL BOOK.*

The story of John Batterson Stetson and how he invented a hat.

Chandra, D., & Comora, M. (2003). *George Washington's teeth* (B. Cole, Illus.). New York: Farrar. (1–4). BIOGRAPHY.

This humorous biography examines George Washington's life through his struggle with bad teeth.

Cine-Ransome, L. (2000). *Satchel Paige* (J. Ransome, Illus.). New York: Simon & Schuster. (All ages). BIOGRAPHY.

A picture-book biography of the great baseball player.

Collins, D. (1999). *Tiger Woods: Golf superstar* (L. Nolte, Illus.). New York: Pelican. (1–3). BIOGRAPHY.*

This book focuses on woods' athletic ability, intelligence, and his positive attitude and demeanor. It documents the prejudice he has encountered, and his ability to overcome it.

Collins, M. (2003). *Airborne: A photobiography of Wilbur and Orville Wright*. Washington DC: National Geographic. (4–8). BIOGRAPHY.

The author chronicles the lives of the Wright Brothers and includes excellent photographs, drawings of planes, and maps.

Delano, M. (2001). *Inventing the future: A photobiography of Thomas Alva Edison*. Washington DC: National Geographic Society. (4–8) BIOGRAPHY.

This photobiography is richly illustrated with photographs.

DesJarlait, P. (1995). *Patrick DesJarlait: Conversations with a Native American artist*. Minneapolis: Runestone Press. (3–8). BIOGRAPHY.

The artist talks about his life and art in this book.

Durbin, W. (1998). *Tiger Woods*. South Burlington, VT: Chelsea. (4–6). BIOGRAPHY.

The author drew on newspaper accounts to write this biography. Durbin emphasizes his precocious skills.

Fleischman, J. (2002). *Phineas Gage: A gruesome but true story about brain science*. Boston: Houghton Mifflin. (All ages). NONFICTION.

The true story of a man whose brain was injured, which led to advances in our understanding of the brain.

Fradin, D. (2002). *The signers: The 56 stories behind the Declaration of Independence*. New York: Walker. (4–8). BIOGRAPHY. *

This book examines the lives of the signers of the Declaration of Independence.

Freedman, R. (1999). *Babe Didrikson Zaharias: The making of a champion*. New York: Clarion. (4–8). BIOGRAPHY.

This is the biography of "the greatest woman athlete of all time."

Fritz, J. (1973). *And then what happened, Paul Revere?* (M. Tomes, Illus.). New York: Coward, McCann. (2–5). BIOGRAPHY.

A humorous tribute to Paul Revere's character.

Fritz, J. (1976). *What's the big idea, Ben Franklin?* (M. Tomes, Illus.). New York: Putnam. (2–4). BIOGRAPHY. *

Fritz begins this book, with Franklin's birth on Milk Street. The theme is his skills as a great inventor and a statesman.

Fritz, J. (1989). *Traitor: The case of Benedict Arnold*. New York: Puffin. (2–4). BIOGRAPHY. *

Fritz explains why Arnold became a traitor and the terrible impact it had on Americans.

Fritz, J. (1991). *Bully for you, Teddy Roosevelt.* New York: Putnam. (2–4). BIOGRAPHY. *

The story of a sickly boy who exercised, worked hard, and became President.

Fritz, J. (1992). *Surprising myself.* New York: Richard Owen. (2–4). AUTOBIOGRAPHY. *

A brief autobiography in which Fritz describes her daily life and how she works.

Fritz, J. (1995). *You want women to vote, Lizzie Stanton?* New York: Putnam. (2–4). BIOGRAPHY. *

Lizzie was a fierce abolitionist who fought for the 19th Amendment.

Fritz, J. (1996). *Can't you make them behave, King George?* New York: Putnam. (2–4). BIOGRAPHY.

The author gives the British view of the Revolution. She shows King George III as frustrated and angry.

Giblin, J. C. (1997). *Charles Lindberg: A human hero.* New York: Clarion. (4–7). BIOGRAPHY.

A well balanced biography of an American hero.

Giblin, J. C. (2000). *The amazing life of Benjamin Franklin.* (M. Dooling Illus.) New York: Scholastic (3–6). BIOGRAPHY.

This biography focuses on Franklin's accomplishments.

Giblin, J. C. (2002). *The life and death of Hitler.* New York: Clarion. (5–up). BIOGRAPHY.

Hitler was probably the most dangerous and destructive 20th-century dictator. He perpetuated the most suffering and misery in the 20th century.

Glass, A. (1998). *Bad guys: True stories of legendary gunslingers, sidewinders, fourflushers, dry gulchers, bushwhackers, preebooters, and downright bad guys and gals of the wild west.* New York: Doubleday. (3–7). BIOGRAPHY.

The title identifies the subjects of this biography.

Gutman, B. (1998). *Tiger Woods: Golf's shining young star.* New York: Millbrook. (4–6). BIOGRAPHY.

This biography focuses on Tiger Woods youth and achievement. This book begins with a crucial tournament in Woods' career. It looks briefly at his childhood and emphasizes his personality.

Ketchum, L. (2000). *Into a new country: Eight remarkable women of the west.* New York: Little Brown. (4–8). BIOGRAPHY.

These women helped people in settling the west.

Krull, K. (2000). *Lives of extraordinary women rulers, rebels (and what the neighbors thought).* New York: Harcourt. (3–4, 5–6). BIOGRAPHY.

This is a book of partial biographies of famous women.

Kunhardt, E. (1993). *Honest Abe.* (M. Zeldis, Illus.). New York: Greenwillow. (1–4). BIOGRAPHY.

Primitive paintings illustrate this biography.

Lalicki, T. (2000). *Spellbinder: The life of Harry Houdini.* New York: Holiday House. (4–8). BIOGRAPHY.

A fascinating biography of the magician which includes many little-known facts.

Lester, H. (1997). *Author: A true story.* Boston: Houghton Mifflin. (1–3). BIOGRAPHY.

Helen Lester shares her life of writing and the struggles involved in getting published.

Lowery, L. (1999). *Aunt Clara Brown: Official pioneer.* Minneapolis: Carolrhoda Books. (2–3). BIOGRAPHY.

Clara Brown was recognized as a pioneer in a time when African Americans and women were not recognized.

Miller, W. (1994) *Zora Hurston and the chinaberry tree.* (C. Van Wright & Y. Hu, Illus.). New York: Leet-Low. (1–3). BIOGRAPHY.

This book focuses on one incident in Zora Hurston's early life.

Myers, W. D. (2001). *The greatest: Muhammad Ali.* New York: Scholastic. (4–8). BIOGRAPHY.

This is the life story of the prize fighter Muhammad Ali and his fight with disability.

Pinkney, A. (2002). *Ella Fitzgerald: The tale of a vocal virtuosa* (B. Pinkney, Illus.). New York: Hyperion. (1–6). BIOGRAPHY.

A cat named Scat Cat Monroe tells the story of Ella Fitzgerald's life. The illustrations are stunning.

Provenson, A., & Provenson, N. (1984). *Leonardo da Vinci: The artist, inventor, scientist.* New York: Viking. (3–7). BIOGRAPHY.

This book describes one year in the life of Leonardo da Vinci.

Ryan, P. M. (2002). *When Marian sang* (B. Selznick, Illus.). New York: Scholastic. (1–4). BIOGRAPHY.

This book shows how Marian Anderson overcame humble beginnings and prejudice to sing.

Say, A. (1993). *Grandfather's journey.* Boston: Houghton Mifflin. (3–6). BIOGRAPHY.

The author compares his life with his grandfather's.

Tallchief, M., with Wells, R. (1999). *Tallchief: America's prima ballerina* (G. Kelley, Illus.). New York: Viking. (All ages). AUTOBIOGRAPHY.

The story of Maria Tallchief, who achieved her dream as one of the world's leading dancers.

References and Books for Further Reading

Carr, J. (1982). What do we do about bad biographies? In *Beyond fact: Nonfiction for children and young people* (pp. 45–63) Chicago: American Library Association.

Coolidge, O. (1974). *The apprenticeship of Abraham Lincoln.* New York: Scribner's.

Fritz, J. (1990). The teller and the tale. In W. Zinsser (Ed.), *Worlds of childhood: The art and craft of writing for children* (pp. 21–46). Boston: Houghton Mifflin.

Harris, V., & McCarthey, S. (2002, Summer). A conversation with James Cross Giblin. *The New Advocate, 15* (3), 175–182.

Hearne, B. (1990). *Choosing books for children: A commonsense approach.* New York: Delacorte.

Hearne, B. (1999). *Choosing books for children: A commonsense approach.* (2nd ed.). New York: Delacorte.

Lukens, R. (1995). *A critical handbook of children's literature* (4th ed.). Glenview, IL: Scott Foresman.

Meltzer, M. (1981). Beyond the span of a single life. In B. Hearne and M. Kaye (Eds.), *Celebrating children's books* (pp. 87–96). New York: Lothrop, Lee, & Shepard.

Meltzer, M. (1987). The reader and the writer. In C. Bauer (Ed.), *The best of the bulletin.* Urbana, IL: National Council of Teachers of English.

Russell, D. (1994). *Literature for Children: A short introduction.* White Plains, New York: Longman.

Sullivan, E. (2002, October/ November). Talking with Jim Arnosky. *Book Links.* Vol. 12. pp. 51–58.

Sutherland, Z., & Arbuthnot, M. H. (1991). *Children and books* (8th ed.). Chicago: Scott Foresman.

Zarnowski, M. (1990). *Learning about biographies.* Urbana, IL: National Council of Teachers of English.

Literature for Children with Real-Life Challenges

12

KEY TERMS

challenged students

exceptional students

inclusion

individual differences

individualized education
plan (IEP)

mainstreaming

GUIDING QUESTIONS

Most of us are confronted daily with challenges of one sort or another. Some of them are merely inconveniences, but others may threaten how we live our lives, our loved ones, or even our safety and well-being. Many children also live with daily challenges of various kinds. As you read this chapter, think about the following questions and try to make connections between what you are reading and the students you teach or will teach.

1. Why might it be important for students to read about the challenges that face some children?

2. How could you, as the teacher, use these books?

3. What principles should you consider when selecting literature that addresses the challenges that children encounter?

4. This subject has more informational books than are found in other chapters. Why might this be so?

5. What other problems and challenges might be addressed in literature for children and young adults?

Children's lives have changed, as have their books. The books shared in this chapter might be described as real-life literature that addresses many different challenges: Children with disabilities, abused children, substance abuse, divorce, and other difficulties (Peck, 1983).

These changes and challenges are having an impact on schools and teachers. Schools today embrace a diverse student population, including those with hearing and sight impairments, impaired mobility, economic disadvantages, cultural differences, giftedness, emotional disabilities, and mental disabilities. These students are no longer segregated because society is becoming more sensitive to the special needs of all people. Sensitivity to the special needs of students escalated when Public Law 94–142 was passed in 1978. This law provides for the education of all children with disabilities and requires that these students be taught in the least restrictive educational environment possible, which often involves *mainstreaming*. In mainstreaming, *exceptional students* spend a large part of the school day in regular classrooms. Each of these students is provided with an *individualized education plan (IEP)* to map out the most suitable education way to meet his/her special needs. *Inclusion* of exceptional children is a major movement in education: the goal is to place *challenged* students in classrooms with fewer students.

The Value of Real-Life Literature

Literature, as this book has emphasized many times, can be a powerful influence in children's lives. Many children who had special challenges growing up can now write about their childhood. Sandra Wilde (1989),

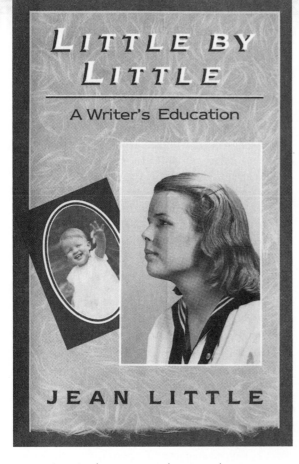

LITTLE BY LITTLE

A Writer's Education

JEAN LITTLE

*Jean Little overcame adversity to become
a successful author.*

a well-known authority in literacy, provides an example in the following quotation:

> My reason for telling this story is to celebrate the power of literature in helping us to know who we really are, and the power of the human spirit to recognize and remember that true self despite pain and adversity. . . . Many years ago, I looked like any other little girl on the outside, but there was something different about me on the inside. My parents were two needy people who didn't know how to love, and I spent much of my childhood being either bullied or casually ignored. . . . Fortunately, I had the public library. (p. 49)

VIGNETTE

Principal Mary Allison hailed Steve Liu as he signed in for the day. "Hi! How are you this fine morning?"

"Good," replied Mr. Liu.

"We need to chat for a few minutes about a new student you'll be getting in a few weeks," Mrs. Allison said.

"This is a lot of notice," Mr. Liu responded.

"You'll probably need it, since this student is legally blind. He can only see the difference between light and dark and will have a tutor. You'll need time to create a good learning environment for everyone," Mrs. Allison replied.

Mr. Liu looked thoughtful. "This should be interesting. I've just started reading Jean Little's autobiography. *Little by Little*. She is virtually blind and still lives a full life. The children enjoyed her book *Different Dragons* so much I decided to read her autobiography to them. They were appalled at the way she was treated by other children."

"Good! Do you think your students could find additional literature, films, and Web sites about blind and partially sighted people?" Mrs. Allison asked.

"I'm sure we can, and the media specialist will be happy to help," he answered.

"Then we can prepare the entire school. This could be the beginning of a schoolwide study of people with special challenges," Mrs. Allison said.

Mr. Liu nodded his agreement, then stopped short. "My kids will really enjoy being at the forefront of this study. We will find ways to integrate the new student as well as find out more about special challenges."

Many people, including teachers, do not intend to be insensitive, but they unwittingly contribute to children's feelings of inadequacy. This is why well-written children's books are so important. They enable students, both those with challenges and those without them, to understand and appreciate themselves and others. Reading about characters who face challenges gives children who have special needs the opportunity to identify with them. Equally important, such literature can cultivate in other students an understanding, empathy, and appreciation of challenged people. Children who have never interacted with persons with disabilities and who are not challenged themselves lack exposure to the difficulties some children experience. Because of this, they may fear children who are different or make fun of them. If they have opportunities to interact with children who are challenged, even if it is only in books and book discussions, they may discover that they have more in common with children with challenges than they first imagined. They may learn to communicate and interact with them honestly and without fear, and grow up to be advocates of those who need to have support. These books can contribute to the richness of the community, both in and out of school.

Selecting and Evaluating Real-Life Literature

When selecting appropriate literature, teachers should consider character portrayal, as well as literary quality (Sage, 1977). Unfortunately, many folk tales depict people with physical deformities as villains or use them to frighten and menace other story characters (Rudman, 1993). Teachers and media specialists must analyze literature with great sensitivity to avoid presenting books that express insensitive attitudes and to present literature that positively addresses the problems children may experience.

However, in a literary work that portrays characters with disabilities, each poem, story, or informational book must have literary merit, or it will not attract readers. Books that are written simply to teach or preach rarely capture readers' interest. (See the section on didacticism in Chapter 8.)

As in all quality literature, characters must be portrayed as complex personalities with strengths, flaws, problems, feelings, and responses. Any characters with disabilities should be clearly integral to the plot and

not an expendable part of the background. Characters with challenges are capable of helping others and of having loving family relationships and friendships. They develop through their experiences, just as individuals without challenges do. Authors must avoid stereotypical behavior in characters with disabilities or challenges and avoid superhuman portrayals, devices often used by some authors to make characters with disabilities more acceptable (Rudman, 1993). Characters with disabilities or challenges must be permitted to have ordinary flaws and to be average, nonspectacular people that readers will care about. The plot must focus on what they can do (Landrum, 1998–1999).

Landrum has developed a guide for evaluating novels written for adolescent readers that include challenged characters. These guidelines are also appropriate for books for younger readers as well. Using her criteria as well as our own, the following standards may be used to choose fiction books that depict challenged characters.

1. Challenged characters are strong or become stronger and more competent through the events.
2. Challenged characters are portrayed through what they can do.
3. Challenged characters are multidimensional characters whose emotions, strengths, and weaknesses are portrayed.
4. Challenged characters are not portrayed as overly heroic or as victims.
5. Challenged characters are portrayed as participating in a family and having friends.
6. Challenged characters' handicaps are accurately portrayed.
7. The plot is realistic and avoids contrived events and miracle cures.
8. The challenged characters experience events similar to the experiences and conflicts of their peer group.
9. All of the events are realistic and uncontrived.
10. The book avoids terms that label the challenged characters.
11. The book should leave the challenged characters with hope.

Similar standards apply to nonfiction books that deal with challenges. They must be realistic and present the disability in a way that is understandable to readers. For example, Pat Thomas's picture book, *Don't Call Me Special: A First Look at Disability,* includes pictures of disabilities on almost every page that encourage children to ask questions and to get reassuring answers. The point is made that people of all ages can have disabilities and that they can live happy and full lives.

Using Books in the Classroom

It may be that teachers need to consider how to use the books in this chapter more carefully than the books in other chapters. Because the characters or experiences portrayed in these books are "different" in some way, children who have not had similar or related experiences may react in inappropriate ways, just as they may react to other children in real life who may be different. They may laugh at the character or situation; they may be afraid that something similar may happen to them; or they may simply dismiss the character or experience as unbelievable. Teachers need to be sensitive both to their students and the books they share so that there is both enjoyment and insight gained.

The following guidelines, based in part on the work of Susan Miller (1997), may be useful to consider.

1. Determine if the problem is one the students can identify with. It needs to be meaningful, interesting, and appropriate for them. They need to make connections to their own lives.
2. Have the students discuss possible solutions. All ideas need to be listened to and respected; a record needs to be kept of the ideas.
3. Discuss the advantages/disadvantages of the possible solutions.
4. Research and find out about the advantages/disadvantages of the possible solutions.
5. Evaluate which solutions might be best and state why.

Children with Challenges

Books for children and young adults featuring characters with special problems are categorized by the specific problems of the characters. They may include physical challenges (hearing impairments, visual impairments, mobility challenges, and albinism), disease and health challenges (HIV/AIDS, diabetes, Alzheimer's disease, leukemia, polio, or mental illness), learning challenges, or challenges that come from outside the person (adoption, abuse, homelessness, disaster, and the death of someone close to the main characters).

In some of the books, the main character is not himself/herself challenged, but must relate to a relative or friend who is challenged. These books may be the ones that students without direct experience connect to most easily.

Most of the books featuring characters who are living with challenges fall into the categories of contemporary realistic fiction, historical fiction, and informational books. Other genre may also include books of this type.

Physical Challenges

Hearing challenges

Children with hearing impairments exhibit a full range of *individual differences*. Their experiences, families, intelligence, and motivation are as diverse as those of other children. Their impairments may range from moderate to severe. Some live in a silent world, whereas others may hear a few sounds. Hearing aids may help some people with hearing impairments to perceive as much sound as possible. However, children whose hearing is impaired usually have distorted or incomplete auditory input even with hearing aids. They may have difficulty producing and understanding speech sounds; words such as *Dan* and *tan* can confuse anyone with impaired hearing. Deaf or hard of hearing children, therefore, require special instruction to learn language.

Issac Millman's *Moses Goes to a Concert* depicts the complex life of children with hearing impairments. In this book, Moses and his deaf classmates enjoy a young people's concert when their teacher gives them balloons so they can feel the vibrations of the music. After the concert, they meet the percussionist, who is also deaf.

In a follow-up book by Issac Millman, *Moses Goes to School,* Moses and his multicultural classmates first learn American Sign Language (ASL) and then learn to read and write spoken English. They are very normal children who use the computer and listen to music and songs. On almost every page, there is a small diagram of Moses signing a simple sentence in ASL.

Another deaf child, Mark, demonstrates the difficulty of connecting with his classmates in Claire

Blatchford's book, *Going with the Flow*. He does finally establish a friendship, which rings true because his friend does not allow him to hog the ball when they play basketball. This book includes author's notes about deafness and sign language.

Laura Rankin's beautiful picture book *The Handmade Alphabet* presents a striking interpretation of the manual alphabet. Her stepson, who is deaf, communicated through lipreading for the first 18 years of his life. He then learned American Sign Language, which allowed him to share ideas fully. Through it, he gained understanding and communication. This book is especially useful in introducing the manual alphabet to children who can hear.

A book for older readers, *Of Sound Mind,* is the story of Theo, the only person in his family who is not deaf. Theo must act as the interpreter for his domineering, sculptor mother; his father, who is ill but more reasonable; and his brother. His conflict between resentment for the demands placed on him and his jealousy when others fill his role seems to be understood by only one person, Ivy, a classmate whose father is also deaf. Jean Ferris's intriguing novel presents a situation most readers have had little experience with.

Vision challenges

Children with visual impairments or blindness do not have the visual input necessary to learn about their world, so they need special instruction and experiences. They need many opportunities to explore concrete objects with their senses of smell, touch, taste, and hearing. Tactile books made from fabric, yarn, buttons, and zippers are excellent learning tools for young children with impaired vision. Pockets in these books can hold cardboard or plastic shapes. Discussion and descriptions of these concrete experiences are essential to building background knowledge and experience. Children who are blind often learn to read Braille and listen to "talking" or recorded books. Fortunately, many more recorded books are available today than ever before. Listening to recorded books extends their experiential background and prepares them to learn to read Braille, or print if they can see large print.

Some people with visual impairments use guide dogs to achieve greater independence, a skill that requires education for the person as well as the dog. *A Guide Dog Puppy Grows Up* by Caroline Arnold follows Honey, a golden retriever, through her training from puppy to guide dog. Each stage of her training is explained with text and photographs. For readers who want to know more about guide dogs, Diana Lawrenson's *Guide Dogs: From Puppies to Partners* is a good choice. General information is given and then the whole process of training is described. Vignettes of the dogs and their new owners are also given.

Several genres include books about children with visual challenges and the ways they have adjusted. These authors sensitize readers to the individual differences among people who have vision loss; their lives are as varied as those of individuals who see.

Alice Carter's informational book *Seeing Things My Way* tells the story of second grader Amanda, who has a brain tumor that caused her to lose some of her vision. She received therapy to learn new skills. Books such as this help children understand that visual impairment does not always mean blindness. Sally Hobart Alexander lost her sight when she was in her 20s. She now travels around the country talking in schools about her frustrations, experiences, and coping skills. She answers questions about daily life and how it feels to be blind. *Do You Remember the Color Blue: And Other Questions Kids Ask about Blindness* provides interesting insights for all readers.

In a realistic fiction book, Louis, who is blind, is lucky to have a close and loving relationship with his grandmother. Before his grandma died, she wrote notes for the family members and hid them in unexpected places. Finding and reading these notes after her death brings the family closer together. All of them, except Louis, find their notes. Not until years later does Louis's granddaughter find his note, located in *The Hickory Chair*, the title of Lisa Rowe Fraustino's book.

A book of historical fiction in the *Dear America* series tells the story of Bess, who lost her sight in a sledding accident. She attends the Perkins School for the Blind and initially has a difficult time adjusting. Readers will learn how people compensate for vision loss in Barry Dennenberg's *Mirror, Mirror on the Wall: The Diary of Bess Brennan—The Perkins School for the Blind 1932*.

Books of biography are often about special individuals who have accomplished great things even though they may be challenged. *Helen Keller: Lighting the Way for the Blind and Deaf* by Carin T. Ford tells the story of Keller's life and accomplishments. Keller is a role model for those who want to become actively involved in helping others.

Mobility and other physical challenges

People with impaired mobility are sometimes identified as orthopedically disabled. They may have impaired legs, arms, or both, or may even have paralyzed body parts. Mobility impairments may originate at birth, through accident, or through illness. Some children are born with cerebral palsy, which can impair mobility quite seriously or very mildly. Likewise, injury to the spinal cord often causes paralysis.

Mobility for people with physical impairments usually requires special equipment such as wheelchairs, walkers, braces, prostheses, and canes. Of course, using this equipment requires therapy and training. In recent years, ramps have been added to buildings to permit better access by people who use this equipment. Likewise, many public places now have restrooms that are accessible to wheelchairs. In the nonfiction book *Some Kids Use Wheelchairs*, Lola Schaefer gives many examples of how and why wheelchairs are used.

Patraicia McMahon's inspirational book, *Dancing Wheels*, describes a dance troupe made up of individuals in wheelchairs and those who stand up. They work hard and prepare for their performance. The story is told from the perspective of two of the dancers, one in a wheelchair and one who is a "stand-up" dancer.

For those who think that people with disabilities cannot compete in sports, reading *Hearts of Gold: A Celebration of Special Olympics and Its Heroes* should change their minds. Sheila Dinn has written a book that is much appreciated by these athletes and should dispel stereotypes of those who are not handicapped.

In Elaine Landau's *Spinal Cord Injuries*, readers can find out about the kinds of injuries and diseases that impact mobility. In reading the case studies of individuals, insight can be gained about possible cures and ways to adjust to the disability, if necessary.

Seeing eye dogs and hearing ear dogs are not the only animals that help people with disabilities. Animals have recently been trained to assist people with impaired mobility as well. Researchers have trained monkeys to prepare food, feed people, pick up the telephone when it rings, pick up things that have been dropped, and even brush people's teeth. Suzanne Haldane tells about some of the ways that monkeys assist people in *Helping Hands: How Monkeys Assist People Who Are Disabled*. The photographs in this book help readers understand how useful monkeys can be.

In the mid-1950s, a polio epidemic left many children crippled or in wheelchairs. In the book *In the Clear*, Pauline goes through dreadful experiences in the hospital but eventually is released. She has an overprotective mother, while her father races her across the ice so she can play hockey in her wheelchair. However, it is her Tante Marie who helps her understand that how she lives her life is really up to her. The theme in Anne Laurel Carter's *In the Clear* transcends the challenge of a wheelchair and helps readers see how each of us is responsible for who we may become.

Some children with disabilities often find making friends is very difficult. Lester, who has cerebral palsy, saves the life of mentally challenged Alfred. These two boys are joined by two others (Myron and Claire) who are also regarded as misfits. The four of them work together on a "get-away boat" in Myron's basement. As they do so, they learn about each other and develop friendships. Jan Slepian's book, *Alfred Summer,* was originally published in 1980; its reissue attests to the story's timelessness.

A very different book about a boy with severe cerebral palsy is Terry Trueman's *Stuck in Neutral.* Shawn is totally dependent on others and is unable to communicate. Everyone around him thinks he is mentally retarded but nothing is further from the truth. He remembers everything he has ever heard and gets enjoyment from being with those around him. He hears his father talking about the possibility of killing him because the father thinks he is in pain, not understanding that his son is a bright person. This book, paired with Susan H. Gray's nonfiction book *Living with Cerebral Palsy,* could be the foundation for significant discussions of ethical issues among older students.

Other kinds of physical challenges

An interesting true story, *The Making of My Special Hand,* tells how a young girl is fitted for a left-hand prosthesis that will allow her to pick up and carry objects as well as throw a ball. Jamee Riggio Heelan presents this topic in such a manner that readers will empathize with her struggle and success.

Stephanie Riggs writes about Josh, who was born with achondroplasia or dwarfism. We read about how

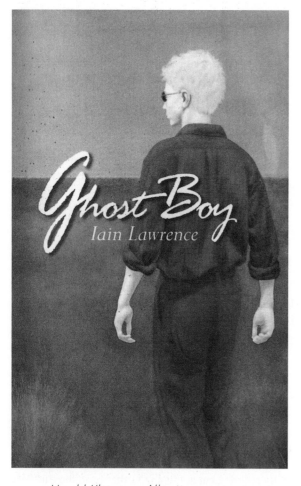

Harold Kline is an Albino—an outcast.

he must get pressurized air into his lungs so he can sleep at night and how he must have his clothes altered so that they fit right. However, what is most important to Josh is how he is able to interact with his friends—playing sports, riding a bike, and becoming involved in school activities. *Never Sell Yourself Short* is an amazing account of a person who has met his physical challenge in a most positive way.

Two books deal with albinism. The first, Elaine Landau's nonfiction book *Living with Albinism,* provides an in-depth look at the topic. The second book is fiction and lets readers more readily identify with this physical challenge. Harold Kline is an albino and an outcast. When the circus comes to town, he joins and thinks he has found a place where he really fits in. He learns, however, that even in the circus there are

two groups—the freaks and eveyone else. In Lain Lawrence's *Ghost Boy,* Harold learns that is it necessary to look inside oneself, rather than at physical appearances, to determine self-worth.

Disease and Health Challenges

Children experience many of the same health challenges as adults. Epilepsy, diabetes, childhood arthritis, leukemia, cystic fibrosis, and heart malfunction are only a few of the diseases that can affect a child's life. In some of the books reviewed here, the characters may not have the disease or health challenge themselves. However, they suffer when those around them do. These books might make the process of identification with characters easier for those without challenges than trying to identify with those who actually have the disease.

Leukemia

Sophie, three years after her younger brother died of leukemia, still obsesses on his memory. She is angry with her father, who left during her brother's illness, and her mother, who has started dating again. She refuses to have a boyfriend or date but finds herself attracted to the son of her mother's new boyfriend. Because of her friendship with Francis, Sophie does a lot of growing up in Garret Freymann-Weyr's *When I Was Older*.

When a new girl, Natalie, joins Dreenie's class, she is so different that everyone tends to ignore her at first. Although she is an African American, her skin is very pale, she wears a hat, and she brings her puppy with her to school. Dreenie and her friend Tuli call her *Bluish* and the three of them become friends. Bluish has leukemia; the girls make a pact that they will not let anything happen to her. Virginia Hamilton's insightful book has disease, religion, and friendship honestly interact.

Leukemia often requires extensive medical treatment and is life threatening. Bone marrow transplants are sometimes used in its treatment, as Diana Amadeo demonstrates in *There's a Little Bit of Me in Jamey*. Brian tells about his concern for his younger brother Jamey, a leukemia victim. He has ambivalent feelings about the situation because he is worried about his brother's terrible illness, yet at the same time he resents the fact that his parents have very little time for him. The doctor then discovers that Brian's bone marrow is a good match for Jamey. The book is very realistic because Brain observes that the transplant is a hope, not a cure.

Diabetes

Three nonfiction books may be used as a basis for discussing diabetes, including the fact that many diabetics must take insulin and have to control their diet. In *You Can't Catch Diabetes from a Friend,* Lynn Kipnis explains diabetes with simple text and photographs. In the second, Alden Carter's *I'm Tougher than Diabetes,* Natalie describes how she manages her type I diabetes. She shows her diabetes kit, which she calls Philomena, and then talks about getting her shots, planning meals as she measures her food, and how she prepares for emergencies. This is a very readable book, with a question/answer section at the end to provide additional information. Diabetes is found from the perspective of Gregory in Carol Peacock's *Sugar Was My Best Food.* After he is diagnosed with diabetes, Gregory describes what his life is like: he feels lonely because he is different. All of these books would be appropriate to use in grades 2 to 6.

Asthma

I'm Tougher than Asthma! talks about asthma from a first person perspective. The author's daughter, Siri Carter, has asthma. She tells readers what it feels like to have an attack, how she manages her condition, and explains her medical treatments in a straightforward way without feeling sorry for herself. As was true in the previously mentioned book by Alder Carter, there is a question/answer section at the end of this book.

HIV/AIDS

AIDS is a health problem of recent origin, but the numbers of AIDS victims are increasing. There are several well-written nonfiction books about HIV/AIDS. *Ryan White: My Own Story* is a good book for youngsters because it tells about AIDS from a child's point of view. The book takes a matter of fact perspective without overdramatizing the disease. Pairing it with Anna Forbes' *Kids with AIDS* would create a nice combination to help students identify with children their age who have the disease.

In Paula McGuire's book *AIDS,* intermediate-grade children can learn the basic facts about the disease, focusing on how HIV is and is not spread. *Children and the AIDS Virus* by Rosmarie Hausherr is a different treatment of this subject. The book is written at two levels, with large print for younger children and smaller print for older children, and looks at the ways children can and cannot contract AIDS.

There are two books, *HIV/AIDS Information for Children: A Guide to Issues and Resources* by Virginia Walter and Melissa Gross, and *AIDS in the 21st Century* by Michelle M. Houle, that can be used as a reference book in the intermediate grades.

One fiction book presents the story of a sixth grader whose life was very much influenced by his principal, Mr. Carr. It was Mr. Carr who encouraged Jason to continue his violin lessons with the hope of playing at Julliard. When Mr. Carr becomes ill, it becomes known that he was a homosexual and is dying from AIDS. Although many of Jason's friends taunt him because of his friendship with Mr. Carr, Jason learns many good lessons. Jane Zalben's *Unfinished Dreams: A Novel* treats a very controversial subject with dignity.

Schizophrenia

Two fiction books for older readers deal with siblings who have schizophrenia. Two sisters, Summer and Lyric, move from Virginia to Detroit with their father. Summer has always been peculiar, but once in Detroit she talks to imaginary people and has periods of paranoia. Lyric is not only embarrassed about Summer's behavior but Summer cannot be left alone, which impacts Lyric's friendships. Finally Summer must be institutionalized, which is very traumatic for the family. Ruth White's sensitive story, *Memories of Summer,* should touch the hearts of all readers.

Betty Hyland's *The Girl with the Crazy Brother* is similar in many ways to the previous book. Dana and her older brother go to a new school. However, Bill's behavior becomes increasingly disturbed. As he becomes worse, he commits himself. As Dana learns to fit in with her friends, she and her family come to terms with Bill's illness.

Learning Challenges

Challenges to learning take many forms, from mild learning disabilities to severe mental retardation. Quality literature that addresses this issue is hopeful, with characters who adjust to their circumstances or make progress through education, therapy, schools, rehabilitation, or determination.

Learning disabilities arise from a number of sources, some of which are unidentifiable. However, learning disabilities prevent many children from experiencing success in school. Jack Gantos has written three books about Joey Pigza, a boy who is hyperactive with ADD. As a result, Joey gets into significant trouble. In the first book, *Joey Pigza Swallows the Key*, Joey's medication wears off after half a day in school and he ends up in a special education room because of his behavior. However, with the help of a supportive case worker and a continuous release patch, Joey is able to return to his old school. In the second book, *Joey Pigza Loses Control,* Joey goes to visit his alcoholic father, who flushes his medications down the toilet because he thinks that Joey is normal. The results are, of course, disastrous. The third book, *What Would Joey Do?,* tells the story of Joey and his blind friend, Olivia, being homeschooled. All three of these books deal with a serious subject with a humorous but sympathetic hero. He is quite a role model for other children with learning disabilities!

Another book, more gentle in nature, is Jean Little's *Birdie for Now*. Dickon, nicknamed Birdie, is an 11-year-old living with his mother, since his father recently left the family. When they move, their apartment backs up on the Humane Society. Birdie has always wanted a dog. His mother is afraid of dogs but Dickon is determined to help train an abused dog and begins to stay focused and on task. His mother realizes that he needs this kind of responsibility to help him grow up and succeed.

Three books about Down syndrome provide insight into this disability. In *Dustin's Big School Day* by Alden Carter, the photoessay shows his productive school day. As shown in the book, some students with learning difficulties have specialized teachers and they are mainstreamed into regular classrooms as well. In Paula Fox's *Radiance Descending*, Paul's brother with Down syndrome embarrasses him, but he discovers that Jacob is nonetheless lovable. Lucille Clifton's *My Friend Jacob* is also about a friendship between two people. Sam is sensitive to the problems of his friend who has Down syndrome, and they discover that they are able to teach each other different things.

Sahara Special by Esma Rajl Codell tells the story of a girl who gets put into a special needs class and is receiving tutoring in the hall. This is not satisfactory, and she is required to repeat fifth grade. Her new teacher is atypical and, under her guidance, Sahara's writing talent is recognized. She begins to make friends and gain maturity.

A kind of learning problem that we often do not hear about is dyscalculia, the inability to do mathematics. In *My Thirteenth Winter: A Memoir* by Samantha Abeel, the author lets readers feel how frustrating it was to have a serious problem of this sort undiagnosed until her early teens. How she coped and dealt with this challenge makes her a good role model for others who may be experiencing similar difficulties.

Three nonfiction books address the subject of dyslexia. The first, geared toward primary children, is Melanie Apel Gordon's *Let's Talk About Dyslexia.* The book provides examples of reading difficulties, as well as hope that the reading difficulties can be overcome. *Dyslexia* by Alvin Silverstein and others describes dyslexia and presents theories about its causes and treatment. This book would be a useful reference book. A book for older readers, Karen Donnelly's *Coping with Dyslexia,* talks about what dyslexia is, learning strategies for dealing with it, and ways to choose a career. Brief biographies are provided about some successful dyslexics.

Jacob is a lovable Down syndrome child.

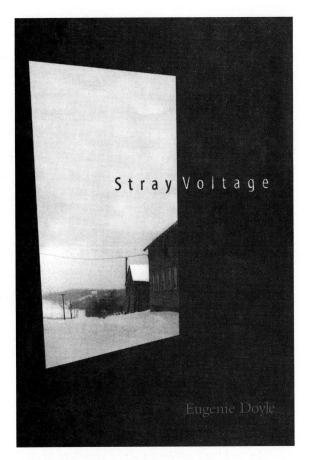

This book tells the story of some of the problems children face in their young lives.

Challenges from Outside the Individual

Very often, children must deal with situations that are not in their control. They may be abused, they may be affected by a disaster such as the bombing of the World Trade Center, or they may have challenges within the family. Situations of this sort require strength and often the support of another adult. The following books are grouped into different categories, but all have a message of hope.

Abused children

Abuse of children, a painful subject, has been addressed very little until recent times. Abuse takes various forms: some children are physically abused, some are sexually abused, some are emotionally abused, and some are neglected. Giving children opportunities to read or hear books about abused characters is important because abused children usually feel they are to blame. Many abused children react with shame and try to protect their abuser. Literature about abused children must not blame the victim or excuse the abusers, although it may offer insight about the abuse. Some abusive adults are also substance abusers who hurt children when they are under the influence of alcohol or drugs.

Two books for younger children are in Linda Sky Grossman's *I'm a Great Little Kid* series. In the first, *Sam Speaks Out,* Sam is not acting like his usual happy self—he finally tells a friend that an adult he knows is tickling and touching him in inappropriate ways. He learns that he must tell others about this kind of behavior. In *A Tale Worth Telling,* David, who is a new boy, finds out that even trusted adults can act in ways that are not right. He has bruises on his arm from when the soccer coach told him he was stupid and grabbed his arm.

The fiction books for older readers take on significant issues. Cynthia Voigt takes on the difficult challenge of writing about a stepfather's sexual abuse and a mother who will not believe it in *When She Hollers.* The protagonist struggles with her problem and tries to talk with a school counselor, and eventually consults with her best friend's father, a lawyer, who cannot give her easy answers. After this she takes control of the situation; she makes clear to her stepfather that he is to leave her alone, and she takes a knife to bed with her. The resolution is not pat or clear, but it is realistic.

Jacqueline Woodson's book *I Hadn't Meant to Tell You This* portrays a friendship between Lena and Marie. Lena finally reveals that her father is sexually abusing her. Lena and her younger sister, Dion, must flee from their father before he starts abusing Dion. Their story continues in the book *Lena.*

Children who are abused when they are young often become the abusers when they are older. In Alex Flinn's powerful but difficult-to-read book, *Breathing Underwater,* Nick has himself been abused by his father. He beats his girlfriend and uses savage tactics to control and isolate her. He ends up in court charged with physical violence, after which he is sent to anger management therapy sessions and is required to keep a journal. This self-examination provides some reason for hope although this is not a happily-ever-after ending.

Nonfiction books also address abuse. Books help both children and adults recognize children's behaviors that indicate abuse and offer advice about what to do if one is the victim of abuse. Margaret

Hyde's *Cry Softly! The Story of Child Abuse* provides lists of organizations that help abused children and their parents. This book helps readers understand the many types of people who abuse children.

Lifestyle challenges

Children whose family structure is different from the traditional two-parent family are apt to feel that they are different because they are in a single-parent family, a family with lesbian/gay parents, in foster care, or may be adopted. However, children in these family structures still have love and support. In Virginia Kroll's *Beginnings: How Families Came to Be,* six different family structures are presented. In each family, the child asks the parent to tell the "story of me." This is a good way for younger children to learn that there is not one "right" kind of family to have; each family is OK even though each is different.

Divorce/separation of parents

Many children today experience pain and unhappiness as a result of their parents' separation. Approximately 50 percent of marriages today end in divorce. Some children live with one parent and have no memory of ever living with both; others live with neither parent. Literature can help them and their friends understand their difficulties.

Middle-grade children, as well as younger children, experience pain and confusion when their parents separate. Readers learn that life goes on after divorce in Elizabeth Feuer's story *Lost Summer.* Lydia goes to camp after her parents divorce and discovers that she has more in common with her sister than she thought once she is drawn into camp life.

Foster homes

Anna feels abandoned even though she has been placed in a foster home. She begins to write in her "explorer's journal" as a way to release her feelings. She does make a friend and is able to discover that she does belong. Adrian Fogelin makes it clear that writing is a powerful tool for healing in *Anna Casey's Place in the World.*

Chance is another child who does not feel that he belongs in his foster home. For him, beginning the butterfly project at school is when he begins to feel friendship and healing. *Chance and the Butterfly* by Maggie deVries is based on a real classroom experience.

Homeless children

Homelessness is a problem for too many children today. In some places, homeless children cannot attend school. When they can attend school, they cannot check books out of a library, and help with homework is usually out of the question. These are just the beginning of their problems. Carol Fenner portrays Ian and his father, a Vietnam War veteran, who are homeless in *The King of Dragons.* When the father simply fails to return one day, Ian is completely on his own.

Judith Berck's nonfiction book *No Place to Be: Voices of Homeless Children* is based on interviews of the homeless children that she got to know. She presents their experiences through their own words and poems, interwoven with her narrative. Lareem speaks about being homeless in this quotation, "The shelter is only another home, it's not another life. It's not like I just moved into another life like an alien . . . the shelter doesn't control who you are" (99–100).

Elizabeth Weitzman helps children understand what it would be like to live in a shelter. *Let's Talk About Staying in a Shelter* provides a realistic view of a situation all children would like to avoid.

Adoption

Many books have recently been published about adoption. Many of these books are about adoptions of children into families of different races and/or from countries other than the United States. For example, *Brown Like Me* by Noelle Lamperti tells the story of an African-American child who is adopted by a white family. She looks for things in her environment that are brown, like she is. In *We Wanted You* by Liz Rosenberg, the interracial parents tell their son, Enrique, how they looked for a child and found him through an international adoption.

Three books tell of children who were adopted from Korea. Eve Bunting, in *Jin Woo,* tells Davey's story and how he is not sure that his parents still love him after adopting a new brother. Jan Czech has written two books about adoption. In *An American Face,* Jessie thinks that when he gets his American citizenship card that he will also get an American face. Annie in *The Coffee Can Kid* has her dad tell her again the story of how she came from Korea. She has a picture of herself as a baby and a letter from her birth mother.

Two books tell about adoptions from China. In *The White Swan Express,* Jean Davies Okimoto and Elaine

Aoki tell the stories of four families in North America waiting for their four baby girls from China. Rose Lewis writes of her experiences going to China to adopt her special baby girl in *I Love You Like Crazy Cakes*.

Jean Little writes an engaging story about Emma and how hard it is to be the big sister to a younger adopted brother. *Emma's Yucky Brother* will be a book that many children with younger siblings can identify with.

Death of a loved one

Dealing with death is difficult for adults; children do not know how to cope with it, either. A good nonfiction book by Sharon Greenlee, *When Someone Dies,* helps children understand the grief and the confusion they may feel after a death has occurred. It is a very readable book, but best used with a supportive adult.

There are two fiction books about a child whose grandparent has Alzheimer's disease. Although the grandparent does not die in the books, their deaths are implicit. Barbara Park has written a very believable story in *The Graduation of Jake Moon*. Jake and his single mom have lived with his grandfather, Skelly, since Jake was an infant. Skelly assumes the functions of a parent by being his room mother and supporting him whenever he needs support. When Skelly is diagnosed with Alzheimer's and his behavior is outrageous, Jake is extremely embarrassed. At Jake's eighth-grade graduation, Skelly "escapes" on the stage: Jake finally realizes that although the behavior is inappropriate, he needs to support his grandfather just as his grandfather supported him.

Linda Jacobs Altman's *Singing with Momma Lou* is the story of the relationship between 9-year-old Tamika and her grandmother. Tamika resents having to go to the nursing home every week, especially since Momma Lou can't even remember her name. Tamika's dad shares Momma Lou's scrapbook, which holds not only the photos of Tamika and her grandma but also artifacts from her grandma's involvement in the Civil Rights Movement. Tamika uses the scrapbook to communicate with Momma Lou.

For younger children, their teacher may almost be like a family member. In *Good Luck Mrs. K,* Louise Borden tells the story of a third-grade class whose teacher gets cancer. The students keep in touch with her throughout her hospitalization by writing notes and letters. After school is out, Mrs. K. comes back to visit the children. The story is based on a real teacher and her class.

Disasters

Fifteen-year-old Green, so named because of her gardening talent, stays home while her family goes to the city to sell their produce. There is a terrible disaster in the city and Green sees it engulfed in flames. Her family doesn't return and Green begins a variety of forms of self-destruction. Finally, she begins to form relationships with others left behind and a slow healing begins. Alice Hoffman's book *Green Angel,* written for older readers, is a reminder that life can change in an instant but that hope is not dead.

Karen Hesse tells the story of a family trying to survive when radiation contaminates the United Sates. They barricade themselves in their basement but, even there, they are not safe from either other survivors or dangers. *Phoenix Rising* is a powerful survival story.

In a book for younger readers, Eve Bunting tells the story of Daniel and his mother, who must leave their apartment during the Los Angeles riots. The illustrations for this Caldecott Award-winning book, *Smoky Night,* are done by David Diaz. They show shattered glass, looting, and burning buildings. Nonetheless, there is a message of hope at the end when Daniel finds his missing cat.

Classroom Activities

A good way to help children who do not have disabilities learn about the difficulties faced by their peers with disabilities is through units that focus on the universal problems they face. These units are also important to students who do have disabilities, because they can identify with the story characters and realize they are not the only people in the world who have encountered problems.

ACTIVITY 12.1   CONNECTING WITH THE PROBLEMS OF STUDENTS WITH DISABILITIES

(IRA/NCTE Standards: 1, 2, 3, 4, 7, 8, 9, 11, 12.)

Purpose

This activity, designed for students in elementary classes, introduces the kinds of adjustments that can be made to help classmates who have sensory or physical disabilities. It can help students understand the feelings of their peers who have disabilities and learn appropriate ways to be their friends. The outcome of this activity is a discussion of disabilities, the feelings of people about their disabilities, and ways to treat people who have disabilities. Middle-grade students can prepare a written handbook of ways that students can help students with disabilities in their classes and those they meet in other places.

Introduction

Before this activity, students should have had some experiences to acquaint them with physical disabilities.

1. Ask children to explain the terms *disability, physical disability, sensory disability*. Create a language-experience chart about the information they volunteer. For fourth graders, ask the children to write their own meanings for these words.

2. Ask the students to make a list of all the physical and sensory disabilities they can think of.

3. Discuss the things that people who have physical and sensory disabilities need to have or do to compensate for their disabilities. For example, ask why some people wear glasses, why some people wear hearing aids, and why others use wheelchairs.

4. Explain that some people make additional adjustments, such as learning Braille, sign language, and so forth, and that the class will be studying about these for the next few weeks.

5. Let the children use some of the equipment used by people who have disabilities so that they can experience the difficulties involved. Bring to class a collection of items such as eye patches, drugstore nonprescription glasses, a wheelchair, a walker, ear plugs, bandages for eyes, arm braces, a boot cast, braces, and crutches. Let the children attempt to take the wheelchair into the bathroom and through doors, use a walker while their legs are in casts, walk with casts, leave ear plugs in for an hour, cover one eye and then both eyes with patches or bandages, and use any other equipment available.

6. After using the equipment, have students write about their feelings and experiences. They may choose to write a letter to a friend, parent, or grandparent or write a journal entry about their feelings. Younger children can dictate rather than write. The students could write and illustrate a class book about their experiences as handicapped people.

7. Students can learn to communicate through the manual alphabet. They may visit with deaf children and try their new skills in communication. Books such as the following are helpful in developing this skill:

Handmade ABC: A Manual Alphabet by Linda Bourke

The Handmade Alphabet by Laura Rankin

Handtalk School by Mary Beth Miller and George Ancona

Handtalk Birthday: A Number and Story Book in Sign Language by Remy Charlip, Mary Beth Miller, and George Ancona

ACTIVITY 12.2   TREES AND FAMILY TREES: AN INTEGRATED UNIT WITH SCIENCE AND MATH

(IRA/NCTE Standards: 1, 2, 3, 4, 5, 6, 7, 9, 10, 11, 12.)

In this unit, students learn to identify many kinds of trees using reference books. Each student identifies and counts the number of different trees in a section of his/her neighborhood. They make bar graphs and determine the percentages of each of the kinds of trees in their section.

During this time students will read many books about different family structures—two parents, single parents (father or mother), gay/lesbian families, adopted families, and so forth. They will make family trees for the characters in each of the books, and then determine bar graphs and percentages of the different kinds of families they have read about. Connections then appear about the diverse kinds of trees in the neighborhood and the diversity found in families. The diversity of both make the world a richer place in which to live. If an atmosphere of trust develops, the students and teacher can also analyze the family structures described in the books they read. (If appropriate, instead of looking at family structures, the students can look at differences in cultures represented in books and in their classroom.)

As culminating activities, the students can write data reports as well as more personal accounts of what they learned. They can also make posters for science fairs or other public display.

The teacher provides guided instruction during all phases of this unit of study, and in all of the content areas.

Resources for Teachers

An issue to consider as teachers plan activities relating to children with challenges is that there may be parents who don't want their children exposed to ideas that are contrary to ones that they hold. If children are reading about lifestyle challenges or even some health challenges, they may be reading about situations parents may not condone. It is hard to conceive of parents who would not want their children to learn about disabilities, but the teacher needs to ascertain if there might be a problem. Some parents might consider these topics to be teaching values.

Teaching values is a controversial educational issue, yet liberals and conservatives alike decry a "moral crisis" among young people. They attribute increased school violence to youngsters who do not know right from wrong. Influential educators such as Thomas Lickona and Nel Noddings have studied these issues. Contentious issues surround values clarification; to wit: Can we actually teach values?

What values should be taught? When should values be taught? Who should teach values? How should values be taught? Although this book cannot resolve these thorny issues, literature can serve as a context for inquiry into values. Books such as Lickona's *Educating for Character* (1992), Noddings' *The Challenge to Care in Schools* (1992), and Andrews' *Teaching Kids to Care* (1994) are helpful resources. For instance, in *Teaching Kids to Care,* Andrews includes units of study and lists of literature for an inquiry approach to values. She includes topics such as appreciation of differences, empathy, compassion, homelessness, consequences of doing right and wrong, gentleness, obedience, self-concept, individuality and independence, honesty, honor, patience, and many others. Many of these topics are addressed in this chapter.

Two books are of particular value when choosing literature including characters with disabilities. *Portraying Persons with Disabilities: An Annotated Bibliography of Fiction for Children and Teenagers* by Friedberg, Mullins, and Sukiennik addresses fiction works (1992), while *Portraying Persons with Disabilities: An Annotated Bibliography of Nonfiction for Children and Teenagers* by Robertson addresses nonfiction (1992). Two references that describe books written before 1990 are *Notes from a Different Drummer* by Baskin and Harris (1977) and *More Notes from a Different Drummer* by Baskin and Harris (1984).

A useful reference for teachers when talking about adoption is Gail Kinn's *Me and My Baby: Parents & Children Talk About Adoption.* She documents the diversity of adoptive families through photographs and interviews. The book can also be used by children with guidance from teachers or parents.

Summary

Every classroom has individuals who are challenged in one way or another. They may vary in social and emotional background, language ability, cultural background, physical ability, and intellectual ability; their family structures may cause them stress; they may face difficulties over which they have no control. These challenges are acknowledged and accepted in contemporary schools more than ever before. The variability in the school population carries with it the responsibility for teachers to make appropriate adjustments in the curriculum and materials. Presenting literature that portrays people with disabilities in a well-balanced manner enables students who do not have disabilities to understand and identify with their peers with disabilities better, and it helps students who do have disabilities to identify with the characters and understand themselves better. Acknowledging that students come to school bringing with them a variety of challenges means that teachers must be sensitive to individual differences and flexible so that all students can learn to their highest potential.

A wide variety of excellent literature is available for educating students about individual differences. All students are individuals, and those who have disabilities or challenges are as varied and individual as students without disabilities or challenges. Quality literature depicts this individuality and does not stereotype characters. Any characters with disabilities are integral to the book; they are not just stuck in to make a point.

Thought Questions

1. Why do you think the portrayal of people with challenges has changed?

2. This subject has more nonfiction books than any other discussed in this book. Why do you think this is true?

3. Can you think of other problems and challenges that should be addressed in children's literature for children?

4. What value does literature about "real life challenges" have for children?

5. Who benefits the most from reading this type of literature; challenged children or those who are not challenged?

Research and Application Experiences

1. Write a short story about a person who has a disability.

2. Choose a topic (type of challenge) and a grade level, then identify books that you could use to develop that topic at the grade level. Then make a card file of these books for future reference.

3. Compare the treatment of a challenge or a disability in two different books. How are they alike? How are they different? Which book did you prefer and why?

4. Interview teachers at primary and intermediate (middle school) grade levels and identify the number of books about challenges they have used in the current school year. Then ask them to identify specific titles that they have used with success.

Children's Literature References and Recommended Books

Note: Books designated with an asterisk (*) are recommended for reluctant readers.

Abeel, S. (2003). *My thirteenth winter: A memoir.* New York: Orchard Books. (5–8). BIOGRAPHY.

  The author writes about her struggle with dyscalculia, a math-related learning disorder.

Alexander, S. (2000). *Do you remember the color blue: And other questions kids ask about blindness.* New York: Viking. (3–6). INFORMATIONAL BOOK.

  Having lost her sight, the author visits schools talking about her blindness.

Altman, L. J. (2002). *Singing with Momma Lou* (L. Johnson, Illus.). New York: Lee & Low. (2–5). CONTEMPORARY REALISTIC FICTION

  Tamika connects with her grandmother who has Alzheimer's through the use of Momma Lou's scrapbook.

Amadeo, D. M. (1989). *There's a little bit of me in Jamey* (J. Friedman, Illus.). Morton Grove, IL: Whitman. (3–6). CONTEMPORARY REALISTIC FICTION

  Brian tells this story about his younger brother Jamey, a leukemia victim. Brian gives his brother a bone marrow transplant, which gives Jamey his best chance to live.

Arnold, C. (1991). *A guide dog puppy grows up* (R. Hewett, Photog.). New York: Harcourt Brace Jovanovich. (2–5). INFORMATIONAL BOOK.*

  This book follows Honey, a golden retriever, through her training from puppy to guide dog. Each stage of training is explained with text and photographs.

Berck, J. (1992). *No place to be: Voices of homeless children.* Boston: Houghton Mifflin. (3–8). INFORMATIONAL BOOK.*

  This book features interviews with homeless children, illustrated with photographs.

Blatchford, C. H. (1998). *Going with the flow* (J. L. Porter, Illus.). Minneapolis, MN: Carolrhoda. (2–4). CONTEMPORARY REALISTIC FICTION.

Fifth-grade Mark, who is deaf, has a difficult time making friends in his new school.

Borden L. (1999). *Good luck Mrs. K.* New York: McElderry. (2–5). CONTEMPORARY REALISTIC FICTION.

The teacher of a third-grade class has cancer.

Bourke, L. (1978). *Handmade ABC: A manual alphabet.* New York: Harvey House. (1–5). INFORMATIONAL BOOK.

This book uses pictures of hands to demonstrate sign language.

Bunting, E. (1999). *Smoky night* (D. Diaz, Illus.). New York: Harcourt. (K–4). PICTURE BOOK.

During the Los Angeles riots, Daniel and his mother must leave their apartment.

Bunting, E. (2001). *Jin Woo* (C. Soentpiet, Illus.). New York: Clarion. (1–4). PICTURE BOOK.

Davy is worried if his parents will still love him when they adopt a baby from Korea.

Carter, A. (1998). *Seeing things my way* (C. S. Carter, Photog.). Morton Grove, IL: Whitman. (K–3). INFORMATIONAL BOOK.

A second grader learns to cope with a brain tumor that is affecting her vision.

Carter, A. (1999). *Dustin's big school day* (D. Young & C. S. Carter, Illus.). Morton Grove, IL: Whitman. (Pres–2). CONTEMPORARY REALISTIC FICTION.

A boy with Down syndrome has an exciting school day.

Carter, A. (2001a). *I'm tougher than diabetes!* Morton Grove, IL: Whitman. (2–5). INFORMATIONAL BOOK.

Natalie describes how she lives with her type I diabetes.

Carter, A. L. (2001b). *In the clear.* Victoria, British Columbia: Orca. (3–5). HISTORICAL FICTION.

Pauline gets polio; with the support of her aunt, she is able to have a fairly normal life even though she uses a wheelchair.

Carter, A., & Carter, S. (1996). *I'm tougher than asthma!* (D. Young, Illus.). Morton Grove, IL: Whitman. (3–6). INFORMATIONAL BOOK.

Siri Carter tells how she lives with asthma.

Charlip, R., Miller, M. B., & Ancona, G. (1987). *Handtalk birthday: A number and story book in sign language.* New York: Four Winds. (K–4). INFORMATIONAL BOOK.

At her surprise birthday party, a deaf woman and her guests communicate using sign language. The book uses photographs for illustrations.

Clifton, L. (1980). *My friend Jacob* (T. Di Grazia, Illus.). New York: Dutton. (1–4). CONTEMPORARY REALISTIC FICTION.*

Sam has a friend, Jacob, with Down syndrome. This story tells how the two friends help each other.

Codell, E. R. (2003). *Sahara special.* New York: Hyperion. (4–7). CONTEMPORARY REALISTIC FICTION.

Sahara's mother takes her out of her special class and she repeats fifth grade with a sensitive, creative teacher.

Czech, J. (2000). *An American face* (F. Clancy, Illus.). Washington, DC: Child Welfare League of America. (K–3). PICTURE BOOK.

Jessie, from Korea, is adopted by American parents.

Czech, J. (2002). *The coffee can kid,* (M. J. Manning, Illus.). Washington, DC: Child Welfare League of America. (K–3). REALISTIC FICTION.

This story focuses on the life of an adopted child from Korea before she was adopted.

de Angeli, M. (1949). *The door in the wall.* New York: Doubleday. (4–9). HISTORICAL FICTION.

Robin has physical impairments in his legs and is mistreated by other children. Eventually he learns to read.

Dennenberg, B. (2002). *Mirror, mirror on the wall: The diary of Bess Brennan—The Perkins School for the Blind, 1932.* New York: Scholastic. (4–7). HISTORICAL FICTION.

After Bess loses her sight she goes to school to learn how to live with her blindness.

deVries, M. (2001). *Chance and the butterfly.* Custer, WA: Orca. (1–4). CONTEMPORARY REALISTIC FICTION.

Chance is unhappy living in a foster home. At school, he finds science fascinating as the class studies butterflies.

Dinn, S. (1996). *Hearts of gold: A celebration of Special Olympics and its heroes.* San Francisco, CA: Blackbirch Publishing. (5–9). INFORMATIONAL BOOK.

A look at the Special Olympics from the time they began in the 1960s to the present time.

Donnelly, K. (2000). *Coping with dyslexia.* New York: Rosen. (4–6). INFORMATIONAL BOOK.

This discussion of how to live with dyslexia includes a chapter about famous people who have dyslexia.

Fenner, C. (1998). *The king of dragons*. New York: McElderry. (4–6). CONTEMPORARY REALISTIC FICTION.

Ian and his father, a Vietnam War veteran, have been homeless for years. When Ian's father fails to return one day, Ian is on his own.

Ferris, J. (2001). *Of sound mind*. New York: Farrar, Straus & Giroux. (6–8). CONTEMPORARY REALISTIC FICTION

Theo has to act as the interpreter for his family, all of whom are deaf. He has a friend who is in a similar situation.

Feuer, E. (1995). *Lost summer*. New York: Farrar. (3–6). CONTEMPORARY REALISTIC FICTION.

After Lydia's parents divorce, she is sent to camp where her sister is a counselor. She learns to make friends and appreciate her sister.

Flinn, A. (2002). *Breathing underwater*. New York: HarperCollins. (6–10). CONTEMPORARY REALISTIC FICTION.

Nick has been abused by his father. When he starts abusing his girlfriend, he is sent to therapy for help.

Fogelin, A. (2002). *Anna Casey's place in the world*. Atlanta: Peachtree. (3–6). CONTEMPORARY REALISTIC FICTION.

Anna has to adjust to living in a foster home; keeping a journal helps.

Forbes, A. (2003). *Kids with AIDS*. New York: Powerkids Press. (4–7). INFORMATIONAL BOOK.

This book presents facts about AIDS; it talks about accepting rather than fearing AIDS.

Ford, C. (2001). *Helen Keller: Lighting the way for the blind and deaf*. Berkeley Heights, NJ: Enslow. (4–7). INFORMATIONAL BOOK.

Helen Keller's accomplishments are presented in this book.

Fox, P. (1997). *Radiance descending*. New York: DK Ink. (3–8). CONTEMPORARY REALISTIC FICTION.

Paul is embarrassed by his brother who has Down syndrome, but he discovers Jacob is nonetheless lovable.

Fraustino, L. R. (2001). *The hickory chair* (B. Andrews, IIlus.). New York: Levine/Scholastic. (3–6). CONTEMPORARY REALISTIC FICTION.

Louis, who is blind, has a special relationship with his grandmother. When she dies, she leaves notes for all the family.

Freymann-Weyr, G. (2000). *When I was older*. New York: Houghton Mifflin. (6–9). CONTEMPORARY REALISTIC FICTION.

Three years after the death of her brother from leukemia, Sophie still has a hard time dealing with the grief.

Gantos, J. (1998). *Joey Pigza swallows the key*. New York: HarperCollins. (4–7). CONTEMPORARY REALISTIC FICTION.

Joey has lots of problems, only one of which is ADHD. When his medications are regulated, he is able to function better.

Gantos, J. (2002a). *Joey Pigza loses control*. New York: HarperCollins. (4–7). CONTEMPORARY REALISTIC FICTION.

Joey goes to stay with his alcoholic dad who thinks Joey can get along without his medication.

Gantos, J. (2002b). *What would Joey do?* New York: Farrar, Straus and Giroux. (4–7). CONTEMPORARY REALISTIC FICTION.

Joey has to deal with significant problems.

Gordon, M. A. (2003). *Let's talk about dyslexia*. New York: Rosen. (1–3). INFORMATIONAL BOOK.

This book about dyslexia is meant for younger readers.

Gray, S. H. (2002). *Living with cerebral palsy*. Chanhassen, MN: Child's World. (4–7). INFORMATIONAL BOOK.

This book discusses cerebral palsy and what it is like to live with the disease.

Greenlee, S. (2002). *When someone dies* (B. Drath, Illus.). Atlanta: Peachtree. (3–6). INFORMATIONAL BOOK.

A counselor suggests ways for children to cope with the issues related to a death.

Grossman, L. S. (2002). *Sam speaks out* (P. Bockus, Illus.). Seattle, WA: Orca. (K–3). CONTEMPORARY REALISTIC FICTION.

Someone has been tickling and touching Sam in inappropriate ways.

Grossman, L. S. (2003). *A tale worth telling* (P. Bockus, Illus.). Seattle, WA: Orca. (K–3). CONTEMPORARY REALISTIC FICTION.

The soccer coach calls David stupid and grabs him, leaving bruises on his arm.

Haldane, S. (1991). *Helping hands: How monkeys assist people who are disabled.* New York: Dutton. (3–7). INFORMATIONAL BOOK.

Through this nonfiction book illustrated with photographs, children learn about the ways that monkeys can help disabled people.

Hamilton, V. (1999). *Bluish.* New York: Scholastic. (4–7). CONTEMPORARY REALISTIC FICTION.

Dreenie makes friends with a new girl who has leukemia.

Hausherr, R. (1989). *Children and the AIDS virus.* New York: Clarion. (3–6). INFORMATIONAL BOOK.*

This book looks at AIDS and the ways that children can and cannot get the disease. The book is written at two levels, with big print for young children and smaller print for older children.

Heelan, J. R. (1998). *The making of my special hand.* Atlanta: Peachtree. (K–3). INFORMATIONAL BOOK.

A young girl born without a hand is fitted for her prosthesis.

Hesse, K. (1994). *Phoenix rising.* New York: Holt. (6–10). MODERN FANTASY.

Set in the future, this story explores radiation contamination throughout the United States. The characters make the issues real for readers.

Hoffman, A. (2003). *Green angel.* New York: Scholastic. (7–10). FANTASY.

After a city is destroyed, those left behind must learn to survive.

Houle, M. M. (2003). *AIDS in the 21st century: What you should know.* Berkeley Heights, NJ: Enslow. (4–6). INFORMATIONAL BOOK.

A good reference book for middle-grade children.

Hyde, M. O. (1980). *Cry softly! The story of child abuse.* Louisville, KY: Westminster Press. (3–6). INFORMATIONAL BOOK.

This book provides a list of organizations that help abused children and their parents. It also helps concerned people to understand that child abuse is not confined to any particular people or class of people in society.

Hyland, B. (2002). *The girl with the crazy brother.* Philadelphia: Xlibris. (7–10). CONTEMPORARY REALISTIC FICTION.

Dana's brother is diagnosed with schizophrenia.

Kinn, G. (2000). *Me and My Baby: Parents & Children Talk About Adoption.* New York: Artisan. (2–4). NONFICTION.

Families and adopted children tell about their experiences.

Kipnis, L. (1983). *You can't catch diabetes from a friend* (R. Benkof, Photog.). Gainesville, FL: Triad Scientific Publishers. (2–6). INFORMATIONAL BOOK.

In simple text and photographs, this book explains diabetes and the daily routines of diabetic children.

Kroll, V. (1994). *Beginnings: How families came to be* (S. Schuett, Illus.). New York: Concept. (K–3). PICTURE BOOK.

Six children from a variety of backgrounds ask the parents to tell "the story of me."

Lamperti, N. (2000). *Brown like me.* Oakland, CA: Words Distributing. (K–3). PICTURE BOOK.

An African-American child adopted by a white family looks for brown in her environment.

Landau, E. (1998). *Living with albinism.* New York: Franklin Watts. (4–7). INFORMATIONAL BOOK.

An in-depth look at albinism, with a section that gives additional references.

Landau, E. (2001). *Spinal cord injuries.* Berkeley Heights, NJ: Enslow. (6–8). INFORMATIONAL BOOK.

A reference book that discusses the nature and treatment of spinal cord injuries.

Lawrence, I. (2000). *Ghost boy.* New York: Dell Laurel-Leaf. (6–10). CONTEMPORARY REALISTIC FICTION.

Harold is an albino. He decides to join the circus but finds that there are two groups there also—the freaks and everyone else.

Lawrenson, D. (1996). *Guide dogs: From puppies to partners.* New York: Allen and Unwin. (4–6). INFORMATIONAL BOOK.

Descriptions of training a guide dog, from birth to being with a partner.

Lewis, R. (2002). *I love you like crazy cakes* (J. Dyer, Illus.). New York: Little Brown. (K–3). PICTURE BOOK.

This book outlines Lewis's experiences of going to China to adopt her baby.

Little, J. (1986). *Different dragons* (L. Fernandez, Illus.). New York: Viking. (3–6). CONTEMPORARY REALISTIC FICTION.

The story of a boy's battle with his fears of darkness, thunderstorms, and dogs. In the process of facing his fears he learns about his brother's and father's fears.

Little, J. (1987). *Little by little: A writer's education*. New York: Viking. (3–6). BIOGRAPHY.

Jean Little's own story about her extraordinary life. She has been nearly blind from birth, but overcame ridicule, rejection, and bullying to find friends and to write poetry and stories.

Little, J. (2002a). *Birdie for now*. Victoria, British Columbia: Orca. (3–6). CONTEMPORARY REALISTIC FICTION.

Dickon has ADHD; when he takes responsibility for training a dog, he begins to take responsibility for himself.

Little, J. (2002b). *Emma's yucky brother* (J. Plecas, Illus.). New York: HarperTrophy. (3-6). FICTION.

Emma's family adopts a little boy, which is difficult for Emma.

McGuire, P. (1998). *AIDS*. Austin, TX: Raintree Steck-Vaughn. (4–6). INFORMATIONAL BOOK.

This book focuses on the basic facts about HIV and AIDS.

McMahon P. (2000). *Dancing wheels*. (J. Godt, Photog.) New York: Houghton Mifflin. (2–5). INFORMATIONAL BOOK.

A dance troupe consists of dancers in wheelchairs as well as those who are "stand-up" dancers.

Miller, M. B., & Ancona, G. (1991). *Handtalk school*. New York: Four Winds. (1–3). INFORMATIONAL BOOK.

Color photographs illustrate this book based on an actual school, its teachers, and its students.

Millman, I. (1998). *Moses goes to a concert*. New York: Farrar, Straus & Giroux. (1–3). INFORMATIONAL BOOK.

Moses and his deaf classmates attend a concert and discover they can feel the instuments' vibrations through balloons.

Millman, I. (2000). *Moses goes to school*. New York: Farrar, Straus & Giroux. (1–3). INFORMATIONAL BOOK.

Moses and his classmates learn American Sign Language before they learn to read and write spoken English.

Okimoto, J. D., & Aoki, E. M. (2002). *The white swan express: A story about adoption* (M. So, Illus.). New York: Clarion. (2–5). INFORMATIONAL BOOK.

Four sets of parents adopt four baby girls in China.

Park, B. (2000). *The graduation of Jake Moon*. New York: Atheneum. (5–8). CONTEMPORARY REALISTIC FICTION.

Jake's grandfather has Alzheimer's disease. Jake is embarrassed by his actions but learns that he still loves his grandfather.

Peacock, C. A., Gregory, A., & Gregory, K. C. (1998). *Sugar was my best friend: Diabetes and me* (A. Levine, Illus.). Morton Grove, IL: Albert Whitman. (3–5). NONFICTION.

After he is diagnosed with diabetes, Gregory describes what his world was like.

Rankin, L. (1991). *The handmade alphabet*. New York: Dial. (1–4). PICTURE BOOK.

This is an alphabet picture book that features the manual alphabet used in sign language. The author explains that her stepson is deaf.

Riggs, S. (2001). *Never sell yourself short*. Morton Grove, IL: Albert Whitman. (6–9). INFORMATIONAL BOOK.

A photo-essay of Josh, who is a "little person."

Rosenberg, L. (2002). *We wanted you* (P. Catalanotto, illus.). Hastings-on-Hudson, NY: Roaring Brook. (K–3). INFORMATIONAL BOOK.

A good book about an interracial family and an international adoption.

Schaefer, L. M. (2000). *Some kids use wheelchairs*. Eden Prairie, MN: Capstone Press. (3–6). INFORMATIONAL BOOK.

A realistic look at children who must use wheelchairs.

Silverstein, A., Silverstein, R. and Silverstein, M. (2001). *Dyslexia*. New York: Watts. (1–3). NONFICTION.

A family tells about their experiences with dyslexia.

Silverstein, A., Silverstein, V., and Nunn, L. S. (2003a). *Asthma*. New York: Franklin Watts. (4–6). INFORMATIONAL BOOK.

This is a reference book about asthma.

Silverstein, A., Silverstein, V., and Nunn, L. S. (2003b). *Diabetes*. New York: Franklin Watts. (4–6). INFORMATIONAL BOOK.

This is a reference book about diabetes.

Slepian, J. (1980). *Alfred summer*. New York: Macmillan. (4–6). CONTEMPORARY REALISTIC FICTION.

Four children, all misfits of one sort or another, work together to make a rowboat. They learn about friendship and that what's inside people is really what is important.

Thomas, P. (2001). *Don't call me special: A first look at disability* (L. Harker, Illus.). Hauppauge, NY: Barron's Educational Series. (K–3). PICTURE BOOK.

A good book to begin discussions about disabilities with younger children.

Trueman, T. (2001). *Stuck in neutral*. New York: HarperCollins. (7–10). CONTEMPORARY REALISTIC FICTION.

Shawn has cerebral palsy and is unable to communicate. His father thinks he is in pain and talks about ending his suffering.

Voigt, C. (1994). *When she hollers*. New York: Scholastic. (4–8). CONTEMPORARY REALISTIC FICTION.

This is a sensitive book about sexual abuse by a stepfather and a mother who will not believe it is happening.

Walter, V. A., & Gross, M. (1996). *HIV/AIDS information for children: A guide to issues and resources*. New York: H. W. Wilson. (5–9). INFORMATIONAL BOOK.

This is a reference book for older students.

Weitzman, E. (1995). *Let's talk about staying in a shelter*. New York: PowerKids Press. (K–5). INFORMATIONAL BOOK.

Kids learn how to adjust to living in a shelter.

White, R. (2000). *Memories of Summer*. New York: Dell Laurel-Leaf. (6–9). CONTEMPORARY REALISTIC FICTION.

Lyric's sister, Summer, develops schizophrenia and has to be put into a mental institution.

White, R., & Cunningham, A. M. (1991). *Ryan White, my own story*. New York: Dial. (6–12). INFORMATIONAL BOOK.

In this account, coauthored by Ryan White, the author tells about Ryan's battle with AIDS, the discrimination he suffered, and his dying. Nevertheless, this is not a depressing book.

Woodson, J. (1994). *I hadn't meant to tell you this*. New York: Delacorte. (6–9). CONTEMPORARY REALISTIC FICTION.

In this book, Lena and her sister face the fact that they must flee their sexually abusive father.

Woodson, J. (1999). *Lena*. New York: Delacorte. (6–9). CONTEMPORARY REALISTIC FICTION.

Lena and her sister, Dion, flee their sexually abusive father. Lena is a protective big sister seeking a place in the world.

Zalben, J. B. (1996). *Unfinished dreams: A novel*. New York: Simon & Schuster. (5–8). CONTEMPORARY REALISTIC FICTION.

The principal in Jason's school has always been the ideal principal. He develops AIDS, which causes problems when some of Jason's friends make fun of him.

References and Books for Further Reading

Andrews, S. (1994). *Teaching kids to care*. Bloomington, IN: ERIC Clearinghouse.

Baskin, R., & Harris, J. (1977). *Notes from a different drummer*. New York: R. R. Bowker.

Baskin, R., & Harris, J. (1984). *More notes from a different drummer*. New Providence, NJ: R. R. Bowker.

Friedberg, J., Mullins, J., & Sukiennik, A. (1992). *Portraying persons with disabilities, Vol. 1* (2nd ed.). New Providence, NJ: R. R. Bowker.

Landrum, J. (1998–1999). Adolescent novels that feature characters with disabilities: An annotated bibliography. *Journal of Adolescent & Adult Literacy, 42*, 284–295.

Lickona, T. (1992). *Educating for character*. New York: Bantam Doubleday Dell.

Miller, S. (1997). *Problem solving safari-blocks*. Everett, WA: Totline.

Noddings, N. (1992). *The challenge to care in schools*. New York: Teachers College Press.

Peck, P. (1983, winter). The invention of adolescence and other thoughts on youth. *Top of the News, 39*(2), 45–47.

Robertson, D. (1992). *Portraying persons with disabilities*. New Providence, NJ: R. R. Bowker.

Rudman, M. K. (1993). *Children's literature: Resource for the classroom*. Norwood, MA: Christopher-Gordon.

Sage, M. (1977). A study of the handicapped in children's literature. In A. S. MacLeod (Ed.), *Children's literature: Selected essays and bibliographies*. College Park: University of Maryland College of Library and Informational Service.

Wilde, S. (1989, November). The power of literature: Notes from a survivor. *New Advocate, 2*, 49–52.

Literature for Children in All Cultures

13

KEY TERMS

cultural consciousness	global literature
cultural diversity	multicultural
culture	literature

GUIDING QUESTIONS

This chapter specifically talks about books and activities to use with children so that they can make connections with the literature, their cultures, and the cultures in the books. As you read, think about the answers to these questions.

1. Why might some readers not make connections with books?

2. Why might it make a difference if readers could see pictures of characters in books that "look like" they do?

3. What might teachers do to assure that the books they use reflect the cultural diversity found in their classrooms, communities, and this country?

4. Do teachers in classrooms where there is little cultural diversity have a responsibility for introducing books about a variety of cultures?

5. What will you, as a member of your culture, need to do to feel comfortable using books that are representative of other cultures?

6. Why do some books contain characters who speak in dialect?

Our country is a mosaic of cultures, which gives our society a richness and patina that we need to respect and cultivate. *Culture* is a design for living—ways of acting, believing, and valuing: it is a shared set of ideas, behaviors, discourses, and attitudes that internally and externally define a social group (Shanahan, 1994). *Cultural consciousness* is awareness of and sensitivity to *cultural diversity* and its contribution to our lives and the larger society. Cultural diversity is a part of our everyday lives—ranging from voice mail systems that offer messages in the language of our choice to information and directions that are printed in several languages. Restaurants and groceries feature foods from all over the world. Our museums and concert halls feature music and art from many cultures. No one can stand apart from culture, and each person is a member of many subcultures within his or her social context. All readers, as cultural beings, are part of a multicultural society. Literature can help children become conscious of culture, cultural traditions, and values. In this chapter, we explore books that will help children acquire sensitivity to and respect for many of the cultures found in this country.

We will use the term *multicultural literature* rather than *culturally conscious literature* because this is the description found in most professional writing. This term can therefore be most easily used to research the topic further. Although multicultural does not have the same connotation as culturally conscious, pragmatically speaking, it is the one that is most familiar and useful to current and future teachers (Henderson, 2003; Newell, 2003). Cultural consciousness often has a political connotation that may imply a different focus than we intend. Even though Shanahan (1994) suggests that "multicultural literature" may not appeal to some people, it is a useful description as long as we do not assume that multicultural refers to "other people": each of us has attitudes that may not be as culturally sensitive as they might be. Multicultural literature demonstrates the complexity of our society and the inescapable conclusion that all readers are cultural beings.

What Is Multicultural Literature?

Grace Enriquez (2001) suggests that there is a wide range of definitions of *multicultural literature*. Some definitions include books that depict minorities and characters from non-mainstream backgrounds, as well as books that depict women, gays, and lesbians. In this chapter, we consider multicultural literature to be literature in any genre that includes a wide range of people and cultures in this country. The study of cultures outside the United States is called global education (Freeman & Lehman, 2001). Books with a global setting are not included here. Multicultural books can help readers explore diversity so that they may gain an understanding of cultures different from their own. Hazel Rochman (1993) makes the point that when we are studying culture, multiculturalism means across cultures and that it does not only refer to people of color. Multicultural literature then includes books that incorporate the experiences of White ethnic and cultural groups as well as diversities of race and religion.

Although we will be focusing specifically on books about a variety of cultural groups in this chapter, books in all of the foregoing chapters have included many of these cultures as well. A point to remember is that multicultural books are found in all genres. We will begin by looking at books about the original Americans, the Native Americans. Their cultures, both past and present, are little known to many of us. Our country is as diverse as it is because of the immigration of people from various countries. Many African Americans, Latinos, and Asian Americans have maintained their cultural traditions although they have lived their

251

Miss Edwards left the group, they had decided that this was a facet of the story that they needed to pursue further.

Miss Edwards also decided that the topic of dialect was one that the class needed to focus on in the future. Perhaps when they studied the aftermath of the Civil War, when many of the slaves went to various parts of Appalachia to live, they could look at the dialect spoken in that region, which could lead into a unit of study that focused more broadly on language use in a variety of settings and cultures. When she went to the Internet to see what might be available, she found a wealth of resources about multicultural books and dialects in different cultures. Many books of traditional literature were on tape so that the children would be able to hear and appreciate the various dialects. When Miss Edwards got excited about a topic, so did her students! This was going to be a wonderful unit of study.

All people of all cultures are a part of our lives.

entire lives in this country. Other cultural groups, such as Jewish, Appalachian, and Amish people, have strong cultural traditions and have also experienced prejudice for their beliefs. There are books of *global literature* about other cultures in this country that could be included in a broader context of cultural studies that are not included here. We hope that reading books about the previously noted cultures will further the goal of developing cultural consciousness and appreciation of these groups.

Why Is Multicultural Literature Important in the Classroom?

Multicultural literature is important in two very different kinds of classroom settings. The first, of course, is in elementary and middle-school classrooms in this country. The second is in classrooms in which pre-service and in-service teachers are learning about teaching. Our hope is that if pre-service and in-service teachers become familiar with multicultural literature, they will become comfortable using it in their classrooms. Teachers are the role models for children; if they read and share multicultural literature, the children will probably read it, too. This could reverse the trend that Ferree and Abbott (2001) found where stu-

dents in elementary classrooms are not reading books about other countries and cultures.

According to the United Nations' demographic data of October 1999, if the earth's population could be reduced to just 100 people, there would be 61 Asians, 12 Europeans, 14 North and South Americans, and 13 Africans. Of these 100 individuals, 70 people would be non-White and 30 would be White (Steiner, 2001). It is obvious that, in a global or a multicultural society, our students need to feel comfortable interacting with people different than they are.

The United States also has a diverse population that is becoming more diverse each year. Some minority groups in some cities are actually the majority group as far as the number of residents is concerned. At the same time, the percentage of White teachers currently is 88 percent and probably will increase (McIntyre, 1997). Many White teachers traditionally have not had a lot of culturally diverse experiences, and many teacher education programs do not provide them, either. This means some teachers may not be aware of the cultural traditions of students from cultural groups different than their own. Sheets (2000) suggests that these teachers are themselves culturally disadvantaged if their experiences are limited. If this is the case, it becomes particularly important that teachers have experiences with multicultural literature. The rationale for teachers becoming familiar with these books is the same as it is for children: Readers are not only able to gain different perspectives but they should also develop an appreciation for the commonalities among people who live differently than they do. As we, as teachers, advocate the use of multicultural and international literature, our own preferences for text and illustrations will be widened and we will become more sensitive.

There are some issues that we need to consider when we read books that are outside of our cultural familiarity. Umber (2002) suggests that "Reading a book written for people of another culture is an interesting experience in itself" (p. 7). This is because words may be unfamiliar and the context may place the readers as "outsiders," which means that they need to infer meanings. They must try to fit in and understand the culture portrayed in the book. This might cause problems if one believes in a transactional view of reading in which "The author isn't boss anymore, but neither is the reader. It's what they come up with together that makes the literary experience" (Sebesta, 2001). As children and their teachers read books that are outside of their personal experiences, they may make inferences different than those anticipated by the author. This is why discussions of multicultural books are important. If readers are able to discuss the incongruities that they read about, insight may develop. They have the chance to be exposed to ideas that may be new to them, and their way of thinking about a cultural group may be impacted in a positive manner.

Multicultural literature can help readers understand both the differences and the similarities among cultures. Writers who use settings readers are not familiar with face a challenge similar to science fiction and fantasy writers: They must "find details vivid enough, but still familiar enough, to illuminate faraway landscapes and people—the struggle to be specific yet universal" (Kurtz, 2001, p. 11). When children read well-written books with adequate details, they are better able to make connections between different cultures and places and their own lives. A strategy that can be used to help readers look at similarities and differences is to use folk and fairy tales. As they read about the books that have different settings, they can see that the human aspects in very different settings are very much alike.

An important reason for using multicultural literature is that "All children need opportunities to see characters like themselves in books, dealing with issues like the ones children face in their own lives" (Copenhaver, 2001). Aoki (1980) writes of the problems of seeing her culture, and therefore herself, stereotypically portrayed in literature as a child. If stereotypes of the race and culture are all an individual finds in books, then the books will have little impact on them. Pat Mora (1995) suggests that all children should see themselves in the picture books that they look at. If they don't, "these children might conclude that there is something the matter with who they are, their skin color, their language, or their family customs and values. If we believe in the power of words and of books, how can we not believe that this invisibility in books can produce psychological scarring?" (p. x).

There are many lists of reasons for using multicultural literature in college of education classrooms, as well as in the classrooms of children and young adults (Ramsey, 1987; Steiner, 2001; Stoodt, 1992). Taking ideas from all of these sources, the following suggestions are made. The use of multicultural literature can:

1. create opportunities for readers to recognize that there are commonalities among all people: we all feel love, fear, joy, and so forth;

2. help readers make connections with individuals in other cultural groups so they may view themselves as members of various groups rather than identifying with just one;

3. increase readers' understanding, appreciation, and respect for different cultures and their contributions;

4. increase the development of positive self-esteem and future goals; and

5. facilitate positive group identity and understanding of personal heritage at the same time readers are learning to respect many different kinds of lifestyles. This encourages a broad range of social relationships, openness, and interest in others.

Guidelines for Choosing Multicultural Literature

As when choosing any other books, multicultural books must be well-written. A book is not necessarily a good choice simply because it has multicultural characters or setting. The following areas need to be evaluated.

1. Is the setting accurate? Does it avoid stereotypes? For example, all African Americans do not live in urban settings. If an urban setting is necessary for the plot, then it would be appropriate; if another setting is better, it should be used.

2. Does the plot draw readers into the story? Unless they are interested in the events, the book will not be read.

3. Are the characters presented without stereotypes? The books should reflect the lives of individual people and not general personality traits that may be associated with an entire group. Consider the roles the characters play. Are males and/or Whites the only problem solvers? Are the characters three-dimensional, ones with whom the readers may identify?

4. Is the theme one that will speak to all readers? Or is it didactic, with the theme overriding the plot?

5. Is the book up-to-date and accurate? Many times older books may not present the most current kinds of situations or information and may include stereotypes. However, a recent publication date does not assure readers that there are no stereotypes.

6. What language is used? Is a dialect used stereotypically or is it one that accurately portrays a cultural group? Is the dialogue authentic?

7. Are the illustrations authentic? Since they can have a great impact on younger readers, they must not be stereotyped.

8. Are the cultural values accurately portrayed? To be able to answer this question, readers must be somewhat familiar with the culture depicted in the books.

Linda Pavonetti (2001) states: "Books mirror our lives. Good books and stories mirror our lives truthfully. . . . Good books speak to Africans, Asians, Europeans, Latinos, Native Americans—women and men. . . They draw readers into a person's life—flaws and feats, triumphs and tragedies. They reflect the humanity in each of us, not just the individual culture we are born into" (p. 70).

Rachel Davis (2000) echoes this perspective. As she explored the potential of literature that impacts the lives of African-American middle-school girls, she

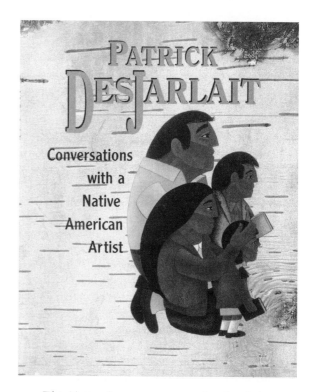

This Native American artist and author helps readers understand his culture.

found that she herself had dismissed her own experiences as an African-American adolescent. For her, as well as the girls in her study, "The literature that mattered most to me as a young girl was literature that allowed me to connect with the experiences occurring in my life at the time" (p. 267).

If we want books to have an impact on the lives of our students, we must choose well-written books. Readers need to be able to make connections between what they are reading and their own lives—whether that may be a situation that they are experiencing or an interest that they have. If there is no connection, or if teachers do not help their students to learn how to make these connections, readers will not value the messages that are implicit in all books. Reading is an intensely personal process and, because of this, well-written books can make a difference in the attitudes of the readers' lives.

As you choose and read some of the books described in this chapter, make your own judgments about whether or not they are "good" books. Multicultural books can be some of your most memorable choices—or they can be trite and insignificant.

Books of Interest

As we look at examples of books that focus on the different cultural groups, there are sometimes other criteria that may be suggested. The previously stated general guidelines can be supplemented by any additional criteria.

Native Americans

Native Americans should not be portrayed as "generic" in nature. Although many tribes had shared values, pictures and text need to focus on specific tribes because each had a specific culture and traditions, defined in part on their location. The setting must be accurately depicted—Native Americans in the northwest had different homes and living styles than did those who lived on the plains. Stereotypes abound in many books about Native Americans, which is why authors who have a Native-American background write some of the best books.

Joseph Bruchac, an Abenaki, has become an important writer of Native-American literature. He is best known for his books of folk lore, but also writes in other genres as well. His autobiography, *Bowman's Store: A Journey to Myself*, is an account of how he came to understand his upbringing, his family, and his heritage. Having this information creates a context for appreciating the more than 60 books he has written for children and adults. *Sacajawea* is the story of the young Shoshone woman who acted as the interpreter and guide for the Lewis and Clark expedition. This book is written from two perspectives, that of Sacajawea and of William Clark, as they describe their trip to Pomp, Sacajawea's son. Bruchac's nonfiction book, *Many Nations: An Alphabet of Native America*, presents 26 beautiful paintings. An issue that might be raised regarding this book is that there is a mixture of historical and contemporary settings that might be confusing to some readers. Nonetheless, with discussions, this is a valuable book for younger readers. Bruchac also has a book of poetry: *Earth Under Sky Bear's Feet: Native American Poems of the Land*. In this book, a grandmother relates the legend of Sky Bear to her granddaughter. As Sky Bear circles the earth, the 12 poems, each from a different tribe, tell what he saw and heard. A book for older readers, *Winter People*, takes place during the French and Indian War. English raiders attacked the Abenaki village and captured Saxso's mother and little sisters. This gives the Native-American perspective of this event, which is usually told from the English view.

Other authors also write books of traditional literature that focus on the legends of Native Americans. Kathy-Jo Wargin wrote two such books that are very well done. The first, *The Legend of the Loon*, is a story of a grandmother and her grandchildren. She shares with them the wonders of nature. The illustrations in this book are also particularly well done. There is a loon(s) hidden in almost all of the paintings. The second, *The Legend of Mackinac Island*, is the story of a large turtle who lived in a world made only of water. When the Great Spirit of the Sky wanted land to be made, the turtle's back was used.

Many times we make connections between Native Americans and buffalo. An interesting fact is that the buffalo were systematically killed until there were few left. Neil Waldman describes, through the voice of a Comanche woman, how five bison were taken from the Bronx and transported to a range in Oklahoma. There they became the "Mother Herd," allowing the repopulation of the bison to begin. *They Came from the Bronx: How the Buffalo were Saved from Extinction* is an appropriate book to use with a wide range of ages, depending on the purpose.

Books of contemporary realistic fiction exist as well. Cynthia Leitich Smith writes of a young girl who is determined to carry on the tradition of her family's women by participating as a *Jingle Dancer* at the next powwow. Although her search for the "jingles" seems a bit mundane, the story of how Jenna uses her family's resources, as well as her community's, to accomplish her goal reflects the important aspects of this culture.

Ben Mikaelsen's *Touching Spirit Bear* is the survival story of 15-year-old Cole Matthews, who has been in trouble most of his life. After he savagely attacks another boy, he is banished to a remote Alaskan island, a punishment based on a Native-American tradition called Circle Justice. He still demonstrates his arrogance there as he destroys his supplies; however, when he tries to kill a Spirit Bear, he is nearly killed. His parole officer, a Tlingit elder who continues to work with him while he is in the hospital and afterwards, helps him come to terms with himself so that emotional as well as physical healing takes place.

Sydele Golston's informational book for older readers, *Changing Woman of the Apache: Women's Lives in Past and Present*, presents the context for the ceremony in which a girl changes from a child to a woman. Following the ceremony, the book presents accounts of all the stages of an Apache woman's life, from childhood through old age. The historical photographs, the source notes, and the bibliography make this a valuable reference book.

Immigrants

Most of us can find connections that relate to ourselves and our families as we read about immigrants. A book in which the connections are particularly easily made is *We Are Americans: Voices of the Immigrant Experience* by Dorothy and Thomas Hoobler. Through documents—letters, diary entries, and oral histories—and photographs, readers are able to appreciate and value the people from all over the world who have come to live in this country.

Three books portray the immigrant experiences of young people through interviews and oral histories. Yale Strom interviewed young immigrants from all over the world to get their views on what it was like to move to this country and how they began to adjust to a new life. *Quilted Landscape: Conversations with Young Immigrants* is an attractive book that should entice readers to pursue this topic. Janet Bode's *New Kids in Town: Oral Histories of Immigrant Teens* is one of her books about teens who have come to this country. In this book, the youngsters talk about fleeing from their homelands and what it is like to move to this country. In *Colors of Freedom: Immigrant Stories*, the teens share their art, recipes, poems, and short stories. Bode talks with those whose ancestors were slaves or slave owners, as well as teens who are themselves immigrants. The book includes questions asked by the Immigration and Naturalization Service as part of the interview process, as well as a sample citizenship test. Middle-school students should be able to identify with many of the young people in these books.

A book to complement those previously noted, *Tenement: Immigrant Life on the Lower East Side* by Raymond Bial, examines the living conditions found in one neighborhood that traditionally has been home to new immigrants. Bial documents the poverty, the politics, and the daily life by providing detailed descriptions and using historical photographs. Even though the area was overcrowded and often unsafe, Bial presents the positive aspects of living there. The book includes a bibliography as well as Web sites that may be used to study this topic further.

All of the previously mentioned books are informational books. Fiction books, especially historical fiction, have also been written about moving to this country. One of the best, especially for middle-school girls, is *A Coal Miner's Bride: The Diary of Anetka Kaminska*, one of the *Dear America* series books, written by Susan Bartoletti. Anetka and her brother come to America, where she is ordered by her father to marry a man who needs a wife to care for him and his three young children. Her life is incredibly hard, death is always a threat, and she herself becomes widowed at age 14. Her life is turned around when she is reunited with a young man who had befriended her. A book for younger readers is John Cech's *My Grandmother's Journey*. It tells the story of the author's grandmother-in-law's life in Russia before the Revolution, after World War II, and upon arriving at Ellis Island.

African Americans

Books about the African-American experience must portray the diverse settings in which real people might live or have lived. In other words, the settings need to be in the north and south, in urban and rural communities, past and present, as well as in places other than the United States. Like books about almost every cultural group, there is not a single African-American culture—the richness created by individuals and their unique situations helps to avoid the stereotypes that may be found in some books.

There have recently been many excellent biographies written about African Americans who have made significant contributions in their areas of expertise. Katherine Krohn's *Ella Fitzgerald: First Lady of Song* tells of the life of one of the great musicians of our times. Ella was discovered at age 15; at that time, she was living on the street. Her voice and her ability to improvise brought her prominence and fame. This book is a good source of other information, as it includes a bibliography, a glossary, and a time line. The audience for another biography of a musician, Roxanne Orgill's *If I Only Had a Horn: Young Louis Armstrong,* is designed for younger readers, who are privileged to find out about Louis's entry into the musical world through the text and illustrations. *Martin's Big Words*, a Caldecott Honor book by Doreen Rappaport, presents events and situations in Martin Luther King's life. Although it is a picture book, it has appeal for all ages. For readers interested in sports, *Hank Aaron* is a picture-book biography of the home run champion. Peter Golenbock shows how Aaron had to overcome prejudice and poverty to meet his goals.

Bad Boy: A Memoir, an autobiography/memoir by Walter Dean Myers, should be on the reading list of all middle-school students and their teachers. Myers, author of many books for children and young adults (for example, *The Glory Field, The Journal of Joshua Loper: A Black Cowboy*, and *Slam!*), tells his own story. He did not have an easy time growing up but did live with a loving adoptive family in Harlem. He shares his memories of his difficulties in school and why he had so much difficulty some years and not others. He even remembers what he was reading and writing. He is an inspiration to all readers.

A collective biography by Andrea Pinkney, *Let it Shine: Stories of Black Women Freedom Fighters*, tells of 10 African-American women who have made a difference in the lives of many people. From Sojourner Truth to Shirley Chisholm, these women have taken extraordinary steps that have created significant changes and made an impact on our society. A similar book, Joyce Hansen's *Women of Hope: African Americans Who Made a Difference*, presents 12 biographies of women who also made contributions to education, social causes, the arts, and science.

There are many well-written informational books by and/or about African Americans. One that is particularly appropriate for middle-school readers is Gail Buckley's *American Patriots: The Story of Blacks in the Military from the Revolution to Desert Storm*. Buckley makes it perfectly clear that the contributions made by African-American men and women have been significant over a very long period of time. Another book that would be useful as middle-school students study history is Jerry Stanley's *Hurry Freedom: African Americans in Gold Rush California*. This was a time and place in which racism and prejudice were rampant; African Americans were frequently taken advantage of and exploited. Even at the time, civil rights efforts were starting, which are documented in the book. The photographs add to the credibility of this text. Dennis Fadin lets readers experience the difficulties of some of the slaves who escaped in his informational book, *Bound for the North Star: True Stories of Fugitive Slaves*. It provides perspectives on the Underground Railroad that may be unknown. A fascinating book, *Breaking Ground, Breaking Silence: The Story of New York's African Burial Ground*, is the account of archeologists studying an African burial site found in Manhattan after an excavation for a new building. Because those of African descent were not allowed to write in the 1600 and 1700s, little is known about this group of people. By studying the artifacts that were found, pieces of their life histories have been reconstructed. Joyce Hansen and Gary McGowan make this subject come alive for readers.

Other informational books share African-American contributions to the arts. Alice McGill has collected 13 lullabies sung to children about the time of the Civil War. *In the Hollow of your Hand: Slave Lullabies* not only is beautifully illustrated, but comes with CD. Belinda Rochelle has collected 20 poems by African-American writers and paired them with 20 works of art by African-American artists. The result is a beautiful book that should be an inspiration to those who read it, as well as an example of how students can combine the two art forms. *Words with Wings: A Treasury of African-American Poetry and Art* is highly recommended.

Well-written historical fiction books also provide insights about African-American experiences. Two books by Elisa Carbone are based on real people and events. *Stealing Freedom* is the story of Ann, a young girl living with her family in slavery. When Ann is separated from her family, she must become more independent than she had been before. She learns to read, cuts her hair to look like a boy, and escapes on the Underground Railroad. *Storm Warriors* takes place in 1895 in North Carolina. Nathan wants to join the all-Black crew of the United States Lifesaving Service. However, racism and prejudice impact the lives of all African Americans: Nathan learns that although his dream of becoming one of the rescuers at sea cannot become reality, he can be of use use saving lives in a different way.

There are many contemporary realistic fiction books that share important aspects of African-American culture. Dinnah Johnson's story of *Quennie Blue* is an example of the storytelling tradition in which a child is helped to imagine the childhood of her grandmother, whose name she shares. The illustrations by James Ransome help readers make the connections between the generations as they read this book and think of their own families.

Most of Sharon Draper's books for young adults are in an urban setting. Many young people find that her books reflect their situations and they are able to identify with the characters and situations. The *Hazelwood High* trilogy has characters who face significant challenges and decisions. In *Tears of a Tiger*, Andy is driving the car in which his friend was killed. Although

Andy gets support from family, friends, and a psychologist, he is not able to live with his guilt. The second book, *Forged by Fire*, focuses on Gerald, who also must face significant questions about his life. The last book, *Darkness Before Dawn*, answers questions about Keisha, Andy's girlfriend, and the relationships she has with people in the previous two books, as well as new characters that cause her to rethink her relationships. These three books have had an impact on a group of readers who have had difficulty finding books that "spoke" to them.

To conclude this section, we share two books, one for younger readers, the other for older ones. *Shades of Black: A Celebration of Our Children* by Sandra Pinkney, with photographs by Myles Pinkney, is a tribute to the concept of similarities/differences. The children photographed are all African American of different shades of black, with a variety of eye colors and hair textures. Although it is a picture book, the concepts are universal and appealing to all ages. Walter Dean Myers presents the stories of a community and the people in it. *145th Street: Short Stories* tell of teens and others who live in this Harlem block. Typical of life in many communities, there are special happenings, unhappy situations, and always things that make us laugh.

Asian Americans

The books shared here reflect the values of the cultures, such as cooperation and a respect for the family and tradition. They, too, are found in all genres.

For younger children, two books tell the story of adoptions from China. *Our Baby from China* by Nancy D'Antonio is a photo essay of her experiences, formatted as a photo album. In the second book, *Mommy Far, Mommy Near* by Carol Peacock, Elizabeth learns about her mother in China and why she was adopted. Both of these books show loving families who very much wanted their new babies from China. Another picture book, *The American Wei* by Marion Pomeranc, tells the story of a young boy who is as excited about losing a tooth as he is about his family taking part in the naturalization process. There are a few notes about the process of naturalization so that children can be introduced to this important topic. Roseanne Thong uses a book about shapes, *Round Is a Mooncake: A Book of Shapes*, to introduce young readers to Chinese culture. This is an intriguing book for older children as well.

Janet Wong, who writes poetry for children, is an Asian American whose family came from Korea and China. Her poetry provides readers with insight into her cultures. In *The Trip Back Home*, Wong writes of visiting her mother's home in Korea when she was a child. She and her mother choose gifts to take, participate in the daily routine, and then receive gifts as they are leaving. *Good Luck Gold and Other Poems* and *A Suitcase of Seaweed and Other Poems* are other books well worth reading; in them, Wong explores her cultural heritage.

Several books of contemporary realistic fiction about Asian Americans exist in which the characters try to balance the expectations of their families and their need to fit in with their friends. Rachina Gilmore tells of Mina, whose East Indian grandfather moves in with her family. Even though she loves him very much, she is both embarrassed by him and angry at her friends who make fun of him. *Mina's Spring of Colors* shows how she was able to come to an understanding of the situation because of her grandfather's wisdom. In *Gold-Threaded Dress*, Oy, a Thai American fourth grader, wants very much to fit in with the popular girls. To do this, she brings her grandmother's ceremonial dress to school. The girls tear the dress and Oy is not only blamed for being the instigator, but she must explain the situation to her mother. Carolyn Marsden has presented a situation that many young people can identify with—the conflict between doing something that may not be acceptable to one's family and the need for acceptance by peers. A similar theme is developed by Marie Lee in *F Is for Fabuloso*, a book for older students. Jin-Ha moves from Korea, attends a middle school, and finds that the customs there are very different from those accepted by her family. She does begin to make friends but the adjustment from one country to another is very difficult.

In a more complex book, An Na's *A Step from Heaven*, the move from Korea to California proves to be devastating to Young Ju's family. The story begins when she is 4 and ends when she leaves for college. The family must live with relatives and Young Ju's parents try to survive on low-paying jobs. Her father is not able to cope and becomes an abusive alcoholic. However, she has the courage to make a decision that impacts her family and there is reason for hope as she leaves for college.

John Son's *Finding My Hat* is as much the story of a Korean family adjusting to life in the United States as it is of Jin-Han Park. His father decides that, to be a success, he must go into business for himself, opening a wig store. This creates an interesting situation for one of Jin-Han's friends. In each vignette, Jin-Han grows up a little more, while we observe his family's racial tensions, parental spats, and friendships. Readers can easily identify with the characters and situations as they begin to understand this family's culture.

Latino/as

Gary Soto, a popular Latino author, suggests that readers need to determine if the author is from the culture. "It can't be done from the outside—it's too hard to get it right" (n.d.). His advice also is to look for books that tell a good story rather than ones that deal with social issues. Books that use Spanish words and phrases generally help to present a realistic view of Latinos.

A series of multicultural books for beginning readers, published by Bebop Books, portray a variety of cultures, not just Latino, and all have an English and a Spanish edition. One book, *Confetti Eggs* by Dani Sneed and Josie Fonseca, shows how to make cascarones, confetti-filled eggs that are a Latino tradition. Another, Lorena Heydenburk's *Seven Cookies*, is the story of a Mexican-American girl and her grandfather making and sharing cookies.

Music is an important part of the Latino culture. Jose-Luis Orozco has selected, arranged, and translated songs for children into two books. *Diez Deditos and Other Play Rhymes and Action Songs from Latin America* is a compilation of finger rhymes and action songs from Spanish-speaking countries. *"De Colores" and other Latin-American Folk Songs for Children* is a collection of folk songs. The lyrics in these books are in both English and Spanish.

Folk tales are also an integral part of the Latino culture. Two are particularly intriguing. Subcomandante Marcos tells *The Story of Colors/La Historia de los Colores*, in which the gods decide to expand the number of colors. The text is in both English and Spanish; the illustrations are in the style of stained glass. Tolerance and respect for diversity are the themes. The author is a Zapatista leader; the NEA later retracted funding for the book. A version of the Tortoise and the Hare is presented in Pat Mora's *The Race of Toad and Deer*. There is more trickery used to win the race than in the traditional story, so a comparison between the two folk tales could be the basis for interesting discussions.

A series of biographies about famous Hispanics has recently become available. The life stories of *Ella Ochoa: The First Hispanic Woman Astronaut*, *Selena Perez: Queen of Tejano Music*, and *Roberto Clemente: Baseball Hall of Famer* are a few of the titles in the *Great Hispanics of our Time* series, written by Maritza Romero. The series is written for younger readers. Gary Soto has also written several biographies, two of which are *Cesar Chavez: A Hero for Everyone* and *Jessie de La Cruz: A Profile of a United Farm Worker*. Jessie de La Cruz was the UFW's first female recruiter. The way she rose from poverty and worked with Cesar Chavez is a fascinating story.

There are two realistic fiction books about Latino migrant workers. Pam Munoz Ryan tells the story of a Mexican girl from a wealthy family in *Esperanza Rising*. After her father is killed, she and her mother have no money, so they travel to California to work in the fields. This extreme change in status causes Esperanza to reevaluate her priorities and, with difficulty, she learns that she can be successful in this new situation as well. *First Day in Grapes* by L. King Perez is the story of Chico, a young migrant boy who begins third grade with much apprehension. However, because of the support of his family and his ability in math, he is able to confront both the bullies from fourth grade and the grouchy bus driver.

Gary Soto's *Taking Sides* looks at issues of loyalty, friendship, racial identity, and prejudice in the context of basketball. When Lincoln Mendoza moves from the barrio to an upper-middle class neighborhood, his basketball skills earn him a place on the team at his new school. However, as the only dark-skinned player on a team of White players, he faces prejudice and discrimination from the other members. However, his greatest challenge comes when his former team from the barrio plays his new team. He must make some very difficult decisions that will impact his life. Another book by Soto, *Baseball in April and Other Stories*, is a collection of 11 short stories about young people living in a Mexican-American neighborhood. They have many of the typical problems of growing up in addition to dealing with poverty.

In *Any Small Goodness: A Novel of the Barrio*, Tony Johnston has Arturo Rodriguez tell the story of living in the barrio of East Los Angeles. He is lucky enough to have the support of a loving family, but tragedies are a regular part of life there. Nonetheless, after tragedies there are positive events, so the book is one in which there is optimism. Spanish words are included in the story, along with a glossary that explains them.

Matthew Olshan bases his book *Finn* on Mark Twain's *The Adventures of Huckleberry Finn.* However, Finn, in this book, is a female and Jim is a pregnant Mexican maid. Their adventures have similarities to the original but are obviously set within the parameters of contemporary life. They face many dangers—beatings, kidnappings, and attempted sexual assault. Readers will find it interesting to do a paired reading between the two books if they want to investigate and compare some of the social issues found in both books.

Frances R. Aparicio's *Latino Voices* collects the writings of many influential and powerful Latino authors. Some of the topics included (homes, families, faith, and work) are ones that have a commonality with all races and cultures, but are presented from the Latino perspective. Other topics specifically deal with issues that are more unique to this culture (language, identity, race, and racial discrimination). She makes the point that, although the U.S. government has labeled them Hispanic, this descriptor erases their "multiple ethnic heritages" (p. 10). *Latino* and *Latina* are the preferred labels. Before each selection of fiction, nonfiction, or poetry, a brief context is presented about the author and/or the piece of writing. Photographs are also used to supplement the text.

Jewish

Books about Jewish culture, as is true of books in all categories, need to entertain, not preach. The plots should not be overshadowed by the theme.

There are some people who may not consider history to be very interesting. Those people, specifically, should read *Strudel Stories* by Joanne Rocklin. In this book, Rocklin recounts the stories of her family history, told while family members are eating apple strudel or working together. While humorous and touching, the stories are historically accurate, which makes them useful as a basis for many interesting classroom activities during which readers can make connections with their own lives.

Two picture books help readers understand some of the Jewish symbols and customs. Sarah Lamstein gives a first-person narrative of the events taking place Friday at sundown through Saturday night in *Annie's Shabbat.* Eve Bunting makes readers a part of a Hanukkah ceremony in which the grandmother tells of her experiences as a 12-year-old in Buchenwald. *One Candle* moves between the present and her time spent in the concentration camp.

In 1993 a rock crashed through the window of a Jewish family who had menorahs displayed in the windows of their home. Two children, one Jewish, one not, and their families were able to involve the whole community in the fight against bigotry and acts of hatred. *The Christmas Menorahs: How a Town Fought Hate* by Janice Cohn is based on actual events in Billings, Montana. It is a wonderful basis for a classroom discussion.

Books of traditional literature also help readers understand other cultures. Leslie Kimmelman shares a version of *The Gingerbread Man* in her book *The Runaway Latkes.* In this story, the latkes run away, with no intention of being eaten. An equally interesting book by Eric Kimmel is based on a traditional Hasidic legend. Gershon never regrets or atones for his mistakes—he just sweeps them into his basement. On Rosh Hashanah he puts them into a bag and dumps them in the Black Sea. Of course, they come back to haunt him and he learns that he must acknowledge his mistakes. *Gershon's Monster: A Story for the Jewish New Year* is one that will be of interest to readers of all ages. The last example is a book of 12 folk tales that take place during different Jewish holidays. Each folk tale is from one to three pages long and is followed by a description of the holiday. *The Day the Rabbi Disappeared: Jewish Holiday Tales of Magic* by Howard Schwartz can be used with young readers as well as older ones.

Karen Levine's *Hana's Suitcase* is based on a Canadian documentary in which a suitcase comes to be a part of the Tokyo Holocaust Education Resource Center. Fumiko Ishioka searches to find information about the owner. The format of the story is that every other chapter is about Hana Brady, who was killed at Auschwitz, and the others are about Fumiko's experiences in trying to find clues about Hana. Hana's brother, George, survived and fills in many details. Each chapter includes photographs, and a CD of the story is also available.

In *With All My Heart, With All My Mind: Thirteen Stories About Growing Up Jewish*, edited by Sandy Asher, well-known writers tell what it was (is and could be) like growing up Jewish. Their stories are set in the past, present, and future; accompanying each story is an interview with the author and a biography. The book makes a real contribution to young adult literature. Some of the authors who have contributed to this book are Jacqueline Dember Greene, Phyllis Shalant, Eric Kimmel, and Susan Beth Pfeffer. This is another book to which readers are able to make connections to the lives of young people who may live in a culture different than their own.

The last book, *Forged in Freedom: Shaping the Jewish-American Experience* by Norman Finkelstein, presents the contributions and the difficulties encountered by Jews in the United States. Although most of the personal accounts are positive, descriptions of anti-Semitism are also presented. The photographs help make the context of each account more realistic. Profiles of famous Jewish Americans are presented, as well as a time line and chapter notes. Reading this book allows non-Jewish readers to have a better understanding of the issues relating to immigration and assimilation. Readers from all cultures have the opportunity to learn about events and issues that are often ignored.

Other Groups

Interracial/multicultural

Recently published books have either been multicultural in nature or are explicitly interracial. These books present a much-needed perspective that can provide insight and acceptance that was perhaps not known in the past.

A wonderful picture book for children of all races is Sandra Pinkney's *A Rainbow All Around Me*, with photographs by Myles Pinkney. This presentation for learning about colors is one in which children can see that all colors and ethnic groups are important. Similarly, Marci Curtis's book *Big Sister, Little Sister* is a celebration of four pairs of multicultural sisters who are having fun as they help each other, play together, and learn together.

There are five notable books for older students. The first is a book in which six 12- and 13-year-olds of different races (Hispanic, Arab, Asian, Caucasian, African American, and Native American) describe how their ethnic backgrounds impact their daily lives. The photographs and first-person narratives present insights that all of us can learn from. *Under Our Skin: Kids Talk About Race* by Debbie Birdseye and Tom Birdseye would be very useful to facilitate discussions in middle-school classrooms.

Kristine Franklin's book of historical fiction, *Grape Thief*, is the story of Slava, nicknamed "Cuss" because he can swear in 14 different languages. Cuss likes school and reading; he does not want to drop out of school and work in the coal mines like his older brothers. However, when they must leave town, the responsibility for the family falls upon his shoulders. He must make decisions about remaining in school and how to support his family.

The three remaining books deal explicitly with individuals who are interracial. In 1999, there was a reunion of Thomas Jefferson's family members at Monticello. DNA tests established that Jefferson and his slave, Sally Hemmings, had been the parents of six children. This book is a product of this reunion, which was attended by both the Jefferson and Hemmings branches of the family. Shannon Lanier, a fifth great-grandson of Jefferson, and photographer Jane Feldman present a fascinating history of this famous man and his descendants in *Jefferson's Children: The Story of One American Family*.

Rain Is Not My Indian Name by Cynthia Leitich Smith is the story of a 14-year-old girl with an interracial heritage. When Galen, her best friend, dies, her whole world falls apart. She isolates herself until her family tries to send her to "Indian Camp." The camp becomes the focus of the town's controversy and Rain becomes the photographer for the local newspaper. Through Rain's journal entries, readers are able to see into her mind and heart, and we feel we are a part of her healing and growth.

TJ is a multiracial teen every coach wants on his team because of his outstanding athletic ability. TJ, however, hates the competition of organized sports and cross-town rivalries. When a teacher convinces him to become the head of the swim team, he collects a group of peers who all seem to be big-time losers. As we read about the abuse and racism he must endure, readers are able to gain insight of this very real character. Chris Crutcher's *Whale Talk* is a book that would be interesting to middle-school students, both boys and girls.

The last book, *Murals: Walls that Sing* by George Ancona, is a photo essay of murals from many cultures. He focuses on murals found in the United States, but also includes those found in Mexico as well as caves in prehistoric France. The graffiti memorials in Harlem, the murals in Boston's Chinatown, and those found in Philadelphia and Chicago all have a story to tell about the connections between the arts and activism. The book is a tribute to multiculturalism.

Amish

Because books about the Amish are written by those who are not themselves members of the culture, readers must remember that the "outsider" perspective, even if sensitively done, is presented. Most of the recently published books are informational, although a few are found in other genres. Also, many of these books are written for younger readers but can be used with older readers as the beginning sources of information for more in-depth studies.

Three books present information about the Amish through the use of photographs and text. Although *Amish Ways* by Ruth Hoover Seitz focuses on Lancaster County, Pennsylvania, the area most highly populated by the Amish, the book also includes photos of other Amish communities. A historical overview is given in which readers learn about some of the values held by this group. *Amish Home* by Raymond Bial takes readers on a tour of a culture that is more like that found in the 1800s than the present. His photographs are of objects and places because the Amish do not like to have their pictures taken. He also shares much interesting information about their way of living and the values by which they live. Phyllis Pellman Good, a native of Lancaster County, Pennsylvania, has written a book that describes the lives and responsibilities of *Amish Children*. The photos of the children and their families help us better understand what it might be like to live in an Amish community. (She has also written an excellent cookbook of recipes adapted from those of Old Order Amish cooks—*The Best of Amish Cooking*!)

Three books written by Richard Ammon and illustrated by Pamela Patrick present other aspects of Amish life. The first, *An Amish Year*, gives an overview of the responsibilities, events, and holidays that occur. The illustrations include quilt designs, and the author's note provides useful information not in the text. In the second book, Ammon shows the important role that horses play: they are used for transportation and farming as well as being an integral part of the whole fabric of Amish life. *Amish Horses* also includes broader aspects of Amish culture as well as a useful glossary. The last of these books shares a very specific event, *An Amish Wedding*, as told from the perspective of the bride's younger sister. Again, the customs and events are realistically described.

The last informational book, *20 Most Asked Questions about the Amish and Mennonites*, is written by Merle Good and Phyllis Pellman Good, who serve as executive directors of the People's Place, an educational center that explores the Amish culture and life. Questions about clothing, ways of living, celebrations, and the similarities and differences between the Amish and Mennonites are addressed. The bibliography is useful as a resource for further study.

A historical fiction picture book by Marguerite De Angeli is particularly interesting. In *Henner's Lydia*, which takes place in the 1930s, Lydia is supposed to be making her hooked mat so she can go to market with her father. She would much rather be doing other things, just as children today would.

Four books of contemporary realistic fiction are set in Amish communities. *Just Plain Fancy* by Patricia Polacco tells the story of two young girls who find an egg that hatches into a peacock. However, the girls are afraid that the bird is too fancy for their "plain" culture. Jane Yolen tells the story of how 8-year-old Matthew helps the men in *Raising Yoder's Barn*. Merle Good tells the story of what happens when a quilt made by Reuben's mother and sisters is stolen off their porch. Instead of reporting the theft to authorities, Reuben's father puts the matching pillow cases on the porch as well. The quilt is returned the next morning in *Reuben and the Quilt*. Although it is unlikely that a young Amish girl would be allowed to travel by herself, Hannah visits Chicago and connects everything she sees with something back home. Her letters tell of her trip in Sarah Stewart's *The Journey*.

Appalachian

The area of "Appalachia" is often considered to be the mountain areas from northern Georgia to southwestern Pennsylvania. The stereotype is that Appalachians are White, rural mountain people. The reality is that some Appalachians are African Americans and Native Americans. Today, people with Appalachian roots are found in every segment of society, not just in the rural mountain areas of the southeast or the urban inner cities. The literature presented here includes books about all of these groups.

To gain an overview of Appalachian lifestyles and customs, Linda Pack's *A Is for Appalachia: The Alphabet Book of Appalachian Heritage* presents, through beautiful illustrations and text, many of the cultural artifacts and customs of this area. It is a book written not just for younger readers but for anyone who wants to learn about this area. To learn about some of the interesting aspects of the early 1800s, a living history museum has been created in Fort New Salem, Virginia. George Ancona has photographed the village and its inhabitants, telling the story through the fictional Davis family. *Pioneer Children of Appalachia* gives readers a window into this time period. A wonderful description of a later period of time, the Great Depression, is given in Kathi Appelt's *Down Cut Shin Creek: The Pack Horse Librarians of Kentucky*. Through the WPA, Franklin Roosevelt created the Pack Horse Library Program. Young women carried books and magazines to people who lived in very rural locations in eastern Kentucky who otherwise would have had no access to a library. A reconstructed description of what might be a typical day for the young women who carried the books makes this era come alive.

Many books of traditional literature are set in Appalachia. Only two will be reviewed here because many of them were published several years ago. Nancy Van Laan's *With a Whoop and a Holler: A Bushel of Lore from Way Down South* is a collection of folk tales. One section is devoted to Appalachian stories. These tales are typical and useful with the other two sections for comparison and contrast. Another collection of folk tales is *Living Stories of the Cherokee*, edited by Barbara Duncan. The language in this book is especially appropriate with the stories told in free verse, which is representative of the style of storytellers.

An original trickster tale, *Aunt Nancy and Cousin Lazybones* by Phyllis Root, tells the humorous story of what happens when Aunt Nancy outwits a lazy relative who comes to stay with her. When she tries to give him chores, like filling the water bucket, he leaves it outside until it rains. Finally Aunt Nancy has had enough. She, herself, does no chores. When Cousin Lazybones realizes that he will have to do some work, he leaves. A mountain dialect is used, which fits in with the setting and the story.

Several books of historical fiction are set in Appalachia. *Bright Freedom's Song* by Gloria Houston tells the story of how escaping slaves were hidden and smuggled to the next safe house on the Underground Railroad. Bright Cameron, a young girl, actively works with her family to make sure that the fleeing slaves move safely north. She is as brave as the adults—both African American and White.

Cornelia Cornelissen's *Soft Rain: A Story of the Cherokee Trail of Tears* is told from the perspective of a 9-year-old who must leave her beloved grandmother behind as her people are moved from North Carolina to Oklahoma. Her family is separated on the trip but most of them are reunited west of the Mississippi. The author includes a description of the background of this horrible forced removal of the Cherokees as well as an extensive bibliography of both fiction and nonfiction books.

The Appalachian African-American experience in the early 1900s in Tennessee is told in Elizabeth Partridge's *Clara and the Hoodoo Man*. This novel, based on the life of Clara Raglan, presents many aspects of the culture that are associated with the mountain traditions. We see her family as they raise and store food, gather ginseng, and celebrate the Juneteenth holiday. Although Clara's mother is afraid of Hoodoo, it is the mountain tradition of the African-American Hoodoo Man who heals her sister when she becomes ill.

In a story set during World War II, 11-year-old Blessing and her grandmother demonstrate the independence associated with living by themselves. After the deaths of Blessing's grandfather, father, and mother, she and her grandmother develop an intensely close and loving relationship. Monnie has filled her life with love, music, and storytelling; together, they garden and do daily chores. Now, however, she is aging, and they both know her death is imminent. Monnie picks out guardians for Blessing to choose from, but Blessing doesn't like any of them. Patricia Hermes writes about a strong-willed girl who faces life, even the unpleasant aspects of it, courageously and on her own in *Sweet By and By*.

Caroline, the youngest of four sisters, lives with her single mom. All of the girls, except for Caroline, seem to have found something that makes them special. Caroline still doesn't know what makes her special. Then *Tadpole*, their musical 13-year-old cousin, shows up. The family discovers that Tadpole is being abused by his guardian and they protect him. Tadpole also sees in Caroline characteristics not noticed by her family, and she finally discovers why she is special, too. The mountain dialect, the positive view of life, and the way that the characters interact make readers care about this family. Ruth White, who is also the author of *Belle Prater's Boy* and *Memories of Summer*, again demonstrates that she is a master storyteller.

Jessie is a 12-year-old who is addressing many issues in her life. She doesn't know who her father is, her best friend Robert needs glasses his family can't afford, and she has a temper that she really can't control. When a VISTA volunteer and photographers come to her small Kentucky town to write a story about poverty, she thinks that she can earn money to pay for Robert's glasses by showing them around. When the article is in the national news, revealing the worst aspects of her town and friends, she is in trouble. Serious issues—alcoholism, poverty, rape—are addressed sensitively in Shutta Crum's *Spitting Image*.

Two books by George Ella Lyon, who grew up in Appalachia, are set in contemporary times. *Momma Is a Miner* tells of a girl whose mother works in the mines. Both realize the dangers of this but the daughter is proud of her mother and her work. There is a mix of information and story. The illustrations in this book are superb and include details that make the setting feel authentic. A novel for older readers, *Gina. Jamie. Father. Bear.*, tells of two girls who live in very different settings with their fathers after their mothers have left them. One lives in Shaker Heights, Ohio; the other in a world that seems ancient. The novel focuses on the girls and their fathers as they try to come to terms with themselves and their families.

Classroom Activities

ACTIVITY 13.1   COMPARING CULTURES

(IRA/NCTE Standards: 1, 2, 9, 11. Read to understand cultures of U.S. and the world; to respect diversity.)

A good way to introduce cultural studies is to discuss culture with children. Explain that *culture* includes manners, feelings about self and other people, religion, right and wrong, education, entering adulthood, holidays, foods, clothes, and games—all the things we learned from our parents, grandparents, friends, neighbors, churches, and schools (Stoodt, 1992).

Ask the children to brainstorm what they have learned from each aspect of their cultures. Make lists of their ideas on the chalkboard or on charts. Organize the material into a chart like the one in Figure 13.1. Older students can create individual charts.

FIGURE 13.1   Chart of cultural teachings.

WHAT I LEARNED FROM MY . . .

Parents	Grandparents	Teachers	Friends	School	Church
To say thank you	To bake cookies	To read	To jump rope	To communicate	To pray

ACTIVITY 13.2   CONTEMPORARY STORIES

(IRA/NCTE Standards: 1, 2, 9, 11. Reading a range of texts to understand U.S. and world cultures. Develop respect for diversity.)

Read aloud a contemporary story from another culture and have the students compare the cultural information with their own lives. A Venn diagram is helpful in making this comparison.

ACTIVITY 13.3   MAPPING CULTURES

(IRA/NCTE Standards: 1, 2, 9, 11. Learn about one's own culture; cultures from various geographic areas.)

Have each student make a map of his or her culture using Figure 13.2 as a model. Culture maps can be the basis for bulletin boards. As students learn about culture, they can create culture maps for characters in stories.

FIGURE 13.2   Culture map. (Students fill in information about their individual culture in the circles.)

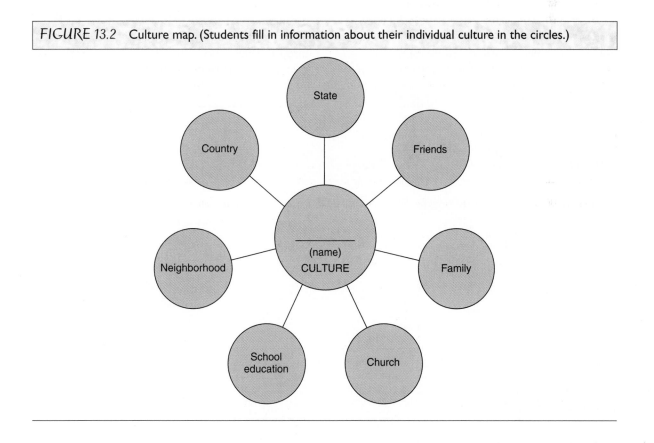

ACTIVITY 13.4 CULTURAL COLLAGES

(IRA/NCTE Standards: 1, 2. About culture.)

Discuss special family ways of celebrating holidays and birthdays, favorite colors, favorite foods, places they have lived, family size and composition, family education, religion, and values. Then students can make collages using magazine pictures (or those drawn by students), squares of colored paper, wallpaper, newspaper, cloth, and objects or symbols that are important to the individual to create collages representing their family's culture.

ACTIVITY 13.5 FAMILY TREES

(IRA/NCTE Standards: 1, 2. Studying the nature of culture)

Create family trees, going as far back into family history as possible. Older students can learn how to research the family genealogy. Studies such as these sometimes give students clues about family ways of doing things that they did not realize had cultural implications. For example, this kind of research led one of the authors to Pennsylvania Dutch connections through family foods, names, and the stories her grandfather told. Faith Ringgold's book *Talking to Faith Ringgold* is very helpful.

ACTIVITY 13.6 COMPARING FOLK TALES

(IRA/NCTE Standards: 1, 2, 9, 11. Read a range of literature to build understanding of various cultures.)

Students can compare the Cinderella story in various cultures, such as *Cinderella* (European), *The Rough-Face Girl* (Native American), and *Yeh-Shen* (Chinese). Figure 13.3 illustrates a comparison chart.

ACTIVITY 13.7 TRADITIONAL STORIES

(IRA/NCTE Standards: 1, 2, 9, 11. Read to identify characteristics of culture.)

Read aloud or have students read three traditional stories or poems from the same culture and identify the recurrent themes and details in these stories. A chart with headings such as those in Figure 13.3 will help them organize their ideas.

FIGURE 13.3 Chart for comparing traditional stories.

Title and Author	Main Character	Setting	Problem	How Solved	Conclusion
Cinderella Marcia Brown	Cinderella	European house and castle	Mean stepmother and stepsisters	The prince finds her and proposes.	They marry and live happily ever after.
The Rough-Face Girl Rafe Martin	An Algonquin girl with a rough face	Native American	The tribe rejects her scarred face	She can see the Invisible Being.	She marries the Invisible Being.
Yeh-Shen: A Cinderella Story from China Ai-Ling Louie	Yeh-Shen	China	Her stepmother kills the fish that is Yeh-Shen's friend and eats it	The fish's magic resides in its bones. The magic provides her with clothing for a festival.	She loses her slipper, and the King searches for her and marries her.
Cendrillon: A Caribbean Cinderella Robert D. San Souci	Cendrillon	Island of Martinique	Mean stepmother and stepsister	Godmother who is washer woman performs magic.	Cendrillon wears slipper and dances with bridegroom.
The Golden Sandal: A Middle-Eastern Cinderella Rebecca Hickox	Maha	Middle East	Mean stepmother and stepsister	Redfish is fairy godmother.	She is saved by a gold sandal; marries Tariq.
The Turkey Girl: A Zuni Cinderella Story Penny Pollock	Turkey girl	Zuni Indian, Western United States	Goes to great feast but does not return in time	Turkeys.	Turkeys are gone.

Summary

The United States has been a multicultural society since its earliest times. Ethnic, linguistic, and racial minorities have made significant contributions to the society we have today. These contributions and the cultural groups who made them need to be appreciated and regarded as an integral part of American life. If firsthand experiences with different cultural groups are not available, reading about them may be the best way to explore and develop an appreciation for this diversity. Well-written multicultural literature can be the vehicle for creating this sensitivity for differences and similarities. This literature can be a key to allowing children and young adults from all backgrounds and cultures to see themselves and how they fit in with other cultural groups. Sensitive teachers have the ability to create equitable educational opportunities for all of their students so that they are able to identify with characters who look like they do and to respect those who do not. Teachers will also learn that the students have much to teach us—if we create the ways to make the children feel safe as they discuss issues of personal and cultural importance to them. If teachers can give children the freedom to discuss and make their own connections, teachers have the freedom and the responsibility to listen and learn (Copenhaver, 2001).

At this time, the beginning of the 21st century, our society is becoming extremely global. Changes are occurring that will continue to impact people throughout the world. The children and young adults may adapt to these changes more easily if they know about and respect cultures other than their own. Using multicultural literature is one practical way this process can begin.

Books on Tape and CD that Have a Multicultural Setting

All of these materials are published by Listening Library, an imprint of the Random House Audio Publishing Group, Old Greenwich, Connecticut.

Crutcher, C., *Whale Talk*
Mikaelsen, B., *Touching Spirit Bear*
Na, A., *A Step from Heaven*
Ryan, P. M., *Esperanza Rising*
Smith, C. L., *Rain Is Not My Indian Name*
White, R., *Belle Prater's Boy*

Awards for Multicultural Literature

In addition to the Coretta Scott King Award and the Pura Belpre' Award, which are described in the Appendix, the following awards are given to multicultural books:

The *Americas Award* is given in recognition of U.S. works of fiction, poetry, folklore, or selected nonfiction published in the previous year in English or Spanish that authentically and engagingly portray Latin America, the Caribbean, or Latinos in the United States.

**www.eduDept/CLAS/outreach.
american.html**

The *Thomas Rivera Award* is given to a distinguished work that authentically reflects the Mexican-American experience.

**www.education.swt.edu/Rivera/
mainpage.html**

The *New Voices Award* was established by Lee & Low books to encourage people of color to write stories for children and submit them to a publisher who strives to diversify the face of children's books.

www.leeandlow.com/home/news/html

Children's Literature References and Recommended Books

Note: Books designated with an asterisk (*) are recommended for reluctant readers.

Ammon, R. (1998). *An Amish wedding* (P. Patrick, Illus.). New York: Atheneum. (1–4). PICTURE BOOK.

This account of an Amish wedding is told from the perspective of the bride's younger sister.

Ammon, R. (2000). *An Amish year* (P. Patrick, Illus.). New York: Atheneum. (1–4). PICTURE BOOK.

A description of the events that occur during a typical year in an Amish community.

Ammon, R. (2001). *Amish horses* (P. Patrick, Illus.). New York: Atheneum. (1–4). PICTURE BOOK.

This book presents a look at the important role of horses in Amish life.

Ancona, G. (1990). *Pioneer children of Appalachia*. Boston, MA: Houghton Mifflin. (3–6). PICTURE BOOK.

This photo essay portrays a living history village in West Virginia.

Ancona, G. (2003). *Murals: Walls that sing.* New York: Marshall Cavendish. (4–7). INFORMATIONAL BOOK.

Text and photographs of the murals found in U.S. cities and in other places in the world create a vision of how art and activism are naturally joined.

Aparicio, F. R. (Ed.). (1994). *Latino voices.* Brookfield, CT: Millbrook Press. (6–10). MIXED GENRE.

A look at Latino life and culture through the use of portions of texts from many fiction, nonfiction, and poetry authors.

Appelt, K. A. (2001). *Down Cut Shin Creek: The pack horse librarians of Kentucky* (J. C. Schmitzer, Illus.). New York: HarperCollins. (4–8). INFORMATIONAL BOOK.

This is the story of early Kentucky librarians.

Asher, S. (Ed.). (1999). *With all my heart, with all my mind: Thirteen stories about growing up Jewish.* New York: Simon & Schuster. (6–10). INFORMATIONAL BOOK.

Thirteen authors share their experiences that describe growing up Jewish.

Bartoletti, S. C. (2000). *A coal miner's bride: The diary of Anetka Kaminska.* New York: Hyperion. (4–6). HISTORICAL FICTION.

Thirteen-year-old Anetka comes to the United States to be the bride of a man with three small children. She soon becomes a widow but is united with the young man she loves.

Bial, R. (1995). *Amish home.* Boston, MA: Houghton Mifflin. (3–7). INFORMATIONAL BOOK.

Photographs and text describe Amish life; no photographs of people are included.

Bial, R. (2002). *Tenement: Immigrant life on the lower east side.* Boston, MA: Houghton Mifflin. (4–8). INFORMATIONAL BOOK.

This book provides a description, with photographs, of an area where immigrants lived in great poverty.

Birdseye, D. H., & Birdseye, T. (1997). *Under our skin: Kids talk about race* (R. Crum, Photog.). New York: Holiday House. (6–8). INFORMATIONAL BOOK.

This book features photographs and essays by six teenagers of different races.

Bode, J. (1995). *New kids in town: Oral histories of immigrant teens.* New York: Scholastic. (6–10). INFORMATIONAL BOOK.

This book features interviews with teenagers who are adjusting to living in the United States.

Bode, J. (1999). *Colors of freedom: Immigrant stories.* New York: Scholastic. (6–10). INFORMATIONAL BOOK.

Teenagers who have come to America recently and those whose ancestors were slaves or slave owners share their stories, poems, and recipes.

Bruchac, J. (1997). *Bowman's store: A journey to myself.* New York: Dial. (7–10). AUTOBIOGRAPHY.

Bruchac tells of his family confusion when he was a child. He learned about prejudice and why his family did not admit to their native roots.

Bruchac, J. (1998a). *Earth under Sky Bear's feet: Native American poems of the land* (T. Locker, Illus.). New York: Scholastic. (K–3). POETRY, TRADITIONAL LITERATURE.

Twelve poems told by a grandmother tell the legend of Sky Bear (the Big Dipper).

Bruchac, J. (1998b). *Many nations: An alphabet of Native America* (R. F. Goetezl, Illus.). New York: Troll. (K–2). INFORMATIONAL BOOK.

Each letter in this book represents a tribe or animal. The diverse nature of Native Americans is explicit in the illustrations and the text.

Bruchac, J. (2000). *Sacajawea.* New York: Harcourt. (4–7). BIOGRAPHY.

Sacajawea's story for her son is told through her eyes and those of William Clark.

Bruchac, J. (2002). *Winter people* (J. Bernadin, Illus.). New York: Penguin Putnam. (6–10). HISTORICAL FICTION.

An Abenaki youth journeys to save his family during the French and Indian War.

Buckley, G. (2002). *American patriots: The story of Blacks in the military from the Revolution to Desert Storm.* New York: Random House. (6–10). INFORMATIONAL BOOK.

A recounting of the long and difficult battle for recognition and promotion of African Americans in the military.

Bunting, E. (2002). *One candle* (W. Popp, Illus.). New York: Joanna Cotler/HarperCollins Childrens. (K–3). PICTURE BOOK.

Flashbacks of Grandma's time in Buchenwald prison are shared during Hanukkah.

Carbone, E. (2001). *Stealing freedom.* New York: Random House. (6–10). HISTORICAL FICTION.

Ann escapes from her cruel mistress on the Underground Railroad. The book is based on the life of a real person.

Carbone, E. (2002). *Storm warriors.* New York: Random House. (6–10). HISTORICAL FICTION.

Nathan wants to join the only African-American crew in the U.S. Lifesaving Service. He chooses a different goal after the experience.

Cech, J. (1998). *My grandmother's journey* (S. McGinley-Nally, Illus.). New York: Simon & Schuster. (K–3). PICTURE BOOK.

A grandmother's story as she lives in Russia and immigrates to the United States through Ellis Island.

Cohn, J. (1995). *The Christmas menorahs: How a town fought hate.* Morton Grove, IL: Albert Whitman. (2–6). CONTEMPORARY REALISTIC FICTION.

When a rock is thrown through the window of a Jewish family, the community rallies to fight bigotry and hate.

Cornelissen, C. (1998). *Soft rain: A story of the Cherokee Trail of Tears.* New York: Bantam. (5–8). HISTORICAL FICTION.

As told from the perspective of a 9-year-old, readers begin to understand the tragedy of the Cherokees' move from North Carolina to Oklahoma.

Crum, S. (2003). *Spitting image.* Boston, MA: Houghton Mifflin. (6–10). HISTORICAL FICTION.

Jessie's intentions are almost always good—but her temper and her "helping" often get her and others into trouble.

Crutcher, C. (2001). *Whale talk.* New York: Green Willow. (7–10). CONTEMPORARY REALISTIC FICTION.

TJ gathers together an unlikely group of peers to form the swim team.

Curtis, M. (2002). *Big sister, little sister.* New York: Puffin. (K–3). INFORMATIONAL BOOK.

This book includes photographs of four pairs of multicultural sisters interacting with each other.

D'Antonio, N. (1997). *Our baby from China.* Morton Grove, IL: Albert Whitman. (K–3). PICTURE BOOK.

This book is a photo essay of the process of adopting a Chinese baby.

De Angeli, M. (1998). *Henner's Lydia.* Scottdale, PA: Herald Press. (1–4). PICTURE BOOK.

Lydia, a young Amish girl, would rather do other things instead of making the mat that is supposed to go to market.

Draper, S. (1996). *Tears of a tiger.* New York: Simon & Schuster. (6–10). CONTEMPORARY REALISTIC FICTION.

Andy is not able to successfully deal with the death of his friend.

Draper, S. (1997). *Forged by fire.* New York: Simon & Schuster. (6–10). CONTEMPORARY REALISTIC FICTION.

This book is the sequel to *Tears of a Tiger.*

Draper, S. (2001). *Romiette and Julio.* New York: Simon & Schuster. (6–10). CONTEMPORARY REALISTIC FICTION.

An African-American girl and a Hispanic boy fall in love; their families and friends work to have them end their relationship.

Draper, S., & Benabib, M. (2002). *Darkness before dawn.* New York: Simon & Schuster. (6–10). CONTEMPORARY REALISTIC FICTION.

Keisha, Andy's girlfriend, is faced with difficult decisions in her struggle to get over Andy's suicide.

Draper, S., & Gabbidon, O'L. (2002). *Double dutch.* New York: Simon & Schuster. (5–7). CONTEMPORARY REALISTIC FICTION.

Three eighth-grade girls want to compete in the Double Dutch Competition and to solve other difficult issues each faces.

Duncan, B. R. (Ed.). (1998). *Living stories of the Cherokee.* Chapel Hill, NC: University of North Carolina Press. (2–10). TRADITIONAL LITERATURE.

Traditional stories of the Native Americans in North Carolina are told.

Fadin, D. (2000). *Bound for the North Star: True stories of fugitive slaves.* Boston, MA: Clarion. (6–10). INFORMATIONAL BOOK.

This book contains documented accounts of escaped slaves.

Finkelstein, N. H. (2002). *Forged in freedom: Shaping the Jewish-American experience.* (6–10). INFORMATIONAL BOOK.

An account of the roles played by Jewish people in the United States, from the time of immigration to the present.

Franklin, K. L. (2003). *Grape thief* (P. Lee, Illus.). Cambridge, MA: Candlewick Press. (6–9). HISTORICAL FICTION.

Cuss has to decide if he will stay in school, which he wants to do, or drop out to help support his family.

Gilmore, R. (2000). *Mina's spring of colors*. Marhkam, Ontario: Fitzhenry & Whiteside. (4–7). CONTEMPORARY REALISTIC FICTION.

When Mina's East Indian grandfather moves in with her family, she is conflicted because he embarrasses her but she doesn't want her friends to make fun of him.

Golenbock, P. (2001). *Hank Aaron* (P. Lee, Illus.). New York: Gulliver. (K–5). BIOGRAPHY.

Hank Aaron overcomes poverty and racism to accomplish his goal of becoming a baseball player.

Golston, S. E. (1996). *Changing woman of the Apache: Women's lives in past and present*. New York: Franklin Watts. (6–9). INFORMATIONAL BOOK.

This book traces the seasons of women's lives from their coming-of-age ceremony through old age.

Good, M. (1999). *Reuben and the quilt* (P. B. Moss, Illus.). Intercourse, PA: Good Books. (2–5). CONTEMPORARY REALISTIC FICTION.

When a quilt is stolen off Reuben's porch, his father puts out the pillow cases as well. The quilt is subsequently returned.

Good, P. P. (2002). *Amish children* (J. Irwin, Photog.). Intercourse, PA: Good Books. K–3. PICTURE BOOK.

The lives of Amish children are described through text and photographs.

Good, P. P., & Good, M. (1995). *20 most asked questions about the Amish and Mennonites*. Intercourse, PA: Good Books. (4–8). INFORMATIONAL BOOK.

This book contains questions, answers, and a bibliography of additional resources about the Amish culture.

Hansen, J. (1998). *Women of hope: African Americans who made a difference*. New York: Scholastic. (5–10). BIOGRAPHY.

Twelve biographies of women who impacted education, social causes, the arts, and science.

Hansen, J., & McGowan, G. (1997). *Breaking ground, breaking silence: The story of New York's African burial ground*. New York: Henry Holt. (5–10). INFORMATIONAL BOOK.

When excavating for a new building in Manhattan, an old burial ground is found and studied.

Hermes, P. (2002). *Sweet by and by*. New York: HarperCollins. (4–7). HISTORICAL FICTION.

Blessing lives with her grandmother, who passes away.

Heydenburk, L. I. (2001). *Seven cookies* (A. Ochoa, Illus.). New York: Bebop Books. (1–2). CONTEMPORARY REALISTIC FICTION.

A Mexican-American girl and her grandfather make and share cookies.

Hoobler, D., & Hoobler, T. (2003). *We are Americans: Voices of the immigrant experience*. New York: Scholastic. (3–7). INFORMATIONAL BOOK.

Diaries, letters, photographs, and oral histories from many immigrant groups present information about those who moved to this country.

Houston, G. (1998). *Bright freedom's song*: A *story of the Underground Railroad*. New York: Harcourt Brace. (4–7). HISTORICAL FICTION.

A young girl and her family help escaping slaves on the Underground Railroad.

Johnson, D. (2000). *Queenie Blue* (J. Ransome, Illus.). New York: Henry Holt. (K–3). PICTURE BOOK.

Queenie imagines the childhood of her grandmother, after whom she is named.

Johnston, T. (2001). *Any small goodness: A novel of the barrio*. New York: Blue Sky/Scholastic. (4–7). CONTEMPORARY REALISTIC FICTION.

Although Turo is supported by his family and friends, tragedies still occur in his East Los Angeles neighborhood.

Kimmel, E. (2000). *Gershon's monster: A story for the Jewish New Year*. New York: Scholastic. (1–6). TRADITIONAL LITERATURE.

This story is based on a Hasidic legend.

Kimmelman, L. (2000). *The runaway latkes*. Morton Grove, IL: Albert Whitman. (K–3). TRADITIONAL LITERATURE.

In the same manner as the Gingerbread Man, the latkes run away so that they are not eaten.

Krohn, K. (2001). *Ella Fitzgerald: First lady of song*. Minneapolis, MN: Lerner. (4–8). BIOGRAPHY.

Ella Fitzgerald was a very private woman. This biography tells the story of her public life.

Lamstein, S. M. (1997). *Annie's Shabbat*. Morton Grove, IL: Albert Whitman. (K–5). CONTEMPORARY REALISTIC FICTION.

Annie participates in the customs of Shabbat.

Lanier, S., & Feldman, J. (2000). *Jefferson's children: The story of one American family*. New York: Random House. (6–10). INFORMATIONAL BOOK.

In 1999, the descendants of Thomas Jefferson held a family reunion at Monticello. Both the Jefferson and the Hemings branches of the family attended.

Lee, M. G. (1999). *F is for fabuloso*. New York: Avon. (5–8). CONTEMPORARY REALISTIC FICTION.

When Jin-Ha moves from Korea to Minnesota, she has many challenges as she adjusts to going to the middle school.

Levine, K. (2002). *Hana's suitcase*. Morton Grove, IL: Albert Whitman. (4–8). BASED ON A DOCUMENTARY.

When the suitcase of a girl killed at Auschwitz is sent to the Tokyo Holocaust Education Resource Center, the teacher explores and finds out about the owner.

Lyon, G. E. (1994). *Momma is a miner*. New York: Orchard. (1–5). CONTEMPORARY REALISTIC FICTION.

A young girl is proud of the work her mother does as a miner.

Lyon, G. E. (2002). *Gina. Jamie. Father. Bear*. New York: Atheneum/Richard Jackson. (6–10). CONTEMPORARY REALISTIC FICTION.

This story is told from the perspectives of two girls whose mothers have left the family. They and their fathers need to come to terms with their pasts and the present.

Marcos, S. (1999). *The story of colors/La historia de los colores*. El Paso, TX: Cinco Puntos Press. (K–3). TRADITIONAL LITERATURE.

A folk tale, written in both English and Spanish, that stresses the importance of diversity and tolerance.

Marsden, C. (2002). *Gold-threaded dress*. Cambridge, MA: Candlewick Press. (3–6). CONTEMPORARY REALISTIC FICTION.

A Thai-American girl tries to join the group of popular girls by bringing her grandmother's ceremonial dress to school.

McGill, A. (2000). *In the hollow of your hand: Slave lullabies* (M. Cummings, Illus.). Boston, MA: Houghton Mifflin. (K–6). INFORMATIONAL BOOK.

A collection of lullabies sung to the children of slaves.

Mikaelsen, B. (2001). *Touching Spirit Bear*. New York: HarperCollins. (7–10). CONTEMPORARY REALISTIC FICTION.

Cole Matthews chooses a Native-American punishment for his wrongdoings, and nearly dies in the process.

Mora, P. (2001). *The race of toad and deer* (Domi, Illus.). Toronto, Canada: Groundwood Books. (K–3). TRADITIONAL LITERATURE.

A version of the folk tale, *The Tortoise and the Hare*.

Myers, W. D. (1994). *The glory field*. New York: Scholastic. (6–10). HISTORICAL FICTION, CONTEMPORARY REALISTIC FICTION.

This book traces the generations of an African-American family from 1753 in Sierra Leone to the present.

Myers, W. D. (1996). *Slam!* New York: Scholastic. (6–10). CONTEMPORARY REALISTIC FICTION.

Basketball was Greg's passion. He wants to be one of the lucky ones who can make it to the top.

Myers, W. D. (1999). *The journal of Joshua Loper: A black cowboy*. New York: Scholastic. (4–6). HISTORICAL FICTION.

This book is a good reminder that many of the cowboys of the west were African American. They often had challenges the White cowboys did not.

Myers, W. D. (2000). *145th street: Short stories*. New York: Delacorte. (6–10). REALISTIC FICTION.

Life in a Harlem neighborhood is celebrated in these 10 stories of everyday life.

Myers, W. D. (2001). *Bad boy: A memoir*. New York: HarperCollins. (4–7). AUTOBIOGRAPHY.

Walter Dean Myers recounts events in his life growing up in Harlem during the 1940s and 1950s.

Na, A. (2002). *A step from heaven*. New York: Penguin Putnam. (7–10). CONTEMPORARY REALISTIC FICTION.

Young Ju's family emigrates from Korea and finds that the move brings unexpected difficulties. In addition to having a hard time adjusting to this country, her father becomes an abusive alcoholic. By the time she leaves for college, she has learned to make difficult decisions and there is hope in her future.

Olshan, M. (2001). *Finn*. Baltimore, MD: Bancfort Press. (7–10). CONTEMPORARY REALISTIC FICTION.

An adaptation of *The Adventures of Huckleberry Finn* in which Finn is a Latina girl.

Orgill, R. (2002). *If I only had a horn: Young Louis Armstrong* (L. Jenkins, Illus.). Boston, MA: Houghton Mifflin. (5–7). BIOGRAPHY.

The story of how Louis Armstrong became a famous musician.

Orozco, J-L. (2001). *"De Colores" and other Latin-American folk songs for children* (E. Kleven, Illus.). New York: Puffin. (K–3). INFORMATIONAL BOOK.

A collection of folk songs from Latin American countries presented in both English and Spanish.

Orozco, J-L. (2002). *Diez Deditos and other play rhymes and action songs from Latin America* (E. Kleven, Illus.). New York: Puffin. (K–3). INFORMATIONAL BOOK.

A collection of finger rhymes and action songs in both English and Spanish.

Pack, L. H. (2002). *A is for Appalachia!: The alphabet book of Appalachian heritage* (P. Banks, Illus.). New York: Harmony House. (1–6). PICTURE BOOK.

Appalachian heritage is explained through the alphabet.

Partridge, E. (1996). *Clara and the Hoodoo Man.* New York: Puffin. (4–8). HISTORICAL FICTION.

Based on the life of a real person, the daily experiences of living in Tennessee in the early 1900s are told in the form of a novel.

Paulsen, G. (1993). *Nightjohn.* New York: Delacorte. (5–9). HISTORICAL FICTION.

When Nightjohn is caught teaching slaves to read, which is illegal, he is tortured.

Peacock, C. A. (2000). *Mommy far, mommy near* (S. C. Brownell, Illus.). Morton Grove, IL: Albert Whitman. (K–3). PICTURE BOOK.

Elizabeth has questions about why she has two mommies—one here and one in China.

Perez, L. K. (2002). *First day in grapes* (R. Casilla, Illus.). New York: Lee & Low. (2–5). CONTEMPORARY REALISTIC FICTION.

Chico's parents are migrant workers, so when he starts school, he is anxious about how he will be accepted. Because of his excellent math ability, he is confident enough to confront the bullies and the grouchy bus driver.

Pinkney, A. (2000). *Let it shine: Stories of Black women freedom fighters* (S. Alcorn, Illus.). New York: Gulliver. (5–10). BIOGRAPHY.

A collective biography of women who have had a significant impact on society.

Pinkney, S. L. (2000). *Shades of black: A celebration of our children* (M. C. Pinkney, Photog.). New York: Scholastic. (PreK–2). PICTURE BOOK.

Photographs of African-American children in which similarities and differences are valued.

Pinkney, S. L. (2002). *A rainbow all around me* (M. C. Pinkney, Photog.). New York: Cartwheel. (K–2). PICTURE BOOK.

Photographs of children and text are used to learn about colors.

Polacco, P. (1990). *Just plain fancy.* New York: Bantam. (3–6). CONTEMPORARY REALISTIC FICTION.

When an egg hatches into a peacock, the girls worry that it is too fancy to be a part of the Amish community.

Pomeranc, M. H. (1998). *The American Wei* (D. DiSalvo-Ryan, Illus.). Morton Grove, IL: Albert Whitman. (K–3). PICTURE BOOK.

Wei is as excited about the tooth fairy coming as he is about his family being naturalized.

Rappaport, D. (2001). *Martin's big words: The life of Dr. Martin Luther King, Jr.* (B. Collier, Illus.). New York: Hyperion. (K–5). BIOGRAPHY.

This book displays paintings of various events in Dr. King's life, along with some of his most famous quotations.

Rochelle, B. (Ed.). (2000). *Words with wings: A treasury of African-American poetry and art.* New York: Amistad Press. (4–10). INFORMATIONAL BOOK.

This book features a collection of poems paired with appropriate artwork.

Rocklin, J. (1999). *Strudel stories.* New York: Delacorte. (2–8). HISTORICAL AND CONTEMPORARY REALISTIC FICTION.

Recounting stories of family history provides a humorous and insightful look at a Jewish family.

Romero, M. (2001a). *Ellen Ochoa: The first Hispanic woman astronaut.* New York: Rosen. (3–5). BIOGRAPHY.

A biography of Ochoa for younger readers.

Romero, M. (2001b). *Roberto Clemente: Baseball hall of famer.* New York: Rosen. (3–5). BIOGRAPHY.

A biography of Clemente for younger readers.

Romero, M. (2001c). *Selena Perez: Queen of Tejano music.* New York: Rosen. (3–5). BIOGRAPHY.

A biography of Selena for younger readers.

Root, P. (1998). *Aunt Nancy and Cousin Lazybones* (D. Parkins, Illus.). Cambridge, MA: Candlewick Press. (K–4). PICTURE BOOK.

This original trickster tale is set in Appalachia.

Ryan, P. M. (2000). *Esperanza rising*. New York: Scholastic. (4–6). CONTEMPORARY REALISTIC FICTION.

After Esperanza's father is killed, she and her mother must move from Mexico to the United States to work in the fields.

Schwartz, H. (2000). *The day the rabbi disappeared: Jewish holiday tales of magic*. New York: Viking. (5–10). TRADITIONAL LITERATURE.

Twelve stories about the Jewish holidays with additional information about each.

Seitz, R. H. (1993). *Amish ways* (B. Seitz, Illus.). Harrisburg, PA: Rb Books. (4–8). INFORMATIONAL BOOK.

This book includes essays and photographs that provide an understanding of the history and daily life of Amish communities in a variety of locations.

Smith, C. L. (2000). *Jingle dancer* (C. Van Wright & Y-H. Hu, Illus.). New York: William Morrow. (K–4). CONTEMPORARY REALISTIC FICTION.

A young Native-American girl wants to participate in the traditional dance but does not have the needed jingles.

Smith, C. L. (2001). *Rain is not my Indian name*. New York: HarperCollins. (6–8). CONTEMPORARY REALISTIC FICTION.

When Rain's best friend dies, she isolates herself until she becomes the photographer for the newspaper covering a town controversy.

Sneed, D., & Fonseca, J. (2001). *Confetti eggs* (M. Cappellini, Photog.). New York: Bebop Books. (1–2). CONTEMPORARY REALISTIC FICTION.

Making cascarones, a Latino tradition, is demonstrated by a girl and boy.

Son, J. (2003). *Finding my hat*. New York: Orchard Books. (4–8). CONTEMPORARY REALISTIC FICTION.

Readers feel that they are a part of Jin-Han's adjustment after his family moves to the United States.

Soto, G. (2000a). *Baseball in April and other stories*. New York: Harcourt. (6–10). CONTEMPORARY REALISTIC FICTION.

This book includes stories of Latino young people growing up in their Mexican-American community in Fresno, California.

Soto, G. (2000b). *Jessie de la Cruz: A profile of a United Farm Worker*. New York: Persea/Norton Books. (6–10). BIOGRAPHY.

The biography of the first female recruiter for the UFW.

Soto, G. (2003a). *Cesar Chavez: A hero for everyone* (L. Lohstoeter, Illus.). New York: Simon & Schuster. (2–5). BIOGRAPHY.

This is the story of the Mexican-American labor leader.

Soto, G. (2003b). *Taking sides*. New York: Harcourt Brace. (4–8). CONTEMPORARY REALISTIC FICTION.

Lincoln Mendoza is a member of a White basketball team that plays his former team from the barrio, placing him in a very difficult situation.

Stanley, J. *Hurry freedom: African Americans in gold rush California*. New York: Crown. (6–10). INFORMATIONAL BOOK.

This book spotlights how African Americans worked under unjust laws during this period of time. Efforts eventually began to be made to change these practices.

Stewart, S. (2001). *The journey*. New York: Farrar, Straus & Giroux. (2–5). CONTEMPORARY REALISTIC FICTION.

Hannah, an Amish girl, takes a trip to Chicago and connects everything she sees with something back home.

Strom, Y. (1966). *Quilted landscape: Conversations with young immigrants*. New York: Scholastic. (5–9). INFORMATIONAL BOOK.

This book includes interviews with young people who are adjusting to life in this country.

Thong, R. (2000). *Round is a mooncake: A book of shapes* (G. Lin, Illus.). San Francisco, CA: Chronicle Books. (K–2). PICTURE BOOK.

Shapes are used to demonstrate aspects of Chinese culture.

Van Laan, N. (1998). *With a whoop and a holler: A bushel of lore from way down south* (S. Cook, Illus.). New York: Atheneum. (3–6). TRADITIONAL.

A collection of Southern lore and folktales.

Waldman, N. (2001). *They came from the Bronx: How the buffalo were saved from extinction*. Honesdale, PA: Boyd's Mill Press. (2–5). PICTURE BOOK.

To repopulate the American range with buffalo, five were transported from the Bronx to Oklahoma.

Wargin, K-J. (Contributor). (1999). *The legend of Mackinac Island*. (G. Van Frankenhuyzen, Illus.). Chelsea, MI: Sleeping Bear Press. (K–5). TRADITIONAL LITERATURE.

The story of how Mackinac Island was formed on the back of a turtle.

Wargin, K. J. (Contributor). (2000). *The legend of the loon*. (G. Van Frankenhuyzen, Illus.). Chelsea, MI: Sleeping Bear Press. (K–5). TRADITIONAL LITERATURE.

Love between grandmothers and grandchildren is reflected in the sound of the loon.

White, R. (2003). *Tadpole*. New York: Farrar, Straus & Giroux. (4–7). HISTORICAL FICTION.

Set in Kentucky in the 1950s, Caroline has a lot of growing up to do. When her cousin who is being abused by his guardian comes to stay with the family, everyone must change.

Wong, J. (1994). *Good luck gold and other poems*. New York: McElderry. (2–6). POETRY.

Poems that touch on cultural differences and similarities.

Wong, J. (1996). *A suitcase of seaweed and other poems*. New York: McElderry. (4–8). POETRY.

Poems for older children are divided into three sections that reflect Wong's heritage—Korean, Chinese, and American.

Wong, J. (2000). *The trip back home*. (B. Jia, Illus.). New York: Harcourt. (K–3). POETRY.

A young child visits Korea, her mother's home.

Yolen, J. (1998). *Raising Yoder's barn*. New York: Little Brown. (K–3). PICTURE BOOK.

Matthew has an important task as the Amish do a barn raising.

References and Books for Further Reading

Aoki, E. M. (1980). Are you Chinese? Are you Japanese? Or are you a mixed-up kid? Using Asian American children's literature. *Reading Teacher, 34*, 382–385.

Copenhaver, J. F. (2001). Listening to their voices connect literary and cultural understandings: Responses to a small group read-aloud of *Malcolm X: A Fire Burning Brightly*. *New Advocate, 14*, 343–359.

Davis, R. T. (2000). African American females' voices in the classroom: Young sisters making connections through literature. *New Advocate, 13*, 259–271.

Enriquez, G. (2001). Making meaning of cultural depictions: Using Lois Lowry's *The Giver* to reconsider what is "multicultural" about literature. *Journal of Children's Literature, 27*, 13–22.

Ferree, A. M., & Abbott, J. A. (2001). *Literature in the elementary classroom: What are they reading and why?* Presentation at the National Council of Teachers of English, Baltimore, MD.

Freeman, E. B., & Lehman, B. A. (2001). *Global perspectives in children's literature*. New York: Allyn & Bacon.

Henderson, D. (2003). Personal communication. Cincinnati, Ohio.

Kurtz, J. (2001). Global nomads in the world of multicultural books. *Journal of Children's Literature, 27*(1), 9–12.

McIntyre, A. (1997). *Making meaning of Whiteness: Exploring racial identity with White teachers*. Albany, NY: State University of New York Press.

Mora, P. (1995). Multicultural Literature. In B. J. Diamond & M. A. Moore, *Multicultural Literacy* (p. ix–xi). White Plains, NY: Longman.

Newell, F. (2003). Personal communication. Cincinnati, Ohio.

Pavonetti, L. M. (2001). Books about children's literature: A mirror for all our students. *Journal of Children's Literature, 27*, 70–80.

Ramsey, P. (1987). *Teaching and learning in a diverse world: Multicultural education for young children.* New York: Teachers College Press.

Rochman, H. (1993). *Against borders: Promoting books for a multicultural world.* Chicago: American Library Association.

Sebesta, A. (2001). What do teachers need to know about children's literature? *New Advocate, 14,* 241–249.

Shanahan, P. (1994). I am the canon: Finding ourselves in multiculturalism. *Journal of Children's Literature, 20,* 1–5.

Sheets, R. H. (2000). Advancing the field or taking center stage: The White movement in multicultural education. *Educational Researcher, 29,* 15–20.

Soto, Gary. (n.d.). *Instructor.* **http://teacher. scholastic.com/lessonrepro/lessonplans/instructor/ multicultural.htm.**

Steiner, S. F. (2001). *Promoting a global community through multicultural children's literature.* Englewood, CO: Libraries Unlimited.

Stoodt, B. (1992, July). *Multicultural children's literature.* Paper presented at the World Congress on Reading, Maui, HI.

Umber, R. (2002). Reading the world and finding connections: A novel by a New Zealand author raises issues relevant to adolescent readers in America. *Signal Journal, 15,* 7–12.

Oral and Silent Literature 14

Key Terms

antiphonal choral
    reading
book-talking
choral reading
creative drama
line-a-child choral
    reading

reader's theater
refrain choral reading
storytelling
unison choral reading

Guiding Questions

1. Why is reading aloud to children important in developing literary experiences?

2. How do oral and silent reading differ?

3. What should you consider when selecting a book to read aloud to your class?

4. At what grade level should teachers stop reading to students?

Reading aloud is the most valuable component of any literature, reading, or language arts program. No other activity has as many benefits. Reading aloud builds a relationship between children and adults;

creates a sense of classroom community; and strengthens literature, language, grammar, vocabulary, and writing skills. Read-alouds motivate students to read and gives them opportunities to express their response to literature (Sipe, 2002). During read-alouds, students listen, question, speak, visualize, and think (Hahn, 2002). In this chapter, we explore the values of oral and silent reading. The vignette on the following page illustrates a read-aloud situation in a second-grade classroom.

Oral and Silent Reading

Oral and silent reading processes are complementary. Reading aloud gives readers the material to construct a network of comprehension techniques for themselves. Readers rely on a foundation of silent reading to prepare for oral interpretation. Silent reading permits them to understand text more rapidly and to think at higher cognitive levels.

Oral reading makes literature accessible to both readers and nonreaders. Oral reading also builds a foundation for learners' responses to literature. Listening to stories frees children from thinking about word identification and word meaning, permitting them instead to think, feel, and respond to the stories, poems, or information they hear. They find thinking critically about literature is easier when it is read aloud, and daily listening to stories improves children's ability to talk about and retell stories (Morrow, 1988).

Discussion, another aspect of oral language, enables readers to respond to literature and to intertwine their own life "stories" with the author's story. It also allows them to reflect on and revise the meaning they derived from the text by hearing and considering others' views about the story's meaning. Oral literature activities enrich children's understanding of the special conventions, devices, and effects of spoken language. In the process, they develop an ear for written language and a sense of the differences between the sound of book language and everyday speech.

Oral Reading Activities

Oral reading activities present natural opportunities for learning without formal instruction. When reading aloud a book such as Michael Rosen's *We're Going on a Bear Hunt,* teachers and children can discuss stories, ask and answer questions, and chant the refrain together: "We're going on a bear hunt. We're going to catch a big one. What a beautiful day! We're not scared." In this warm, supportive environment, children associate reading with pleasure; they begin to see reading as an activity to be enjoyed and valued. They also acquire a foundation for learning to read (Naylor & Borders, 1993).

Providing time to read aloud to children in the school is vital. Children at all grade levels, including high school, should hear good literature read aloud daily. Reading aloud gives listeners of all ages opportunities for shared responses to literature—whether social, emotional, or intellectual. Perfect (1999) points out that a sense of community develops when a group shares the experience of listening to a book read aloud.

As children grow in their ability to read, many will choose to read a story they have heard read aloud. This author first observed this phenomenon when reading *Little House on the Prairie* by Laura Ingalls Wilder. The students checked out every copy in the library and parents reported they had to buy copies for their children. They read along silently as I read the story aloud. After completing this book, the students asked me to read the other books in this series. In this way, the experience of oral reading is not unlike throwing pebbles into a pond; the story creates an impetus for reading more.

VIGNETTE

Callie Rogers held up an unopened picture book after she turned off the classroom lights to get her students' attention. They had learned this was a time for quiet attention and for sitting on the literature rug.

Callie had written the title and author of the read-aloud book on the chalkboard. She asked the children whether they had ever seen a dragon, and several children described the dragons they had seen. She displayed the book and asked the children to describe the dragon on the cover in their own words. She then read the title, *The Dragon Machine,* and the author's name, Helen Ward. She explained the protagonist's name was George, showed them the first double-page spread, and asked them why they thought the title was *The Dragon Machine.* They successfully predicted the book's plot and the characters from the title page.

After a class discussion, Callie said, "Let's see if your predictions are like the story. As I read the story, think about the way George felt at the beginning, in the middle, and at the end of the story." She also asked the children to identify George's problem in the story.

As she finished the first part of the book, Callie stopped and asked the students, "How did George feel at the beginning of the story?"

Quinton answered, "He felt ignored and overlooked."

"No," Annie said. "He felt sad."

Callie asked, "Do you think he could feel both ignored and overlooked as well as sad?"

After some discussion, the children decided that situation was possible. Then Callie asked, "How were George and the dragon alike?"

(continued)

279

Andrew created this picture of a dragon machine after he heard the story.

A big sister likes to read to her brothers.

Jessica answered, "He was unnoticed, just like George."

She then asked, "Have you ever felt like George and the dragon?"

The children explored the feelings of George and the dragon. George's imagination was a major part of the discussion. Some students were convinced that the events were real.

After completing the story, Callie asked, "Why did George build the dragon machine?" The students engaged in extensive discussion because the dragon machine fascinated them. All the students enjoyed the stunning illustrations, but disagreed about the dragon count. Callie asked the children to take turns looking at the book and counting the dragons. Will suggested they define what constituted a dragon, because in some illustrations they saw only a tail or a paw. The students asked if they could read other dragon books, so Callie asked the librarian/media specialist for assistance.

After hearing Mildred Taylor's *Roll of Thunder, Hear My Cry,* the story of an African-American family's plight in Mississippi during the Great Depression, middle-school children may elect to read this book on their own. They may also choose to read Mildred Taylor's other books, such as *The Friendship* or *The Gold Cadillac.*

Selecting Material for Reading Aloud

Read-alouds give teachers a chance to read quality literature that children might not choose for themselves or that they might be unable to read. Read-aloud materials are not confined to books; they can also include magazine articles, short stories, poems, newspaper articles, or anything of interest to both reader and listener. Read-aloud materials should be chosen carefully, in order to motivate children. The criteria for good read-aloud materials mandates that the work:

1. be of high literary quality from a variety of genres;
2. be appropriate to the age and developmental level of children;
3. be interesting enough to hold children's attention;
4. have strong plot lines and characters with whom children can identify, if fiction;
5. have accurate information, if nonfiction;
6. have a concrete subject related to children's experiences in poetry; and
7. be up to two or more reading levels above the grade level of the children, so long as the material interests them.

Read-aloud literature may be confined to fiction or poetry, but all genres can result in interesting read-alouds. Traditional literature is, of course, always a favorite read-aloud because these tales lend themselves to oral presentation. Traditional literature interests a wide age range of listeners. Steven Kellogg's *I Was Born About 10,000 Years Ago* is a well-loved tall tale that appeals to many children. Jon Muth's *Stone Soup,* which is set in China, is bound to please primary grade students. Elementary level students like Sherry Garland's *Children of the Dragon: Selected Tales from Vietnam.* Middle-grade students will enjoy Angel Vigil's *The Corn Woman,* a collection of stories and legends of the Hispanic Southwest.

Many adults and children enjoy the humor in a book such as David Wisniewski's *The Secret Knowledge of Grown-Ups,* and the laughter can continue with Jan Carr's *Swine Divine* and Denys Cazet's *Minnie and Moo Go Dancing.* Laughter is definitely the product of reading the poems in Douglas Florian's *Laugh-eteria.* Young children will also enjoy the rhyming text in Mem Fox's *Boo to a Goose.* Children in Grades 2 through 4 will appreciate Lloyd Alexander's *Gypsy Rizka,* which generates laughter with its perils-of-Pauline type story. In this episodic chapter book, one chapter sets up the joke and the next one resolves it.

Popular primary-grade read-alouds include *Baloney (Henry B)* by Jon Scieszka, *The Bug Scientists* by Donna Jackson, *Peanut's Emergency* by Cristina Salat, *The White Swan Express: A Story About Adoption* by Jean Davies Okimoto and Elaine M. Aoki, and works by Leo Lionni, Tomie dePaola, Arnold Lobel, and poems by Shel Silverstein and Jack Prelutsky.

Successful intermediate-grade read-alouds include *Island of the Blue Dolphins* by Scott O'Dell, *Mrs. Frisby and the Rats of NIMH* by Robert C. O'Brien, and *Bud, Not Buddy* by Paul Christopher. Biographies and nonfiction books are excellent read-alouds for every grade level. Biographies, such as Robert Burleigh's *Black Whiteness: Admiral Byrd Alone in the Antarctic,* are ideal for reading aloud. *The Amazing Life of Benjamin Franklin* by James Cross Giblin is another great read-aloud for middle-grade students.

The lively text of Joy Cowley's informational book *Red-Eyed Tree Frog* makes this a riveting read-aloud adventure for children in Grades 1 through 3. Children will acquire information about water. Nonfiction read-alouds for primary children also might include books such as Candace Fleming's *The Hatmaker's Sign: A Story by Benjamin Franklin,* which may be considered historical fiction although it is based on an anecdote found in Thomas Jefferson's papers and has a wonderful read-aloud quality.

Planning a Read-Aloud Session

Reading aloud is a sharing time. The reader selects the material, arranges the physical setting so that readers can see and hear, and looks over the materials. When reading picture books, the reader shows the illustrations at the same time he or she is reading.

A read-aloud session has three major components. First, the teacher will introduce the book, identify the author and illustrator, and help the listeners connect with the book. Second, the teacher reads the selection, initially for understanding and appreciation; however, teachers or librarians may stop reading to encourage prediction or to connect a character, an incident, or a problem to literature students have previously read or heard. Third, depending upon the particular book in question, the teacher may conduct a follow-up discussion during which the children may raise questions or the teacher may introduce discussion points. Figure 14.1 illustrates this read-aloud model.

Activities like the following give children a chance to respond to literature, while strengthening oral and silent reading.

FIGURE 14.1   Read-aloud example for third grade.

The Little Ships: The Heroic Rescue at Dunkirk in World War II
BY LOUISE BORDEN
ILLUSTRATED BY MICHAEL FOREMAN

Introduction: Louise Borden has written a number of books, including *Goodbye, Charles Lindbergh: Based on a True Story* and *A. Lincoln and Me.* The illustrator of *The Little Ships,* Michael Foreman, has also illustrated other books about war.

This is a true story that happened during World War II. Soldiers from the United States and other Allied countries were stranded on the beaches at Dunkirk. (Teachers may bring in a map of Europe and place a star by Dunkirk so children can see where this happened.) The book tells how the troops were saved.

During reading: The reader may choose to stop and ask children to predict future events, although this is not necessary with every book. The teacher might also ask the children to identify who is telling the story.

Following reading: The teacher should conduct a discussion using the following questions:

- Why do you think the author called this book *The Little Ships* when many of these vessels were boats rather than ships?
- Who were the heroes in this story? What kind of heroism did they demonstrate?
- Can you think of any other books or characters that are similar to *The Little Ships?* How are they similar?
- What was the "miracle of Dunkirk"?
- What image does the phrase "silent parade over the waters" bring to your mind?

Reader's Theater

"Reader's theater is a great way to develop children's meaningful and fluent reading" (Martinez, Roser, & Strecker, 1998–1999). *Reader's theater* is oral delivery of stories, poetry, biography, or information by two or more readers who characterize and narrate clearly and expressively. The performers must understand the literature they are presenting so that they can structure the development of character and plot. "Reader's theater is . . . a staged program that allows the audience to create its own images through the skilled performance of the readers" (McCaslin, 1990, p. 263). The simplicity of reader's theater makes it so appealing and motivating that students enjoy practicing their oral reading. However, reader's theater does not require rehearsal or elaborate staging.

In reader's theater, the cast may be large or small. If necessary, one individual may read several parts. During the presentation, the entire cast remains on stage, reading the various assigned portions (McCaslin, 1990). Movement is minimal, and actions are suggested through simple gestures and facial expressions. Readers usually take formal positions behind lecterns or sit on stools, often turning their backs to the audience to show that they are absent from a scene. In addition, readers may turn around or lower their heads when not participating in a scene.

Selecting Material

Students who are becoming fluent readers need manageable texts in which to practice. Many types of literature are well-suited to reader's theater presentations. In some instances, related materials may be mixed in the presentation. For example, a poem and a story with related themes can be performed together. Manna (1984) suggests that reader's theater stories should have these characteristics:

1. an interesting, fast-paced story with a strong plot;
2. a lot of dialogue;
3. recognizable and believable characters;
4. plausible language; and
5. a distinct style.

Clearly, teachers may choose from among many appropriate pieces of literature, including the following suggestions.

- *The Princess and the Pea* by Hans Christian Andersen, illustrated by Paul Galdone
- *The Golly Sisters Ride Again* by Betsy Byars
- *All the Way to Lhasa: A Tale from Tibet* by Barbera Berger
- *Henny Penny* by Paul Galdone
- *The Water Gift and the Pig of the Pig* by Jacqueline Martin
- *Stone Soup* by Jon Muth
- *The Recess Queen* by Alexis O'Neill
- *Rolling Harvey Down the Hill* by Jack Prelutsky
- *The Relatives Came* by Cynthia Rylant
- *I Am the Cat* by Alice Schertle, illustrated by Robert Buehner
- *Bartholomew and the Oobleck* by Dr. Seuss
- *Horton Hatches the Egg* by Dr. Seuss
- *Raising Sweetness* by Diane Stanley
- *The Widow's Broom* by Chris Van Allsburg

Planning a Reader's Theater Performance

After selecting a piece of literature for the performance, the next step in reader's theater is identifying who will read which part. Use a colored marker to identify the various parts. If the piece is too long, have the readers choose the scenes that convey the piece's concept or theme rather than read the entire selection. The readers sit on stools in a circle, turning around on the stools so their backs face the audience when they are not participating in a scene. In somewhat more-elaborate staging, a spotlight may be focused on the individual who is reading. Students may sit or stand side-by-side, with the narrators at one side and closer to the audience.

Readers should practice reading in a comfortable, relaxed manner at a pace that moves the scene along, but not so rapidly that the audience is lost. Careful reading and discussion of the text enables readers to interpret the literature. The accompanying box, entitled "A Report on a Reader's Theater Performance," illustrates a fifth-grade class preparing for a reader's theater performance.

Storytelling

Some stories are for reading aloud and some are for telling. *Storytelling*, which was introduced in Chapter 6, is a powerful, magical way of introducing and ex-

A Report on a Reader's Theater Performance

The students chose to read *Where the Lilies Bloom* by Vera and Bill Cleaver. Eight readers took the parts of Mary Call, the protagonist; Devola, her older sister; Roy Luther, the father; Kiser Pease, the landlord and neighbor; Mary Call's younger brother and sister; the storekeeper who buys herbs from Mary Call; and a neighbor. The readers used stools in a circle so they could turn their backs to the audience when not participating.

They identified the following scenes as key to understanding the story.

1. Mary Call and Roy Luther discuss his impending death and burial in the grave he has prepared.
2. Mary Call and the children pretend their father is ill when a neighbor comes to call.
3. Mary Call and Devola care for Kiser Pease when he is ill.
4. Mary Call and the storekeeper interact when Mary Call sells herbs.
5. Kiser Pease brings his car to the Luther's so that Devola can sit in it.
6. Kiser Pease asks Devola to marry him.
7. Mary Call pretends she wants to marry Kiser.
8. Devola takes charge and decides to marry Kiser.

The readers decided to serve herb tea after their performance because Mary Call earns a living for her family by gathering herbs. They also planned to read the sequel to this story, *Trial Valley.*

---

ploring literature, as storytellers make stories come to life. Ruth Sawyer (1962), who traveled around the world to discover stories and storytellers, calls storytelling a folk art. Storytellers have preserved our past and transmitted it orally to new generations. Oral literature includes stories, poems, and information told aloud to another person or persons.

Unlike writers, who do not have a chance to interact directly with their readers, storytellers have a live, listening audience with whom to interact. Listeners hear voice effects and see their storyteller move, bend, and breathe. "As the teller looks right at the listeners, eyes meet and an interactive communication exists between them" (Livo & Rietz, 1986, p. xi).

The oral story is soft and malleable, yielding to the pleasures of the audience. Its language is not the precise and unchanging form of the written story created by a single author, but the evolving, flowing language of the community (Barton, 1986). Storytelling is natural to human beings because it helps us remember and understand things that have happened; it teaches us how to behave, as well as how not to behave. It stimulates our imagination: As the storyteller spins a tale, the listeners create mental pictures of the characters, the setting, and the story events.

Storytelling in the Classroom

Oral language precedes written language in children's development. Children learn to talk and to explain, a form of storytelling, before they learn to read and write stories. Storytelling motivates children to read and write themselves, as shown in the accompanying box on page 284, and provides a model for children's own writing.

Children participate in storytelling by telling their own stories and joining in on repeated phrases when others are telling stories. Hearing and telling different types of stories develops their awareness and comprehension of the various forms of narrative. In this way, storytelling develops thinking abilities (Roney, 1989).

Teachers can tell stories to introduce literature, to help children learn about stories, to develop children's listening and speaking skills, and to model storytelling behavior. Teachers can also help their students learn to tell stories.

The Internet is a rich source of storytelling ideas and suggested materials. At some sites, students can actually hear storytellers sharing their favorite stories. For example, **www.themoonlitroad.com** is an excellent site, and the Storytelling FAQ at **www.timsheppard. co.uk/story** is another helpful site.

A Storytelling Experience

Jim Phillips told his first graders to make a story circle on the rug in his classroom; then he sat down on a low chair and opened the book *Brown Bear, Brown Bear* by Bill Martin. He held the book so the children could see it, told them the title and the author's name, and started reading.

"Brown Bear, Brown Bear, What do you see?" "I see a red bird looking at me."

Mr. Phillips read through the entire cumulative tale, in which each animal or bird sees another. When he finished, the children pleaded for him to read it again and he did. After the second reading, Mr. Phillips told the children they were going to make a story. They immediately asked how.

He answered, "You are going to think of new animals for the *Brown Bear, Brown Bear* story. I'll begin with 'Blue Jay, Blue Jay, What do you see?' Now, Lauren, tell us what the Blue Jay sees."

After thinking for a few moments, Lauren said, "I see a pink butterfly looking at me."

Mr. Phillips said, "Pink butterfly, pink butterfly, What do you see? Tony, tell us what the pink butterfly sees."

Tony said, "I see a striped zebra looking at me!"

Mr. Phillips and the children continued until they had completed a story, then they retold it. Afterward, Mr. Phillips said, "I am going to write your story on this chart, so you can remember it. While I am writing your story on a chart, you can draw pictures of the animals and birds that you thought of for the story and we will paste them to the chart pages."

Later in the day, he noticed that a number of the children were writing and illustrating their own *Brown Bear* stories. When the children completed their individual stories, they read them to their classmates.

Selecting Material

The first step in storytelling is selecting a story to learn. Traditional literature is a good starting point. Books such as *Teaching Through Stories: Yours, Mine, and Theirs* (Roe, Alfred, & Smith, 1998) are helpful to teachers and students. Begin with an appealing version of a traditional story that you already know, such as *Cinderella, Three Billy Goats Gruff,* or *Stone Soup.* The most important factor in choosing a story for telling is that you enjoy it.

As a beginning storyteller, a simple story will give you security as you begin. Storytellers need not feel confined to traditional stories, however. Modern tales such as Judith Viorst's *Alexander and the Terrible, Horrible, No Good, Very Bad Day* is a delightful story that has broad appeal. You will find the following authors helpful because they retell traditional stories and write stories in a traditional literature style.

- *Dichos: Proverbs and Sayings from the Spanish* by Charles Aranda
- *I, Houdini: The Autobiography of a Self-Educated Hamster* by Lynne Reid Banks, illustrated by Terry Riley
- *The Three Little Pigs* by Jean Claverie
- *Look What Happened to Frog: Storytelling in Education* by Pamela Cooper and Rives Collins
- *Hairyman* by David Holt
- *Jack and the Beanstalk* by Steven Kellogg
- *Black Folktales* by Julius Lester
- *The Tales of Uncle Remus: The Adventures of Brer Rabbit* by Julius Lester
- *The Giver* by Lois Lowry
- *The Boy Who Loved Frogs* by Jay O'Callahan
- *Little Heroes* by Jay O'Callahan
- *The Recess Queen* by Alexis O'Neill
- *Stories and Songs for Little Children* by Pete Seeger
- *Baseball in April and Other Stories* by Gary Soto

Planning Storytelling

The main ingredient in planning storytelling is learning the story. Storytelling confidence comes with story familiarity. Storytellers should know their story well. Learning the framework of a story provides a skeleton to follow in telling it. The storyteller should learn any phrases that are repeated or important to the story. Once these elements are learned, practice telling the story several times to help polish the presentation.

Learning the framework of a story is easy. As discussed in Chapter 2, stories are orderly and conform to structure rules recognized as story structure or story grammar (Livo & Rietz, 1986). Stories that conform to the expected structure are easier to recall and to understand (Downing & Leong, 1982).

Story patterns help readers comprehend literature; they also give form to writing. Story patterns can be mapped or diagrammed to assist storytellers in recalling and interrelating the ideas and events of a story. Story patterns and maps are especially helpful in teaching children to prepare stories for storytelling. Figure 14.2 illustrates a structural map of the story

"The Wide-Mouthed Frog." The following techniques will help teachers and children with storytelling.

1. When preparing to learn a story for storytelling, a week or so in advance, read several stories. The story that comes back to you most frequently is the one to learn.

2. Divide the story into beginning, middle, and end. Learn the story in segments, such as separate scenes or units of action. Learn the story structure

---

FIGURE 14.2   Story grammar for "The Wide-Mouthed Frog."

Setting:

 The wide-mouthed frog and his wife live beside a pond with their newborn babies.

The Problem:

 The wide-mouthed frog babies are hungry. Mrs. Wide-Mouthed Frog sends her husband out to get food for the babies.

The Events:

 1. Mr. Wide-Mouthed Frog meets a goat and asks him what his babies eat. The goat recommends tin cans, which the wide-mouthed frog rejects.
 2. He meets a cat who recommends mice.
 3. He meets a duck who recommends milk.
 4. He meets a horse who recommends grain.
 5. He meets an owl who recommends wide-mouthed frogs.

Resolution:

 The wide-mouthed frog narrows his mouth and says, "Oooooooohhhhhh."

Literature becomes a living story when a storyteller talks.

A Storyteller's Version of "The Wide-Mouthed Frog"

Mr. and Mrs. Willie T. Wide-Mouthed Frog lived beside a pretty pond with blue water and white lily pads. They were thrilled to have three beautiful green babies. But the babies were always hungry and crying. Mrs. Wide-Mouthed Frog was tired of hunting for food, so she told her husband to go out and hunt food for their hungry babies. Mr. Willie T. Wide-Mouthed Frog set out to find food. He hopped around the beautiful blue pond.

He met a goat and stopped. "Hello, Goat, I'm a wide-mouthed frog, and I'm hunting food for my babies. What do your babies eat?"

"My babies eat tin cans. They chew them right up."

"Oh! Wide-mouthed frog babies can't eat tin cans. Thank you."

The frog hops on. He meets a cat.

"Hello, Cat, I'm a wide-mouthed frog, and I'm hunting food for my babies. What do your babies eat?"

"My babies eat mice. They chew them up bones and all."

"Wide-mouthed frog babies can't eat mice. Thank you."

The frog hops on. He meets a horse and stops.

"Hello, Horse, I'm a wide-mouthed frog and I'm hunting food for my babies. What do your babies eat?"

"My babies eat grain. They grind it up with their teeth."

"Wide-mouthed frog babies can't eat grain. Thank you."

The frog hops on. He meets a duck and stops.

"Hello, Duck, I'm a wide-mouthed frog, and I'm hunting food for my babies. What do your babies eat?"

"My babies eat worms. They wash them down with water."

"Wide-mouthed frog babies can't eat worms. Thank you."

The frog hops on. He sees on owl in a tree and stops.

"Hello, Owl, I'm a wide-mouthed frog, and I'm hunting food for my babies. What do your babies eat?"

"My babies eat wide-mouthed frogs."

The frog sucks his mouth into a narrow little circle and says, "Oooohhhh!" and then hurries home.

---

in order, but do not memorize it. The ways of dividing a story differ from storyteller to storyteller. One way of dividing *The Three Little Pigs* is:

- *Part 1.*   The three little pigs set out to find their fortune. One builds a house of straw, the next builds a house of sticks, and the third builds a house of bricks.

- *Part 2.*   The wolf eats pigs one and two and goes after the third one.

- *Part 3.*   The pig sends the wolf to an apple orchard and a fair and then outwits him. The wolf ends up in the kettle.

3. Do not memorize the exact words of a story, but do learn any special catch phrases and use them in telling the story. Catch phrases are phrases that may appear several times within the story or that the story hinges on, such as "I'll huff and I'll puff and I'll blow your house down" in *The Three Little Pigs*.

4. Don't worry about using the same words every time you tell the story.

5. Be expressive in storytelling, but do not be so dramatic that you overshadow the story itself (Morrow, 1988).

6. Practice telling the story several times before actually telling it to an audience to get comfortable with saying the story aloud and with the sound of your own voice.

7. Tape record yourself. Wait a day or two to listen to the tape so you can be objective. When you evaluate the tape, think about the parts of the story and identify those that need changing or expanding. Does your voice sound pleasing? Do you speak at a speed that is appropriate to the story?

8. Look directly at your audience when you are telling the story.

9. The story should not be longer than 10 minutes. You will find helpful materials through the Internet and storytelling associations. The National Storytelling Network (NTN) is located in Jonesborough, Tennessee. It has a Web site, **www.storynet.org**, a magazine, many storytelling materials, and it spon-

sors storytelling events such as "Tellabrations" on the Saturday before Thanksgiving. This international event takes place in elder hostels, on airplanes, in schools and colleges, in museums, and wherever people gather. Whenever you access the NTN Web site, you will discover a plethora of storytelling sites from around the world. East Tennessee State University has a storytelling program with coursework. It also publishes *Storytelling World*.

Storytelling Variations

Sitting in front of an audience and using only voice and expressions is not the only way to tell a story. Storytelling can be varied in many ways to give novelty to tried-and-true stories. Variations also can be used cooperatively with children to give them greater involvement with the story.

Flannel board stories

When telling stories with flannel boards, the teller sits or stands by a board covered with flannel. Cutouts of characters backed with flannel are placed on the board as they appear in the story. Some storytellers may lay the flannel board on a table to prevent the figures from falling. Children enjoy taking turns telling stories with a flannel board.

Flannel board stories should not have large numbers of characters or complex actions. After selecting a story, the teller decides which parts to show and which to tell. For example, in preparing *Goldilocks and the Three Bears*, the teller or students could make figures for Goldilocks, the three bears, three sizes of bowls, three sizes of chairs, and three sizes of beds; some tellers may like to have a broken bowl and a broken chair to illustrate the story further. These figures can be used to present the entire story; details and actions do not have to be portrayed. The characters can be drawn or painted on cardboard, construction paper, or any other convenient material. After cutting them out, back them with flannel or sandpaper so they will stick to the flannel board. Use yarn, buttons, or fabric to decorate and develop the characters. The board can be covered with flannel, although indoor-outdoor carpeting also makes a very satisfactory backing. Figures cling to it and it wipes clean.

Prop stories

Props such as hats, canes, stuffed animals, boxes, rocks, toys, and fruit can enhance storytelling. Beans, a small harp, and a china or plastic hen are excellent props for *Jack and the Beanstalk*. The props give the storyteller and the audience a focal point and help the storyteller remember the story.

Music stories

Some stories are excellent when told with background music. For example, *Jack and the Beanstalk* sounds wonderful when told with the music "In the Hall of the Mountain King" from *Legends in Music* by the Bowmar Orchestral Library playing in the background. RCA Victor has an *Adventures in Music* record library for elementary schools that includes excellent selections for story background music. Musical storytellers may also play their own accompaniment.

Cut stories

Cut stories are told while the storyteller cuts out a piece of paper to form a character or object in the story. The figures may be drawn ahead of time on construction paper to make the cutting easier (Morrow, 1979). Some teachers are sufficiently skilled to fold the paper and cut multiple figures while storytelling. Many picture books and folktales are good choices for cut stories because the teller can also cut objects to accompany the story. For example, a gingerbread boy cutout could accompany the story *The Gingerbread Boy*, or a pancake could accompany *The Pancake*.

Choral Reading

Choral reading is an oral literary activity in which several readers read a selection in unison with the direction of a leader. This ancient technique has been in use for centuries. For example, choral reading was an important element of Greek drama. Researchers found evidence of choral speaking in ancient religious ceremonies and festivals, and it is still used for ritualistic purposes in church services and on patriotic occasions (McCaslin, 1990). Ross (1972) points out that choral reading was used in early schools because there were not enough books.

Choral reading involves listening and responding to language. Through participating in choral reading, students learn the sounds of language, predictable language patterns, and the rhythm and melody of language, which enhances their understanding (Miccinati, 1985). After choral reading experiences, children are better able to predict the words and phrases that follow one another.

The purpose of choral reading is to convey meaning through sound, stress, duration, and pitch. Choral reading also develops diction and the enunciation of speech sounds. Choral reading is a group activity that gives students opportunities for social cooperation. In a group activity such as this, students can participate without feelings of self-consciousness. Choral reading knows no age limits—kindergarten children enjoy it, as do high school students.

Selecting Material

Choral reading in the elementary classrooms can begin with short nursery rhymes in kindergarten. Rhythm and rhyme are the important factors in nursery rhymes, which help children remember them. Material for choral reading should be meaningful, have a strong rhythm, and have an easily discernible structure. The following list includes only a few of the selections that make interesting choral readings.

- "So Long as There's Weather" by Tamara Kitt
- "Godfrey, Gordon, Gustavus Gore" by William B. Rand
- "The Umbrella Brigade" by Laura Richards
- *I Know an Old Lady Who Swallowed a Fly* by Glen Rounds
- *Train Song* by Diane Siebert
- *Truck Song* by Diane Siebert
- *Laughing Time: Collected Nonsense* by William Jay Smith
- *Peanut Butter and Jelly* by Nadine Westcott

Planning a Choral Reading

When initiating a choral reading activity, prepare the students by giving them time to read the material silently, and then read it aloud to themselves or their peers. After reading, discuss the literature to ensure comprehension. Once the students understand the selection, they can practice reading it orally. Teachers can help young children respond to language rhythms by clapping or tapping to the rhythm. Initially, the teacher may chant most of the rhyme and have the children chime in only on the last line or a repeated refrain. Use a single selection with various choral reading methods so students learn about the various ways of expressing meaning. After students have experiences with the various choral reading types, they can choose selections and plan their own choral readings.

Four common types of choral reading exist: refrain, line-a-child, antiphonal, and unison. The easiest to learn is *refrain choral reading*, in which the teacher reads most of the lines and the students read the refrain. In *line-a-child choral reading*, individual students read specific lines while the entire group reads the beginning and ending of the selection. *Antiphonal* or *dialogue choral reading* is most appropriate for middle- or intermediate-level students. It enables readers to explore the pitch and duration of sound. Boys, girls, and groups vary their pitches and sound duration for different parts of the selection.

Unison choral reading is the most difficult approach because the entire group speaks all of the lines. Without seeking perfection, the participants must practice timing so they are simultaneously producing words and sounds. Combinations of all of these types may be used for a single selection.

Tamara Kitt's poem "So Long as There's Weather" is a fine children's choice for choral reading. The spare use of words, frequent pauses, sound effects, emphasized words, and short lines ranging from one to five syllables create a feeling of changing weather and a child's joy in all kinds of weather. The appeal of this poem for children makes it an excellent choice for choral reading. Alert the students to the fact that dashes in the text represent pauses and that the emphasized words and pauses make the choral reading more interesting. A choral reading experience involving "So Long as There's Weather" for primary-grade children might proceed as indicated in the following steps.

1. The teacher begins with crashing cymbals to simulate thunder or with water poured from container to container to simulate rain.
2. The teacher reads the first verse.
3. The children read the second verse in unison from a chart.
4. The teacher or a child who has practiced reads the third verse.
5. The children read the fourth verse in unison from a chart.
6. On the emphasized words in the fourth verse, designated children crash cymbals together.

As children develop their understanding of chanting in unison, they can move to longer selections. *Peanut*

Butter and Jelly by Nadine Westcott is an excellent longer piece for choral reading. After children learn to chant this play-rhyme, the teacher can introduce the hand-clap and knee-slap motions that accompany it. Later, the teacher may choose to divide the poem into parts to be read by different groups.

Creative Drama

Creative drama is informal drama created by the participants (McCaslin, 1990). This kind of drama is improvisational and process-centered. It may be based on a story with a beginning, a middle, and an end. It may, however, be an original plot that explores, develops, and expresses ideas and feelings through dramatic enactment. The players create the dialogue whether the content is a well-known story or an original plot. "With each playing, the story becomes more detailed and better organized, but it remains extemporaneous and is at no time designed for an audience," which avoids rehearsal and memorization (McCaslin, 1990, p. 5).

Reenactments allow each member of the group an opportunity to play various parts and to be part of the audience for others. Scenery and costumes have no place in creative drama, although an occasional prop or piece of costume may be permitted to stimulate the imagination (McCaslin, 1990). Similarly, readers have no written script to follow. Creative drama emphasizes spontaneity and improvisation, although involvement in creative drama may lead students to write a script for a play later. When dialogue is written, the nature of the drama changes. Written drama can be very rewarding, as children enjoy the creative writing involved in such enterprises.

Creative drama yields fun, understanding, and learning, as well as other benefits. As children improvise in acting out a story, an episode from a story, or an experience of their own, they comprehend and express the important details of plot, character, word meanings, story sequence, and cause-and-effect relations (Miccinati, 1985). This makes story characters and story action more concrete and comprehensible. In acting out stories, they use their bodies, voices, and movements to enact literature; translating words into action encourages children to interpret and respond to literature. Dramatization increases vocabulary, syntactic flexibility, and the ability to predict aspects of the story.

Creative drama also makes strong contributions to the growth of children's communication effectiveness (Busching, 1981). It requires logical and intuitive thinking; it personalizes knowledge and yields aesthetic pleasure (Siks, 1983). Drama gives children opportunities to experiment with words, emotions, and social roles. Heathcote (1983) believes that drama expands children's understanding of life experiences and that it leads them to reflect on particular circumstances and make sense out of their world in a deeper way.

Selecting Material

A dramatized story can make a lasting impression. Both folk tales and modern stories provide fine opportunities for acting. Believable characters, a well-constructed plot, and a worthwhile theme make for engrossing drama. Any story, episode, or event that children have enjoyed is a likely candidate for dramatization. Students of all ages enjoy acting out versions of the same story and comparing them. For example, they might act out three versions of *Cinderella* and compare the characterization, plot, and setting. Perhaps a few suggestions of specific stories for dramatization will stimulate you to think of others.

Children enjoy dramatizing many traditional stories they have heard again and again, such as Brett Johnson's *Jack Outwits the Giants* or a version of *Little Red Riding Hood* for Grades kindergarten through 3. Middle-grade students enjoy stories such as *Bunnicula* by Deborah and James Howe, *The Pushcart War* by Jean Merrill, and *The Book of Three* by Lloyd Alexander.

Planning Creative Drama

Guidelines like the following will help teachers create many opportunities for children to participate in short, unstructured drama.

1. Although props are not necessary, many teachers gather a collection of props for dramatic plays. Jewelry, fabric, hats, canes, clothing, and Halloween costumes are useful props.
2. Select a story or have the children select a favorite story. A book that includes a large number of characters gives more children opportunities to participate.
3. Discuss the main events with the students. Identify and sequence the events to be included. You may wish to outline the events using a story map.

4. Identify the characters in the story. Discuss their actions, attitudes, and feelings. Explain that the children should act the way they think the character walked, talked, and so on.

5. Discuss the action in each scene and give the children opportunities to practice it. They may need to pretend to walk in heavy boots or need to practice expressive gestures such as walking happily, sadly, or so forth. Pantomime (discussed next) is a way of preparing children to move in expressive ways.

6. Assign character roles to class members. Ask the participants to think about and visualize the characters. Children who do not want to participate can be directors or stage managers.

7. Give the audience a purpose for watching the play. For example, ask them to observe characterization, character development, or plot development.

8. Dramatize the story.

9. Discuss the dramatization.

10. Recast the characters and play the story again.

Pantomime

"Pantomime is the art of conveying ideas without words"; it sharpens children's perceptions and stimulates the imagination as the players try to remember actions and characters (McCaslin, 1990, p. 71). Children can pantomime stories as another child or the teacher reads them. They may create a character from literature or one of their own invention. Music can set the mood for people marching in a parade, horses galloping, toads hopping, cars racing on a track, or children skipping on a sunny spring day (McCaslin, 1990). Older children also enjoy pantomime, and children who have limited knowledge of English or who have speech and hearing problems can participate in it.

Puppets

Puppet shows are dramas in which the actors are puppets that come to life with the assistance of a puppeteer. Children enjoy making puppets and becoming puppeteers. Puppets are excellent for children who are shy because they can express themselves through the puppet. They also work well with children who are reluctant to participate in creative drama. A puppet show allows children to dramatize their favorite books, as

FIGURE 14.3   Student-made puppets.

Stick puppet

Paper plate puppet

Sock puppet

Styrofoam-cup puppet

Cloth or hand puppet

Paper-bag puppet

well as scripts they have written. Puppetry stimulates the imagination of the children who are creating puppets and planning to dramatize a story. Children practice cooperation as they work with others to make puppets and puppet productions.

The stage can be quite simple—a youngster kneeling behind a table and moving an object along the edge of it—or as elaborate as imagination and skill can make or buy it. Similarly, you can provide commercially produced puppets, or children can make their own, possibly nothing more than a bandanna wrapped around the first three fingers so that the thumb and little finger are the arms (McCaslin, 1990). Figure 14.3 features some of the puppets students can construct (Stoodt, 1988, p. 119).

- *Stick puppets.*   Draw the character on tagboard, cardboard, or construction paper and decorate it with yarn, sequins, and tissue paper. Cut out the figure and attach it to a stick, tongue depressor, or dowel for manipulation.

- *Paper plate puppets.* Draw faces on paper plates and decorate them with yarn for hair. Glue the plates on sticks, dowels, or rulers for manipulation.
- *Sock puppets.* Add yarn hair, button eyes, and felt bits for a nose, ear, or other features to the toe end of a sock. Put your hand inside the sock for manipulation.
- *Styrofoam-cup puppets.* Decorate a cup as a character and attach the completed puppet to a stick or dowel for manipulation.
- *Cloth puppets.* Sew fabric to fit over a child's hand. Decorate it to create a character.
- *Paper-bag puppets.* Draw the character on the bag and put the bag over your hand to manipulate it, using the folded bottom of the bag for the mouth area; or decorate the bag as the character, stuff it with newspaper or cotton, and put a stick, dowel, or ruler into the neck of the bag and tie it shut, turning it upside down and using the stick for manipulation.

Some helpful puppeteering references include *Storytelling with Puppets* by Connie Champlin and Nancy Renfro (1985), *Making Puppets Come Alive* by Larry Engler and Carol Fijan (1973), and *The Consultant's Notebook* by Puppeteers of America (1989).

Book-talks

Book-talks are akin to storytelling but have a somewhat different purpose: motivating children to read. Both children and teachers should regularly share their favorite books through book-talks.

Book-talks should be based on books the teller really enjoys; otherwise, attracting readers for the book will be difficult. To prepare for the book-talk, read the book, think about the things that make it work, and listen to the voice of the book. Put the book aside and do other things. The parts that come back to you over the next few days will be the ones to include in your talk.

Book-talks may include one or more books. A common subject or theme—animals, war, survival, terror, love, secrets, outsiders—can link multiple books. A variety of reading levels, genres, and cultures will appeal to a wide range of reading interests and push readers a little beyond where they might go on their own (Rochman, 1989). Book-talks usually follow one of three styles: (a) tell highlights of the book, (b) read highlights from the book, or (c) combine telling and reading. For instance, a book-talk on Peter Dickinson's *Eva* might begin by telling about the hospital scene with the sobbing mother and Eva's confusion as she comes out of a coma, followed by reading a quotation in which Eva talks about living in a chimpanzee's body: "You had to awaken and open your eyes and see your new face and like what you saw. You had to make the human greeting and the chimp greeting and mean them."

Evaluating Oral Story Experiences

"Experience without reflection is hollow" (Cooper & Collins, 1992, p. 3). Guided discussion gives children an opportunity to reflect on oral experiences, respond to them, offer support to their classmates, and think about future experiences. They can also be used to elicit constructive criticism. For instance, questions such as the following, partially suggested by Cooper and Collins, could be used to evaluate a creative drama.

1. What did you like best about this play?
2. When was the imagination really at work?
3. When were the characters most believable?
4. What did you learn from the play that you did not know from the telling?
5. What did you learn about the important ideas in this story?
6. Did we leave out anything in this playing?
7. What would you like to try in our next playing of the scene?
8. What other things could our characters do or say?
9. How can we make our playing even more believable?

Silent Reading

Understanding is the goal of all reading, whether one is being read aloud to, reading silently, or reading aloud for an audience. All reading is an interactive process. Silent reading becomes more fluent with practice. In silent reading, students can more readily perceive ideas in the text. Children who read more show large differences in their reading abilities as a result of their practice (Fractor,

Woodruff, Martinez, & Teale, 1993). Silent reading, which precedes reading aloud to others, permits readers to focus on meaning without being overly involved with pronouncing words. Oral reading requires readers to think ahead of their voices and prepare to pronounce the next word or phrase, a skill that develops over time with extensive practice in silent reading.

Literature Circles

Literature circles are small, temporary discussion groups who have chosen to read the same story, poem, article, or book. Each group member prepares to take specific responsibilities in the discussion and the participants come to group with the notes they have taken to help them with their responsibilities. The literature circles have regular meetings, with the discussion roles rotating for each meeting. After they finish a book, the circle members plan to share the highlights of their reading with others in the classroom or school. They then form different groups, select another reading, and begin a new cycle. After the readers learn to sustain their discussions, they may drop the specific roles in the discussion (Daniels, 1994).

The goal of literature circles is to create open, natural conversations about books students have read. Divergent, open-ended, interpretive questions and critical reading questions encourage reader response and discussion. Questions such as the following encourage readers to read, process, savor, and share their personal response. When organizing literature circles, teachers give students sample questions to help them begin, but teachers point out that the best discussion questions come from their own thoughts, feelings, and concerns. The following are sample questions (Daniels, 1994).

- What was going through your mind while you read this?
- What was discussed in this (a specific) part of the book?
- Can someone briefly summarize today's reading?
- Did today's reading remind you of any real-life experiences?
- What questions did you have when you finished this section?
- Did anything in the book surprise you?
- What are the one or two most important ideas in the book?

- Predict some things you think will be talked about next.

Children participating in literature circles may choose passages to be shared using these guidelines: important, surprising, funny, confusing, informative, controversial, well-written, and thought-provoking (Daniels, 1994). We recommend that you read Harvey Daniels' book because it provides excellent ideas based on teachers' experiences in developing reading circles. Another helpful book for students in middle school is *You Gotta Be the Book* by Jeffrey D. Wilhelm.

Book and Breakfast

Book and Breakfast has been implemented in Chesterfield County, Virginia, schools. Participants in this program read designated books and discuss them, with volunteer mothers leading the discussion. The volunteer leaders read the book and are provided a discussion guide. The discussions take place before school and the students have breakfast while talking about their books. Both students and volunteer discussion leaders enjoy Book and Breakfast.

Uninterrupted Sustained Silent Reading (USSR-DEAR-SSR)

Uninterrupted sustained silent reading (USSR), also known as drop everything and read (DEAR) or sustained silent reading (SSR), is usually regarded as a logical counterpart to daily oral reading. USSR is predicated on the idea that teachers regularly involve children in learning the skills of reading, but they often overlook giving children time to practice reading, thereby developing reading fluency. USSR also makes children aware that reading and books are important; it allows them to experience whole books rather than fragments, and it gives them practice in sustaining attention, thinking, and reading.

Effective USSR programs require a foundation of reading materials broad enough to be appropriate to the age, development, and reading levels of all the children involved. These materials may include books, periodicals, magazines, newspapers, reference books, and any other type of reading material that might interest the children. They should be in the classroom library where children can readily obtain them. Select books from the school library and obtain extended loans from the local public library to stock classroom shelves.

When developing a USSR program, teachers should first explain the purpose and procedures. The students should understand that they may bring reading material to class or select from the classroom library, but they are not to move around the room, draw, talk, or do anything other than read. Everyone reads; teachers should allow no interruptions and require no reports on their reading.

At the outset, allocate 5 to 10 minutes for first and second graders and 10 to 15 minutes for third through sixth graders. The time can gradually be increased as children grow more comfortable with the process. The time of day for USSR varies among schools and teachers. Some schools have programs that involve everyone in the school reading at the same time. In other schools, individual teachers schedule USSR when it fits best in their schedules. Some teachers have students maintain records of their reading through a log of titles, number of pages read, or through a reading journal. Some teachers give the students time to share poems or excerpts from their reading.

Fostering Silent Reading

The best way teachers can foster silent reading is to provide many opportunities for silent reading such as USSR. Silent reading, however, is not a directly observable skill. Teaching children how to read silently through guided silent reading is important, as is providing opportunities for readers to respond to silent reading through discussion and other activities.

Guided silent reading

Teachers should begin by guiding children to read silently or "read with their eyes," then encouraging them to think about what they read as they read it. Demonstrate the thinking that occurs during silent reading by means of a "think-aloud," in which the teacher or a fluent reader verbalizes what occurs in their minds while they silently read. For example, reading "A treasure hunt—today's the day. Come on in and you can play!" (Cauley, *Treasure Hunt*) might lead a reader to think of questions such as the following:

- What kind of a treasure hunt?
- What is the treasure?

- Is it a Saturday or summer vacation, because these children should be in school?
- Who are they inviting to the treasure hunt?

These demonstrations guide students toward understanding how to think as they read silently—which simply admonishing them to think does not do—and enhance their response to literature.

Perhaps the most important step to developing silent reading skill is helping readers develop authentic purposes for silent reading. Silent reading that is active and purposeful enhances understanding and response. Again, purpose in reading is not directly observable, so teachers must guide readers' understanding and development of purpose. Teachers can model purposeful silent reading with a group through a read-aloud activity, as shown here with *Splash!* by Ann Jonas:

1. Introduce the book to the children by reading the title, *Splash!*, and asking what they think the story will be about. Such anticipation activities will give the students something to think about as they read—a purpose.

2. Write the children's responses on the chalkboard and ask them to think, as they hear the story, whether the splash in the story is what they expected. This will develop their sense of listening purpose and help them to actively and purposefully listen as you read.

3. Ask the children which character in the story they liked best. Answering this question develops purpose because readers see the story through the eyes of characters they like, which focuses their attention.

4. Ask them why they think Ann Jonas wrote this book. Thinking about why the author wrote the book will allow them to compare the author's purpose in writing with their purpose in listening and will develop their understanding of purpose.

Prereading discussions and purposeful listening activities such as these connect readers and books. Purposes based on children's own questions are the most useful and understandable. Encourage students to read the entire piece, so they can respond to the complete work. Figure 14.4 shows a web of student questions generated from the title of Dick King-Smith's *All Pigs Are Beautiful*

FIGURE 14.4   Web of student-generated questions for the title *All Pigs Are Beautiful*.

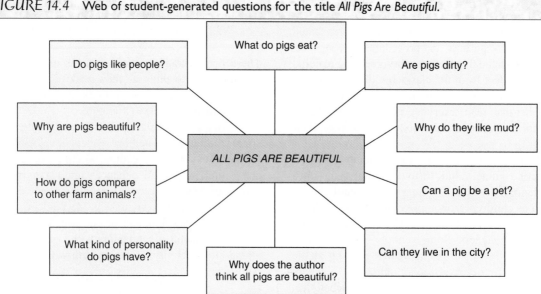

Responding to Silent Reading

Students can respond to and organize their silent reading in many ways. Class discussion is a tried-and-true method of allowing some children to respond to their reading. Prompts (discussed in Chapter 3) are useful in eliciting oral and written responses. Reflecting about a story and participating in written dialogues and discussions develop comprehension. Participating in a community of readers, dramatizing a story, or preparing for literature circles also gives opportunities for response and peer feedback. Individual response could include completing a story grammar of the book or choosing a character and explaining why this individual is their favorite. Figure 14.4 illustrates a third-grade reader's response to *All Pigs Are Beautiful*.

Classroom Activities

ACTIVITY 14.1   RAINY'S POWWOW

(IRA/NCTE Standards: 1, 4, 7, 9. Students read a variety of materials; conduct research, respect cultural practices.)

Introduction

In this tale of self-discovery and acceptance, a young girl learns that she must listen to and follow her own heart. The Thunderbird Powwow is about to begin, and Rainy still does not know what style of dance to choose so that she can be given her own special name. She asks Grandmother White Hair (who had been a traditional dancer), the Powwow Princess (who is a shawl dancer), and her friend Celeste (who is a jingle dancer) what it feels like to dance in their chosen styles, but none of these seem right for Rainy. As the dancing begins, Rainy enters the arena, but she is too shy to move. Then, listening to the drumbeats, Rainy moves with the rhythm and keeps on dancing even when the music stops. The sound of laughter gradually reaches Rainy, who flees the dance floor, embarrassed and humiliated. Grandmother White Hair's words comfort her, but it is the eagle's gift that gives Rainy her special name and the inspiration to choose her own dance.

ACTIVITY 14.2   SOARING WITH THE EAGLES

This activity can be an individual project, incorporated into cooperative grouping, or completed with partners working together. For younger students, show pictures of eagles and orally lead a fact-finding discussion about the birds. As a class, brainstorm the facts chosen to be included in the eagle books, then have students write the same facts in their booklets. The layered booklets must be made ahead of time and distributed when the students have chosen their six facts. Ask students to write a title for their booklets and illustrate the covers.

Book Connection

"Little Sister," Saleen said. "An eagle circled the arbor during the dance and dropped this in your path. In this way the eagle has honored you with a name. White Plume Dancing, this is your eagle feather."

Information

Eagles are very important to the spiritual traditions of Native North Americans. The birds are celebrated as animals of power, strength, and grace. The symbolism of eagles can be seen throughout the United States. As in the book, the eagle feather is honored in Native-American headdresses as well as eagle totems, arrows, myths, and dances. Eagle feathers are cherished and celebrated.

Activity

Research information about eagles. Create your own "layered" eagle fact book complete with illustration.

- Research information about eagles from books, movies, magazines, and the Internet.
- After reviewing your newfound information, create a booklet by choosing six of your favorite facts about eagles and listing them on separate pieces of paper. You'll need a paper cutter, stapler, and ruler.
- Each eagle fact should be written in sentence form on the bottom of each layered page. Regular 8½″ × 11″ paper works well if complete sentences are used. The remainder of the page is used for illustrations; thus, the last page of the booklet has the most room for illustrations. There will be a total of seven pieces of white paper stapled together at the top. The cover will be four inches in length, and the attached pages will be increased in length by one inch from the previous page. Each flap will lift up to reveal the illustration underneath. (Smaller versions of this layered booklet are also fun for students!)
- When the booklet is complete, you should be able to read all the eagle facts without lifting the pages!
- Share your book with a friend!

ACTIVITY 14.3   POWWOW HEADPIECES

Book Connection

"They watched the soldiers march by solemnly, holding flags high over their heads. Then came the traditional dancers slowly, in buckskin and feathers, porcupine quills, shells, beads—all things from nature."

Activity

Create your own powwow headpiece using items found on a nature walk.

- Before starting out on a nature scavenger hunt, make a list of the items you will be searching for. (Keep in mind you will need small, light objects.)

- Discuss the possibilities of what you may find on your walk.
- Discuss the difference between litter and objects in nature.
- Review the necessary safety rules before beginning your nature walk. Try to plan your walk outside of the school playground where you are more likely to find things in their natural state.
- Bring a paper lunch sack with you to collect your items.
- Upon returning from the nature walk, list your newfound treasures on paper. Compare both the prediction list and the new list. Were you

surprised by some of the items you found? Were you unable to find any items on your prediction list?

- Choose one or two items from your bag and describe them to a classmate using as many descriptive words as possible.
- Use a two-inch-wide tag board band as a basic pattern for the headpiece. Make sure the band will fit around your head, but do not staple the ends together until the project is complete. Use your items from nature, as well as additional materials, to create a unique and colorful headpiece!

Sample List of Things Found in Nature

- feathers
- dirt
- shells
- flowers
- seeds
- grass
- thorns
- berries

- quills
- bark
- pebbles
- leaves
- sticks
- nuts
- sand
- bone

Suggested Additional Materials

- construction paper
- glue
- stapler
- crayons
- string
- paint
- scissors
- yarn
- tag board
- sequins

Summary

Oral and silent reading strategies give students opportunities to experience literature and to respond to it in highly motivating situations. Comprehension is the focus of both oral and silent reading. In many instances, oral and silent reading are integrated because children who are preparing for oral activities read silently in anticipation of oral reading. One of the major differences between oral and silent reading is that oral readers must think of word pronunciation and produce the appropriate sounds for a word. This makes oral reading a slower process than silent reading.

Interpreting written literature for the appreciation of listeners is the purpose of oral reading. Oral reading has a variety of other purposes; for example, in the early years of school, children have limited reading abilities that restrict their experiences with books, but oral activities like those presented in this chapter enhance their understanding and appreciation of literature. Moreover, these activities develop children's ear for the sound of written language and their understanding. In choosing literature for oral activities, teachers need to consider how it sounds.

Thought Questions

1. Why are the oral activities motivating for children?
2. How do oral reading activities develop literacy?
3. Which oral reading activities will you use most often? Why?
4. Why do you think some teachers neglect reading aloud?
5. Why should a teacher feel that reading aloud to children is important?

Research and Application Experiences

1. Choose a poem and plan a choral reading for it that involves individual and unison reading.
2. Prepare *Alexander and the Terrible, Horrible, No Good, Very Bad Day* by Judith Viorst for oral reading. Then make a tape of your reading for your own analysis.
3. Make a story map for the story. This map can serve as your guide for telling this story.

4. Invent five descriptive phrases for the characters in *Goldilocks and the Three Bears*. These phrases should add color and dramatic appeal to the story when it is told aloud.

5. Choose a story for a flannel board presentation, prepare a script, and make the flannel board and the characters. Then present it to a group of children. Write about your experiences.

6. Choose a story for a puppet dramatization. Plan the script, make the puppets, and practice the presentation. Present it to a group of children. Write about your experiences.

7. Find storytelling on the Internet and listen to a story told by a professional storyteller.

Children's Literature References and Recommended Books

Note: Books designated with an asterisk (*) are recommended for reluctant readers.

Alexander, L. (1964). *The book of three.* New York: Holt Rinehart & Winston. (4–8). FANTASY.

A story of magic and amazing feats.

Alexander, L. (1999). *Gypsy rizka.* New York: Dutton. (3–6). FANTASY.*

A hilarious, perils-of-Pauline story. The episodic chapters lend themselves to reading chapter by chapter.

Anderson, H. C. (1978). *The princess and the pea* (P. Galdone, Illus.). New York: Seabury. (1–3). TRADITIONAL LITERATURE.

The story of a delicate princess who could feel a pea under hundreds of mattresses.

Aranda, C. (1993). *Dichos: Proverbs and sayings from the Spanish.* Santa Fe, NM: Sunstone. (4–8). TRADITIONAL LITERATURE.

The content of this book will be familiar to people familiar with the Spanish language.

Asch, F. (1995). *Water.* New York: Harcourt Brace. (K–3). NONFICTION.*

This informative book tells about water and its values.

Bania, M. (2002). *Kumak's house: A tale of the far north.* Alaska Northwest Books/Graphic Arts Center Publishing. Toronto, Canada. (1–3). TRADITIONAL LITERATURE.

A humorous tale from the Inupiat Eskimo culture.

Banks, L. R. (1988). *I Houdini: The autobiography of a self-educated hamster* (T. Riley, Illus.). New York: Doubleday. (3–6). FANTASY.

Houdini escaped the pet store and learned about life.

Base, G. (2001). *The water hole.* New York: Harry Abrams. (2–7). PICTURE BOOK.

A counting book that points up the importance of water.

Berger, B. (2002). *All the way to Lhasa: A tale from Tibet.* New York: Philomel. (K–4). TRADITIONAL LITERATURE.

A Tibetian parable about people traveling and an old woman advises you get there by putting one foot in front of the other.

Borden, L. (1997). *The little ships: The heroic rescue at Dunkirk in World War II* (M. Foreman, Illus.). New York: McElderry. (3–6). HISTORICAL FICTION.*

This book Tells the story of the rescue of American troops at Dunkirk.

Burleigh, R. (1998). *Black Whiteness: Admiral Byrd alone in the Antarctic* (W. L. Krudop, Illus.). New York: Atheneum. (3–8). BIOGRAPHY.

This book is told through entries in Admiral Byrd's journal; it includes beautiful illustrations.

Byars, B. (1994). *The Golly sisters ride again* (S. Truesdell, Illus.). New York: HarperCollins. (1–3). HISTORICAL FICTION.*

Hilarious sisters make their mark in the old west.

Carr, J. (1999). *Swine divine* (R. Bender, Illus.). New York: Holiday House. (1–4). FANTASY.

Farmer Luke bathes Rosie the pig, but she prefers mud.

Cauley, L. B. (1994). *Treasure hunt.* New York: Putnam. (1–3). REALISTIC FICTION.*

A clever mystery for younger children.

Cazet, D. (1998). *Minnie and Moo go dancing.* New York: DK Publishing. (1–4). FANTASY.*

Two cows dress up to go dancing with funny results.

Cherry, L., & Plotkin, M. J. (1998). *The Shaman's apprentice.* New York: Harcourt Brace. (2–5). REALISTIC FICTION.

Kamanya lives in the Amazon rain forest. After the Shaman saves his life, he wants to be a Shaman.

Christopher, P. (2002). *Bud not buddy.* New York: Yearling/Doubleday (4–7). HISTORICAL FICTION.

Bud is a 10 year old who is in the foster care system during the 1930's.

Claverie, J. (Reteller). (1989). *The Three Little Pigs.* New York: North South (K–3). TRADITIONAL.

A storyteller's unique version of the three little pigs.

Cleaver, V., & Cleaver, B. (1969). *Where the lilies bloom* (J. Spanfeller, Illus.). New York: Harper & Row. (5–8). REALISTIC FICTION.

Mary Call, a 14-year-old, has to care for her family after her father's death.

Cleaver, V., & Cleaver, B. (1977). *Trial valley*. Philadelphia: Lippincott. (5–8). REALISTIC FICTION.

In the sequel to *Where the Lilies Bloom*, Mary Call's sister marries the evil neighbor and an abandoned child comes to live with Mary Call.

Cowley, J. (1999). *Red-eyed tree frog* (N. Bishop, Illus.). New York: Scholastic. (1–3). NONFICTION.

This lively text contains exquisite illustrations.

Dickinson, P. (1988). *Eva*. New York: Delacorte. (6–9). SCIENCE FICTION.

Eva's body is destroyed, so her brain is implanted in the body of a chimpanzee. This book features fascinating plot and superb characterization.

Fleming, C. (Reteller). (1998). *The hatmaker's sign: A story by Benjamin Franklin* (R. A. Parker, Illus.). New York: Orchard. (1–3). HISTORICAL FICTION.

Benjamin Franklin told this story to Thomas Jefferson.

Florian, D. (1999). *Laugh-eteria*. New York: Harcourt. (3–6). POETRY.

This book is a collection of hilarious poems.

Fox, M. (1998). *Boo to a goose* (D. Miller, Illus.). New York: Dial. (K–2). PICTURE BOOK, REALISTIC FICTION.

A child will do anything except say "boo" to a goose.

Galdone, P. (Reteller). (1984). *Henny Penny*. Boston: Houghton Mifflin. (K–2). TRADITIONAL LITERATURE.*

This is a retelling of the well-known tale of a hen who believes the sky is falling.

Garland, S. (2001). *Children of the dragon: Selected tales from Vietnam* (T. Hyman, Illus.). New York: Harcourt. (1–4). TRADITIONAL LITERATURE.

These tales are traditional to Vietnam.

Giblin, J. C. (2000). *The amazing life of Benjamin Franklin* (M. Dooling, Illus.). New York: Scholastic. (3–7). BIOGRAPHY.

A biography of Franklin, focusing on his achievements.

Greaves, M. (Reteller). (1990). *Tattercoats*. New York: Potter. (1–3). TRADITIONAL.

This is a version of the Cinderella tale.

Guthrie, W. (1998). *This land is your land* (K. Jakobsen, Illus.). New York: Little Brown. (K–4). PICTURE BOOK, POETRY.

This book presents Woodie Guthrie's view of America.

Heard, G. (2002). *This place I know: Poems of comfort*. Cambridge, MA: Candlewick Press. (1–5). POETRY.

These poems provide words of comfort for children.

Holt, D. (1994a). *Hairyman*. Fairview, NC: High Windy Audio. (All ages). TRADITIONAL LITERATURE.

The traditional tale of Hairyman.

Holt, D. (1994b). *Tailybone*. Fairview, NC: High Windy Audio (All ages). TRADITIONAL LITERATURE.

This is a well-known Appalachian tale.

Howe, D., & Howe, J. (1979). *Bunnicula* (A. Daniel, Illus.). New York: Atheneum. (2–4). FANTASY.

The author of this fantasy about a vampire rabbit is a dog.

Jackson, D. (2002). *The Bug Scientists*. New York: Houghton Mifflin. (2–4). NONFICTION.

Excellent photos of unusual bugs.

Johnson, P. (2002). *Jack outwits the giants*. New York: McElderry. (1–3). TRADITIONAL LITERATURE.

This is a traditional "Jack" tale from the Appalachians.

Jonas, A. (1995). *Splash!* New York: Greenwillow. (K–2). PICTURE BOOK.

Animals and children splash in a pool while adding and subtracting.

Kellogg, S. (Reteller). (1991). *Jack and the beanstalk*. New York: Morrow. (K–4). TRADITIONAL LITERATURE.

This is a version of the traditional fairy tale.

Kellogg, S. (Reteller). (1996). *I was born about 10,000 years ago*. New York: Morrow. (K–5). TRADITIONAL LITERATURE.

This is an exuberant tall tale.

King-Smith, D. (1993). *All pigs are beautiful* (A. Jeram, Illus.). Cambridge, MA: Candlewick Press. (1–4). PICTURE BOOK.

The author shares his love of pigs.

Kitt, T. (1988). So long as there's weather: In B. S. de Regniers, E. Moore, M. M. White, & J. Carr (Eds.), *Sing a song of popcorn*. New York: Scholastic. (K–6). POETRY.

A wide ranging collection of poems.

Lester, J. (1968). *To be a slave* (T. Feelings, Illus.). New York: Dial. (5–12). NONFICTION.

This book features descriptions of slave life based on interviews with former slaves.

Lester, J. (1969). *Black folktales* (T. Feelings, Illus.). New York: Baron. (3–12). TRADITIONAL LITERATURE.

This is a wonderful collection for oral reading.

Lester, J. (1987). *The tales of Uncle Remus: The adventures of Brer Rabbit* (J. Pinkney, Illus.). New York: Dial. (3–6). TRADITIONAL LITERATURE.

This is an updated version of the Uncle Remus tales.

Littlechild, G. (1993). *This land is my land*. San Francisco: Children's Book Press. (3–6). BIOGRAPHY.

The author tells about his life through his art.

Louie, A. L. (Reteller). (1982). *Yeh Shen: A Cinderella story from China* (E. Young, Illus.). New York: Philomel. (1–3). TRADITIONAL LITERATURE.

A Chinese version of the traditional Cinderella tale.

Lowry, L. (1993). *The giver*. Boston: Houghton Mifflin. (5–8). FANTASY.

This story is based on a seemingly ideal society.

Martin, B. (1967). *Brown Bear, Brown Bear, What Do You See?* (E. Carle, Illus.). New York: Holt. (K-2). PICTURE BOOK.

A repetitive tale.

Martin, J. B. (2003). *The water gift and the pig of the pig* (L. Wingerter, Illus.). Boston: Houghton Mifflin. (1–3). FANTASY.

When Isabel's grandfather, a water man, loses his confidence, Isabel and her pet pig help him. The book contains lyric language and has a folk-inspired feel.

Merrill, J. (1964). *The pushcart war* (R. Solbert, Illus.). New York: Scott. (4–8). FANTASY.

The story of a war between pushcarts and trucks in New York.

Milne, A. A. (1926). *Winnie-the-Pooh* (E. H. Shepard, Illus.). New York: Dutton. (1–5). FANTASY.

The adventures of Pooh and his friends.

Muth, J. (2003). *Stone soup*. New York: Scholastic. (1–3). TRADITIONAL LITERATURE.

Stone soup is set in China, and the instigators are monks.

O'Brien, R. C. (1974). *Mrs. Frisby and the rats of NIMH* (Z. Bernstein, Illus.). New York: Atheneum. (4–8). FANTASY.

Intelligent rats escape the National Institute of Mental Health.

O'Callahan, J. (1994a). *Little Heroes*. Fairview, NC: High Windy Audio. (1–3). TRADITIONAL.

Stories about little heroes like Tom Thumb.

O'Callahan, J. (1994b). *The boy who loved frogs*. West Tilbury, MA: Vineyard Video. (1–3). TRADITIONAL LITERATURE.

This is an audio version of the traditional tale.

Okimoto, J. and Aoki, E. (2002). *The white swan express: A story of adoption*. New York: Clarion. (K–3). REALISTIC FICTION.

The story of three Chinese baby girls who are adopted.

O'Dell, S. (1960). *Island of the blue dolphins*. Boston: Houghton Mifflin. (4–6). HISTORICAL FICTION.

The story of a girl who survives alone on a Pacific island.

O'Neill, A. (2002). *The recess queen* (L. Huliska-Beith, Illus.). New York: Scholastic. (1–4). REALISTIC FICTION.

Mean Jean is the recess queen until a new girl moves in.

Prelutsky, J. (1980). *Rolling Harvey down the hill* (V. Chess, Illus.). New York: Greenwillow. (K–3). POETRY.

Children will enjoy this humorous poetry.

Raczek, L. T. (1999). *Rainy's powwow* (G. Bennett, Illus.). Flagstaff, AZ: Rising Moon. (2–5). REALISTIC FICTION.

Rainy, a Native American, is thrilled to attend her first powwow.

Rand, W. B. (1951). Godfrey, Gordon, Gustavus Gore. In M. H. Arbuthnot (Comp.), *Time for poetry*. Glenview, IL: Scott Foresman. (K–6). POETRY.

An anthology of poetry on many subjects.

Richards, L. (1951). The umbrella brigade. In M. H. Arbuthnot (Comp.), *Time for poetry*. Glenview, IL: Scott Foresman. (K–6). POETRY.

This is a rhythmic poem for a rainy day.

Rosen, M. J. (Ed.). (1989). *We're going on a bear hunt* (H. Oxenbury, Illus.). New York: McElderry. (K–2). REALISTIC FICTION.

Repetitious language encourages listeners' participation.

Rounds, G. (1990). *I know an old lady who swallowed a fly*. New York: Holiday. (1–6). TRADITIONAL LITERATURE.

A cumulative rhyme.

Rylant, C. (1985). *The relatives came* (S. Gammell, Illus.). New York: Bradbury. (2–4). REALISTIC FICTION.

A visit from the relatives changes sleeping and eating arrangements.

Salat, C. (2002). *Peanut's emergency*. (T. Lyon, illus.). Boston, MA: Charles Bridge. (K–2). REALISTIC FICTION.

Peanut's mother has car problems so she is late to pick up Peanut.

Schertle, A. (1999). *I am the cat* (M. Buehner, Illus.). New York: Lothrop, Lee & Shepard. (1–4). POETRY.

This book features poems about cats.

Scieszka, J. (2001). *Baloney* (Henry L. Smith, Illus.). New York: Viking. PICTURE BOOK.

An alien boy is late for school and has a wild story to tell.

Seeger, P. (1994). *Stories and songs for little children.* Fairview, NC: High Windy Audio. (K–2).

Recordings of Seeger's stories and songs for young children.

Seuss, Dr. (1940). *Horton hatches the egg.* New York: Random House. (1–4). FANTASY.

An old Dr. Seuss story that children love.*

Seuss, Dr. (1949). *Bartholomew and the oobleck.* New York: Random House. (1–4). FANTASY.

This is another delightful Dr. Seuss story.*

Siebert, D. (1984). *Truck song* (B. Barton, Illus.). New York: Crowell. (1–4). POETRY.

In this book, the rhythm of trucks comes through the poetry.

Siebert, D. (1990). *Train song* (M. Wimmer, Illus.). New York: Crowell. (1–4). POETRY.

Train rhythm is the theme of this poetry.

Sloat, T. (2001). *The hungry giant of the tundra.* (R. Sloat, Illus.). Edmonds, WA: Alaska Northwest Books. (K–3). TRADITIONAL.

This well-known tale has a hungry giant and disobedient children who escape using their wits.

Smith, W. J. (1990). *Laughing time: Collected nonsense* (F. Krahn, Illus.). New York: Farrar, Straus & Giroux. (1–5). POETRY.

This is a collection of hilarious poetry.*

Soto, G. (1990). *Baseball in April and other stories.* New York: Harcourt Brace. (3–5). REALISTIC FICTION.

This book contains stories about spring practice for baseball.

Stanley, D. (1999). *Raising sweetness* (G. B. Karas, Illus.). New York: Putnam. (1–4). REALISTIC FICTION.

This is a humorous family story.*

Steptoe, J. (2003). *The Jones family express.* New York: Lee & Low. (K–4). REALISTIC FICTION.

This family story is told through Steven's collection of Aunt Carolyn's humorous post cards.

Stevens, J. R. (1999). *Twelve lizards leaping* (Mau, Illus.). Flagstaff, AZ: Rising Moon. (K–2). PICTURE BOOK.

This story is take-off on the traditional Christmas carol.

Taylor, M. D. (1976). *Roll of thunder, hear my cry.* New York: Dial. (5–9). HISTORICAL FICTION.

Set in the 1930s, a Black family seeks to retain pride and integrity in this story.

Van Allsburg, C. (1992). *The widow's broom.* Boston: Houghton Mifflin. (4–7). FANTASY.

This is a story of superstition and prejudice. The widow wants to keep the broom, but Spivey wants to get rid of it.

Vigil, A. (Reteller). (1994). *The corn woman.* Englewood, CO: Libraries Unlimited. (5–8). TRADITIONAL LITERATURE.

This book contains stories from the southwestern United States.

Viorst, J. (1972). *Alexander and the terrible, horrible, no good, very bad day.* (J. Cruz, Illus.). New York: Atheneum. (K–6). PICTURE BOOK, REALISTIC FICTION.

Alexander has a bad day, which happens even in Australia.

Ward, H. (2003). *The dragon machine* (W. Anderson, Illus.). New York: Dutton. (K–3). FANTASY.

George finds a dragon who befriends him. He begins to accumulate dragons and builds a dragon machine.

Westcott, N. B. (1987). *Peanut butter and jelly.* New York: Dutton. (K–2). POETRY.

This book features a traditional play-rhyme.

Westcott, N. B. (1990). *I know an old lady who swallowed a fly.* New York: Dutton. (1–6). POETRY.

This book features a traditional play-rhyme.

Wilder, L. I. (1953). *Little house on the prairie* (G. Williams, Illus.). New York: Harper. (3–6). HISTORICAL FICTION.*

This book tells the story of the Ingalls family.

Wisniewski, D. (1998). *The secret knowledge of grown-ups.* New York: Lothrop, Lee & Shepard. (K–4). FANTASY.*

The author opens secret files, hidden from kids for thousands of years.

References and Books for Further Reading

Barton, B. (1986). *Tell me another*. Portsmouth, NH: Heinemann.

Busching, B. (1981, March). "Reader's theater": An education for language and life. *Language Arts, 58*, 330–338.

Champlin, C., & Renfro, N. (1985). *Storytelling with puppets*. Chicago: American Library Association.

Cohen, D. (1968). The effect of literature on vocabulary and reading achievement. *Elementary English, 45*, 209–213, 217.

Cooper, P., & Collins, R. (1992). *Look what happened to frog: Storytelling in education*. Scottsdale, AZ: Gorsuch Scarisbrick.

Daniels, H. (1994). *Literature circles: Voice and choice in the student-centered classroom*. York, ME: Stenhouse.

Downing, J., & Leong, C. K. (1982). *Psychology of Reading*. New York: Macmillan.

Engler, L., & Fijan, C. (1973). *Making puppets come alive*. New York: Taplinger.

Fractor, J. S., Woodruff, M. C., Martinez, M. G., & Teale, W. H. (1993). Let's not miss opportunities to promote voluntary reading: Classroom libraries in the elementary school. *Reading Teacher, 46*, 476–484.

Golden, J. M. (1984). Children's concept of story in reading and writing. *Reading Teacher, 37*, 578–584.

Hahn, M. L. (2002). *Reconsidering read-aloud*. Portland, ME: Stenhouse.

Heathcote, D. (1983). Learning, knowing, and languaging in drama: An interview with Dorothy Heathcote. *Language Arts, 73*, 8.

Lenz, L. (1992). Crossroads of literacy and orality: Reading poetry aloud. *Language Arts, 69*, 597–603.

Lester, J. (1988). The storyteller's voice: Reflections on the rewriting of Uncle Remus. *New Advocate, 1*, 143–147.

Livo, N. J., & Rietz, S. A. (1986). *Storytelling process and practice*. Littleton, CO: Libraries Unlimited.

Manna, A. L. (1984). Making language come alive through reading plays. *Reading Teacher, 52*, 326–334.

Martinez, M., Roser, N., & Strecker, S. (1998–1999). I never thought I could be a star: A reader's theater ticket to fluency. *Reading Teacher 52*, 326–334.

McCaslin, N. (1990). *Creative drama in the classroom* (5th ed.). New York: Longman.

Miccinati, J. (1985). Using prosodic cues to teach oral reading fluency. *Reading Teacher, 39*, 206–212.

Morrow, L. M. (1979). *Super tips for storytelling*. New York: Scholastic.

Morrow, L. M. (1988). Young children's responses to one-to-one story readings in school settings. *Reading Research, 23*, 89–107.

Naylor, A., & Borders, S. (1993). *Children talking about books*. Portsmouth, NH: Heinemann.

Perfect, K. A. (1999). Rhyme and reason: Poetry for the heart and head. *Reading Teacher, 52*, 728–737.

Puppeteers of America. (1989). *The consultant's notebook*. Chicago: Puppeteers of America.

Purcell-Gates, V. (1988). Lexical syntactic knowledge of written narrative held by well-read-to kindergartners and second graders. *Research in Teaching English, 22*, 128–160.

Rochman, H. (1989). Booktalking: Going global. *Horn Book, 58*, 30–35.

Roe, B., Alfred, S., & Smith, S. (1998). *Teaching through stories: Yours, mine, and theirs*. Norwood, MA: Christopher-Gordon.

Roney, R. C. (1989). Back to the basics with storytelling. *Reading Teacher, 42*, 520–523.

Sawyer, R. (1962). *The way of the storyteller*. New York: Harper & Row.

Siks, G. (1983). *Drama with children* (2nd ed.). New York: Harper & Row.

Sipe, L. R. (2002, February). Talking back and taking over: Young children's expressive engagement during storybook read alouds. *The Reading Teacher, 55* (5), 476–483.

Stoodt, B. D. (1988). *Teaching language arts*. New York: Harper & Row.

Teale, W. H., & Martinex, M. (1987). *Connecting writing: Fostering emergent literacy in kindergarten children*. Technical Report No. 412. San Antonio, TX: University of Texas at San Antonio.

Wilhelm, J. D. (1997). *You gotta be the book*. New York: Teachers College Press.

Engaging with and Responding to Children's Literature

GUIDING QUESTIONS

Think about your responses to the different genres of literature you read. Do you have a favorite genre? What element of literature arouses your strongest response? As you read this chapter, think about the following questions.

1. What is engaged reading? Describe it in your own words.

2. What is the response process? Describe it in your own words.

3. How can teachers nurture children's response to literature?

When readers open a book, they accept an invitation to collaborate with the author or the illustrator, to explore existing meanings as well as to forge new meanings. No matter how excellent the writing may be, a book is never complete until someone reads it and brings it to life. Readers not only use what is in the text—words and their meanings—but also the meanings they bring to the text (Musthafa, 1996; Thacker, 1996).

Response, the way readers react and feel about a book or books, is built on readers' interpretations of literature. Their response may range from quiet pleasure to excitement to hurling a book across the room. Engaged readers have the strongest response to literature—they get lost in a story, and can't wait to find out what happens.

Engaged readers get excited when they read new ideas. The readers' purpose or stance, and individual meaning or envisionment, also influence their response. Moreover, they create meaning through intertextual connections among the books they enjoy and their life experiences, as illustrated in the vignette on the following page.

Engagement with Literature

The children in the vignette demonstrated engagement and response. They engaged with and responded to their books. Engaged readers actively pursue meaning from the first instant of reading. They focus on the text, constantly building and synthesizing meaning, notic-

Sarah drew this lighthouse after reading Birdie's Lighthouse as part of a lighthouse unit. She also visited some lighthouses on the Web.

ing words, and attending to the images and emotions created in the text. As they make sense of the written language, they either confirm or cancel their predictions of meaning. Teachers and librarians build children's engagement and response through the books they select, the way they introduce books, and the literary experiences they create (Chambers, 1996).

VIGNETTE

Jane Morrison, a third-grade teacher, introduced poetry, fiction, and non-fiction related to the students' interests, as well as the language arts standards for third grade. She book-talked the books she had collected, and the students started reading their chosen books. During the day's lesson, she moved around the classroom, discussing individual children's choices with them.

Christopher reported that he read Jerdine Nolen's *Raising Dragons*. "This book is really good! The dragon is a good guy. He helped the family solve their problems, and he had a bunch of adventures. I wish I could find a dragon egg."

"What would you like to read next?" Ms. Morrison asked.

"I want to read *Dinosaurs Forever* by William Wise because it looks like a funny book. After that, I am going to read *Dinosaurs with Feathers: The Ancestors of Modern Birds* by Caroline Arnold. Mrs. Miller (the media specialist) said that it's a good nonfiction book."

In another part of the classroom, Annie sat engrossed in Deborah Hopkinson's *Birdie's Lighthouse*. Annie looked up as Kayla asked, "Is that a good book?"

"Oh, yes!" she answered. "Birdie is so smart! I really like the way she keeps her head and struggles so hard to keep the lighthouse burning when her father is sick. I saw a lighthouse in North Carolina last summer. I want to read *The Light at Tern*

(continued)

303

Rock by Julia Sauer next because Miss Morrison talked about it. Plus, I want to get on the Internet and learn more about lighthouses."

Jimmy and Patsy sat on the floor constructing something with paper. The teacher assistant observed them for a time, then asked, "What are you making?"

"We just finished reading Gail Gibbons' book, *Catch the Wind!* and it has directions for making a cool kite, so we're making it. Then we're going to read a book about Japanese kites."

"Do you enjoy flying kites?"

"Oh, yes! We fly kites at the beach."

Stance

All readers have a purpose for reading, or *stance* (Holland, Hungerford, & Ernst, 1993). Whether they are reading assigned text for knowledge or reading for pleasure, adopting a stance is an active process that indicates what the reader is paying attention to while reading. A reader's stance shows what has caught the reader's attention (Many, 1996). Two major stances exist in literature: aesthetic and efferent.

Aesthetic and Efferent Reading

Aesthetic reading

Aesthetic readers focus attention on pleasurable, interesting experience for its own sake. Aesthetic readers center on the sound and rhythm of the words and the personal feelings, ideas, and attitudes created during reading (Rosenblatt, 1982). Children create new experiences as they live through the literature: participating in the story, identifying with the characters, and sharing their conflicts and their feelings, a process Judith Langer identifies as *envisionment* (1992). Excellent fiction and nonfiction both have aesthetic values because the authors' language style expresses meaning. The language in some books such as poetry is obviously aesthetic. For instance, *John Coltrane's Giant Steps,* remixed by Chris Raschka, creates an unique literary experience by combining John Coltrane's composition, "Giant Steps," with color and art in a picture book.

Efferent reading

The *efferent reading* stance focuses on the meanings and ideas in the text (Rosenblatt, 1982). Readers have

FIGURE 15.1   Reading stance continuum.

Mostly aesthetic	Half efferent, half aesthetic	Mostly efferent

a narrow focus as they seek information, directions, solutions, and conclusions in efferent reading. Rosenblatt points out, however, that a reading event may fall anywhere on a continuum between the aesthetic and the efferent poles. Therefore, a stance cannot be only aesthetic or only efferent, because most reading experiences have elements of both (see Figure 15.1).

Envisionment: Individual Meaning

Authors' words and sentences stimulate readers' memories, associations, thoughts, and questions, which enhance comprehension (Barksdale-Ladd & Nedeff, 1997; Probst, 1992). Langer uses the word *envisionment* to refer to this reader-derived meaning. Envisionments are created as the individual reads and enters into the story, creating his or her vision of the text (Langer, 1992).

The box, *Envisioning "The New Kid on the Block,"* describes how one reader creates meaning from Jack Prelutsky's poem. Another reader might emphasize different words and fill in gaps in meaning from a dissimilar set of world experiences, creating an entirely different envisionment of the poem. This reader might not know any bullies or might not even know what the word *bully* means. A reader well-acquainted with Jack Prelutsky's poetry will have different expectations of the poem than one who is not.

Response to Literature

Response to literature is many things: what readers make of a text as they read, how it comes alive and becomes personal; what happens during reading; and how readers feel and react to what they have read. Response is also the pleasure and satisfaction readers feel and the way they display these feelings (Barton, 2001; Blake, 1995; Langer, 1995). Literary experience does not stop with the book's last page (Martinez & Nash, 1991; Rosenblatt, 1978). The readers continue to respond as they rethink and reread the book or parts of the book, or even read another book that is somehow

Envisioning "The New Kid on the Block"

In Jack Prelutsky's poem, "The New Kid on the Block," I first read that the new kid is *real tough*. These words create a mental image of a muscular bully. The next few lines tell how the new kid *punches hard, pulls hair,* and *likes to fight,* which elaborates on my envisionment of a neighborhood bully. The poet then describes the bully's be-havior with the words *swiped* and *bad,* so my interaction with the text develops further with the fact that the bully is also unpleasant to my envisionment. However, the surprise in the last line of the poem makes me reconsider my earlier envisionments: "I don't care for *her* at all."

---

related. The reader's feelings remain and continue to evolve after completing the book, sometimes long after the book is read (Rosenblatt, 1978; Stoodt & Amspaugh, 1994). A child who has read *The Stray Dog* by Marc Simont may choose another book about dogs or visit an animal shelter and remember the story. Another possibility is that the child will remember the story and write his or her own story (Wollman-Bonilla & Werchaldo, 1999). Response includes both intertextuality and stance. During this process, readers create intertextual connections.

Intertextuality: Individual Connections

Literature is woven with quotations, references, and echoes of prior literary experiences that give it virtually unlimited meaning (Barthes, 1975). Meaning in each new book one reads is enriched in some measure by the shadows of previously read texts. This process, called *intertextuality*, means interpreting one text by means of another (Hartman, 1992; Lundin, 1998). Two or more texts, written or oral, are involved in the intertextuality process (Bloome & Bailey, 1992) and may include films, books, class lectures, Internet sites, conversations, and videos (Hartman, 1992).

The *Cinderella* story gives readers intertextual connections for understanding San Souci's *The Talking Eggs.* Readers of this story usually recognize the plot and character are similar to *Cinderella.* In *The Talking Eggs,* a widow, her bad-tempered daughter Rose, and her sweet and kind daughter Blanche are the main characters. The story is set in the rural south rather than a palace, and the magic character is an old woman who blesses Blanche. In the end, the widow and her bad-tempered daughter run into the woods, chased by whip snakes, toads, frogs, yellow jackets, and a big gray wolf.

Heckedy Peg, inspired by a sixteenth-century game still played by children today, is about seven children, a wicked witch's intrusion into their lives, and a spell that only their mother can break.

Research reveals that readers enlist an incredible diversity among the links they make between current and previous reading. The most common intertextual links include genre, character, and plots (Cairney, 1990). As in creating meaning, readers apply intertextuality differently from one individual to the next. Although reading exactly the same stories, readers nonetheless identify different links for making meaning. We cannot predict intertextual links with confidence, but we can encourage children to compare *plots*, characters, settings, and so forth from story to story.

Understanding Response

In the opening vignette, Jimmy and Patsy chose to read a book about kites because they had enjoyable experiences with kites. Their previous reading and knowledge created intertextual links that helped them construct meaning. They acquired some new knowledge after reading *Catch the Wind!*, built kites, and planned to read more books about kites. All of these responses to literature extended their efferent experience.

Dimensions of Response

The various facets of response include sound, event, world, and author style, which are explored in this section.

Sound is a natural response for children, who respond to a book's words and rhythms of language. They hear the text in their head as they read, listening to the dialogue as they would conversation. This is why "reading aloud to children of all ages is vital . . . because this is the way we learn how to turn cold print into a dramatic enactment in the theater of our imagination" (Chambers, 1996, p. 169). The dialogue in Hilary

The beauty of Christmas and the winter world are shown in the pictures and words.

McKay's *Saffy's Angel* is like that heard in many families, so readers respond to the sounds of family talk.

Readers who respond to *event* are sensitive to the forms of story, poem, or nonfiction. They can anticipate events, characters, and setting when they read. They expect stories to have characters, settings, problems or conflicts, and efforts to solve problems. Experienced readers have learned that events increase suspense in a story, and that characters usually have conflicts as they try to solve problems. Their expectations are based on genre, story elements, story grammar, poetic form, and expository grammars, which are discussed in Chapter 3.

Children identify with story characters, which is why they enjoy reading about people near their own age or those a bit older. Children who enjoy dramatic play will enjoy acting out the role of wolf or boy in Bob Hartman's book, *The Wolf Who Cried Boy*. They may reshape and revise this story to fit their own envisionment.

Author style is the quality of writing and the way the author creates plot, characters, setting, and theme. "To enter and hold the mind of a child or a young person is one of the hardest of all writers' tasks" (Zinsser, 1990). Young readers do not have the authors' breadth of experience, but they have enough experience to recognize a writer who fails to respect their experience and intelligence. They identify and reject shallow books or didactic, preachy books.

The *world* response occurs when readers respond to sound, event, and author style. For instance, when reading Judith Viorst's poem "If I Were in Charge of the World," children connect it with their own lives and with other literature that has similar themes. The alliterative phrases in this poem create sounds that resonate with children such as "healthy hamsters" and "basketball baskets." Children who have allergies identify with the author's desire to "cancel" allergy shots, and both children and adults identify with the poet's desire to eliminate "Monday mornings." Anyone who has had pet hamsters can relate to the author's desire for "healthy hamsters." Viorst consistently enters the children's world with her stories and poems.

Truth is a critical quality in children's books, even when the story is not literally true. E. B. White (1970) said of his own writing: "I have two or three strong beliefs about the business of writing for children. I feel I must never kid them about anything. I feel I must be on solid ground myself. I also feel that a writer has an obligation to transmit, as best as he can, his love of life, his appreciation for the world. I am not averse to departing from reality, but I am against departing from the truth" (p. 544). Fine writers express truth as they understand it, through fiction, poetry, or nonfiction. Truth in literature is also expressed in the integrity of the transaction between the writer and the reader (Zinsser, 1990). When the writer's truth resonates with the child's truth, the reader responds to the author's storytelling skill.

Truth is the foundation of Mary Hoffman's picture book *Amazing Grace,* in which one classmate tells Grace that she cannot be Peter Pan in the school play because she is a girl, and a second classmate says that she cannot be Peter Pan because she is Black. The truth of a book must be an integral feature; to omit the truth or to tiptoe around it is dishonest. Children respond to honest characters such as Grace, as well as their creators.

Literature as a Means of Knowing

Literary thinking develops readers' learning and knowledge (Probst, 1992). Literature plays four roles in the curriculum. These ways of knowing include: knowledge about self, knowledge about others, knowledge about books, and knowledge about contexts.

Self

First, the reader learns about self through literature when he or she recalls experiences related to the text and integrates them with the text, thereby developing self-understanding. For instance, after reading *The Stray Dog* by Marc Simont, 7-year-old Julia recalled family picnics and going to an animal shelter to adopt their dog. Through this association, she realized that the family in the book was like her own.

Others

Children also begin to realize that other readers have different experiences. For instance, Julia's classmate, Josh, said the family portrayed in *The Stray Dog* was not real because he could not relate to their activities. Both Julia and Josh discovered new ideas about one another from this experience and deepened their understanding of the book.

Books

Literary thinking helps readers understand books and literary devices used by authors to stimulate readers' thinking. For instance, Hilary McKay creates distinctive characters using authentic dialogue in her book *Saffy's Angel.* Saffy, the central character, discovers that she is adopted and that her siblings are actually cousins. Through humor, subplots, and characters, readers come to understand how authors express meaning.

Contexts

Literature helps learners know about different contexts. For instance, in *Good-bye, 382 Shin Dang Dong* by Frances Park and Ginger Park, a Korean child, Jangmi, and her family move. The author helps readers understand that Jangmi is sad about leaving her grandparents, cousins, and friends to move to a strange new place. Jangmi's context leads her to view her new home as strange and different. Each of these readers brings a different context or background to the book, depending on the extent of his or her personal experiences. Discussion helps readers clarify and activate their contexts.

Author's Meaning

Authors write because they have something to communicate. They may write to share information, points of view, beauty, and stories. Meaning in literature is expressed in several unique ways (Langer, 1992): through written language style; the conventions of language; genre; and literary structures such as characters, setting, plot, theme, and so forth, which were introduced in earlier chapters. These distinct patterns of thinking entail readers relating prior knowledge, experiences, and the text to understand genre and the elements of literature (Langer, 1992).

Outstanding children's writers have the ability to communicate with children on their own level—to respect their experience and understanding. The key to their success is their ability to make the stories come to life (Zinsser, 1990, p. 1). Children's authors seem to be able to remember what it feels like to be a child and how the world looks when the main character is three feet tall. These writers are able to create images, language, characters, plots, themes, and settings that ring true to children. These authors relate to and respect their experiences (Thacker, 1996). When readers respond to an author's style, characters, and so forth, they are motivated to read more books by the author. Response to authors becomes a powerful force in readers' engagement with literature.

Guiding Response (Level 1)

Nurturing children's response to literature means creating pleasurable experiences with books in a warm, accepting setting. Chambers (1996) sums up the literary experience as one in which adults and children share what they read and discover together what is "entertaining and revealing, recreative, re-enactive, and engaging" (p. 40). The focus of a literary experience is discovering the meaning, thinking about it, and discovering the reader's feelings about the experience. According to Chambers, literature is an experience "to be entered into, to be shared and contemplated" (p. 39).

Literary experiences stimulate the growing mind (Langer, 1992). The major reason for providing children with literary experiences is to help them read with more pleasure and understanding. "Helping children to read for themselves, widely, voraciously, and indiscriminately" is something every adult can do (Chambers, 1996, p. 48). Although we cannot directly teach literature to children, we can set the stage for them to experience literature so they actively construct their own knowledge and beliefs. There is no one correct interpretation of a literary work, but rather multiple interpretations, each of which is profoundly dependent on the reader's experience (Daniels, 2002). Literature loses its appeal when it is misused. For example, asking many pointless questions is one type of misuse. Another is teaching phonics rules. As teachers we must focus on "big ideas," response, and the elements of literature. A child writing a letter to a friend to tell why she liked a book or an author is a response. The literary experience is not a quest for a predetermined right answer. The process of making meaning is not one of learning a correct interpretation prescribed by an authority in the field (Langer, 1995).

Teachers can create a literate environment that encourages children to connect with books and build the background needed for understanding (McClure & Kristo, 1996). They can encourage readers to engage with and respond to books, films, and tapes and provide opportunities to express their responses. Figure 15.2 presents the components of literary experience.

Warm, Literate Environment (Level 2)

A warm, literate environment sets the stage for children's engagement with and response to literature through providing and introducing books for children to hear, read aloud, or read silently, and through stimulating their thinking beyond the book. Both centralized school libraries and classroom library centers are essential to literacy experiences. The classroom reading center gives children immediate access to literature. Adults create warm, literate environments when they have books and magazines in the home, media center, and library. Pleasing arrangements of books, displays, posters, and bulletin boards in the media center invite children to sample literature.

Community of Response (Level 1)

When readers think, rethink, reread, discuss, and write about books, they discover what a book means to them and how they feel about it (Hill, 2000). They infer, interpret, and think critically as they revise and sharpen their understanding of the text. Although response is individual, *community* discussions encourage individuals to share their unique verbal, artistic, dramatic, and written interpretations of and responses to literature, as well as exploring authors' writing style and literary conventions (Jewell & Pratt, 1998–1999).

Communities of response give children opportunities to build their own understanding of literature and raise their own questions rather than focusing on questions created by someone with different experiences and knowledge (Daniels, 2002). Although each reader creates a unique understanding of text, each relies on common understandings and language for discussions and sharing responses. Shared understandings emerge from a mutual focus in a community of response. In a community of readers discussion, students can agree that stories include plot and character, and they can agree about the identity of the principal character, but they may disagree about character motivation, which is open to individual interpretation.

As children share their individual understandings with one another, they learn that a story can have many interpretations. One person's interpretation of an incident or a character might not occur to another individual without the opportunity for discussion. They may not agree after sharing various interpretations, but they learn how perceptions of a single text can differ due to varying experiences.

Story structures such as plot, setting, characterization, theme, and author style are common understandings that readers share, just as main ideas and supporting details are common understandings they share about non-

FIGURE 15.2 Dimensions of creating literary experience.					
Processes for enhancing literary experience	**Ways of Organizing Literature Study**				
	Genre studies	**Studies of outstanding books**	**Studies of the elements of literature**	**Illustrator studies**	**Author studies**
Read aloud Reader's Theater	x	x	x		x
Read silently	x	x	x	x	x
Drama	x	x		x	
Writing	x	x	x	x	x
Art	x	x	x		
Music	x	x	x	x	
Discussion	x	x	x	x	x
Movement		x		x	

Dimensions of creating literary experience.

A First-Grade Literature Experience

INTRODUCTION

Ms. Osaka showed her first-grade students a picture of a mouse to introduce them to Rose Fyleman's poem "Mice." After reading the first line of the poem, she asked them what reasons they thought the poet would give for saying that mice were nice, and she listed their reasons on the chalkboard. She then read the entire poem aloud.

DISCUSSION AND UNDERSTANDING

After reading the poem through a second time when the children asked to hear it again, Ms. Osaka asked them what the poet said she liked about mice. She listed their responses next to the earlier list on the board. Several children said their families did not like mice, so Ms. Osaka let the class discuss those reasons as well.

Afterward, she asked the students what kind of words the poet used to help listeners see mice in their mind. Some of the children recognized "scurrying" words in the poem.

RESPONSE ACTIVITIES

Ms. Osaka asked the children to think about the things they could do to show another person how they felt about this poem. Many of the children chose to draw pictures. Some of them selected mouse puppets and acted out the poem. Some others remembered the book *Whose Mouse Are You?* by Robert Kraus and asked the teacher to read it again.

DISCUSSION PROMPTS

1. What was important about this book?
2. How did the story make you feel?
3. What does the story remind you of in your own life?
4. What other books (TV, movies, videos, etc.) does this book remind you of?

fiction. Genre characteristics are another source of agreement. Identifying a book as historical fiction, poetry, or nonfiction is a relatively concrete task. Without shared understandings "there would never be the sort of agree-ment that makes a book well-loved or well-hated. Children as well as adults seem to seek this commonality" (Sebesta & Iverson, 1975, p. 412). They talk over their thoughts and reactions to a best-selling book, a television show, or a play; they may even argue the finer points of the piece. Chambers (1996) says the need to re-create the story in our own words is so strong that "when two friends discover they have both read and enjoyed the same book their talk often consists simply of sharing retellings: 'I especially liked that part where. . . .'" These discussions clarify understanding and response; therefore, the community of response is an important issue for those who work with children.

Engaging with Literature

The purpose of *engagement* activities is to get students immersed, engrossed, absorbed, and totally involved in literature (Macon, Bewell, & Vogt, 1991, p. 3). Engagement activities focus on what the story, poem, or nonfiction is really about so that readers can understand and respond to it. The following are some typical engagement activities.

- discussion of genre
- writing or discussing story grammar
- creating a story map
- predicting story events
- comparing/contrasting characters, settings, and so forth (Venn diagram)
- problem solving related to a book
- creating plot maps
- creating a story summary
- creating a story pyramid
- creating character maps
- answering student-generated questions
- reading author studies
- identifying new facts gleaned from reading
- researching topics

Nurturing Response

All of the experiences authors have influence their writing. Paula Fox explains: "It is my view that all the moments and years of one's life are part of any story that one writes" (Elleman, 1991, p. 48). Studying authors and illustrators yields many benefits. Readers who know something about the person who wrote or illustrated a literary work have a better understanding of it. Finding connections between books and their creators challenges children to think in new ways. Because an author's experiences influence their writing so heavily, knowing about the author greatly enhances the response process.

Hank, the dragon, hatches from an egg and saves the day for his farm family.

Response activities sustain the reader–text interaction and nurture literary development (Martinez & Nash, 1991). Response may be written or oral, formal or informal, and may make use of a variety of media. Readers need opportunities for varied responses to literature through activities before reading, during reading, and after reading. In later sections, we explain strategies and activities for introducing books, experiencing books, and encouraging response to literature.

Introducing Books

Introductions may be elaborate or very simple. They may consist of a question, discussion, or picture; a comparison to another book, a film, or a piece of music; reading the opening paragraph or paragraphs; presentation of an object that symbolizes some aspect of the book; or a teacher, librarian, or student book-talk. Introductions arouse children's interest in the text and give them background that enriches their comprehension. The teacher, parent, or librarian acquaints children with the genre, content, structure, and language of the text (Langer, 1995). Children usually meet the main character and identify the setting during the introduction.

After reading Raising Dragons, Kyle and his friends dramatized the story.

The first step in planning a book introduction is considering what readers need to know to understand the book. To understand a fantasy such as Marjorie Priceman's *My Nine Lives by Clio,* readers have to imagine places and people outside of their experience. In addition, following the story as it switches from century to century can be a challenge. A good introduction can include a discussion of the superstition that cats have nine lives. Likewise, the skilled author makes us believe that a cat could write a book. Readers form different expectations for a book introduced as a fantasy, such as *My Nine Lives by Clio,* than for a book introduced as realistic fiction or poetry.

Creating a relationship between a piece of literature and previous reading develops intertextuality and facilitates response. Use Uri Shulevitz's *snow* to introduce Jacqueline Martin's *Snowflake Bentley.* This will prepare children for Snowflake Bentley's intensity when studying snowflakes. Literary experience is not based on a single book, but the ideas, experiences, and understandings that come from reading many books. Children can learn to preview books themselves from the techniques used to introduce books to them. By the time students reach the middle grades, they are ready to independently explore a book before reading and know that the dust jacket usually provides background information.

Experiencing Books

After the introduction, the children read or listen to the book or poem. After reading the entire story, article, poem, or informational piece, children are ready to explore it in discussion or response activities. Understanding grows as readers follow the unfolding of character, the story problem and its resolution, or the full development of the theme. This is the way they learn how the story works or the way the informative pieces fit together.

Readers who immerse themselves in the literature gradually build an understanding of the piece, identifying and coming to understand the main character's personality. As the story unwinds, readers recognize the escalating tension in the plot, the cause and effect, and the problem or conflict that builds suspense. Readers who ask themselves "why" and "who" can relate literature to their own experiences, which increases their comprehension.

Through the comprehension of both narrative and informational text, children build a knowledge base about our world (Gambrell & Almasi, 1996). Understanding is related to *inferencing* or interpretation of literature, which is concerned with meanings that are not directly stated in the text. The author suggests and hints at ideas rather than stating them directly, and the reader must interpret the author's words to understand the intended meaning. Authors cannot tell readers everything: the stories would be too long and the detail would make them too boring. Authors must rely on their audience to fill in the empty spaces. In Louis Sachar's *Holes,* when Mr. Sir tells Stanley, "This isn't a Girl Scout Camp" (p. 14), the author is telling the reader that Camp Green Lake is a bad place. Mr. Sir also tells Stanley that he is going to be thirsty for the next 18 months. The reader can interpret these statements to mean that this is a really hard place.

Critical thinkers make judgments about the quality, value, and validity of text. They evaluate the accuracy of the material, synthesize information, make comparisons and inferences, and suspend judgment until they have all the information they need. Critical readers recognize the author's purpose, point of view, and use of language. They distinguish fact from opinion and test the author's assertions against their own observations, information, and logic. For instance, a critical reader would probably conclude that Stanley was in a much worse place than he realized. At this point, students are ready to engage in activities and experiences based on their understanding of literature.

The activities described in this section may be conducted as individual activities, small-group activities, or whole class activities. Pencil-and-paper activities help students organize and remember their thoughts for discussion. Activities should be varied, because even the most interesting ones become boring when overused. The major purpose in exploring literature should be simply to read.

Discussion

Discussion is an integral part of developing understanding and engagement with literature. Engaging in discussions about text can help students become part of the active conversation that is reading: the conversation between the reader and text, between text and community, and among readers (Bloem & Manna, 1999; Borders & Naylor, 1993; Musthafa, 1996). The questions raised with others in the discussion process and the teacher's thoughtful questions increase comprehension and foster cognitive development. Thoughtful discourse gives students many occasions to raise questions and make comments about the literature they read (Jewell & Pratt, 1998–1999). Friendly debate regarding various reactions fosters readers' response to literature (Larrick, 1991).

The teacher's role is to facilitate discussion, keep it going, encourage full participation, and inspire children to talk about literature. Thoughtful questions based on listening to the voice of the book facilitate discussion. The most useful questions are broad and open-ended because these questions help students develop a sense of the entire story, poem, or informational piece. Focusing on a few significant ideas will stimulate greater understanding and discussion, while focusing on trivial and obvious ideas leads to brief answers that are often as simple as "yes" and "no."

A few thoughtful questions, especially those that the students ask, will stimulate a good discussion. The inquisition approach of asking many, many questions is guaranteed to destroy children's response to literature. One teacher who commented "I feel like I have

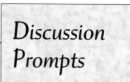 

Discussion Prompts

Kelly's (1990) prompts:

1. What did you notice about the story?
2. How did the story make you feel?
3. What does the story remind you of in your own life?

Borders and Naylor's (1993) prompts:

1. Talk about what you notice in the story, which may include any aspect of the book such as text, format, illustrations, characters, and so forth. Children will notice things that teachers never noticed.
2. Talk about how the story makes you feel. When members of a group share feelings and thoughts they bond, and the group is a safer place to explore issues.
3. Talk about what the story reminds you of in your own life. Our own experiences help us understand a book and the book helps us understand our experience.

wrung the life out of this book and neither the students nor I ever want to see it again" has assuredly overanalyzed the book and ensured that her students did not enjoy it, even though it is a favorite of many children who were not subjected to overteaching or overanalysis.

Discussions that focus on the characters suggest that readers wonder what kind of person the main character will turn out to be (Hansen, 1991). The well-developed characters in Katherine Paterson's books invite this kind of response. When focusing on character, develop questions to guide students' thinking, such as:

- What kind of character is the main character?
- What words describe the character?
- What character have you read about that is like the main character in this book? How are they alike?
- Do you know anyone who is like the main character? How so?

Some books are plot driven, so students read for the story events or the adventures. Many of these stories are action packed and have story events that build suspense. Guiding children's response to these stories could involve questions such as:

- What events create suspense?
- What is the main problem or conflict in this story?
- What is the climax of this story?
- How is the problem or conflict solved?

Prompts, such as the ones listed in the Discussion Prompts box, can elicit children's oral and written responses to literature. Using these prompts for a full year in a third-grade class shows that the students are more actively involved in learning and more enthusiastic about literature than their peers, with an observable difference in fluency and increased reflection of emotional involvement as the students use the process (Kelly, 1990). Adapting the prompts to statements shows that they are effective for discussion and that prompts are more effective the more they are used. Children as young as age 3 respond to the prompts; moreover, the children involved in the latter study used the prompts on the teachers and asked what they noticed in the story (Borders & Naylor, 1993).

Writing

Students who read well usually write well because they have a command of language, vocabulary, and literary knowledge. Reading gives students models for organizing writing and language to express their thoughts. The response journal is one of many appropriate writing response activities.

Literature response journals

Literature response journals, also called reading journals, reading logs, and dialogue journals, are a form of response activity that leads students to engage with literature. The journals consist of students writing down their thoughts about their reading. It is a place to explore thoughts, discover reactions, and let the mind ramble. Response journals are an effective means of linking writing and thinking with the active reading process (Barone, 1990; Raphael & McMahon, 1994). Some students find it difficult to get started writing in their journal, or they may say the same things again and again, so plan ways to encourage their responses when they seem to have difficulty thinking of something to write.

Janet Hancock (1991) reported an analysis of a sixth-grade girl's literature response journal. The journal revealed the student's personal meaning-making process as well as insights into her personal feelings, which the teacher had rarely seen. This student was encouraged to record all of the thoughts going on in her head as she read the book and not concern herself with correct spelling or the mechanics of writing because the objective was to capture her thoughts. Her entries were classified in these ways: (a) character interaction, (b) character empathy, (c) prediction and validation, (d) personal experiences, and (e) philosophical reflections. When writing about character interaction, the student wrote comments directly to the character she was reading about. The researcher noted her responses were of the quality of reading and writing that teachers hope to inspire. After the student wrote entries, the researcher made encouraging, nonevaluative responses that motivated her. She then tried to repeat the kind of writing to which teachers responded.

Literature response journals can have several formats. A few are suggested here, but teachers can try anything that fits the situation. Langer (1992) suggests a two-part journal with a student entry on one side and the teacher's response (or the response of another student) on the other side (see the sample entry in Figure 15.3).

FIGURE 15.3 **Two-part literature response journal.**

Book: *The Village that Vanished* by Ann Grifalconi, Illustrated by Kadir Nelson

Notes	Comments
African folk tale	The art is stunning, and creates story mood.
The story is written in the style of an African storyteller (griot).	The wonderful colors help the mood.
The Slavers shoot guns and capture unarmed farmers. Abikanile's villagers make their village look as if no one lives there and they escape, but they need a miracle to cross the river between them and safety.	

FIGURE 15.4   A sample story map for *Bloomability* by Sharon Creech.

Main characters: The main characters are Dinnie, her Aunt Sandy and Uncle Max, and her school friends, Lila and Guthrie.

Setting: Most of the story takes place in Switzerland and at a Swiss Boarding School.

Story Problem: Dinnie's father constantly moves the family, so she has few possessions and no friends. She does not want to move to Switzerland.

Story event 1:   Dinnie's aunt and uncle take her to Switzerland to attend boarding school.

Story event 2:   She makes friends.

Story event 3:   She discovers the beauty of nature.

Problem solution: She makes friends who help her find her place in the world and the possibilities (bloomabilities) of her life. She discovers the beauty of Switzerland.

Theme: The value of friendship and the possibilities of life.

Another format, which Langer suggests and which Stoodt and Amspaugh (1994) researched, shows that children's responses change over time as they relate new information, feelings, and ideas to previous knowledge. An immediate response is more detailed, whereas longer reflection permits children to relate these data to a larger context. In this journal format, the students make entries under three headings: immediate reaction, later reaction, and reading and writing. A third approach is for students to make comments in the journal and then pass it to another student who has read the book to respond to the comments.

Research that Raphael and McMahon (1994) conducted identified reading log entry possibilities that can be useful. These possibilities include character maps, wonderful words, pictures, special story parts, sequences of events, book/chapter critique, relating the book to oneself, and author's writing techniques and language use. After reading nonfiction books, some students become so interested in the information that they want to learn all they can about the subject, which could lead to writing an article about it. Students may decide to develop their own original information and create a nonfiction book to share with classmates. Writing response activities are unlimited.

Oral Language

Dramatic activities are important response activities for children. These activities, explored in Chapter 14, give children opportunities to act out their interpretations of characters and events and see how the action evolved.

Maps and Charts

Literature may be mapped or charted (sometimes through *diagrams*) as a means of summarizing and organizing thoughts and responses to the text. Many kinds of maps and charts are available.

Story maps

The sample story map in Figure 15.4 is based on Sharon Creech's *Bloomability*. A *story map* is a diagram of a story grammar. Readers complete the various parts of the map based on the story structure (grammar) of the book they have read.

Character maps

Character maps focus on the main character in a story. They assist children in developing a more thorough understanding of story characters and their actions, thereby helping readers identify character traits (Toth, 1990). They also serve to summarize the story. Students write, or cut and paste, the character's name on the map. They then write in the qualities (e.g., honesty, loyalty, bravery) that character exhibits. Finally, they identify the actions that support the qualities identified. This activity can be varied by having students draw pictures or

FIGURE 15.5   Character map based on *Amazing Grace*.

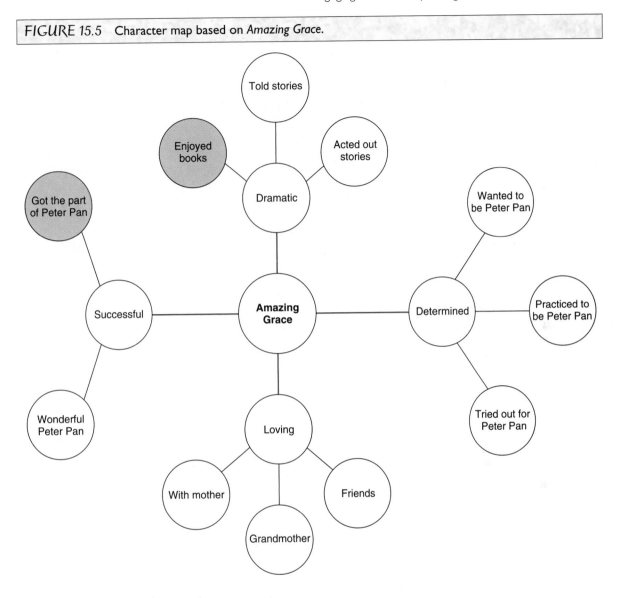

locate magazine photographs that illustrate a character's behavior. Figure 15.5 shows a sample character map based on Mary Hoffman's *Amazing Grace*.

Units

A literature response unit focuses on clusters of books that have some common element (e.g., theme, genre, author). Each unit includes children's books to be read over a specified period of time, and the unit guide includes background information and suggestions for sharing and discussing books as well as response activ-

ities. The organization of the units provides a framework for children to discover the connections among literature selections. Chapter 16 discusses units further.

Plot relationships charts

The plot relationships chart shown in Figure 15.6 for Candace Fleming's book *When Agnes Caws* is similar to one developed by Barbara Schmitt and Marilyn Buckley (1991). It categorizes story information under four headings: *somebody, wanted, but,* and *so*. The chart guides children as they identify the major

FIGURE 15.6   A sample plot relationships chart for *When Agnes Caws.*

When Agnes Caws			
Somebody	Wanted	But	So
Agnes	to spot the pink-headed duck	Evil Professor tried to foil Agnes	Agnes used bird-calling skills to outwit him

elements of a selection they have heard or read and helps them understand relationships between characters, problems, and solutions.

Story pyramids

A *story pyramid* (Waldo, 1991) gives students a convenient way to summarize a story. Each line of the pyramid gives specific information about the story in a specific number of words: the first line has one word, the second line has two words, and so forth. Figure 15.7 shows a sample pyramid based on Patricia MacLachlan's *Journey.* The lines of the pyramid force the student to encapsulate the plot, and should describe the following:

1. the main character's name
2. the main character
3. the setting
4. the problem
5. one main event
6. a second main event
7. a third main event
8. a solution to the problem

Prediction charts

Prediction charts guide children to predict what will happen next as they move through a story. Prediction charts guide readers to activate prior knowledge and establish purposes for reading (Hammond, 1991). When using a prediction chart, the teacher introduces the book to students. Students predict orally or in writing what will happen next in the story. They also summarize what actually did happen and compare the results to their predictions. This can be an individual or group activity. Younger children who are not able to write can dictate their predictions. For longer books, predictions can be broken into smaller parts (Part

I, Part II, Part III) or into the book's chapters. Figure 15.8 shows a sample prediction chart based on *Keeper of the Doves* by Betsy Byars.

Knowledge charts

Knowledge charts are quite useful with nonfiction, but they also apply to fictional materials. The purpose of knowledge charts is to engage and focus students' reading, as well as to help them access the knowledge they already have regarding the topic. If students do not have previous knowledge regarding a particular topic, then as part of this study teachers need to help them acquire background knowledge. Figure 15.9 shows a sample knowledge chart based on J. Lynett Gillette's *Dinosaur Ghosts.*

Author and Illustrator Studies

Author studies can motivate students as well as stimulate their response to a favorite author's work. Author and illustrator studies also motivate children to read and to continue reading (Jenkins, 1999).

Reading a body of work

The body of an author's work differs from a single work. Students can compare genre, subject, characters, plot, theme, and style in examining all of the author's books. This will help them understand the body and significance of a single author's work. For instance, James Howe's work was humorous fantasy, such as *Bunnicula,* until his first wife's death, when his writing took a more serious turn, as seen in *The Hospital Book.* Reading all of an author's books in the order of publication helps readers understand the ways in which the author's work has changed over time. They may also consider whether the body of work is diverse or seems to follow a single thread. Figure 15.10 compares some of the writings of Lois Lowry.

FIGURE 15.7 A sample story pyramid for *Journey*.

1	Journey
2	young boy
3	farm fields barn
4	wants to see mother
5	mother sends money no words
6	Journey adopts a cat named Bloom
7	Journey discovers torn photographs of his family
8	grandfather finds negatives, Journey becomes photographer, replaces photographs

Adapted from Waldo, 1991.

FIGURE 15.8 A sample story prediction chart for *Keeper of the Doves* by Betsy Byars.

	What Do You Really Think Will Happen?	What Did Happen?
Part I		Amen the protagonist is afraid of Mr. Tominski who keeps the doves. I think she will get in trouble because of her fear and restlessness.
Part II		Grandma's visit will help Amen get over her fear.
Part III		Amen will put her face to the future.

FIGURE 15.9 A sample knowledge chart based on *Dinosaur Ghosts* by J. Lynett Gillette.

Prior Knowledge About Dinosaurs	New Knowledge About Dinosaurs
1. Dinosaurs lived long ago.	1. Coelophysis lived in New Mexico.
2. Some dinosaurs ate plants.	2. They lived 225 million years ago.
3. Some dinosaurs ate meat.	3. Coelophysis lived in large herds.
4. Dinosaurs were big and little.	4. Something killed many of these dinosaurs at the same time.
5. They hatched from eggs.	5. Scientists did detective work to unravel the mystery.
6. Their fossils were discovered at Ghost Ranch.	6. The best theory they came up with is a drought and a flood killed them.

Studying influences on illustrators

Artists who illustrate children's books usually have their own favorite artists. For example, Maurice Sendak (1988) identifies Randolph Caldecott, George Cruikshank, and Boutet de Monvel as favorites. Students can study an illustrator by (a) studying the illustrator's books, (b) identifying some of the major influences on the illustrator's work, and (c) comparing the various works of the illustrator. They can consider concepts such as color choice and use, style, medium, size, and shape.

Becoming an author expert

Reading an author's works, as well as finding articles, interviews, book reviews, and Internet sources of information about him or her helps students become experts about their favorite author. A student can become expert on his or her favorite authors or illustrators by reading their works and finding articles, interviews, book reviews, and other sources of information about them. After becoming expert on a particular author, the student may write magazine or newspaper articles about the author or write and design a new dust jacket

---

FIGURE 15.10   Examining an author's body of work.

Book:	*The Giver* by Lois Lowry (science fiction)		Setting:	Denmark, World War II.
Plot:	In a Utopian society where people do not want to make decisions, one person, a receiver, keeps all the memories of history. When a new receiver is being trained, he learns about war, hate, snow, trees, and color that are no longer in society.		Theme:	Courage in helping friends.
			Style:	Family conversations, especially between parents, are authentic and make the events real. The story has a vivid setting and memorable characters, especially Ann Marie.
Character:	The main character is Jonas, a young boy who is about to receive his life's assignment. However, he discovers pain as a result of learning about evil.			Both families show empathy for one another. Ann Marie demonstrates outstanding, believable courage and enterprise to help her friend.
Setting:	Utopian society.		Book:	*Rabble Starkey* by Lois Lowry (realistic fiction)
Theme:	Jonas learns that even a Utopian society with no disease, crime, and rudeness lacks something.		Plot:	Rabble (Parable Ann) and her mother (Sweet Hosanna) were deserted by her father.
Style:	Mystic style; the characters accept this world that is strange to readers, who accept it because the story characters accept it. It includes memorable characters and a vivid setting.			Rabble hopes for a more permanent and conventional family, but she learns a great deal about family through the events in the story.
			Character:	The main character is Rabble Starkey.
Book:	*Number the Stars* by Lois Lowry (historical fiction)		Setting:	A small Appalachian town.
			Theme:	Love of family, and mental illness.
Plot:	The Johansen family helps their Jewish friends, the Rosens, protect their daughter, Ellen.		Style:	Realistic fiction; the central characters are memorable, as are the many characters who inhabit the small Appalachian town. The characters' personalities and actions are very believable.
Character:	The main characters are Ann Marie Johansen and Ellen Rosen.			

---

for a favorite book. In the persona of the author or illustrator, the student may participate in interviews, round-table discussions, or television talk shows staged by the class. Students can take turns conducting the interviews or directing the discussion and film the interviews or talk shows, if possible.

Studying how book illustration has changed

Study the illustrations in the book *75 Years of Children's Book Week Posters* by the Children's Book Council (1994). Compare the posters with book illustrations by the same artist, considering how the posters and slogans have changed over the years. Students can then design book week posters and slogans.

Learning about authors

Divide the class into three groups. Group 1 will read books written by the author, Group 2 will read articles or reference materials about the author, and Group 3 will read reviews of books written by the author. After the reading is completed, the students will share their information in discussion as a means of developing their understanding and appreciation of the author's work.

Studying author technique

Gaining a deeper understanding of an author's technique not only helps students understand the author, but is beneficial in developing their own writing skills. Students can investigate an author's technique in several ways, including:

1. Use a single book to study a specific technique; for instance, explore the techniques Louis Sachar used to create Stanley in *Holes*.

2. Compare a specific technique in several books by the same author; for instance, study setting in Pamela Service's books, such as *Stinker from Space*, and the techniques she uses to develop it.

3. Compare how different authors achieve the same goal; for instance, study dialogue in books by two authors to see how each author develops character through conversation.

Profiling an author

Learning about authors and their interests helps readers understand how they get story ideas. After studying

A Biographical Profile: James Cross Giblin

James Cross Giblin served as editor and publisher at Clarion Books for more than 20 years. He has also published books with several other publishers. Many of his books are nonfiction, and he points out that organizing and shaping facts into readable, interesting prose require all the skills of a storyteller (Giblin, 1990).The focus of his books usually is unusual aspects of history or information, but he always blends his research with wit and drama.

He explains how he gets his writing ideas in *Writing Books for Young People* (1990). He came up with the idea for *Chimney Sweeps* after meeting a chimney sweep on an airplane. In fact, he asked his new acquaintance to read the book manuscript for accuracy. Another book, *The Truth About Santa Claus,* resulted from seeing a picture of a contemporary Santa Claus juxtaposed next to his tall, thin ancestor, St. Nicholas. Giblin points out that an idea should not only be interesting to the writer, but it must also be an idea to which the writer is willing to devote a year or more. Six months of research and six months or more of writing and rewriting represent a major commitment of time and energy.

When researching a topic, Giblin looks for dramatic or amusing anecdotes that will bring the subject to life for young readers. His readers will attest to his successful use of this technique. For example, in *From Hand to Mouth* he tells how Cardinal Richelieu had his knives ground down so the points could not be used for picking teeth. When researching *The Riddle of the Rosetta Stone,* he found previously unpublished photographs to use in the book. These unusual angles on topics are a hallmark of his writing.

James Cross Giblin was awarded the Robert F. Sibert Informational Book Award in 2003 for *Adolf Hitler.* His goal in this book was to demonstrate that Hitler was a more complex person than is usually portrayed. He achieved this by posing three questions: "What sort of man could plan and carry out such horrendous schemes, win support for his deadly ventures, and why did no one stop him until it was almost too late?"

an author or illustrator through one of the methods described in the previous activities, students can write biographical profiles to summarize their research. The profile of James Cross Giblin (see accompanying box) describes some of his strategies for selecting and developing ideas.

Classroom Activities

ACTIVITY 15.1   SAMPLE BOOK INTRODUCTION FOR HISTORICAL FICTION

(IRA/NCTE Standards: 2, 3, 7, 8. Students will read and comprehend a variety of literature from various periods and use various media to gather and synthesize data.)

Book: *Fair Weather* by Richard Peck. Synopsis (for teachers):This historical fiction is set in 1893, the year of the World's Columbian Exposition. The central character, Rosie, is 13 years old. Rosie and her farm family are invited to Chicago to visit with Aunt Euterpe and attend the Exposition, considered the wonder of the age.The life of each family member changes forever due to their experiences. Many new and modern products were introduced at the Columbian Exposition; in addition, it generated new experiences. The focus of this literary experience is to reflect on this quotation from the book: "It was the last day of our old lives, and we didn't even know it." Another valuable focus is to analyze character growth and historical setting.The following topics will aid in the discussion and help children apply new insights gained to their own lives.

1. Identify the reasons that the characters thought this was the last day of their old lives. Students can also think of an event that affected their own lives in the way of this quotation. (Some readers have compared it to 9–11.)

2. Analyze the central character and character growth (the causes and effects of character growth, as well as the relationship of setting to character development).

3. Contrast the farm family with Aunt Euterpe, the city aunt.

These steps provide organization for introducing a book:

1. Introduce Rosie, and read a description of her and her feelings about going to Chicago.
   A. Ask students if they know any children who have gone to the Olympics or a World Fair.
   B. Explain the kinds of displays and shows that would occur at a World Fair.
   C. Read the quotation on page 1 and show the book cover.

   D. Show the pictures on pages 37, 71, 96, and 121.
   E. How do the views of country people differ from those of city folk?

2. If students read the story silently, discussion will prepare them to read with greater understanding.

3. Discuss the story with the students, stimulating them to think about the story. Follow-up discussion takes place after the students have read the entire story, focusing on the following:
   A. Which character changed the most? Why?
   B. Which exhibit at the Exposition interested you the most? Why?

4. Use extension activities to allow students to respond to the story. One class researched World Fairs and identified the kinds of exhibits and people that they would probably find in a current exposition after reading the work.

5. How would a trip to a World Fair today compare to the one in this book?

ACTIVITY 15.2   SAMPLE BOOK INTRODUCTION FOR AN INFORMATIONAL BOOK.

(IRA/NCTE Standards: 2, 3, 7. Students will read and comprehend a variety of genre.)

Book: *Cave* by Diane Siebert; Illustrations by Wayne McLoughlin. Synopsis (for teachers): This book gives readers the experience of visiting a cave. The author writes in the first person as this quote illustrates, "I am the cave, So cool and Dark, Where time, unending Leaves its mark" (p. 1). The rich text makes readers feel as if they are in the cave, and the luminous paintings capture the feeling of being underground.

1. Introduce *Cave*.
   A. The photographs, the author's note, and the dust jacket give background information that establishes the author's credentials and experiences.
   B. The irresistible paintings in this book are the best introduction. Let students browse through the pictures and discuss the mood that the paintings create. Students may use words such as *mysterious, caverns, magic,* and *underground.*

   C. Give background information and statistics about caves and caverns found in their state or locale.

2. Have students listen to the book while looking at the illustrations.

3. Discuss the book, focusing on the relationship between the language and the illustrations.
   A. Ask students to think about and discuss their experiences in caves and caverns and compare them to the experience presented in the book.
   B. Ask students to identify sensory words the author used to create the feeling of a cave.
   C. Show the students photographs of places or experiences and ask them to choose one photo to write about in a way that would give the readers the feeling of being there.

4. Use extension activities to allow students to respond to the story.

Summary

This chapter explores children's understanding of and response to literature. The ultimate response, of course, is pleasure in reading. Engagement, stance, and intertextuality are involved in response. Teachers and librarians can guide children's literary experiences and inspire their response to literature by selecting good literature and creating a warm, literate environment. They can introduce literature, provide activities to develop understanding, and encourage follow-up activities to enhance response, including discussion, writing, drama, and further reading. Focusing on text meaning to address students' reading purpose enhances their response to literature. This is influenced by the child's stance or purpose for reading. Each reader has an individual understanding of and response to literature based upon his or her experiences and interactions with the text; however, students must also have the knowledge that enables them to share their understanding and discuss their response with a community.

Thought Questions

1. Discuss the response process that you observe in a classroom.
2. Identify the response activities that you would like to use in your own classroom.
3. What is meant by response to literature?
4. Why is response to literature important?
5. What is the teacher's role in creating literary experiences?
6. Why is discussion central to literary experience and response?
7. How are author studies related to response?
8. What is the librarian's role in creating literary experiences?

Research and Application Experiences

1. Read a book to a group of children and observe their responses to it. Note facial expressions, attentiveness, and comments. Write a paper that describes their responses. Tape-record your reading, if possible. Identify the responses that are characteristic to the grade level of the children in the experience.
2. Read a book to a small group of children. Have each child retell the story individually and tape-record them, if you can. How are their understandings alike? How are they different?
3. Create a discussion plan that fosters children's questions and comments about a book rather than a teacher-directed discussion. Conduct this discussion with a group of children and tape it for further analysis.
4. With one student or a small group of students, conduct a teacher-directed discussion. Using the same book and a different student or group, hold a student-focused discussion. Tape both discussions and compare them.

   A. Which discussion involved the most students?
   B. Which discussion revealed the greatest depth of understanding?
   C. Which students appeared to be the most interested in the book?
   D. How were the discussions similar?
   E. How were the discussions different?

5. Use one of the maps or charts presented in this chapter as an introduction or a follow-up to a book with a group of children. Bring the maps or graphics that the students developed to class and discuss them.
6. Make plans for introducing three books to a group of children, using a different technique for each. Identify the introduction needed for each book (e.g., character introduction, plot introduction, setting introduction, or story problem or conflict introduction).
7. Plan questions that could be used to guide the discussion of a book. If possible, conduct the discussion with a group of children and tape it for further analysis.
8. Select three books that are related that could be used together in the classroom.
9. Select five books that would stimulate language development.

Children's Literature References and Recommended Books

Note: Books designated with an asterisk (*) are recommended for reluctant readers.

Arnold, C. (2001). *Dinosaurs with feathers: The ancestors of modern birds* (L. Caple, Illus.). New York: Clarion. (3–6). NONFICTION.

The author traces the relationship between dinosaurs and birds.

Creech, S. (1998). *Bloomability.* New York: HarperCollins. (4–8). CONTEMPORARY REALISTIC FICTION.

Dinnie's aunt and uncle whisk her off to a private school in Switzerland where she discovers her place in the world and the value of friendship.

Fleming, C. (1999). *When Agnes caws* (G. Potter, Illus.). New York: Atheneum. (K–3). MODERN FANTASY.

Agnes, an accomplished bird caller, travels to the Himalayan Mountains to spot the elusive pink-headed duck. Instead, she encounters a villain.

Fyleman, R. (1931). Mice. In *Fifty-one new nursery rhymes.* New York: Doubleday. (1–3). POETRY.

This is a poem about mice and their activities in homes.

Gibbons, G. (1989). *Catch the wind!* New York: Little, Brown. (K–3). NONFICTION.

When visting a kite shop, these children learn all about kites.

Giblin, J. C. (1982). *Chimney sweeps* (M. Tomes, Illus.). New York: Crowell. (3–6) NONFICTION*.

This book is packed with little-known information about chimney sweeps.

Giblin, J. C. (1985). *The truth about Santa Claus.* New York: Crowell. (3–6). NONFICTION.

Santa Claus myths and traditions are the focus of this book.

Giblin, J. C. (1987). *From hand to mouth.* New York: Crowell. (3–6). INFORMATIONAL BOOK.

This book presents a historical study of eating implements.

Giblin, J. C. (1990). *The riddle of the Rosetta stone.* New York: Crowell. (3–6). INFORMATIONAL BOOK.

A history of the Rosetta Stone illustrated with pictures.

Giblin, J. C. (2002). *Adolf Hitler.* New York: Clarion. (5–9). INFORMATIONAL BOOK.

Hitler is portrayed as a complex person in this engrossing and absorbing biography.

Gillette, J. L. (1997). *Dinosaur ghosts* (D. Henderson, Illus.). New York: Dial. (3–7). INFORMATIONAL BOOK.

This informational book tells about a speedy little dinosaur called Coelophysis and how his bones are found.

Grifalconi, A. (2002). *The village that vanished* (K. Nelson, Illus.). New York: Dial. (2–4). TRADITIONAL LITERATURE.

An African folk tale about villagers who feared the slavers, so they made their village disappear. They escaped into the jungle, but encountered problems.

Hartman, B. (2002). *The wolf who cried boy* (T. Raglin, Illus.). New York: Putnam. (1–3). PICTURE BOOK.

Little Wolf wants boy for dinner, but his parents can't find any. He tells them he saw a boy in the woods, but he really had not. Later he sees an entire boy scout troop, but his parents do not believe him.

Hoffman, M. (1991). *Amazing grace* (C. Binch, Illus.). New York: Dial. (1–3). CONTEMPORARY REALISTIC FICTION.

Grace loves to pretend and hopes to be Peter Pan in the school play, but she first has to overcome prejudice.

Hopkinson, D. (1997). *Birdie's lighthouse* (K. B. Root, Illus.). New York: Atheneum. (K–3). HISTORICAL FICTION.

Birdie keeps the lighthouse lamps burning when her father falls ill during a storm.

Howe, D., & Howe, J. (1979). *Bunnicula: A rabbit tale of mystery* (A. Daniel, Illus.). New York: Atheneum. (K–5). MODERN FANTASY.

The hilarious story of three pets: Harold, a dog; Chester, a cat; and Bunnicula, a suspicious bunny.

Howe, J. (1994). *The hospital book* (M. Warshaw, Photog.). New York: Morrow. (3–7). INFORMATIONAL BOOK.

This book introduces all aspects of the hospital experience to children.

Lowry, L. (1987). *Rabble Starkey.* Boston: Houghton Mifflin. (4–7). REALISTIC FICTION.

Rabble Starkey was given a Bible name, Parable Ann, to stave off trouble. This book is the story of her 12th year of life in a small Appalachian town. This is a story of family, growth, and change.

Lowry, L. (1989). *Number the stars*. Boston: Houghton Mifflin. (4–6). HISTORICAL FICTION.

Ann Marie Johansen bravely protects her Jewish friend during the Nazi occupation of Denmark.

Lowry, L. (1993). *The giver*. Boston: Houghton Mifflin. (5+). SCIENCE FICTION, FANTASY.

This story is set in a Utopian society where everyone has a job, and every family has a father, mother, and two children: a boy and a girl. There is no disease, crime, or rudeness, and there is much laughter and joy.

MacLachlan, P. (1991a). *Journey*. New York: Delacorte. (2–5). CONTEMPORARY REALISTIC FICTION.

Journey and his sister, Cat, live with their grandparents because their mother has gone away. Journey has difficulty adjusting when his mother sends money but no words.

MacLachlan, P. (1991b). *Three Names* (A. Pertzoff, Illus.). New York: HarperCollins. (2–4). CONTEMPORARY REALISTIC FICTION.*

Three Names is a dog who has three names because different people in the family have different names for him.

Martin, J. B. (1998). *Snowflake Bentley* (M. Azarian, Illus.). Boston: Houghton Mifflin. (1–3). BIOGRAPHY.

Wilson Bentley researches snowflakes through photography.

McKay, H. (2002). *Saffy's angel*. New York: Margaret K. McEldery. (3–5). REALISTIC FICTION.

Saffy learns that she is adopted and her siblings are actually cousins. She then sets out to find her mother's last home, which of course disturbs her family. A chaotic family situation, humor, and excellent characterizations make this book notable.

Miller, C. G., & Berry, L. A. (1989). *Coastal rescue*. New York: Atheneum. (4–6). INFORMATIONAL BOOK.

This informational book addresses the coastal crises of erosion and coastal resources in the United States.

Nolen, J. (1998). *Raising dragons* (E. Primavera, Illus.). New York: Silver Whistle/Harcourt Brace. (K–2). MODERN FANTASY, PICTURE BOOK.

A little girl finds an egg that hatches into a dragon that becomes her friend.

Park, F., & Park, J. (2002). *Good-bye, 382 Shin Dang Dong* (Yangsook Choi, Illus.). Washington DC: National Geographic. (1–3). REALISTIC FICTION, PICTURE BOOK.

A Korean youngster and her family leave their home in Korea to make a new home in the United States. She is sad to leave her friends, grandparents, and cousins for a strange place.

Peck, R. (2001). *Fair weather*. New York: Dial. (4–7). HISTORICAL FICTION.

The story of Rosie Beckett's family and their trip to the World's Columbian Exposition in 1893. Rosie and her family are country relatives of Aunt Euterpe, who lives in Chicago and invites them to the Exposition.

Prelutsky, J. (1984). *The new kid on the block*. New York: Greenwillow. (1–6). POETRY.

This collection of poems introduces unusual things such as jellyfish stew, a bounding mouse, a ridiculous dog, and a boneless chick, to name a few.

Priceman, M. (1998). *My nine lives by Clio*. New York: Atheneum. (1–3). MODERN FANTASY.

A cat's journal about her nine extraordinary lives in nine historical periods.

Raschka, C. (2002). *John Coltrane's giant steps*. New York: Atheneum. (1–6). PICTURE BOOK.

This book presents John Coltrane's composition "Giant Steps" through language and illustrations.

Sachar, L. (1998). *Holes*. New York: Farrar, Straus & Giroux. (4–7). CONTEMPORARY REALISTIC FICTION.

This Newbery Award and National Book Award book tells the story of Stanley Yelnats and his bad-luck family.

San Souci, R. (1989). *The talking eggs* (J. Pinkney, Illus.). New York: Dial. (1–4). TRADITIONAL LITERATURE.

This is a colorful version of the Cinderella story.

Sauer, J. (1994). *The light at Tern Rock*. New York: Puffin. (3–6). HISTORICAL FICTION.

Ronnie and his aunt tend the Tern Rock lighthouse while the keeper takes a vacation. However, the keeper does not return.

Service, P. (1989). *Stinker from space*. New York: Scribner. (3–6). MODERN FANTASY.

When space warrior Tsynq Yr crashes his space vehicle, he must find a body to use and a power source for his return trip.

Shulevitz, U. (1998). *Snow*. New York: Farrar, Straus & Giroux. (K–2). PICTURE BOOK, CONTEMPORARY REALISTIC FICTION.

An exquisite picture book that shows a child's optimism in the face of adults' view of snow.

Siebert, D. (2000). *Cave* (W. McLoughlin, Illus.). New York: HarperCollins. (3–6). NONFICTION.

The author creates the feeling of a cave through language, and the mood is further developed through the paintings that illustrate the book.

Simont, M. (2001). *The stray dog*. New York: HarperCollins. (1–3). REALISTIC FICTION/PICTURE BOOK.

A family picnic leads children to play with a stray dog. After returning home, they realize that they want to adopt the dog. Therefore, they return to the park and find the dog.

Viorst, J. (1981). *If I were in charge of the world and other worries* (L. Cherry, Illus.). New York: Atheneum. (1–6). POETRY.

Poems about everyday children's everyday problems. The compilation includes topics such as goodbye, wicked thoughts, thanks and no thanks, facts of life, and night.

Wise, W. (2000). *Dinosaurs forever* (L. Meinsinger, Illus.). New York: Dial. (2–4). POETRY.

This collection of poems provides humorous information about specific dinosaurs. The dinosaurs are a mixture of real and make-believe breeds.

References and Books for Further Reading

Barksdale-Ladd, M. A., & Nedeff, A. R. (1997). The worlds of a reader's mind: Students as authors. *Reading Teacher, 50,* 564–573.

Barone, D. (1990). The written responses of young children: Beyond comprehension to story understanding. *New Advocate, 3,* 49–56.

Barthes, R. (1975). *The pleasure of the text*. London: Jonathan Cape.

Barton, J. (2001). *Teaching with children's literature*. Norwood, MA: Christopher-Gordon.

Blake, R. W. (1995). *From literature-based reading to reader response in the elementary classroom*. Paper presented at the Annual Meeting of the National Council of Teachers of English, San Diego, CA.

Bloem, P. L., & Manna, A. (1999). A chorus of questions: Readers respond to Patricia Polacco. *Reading Teacher, 52,* 802–809.

Bloome, D., & Bailey, F. M. (1992). Studying language and literature through events, particularity, and intertextuality. In R. Beach (Ed.), *Multidisciplinary perspectives on literacy research* (pp. 181–210). Urbana, IL: National Conference on Research in English.

Borders, S., & Naylor, A. (1993). *Children talking about books*. Phoenix, AZ: Oryx.

Cairney, T. (1990). Intertextuality: Infectious echoes from the past. *Reading Teacher, 43,* 478–484.

Chambers, A. (1996). *The reading environment*. Portland, ME: Stenhouse.

Children's Book Council. (1994). *75 years of children's book week posters*. New York: Knopf.

Daniels, H. (2002). *Literature circles*. Portland, ME: Stenhouse.

Elleman, B. (1991). Paula Fox's *The village by the sea. Book Links, 1,* 48–50.

Gambrell, L., & Almasi, J. (Eds.). (1996). *Lively discussions! Fostering engaged reading*. Newark, DE: International Reading Association.

Giblin, J. C. (1990). *Writing books for young people*. Boston: The Writer.

Hammond, D. (1991). Prediction chart. In J. Macon, D. Bewell, & M. Vogt (Eds.), *Responses to literature* (p. 3). Newark, DE: International Reading Association.

Hancock, K. J. (1991). *Teaching with picture books*. Portsmouth, NH: Heinemann.

Hansen, J. (1991, Spring). I wonder what kind of person he'll be. *The New Advocate,* 89–100.

Hartman, D. K. (1992). Eight readers reading: The intertextual links of able readers using multiple passages. *Reading Research Quarterly, 27,* 122–133.

Hill, S. (2000). *Guiding literacy learners*. Portland, ME: Stenhouse.

Holland, K., Hungerford, R., & Ernst, S. (1993). *Journeying: Children responding to literature*. Portsmouth, NH: Heinemann.

Jenkins, C. B. (1999). *The allure of authors: Author studies in the elementary classroom*. Portsmouth, NH: Heinemann.

Jewïell, T., & Pratt, D. (1998–1999). Literature discussions in the primary grades: Children's thoughtful discourse about books and what teachers can do to make it happen. *Reading Teacher, 52,* 842–855.

Kelly, P. R. (1990), Guiding young students' responses to literature. *Reading Teacher 43,* 464–476.

Langer, J. (1992). Rethinking literature instruction. In J. Langer (Ed.), *Literature instruction: A focus on student response* (pp. 35–53). Urbana, IL: National Council of Teachers of English.

Langer, J. (1995). *Envisioning literature: Literary understanding and literature instruction.* New York: Teachers College Press.

Larrick, N. (1991). Give us books! . . . But also . . . . Give us wings! *New Advocate, 2,* 77–84.

Lewis, C. S. (1961). *An experiment in criticism.* Cambridge, England: Cambridge University Press.

Lundin, A. (1998). Intertextuality in children's literature. *Journal of Education for Library and Information Science, 39,* 210–213.

Macon, J. M., Bewell, D., & Vogt, M. E. (1991). *Responses to literature.* Newark, DE: International Reading Association.

Many, J. (1996). Exploring the influences of literature approaches on children's stance when responding and their response complexity. *Reading Psychology, 17,* 1–41.

Martinez, M., & Nash, M. F. (1991). Bookalogues: Talking about children's books. *Language Arts, 68,* 140–147.

McClure, A. A., & Kristo, J. V. (Eds.). (1996). *Books that invite talk, wonder, and play.* Urbana, IL: National Council of Teachers of English.

McMahon, S., & Raphael, T. (1994). The book club program: Theoretical and research foundations. In S. McMahon, T. Raphael, V. Goatley, & L. Pardo (Eds.), *The book club connection.* New York: Teachers College Press.

Musthafa, B. (1996). *Nurturing children's response to literature in the classroom context.* ERIC NO: ED398577.

Probst, R. (1992). Five kinds of literary knowing. In J. Langer (Ed.), *Literature instruction: A focus on student response* (pp. 54–77). Urbana, IL: National Council of Teachers of English.

Raphael, T., & McMahon, S. (1994). Book club: An alternative framework for reading instruction. *Reading Teacher, 48,* 102–116.

Rosenblatt, L. M. (1978). *The reader, the text, the poem: The transactional theory of the literary work.* Edwardsville: Southern Illinois University.

Rosenblatt, L. M. (1982). The literary transaction: Evocation and response. *Theory into Practice, XXI,* 268–277.

Schmitt, B., & Buckley, M. (1991). Plot relationships chart. In J. Macon, D. Bewell, & M. Vogt (Eds.), *Responses to literature.* Newark, DE: International Reading Association.

Sebesta, S., & Iverson, W. J. (1975). *Literature for Thursday's child.* Chicago: Science Research Associates.

Sendak, M. (1988). *Caldecott and co.: Notes on books and pictures.* New York: Farrar, Straus & Giroux.

Stoodt, B., & Amspaugh, L. (1994, May). *Children's response to nonfiction.* Paper presented to the Annual Meeting of the International Reading Association, Toronto, Canada.

Thacker, D. (1996). The child's voice in children's literature. In *Sustaining the vision: Selected papers from the annual conference of the International Association of School Librarianship,* Worcester, England, July 1995.

Toth, M. (1990). Character map. In J. Macon, D. Bewell, & M. Vogt (Eds.), *Responses to literature K–8.* Newark, DE: International Reading Association.

Waldo, B. (1991). Story pyramid. In J. Macon, D. Bewell, & M. Vogt (Eds.), *Responses to literature.* Newark, DE: International Reading Association.

White, E. B. (1970). Laura Ingalls Wilder Award Acceptance Speech. *Horn Book, 56,* 540–547.

Wollman-Bonilla, J., & Werchadlo, B. (1999). Teacher and peer roles in scaffolding first graders' responses to literature. *Reading Teacher, 52,* 598–608.

Zinsser, W. (Ed.). (1990). Introduction. In *The art and craft of writing for children* (pp. 1–21). Boston: Houghton Mifflin.

Unit Studies: Literature and Learning

16

KEY TERMS

book clusters
connections
core literature
inquiry

integrated units
semantic map
units

GUIDING QUESTIONS

You were fortunate if you were among the students who had a teacher that introduced literature, read aloud, and integrated literature with the curriculum. Not all students have been as lucky. As you study this chapter, think about these questions.

1. What are the benefits of using literature as a resource for pleasure and instruction?

2. What problems might a teacher encounter in developing literature-related instruction?

3. How can a book "cluster" help teachers?

Literature is a rich teaching resource. The goal with literature is to alert current and prospective teachers about ways of connecting students with literature to enhance their learning. This chapter synthesizes and organizes the understandings developed in the preceding chapters. We include practical, usable guides and units in this chapter. Our text and the associated Internet site are resources for identifying books that address the themes and topics of interest to children.

Units, Themes, and Topics

A unit is a collection of lessons and an organizing framework. Well-developed units motivate students toward in-depth study of a topic, book, issue, person, idea, or theme. A unit identifies the goals (standards or objectives), experiences, activities, and materials the teacher plans to develop through the theme. Students use reading, writing, talking, listening, and thinking as tools to discover relations and to link new connections with prior understandings. The length of time involved in a study may be one hour, one day, one week, or longer.

This text uses the term *theme* to identify the meaning, focus, or central idea of a unit of study, such as racial tension, loneliness, or survival. Topics such as the solar system, the water cycle, and endangered species are appropriate for topical units. The box on page 329 identifies the focus and framework of a given unit.

In unit studies, students and teachers investigate themes and topics in various ways. Students who are independent readers can study textbooks, magazines, and reference books, while emergent readers can rely on stories and information read aloud. Discussion contributes to the thinking process about a topic, as does writing. In addition, many teachers encourage students to write in learning logs. During units, students usually

This is an alphabet book for Americans.

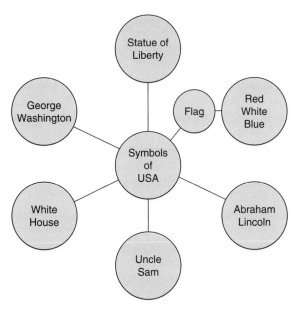

Semantic Web for Symbols of the USA

VIGNETTE

Dawn Michaels' Third Grade

Several students in Dawn's third-grade class had fathers in the armed forces, so she decided to develop a unit entitled "What makes us Americans?" Her goal was to explore symbols, landmarks, documents, and people related to our country. The books she chose for the unit ranged from easy to difficult, so that all students could find reading material suited to their taste. She identified the following IRA/NCTE Standards to guide her study: reading a wide range of materials, understanding the United States, acquiring new information, applying a wide range of strategies, writing, spelling, punctuation, listening, speaking, generating questions, and using technology and libraries (IRA/NCTE Standards: 1, 3, 4, 5, 6, 7, 8, 10, 11, 12).

To kick the unit off, she invited Noah's army father to talk with the students. In subsequent weeks, she invited other fathers who were in the armed forces.

Dawn read selections from Caroline Kennedy's *A Patriot's Handbook* to introduce the unit's literature and its basic concepts. She read "You're a Grand Old Flag" by George M. Cohan, "The Pledge of Allegiance," and the story of the pledge. She then asked, "What are some symbols of America?" After explaining the word *symbols* for some of the students, they began to identify symbols.

Chris said, "Soldiers and sailors are symbols."

"So is the flag," Delonta suggested.

"Red, white, and blue," Emily offered.

The students concluded with these symbols: eagle; flag; red, white, and blue; Statue of Liberty;

(continued)

soldiers, sailors, and marines; and the Pledge of Allegiance. Dawn gave the students a blank semantic web with the word *American* in the center to complete as they worked through the unit. She then book-talked the selected literature for the unit, which included:

The Pledge of Allegiance by Francis Bellamy

America Is. . . . by Louise Borden

We the Kids: The Preamble to the Constitution of the United States by David Catrow

America: A Patriotic Primer by Lynn Cheney

Don't Know Much About American History by Kenneth Davis

The Declaration of Independence by Sam Fink

Old Glory: An American Treasure by Robert Lang

The Story of the Statue of Liberty by Betsy Maestro

Uncle Sam and Old Glory: Symbols of America by Christopher Manson

Celebrate America: In Poetry and Art by N. Panzer

The Flag We Love by Pam Munoz Ryan

One Nation: America by the Numbers by Devin Scillian

A is for America by Devin Scillian

Lily and Miss Liberty by Carla Stevens

The Story of the White House by Kate Waters

CD: *A is for America* by Devin Scillian, Sleeping Bear Press

RELATED WEB SITES

National Geographic World [http://Nationalgeographic.com/media/world]

Library of Congress (Type this term into your browser and it will pull up this site.)

Smithsonian (Type this term into your browser to locate the site.)

Mathematics

The book *One Nation: America by the Numbers* is an excellent beginning point for re-

lating math to a study of the United States. Students can create their own "America by Numbers."

Language Arts

Explore the word *symbols,* the meaning of symbols, the reasons that Americans have certain symbols, and identify common symbols of our country. Have students write in their journals after reading, and research selected topics and symbols.

Social Studies

This unit focuses on history and patriotism.

Fine Arts

Students should view relevant art for Americans, along with related poetry, in *Celebrate America: In Poetry and Art*. They may contact regional and local art museums to order prints and slides for classroom display. Some students may choose to make their own artistic treatment of American symbols and choose poetry to accompany their work. Tapes of patriotic music will also enhance children's understanding.

Closure

At the end of each day, students will discuss their experiences and write in their learning logs. When the study is completed, they may choose to share products developed during the unit.

participate in individual and group activities and projects related to the topic. Teachers frequently incorporate the arts (music, drama, and visual arts) into the unit. In many instances, science, math, and social studies are relevant to the unit. These connections offer opportunities for both direct and indirect teaching of the skills and strategies that we expect students to accomplish.

Units are intensive learning experiences. Teachers and/or students may generate theme units or topic units. Some educators call student-generated units *theme cycles* (Altwerger & Flores, 1994). Developing units that address student interests motivates them and gives them a sense of ownership. However, both types of units are valuable. The suggested theme and topics in the box on page 330 can be used for many grade levels by simply selecting different books.

Theme Unit

Focus: Time Fantasy for Upper Elementary

Standards: To develop students' concepts of fantasy and the rules of well-written fantasy

To develop students' concepts of time and space as they are related to time fantasy

To develop students' ability to compare and contrast

IRA/NCTE Standards: 1,2,3,7

PART I. TEACHER-PLANNED WHOLE-CLASS READING AND VIEWING

Teacher Read-Aloud:	*A Wrinkle in Time* by Madeleine L'Engle
Group or Partner Reading:	*Tom's Midnight Garden* by Philippa Pearce
	Playing Beatie Bow by Ruth Park
	"Flying Saucers" nonfiction magazine article
Music:	appropriate to the past or future
Art:	art of the period

PART II. OVERVIEW OF LITERATURE PRESENTATION

Introduce the unit with a discussion of time travel. Ask the students questions such as:

1. Do you think people can travel through time?
2. If you could travel through time where would you go and what time period would you choose?
3. What are the advantages of time travel?
4. What are the disadvantages of time travel?

In addition to discussion, have students write their thoughts about these questions. Then have them think of questions they would like to have answered. Create time capsules with paper towel rollers or some similar container. Seal the containers and store them until the unit is complete.

The teacher will read *A Wrinkle in Time* aloud over a three-week period. When the book is fin-ished, have students read in small groups or in pairs one of the titles listed for group or partner reading in Part I. Additional related reading is listed at the end of this unit.

The beginning point when devising a literature unit is to determine the focus of the project. Next, locate and sequence relevant material and develop appropriate experiences. Choosing the focus may be the most difficult aspect of the process because it demands a fairly broad familiarity with the world of children's literature and an understanding of the structure of the discipline. Units can be formulated around topic, form, structure, or theme (Johnson & Louis, 1990).

Have students work in small groups or pairs and assign a novel to be read by a specified date. Ask each group or pair of students to prepare analyses of their novels to share with the rest of the class. All students should be prepared to contribute to the comparison chart.

RELATED READINGS

- *Stonewords* by Pam Conrad
- *Eva* by Peter Dickinson
- *A Swiftly Tilting Planet* by Madeleine L'Engle
- *A Traveler in Time* by Alison Uttley
- *Ella Enchanted* by Gail Levine

CURRICULAR CONNECTIONS

Math. Have students discuss the role of math in space travel and how math relevant to space relates to their current math instruction.

Social studies. Describe the lifestyle and values of the people in the various stories. Have the students identify what kinds of things they need to consider when describing a society and its values.

Writing. Instruct students to keep reading journals in which they write a response to a novel they read.

Students also may use art, or music, or both to express their responses to the novels.

Topics for Units

HOLIDAYS ACROSS CULTURES

New Year's	Flag Day
Christmas	Memorial Day
Kwanzaa	Arbor Day
Hanukkah	

CONCEPTS

being a friend/having friends	journeys around the world
what do your senses tell you?	journeys around our state
how many kinds of courage are there?	journeys around our country
heroes	what makes you laugh?
superheroes	what is a family?
space	conservation
communities	growing

ARTISTS AND WRITERS

Steven Kellogg	Trina Schart Hyman
Avi	Lois Ehlert
Pam Conrad	Katherine Paterson
Marc Brown	Tomie de Paola

CURRENT EVENTS

disasters	hurricanes
floods	blizzards
earthquakes	random acts of kindness
senseless acts of beauty	senseless acts of violence

CURRICULUM TOPICS (CONSULT YOUR OWN CURRICULUM)

addition	multiplication
great sentences from literature	great paragraphs from literature
water cycle—where has all the rain gone?	nutrition—you are what you eat
interpreting maps—where in the world are you going?	rain forests—what do rain forests have to do with me?
weather—it's raining cats and dogs	genre (traditional literature, poetry, biography, etc.)

Jean Dickinson (1995) reports that her fifth- and sixth-grade students, who used picture books, novels, and textbooks to explore World War II, developed these reading strategies:

1. to visualize while reading
2. to use prior knowledge
3. to reread interesting and exciting parts and parts with especially interesting language
4. to ask questions about what they read
5. to make predictions
6. to discuss books with friends
7. to find ideas for writing
8. to look beyond the cover
9. to relate books to other books they have read and to books by the same author
10. to put themselves in the story
11. to know when they do not understand something in the book
12. to read the rest of a paragraph to figure out word meanings

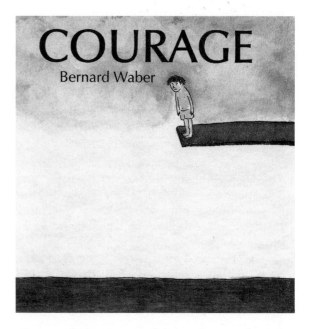

Courage illustrates some of the many types of courage that may be studied in a unit.

Planning Units

When choosing the unifying theme or topic for a unit, the teacher should consider curriculum goals, standards, and objectives. For instance, first-grade teachers are usually accountable for emergent reading and writing, as well as developing concepts of family, friends, and holidays, among others.

Consider what the students already know and what they need to know about the selected topic or theme. In addition to prior knowledge, teachers may consider the students' interests because this motivates them and provides a sense of ownership. Other considerations include the students' learning needs, developmental levels, and previous experiences. Building background experiences for the theme or topic is necessary for students who lack them.

The resources available for students are another consideration. A good supply of well-written books is essential. The books must, of course, address the unit topic or theme, and match the students' range of reading levels. Both print and nonprint media develop children's knowledge base and understanding. Videos, films, pictures, computer programs, and Web sites are useful in units. Guest speakers or people who can demonstrate skills or materials also add interest to units.

Teachers should plan read-alouds, as well as book-talks, on the books selected for the unit. Book-talks provide students with the information they need when choosing the books they want to read.

When planning units, teachers may include opportunities for art, music, writing, and similar experiences as a means of responding to literature (Weston, 1993). The box on page 332 shows some of the possibilities for response experiences with literature-based units. The box on page 334 provides a form to summarize the unit plan.

Making Connections Through Inquiry

Knowledge only gives the illusion of residing in books. It actually develops through discussing, questioning, and writing about literature. Discussion is a social process that strengthens learning and response. It also helps readers make sense of new information (Copenhaver, 1993). Although learners can arrive at a meaning alone, they do so more often through collaboration (Barnes, 1995).

To investigate their questions, students listen, read, write, view films, listen to audiotapes, use the Internet, and watch television; they also consult with people who have special knowledge related to the questions. They may conduct their own experiments, such as a group of kindergarten students did when investigating insects to find out which insects crawled fastest. All of these approaches to investigation and more can be applied.

The beginning or access point for *inquiry* is identifying students' knowledge about a topic. Brainstorming is an effective strategy for summarizing existing knowledge. Students can also create individual webs of knowledge. Figure 16.1 shows a web of prior knowledge for the theme of friends, created by a second-grade class. The teacher decided to initiate inquiry with the question, "Why do we like to do things with friends?" Figure 16.2 summarizes the unit activities of teachers and students, and Figure 16.3 is a planning guide.

Shared Book Experiences

Obviously, accessing literature is necessary for incorporating literature in the curriculum and units. Teachers should plan to read books aloud and to identify books that reflect a range of readability, so that students can independently read those books. The following guidelines will help teachers plan.

1. Select the *core literature* (literature central to the unit theme or topic) carefully. The literature should reflect a wide range of readability. Book-talk each book to help students select those they wish to read.

2. Read the book or books aloud, encouraging the students to discuss what is happening (Jacque, 1993).

3. Have the students use response journals, literature logs, or interactive journals. In response journals, students write about their feelings, specifically *connections* to their lives and to other literature. In a literature log, students discuss their understanding of the elements of literature. In an interactive journal, the student writes and the teacher responds and/or asks questions.

4. Divide the class into four cooperative groups and have each group read a different book. Conduct a book-talk for each of the books in advance to

Response Experiences for Literature-Based Units

Language Arts

LISTENING

- Listening exercises using passages with outstanding language
- Visualize scenes from the book
- Listen for sensory images
- Identify story or text structures
- Retell a story
- Speakers on special subjects

SPEAKING

- Discuss the book in a group
- Discuss the book using student-generated questions
- Tell the story as a news report
- Tell a student-composed story

READING

- Use reader's theater for all or part of a story or poem
- Read or story tell cultural variations of a traditional story
- Read and compare to other books

WRITING

- Write an original story with the same pattern
- Write the story as a play
- Write more about a character or add a new character

- Write song lyrics based on the story
- Keep a journal of feelings, ideas, parallels evoked as a result of story reading or listening

SCIENCE

- Study the habitat of the story
- Create an experiment to solve a story problem or mystery
- Think about how science is related to the book
- Relate scientific method to the book

SOCIAL STUDIES

- Research the country, people, geography, history, anthropology of the setting
- Study the descriptions of places

PHYSICAL EDUCATION

- Create a dance of a scene in a story or a poem

MATH

- Discuss the math concepts that appear in the story

FINE ARTS

- Create a mural depicting scenes from the story
- Draw a picture story map
- Make puppets
- Dramatize one character

---

help children choose a book that appeals to their interests.

5. Have various groups or individuals read a book and retell the high points of the parts they read.

Assessing Unit Experiences

Assessment is an integral part of instruction. The purpose of assessment in literature is to gather informa-

tion regarding students' growth in understanding and appreciating literature. Sources of information regarding student progress include work samples, journal entries, projects and displays, individual conferences, oral presentations, portfolios, and student observation forms. Portfolio assessment is a type of informal evaluation that involves student input. Portfolios may include work samples, checklists, and assignments specifically designed to collect information (Meinback, Rothlein, & Fredericks, 2000).

FIGURE 16.1   Friends web.

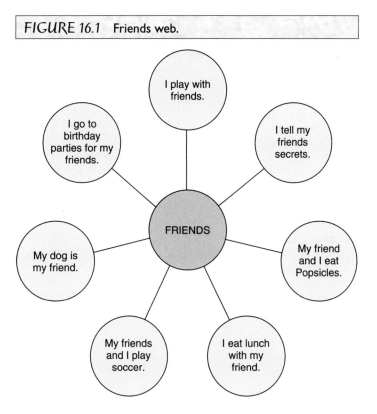

FIGURE 16.2   Unit activities.

Teacher Activities

Plan:
  Identify theme or topic
  Connect to literature and/or knowledge
  Identify Standards
Select: literature, Web sites, videos, audios, activities
Accept children's ideas
Engage children in meaningful activities as time allows.
Initiating activities
  Closure (Culmination)
  Evaluation/Assessment

Student Activities

Ask questions
Apply background
Focus-relate
Listen, read, think, write
Discuss complete required work.
Do optional activities as time allows.

When using a literature checklist, the student should:

- identify the beginning, middle, and ending of stories;
- recognize the central character in a story;
- follow the sequence of events in a story;
- recognize the literary elements (plot, character, setting, theme, style);
- understand and follow plot; and
- choose to read for pleasure.

FIGURE 16.3   Unit planning guide

Planning Guide

Theme or Topic: _____

Standards or Objectives: _____

Questions:

Literature and Media Selections:

Students to learn (knowledge, skills, response):

Prereading (initiating activities):

During reading (activities):

Following reading (activities): Include literature log.

Evaluation/assessment strategies:

Classroom Activities

Teaching with literature is not a specific method or process based on hard-and-fast rules. Literature experiences can be molded and adapted to fit local curricula and students. One of the most powerful ideas in teaching literature in units is to constantly seek connections. Students should think about connections in plot, characters, themes, setting, and style.

This section of the chapter is devoted to actual units that classroom teachers have developed, used, and refined. These units are organized around different formats, some narrative and others outlined. You may choose to use all or part of any unit or activity in your own teaching. Activity 16.7 illustrates a *book cluster;* additional book clusters are included on our Internet site.

ACTIVITY 16.1   DAY AND NIGHT (KINDERGARTEN, FIRST GRADE, SECOND GRADE)

(IRA/NCTE Standards: 2, 3, 7, 12. Students will use a range of strategies to comprehend, evaluate and appreciate text.)

This unit provides a variety of activities. When planning a thematic unit, consider the students' interests and the activities they enjoy. You should consult the State Standards for your grade level and identify specific curricular goals and objectives from each of the content areas that correspond to the unit.

This unit explores day and night. The students will learn how to explain, both verbally and nonverbally, why we have day and night. Many other skills can also be developed during this study, such as the concept of telling time to the hour and half-hour; reviewing counting and number identification of 0–12; and reviewing seasons, months of the year, and days of the week. Children may use a sundial for the first time and create a crude sundial for themselves. Children will have fun discovering shadows and measuring their own shadows during different times of the day. Each of the mini-lessons in this unit can be taught separately as a stand-alone experience. The goals that meet state standards follow.

Topic: Day and Night

Goals

1. To help children understand that day and night are caused by the rotation of the earth. (Science)
2. To introduce the concepts of the sun, moon, stars, and the planet Earth. (Science)
3. To introduce the concept of telling time using various instruments (sundial, clock, calendar). (Math)
4. To explore literary understandings of plot, character, and setting. (Language arts)

Skills to Develop

Mathematics

- counting from 0–12 (review)
- telling time—compare/contrast a clock, calendar, and sundial
- identifying numbers from 0–12 (review)
- telling time to the hour and half-hour (introduction)

Reading

- sequencing (story events)
- letter identification: Mm, Ss, Dd, Nn
- rhyming words (continued)
- phonemic awareness: m, s, d, n

Writing

Children dictate stories to their teacher or write their own responses to these books: *Sounds All Around*, *Night in the Country*, *Me and My Shadow*, and *Stella and Roy Go Camping*.

Literature

- journals
- logs
- shared writing

Science

- day/night
- constellations
- earth, sun, stars, moon
- rotation or turning
- shadows
- seasons with respect to day/night

Social Studies

- things we do during the day/night
- days of the week
- careers that require working at night
- months of the year
- culture

Fine Arts

- tracing shadows
- nighttime pictures using black wash paint
- daytime pictures
- constellation patterns

Physical Education

Focus on circle games that move clockwise ("Duck, Duck, Goose"; "With Stars"; "Farmer in the Dell"; "London Bridge").

Introduction

Thought Question

Why do we have day and night? Record student responses on chart paper.

Mini-Lesson One

Use Keiko Narahashi's book *I Have a Friend* to introduce the concept of shadows. After reading, have children go out and find their shadows. With a friend, they can use a nonstandard unit of measurement (jump ropes or blocks) to measure one another's shadows. Compare the height of the shadow with the child's actual height. Repeat this activity at another time of day. Discuss the concepts of taller and shorter and ask the children why they have shadows. Record their responses.

Mini-Lesson Two

Read Frank Asch's story *Bear Shadow*.

Discussion Questions

- Why did the bear want to lose his shadow?
- What things did he do to lose his shadow?
- How would you lose your shadow?
- Draw a picture of where you might go so your shadow would not find you.

Activities

- Have children dictate a story about losing their shadow.
- Trace children's shadows outside on butcher paper. Have the children come inside and paint their shadows to show the clothing they are wearing.
- Have children write a story about something they and their shadow like to do together.
- Using paper clocks, show the children the time they went outside to trace their shadows.
- Play the recording "Paper Clocks" by Hap Palmer.
- Discuss the events of a school day. Using the clock, show the time children get up in the morning, eat breakfast, start school, have circle time, go outside to play, and so forth. Let children experiment with clocks to show when they do certain things at home. *The Grouchy Ladybug* by Eric Carle may be read in a small group, after which it is placed on a table so that children can access it.

Learning About Daytime

Mini-Lesson Three

Read Ragnhild Scamell's *Rooster Crows*. Discuss why the rooster could not get the sun to come up at the stroke of midnight, and show this time on the clock. Explain that we have day and night because the earth rotates or turns. When the earth turns, part of it is exposed to the sun and the other part is not. Using a globe, help the children locate your state and mark it with a sticker.

Gently turn the globe so that the children can see the earth rotate or turn. Let the children practice rotating the globe. Have one child hold a flashlight on the part of the globe with the students' state. Explain that the sun is a star and it does not move; rather, the earth slowly rotates or turns. As it turns and the sun is no longer pointing directly at the state, it is becoming afternoon. As the earth turns we no longer face the sun and it is nighttime. Let children take turns holding the flashlight (the sun) and turning the globe (Earth).

Mini-Lesson (Follow-up)

Discuss shadows by asking the children questions like these:

> Can you see your shadow when it is cloudy?
> Can you see your shadow when it rains?
> What makes it possible to see your shadow? (The sun)
> What planet do we live on?
> Why do we have day and night?

Mini-Lesson Four

Share Audrey Wood's *The Napping House* with the students. After several readings students will enjoy predicting what is coming next. The children can dramatize the story with puppets. Read Barbara Berger's *Grandfather Twilight* to the students. Discuss what the pearl in the story represents (the moon). This will lead into the study of night.

Have the children do a shared writing activity. For example, the children can write to their parents explaining their experiences and what they learned.

Learning About Nighttime

Mini-Lesson Five

Have the children observe the night sky. Ask them to record everything they see. They can do this for several evenings. During circle time, have the children tell what they saw and record their information. Categorize and count the different things. Discuss what the moon looked like. Introduce the phases of the moon with Frank Asch's book *Moon Bear.* Have children compare the moon they saw with the one in the story. Have children draw the phases of the moon on the calendar as they observe them in the night sky.

Group Activities

Share picture books of constellations. Show the children that the constellations make patterns in the sky. Tell them how long ago people used these patterns to help find their way. Help children recreate the pattern of the Big Dipper and Little Dipper. Place glue-backed stars on black paper as they appear in the night sky (copy the pattern from the constellation book). Use chalk to connect the stars so that children can see the pattern. Repeat this activity using other stars.

Have children cut out pictures of activities that are done during the day and others that are done at night; then sort and paste the pictures onto poster board. Record words and phrases that are dictated about the pictures. (One half of the poster board can be yellow and the other half black to simplify the sorting process for students. It also helps to have some pictures already available for children to cut if they are unable to locate any pictures in magazines.)

Introduce /Ss/ for stars. Have children look for /s/ on stars. Use sand trays to trace the letter /s/. Discuss the /s/ sound. Help children identify words beginning with the /s/ sound. Use a dictionary to help children associate pictures with the letter and sound. (Repeat this activity with other letters when appropriate.)

Mini-Lesson Six

Introduce Margaret Wise Brown's *Goodnight Moon.* Read the story several times. Begin leaving out the final word in the second sentence and have children supply it. Pull out pairs of rhyming words and illustrate each on an index card. Have children practice putting the pairs of words together.

Group Activities

Read Mem Fox's *Time for Bed.* Study the end papers. Listen for pairs of rhyming words. Help the children find the rhyming words. Create a book of rhyming words consisting of things associated with day and night. Encourage the students to make end papers for their books. Make nighttime pictures using crayons. Use a tempera paint wash to cover the pictures. Have children dictate sentences about things they like to do at night.

Read Frank Asch's *Happy Birthday, Moon.* Help the children learn their birthdays. Discuss the book, asking what kind of present the children would give the moon. Discuss the idea of an echo, which is introduced in this story. Then have children make a birthday board with their birthdays and the birthdays of family members.

Mini-Lesson Seven

Read Cynthia Rylant's *Night in the Country.* Have the children listen to and record the night sounds of the city. Share these during circle time. Compare the night sounds of the city and the night sounds of the country.

Group Activities

Share Pat Hutchins' *Good, Night, Owl!* Have the students cut out figures of the animals that keep the owl awake. Put flannel or sand paper on the back of the figures so you can use them on a flannel board. The children can practice retelling the story using the flannel board animals to sequence the retelling.

Additional Books for the Unit:

- *What the Moon Is Like* by Franklin M. Branley
- *Turtle Day* by Douglas Florian
- *Star, Little Star* by Lonnie George
- *The Moon and You* by E. C. Krupp
- *Under the Moon* by Joanne Ryder

ACTIVITY 16.2   EVERYBODY LOVES A GOOD MYSTERY—GRADE LEVELS 4–7

(IRA/NCTE Standards: 2, 3, 4, 5, 6, 7, 11, 12.)

Mysteries have wide appeal for all ages; furthermore, they give teachers opportunities to develop a sequence of story events, analysis, inferencing, critical thinking, problem solving, vocabulary, and drawing conclusions.

Objectives

1. Students will read a mystery.
2. Students will learn strategies for solving the mystery.
3. Students will identify the problem, clues, and perpetrator.
4. Students will refine their literary knowledge of plot, characterization, and motivation.

Mystery

In *The Mysterious Matter of I. M. Fine* by Diane Stanley, Franny, a fifth grader, is concerned because her classmates have psychosomatic illnesses and delusions after reading middle-grade horror novels called "Chillers." Franny and her friend, Beamer, decide to find the author of the books and stop her.

Introduction

1. Ask the students if they have ever experienced a mystery. Discuss their responses.
2. Read the first three chapters of the book aloud to the class.
3. Introduce these words: alibi, clue, deduction, delusions, evidence, perpetrator, psychosomatic illness, suspects, and witness. Apply these terms to the first three chapters of the book.
4. What is the mystery in this book? Identify the sequence of events up to this point.
5. Identify the central character and describe her.
6. Explain the steps to analyzing a problem (in this instance, a mystery).

Silent Reading in Small Groups

Organize groups of four or five to read the story. After the students complete it, discuss the following questions and write out the answers. Students can work out the answers as a group or assign different individuals to answer different questions.

1. Describe the main characters in the mystery, explaining how each is related to the mystery.
2. Identify the important clues to the mystery.
3. What was the most important clue to the mystery?
4. What is the solution to the mystery?
5. How did you analyze the problem? (Work backwards to the beginning, make guesses that you can support with information from the book, and draw a web of facts, events, and characters. Draw a web of clues.)
6. How did the characters in the book solve the problem (mystery)?

Additional Mysteries

We recommend that students read additional mysteries, so they can use their newly developed knowledge and understanding. The asterisk (*) indicates mysteries that will appeal to challenged readers. The numbers in parentheses indicate grade levels.

Cutler, J. *'Gator Aid.* (4–6).*

Hoobler, D., & Hoobler, T. *The Ghost in the Tokaido Inn.* (4–6).

Konigsburg, E. L. *Silent to the Bone.* (4–6).

Littke, L. *Lake of Secrets.* (6–9).

Manns, N. *Operating Codes.* (6–9).

Martin, T. *A Family Trait.* (4–6).

Naylor, P. *Bernie Magruder & the Bats in the Belfry.* (4–7).

Nickerson, D. *How to Disappear Completely and Never Be Found.* (6–9).

Stanley, G. *The Cobweb Confession.* (All).*

Stenhouse, T. *Across the Steel River.* (5–8).

Internet Sites

We highly recommend the following Internet sites. You can obtain copies of mysteries for children that are a quick read plus explanations of how the mystery was solved. Students can compare their solutions with the professionals. Students are encouraged to write mysteries and to learn from them. The sites are MysteryNet's Kids Mysteries at **http://kids.mysterynet.com** and Kids Love a Mystery.com at **www.kidsloveamystery.com.**

ACTIVITY 16.3   COUNTING (SECOND, THIRD, OR FOURTH GRADE)

(IRA/NCTE Standards: 2, 3, 4, 5. Students Learn to comprehend various genre, use language to accomplish purposes.)

This unit, which focuses on various ways of counting and the importance of math, is presented in a unit map.

Questions
- What do you want or need to count?
- What is the best way to count that thing?

Math
- Why do we need to count things?
- What kinds of things need to be counted?
- What is one-to-one correspondence?

Writing
- Think of a new way to count and write it down.

Art
- Make illustrations and art to go with the project.

Social Studies
- Why is counting people important?
- What do we call it when we count people?

- What is a poll?
- Why do we conduct polls?

Literature
- *The Search for Delicious* by Natalie Babbitt
- *Ten Seeds* by Ruth Brown
- *The Father Who had 10 Children* by Benedicte Guettier
- *The Toothpaste Millionaire* by Jean Merrill
- *Counting Jennie* by Helena Clare Pittman
- *Arithmetickle* by Patrick Lewis
- *Math Curse* by Jon Scieszka and Lane Smith

ACTIVITY 16.4   NATIVE AMERICAN FOLK TALES (THIRD GRADE)

(IRA/NCTE Standards: 2, 3, 4, 6, 9. Students read a variety of genre from various periods, develop comprehension, use language for a variety of purposes.)

Topic: Native American Folk Tales

Objectives
1. To learn the characteristics of the folk tale genre.
2. To identify Native-American values through their folk tales.
3. To develop vocabulary related to the Native-American culture.

Background Information
Storytellers originally told folk tales; this is why they differ from other genres. Storytellers knew their stories and often told them to people who could not read or write. Traditional stories entertained, taught lessons, and helped listeners learn about their culture. Folk tales were very important in transmitting culture. These tales help us know how Native Americans lived and what was important to them.

Literature for this Unit:
- *Baby Rattlesnake* by Te Ata. This teaching tale is written at an independent reading level for third grade.
- *Ma'ii and Cousin Horned Toad* by Shonto Begay. The author, a Navajo, tells his own favorite childhood tale in this book.
- *Iktomi and the Berries: A Plains Indian Story* by Paul Goble. Read aloud to introduce Native-American storytelling to students.
- *Mystic Horse* by Paul Goble. This Pawnee tale has themes of courage and transformation.
- *The Great Buffalo Race: How the Buffalo Got His Hump: A Seneca Tale* retold by Barbara Juster Esbensen. This tale explains how the buffalo got its hump. It is a good read-aloud.

- *Sky Dogs* by Jane Yolen. This read-aloud explains why Native Americans first thought horses were dogs.
- *The Mud Pony: A Traditional Skidi Pawnee Tale* by Caron Cohen. This story shows the importance of horses in the Native-American culture. Children can read this one.
- *Rainbow Crow: A Lenape Tale* by Nancy Van Laan. This is good read-aloud.
- *The Rough-Face Girl* by Rafe Martin. This is a tale from both the Algonquin and Comanche. This *Cinderella* story is a good read-aloud for comparison with other *Cinderella* versions.
- *Navajo: Visions and Voices Across the Mesa* by Shonto Begay. The talented Navajo artist combines his art with his prose and poetry in this book.

Before the Unit

Introduce a map that shows where the various Indian tribes lived. Discuss the term *Native American* and the reasons for it. Brainstorm the words *Indian* and *Native American* to tap into children's experiences. They may have movie and television ideas of Indians that can be dispelled through this unit.

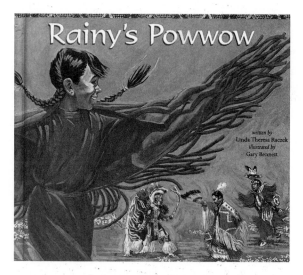

This story is an excellent choice for a Native American unit.

Discussion Questions
Prereading

- What do you think a "teaching tale" is?
- Have your parents ever told you a teaching tale? What about?
- As you read one of these stories, think about who is teaching something and who is supposed to learn something.

Postreading

- What lesson do you think the characters were supposed to learn?
- What did you notice in these stories?
- Did any of the stories remind you of other books you have read or television shows you have seen?
- What questions would you like to ask the characters in these stories?

Extensions for Response

- Summarize one of the stories orally or in writing.
- Describe the setting of one of the stories.
- Tell what you learned about Native Americans from these tales. Tell or write what makes you think this.
- Look at the Seneca page borders in *The Great Buffalo Race* and create the borders you would like if you were a Native American.
- Have the children draw numbers and participate in small-group sharing according to the number they drew. In the small groups, ask them to:
  1. Retell a favorite part of the story.
  2. Identify the words that describe the main character.
  3. Tell two new things learned from one story.
  4. Summarize the story.

ACTIVITY 16.5   PIRATES (THIRD OR FOURTH GRADE)

Topic: Pirates

(IRA/NCTE Standards 3, 4, 7: Comprehension, use a variety of strategies, apply language to print and non print texts.)

Title and author: _____

Problem: _____

Resolution: _____

Main character: _____

What was the reward? _____

Who received the reward? _____

What did you learn about Native Americans? _____
_____

Objectives

- To study oceans through pirate routes.
- To study the difference between saltwater and fresh water.
- To learn about the importance of vitamin C and how sailors got vitamin C.
- To learn why pirates needed math to figure out where they were and to plot their route.
- To learn pirate songs.
- To learn pirate words and language.

Questions

1. Why did pirates live on ships? Did they always live on ships? Can you be a pirate if you do not live on a ship?
2. Why do pirates wear funny clothes?
3. How did they get their treasure?
4. Did they help other people?
5. How do you become a pirate?
6. Why do they use funny words?
7. Did all the pirates live long ago? Do pirates exist today?
8. Why did people become pirates?
9. Can girls be pirates?

Literature

- *Tough Boris* by Mem Fox
- *Pirates: Robbers of the High Seas* by Gail Gibbons
- *One-Eyed Jake* by Pat Hutchins
- *Pirates* by Drew Lamm
- *Pirate Diary: The Journal of Jake Carpenter* by Richard Platt
- *Do Pirates Take Baths?* by Kathy Tucker
- *The Ballad of the Pirate Queens* by Jane Yolen

ACTIVITY 16.6   INVENTORS (FOURTH OR FIFTH GRADE)

(IRA/NCTE Standards: 2, 3, 4, 7. Read a variety of genre, develop comprehension, adjust use of spoken and written language.)

Topic: Inventors

Questions

- What is the best invention in the world?
- What is an invention that changed the world?
- What is creativity?

Math

- Measurement
- Computers
- Probability

Thinking

- Classify inventions

Science

- Identify important scientific inventions

Writing

- Write to the U.S. Patent Office to get information about obtaining patents.
- Write about a needed invention that would improve your life.

Social Studies

- How did these inventions change life in the United States: automobiles, telephones, computers, computer chips?

Reading

- Review biographies of famous inventors and some who are not so famous—what made these people creative?

Literature

- *The Wright Brothers: How They Invented the Airplane* by Russell Freedman
- *Ice Cream Cones for Sale* by Elaine Greenstein
- *The Amazing Thinking Machine* by Dennis Haseley
- *Outward Dreams: Black Inventors and Their Inventions* by Jim Haskins
- *Mistakes That Worked: 40 Familiar Inventions and How They Came to Be* by Charlotte Foltz Jones
- *The Many Lives of Benjamin Franklin* by Mary Osborne
- *Pinkerton: America's First Private Eye* by Richard Wormser
- *100 Inventions That Shaped World History* by Bill Yenne

ACTIVITY 16.7   BOOK CLUSTERS

Book clusters are groups of books under a common theme or topic with a range of reading difficulty that teachers can use to develop units. The following example is a cluster of sports books.

Adler, D. (1997). *Lou Gehrig: The luckiest man.* Harcourt. (3–5). PICTURE BOOK, BIOGRAPHY.

Bunting, E. (1997). *Trouble on the t-ball team.*

Clarion. (K–3). FICTION.

Green, M. (2002). *A strong right arm: The story of Mamie "Peanut" Johnson.* Dial. (4–8). BIOGRAPHY.

Layden, J. (1997). *NBA game day.* Scholastic. (2–6). NONFICTION.

Telander, R. (2002). *String music.* Cricket. (4–6). FICTION.

Summary

This chapter guides readers' synthesis of their learning about children's literature. Using literature in the classroom, reading aloud daily, and using an integrated curriculum, inquiry learning, units, and assessment are the focus of this chapter. Units are intensive learning experiences that help students make connections as they learn. Integrated units develop language skills within a context that may involve social studies, math, science, the arts, music, and physical education. Inquiry learning focuses on students' questions as powerful stimulators of learning. Units may focus on curriculum topics, themes, authors/illustrators, current events, concepts, or student-generated ideas. A unit plan serves as a road map for teachers, which may be revised as it is used.

Thought Questions

1. What components should teachers consider when developing units? Can you think of any additional considerations?
2. Describe a unit in your own words.
3. What is the purpose of literature assessment?
4. How are reading aloud to children and their own silent reading related to inquiry units?

Research and Application Experiences

1. Prepare a complete unit for a grade level of your choice. Teach your unit, if possible.

2. Prepare a unit that could be integrated with a specific unit in a basal reader of your choice.

3. Consult a curriculum guide or the standards for your state and list the unit topics or themes appropriate for the grade level you teach or hope to teach.

4. Read a unit ideas book and decide which units you would be interested in using and why you would use these.

5. Write a narrative plan for inquiry instruction and get children to raise important questions.

6. Determine what literature-related items you think should be included in a portfolio for your class or the class you plan to teach. Explain why you would choose these items.

Children's Literature References and Recommended Books

Note: Books designated with an asterisk (*) are recommended for reluctant readers.

Asch, F. (1978). *Moon bear.* New York: Scribner's (PreK–1). PICTURE BOOK.

Bear thinks he sees a bear in the moon.

Asch, F. (1985). *Bear shadow.* Upper Saddle River, NJ: Prentice Hall. (PreK–1). PICTURE BOOK.

Little Bear sees his shadow and is fascinated.

Asch, F. (2000). *Happy birthday, moon.* New York: Simon & Schuster. (PreK–1). PICTURE BOOK.

In this book, a birthday celebration leads to a discussion of moons.

Ata, T. (1989). *Baby rattlesnake* (L. Moroney, Adapt.; V. Reisberg, Illus.). San Francisco: Children's Book Press. (1–2). TRADITIONAL LITERATURE.

This is a Native-American teaching tale.

Babbitt, N. (1969). *The search for delicious.* New York: Farrar, Straus & Giroux. (3–6). MODERN FANTASY.

The king searches for the meaning of *delicious.*

Begay, S. (1992). *Ma'ii and cousin horned toad.* New York: Scholastic. (1–3). TRADITIONAL LITERATURE.

This is a traditional Navajo story about the coyote trickster.

Begay, S. (1994). *Navajo: Visions and voices across the mesa.* New York: Scholastic. (2–6). POETRY, PICTURE BOOK.

Shonto Begay combines his art with his prose and poetry in this book.

Bellamy, F. (2001). *The Pledge of Allegiance.* New York: Cartwheel Books. (1–4). NONFICTION.

Colorful photographs illustrate the pledge and our country.

Berger, B. (1996). *Grandfather Twilight.* New York: Puffin. (K–3). PICTURE BOOK.

Grandfather twilight goes through the forest bringing the miracle of night.

Borden, L. (2002). *America is. . .* (S. Schuett, Illus.). New York: McElderry. (2–4). NONFICTION.

This picture book expresses that America is our home and shows the diversity of the 50 states.

Branley, F. M. (1986). *What the moon is like* (T. Kelley, Illus.). New York: Harper & Row. (1–3). INFORMATIONAL BOOK.

This is a simple, informational book.

Brown, L. K., & Brown, M. (1992). *Dinosaurs to the rescue! A guide to protecting our planet.* New York: Little, Brown. (2–6). INFORMATIONAL BOOK.

This informational book is a guide to conservation.

Brown, M. W. (1947). *Goodnight moon* (C. Hurd, Illus.). New York: Harper & Row. (PreK–1). PICTURE BOOK.

A young child wishes goodnight to everything in his room and to the moon.

Brown, R. (2001). *Ten Seeds.* New York: Knopf. PICTURE BOOK. (K–2).

This seed-planting story introduces subtraction.

Cannon, A. (2003). *On the go with Pirate Pete and Pirate Joe* (E. Smith, Illus.). New York: Viking. (1–3). FANTASY.

The story of two pirates, one tall and thin and one short and round, who like to dance.

Carle, E. (1977). *The grouchy ladybug.* New York: Thomas Crowell. (K–2). PICTURE BOOK.

The grouchy ladybug tries to fight with everyone she meets, but makes a friend.

Catrow, D. (2002). *We the kids: The Preamble to the Constitution of the United States.* New York: Dial. (3–6). NONFICTION.

This is a sort of "how-to" book showing how to have happiness, safety, and comfort.

Cheney, L. (2002). *America: A patriotic primer* (Glasser, Illus.). New York: Simon & Schuster (2–4). NONFICTION.

This book contains alphabetical information about our country.

Cohen, C. L. (Reteller). (1988). *The mud pony: A traditional Skidi Pawnee tale* (S. Begay, Illus.). New York: Scholastic. (1–3). TRADITIONAL LITERATURE.

A Pawnee boy makes a pony from mud, which comes to life.

Cutler, J. (1999). *'Gator aid* (T. Pearson, Illus.). New York: Farrar, Straus & Giroux. (4–6). REALISTIC FICTION/MYSTERY.*

Edward believes he sees an alligator, but no one believes him. He has to solve the mystery.

Davis, K. (2003). *Don't know much about American history*. New York: Harper. (3–6). NONFICTION.

Interesting facts and ideas about American history.

Dorros, A. (1990). *Me and my shadow*. New York: Scholastic. (1–3). CONTEMPORARY REALISTIC FICTION.

The author explores the concepts of shadows.

Erlback, A. (1997). *The kids' invention book*. Minneapolis, MN: Lerner. (2–5). NONFICTION.

This book suggests science fair projects that could grow into products for manufacture.

Esbensen, B. J. (Reteller). (1994). *The great buffalo race: How the buffalo got his hump: A Seneca tale*. New York: Little, Brown. (1–3). TRADITIONAL LITERATURE.

This pourquoi tale explains how the buffalo got its hump.

Fink, S. (2002). *The Declaration of Independence*. New York: Scholastic. (4–up). NONFICTION.

The author breaks the document into phrases and explains them with historically accurate illustrations.

Florian, D. (1989). *Turtle day*. New York: Crowell. (1–3). INFORMATIONAL BOOK.

This book helps children learn about turtles and reptiles.

Ford, B. (1989). *Walt Disney*. New York: Walker. (4–8). BIOGRAPHY.

This biography of Walt Disney provides children with insight about the man.

Fox, M. (1989). *Night noises* (T. Denton, Illus.). New York: Harcourt Brace Jovanovich. (K–2). PICTURE BOOK.

This story is about the sounds of animals at night.

Fox, M. (1994). *Tough Boris* (K. Brown, Illus.). New York: Harcourt Brace Jovanovich. (2–4). PICTURE BOOK.

This book is about Boris, a pirate who is not so tough.

Fox, M. (1997a). *Time for bed* (J. Dyer, Illus.). New York: Harcourt Brace Jovanovich. (PreK–1). PICTURE BOOK.

All of the animals are ready for bed in this book.

Fox, M. (1997b). *Whoever you are* (L. Straub, Illus.). New York: Harcourt. (K–4). PICTURE BOOK.

The author illustrates the importance of each individual.

Freedman, R. (1991). *The Wright brothers: How they invented the airplane* (W. Wright & O. Wright, Photog.). New York: Holiday House. (3–8). BIOGRAPHY.

An excellent biography of the *Wright Brothers* and the Wright brothers' quest to fly. Photographs from the time add realism to the presentation.

Friedman, A. (1994). *The king's commissioners*. New York: Scholastic. (2–5). MODERN FANTASY.

Commissioners of the king find a mathematical solution to their problems.

George, L. (1992). *Star, little star*. East Rutherford, NJ: Grosset and Dunlap. (K–2). POETRY.

This is a book of poetry about night and sleeping.

Gibbons, G. (1992). *Recycle! A handbook for kids*. New York: Little, Brown. (2–5). INFORMATIONAL BOOK.

This book suggests specific recycling projects.

Gibbons, G. (1993). *Pirates: Robbers of the high seas*. New York: Little, Brown. (2–5). INFORMATIONAL BOOK.

Facts are presented about pirates in this descriptive book.

Goble, P. (2003). *Mystic horse*. New York: Harper Collins. (K–4). TRADITIONAL LITERATURE.

Pawnee story about a boy and his Grandmother who rescue a sickly horse.

Goble, P. (Reteller). (1989). *Iktomi and the berries: A Plains Indian story*. New York: Orchard. (K–6). TRADITIONAL LITERATURE.

A trickster story from the Lakota Sioux.

Greenstein, E. (2003). *Ice cream cones for sale*. New York: Scholastic. (1–3). REALISTIC FICTION.

This book tells the story of the first ice cream cones.

Guettier, B. (1999). *The father who had 10 children*. New York: Dial. (1–3). REALISTIC FICTION.

The father of 10 children has to count by ones, twos, fives, and tens.

Haseley, D. (2002). *The amazing thinking machine.* New York: Dial. (4–6). REALISTIC FICTION.

The central character invents the thinking machine to support his family.

Haskins, J. (1991). *Outward dreams: Black inventors and their inventions.* New York: Walker. (5–8). INFORMATIONAL BOOK.

This book details significant accomplishments of African Americans that have been omitted from traditional history books.

Hoobler, D., & Hoobler, T. (1999). *The ghost in the Tokaido inn.* New York: Philomel. (4–7). HISTORICAL FICTION, MYSTERY.

In this complex mystery set in 18th-century Japan, a boy solves a crime to improve his status.

Hutchins, P. (1972). *Good night, owl!* New York: Macmillan. (K–2). PICTURE BOOK.

A cumulative tale about night and going to sleep.

Hutchins, P. (1979). *One-eyed Jake.* New York: Greenwillow. (1–3). PICTURE BOOK.

This book is about one-eyed Jake, a mean-looking pirate.

Jones, C. F. (1991). *Mistakes that worked: 40 familiar inventions and how they came to be* (J. O'Brien, Illus.). New York: Doubleday. (4–8). INFORMATIONAL BOOK.

This book presents the stories behind 40 things that were invented or named by accident.

Kennedy, C. (2003). *A patriot's handbook.* New York: Hyperion. (1–7). VARIETY OF GENRES.

The author has collected a variety of readings.

Konigsburg, E. (2000). *Silent to the bone.* New York: Atheneum. (4–7). REALISTIC FICTION, MYSTERY.

A 13-year-old boy is accused of dropping his baby sister. The father tries to solve the mystery.

Krulik, N. E. (1991). *My picture book of the planets.* New York: Scholastic. (1–3). INFORMATIONAL BOOK.

This book introduces the planets to young children.

Krupp, E. C. (1993). *The moon and you* (R. R. Krupp, Illus.). New York: Macmillan. (1–3). CONTEMPORARY REALISTIC FICTION.

This book presents a bedtime story about a child and the moon.

Lamm, C. D. (2001). *Pirates* (S. Schuett, Illus.). New York: Hyperion. (1–3). FANTASY.

Ellery reads a scary book to her younger brother, Max.

Lang, R. (1999). *Old glory: An American treasure* (S. Winget, Illus.). Delafield, WI: Lang Books. (All ages). NONFICTION.

The history of America and the flag told with exquisite paintings.

Lewis, P. (2002). *ARITHME-TICKLE.* New York: Harcourt. (1–4). PICTURE BOOK.

A collection of even numbers and of odd Riddle rhymes.

Littke, L. (2002). *Lake of secrets.* New York: Holt. (6–9). REALISTIC FICTION.

Carlene has a lost brother, and she has peculiar experiences that she needs to solve.

Lyons, M. E. (1992). *Letters from a slave girl: The story of Harriet Jacobs.* New York: Scribner's. (4–7). HISTORICAL FICTION.

The experiences of a slave girl are written in the form of letters.

Maestro, B. (1989). *The story of the Statue of Liberty* (G. Maestro, Illus.). New York: Harper. (1–3). NONFICTION.*

This book explains the Statue of Liberty.

Manns, N. (2001). *Operating codes.* New York: Little, Brown. (6–9). REALISTIC FICTION, MYSTERY.

After moving into a new home, Graham discovers ghosts and mysteries.

Manson, C. (2000). *Uncle Sam and Old Glory: Symbols of America.* New York: Atheneum. (2–up). NONFICTION.

This book identifies and explains 15 American symbols, including the Liberty Bell and Uncle Sam.

Martin, R. (1992). *The rough-face girl* (D. Shannon, Illus.). New York: Putnam. (K–4). TRADITIONAL LITERATURE.

This tale, from both the Algonquin and Comanche Indians, is the Native-American version of *Cinderella.*

Martin, T. (1999). *A family trait.* New York: Holiday House. (4–7). REALISTIC FICTION, MYSTERY.

Mae Watson solves the mystery of a neighbor's death and other family mysteries.

Merrill, J. (1972). *The toothpaste millionaire.* Boston: Houghton Mifflin. (4–7). CONTEMPORARY REALISTIC FICTION.

In this book, a homemade toothpaste project becomes very profitable.

Narahashi, K. (1987). *I have a friend.* New York: McElderry. (PreK–3). CONTEMPORARY REALISTIC FICTION.

Some children have dolls, pets, or toys as friends; this boy has a shadow as a friend.

Naylor, P. (2003). *Bernie Magruder & the bats in the belfry*. New York: Atheneum. (4–7). REALISTIC FICTION.

A town is plagued by a provision in Eleanor Scuttlefoot's will, so Bernie Magruder and his companions set out to solve the mystery.

Nickerson, S. (2002). *How to disappear completely and never be found*. New York: HarperCollins. (6–9). REALISTIC FICTION, MYSTERY.

Margaret lives with a mother who doesn't talk about the past. She then discovers a mystery.

Osborne, M. P. (1990). *The many lives of Benjamin Franklin*. New York: Dial. (4–8). BIOGRAPHY.

The author focuses on Franklin as a scientist, statesman, diplomat, and inventor.

Panzer, N. (Ed.). (1994). *Celebrate America: In poetry and art*. New York: Hyperion. (3–8). PICTURE BOOK.

Art and poetry are thematically arranged. The art is from the National Museum of American Art at the Smithsonian.

Pfeffer, W. (1999). *Sounds all around* (H. Keller, Illus.). New York: HarperCollins. (K–3). INFORMATIONAL BOOK.

This book teaches young children the science of sound and how we use sound.

Pittman, H. C. (1994). *Counting Jennie*. Minneapolis: Carolrhoda. (1–3). PICTURE BOOK.

In this picture book, Jennie counts everything she sees.

Platt, R. (2001). *Pirate diary: The journal of Jake Carpenter* (Riddell, Illus.). New York: Candlewick Press. (3–6). HISTORICAL FICTION.

This story is written like a pirate's journal of his experiences.

Raffi. (1992). *Raffi songs to read*. New York: Crown. (PreK).

This is a cassette tape containing songs to help children learn the rhythm of language. Printed text for the tape is available.

Rector, R. (2002). *Tria and the great star rescue*. New York: Delacorte. (4–7). FANTASY, MYSTERY.

Tria lives in a futuristic home with a holographic friend. She and her friend must discover what a group of criminals are looking for.

Ryan, P. (2000). *The flag we love* (F. Masiello, Illus.). New York: Charlesbridge. (1–6). NONFICTION.*

This book identifies the national symbol and what it stands for.

Ryder, J. (1989). *Under the moon* (C. Harness, Illus.). New York: Random House. (PreK–K). PICTURE BOOK.

Mama mouse teaches her child special things such as how to use his nose.

Rylant, C. (1986). *Night in the country* (M. Szilagyi, Illus.). New York: Bradbury. (1–3). PICTURE BOOK.

This book is a beautifully illustrated exploration of night.

Scamell, R. (1994). *Rooster crows* (J. Riches, Illus.). New York: Tambourine. (1–3). PICTURE BOOK.

A placid rooster bets he can crow the sun up.

Sciezka, J. & Smith, L. (1995). M*ath curse*. New York: Viking. (2–7). PICTURE BOOK.

Readers learn how every thing is a math problem.

Scillian, D. (1995). *A is for America* (P. Carroll, Illus). Chelsea, MI: Sleeping Bear Press, (1–4). NONFICTION.

An Alphabet Book about the U.S.

Scillian, D. (2000). *One nation: America by the numbers* (P. Carroll, Illus.). Chelsea, MI: Sleeping Bear Press. (All ages). NONFICTION.

This counting book for all ages includes U. S. trivia related to numbers.

Stanley, D. (2001). *The mysterious matter of I.M. Fine*. New York: HarperCollins. (4–8). REALISTIC FICTION, MYSTERY.

Franny realizes that classmates who read "Chillers" develop problems, so she decides to solve the mystery.

Stanley, G. (2001). *The cobweb confession* (S. Murdocca, Illus.). New York: Aladdin. (All ages). REALISTIC FICTION, MYSTERY.*

A science teacher and his students solve mysteries.

Stenhouse, T. (2001). *Across the steel river*. Toronto, Canada: Kids Can. (5–8). REALISTIC FICTION.

This book describes a friendship between Will Samson and Siksika, a Blackfoot Indian. When a local hero is beaten, the boys solve the mystery.

Stevens, C. (1993). *Lily and Miss Liberty*. New York: Little Apple. (3–5). HISTORICAL FICTION.

A girl and her father discuss the Statue of Liberty and how it was contributed by the French.

Stevens, J. R. (1999). *Carlos and the carnival* (J. Arnold, Illus.). Flagstaff, AZ: Rising Moon. (K–4). CONTEMPORARY REALISTIC FICTION.

Carlos shows how he and his Latino friends celebrate Carnival.

Tucker, K. (1994). *Do pirates take baths?* (N. B. Westcott, Illus.). Morton Grove, IL: Albert Whitman. (1–3). PICTURE BOOK.

In this humorous story, children learn that even pirates take baths.

Uttley, A. (1964). *A traveler in time* (C. Price, Illus.). New York: Viking. (3–6). MODERN FANTASY.

Van Laan, N. (Reteller). (1989). *Rainbow crow: A Lenape tale* (B. Vidal, Illus.). New York: Knopf. (1–3). TRADITIONAL LITERATURE.

A tale about a humorous and cunning crow.

This traditional tale is about a smart crow.

Waters, K. (1992). *The Story of the White House.* New York: Scholastic. (K–3). PICTURE BOOK.

This is a photo essay about the white house.

Wood, A. (1984). *The napping house* (D. Wood, Illus.). New York: Harcourt Brace Jovanovich. (K–2). PICTURE BOOK.

A child and a number of animals go to sleep in Granny's bed.

Wormser, R. (1990). *Pinkerton: America's first private eye.* New York: Walker. (5–8). INFORMATIONAL BOOK.

This book begins with Pinkerton growing up in the slums of Glasgow.

Yenne, B. (1993). *100 inventions that shaped world history.* San Francisco: Bluewood Books. (3–6). INFORMATIONAL BOOK.

This book identifies and tells about 100 important inventions.

Yolen, J. (1990). *Sky dogs* (B. Moser, Illus.). New York: Harcourt Brace Jovanovich. (K–4). TRADITIONAL LITERATURE.

The story is about how the Blackfoot Indians got horses.

Yolen, J. (1995). *The ballad of the pirate queens* (D. Shannon, Illus.). New York: Harcourt Brace Jovanovich. (3–8). MODERN FANTASY.

This picture book is about two female pirates and their exploits.

References and Books for Further Reading

Altwerger, B., & Flores, B. (1994). Theme cycles: Creating communities of learners. *Primary Voices K–6, 2,* 2–6.

Barnes, D. (1995). Talking and learning in classrooms: An introduction. *Primary Voices K–6, 3,* 2–7.

Copenhaver, J. (1993). Instances of inquiry. *Primary Voices K–6, 1,* 6–12.

Dickinson, J. (1995). Talk and picture books in intermediate classrooms. *Primary Voices K–6, 3,* 8–14.

Fredericks, A. (1991). *Social studies through children's literature.* Englewood, CO: Teachers' Ideas Press.

Harste, J. (1993). Inquiry-based instruction. *Primary Voices K–6, 1,* 2–5.

Hartman, D. K. (1992). Eight readers reading: The intertextual links of able readers using multiple passages. *Reading Research Quarterly, 27,* 122–123.

Hughes, S. (1993). The impact of whole language on four elementary school libraries. *Language Arts, 70,* 521–530.

Jacque, D. (1993). The judge comes to kindergarten. In *Journeying: Children responding to literature* (pp. 43–53). Portsmouth, NH: Heinemann.

Johnson, T., & Louis, D. (1990). *Bringing it all together: A program for literacy.* Portsmouth, NH: Heinemann.

Kimeldorf, M. (1994). *A teacher's guide to creating portfolios.* Minneapolis, MN: Free Spirit.

Laughlin, M., & Swisher, C. (1990). *Literature-based reading.* Phoenix, AZ: Oryx Press.

Meinback, A., Rothlein, L., & Fredericks, A. (2000). *The complete guide to thematic units: Creating the integrated curriculum* (2nd ed.). Norwood, MA: Christopher-Gordon.

Peterson, B. (1991). Selecting books for beginning readers. In D. Deford, C. A. Lyons, and G. S. Pinnell (Eds.), *Bridges to literacy: Learning from reading recovery.* Portsmouth, NH: Heinemann.

Rosenblatt, L. M. (1983). *Literature as exploration.* New York: Noble and Noble.

Walmsley, S. (1994). *Children exploring their world.* Portsmouth, NH: Heinemann.

Weaver, C., Chaston, J., & Peterson, S. (1993). *Theme exploration.* Portsmouth, NH: Heinemann.

Weston, L. (1993). The evolution of response through discussion, drama, writing, and art in a fourth grade. In K. Holland, R. Hungerford, and S. Ernst (Eds.), *Journeying: Children responding to literature* (pp. 137–150). Portsmouth, NH: Heinemann.

Appendix

BOOK AWARDS

The Caldecott Medal

This award, sponsored by the Association for Library Service to Children division of the American Library Association, is given to the illustrator of the most distinguished picture book for children published in the United States during the preceding year. Only U.S. residents or citizens are eligible for this award.

2004   *The Man Who Walked Between the Towers* by Mordio Gerstein. Roaring Brook/Millbrook.

2003   *My Friend Rabbit* by Eric Rohmann. Roaring Brook Press/Millbrook Press.

2002   *The Three Pigs* by David Wiesner. Clarion/Houghton Mifflin.

2001   *So You Want to Be President?* by Judith St. George, illustrated by David Small. Philomel.

2000   *Joseph Had a Little Overcoat* by Simms Taback. Viking.

1999   *Snowflake Bentley* by Jacqueline Briggs Martin, illustrated by Mary Azarian. Houghton Mifflin.

1998   *Rapunzel* retold by Paul O. Zelinsky. Dutton.

1997   *Golem* by David Wisniewski. Clarion.

1996   *Officer Buckle and Gloria* by Peggy Rathmann. Putnam.

1995   *Smoky Night* by Eve Bunting, illustrated by David Diaz. Harcourt.

1994   *Grandfather's Journey* by Allen Say. Houghton Mifflin.

1993   *Mirette on the High Wire* by Emily Arnold McCully. G. P. Putnam.

1992   *Tuesday* by David Wiesner. Clarion.

1991   *Black and White* by David Macaulay. Houghton Mifflin.

1990   *Lon Po Po: A Red-Riding Hood Story from China*. Translated and illustrated by Ed Young. Philomel.

1989   *Song and Dance Man* by Karen Ackerman, illustrated by Stephen Gammell. Knopf.

1988   *Owl Moon* by Jane Yolen, illustrated by John Schoenherr. Philomel.

1987   *Hey, Al* by Arthur Yorinks, illustrated by Richard Egielski. Farrar.

1986   *The Polar Express* by Chris Van Allsburg. Houghton Mifflin.

1985   *Saint George and the Dragon* retold by Margaret Hodges, illustrated by Trina Schart Hyman. Little, Brown.

1984   *The Glorious Flight: Across the Channel with Louis Blériot* by Alice and Martin Provensen. Viking.

1983   *Shadow* by Blaise Cendrars, translated and illustrated by Marcia Brown. Scribner's.

1982   *Jumanji* by Chris Van Allsburg. Houghton Mifflin.

1981   *Fables* by Arnold Lobel. Harper.

1980   *Ox-Cart Man* by Donald Hall, illustrated by Barbara Cooney. Viking.

1979   *The Girl Who Loved Wild Horses* by Paul Goble. Bradbury.

1978   *Noah's Ark* by Peter Spier. Doubleday.

1977   *Ashanti to Zulu: African Traditions* by Margaret Musgrove, illustrated by Leo and Diane Dillon. Dial.

1976   *Why Mosquitoes Buzz in People's Ears* retold by Verna Aardema, illustrated by Leo and Diane Dillon. Dial.

1975   *Arrow to the Sun* adapted and illustrated by Gerald McDermott. Viking.

The Newbery Award

This award, sponsored by the Association for Library Service to Children division of the American Library Association, is given to the author of the most distinguished contribution to children's literature published during the preceding year. Only U.S. citizens or residents are eligible for this award.

2004 *The Tale of Despereaux* by Kate Di Camillo, illustrated by Timothy Basil Ering. Candle Wick Press.

2003 *Crispin: The Cross of Lead* by Avi. Hyperion.

2002 *A Single Shard* by Linda Sue Park. Clarion/Houghton Mifflin.

2001 *A Year Down Yonder* by Richard Peck. Dial.

2000 *Bud, Not Buddy* by Christopher Paul Curtis. Delacorte.

1999 *Holes* by Louis Sachar. Farrar Straus.

1998 *Out of the Dust* by Karen Hesse. Scholastic.

1997 *The View from Saturday* by E. L. Konigsburg. Atheneum.

1996 *The Midwife's Apprentice* by Karen Cushman. Clarion.

1995 *Walk Two Moons* by Sharon Creech. Harper-Collins.

1994 *The Giver* by Lois Lowry. Houghton Mifflin.

1993 *Missing May* by Cynthia Rylant. Jackson/Orchard.

1992 *Shiloh* by Phyllis Reynolds Naylor. Atheneum.

1991 *Maniac Magee* by Jerry Spinelli. Little, Brown.

1990 *Number the Stars* by Lois Lowry. Houghton Mifflin.

1989 *Joyful Noise: Poems for Two Voices* by Paul Fleischamn. Harper.

1988 *Lincoln: A Photobiography* by Russell Freedman. Clarion.

1987 *The Whipping Boy* by Sid Fleischman. Greenwillow.

1986 *Sarah Plain and Tall* by Patricia MacLachlan. Harper.

1985 *The Hero and the Crown* by Robin McKinley. Greenwillow.

1984 *Dear Mr. Henshaw* by Beverly Cleary. Morrow.

1983 *Dicey's Song* by Cynthia Voigt. Atheneum.

1982 *A Visit to William Blake's Inn: Poems for Innocent and Experienced Travelers* by Nancy Willard, illustrated by Alice and Martin Provensen. Harcourt.

1981 *Jacob Have I Loved* by Katherine Paterson. Crowell.

1980 *A Gathering of Days: A New England Girl's Journal, 1830–1832* by Joan Blos. Scribner's.

1979 *The Westing Game* by Ellen Raskin. Dutton.

1978 *Bridge to Terabithia* by Katherine Paterson. Crowell.

1977 *Roll of Thunder, Hear my Cry* by Mildred D. Taylor. Dial.

1976 *The Grey King* by Susan Cooper. McElderry/Atheneum.

1975 *M. C. Higgins, the Great* by Virginia Hamilton. Macmillan.

Coretta Scott King Awards

These awards, founded to commemorate Dr. Martin Luther King, Jr., and his wife, Coretta Scott King, for their work in promoting peace and world brotherhood, are given to an African-American author and, since 1974, an African-American illustrator whose children's books, published during the preceding year, made outstanding inspirational and educational contributions to literature for children and young people. The awards are sponsored by the Social Responsibilities Round Table of the American Library Association.

2004 Author: *The First Part Last* by Angela Johnson. Simon & Schuster
Illustrator: *Beautiful Black bird* by Ashley Bryan. Atheneum.

2003 Author: *Bronx Masquerade* by Nikki Grimes. Dial.
Illustrator: *Talkin' About Bessie: The Story of Aviator Elizabeth,* illustrated by E. B. Lewis. Orchard.

2002 Author: *The Land* by Mildred Taylor. Peng Putnam.
Illustrator: *Goin' Someplace Special,* illustrated by Jerry Pinkney. Atheneum.

2001   Author: *Miracle's Boys* by Jacqueline Woodson. Putnam.

Illustrator: *Uptown* by Bryan Collier. Henry Holt.

2000   Author: *Bud, Not Buddy* by Christopher Paul Curtis. Delacorte.

Illustrator: *In the Time of the Drums,* illustrated by Brian Pinkney. Text by Kim Siegelson. Hyperion.

1999   Author: *Heaven* by Angela Johnson. Simon & Schuster.

Illustrator: *I See the Rhythm,* illustrated by Michele Wood. Text by Toyomi Igus. Children's Book Press.

1998   Author: *Forged by Fire* by Sharon M. Draper. Atheneum.

Illustrator: *In Daddy's Arms I Am Tall: African Americans Celebrating Fathers,* illustrated by Javaka Steptoe. Lee & Low.

1997   Author: *Slam!* by Walter Dean Myers. Scholastic.

Illustrator: *Minty: A Story of Young Harriet Tubman,* illustrated by Jerry Pinkney. Text by Alan Schroeder. Dial Books for Young Readers.

1996   Author: *Her Stories* by Virginia Hamilton, illustrated by Leo and Diane Dillon. Scholastic/Blue Sky Press.

Illustrator: *The Middle Passage: White Ships Black Cargo* by Tom Feelings. Introduction by John Henrik Clarke. Dial.

1995   Author: *Christmas in the Big House, Christmas in the Quarters* by Patricia C. and Frederick L. McKissack, illustrated by John Thompson. Scholastic.

Illustrator: *The Creation,* illustrated by James E. Ransome. Text by James Weldon Johnson. Delacorte.

1994   Author: *Toning the Sweep* by Angela Johnson. Orchard.

Illustrator: *Soul Looks Back in Wonder*, illustrated by Tom Feelings. Text edited by Phyllis Fogelman. Dial.

1993   Author: *The Dark-Thirty: Southern Tales of the Supernatural* by Patricia McKissack, illustrated by Brian Pinkney. Knopf.

Illustrator: *The Origin of Life on Earth: An African Creation Myth,* illustrated by Kathleen Atkins Wilson. Retold by David Anderson. Sights Production.

1992   Author: *Now Is Your Time! The African-American Struggle for Freedom* by Walter Dean Myers. HarperCollins.

Illustrator: *Tar Beach* by Faith Ringgold. Crown.

1991   Author: *Road to Memphis* by Mildred D. Taylor. Dial.

Illustrator: *Aïda,* illustrated by Leo and Diane Dillon. Retold by Leontyne Price. Harcourt.

1990   Author: *A Long Hard Journey* by Patricia and Frederick McKissack. Walker.

Illustrator: *Nathaniel Talking,* illustrated by Jan Spivey Gilchrist. Text by Eloise Greenfield. Black Butterfly Press.

1989   Author: *Fallen Angels* by Walter Dean Myers. Scholastic.

Illustrator: *Mirandy and Brother Wind,* illustrated by Jerry Pinkney. Text by Patricia McKissack. Knopf.

1988   Author: *The Friendship* by Mildred D. Taylor, illustrated by Max Ginsburg. Dial.

Illustrator: *Mufaro's Beautiful Daughters: An African Tale,* retold and illustrated by John Steptoe. Lothrop.

1987   Author: *Justin and the Best Biscuits in the World* by Mildred Pitts Walter. Lothrop.

Illustrator: *Half a Moon and One Whole Star,* illustrated by Jerry Pinkney. Text by Crescent Dragonwagon. Macmillan.

1986   Author: *The People Could Fly: American Black Folktales* by Virginia Hamilton, illustrated by Leo and Diane Dillon. Knopf.

Illustrator: *The Patchwork Quilt,* illustrated by Jerry Pinkney. Text by Valerie Flournoy. Dial.

1985   Author: *Motown and Didi* by Walter Dean Myers. Viking.

Illustrator: No award.

1984   Author: *Everett Anderson's Goodbye* by Lucille Clifton. Holt.

Illustrator: *My Mama Needs Me,* illustrated by Pat Cummings. Text by Mildred Pitts Walter. Lothrop.

1983   Author: *Sweet Whispers, Brother Rush* by Virginia Hamilton. Philomel.

Illustrator: *Black Child* by Peter Magubane. Knopf.

1982   Author: *Let the Circle be Unbroken* by Mildred Taylor. Dial.

Illustrator: *Mother Crocodile: An Uncle Amadou Tale from Senegal*, illustrated by John Steptoe. Adapted by Rosa Guy. Delacorte.

1981   Author: *This Life* by Sidney Poitier. Knopf.

Illustrator: *Beat the Story-Drum, Pum-Pum* by Ashley Bryan. Atheneum.

1980   Author: *The Young Landlords* by Walter Dean Myers. Viking.

Illustrator: *Cornrows*, illustrated by Carole Byard. Text by Camille Yarbrough. Coward.

1979   Author: *Escape to Freedom* by Ossie Davis. Viking.

Illustrator: *Something on My Mind*, illustrated by Tom Feelings. Text by Nikki Grimes. Dial.

1978   Author: *Africa Dream* by Eloise Greenfield, illustrated by Carole Byard. Crowell.

Illustrator: *Africa Dream*, illustrated by Carole Byard. Text by Eloise Greenfield. Crowell.

1977   Author: *The Story of Stevie Wonder* by James Haskins. Lothrop.

Illustrator: No award.

1976   Author: *Duey's Tale* by Pearl Bailey. Harcourt.

Illustrator: No award.

1975   Author: *The Legend of Africana* by Dorothy Robinson. Johnson Publishing.

Illustrator: No award.

Robert F. Sibert Informational Book Medal

This award was established by the Association for Library Service to Children in 2001. It is awarded annually to the author of the most distinguished informational book published during the preceding year.

2003   *The Life and Death of Adolf Hitler* by James Cross Giblin. Clarion.

2002   *Black Potatoes: The Story of the Great Irish Famine, 1845–1850* by Susan Bartoletti. Houghton Mifflin.

2001   *Sir Walter Raleigh and the Quest for El Dorado* by Andrea Warren. Clarion.

Nonfiction Awards: Orbis Pictus Award

The Orbis Pictus Award for Outstanding Nonfiction for Children was established by the National Council of Teachers of English (NCTE) in 1990 to promote and recognize excellence in the field of nonfiction writing.

2004   *An American Plague: The True and Terrible Story of the Yellow Fever Epidemic of 1793* by Jim Murphy. Clarion Books.

2003   *When Marian Sang: The True Recital of Marian Anderson: The Voice of a Century* by Pam Munoz Ryan. Scholastic.

2002   *Black Potatoes: The Story of the Great Irish Famine, 1845–1850* by Susan Bartoletti. Houghton Mifflin.

2001   *Hurry Freedom: African Americans in Gold Rush California* by Jerry Stanley. Crown.

2000   *Through My Eyes* by Ruby Bridges, edited by Margo Lundell. Scholastic.

1999   *Shipwreck at the Bottom of the World: The Extraordinary True Story of Shackleton and the Endurance* by Jennifer Armstrong. Crown.

1998   *An Extraordinary Life: The Story of a Monarch Butterfly* by Laurence Pringle, paintings by Bob Marstall. Orchard.

1997   *Leonardo da Vinci* by Diane Stanley. Morrow.

1996   *The Great Fire* by Jim Murphy. Scholastic.

1995   *Safari Beneath the Sea* by Diane Swanson. Sierra Club Books.

1994   *Across America on an Emigrant Train* by Jim Murphy. Clarion.

1993   *Children of the Dust Bowl: The True Story of the School at Weedpatch Camp* by Jerry Stanley. Crown.

Honor Books

1993   *Come Back Salmon: How a Group of Dedicated Kids Adopted Pigeon Creek and Brought it Back to Life*. Harper Collins. Sierra Club.

Honor Books

1992   *Flight: The Journey of Charles Lindberg* by Robert Burleigh and Mike Wimmer. Philomel *Now is Your Time!* by Walter Dean Myers. HarperCollins. *Prarie Vision: The Life and Times of Soloman Butcher* by Pam Conrad.

Franklin Delano Roosevelt by Russell Freedman. Clarion.

Honor Books

1991 *Arctic Memories* by Normee Ekoomiak. Holt.

Seeing Earth from Space by Patricia Lauber. Orchard.

Honor Books

1990 *The Great Little Madison* by Jean Fritz. Putnam.

The News About Dinosaurs by Patricia Lauber. Bradbury.

The Great American Gold Rush by Rhoda Blumberg. Bradbury.

Other nonfiction awards not listed are: the Boston Globe–Horn Book Award; the Carter B. Woodson Book Award; the Children's Book Guild Nonfiction Award; the Christopher Awards; and the Eva L. Gordon Award for Children's Science Literature.

Pura Belpré Award

The Pura Belpré Award is given every two years by the Association for Library Service to Children (ALSC) and the National Association to Promote Library Services to the Spanish Speaking (REFORMA).

The award honors Latino writers and illustrators whose work best portrays, affirms, and celebrates the Latino cultural experience in a work of literature for youth. The award was named in honor of Pura Belpré, the first Latina librarian of the New York Public Library. The first awards, given in 1996, were selected from books published between 1990 and 1995.

2004 Text: *Before We Were Free* by Julia Alvarez. Knopf.

Illustration: *Just a Minute: A Tricks and Counting Book*. Chronicle Books.

2002 Text: *Esperanza Rising* by Pam Munoz Ryan. Scholastic.

Illustration: *Chato and the Party Animals* by Gary Soto. Putnam.

2000 Text: *Under the Royal Palms: A Childhood in Cuba* by Alma Flor Ada. Atheneum.

Illustration: *Magic Windows: Cut Paper Art and Stories* by Carmen Lomas Garza. Children's Book Press.

1998 Text: *Parrot in the Oven: Mi Vida* by Victor Martinez. Joanna Cotler Books/HarperCollins.

Illustration: *Snapshots from the Wedding*, illustrated by Stephanie Garcia. Text by Gary Soto. Putnam.

1996 Text: *An Island Like You: Stories of the Barrio* by Judith Ortiz Cofer. Melanie Kroupa/Orchard.

Illustration: *Chato's Kitchen*, illustrated by Susan Guevara. Text by Gary Soto. Putnam.

Glossary

Aesthetic reading pleasurable, interesting reading done for its own sake.

Alliteration literary device based on repetition of consonant sounds.

Animal fantasy stories in which animals act and interact like human beings.

Antagonist a character in a story who is in conflict with the main character or protagonist.

Assonance the close repetition of middle vowel sounds between different consonant sounds.

Audio book/s Books that are recorded for listening.

Authentic activities activities that have meaning for the students engaged in them.

Authentic biography biography based entirely on the actual words and experiences of the subject. There are no imagined conversations or events.

Author the title given to the person who writes the text in books.

Autobiography a category of biography written by the subject of the book.

Ballads rhymes and rhythms set to music, centering on a single character in a dramatic situation.

Benchmark a term describing an exemplary book that is used as a standard of quality for comparing other similar books.

Bibliotherapy helping with books.

Biography the story of a particular person's life. In biography, authors conduct careful research in order to explore and record the lives and significant acts and accomplishments of a person. Three styles of biography are typical. For children (a) **authentic biography** is based on documented words, speeches, and writing of the subject; (b) the **biographical fiction style** of biography permits the author to create conversations and portray the everyday life of the subject, but these details are based on thorough historical research into the subject's character and life as well as the time in which the person lived; and (c) when writing **fictionalized biography**, the author takes greater latitude in creating a story around the actual life of a subject.

Book cluster groups of books based on common theme or subject.

Book-talking the act of telling or reading highlights of a book without revealing its entire plot. The purpose of book-talking is to motivate others to read a book.

Caldecott Medal an award presented each year by the American Library Association to the creator of an outstanding picture book.

Catharsis books that help work out emotions.

Censorship the act of controlling what literature is available to be read in any given setting. Censors may attempt to remove books from library shelves because they believe the works in question violate particular values, religious beliefs, or good taste.

Challenged students individuals who face difficulties in educational situations.

Chapter books relatively short books divided into chapters with more text than pictures. They are intended for readers who are ready to read longer books than picture books.

Character maps a strategy for developing students' understanding of character development in a story.

Characters the people in a story, comparable to actors in movies or on stage. Their actions, thoughts, and conversations tell the story.

Choral reading an oral literary activity in which a selection from literature is read by several persons in unison with the direction of a leader. The most common types of choral reading are: (a) refrain, in which the teacher reads most of the lines and the children read the refrain; (b) line-a-child choral reading, in which individual students read specific lines, while the entire group reads the beginning and ending of the selection; and (c) antiphonal or dialogue choral reading, based on boys and girls (sometimes in groups) varying their voices to speak different parts of a selection.

Classroom sets   multiple copies of trade books for classroom use.

Climax   the high point of a story when conflicts are resolved.

Community of readers   term that denotes shared understandings within a group of readers who discuss ideas about the same books.

Concept books   books that explore the various facets of a particular concept and in the process develop a reader's understanding of it. Geometric shapes, nature, and maps are some of the subjects of concept books.

Concrete poetry   poetry written in the shape of the topic; a poem about a boat, for example, would be written in the shape of a boat.

Conflict   the result of difficulties or opposing views between characters in a story. Conflict gives a story the tension that makes it interesting. There are a number of types of conflict, such as conflict within an individual, between individuals, or between an individual and nature.

Connections   the process of identifying ways that books are related to one another and to the experiences of the reader.

Connotative meaning   inferred meaning as opposed to literal meaning. It is meaning deduced from "reading between the lines."

Contemporary (realistic fiction)   events and settings that readers recognize as being in the present.

Core literature   literature that is the focus of a unit study.

Creative drama   informal drama created by the participants in the drama. It is improvisational and process-centered: The players create the dialogue and there are no written scripts to follow.

Culturally conscious literature   literature that recognizes the importance of culture and shows respect for people of all cultures and races.

Cultural diversity   society that includes people from many cultures and races.

Culture   the context in which children develop. Culture is comprised of the values and customs that form an identifiable heritage.

Cumulative stories   refers to stories that accumulate. Events build on events and phrases build on phrases, leading to a climax, at which point the accumulation falls apart.

Denouement   the falling action that occurs after the climax.

Developmentally appropriate   a phrase describing instruction that is compatible with the learner's stage of development.

Didacticism   obvious moral messages or values that some authors believe should be taught directly.

Diversity background   the student population of today's schools is more varied than in the past. Diversity arises from many sources, including ethnicity as well as emotional and physical development.

Early literacy experiences   experiences with literature that are had through listening to stories and handling books and writing materials.

Efferent reading   has a narrow focus and depends upon the reader's purpose; for example, efferent reading may be done to seek specific information such as directions.

Element of literature   the structural elements of fiction that include plot, characterization, setting, style, and theme.

Emergent literacy   refers to the beginning stages of learning to read and write.

Enchanted realism   has elements of both fantasy and high fantasy. These stories include magic objects, characters, or events that appear in a realistic world, creating suspense and intrigue in the story.

Engaging with literature   describes readers' response to reading in which readers' minds, interests, and feelings connect with the ideas in a text. It connotes an understanding and an emotional response to what is read.

Envisionment   the unique meaning each reader creates when reading; each reader has slight to significant differences in interpretation.

Epic   a story of a person's life and death told in poetic form.

Episode   the name given to a small plot within a larger one. It usually occurs in a single chapter within a book. In some books, each chapter is an episode.

Exceptional   a descriptive word for individual differences that fall outside the average, or bell curve. Exceptional students need adjustments in their instruction in order to achieve their potential.

Experiencing literature reading with pleasure and with understanding.

Exposition literature that explains.

Fable a story about an animal that teaches a lesson.

Fact frames a strategy for organizing the facts that one acquires from reading.

Family literacy reading and writing that occur in the home.

Fantastic element an impossible element in a story; something that could not really happen such as a person or animal that does not really exist, or an aberration of some other aspect of the laws of the real world.

Fantasy a genre of literature that is based on make-believe elements; it may include such factors as characters, place, events, and time.

Figurative language has a nonliteral meaning; it may include similes, metaphors, hyperbole, and personification.

Folk tales pieces of literature that mirror the mores and values of a culture; they are passed down from generation to generation and have no identifiable author.

Foreshadowing a stylistic device employed to hint at future actions or events.

Free verse poetry that does not follow a traditional form in that it does not have a regular rhythm or meter, nor does it usually rhyme.

Genre classifications of literature that share the same basic characteristics. The genre of children's literature includes picture books, poetry, fantasy, traditional literature, historical fiction, realistic (contemporary) fiction, biography, and nonfiction.

Global literature these books reflect the global community in which we live.

Great books those books that have lived through several generations, usually because they express universal truths; people in different situations and circumstances can relate to the way these truths are expressed.

Haiku a poetic form that originated in Japan and refers to nature and the seasons; it is patterned poetry of 17 syllables in which the first line contains five syllables, the second contains seven, and the third contains five.

High fantasy complex fantasy that is grouped into heroic fantasy and science fiction.

Historical fiction found in books in which the setting is in the past. Events and characters are realistic, and set-ting and background are true to a particular time period, but descriptions, and sometimes characters, are made up. Characters behave and react the way one would expect of people in the time period in which the story is set.

Illustrated books books in which illustrations are used to supplement the text.

Illustrators artists who create the illustrations for books. These artists create pictures that interpret the text; sometimes illustrations tell the whole story, as in worldless picture books.

Imagery images that are created in the mind through the use of language; imagery appeals to the senses of sight, sound, touch, and smell.

Inclusion a plan for teaching educationally handicapped students in the regular classroom rather than segregating them in special education classrooms.

Individual differences variations from one individual to another.

Individualized education plan (IEP) the plan developed by teachers, administrators, parents, and special educators to guide the education of students.

Inferencing interpretation of literature based on meanings that are not directly stated in a text; readers must "fill in the empty spaces."

Informational books books that explain, impart knowledge, or describe persons, places, things, or events.

Inquiry the process of searching for information, ideas, and truth about questions the student has raised.

Inside perspective a perspective of a culture from a member inside that culture.

Integrated units units that address various subjects and literacy processes included in the elementary curriculum.

Interests topics and experiences toward which individuals gravitate because they are motivated. Interests are usually developed and cultivated through experience.

Intertextuality the process of interpreting one text by connecting the ideas in it with the ideas in all other previously read texts.

KWL chart an activity that identifies what the reader knows about the topic, what he wants-to-learn and finally what he learns.

Legends stories that are often based on an actual historical figure whose deeds and exploits have been embellished.

Life-cycle books   books that explain and illustrate the life cycles of animals, insects, and so forth.

Literary fairy tales   stories that use the folk tale style although they were written by an author rather than emerging from the oral tradition.

Literary conventions   elements of form, style, or content. These fundamental patterns, conventions, or universals occur in both children's and adult literature.

Literary criticism   is concerned with identifying the quality of literature. It falls into three categories: text-centered, child-centered, and issues-centered.

Literary quality   describes well-written literature that has well-developed plots, themes, characterization, setting, and style. Nonfiction has literary quality when it is accurate, well-written, and interesting. It presents main ideas and supporting details, differentiates theories from facts, and has illustrations that are appropriate to the subject.

Literate environment   a place where reading and writing are used for authentic purposes; many kinds of reading and materials are available in such a place.

Literature   a body of written works, an art form in which language is used in creative, artistic ways.

Mainstreaming   a practice that places exceptional students in the regular classroom.

Metaphor   a figure of speech comparing two items that says one thing is the other.

Modern fantasy   stories that take for granted not only the realities of the world that we see and feel, but also the supernatural aspects that lead to all sorts of possibilities; fantasies have identifiable authors.

Multicultural literature   portrays the diversity of the population.

Multiculturalism   the process of developing sensitivity to the various cultures comprising a community, state, country, and world.

Myths   stories that explain the origin of the world and natural phenomena.

Narrative poetry   tells a story; it includes the story elements of plot, character, setting, and theme.

Newbery   the name given to a medal that is awarded annually by the American Library Association to an outstanding children's book.

Nonfiction books   those in which all the information presented is true, such as a biography. No fictional elements are included in nonfiction.

Nonsense poetry   composed in lyric or narrative form, this poetry is playful and does not conform to what is expected; it pokes fun at what is usually taken seriously.

Partial biographies   focuses on a particular part of a person's life. For example, a partial biography focuses on a subject's childhood or adult life.

Personification   attributes human characteristics to something that does not actually have these qualities.

Physical disability   refers to the condition of an individual who has learning challenges because of physical exceptionalities.

Picture books   these books tell stories by integrating language and pictures. Some picture books, however, are wordless.

Plot   the plan and structure of the story. Plots usually consist of introductory material, a gradual building of suspense, a climax, the falling of action, and the culmination.

Plot frames   strategies that help readers understand the plot line of a story.

Poetry   literature in its most intense, imaginative, and rhythmic form, which expresses and interprets the essence of experience through language; it is not the same as "verse."

Popular literature   in vogue at a particular time, it is usually characterized as a fad that enjoys a period of popularity and then disappears. Popular literature is produced very quickly and lacks the literary quality that would inspire readers to read and reread it.

Pourquoi   a story that explains why things are the way they are.

Prediction   chart-guide readers to anticipate text which improves comprehension.

Problem resolution   refers to the way conflicts and story problems are resolved.

Protagonist   This character in a story is usally the main character or hero of the book. Readers identify with this "good guy" character.

Racial and ethnic stereotyping   based on the assumption that all members of a racial or ethnic group have the same characteristics. The characteristics assumed in stereotypes are usually negative views of people. Stereotyping interferes with the ability to see individuals as human beings.

Readability   the level at which a person can read a book (or other printed text) with comprehension.

Reader's theater an oral presentation of literature—the oral delivery of stories, poetry, biography, or information by two or more readers who characterize and narrate clearly and expressively.

Realistic fiction fiction that is written true to the physical and factual details of a particular time period. The problems that characters encounter are related to the realities of life during that time.

Response what readers take to a text, what happens during reading, how they feel about what they have read, how it becomes alive and personal, and the ways these feelings are displayed.

Rhythm the patterned flow of sound in poetry.

Schemata expectations based on experience. Readers expect stories to have characters, setting, and so forth. These are schemata for stories.

Science fiction stories created around events and problems that would not have happened without the scientific content.

Setting the time and place of the story.

Sexual stereotyping assumes that all men or all women behave in certain ways (for example, that all women are weak and all men are strong). Sexual stereotyping functions in a negative way and interferes with the ability to appreciate individuals as human beings.

Simile a figure of speech using the words *like* or *as* to compare one thing to another.

Social studies one of the primary content areas studied in schools; some of the subjects within this discipline are history, geography, and anthropology.

Stance the purpose or purposes a reader has for reading. It gives form to the literacy experience as well as the mode for expressing a response.

Story frames strategy for developing students' understanding of story structure.

Story grammar refers to story structure.

Story map the story map illustrates the story structure.

Storytelling the act of telling stories. Many storytellers tell traditional stories that they have heard from other storytellers, and they often read and memorize stories and retell them.

Style the way an author uses language and symbols to express ideas.

Survey nonfiction a form of nonfiction that gives readers a broad overview of a topic rather than in-depth information.

Teacher-generated themes those themes that teachers identify or suggest.

Theme the universal meaning (big idea) that the author expresses through a literary work.

Touchstone books books of such excellent quality that they become a standard for evaluating other books.

Trade books books that are not textbooks.

Traditional literature literature based on oral tradition. *Little Red Riding Hood,* is an example of a traditional story.

Transaction the interaction between a text and a reader in which both are modified and changed.

Unit an organizing framework for children's inquiry and study.

USSR (uninterrupted sustained silent reading) sometimes called DEAR (drop everything and read), it is a specific period set aside for reading. Everyone in the class reads, including the teacher. In some schools, this is a school-wide reading time.

Values clarification literature that encourages readers to examine their own values.

Visual art evokes both cognitive and aesthetic understanding and response.

Visual literacy a major avenue of communication in which understanding is gained visually by interpreting information presented on billboards, signs, television, pictures, and photographs.

Wordless picture book describes a book in which the story is told entirely through the use of illustrations.

Subject Index

Author/Title Index

Credits

Page 2, Cover from *Epossumondas* by Coleen Salley, Illustrated by Janet Stevens. By permission of Harcourt Brace & Co.

Page 4, Cover from *ArithmeTickle* by J. Patrick Lewis. By permission of Harcourt Brace & Co.

Page 8, Jacket of *Little Penguin's Tale,* written and illustrated by Audrey Wood. By permission of Harcourt Brace & Co.

Page 9, Cover from *Miss Alaineus* by Debra Frasier. By permission of Harcourt Brace & Co.

Page 11, *Standards for the English Language Arts,* by the International Reading Association and the Council of Teachers of English, Copyright 1996 by the International Reading Association and the National Council of Teachers of English. Reprinted with permission.

Page 19, Dust jacket cover from *Weird Friends* by Jose Aruego and Arlane Dewey. By permission of Harcourt Brace & Co.

Page 21, Cover from *The Bug Scientists* by Donna M. Jackson. Copyright © 2002 by Donna M. Jackson. Reprinted by permission of Houghton Mifflin Company. All rights reserved.

Page 23, Cover from *Gooney Bird Greene* by Lois Lowry, illustrated by Middy Thomas. Jacket art copyright © 2002 by Houghton Mifflin Company. Reprinted by permission of Houghton Mifflin Company. All right reserved.

Page 30, Cover from *Home: A Journey Through America,* written and illustrated by Thomas Locker. By permission of Harcourt Brace & Co.

Page 41, Cover from *The Captain's Dog* by Roland Smith. By permission of Gulliver Harcourt.

Page 43, Jacket cover of *Belle Prather's Boy* by Ruth White. Used by permission of Random House Children's Books, a division of Random House, Inc.

Page 44, Cover from *A Caldecott Celebration* by Leonard S. Marcus. By permission of Walker and Co.

Page 45, Jacket cover of *A Single Shard* by Linda Sue Park. Used by permission of Random House Children's Books, a division of Random House, Inc.

Page 53, Cover from *What Jamie Saw* by Carolyn Coman, copyright © 1995 by Brock Cole. By permission of Front Street, Inc.

Page 63, Cover from *And the Dish Ran Away with the Spoon* by Janet Stevens and Susan Stevens Crummel. By permission of Harcourt Brace & Co.

Page 64, 65, Cover and one interior illustration from *In the Haunted House* by Eve Bunting, illustrated by Susan Meddaugh. Illustrations copyright © 1990 by Susan Meddaugh. Reprinted by permission of Clarion Books/Houghton Mifflin Company. All rights reserved.

Page 67, Illustrations from *The Napping House* by Audrey Wood, illustrated by Don Wood. Text copyright © 1984 by Audrey Wood. Illustrations copyright © 1984 by Don Wood. By permission of Harcourt Brace & Co.

Page 68, Cover of *Bye, Bye!* by Nancy Kaufmann. Pictures by Jung-Hee Spetter. By permission of Front Street.

Page 71, *Alberto the Dancing Alligator Text* © 2002 by Richard Waring. Illustrations © 2002 by Holly Swain. Reproduced by permission of the publisher Candlewick Press, Inc., Cambridge, MA.

Page 76, Copyright © 1983 by Trina Schart Hyman. All rights reserved. Reprinted from *Little Red Riding Hood* by permission of Holiday House, Inc.

Page 89, Dust jacket from *Carver a Life in Poems* by Marilyn Nelson. By permission of Front Street.

Page 90, Cover from *Insectlopedia* by Douglas Florian. By permission of Harcourt Brace & Co.

Page 95, Cover of *This Land is Your Land* by Woodie Guthrie and paintings by Kathy Jakobsen, by permission of Little, Brown and Company.

Page 97, Jacket illustration of *Still as a Star* by Lee Bennett Hopkins, illustrated by Karen Milone. By permission of Little, Brown and Company.

Page 107, Poetry festival invitation. Reprinted by permission of M. Richardson.

Page 115, Cover from *Domitila: A Cinderella Tale from the Mexican Tradition* by Jewell Reinhart Coburn. Illustration by Connie McLennan. By permission of Shen's Books.

Page 116, Cover from *Jack and the Giant,* written by Jim Harris, by permission of Rising Moon.

Page 119, Cover from *The Marvelous Mouse Man* by Mary Ann Hoberman. By permission of Harcourt Brace & Co.